Art through the Ages

seventh edition

I Ancient, Medieval, and Non-European Art

revised by Horst de la Croix
SAN JOSE STATE UNIVERSITY

and Richard G. Tansey
SAN JOSE STATE UNIVERSITY

Gardner's Art through the Ages

seventh edition

I Ancient, Medieval, and Non-European Art

Harcourt Brace Jovanovich, Publishers

SAN DIEGO   NEW YORK   CHICAGO   ATLANTA   WASHINGTON, D.C.
LONDON   SYDNEY   TORONTO

COVER ART: Detail, *Icon of the Virgin and Child,* sixth century. Encaustic painting, sacristy, Santa Francesca Romana, Rome.

Copyright © 1980, 1975, 1970, 1959, copyright 1948, 1936, 1926 by Harcourt Brace Jovanovich, Inc.

Copyright renewed 1954 by Louise Gardner.

Copyright renewed 1964, 1976 by Harcourt Brace Jovanovich, Inc.

Chapter-opening illustrations by Veit-Martin Associates and Martin Eichtersheimer, and by Philip Ressner.
Architectural drawings by Felix Cooper and others.
Maps and chronology revisions by Jean-Paul Tremblay.

Excerpts from "The Hollow Men" and "Preludes, II" by T. S. Eliot are reprinted from his volume *Collected Poems 1909-1962* by permission of Harcourt Brace Jovanovich, Inc.

ISBN: 0-15-503758-7 (hardbound)
        0-15-503759-5 (paperbound, Vol. I)
        0-15-503760-9 (paperbound, Vol. II)

Library of Congress Catalog Card Number: 79-65963 (hardbound)
                                          79-89052 (paperbound)
Printed in the United States of America

preface

Since publication of the first edition in 1926, Helen Gardner's *Art through the Ages* has been a favorite with generations of students and general readers, who have found it an exciting and informative survey. Miss Gardner's enthusiasm, knowledge, and humanity have made it possible for the beginner to learn how to see and thereby to penetrate the seeming mysteries of even the most complex artistic achievements. Every effort has been made in this volume to preserve her freshness and simplicity of style and, above all, her sympathetic approach to individual works of art and to the styles of which they are a part.

Miss Gardner completed the third edition shortly before her death in 1946. The fourth was prepared in 1959 by Professor Sumner Crosby and his colleagues at Yale University. Our fifth edition was published in 1970 and the sixth in 1975. We were led to prepare this seventh edition by the popularity of those earlier editions and by suggestions we received for further improvement.

In this edition, in addition to emendations made throughout the book, the chapters on Medieval, Renaissance, and Baroque art have been thoroughly revised and expanded. The chapters on the eighteenth, nineteenth, and twentieth centuries have been enlarged to accommodate matter from new studies and interpretations and are presented, we believe, with improved continuity and organization. There are, of course, corresponding increases in the number of illustrations. A new feature of considerable importance is the integration of color illustrations so that they are no longer bound in isolated groups, distant from their citations, but appear in sequence among the black-and-white illustrations.

Although in some cases, like that of North American Indian art, a sure chronology is impossible, it remains our conviction that a chronological presentation is still the best for introducing the history of art, and, as in previous editions, this bias is reflected in our use of a linear chronology to open most chapters and in our use of time-lines—short elaborated sections of a chapter chronology that are keyed into the text at the point or periods on which they focus. Most chapters also open with a map that is related to the accompanying chronology; small drawings of key monuments, shown on the chronology, also appear on the map, thus orienting the various works in space as well as time.

In making a balanced historical introduction to the art of the whole world, which *Art through the Ages* uniquely achieves, the hardest task is selection—in effect, limitation—of the monuments to be discussed and illustrated. Though a corpus of monuments essential to the art-history survey course has long been forming, and though there seems to be considerable agreement as to what constitutes it, there will naturally be differences of choice deriving from differences of emphasis. While this is as it should be, radical departure from the corpus might well obliterate the outlines of the study. To avoid the random, systemless distribution of material that might result, we have generally adhered to the corpus, occasionally introducing monuments not well known or not customarily treated in a survey. Our aim throughout has been to present and interpret works as reflections of an intelligible development rather than merely as items of a catalogue or miscellany. We have tried particularly to give coherence to the vast assortment of materials by stressing—in the descriptions of sculpture and painting—the theme of representation as it passes through the many historical variations behind which operate the crucial transformations of humankind's view of itself and the world.

The treatment of the art of the non-European world now follows immediately that of the Middle Ages. This shift from its former position, which makes the text more readily adaptable to quarter- as well as semester-based courses, has its rationale in the fact that much of the non-European art available to us is from time periods that parallel roughly those of the Middle Ages. Some stylistic similarities may also be seen between medieval art and certain non-European works—Chinese sculpture, for example, of the fifth to seventh centuries.

A work as extensive as a history of world art could not be undertaken or completed without the counsel and active participation of experts in fields other than our own. In some cases this took the form of preparation of chapters or portions of chapters; in others, of reviews of work in progress or already prepared. For such contributions to this edition we offer our sincere thanks to Professor James Ackerman, Harvard University; Professor Louise Alpers Bordaz, Columbia University; Professor Jacques Bordaz, University of Pennsylvania; Professor James Cahill, University of California, Berkeley; Mr. Patrick Cardon, New York; Professor Herbert M. Cole, University of California, Santa Barbara; Professor George Corbin, Lehman College, City University of New York; Professor Oleg Grabar, Harvard University; Professor M. F. Hearn, University of Pittsburgh; Professor Howard Hibbard, Columbia University; Professor Joel Isaacson, University of Michigan; Professor Robert A. Koch, Princeton University; Professor William L. MacDonald, Smith College; Professor A. Dean McKenzie, University of Oregon; Professor Edith Porada, Columbia University; Professor Bruce Radde, San Jose State University; Professor Raphael X. Reichert, California State University at Fresno; Professor Grace Seiberling, University of Rochester; Dr. Peter Selz, University of California, Berkeley; Professor David Simon, State University of New York, Cortland; Dr. Martin S. Stanford, New York; Professor Richard Vinograd, Columbia University; Professor Joanna Williams, University of California, Berkeley; and the Art History Department, Herron School of Art, Indiana University-Purdue University at Indianapolis. We owe a special debt of gratitude to Luraine Tansey, art librarian and slide consultant, who compiled the bibliography and made valuable suggestions on its content. Harriet Frankel was her typist.

Philip Ressner, at Harcourt Brace Jovanovich, has now been our editor for three editions of this book; he has done his task with a skill, diligence, and good humor that honor his profession and his house. His colleague, Andrea Haight Lévy, has been indefatigably efficient in the management of the enormously detailed manuscript. Among the many others contributing their efforts, in often exacting roles, were Anna Kopczynski, designer of the book; Robert Karpen, production manager; Carla Wiltenburg and Dodie Shaw, art editors; and Dorothea von Elbe, assistant to the designer. Invaluable was the personal and extensive attention given the whole project by John Johnston, Director of Production.

We should like, as we thank all those who have helped immeasurably in the production of this book, to affirm that we alone are responsible for whatever may be its deficiencies.

HORST DE LA CROIX

RICHARD G. TANSEY

contents

A Note on the Paperbound Version

This volume is one of two that constitute the paperbound version of *Gardner's Art through the Ages,* Seventh Edition. The two volumes exactly reproduce the text of the one-volume version, including its pagination. The first of these volumes contains Part One, The Ancient World; Part Two, The Middle Ages; and Part Three, The Non-European World. The second contains Part Four, The Renaissance and the Baroque and Rococo; and Part Five, The Modern World. The Introduction, all appendixes, and the index appear in both volumes. The two-volume printing, then is intended for those who have occasion to use only half of *Art through the Ages.* The differences between the one-volume and the two-volume versions of the book are differences in form only.

Art through the Ages

seventh edition

I Ancient, Medieval, and Non-European Art

introduction

The goal of art history, the subject of this book, is the discerning appreciation and enjoyment of art, from whatever time and place it may have come, by whatever hands made. Outside the academic world the terms *art* and *history* are not often so juxtaposed. People tend to think of history as the record and interpretation of past (particularly political) human actions, and of art—quite correctly—as something *present* to the eye and touch, which, of course, the vanished human events that make up history are not. The fact is that a visible and tangible work of art is a kind of *persisting event*. It was made at a particular time and place by particular persons, even if we do not always know just when, where, and by whom. Though it is the creation of the past, it continues to exist in the present, long surviving its times; Charlemagne has been dead for a thousand years, but his chapel still stands at Aachen.

THE BASES OF ART HISTORY

Style

The time a work of art was made has everything to do with the way it looks—with, in one key term, its *style*. In other words, the style of a work of art is a function of its historical *period*. The historiography of art proceeds by sorting works of architecture, sculpture, and painting into stylistic classes on the bases of their likenesses and the times or periods when they were produced. It is a fundamental working hypothesis of art history that works produced at the same time (and, of course, the same place) will generally have common stylistic traits. Of course all historiography assumes that events derive their character from the time in which they happen (and perhaps from their "great men," also products of their time); thus we can speak of the Periclean Age, the Age of Reason, even—as with the title of a recent historical work—the Age of Roosevelt. We must also know the time of a work if we are to know its meaning, to know it for what it is. Yet if the work of art still stands before us, persisting from the past, is this not sufficient? By virtue of its survival, is not the work in a sense *independent* of time? May not a work of art speak to people of all times as long as it survives? The key to the question is the word "speak." Indeed, it may speak, but what is its language? What does it say to us? Art may be more than a form of communication, yet it is certainly that; and it is the business of art history to learn the "languages" of the art of many different periods as they are embodied in the monuments from their respective times. We can assume that artists in every age expressed in their works a meaning of some sort intelligible to themselves and others. One can get at that meaning only by setting a particular work in relation to others like it that were made about the same time. From works grouped in this way we can infer a community of meaning as well as of form; we will have outlined, then, a style. In a chronological series of works having common stylistic features, one may find that the later and the earlier works show stylistic *differences* as well. The art historian tends to think of this phenomenon as reflecting an evolution, a *development*.

It is obvious that before one can infer stylistic development it is necessary to be sure that the chronological sequence is correct, that each monument is correctly dated; without this certainty art-historical order and intelligibility are impossible. Thus an indispensable tool of the historian is *chronology*, the measuring scale of historical time; without it there could be no history of style, only a confusion of unclassifiable monuments impossible to describe in any sequence of change.

The table of contents of this book reflects what is essentially a series of periods and subperiods arranged in chronological order, the historical sequence that embraces the sequence of art styles. Until the later eighteenth century the history of art was really a disconnected account of the lives and works of individual artists. Now we regard it as a record of the dynamic change of styles in time, the art of individual masters being substyles of the overall period styles. Although one speaks of "change" in the history of art, the objects themselves obviously do not change; as we have said, they persist, although each will of course suffer some material wear and tear with time. But the fact that works of art from one period look different from those of other periods leads us to infer that *something* changes. This something can only be the points of view of the human makers of works of art with respect to the meaning of life and of art. Modern historiography is much influenced by modern philosophies of change and evolution and, from the terms and data of biological science, our modern history of art was bound to borrow a sense of continuous process to help explain art-historical change.

In art history, as in the sciences and in other historical disciplines, we have gone far in knowing a thing once we have classified it. Art historians, having done this, resemble experienced travelers who learn to discriminate the different "styles" peculiar to different places. Such travelers know that one must not expect the same style of life in the Maine woods as on the Riviera, and when they have seen a great many places and peoples—like art historians who are familiar with a great many monuments—they are not only at ease with them, but can be said to know and appreciate them for what they are. As their experience broadens so does their discrimination, their perception of distinctive differences. As world travelers come to see that the location contributes to the unique quality and charm of a town, so students of art, viewing it in the historical dimension, become convinced that a work's peculiar significance, quality, and charm are a function of the time of its making.

But is not the historical "placing" of a work of art, so visibly and tangibly present, irrelevant to the *appreciation* of it? After all, is not art-historical knowledge *about* a work of art something different from direct experience of it? The answers lie in the fact that uninstructed appreciators, no matter how sincere, will still approach a work with the esthetic presuppositions of their own time rather than those of the time of the work itself. Hence, their presuppositions can be tantamount to prejudices, so that their appreciation, even if genuine, may well be for the wrong reasons; it will, in fact, be undiscerning and indiscriminate, so that dozens of works of art may be viewed in the same way, without any savor of the individual significance and quality of each. Thus, as a work of art is intended for a particular audience at a particular time and place, so may its *purpose* be quite particular, and its purpose necessarily enters into its meaning. For example, the famous *Vladimir Madonna* (FIG. 7-57, p. 252) is a Byzantine-Russian icon, a species of art produced not as a work of "fine art" so much as a sacred object endowed with religio-magical power. It was considered, moreover, the especially holy picture of Russia that miraculously saved the city of Vladimir from the hosts of Tamerlane, the city of Kazan from the later Tartar invasions, and all of Russia from the Poles in the seventeenth century. We may admire it for its innate beauty of line, shape, and color, its expressiveness, and its craftsmanship, but unless we are aware of its special historical function as a wonderworking image we miss the point. We can admire many works of art for their form, content, and quality, but we need a further characterizing experience; otherwise we are admiring very different works without discriminating their decisive differences. We shall be confused and our judgment faulty.

While our most fundamental way of classifying works of art is by the time of their making, classification by *place of origin* is also crucial. In many periods a general style, Gothic for example, will have a great many regional variations: French Gothic architecture is strikingly different from both English and Italian Gothic. Differences of climate helped to make French Gothic an architecture without bearing walls (and with great spaces for stained-glass windows) and Italian Gothic an architecture with large expanses of wall wonderfully suited to mural painting. Art history, then, is also concerned with the spread of a style from its place of origin. Supplementing time of origin with place of origin thus adds another dimension to the picture of art monuments in the process of stylistic development.

The *artist*, of course, provides a third dimension in the history of art. As we have noted, early "histories" of art, written before the advent of modern concepts of style and stylistic development, were simply biographies of artists. Biography as one dimension is still important, for through it we can trace stylistic development within the artists' careers. We can learn much from contemporaneous historical accounts, from documents such as commission contracts, and from the artists' own theoretical writings and literary remains. All of this is of use in "explaining" their works, though of course no complete "explanation" exhausts the meaning of them. Relationships to their predecessors, contemporaries, and followers are describable in terms of the concepts *influence* and *school*: Artists are likely to have been influenced by their masters, and then to have influenced or been influenced by their fellows working somewhat in the same style at the same time and place. We designate a group of such artists as a school, by which we mean not an academy, but a time-place-style classification. Thus we may speak of the Dutch School of the seventeenth century and, within it, of subschools like those of Haarlem, Utrecht, and Leyden.

Iconography

Thus the categories of time and place, the record of the artist, influences, and schools—all are used in composition of the picture of stylistic development. Another kind of classification, another key to works of art, is *iconography*—the study of the subject matter of and symbolism in works of art. By this approach paintings and sculptures are grouped in terms of their themes rather than their styles, and the development of subject matter becomes a major focus of critical study. Iconographical studies have an ancillary function in stylistic analysis since they are often valuable in tracing influences and in assigning dates and places of origin.

Historical Context

Another, very broad, source of knowledge of a work of art lies outside the artistic region itself, yet encloses it and is in transaction with it. This is the *general historical context*—the political, social, economic, scientific, technological, and intellectual background that accompanies and influences the specifically art-historical events. The fall of Rome, the coming of Christianity, and the barbarian invasions all had much to do with stylistic changes in architecture, sculpture, and painting in the early centuries of our era. The triumph of science and technology has everything to do with the great transformation of the Renaissance tradition that takes place in what we call modern art, the art of our own time. The work of art, the persisting event, is after all a historical document.

THE WORK OF ART

The work of art is an object as well as a historical event. To describe and analyze it we use categories and vocabularies that have become more or less standard and that are indispensable for understanding this book.

General Concepts

Form, for the purposes of art history, refers to the shape of whatever is the "object" of art; in the made object it is the shape that the expression of content takes. To create forms, to make a work of art, artists must of course shape materials with tools. Of the many materials, tools, and processes available, each has its own potentialities and limitations, and it is part of the artists' creative activity to select the ones most suitable to their purpose. The technical processes they employ as well as the distinctive, personal way they handle them, we call their *technique.* If the material artists use is the substance of art, technique is their individual manner of giving that substance form. Form, technique, and material are interrelated, as can be readily seen in a comparison of the marble statue of Apollo from Olympia (FIG. 5-36, p. 128) with the bronze *Charioteer* from Delphi (FIG. 5-33, p. 127). The *Apollo* is firmly modeled in broad, generalized planes reflecting the ways of shaping stone that are more or less dictated by the character of that material and by the tool used—the chisel. On the other hand, the *Charioteer*'s fineness of detail, the crisp, sharp folds of the drapery, reflect the qualities inherent in cast metal. However, a given medium (the material used) can lend itself to more than one kind of manipulation. The technique of Lehmbruck's bronze *Seated Youth* (FIG. 1), for example, contrasts strikingly with Rodin's *The Thinker* (FIG. 2), also bronze. The surfaces of Lehmbruck's figure are smooth, flowing, quiet, while those of Rodin's are rough, broken, and tortuous. Here it is not so much the bronze that determines the form as it is the sculptor's difference of purpose and of personal technique.

Space, in our common-sense experience, is the bounded or boundless "container" of masses of objects. For the analysis of works of art we regard it as bounded and susceptible of esthetic and expressive organization. Architecture provides our commonest experience of the actual manipulation of space, while the art of painting frequently has had the purpose of projecting upon a two-dimensional surface an image (or illusion) of the three-dimensional spatial world we move in.

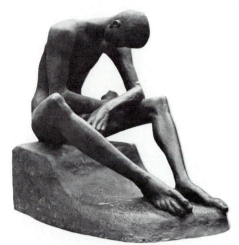

1   WILHELM LEHMBRUCK, *Seated Youth,* 1918. Bronze. Wilhelm-Lehmbruck-Museum, Duisburg.

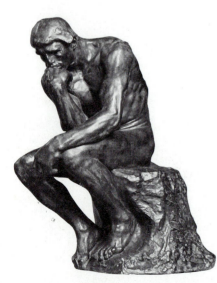

2   AUGUSTE RODIN, *The Thinker,* 1880. Bronze. Metropolitan Museum of Art, New York (gift of Thomas F. Ryan, 1910).

Area and *plane*, terms that describe limited, two-dimensional space, generally refer to surface. A plane is flat, two-dimensional—like this page and like elements dealt with in plane geometry, such as a circle, square, triangle. An area, also describable in terms of plane geometry, is often a plane or flat surface that is enclosed or bounded. Bernini, when he defined the essentially plane surface in front of St. Peter's by means of his curving colonnades, created an area (FIG. 19-3, p. 633).

Mass and *volume*, in contradistinction to plane and area, describe three-dimensional space. In both architecture and sculpture, mass is the bulk, density, and weight of matter in space. Yet the mass need not be solid; it can be the exterior form of enclosed space. For example, "mass" can apply to a pyramid (FIG. 3-7, p. 69), which is essentially solid, or to the exterior of the Hagia Sophia (FIG. 7-38, p. 241), which is essentially a shell enclosing vast spaces. Volume is the space that is organized, divided, or enclosed by mass. It may be the spaces of the interior of a building or the intervals between the masses of a building or between those of a piece of sculpture, ceramics, or furniture. Volume and mass describe the exterior as well as the interior forms of a work of art—the forms of the matter of which it is composed *and* the forms of the spaces that exist immediately around that matter and interact with it. For example, in the Lehmbruck statue (FIG. 1) referred to above, the expressive volumes enclosed by the attenuated masses of the torso and legs play an important part in the open design of the piece. The absence of enclosed volumes in the Rodin figure—equally expressive—closes the design, making it compact, heavy, and locked-in. (Yet both works convey the same mood—one of brooding introversion.) These forms—the closed and the open—manifest through the history of art, demonstrate the intimate connection between mass and the space that surrounds and penetrates it.

In the definition of mass and volume, *line* is one of the most important yet most difficult terms to comprehend fully. In both science and art line can be understood as the path of a point moving in space, the track of a motion. Because the directions of motions can be almost infinite, the quality of line can be incredibly various and subtle. It is well known that psychological responses attach to the direction of a line—a vertical line being positive, a horizontal one passive, a diagonal suggestive of movement, energy, or unbalance, and so on. Hogarth regarded the serpentine or S-curve line as the "line of beauty." Our psychological response to line is also bound up with our esthetic sense of its quality. A line may be very thin, wirelike and delicate, giving a sense of fragility, as in Klee's *Twittering Machine* (FIG. 22-31, p. 833). Or it may alternate quickly from thick to thin, the strokes jagged, the outline broken, as in a 600-year-old Chinese painting (FIG. 12-18, p. 392); the effect is of vigorous action and angry agitation. A gentle, undulating but firm line, like that in Picasso's *Bathers* (FIG. 3), defines a *contour* that is restful and quietly sensuous. A contour continuously and subtly contains and suggests mass and volume. In the Picasso drawing the line is distinct, dark against the white of the paper. But line can be felt as a controlling presence in a hard edge, profile, or boundary created by a contrasting area even when its tone differs only

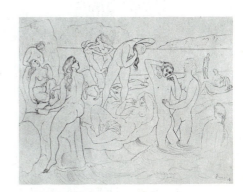

3 PABLO PICASSO, detail of *Bathers*, 1918. Pencil drawing. Fogg Art Museum, Harvard University (bequest of Paul J. Sachs).

slightly from that of the area it bounds. A good example of this is to be seen in the central figure of the goddess in Botticelli's *Birth of Venus* (FIG. 16-61, p. 517).

When a line serves as an element along which forms are organized, it is known as an *axis*. The axis line itself need not be evident, and there may be several (usually with one dominant), as in the layout of a city. Though we are most familiar with directional axes in urban complexes, they occur in all the arts. A fine example of the use of axis in large-scale architecture is the plan of the Palace of Versailles and its magnificent gardens (FIG. 19-70, p. 679). Axis—vertical, horizontal, or diagonal—is also an important compositional element in painting.

Perspective, no less than axis, is a method of organizing forms in space, yet we use perspective mainly in creating an illusion of depth or space on a two-dimensional surface. Conditioned by exposure to Western single-point perspective, an invention of the Italian Renaissance (see pp. 526–56), we tend to see perspective as a systematic ordering of pictorial space in terms of a single point—a point where those lines converge that mark the diminishing size of forms as they recede into the distance (FIG. 17-19, p. 538). Renaissance and Baroque artists created masterpieces of perspective illusionism. In Leonardo's *Last Supper* (FIG. 4), for example, the lines of perspective (dashed lines) are handled so that they converge on Christ and, in the foreground, project the picture space into the room on whose wall the painting appears, creating the illusion that the space of the picture and of the room are continuous. Yet we must remember that Renaissance perspective is only one of several systems for depicting depth. Others were used in ancient Greece and Rome, and still others, in the East. Some of these other systems, as well as Renaissance perspective, continue to be used. There is no final or absolutely correct projection of what we "in fact" see.

4 LEONARDO DA VINCI, *The Last Supper, c.* 1495-98. Fresco. Santa Maria delle Grazie, Milan. Perspective lines are dashed; lines indicating proportions are solid white or black.

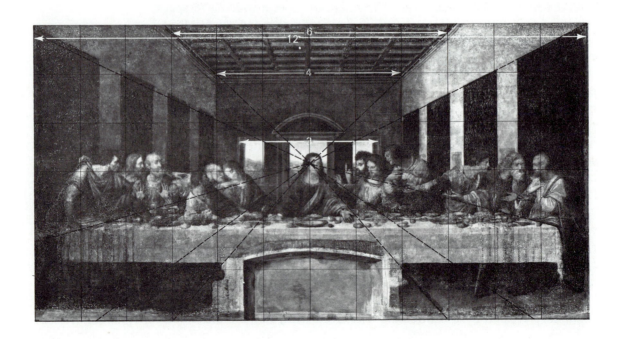

Proportion deals with the relationships (in terms of size) of the parts of a work. The experience of proportion is common to all of us: We seem to recognize at once when the features, say, of the human face or body are "out of proportion," if the nose or ears are too large for the face or the legs too short for the body. An instinctive or conventional sense of proportion leads us at once to regard the disproportionate as ludicrous or ugly. Proportion, formalized, is the mathematical relationship in size of one part of a work of art to the others within the work, as well as to the totality of the parts; it implies the use of a denominator common to the various parts. Recently it has been shown that the major elements of Leonardo's *Last Supper* show proportions found in harmonic ratios in music—12:6:4:3 (FIG. 4). These figures (with the greatest width of a ceiling panel taken as one unit) are the widths, respectively, of the painting, the ceiling (at the front), the rear wall, and the three windows (taken together and including interstices); they apply as well to the vertical organization of the painting. Leonardo found proportion everywhere, "not only in numbers and measures, but also in sounds, weights, intervals of time, and in every active force in existence."[1] The ancient Greeks, who thought beauty to be "correct" proportion, sought a canon (or rule) of proportion, not only in music, but also for the human figure. The famous canon of Polycleitos (p. 138), expressed in his statue of Doryphoros (FIG. 5-54, p. 137), long provided an exemplar of correct proportion. But it should be noted that canons of proportion differ from time to time and culture to culture and that, occasionally, artists have deliberately used disproportion. Part of the task of the students of art history is to perceive and adjust to these differences as they try to understand the wide universe of art forms. Proportional relationships are often based on a *module*, a dimension of which the various parts of a building or other work are fractions or multiples. It might be the diameter of a column, the height of the human body, an abstract unit of measurement. For example, the famous "ideal" plan of the ninth-century monastery of St. Gall (FIG. 8-14, p. 285) has a modular base of $2\frac{1}{2}$ feet, with all parts of the structure multiples or fractions of this dimension.

Scale (like proportion) refers to the dimensional relations of the parts of a work to its totality (or of a work to its setting) but usually in terms of appropriateness to use or function. We do not think a private home need be high as an office building, nor an elephant's house at the zoo the size of a hencoop—or vice versa. This sense of scale is necessary for the construction of form in all the arts. Most often, but not necessarily, it is the human figure that gives the scale to form.

Form, with which we began this list of fundamental concepts, is mediated primarily by *light*. The function of light in the world of nature is so pervasive that we often take it for granted, and there are few who realize the extraordinary variations wrought by light alone—

---

[1] Thomas Brachert, "A Musical Canon of Proportion in Leonardo da Vinci's *Last Supper*," *Art Bulletin*, vol. 53, no. 4 (December 1971), pp. 461–66.

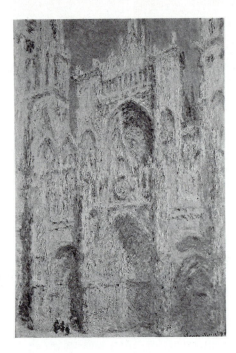
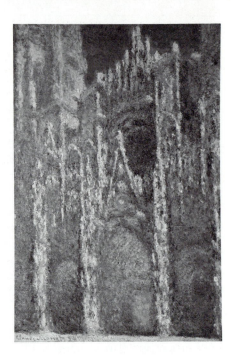

5 CLAUDE MONET, façade of Rouen Cathedral, *c.* 1880. Left, National Gallery of Art, Washington, D.C. (Chester Dale Collection); right, Museum of Fine Arts, Boston (bequest of Hanna Marcy Edwards).

6 Effect of adjacent value on apparent value. Actual value of center bar is constant.

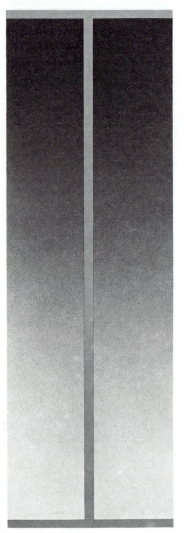

whether natural or artificial—on our most familiar surroundings, as daylight, for example, changes with the hour or season. Few realize fully the extent to which light affects and reveals form. One who did was the French artist Monet (pp. 276-77), who painted the reflections in a waterlily pond according to their seasonal variations, and in a series of more than twenty canvases of the façade of the cathedral of Rouen revealed its changing aspect from dawn until twilight in different seasons (FIG. 21-64 and FIG. 5). Light is as important for the perception of form as is the matter of which form is made.

One function of light is *value.* In painting, and in the graphic arts generally, value refers to lightness, or the amount of light that is (or appears to be) reflected from a surface. Value is a subjective experience, as FIGURE 6 shows. In absolute terms—if measured, say, by a photoelectric device—the center bar in this diagram is uniform in value. Yet where the bar is adjacent to a dark area, it *looks* lighter, and where adjacent to a lighter area, darker. Value is the basis of the quality called *chiaroscuro—chiaro* (light), *scuro* (dark)—which refers to gradations between light and dark that produce the effect of *modeling,* or of light reflected from three-dimensional surfaces, as exemplified in Leonardo's superb rendering of *The Virgin and St. Anne* (FIG. 17-2, p. 528).

In the analysis of light an important distinction must be made for the realm of art: Natural light, or sunlight, is whole or additive light, whereas the painter's light in art—the light reflected from pigments and objects—is subtractive light. Natural light is the sum of all the wavelengths composing the visible spectrum, which may be disassembled or fragmented into the individual colors of the spectral band. (Recent experiments with lasers—*l*ight *a*mplification by *s*timulated *e*mission of *r*adiation—have produced color of incredible brilliance and intensity, opening possibilities of color composition until now not suspected. The range and strength of color produced in this way approach, though at considerable distance, those of the sun.)

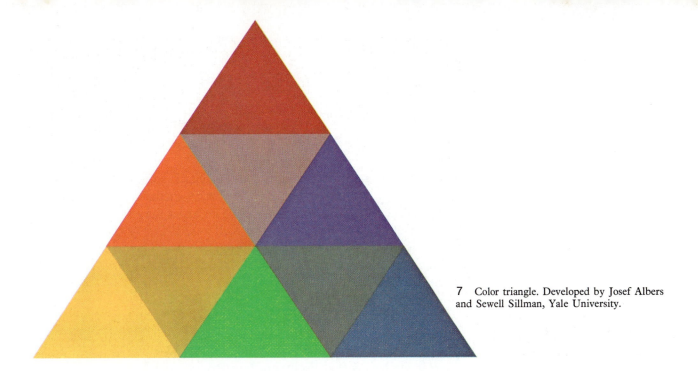

7 Color triangle. Developed by Josef Albers and Sewell Sillman, Yale University.

Although the esthetics of color is largely the province of the artist and can usually be genuinely experienced and understood only through intense practice and experimentation, some aspects are susceptible of analysis and systematization. Paint pigments (as well as those of the human body) produce their individual colors by reflecting a segment of the spectrum while absorbing all the rest. "Green" pigment, for example, subtracts or absorbs all the light in the spectrum except that seen by us as green, which it reflects to the eye. (In the case of transmitted rather than reflected light, the coloring matter—as in stained glass—blocks or screens out all wavelengths of the spectrum but those of the color one sees.) Thus, theoretically, a mixture of pigments that embraced all the colors of the spectrum would subtract all light—that is, it would be black; actually, such a mixture of pigments never produces more than a dark gray. (See the discussion of complementary colors below.)

The name of a color is its *hue*—red, blue, yellow. Although the colors of the spectrum merge into each other, artists usually conceive of their hues as distinct from each other, and this gives rise to many different devices for representing color relationships. There are basically two variables in color—the apparent amount of light reflected and the apparent purity, and a change in one must produce a change in the other. Some terms for these variables are (for lightness) *value* (see above) and *tonality*, and (for purity) *chroma, saturation,* and *intensity.*

One of the more noteworthy diagrams of the relationships of colors is the triangle (FIG. 7), once attributed to Goethe, in which red, yellow, and blue (the *primary colors*) are the vertexes of the triangle, and orange, green, and purple (the *secondary colors,* which result from mixing pairs of primaries) lie between them. Colors that lie opposite each other (such as red and green) are called *complementary,* since they complement, or complete, one another, each absorbing those colors that the other reflects, leaving a neutral, or gray (theoretically, black), when mixed in the right proportions. The inner triangles are products of such mixing.

Color also has a psychological dimension, red and yellow, quite naturally, having connotations of warmth, and blue and green, coolness. Generally, *warm colors* seem to advance, and *cool colors,* to recede.

The quality of a surface—rough, smooth, hard, soft, shiny, dull—as revealed by light is *texture.* The many painting media and techniques permit creation of a variety of textures. The artist may simulate the texture of materials represented, as in Kalf's *Still Life* (FIG. 19-59, p. 671), or create arbitrary surface differences, even using materials other than canvas, as in Picasso's *Still Life with Chair-caning* (FIG. 22-15, p. 819).

Specialized Concepts

The terms we have been discussing have connotations for all the visual arts. Certain observations, however, are relevant to only one category of artistic endeavor—to architecture only, or to painting, or to sculpture.

IN ARCHITECTURE

Works of architecture are so much a part of our environment that we accept them as given, scarcely noticing them until our attention is summoned. People have long known how to enclose space for the many purposes of life. Of all the arts it is in architecture that the spatial aspect is most obvious. The architect makes groupings of enclosed spaces and enclosing masses, keeping always in mind the function of the structure, its construction and materials, and of course its design, the correlative of the other two. We experience architecture both visually and by motion through and around it, so that architectural space and mass are given to our perception together. The articulation of space and mass in building is expressed graphically in several ways; the principal ones follow.

A *plan* is essentially a map of a floor, showing the placement of a structure's masses and, therefore, the spaces they bound and enclose (FIG. 7-41, p. 243). A *section,* like a vertical plan, shows placement of the masses as if the building were cut through along a plane—often one that is a major axis of the building (FIG. 3-8, p. 69). An *elevation* is a head-on view of an external or internal wall, showing its features and often other elements that would be visible beyond or before the wall (FIG. 5-50, p. 135).

Our response to a building can range from simple comfort to astonishment and awe, and such reactions are products of our experience of a building's function, construction, and design. We react differently to a church, a gymnasium, and an office building. For one thing, the very movements required of us in order to experience one building will differ widely and profoundly from those required to experience another. These movements will be controlled by the continuity—or discontinuity—of the plan, or by the placement of its axes. For example, in a central plan—one that radiates from a central point, as in the Pantheon in Rome (FIG. 6-50, p. 192)—we perceive the whole spatial entity at once, while in the long axial plan of a Christian basilica (FIG. 7-25, p. 231) or a Gothic cathedral (FIG. 10-17, p. 326) our attention tends to focus on a given point—the altar at the eastern end of the nave. Mass and space can be so interrelated as to produce effects of great complexity, as, for example, in the Byzantine church of the Katholikon (FIG. 7-45, p. 245) or Le Corbusier's church at Ronchamp (FIG. 22-104, p. 878). Thus, our experience of architecture will be the consequence of a great number of material and formal factors, including training and knowledge and our perceptual and psychological makeup, which function in our experience of any work of art.

The architect must have the sensibilities of a sculptor and of a painter and in establishing the plan of a building must be able, as well, to use the instruments of a mathematician. As architects resolve structural problems they act as—or with—engineers cognizant of the structural principles underlying all architecture (FIG. 8). Their major responsibilities, however, lie in the manner in which they interpret the *program* of the building. We are not talking in architectural terms when we describe a structure simply as a church, a hospital, an airport concourse, a house. Any proposed building presents an architect with problems peculiar to it alone—problems related to the site and its surroundings, the requirements of the client, and the materials available, as well as the function of the building. A program, then, deals with more than function; it addresses itself to all the problems embodied in a specific building.

IN SCULPTURE

Like architecture, sculpture exists in the three-dimensional space of our physical world. But sculpture as image is closer to painting than is architecture. Until recently, sculpture has been primarily concerned with the representation of human and of natural forms in tangible materials, which exist in the same space as the forms they represent. Sculpture may also embody visions and ideals and has consistently presented images of deities and of people in their most heroic as well as most human aspects (FIGS. 17-22, p. 524, and 5-66, p. 145). Today sculpture often dispenses with the figure as image, and even with the image itself, producing new forms in new materials and with new techniques (FIGS. 22-85 to 22-97, pp. 866–73).

Sculpture may be intimately associated with architecture, often to such a degree that it is impossible to disassociate them (FIG. 10-14, p. 325). Sculpture is called *relief* sculpture (FIG. 3-37, p. 87) when it is attached to a back-slab or back plate; *high relief* if the figures or design project boldly (FIG. 5-68, p. 146); *low relief*, or *bas-relief*, if they project slightly (FIG. 3-37, p. 87).

Sculpture that exists in its own right, independent of any particular

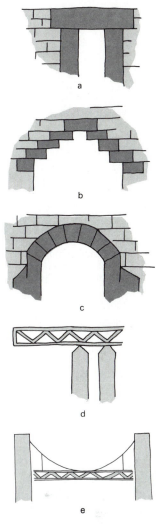

8 Basic structural devices: *a*, post and lintel; *b*, corbeled arch; *c*, arch; *d*, cantilever; *e*, suspension.

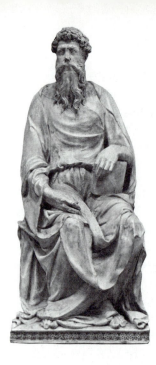

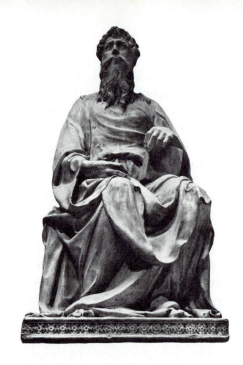

9 DONATELLO, *St. John the Evangelist,* 1412–15. Marble. Museo del Duomo, Florence. Left, as seen in museum; right, as intended to be seen on façade of the cathedral of Florence.

architectural frame or setting (FIG. 17-49, p. 562), is usually referred to as *freestanding* sculpture or "sculpture in the round," although there are many occasions in the art of Greece and of the Renaissance when freestanding sculpture is closely allied to architecture. Indeed, sculpture is such a powerful agent in creating a spatial as well as an intellectual environment that its presence in city squares or in parks and gardens is usually the controlling factor in their "atmosphere" or general effect (FIG. 19-79, p. 684).

Some statues are meant to be seen as a whole—to be walked around (FIG. 17-49, p. 562). Others have been created to be viewed only from a restricted angle. How a sculpture is meant to be seen of course has to be taken into account by the sculptor, and by those who exhibit the work. FIGURE 9 illustrates the effect of ignoring this. The upper photograph is taken directly from the front, as the piece is now seen in the museum, whereas the lower one is taken from below, at approximately the same angle from which the statue was originally meant to be seen in its niche on the façade of the cathedral of Florence.

In sculpture, perhaps more than in any other medium, textures, or tactile values, are important. One's first impulse is almost always to handle a piece of sculpture, to run one's finger over its surfaces. The sculptor plans for this, using a great variety of surfaces from rugged coarseness to polished smoothness (FIGS. 10-51, p. 374, and 16-50, p. 509). Textures, of course, are often intrinsic to a material, and this influences the type of stone, wood, plastic, clay, or metal that the sculptor selects. There are two basic categories of sculptural technique—*subtractive* and *additive.* Carving, for instance, is a subtractive technique, in that the final form is a reduction of the original mass (FIG. 10). Additive sculpture, however, is built up, usually in clay around an armature. The piece so made is fired and used to make a mold in which the final work is cast in a material such as bronze (FIG. 16-52, p. 511). Casting is a popular technique today, as

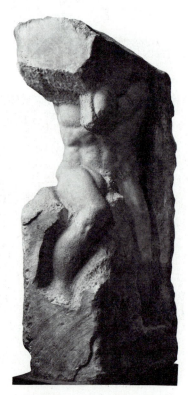

10 MICHELANGELO, *Unfinished Bound Slave,* 1519. Marble. Accademia, Florence.

is direct construction of forms by the welding of shaped metals (FIG. 22-86, p. 867), also an additive technique.

Within the sculptural family must be included ceramics and metalwork, and numerous smaller, related arts, all of which employ very specialized techniques with their own distinct vocabularies. These will be considered as they arise in the text.

IN THE PICTORIAL ARTS

While the forms of architecture and sculpture exist in the actual, three-dimensional space, the forms of painting (and of its relatives, drawing, engraving, etc.) exist almost wholly on a two-dimensional surface on which the artist creates an illusion—something that replicates what we see around us or something that is unique to the artist's imagination and that has little correspondence to anything seen in the optical world. Human discovery of the power to project illusions of the three-dimensional world upon two-dimensional surfaces goes back thousands of years and marks an enormous step in the control and manipulation of things perceived. To achieve this illusion the artist configures images or representations drawn from the world of common visual experience. Throughout the history of art this has been interpreted in almost infinite variety; yet doubtless there is much that all people *see* in common and can agree on: the moon at night, a flying bird, an obstacle in one's path. They may differ, though, in their interpretation of the seen; for seeing, and then representing what is seen, are very different matters. The difference between seeing and representing determines the variability of artistic styles, both cultural and personal. For what we *actually* see—that is, the optical "fact"—is not necessarily reported in what we represent. In other words, for art there is and need be but little agreement about the likeness of things to the representations of them. This makes a persisting problem in the history of art: How are we to interpret or "read" images or replicas of the seen? Is there a "correct" vision of the "real" world?

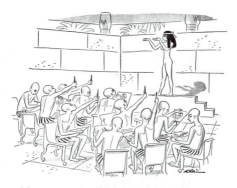

11 ALAIN, drawing. Copyright 1955 by The New Yorker Magazine, Inc.

THE PROBLEM OF REPRESENTATION

The conundrum of seeing something and making a representation of it is artfully illustrated in FIGURE 11, a cartoon of an ancient Egyptian life-drawing class that Gombrich uses to introduce his invaluable work *Art and Illusion*. The cartoon and the actual representation of an Egyptian queen (FIG. 12) raise many questions: Did Egyptian artists copy models exactly as they saw them? (That is, did Egyptians actually *see* each other in this way?) Or did they translate what they saw according to some formula dictated by conventions of representation peculiar to their culture? Would we have to say—if what was seen and what was recorded were optically the same—that is the way Egyptians must have looked? Or wished to look? Beginning students usually have questions somewhat like these in mind when they perceive deviation, in historical styles, from the recent Western realism to which they

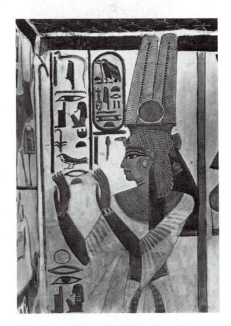

12 *Queen Nofretari*, from her tomb at Thebes, *c.* 1250 B.C. Detail of a painted bas-relief.

15

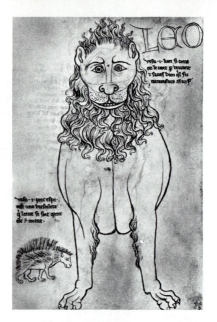

13 VILLARD DE HONNECOURT, *Lion Portrayed from Life*, c. 1230–35. Drawing. Cabinet des Manuscripts, Bibliothèque Nationale, Paris.

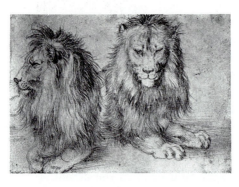

14 ALBRECHT DÜRER, *Two Lions*, c. 1521. Drawing. Staatliche Museen Preussischer Kulturbesitz, Kupferstichkabinet Berlin.

have been conditioned. They will ask whether the Egyptians or others were simply unskilled at matching eye and hand, so to speak, and could not draw from what they saw. But this would be to presuppose that the objective of the artist has always been to match appearances with cameralike exactitude. This is not the case, nor is it the case that artists of one period "see" more "correctly" and render more "skillfully" than those of another. It seems rather to be the case that artists represent what they *conceive* to be real rather than what they *perceive*. They bring to the making of images conceptions that have been instilled in them by their cultures. They understand the visible world in certain unconscious, culturally agreed-upon ways, and thus bring to the artistic process ideas and meanings out of a common stock. They record not so much what they *see* as what they *know* or *mean*. Even in the period of dominant realism in recent Western European art, great deviations from camera realism have set in. Moreover, in our everyday life there are images familiar to all of us that distort optical "reality" quite radically; consider, for one example, those of the ubiquitous comic strip.

Solutions to the problem of representation compose the history of artistic style. It is useful to examine some specimens of sharp divergence in representational approach. Compare, for example, the lion drawn by the medieval artist Villard de Honnecourt (FIG. 13) and lions drawn by the Renaissance artist Albrecht Dürer (FIG. 14). In the de Honnecourt lion, which, it is important to notice, the artist asserts was drawn from life, we have a figure entirely adequate for identification, yet preconceived in the formulas of its time and constructed accordingly. Dürer's lions, drawn some three centuries later, obviously make a much different report of what the artist is seeing or has seen. So do the Assyrian lions of the hunting reliefs (FIG. 2-29, p. 54), the lion of the Ishtar Gate processional way (FIG. 2-30, p. 55), the lion in Rousseau le Douanier's *Sleeping Gypsy* (FIG. 21-85, p. 795), or (in a slight shift of species) Barye's sculpture of a jaguar in his *Jaguar Devouring a Hare* (FIG. 21-8, p. 730). In each case personal vision joins with the artistic conventions of time and place to decide the manner and effect of the representation. Yet even at the same time and place—for example, nineteenth-century Paris—we can find sharp differences in representation where opposing personal styles, those of Ingres and Delacroix, are recording the same subject (FIGS. 21-26 and 21-27, p. 744).

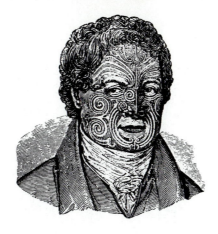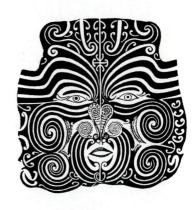

15 *The Maori Chief Tupai Kupa, c.* 1800.
Left, after a drawing by John Sylvester;
right, a self-portrait. From
The Childhood of Man by Leo
Frobenius, 1909. Reproduced by
permission of J. B. Lippincott
Company.

A final example will underscore the relativity of vision and representation that differences in human cultures produce. We recognize, moreover, that close matching of appearances has mattered only in a few times and places. Although both portraits (FIG. 15) of a Maori chieftain, one by a European, the other by the chieftain himself, reproduce his facial tatooing, the first portrait is a simple commonplace likeness that underplays the tatooing. The latter is a statement by the chieftain of the supreme importance of the design that symbolizes his rank among his people. It is the splendidly composed insignia that is his image of himself, the European likeness being superficial and irrelevant to him.

Students of the history of art, then, learn to distinguish the works before them by scrutinizing them closely in the context of their time and place of origin. But this is only the beginning. The causes of stylistic change in time are mysterious and innumerable; and it is only through the continuing process of art-historical research that we can hope to make the picture even fragmentarily recognizable, never complete. Incomplete though the picture is, the panorama of art, changing in time, lies before the students; and, as their art-historical perspective gains depth and focus, they will come to perceive the continuity of the art of the past with that of the present. It will become clear that one cannot be understood without the other, and that our understanding of the one will constantly change with changes in our understanding of the other. The great American poet and critic T. S. Eliot has cogently expressed this truth for all of art in a passage that suggests the philosophy and method of this book:

> . . . what happens when a new work of art is created is something that happens simultaneously to all the works of art which preceded it. The existing monuments form an ideal order among themselves, which is modified by the introduction of the new (the really new) work of art among them. . . . Whoever has approved this idea of order . . . will not find it preposterous that the past should be altered by the present as much as the present is directed by the past.[2]

[2] "Tradition and the Individual Talent" in *Selected Essays 1917–1932*, by T. S. Eliot (New York: Harcourt Brace Jovanovich, 1932), p. 5.

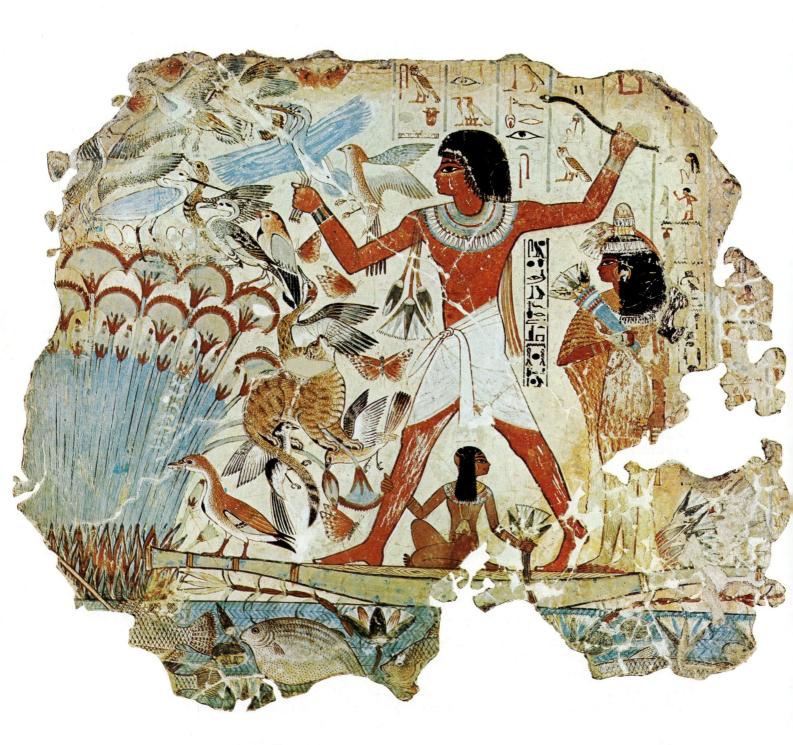

Wall painting from the
tomb of Nebamun(?),
Thebes, *c.* 1450 B.C.

part one
The Ancient World

The Christian civilizations of the Western world early distinguished an ancient past from a new age—the times, respectively, before and after Christ. For them the ancient world—the world of the Old Testament—had the character of a preparation; it was related to the new era as promise to fulfillment. This slightly condescending view toward antiquity changed during the Renaissance, when scholars and artists deeply admired especially the Greek and Roman past and often debated the question of which was superior, the "ancient" or the "modern." Interest in Greco-Roman antiquity was broadened later to take in the great civilizations that had preceded it—those of the pre-Greek Mediterranean, Egypt, the Near East, and the very remote, prehistoric cave cultures of western Europe.

From the end of the eighteenth century to the present, archeologists and art historians, with ever improving methods of investigation, have recovered great tracts of forgotten history to fill out with increasing accuracy our picture of the distant past. Within the past three decades evidence has been brought forward of the existence of civilizations that flourished as early as 7000 B.C., and the sequence of development that viewed early Egypt and Mesopotamia as having concurrent existence has been shown to be incorrect, Mesopotamia, in fact, having preceded Egypt by many centuries.

Historical perspective is likely to produce a distortion of view akin to that of the early Christian depreciation of the pre-Christian world. Until we have become familiar with the ancient world, it seems to us simply *that*—ancient, exceedingly old—and we imagine it in terms and images of faded inscriptions, dusty ruins, fallen idols, and long-outdated institutions. More properly we should see *ourselves* as ancient—that is, as living in the later eras of a great epoch at whose beginning, thousands of years ago, some of our most fundamental beliefs, institutions, folkways, and art and science had their inception.

The precarious, furtive life of the cave-dwelling hunter and later nomadic herdsman was, with the development of agriculture and the widespread domestication of animals, succeeded by the more sedentary, predictable, and ordered life of village farmers. Aside from the technological revolutions of our times, this leap from food-gathering to food production brought perhaps the most significant transformation of the human condition and made possible all that has followed. In Mesopotamia, Asia Minor, and Egypt more complex forms of human community were created—cities, city-states, and kingdoms. Formal religion and codes of law were developed to regulate the relationships among men and between gods and men. Writing was invented, as well as numbers and the art of calculation. The courses of the stars were plotted in order to predict the seasons and the times for planting and harvesting. Architecture, sculpture, and painting flourished in the service of kingly magnificence. The sacred books of Judaism and Christianity were produced in the shadow of mighty and hostile empires, and the legacy of Israel, which has contributed so much to the formation of the Western spirit, was preserved through all the vicissitudes of a remarkable people.

It was with the Greeks that there emerged what might be called the specifically Western intelligence, with its respect for reason, scientific inquiry, the physical concept of nature, and the humanistic view of man. The city-states of Greece were more than seats of commerce and government, and the loyalties of the citizens of each had social, educative, and local religious bases as well. It was in some of these city-states—Athens in particular—that democracy, though in a limited form, first evolved. Thus, about twenty-five hundred years ago, Athens had a government that was largely in the hands of a council of citizens, who were chosen by lot, and a kind of legislative assembly composed of all citizens—though citizenship did not extend to women or to the slaves who made up nearly half the population.

With the repulse of the Persian invaders in the fifth century B.C., the Greeks inaugurated the first authentic phase of European culture, the content and spirit of which, commingled with Hebraism, is still largely with us in our patterns of life and thought.

Rome, never matching the Greek achievement in intellectual and artistic culture, yet produced the greatest empire of the ancient world. In a period of eight hundred years it passed from its beginnings as a trading center under Etruscan kings to the zenith of its empire, when it extended from what are now the borders of Scotland to Jordan and to the far shores of the Black Sea, asserting its hegemony over a multitude of peoples and lands. The dynamic and aggressive Roman spirit was reflected in and supported by an astonishing military machine and technology, although Roman control over diverse peoples was exercised as much by the encouragement of their participation in the empire as in the naked assertion of Roman power. The Romanization of western Europe—through the Roman genius for government and the "Roman Peace"—has still much to do with the character of Europe, and the Roman ideal of a single, peaceful community of all mankind is very much in our view today.

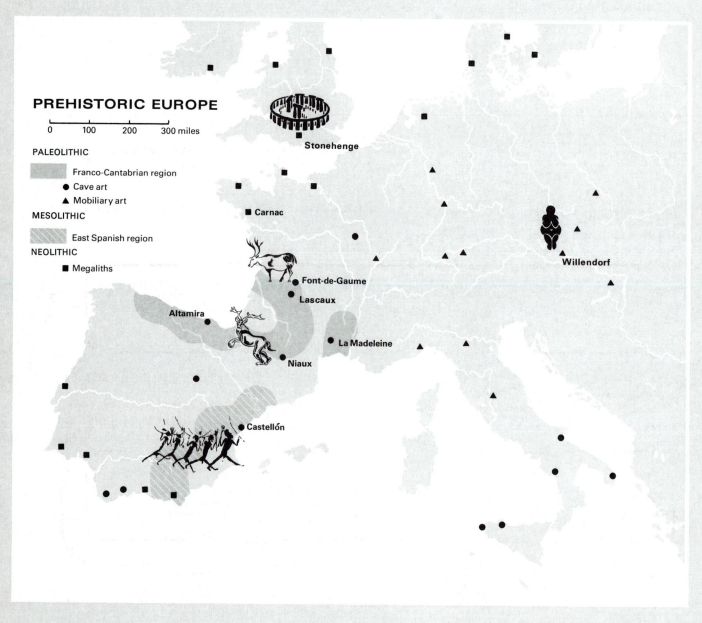

PREHISTORIC EUROPE

0   100   200   300 miles

PALEOLITHIC

Franco-Cantabrian region

● Cave art

▲ Mobiliary art

MESOLITHIC

East Spanish region

NEOLITHIC

■ Megaliths

Stonehenge

Carnac

Font-de-Gaume

Lascaux

Altamira

La Madeleine

Niaux

Castellón

Willendorf

chapter one

22

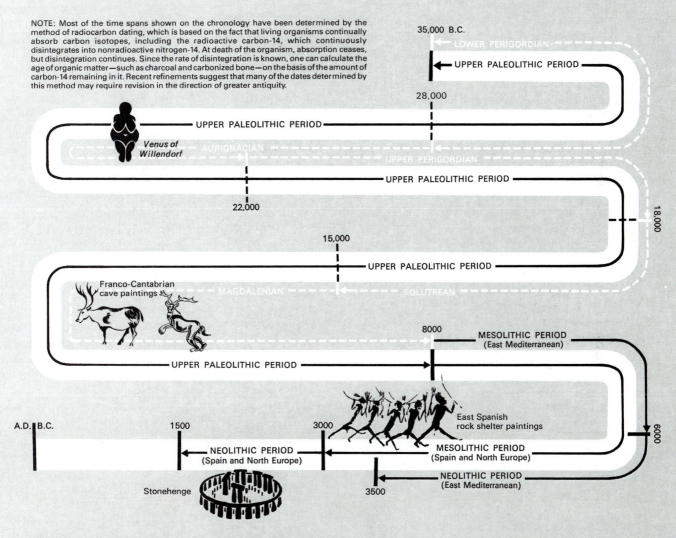

NOTE: Most of the time spans shown on the chronology have been determined by the method of radiocarbon dating, which is based on the fact that living organisms continually absorb carbon isotopes, including the radioactive carbon-14, which continuously disintegrates into nonradioactive nitrogen-14. At death of the organism, absorption ceases, but disintegration continues. Since the rate of disintegration is known, one can calculate the age of organic matter—such as charcoal and carbonized bone—on the basis of the amount of carbon-14 remaining in it. Recent refinements suggest that many of the dates determined by this method may require revision in the direction of greater antiquity.

35,000 B.C.

LOWER PERIGORDIAN

UPPER PALEOLITHIC PERIOD

28,000

UPPER PALEOLITHIC PERIOD

Venus of Willendorf

AURIGNACIAN

UPPER PERIGORDIAN

UPPER PALEOLITHIC PERIOD

22,000

18,000

15,000

UPPER PALEOLITHIC PERIOD

Franco-Cantabrian cave paintings

MAGDALENIAN

SOLUTREAN

8000

MESOLITHIC PERIOD (East Mediterranean)

UPPER PALEOLITHIC PERIOD

East Spanish rock shelter paintings

A.D. B.C.

1500

3000

6000

NEOLITHIC PERIOD (Spain and North Europe)

MESOLITHIC PERIOD (Spain and North Europe)

Stonehenge

NEOLITHIC PERIOD (East Mediterranean)

3500

The Birth of Art

HAT GENESIS is to the biblical account of the fall and redemption of man, early cave art is to the history of his intelligence, imagination, and creative power. In the caves of southern France and of northern Spain, discovered only about a century ago and still being explored, we may witness the birth of that characteristically human capability that has made man master of his environment—the making of images and symbols. By this original and tremendous feat of abstraction upper Paleolithic men were able to fix the world of their experience, rendering the continuous processes of life in discrete and unmoving shapes that had identity and meaning as the living animals that were their prey. Like Adam, Paleolithic man gathered and named the animals, and the faculty of imagination came into being along with the concepts of identity and meaning.

In that remote time during the last advance and retreat of the great glaciers man made the critical breakthrough and became wholly human. Our intellectual and imaginative processes function through the recognition and construction of images and symbols; we see and understand the world pretty much as we are taught to by the representations of it familiar to our time and place. The immense achievement of Stone Age man, the invention of representation, cannot be exaggerated.

THE LATER OLD STONE AGE (UPPER PALEOLITHIC)

The physical environment of the cave peoples during the long thousands of years would not, one imagines, be favorable to the creation of an art of quality and sophistica-tion since survival alone would seem to have required most of their energies. Though the Aurignacian period began between the early and main advances of the last glaciers and for a while was temperate, it grew cold toward its end. The great ice sheet advanced south from Scandinavia over the plains of north central Europe, and glaciers spread down from the Alps and other mountain ranges to produce a tundra and forest-tundra climate. With the end of the Magdalenian period began the final recession of the ice and the onset of temperate weather. In the cold periods, man, the hunter and food-gatherer, took refuge in caves, and it was here that Cro-Magnon man, who first appeared during the Aurignacian period, replacing Neanderthal man, took the remarkable turn that made him not simply a fabricator of stone tools, but an artist.

Cave Art

The first example of cave art was discovered—by amateurs and by accident—in 1879 near Santander in northern Spain. Marcelino de Sautuola, a local resident interested in the antiquity of man, was exploring the Altamira Caves on his estate, in which he had already found specimens of flint and carved bone. With him was his little daughter. Since the ceiling of the debris-filled cavern was only a few inches above the father's head, it was the child who was first able to discern, from her lower vantage point, the shadowy forms of painted beasts on the cave roof. De Sautuola was the first modern man to explore this cave and he was certain that these paintings dated back to prehistoric times. Archeologists, however, were highly dubious of their authenticity, and at the Lisbon Congress on Prehistoric Archeology in 1880 the Altamira paintings were officially dismissed as forgeries. But in 1896, at Pair-non-Pair in the

1-1 *Hall of Bulls,* left wall, Lascaux, c. 15,000–13,000 B.C. Dordogne, France.

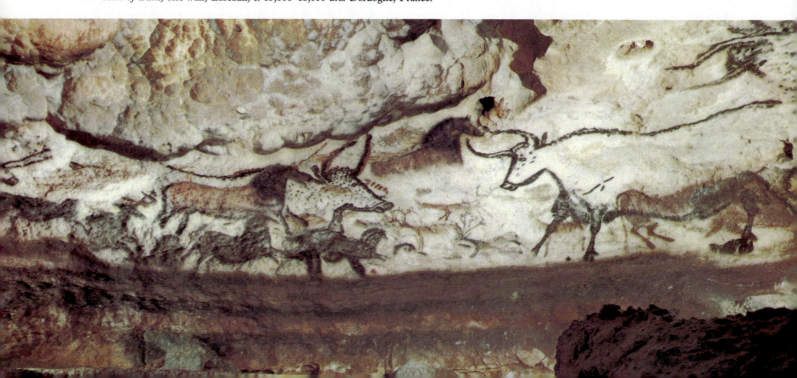

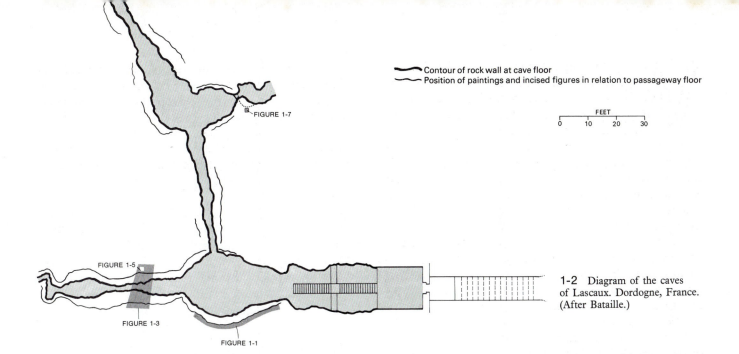

Contour of rock wall at cave floor
Position of paintings and incised figures in relation to passageway floor

FEET
0   10   20   30

FIGURE 1-7

FIGURE 1-5

FIGURE 1-3

FIGURE 1-1

1-2 Diagram of the caves of Lascaux. Dordogne, France. (After Bataille.)

Gironde district of France, paintings were discovered partially covered by calcareous deposits that would have taken thousands of years to accumulate; these paintings were the first to be recognized as authentic by experts. The conviction grew that these remarkable works were of an antiquity far greater than man had ever dreamed. In 1901 Abbé Breuil, dean of archeologists of the prehistoric, discovered and verified the cave art of Font-de-Gaume in Dordogne, France. The skeptics were finally convinced.

The caves at Lascaux, near Montignac, also in the Dordogne region of France, were discovered accidentally in 1940 by two young boys who were playing in a field. Their dog, following a ball, disappeared into a hole, and the boys, hearing barking from below, followed the animal down into the caves. Their lighted matches revealed magnificent drawings of animals, now generally regarded as the most outstanding of all known prehistoric art (FIG. 1-1).

While these paintings survived more than 15,000 years in the sealed and dry subterranean chambers, many have deteriorated rapidly since the caves were opened to the public in recent decades. At Lascaux, for example, it was found that moisture and carbon dioxide exhaled by hordes of visitors settled on the walls and encouraged the growth of fungi destructive to the paintings. To avoid further damage, the cave has been closed to the public.

The Lascaux caverns (FIG. 1-2), like the others, had been subterranean water channels, a few hundred to some four thousand feet long. They are often choked, sometimes almost impassably, by faults or by deposits such as stalactites and stalagmites. Far inside these caverns, well removed from the cave mouths that he chose for habitation, the hunter-artist engraved and painted on the walls pictures of animals—mammoth, bison, reindeer, horse, boar, wolf. For light he must have used tiny stone lamps filled with marrow or fat, with a wick, perhaps of moss. For drawing he used chunks of red and yellow ocher, and for painting he ground these same ochers into powder that he blew onto the walls or mixed with some medium, perhaps animal fat, before applying. A large flat bone may have served him as a palette; he could make brushes from reeds or bristles; he could use a blowpipe of reeds to trace outlines of figures and to put pigments on out-of-reach surfaces; and he had stone scrapers for smoothing the wall and sharp flint points for engraving. Such were the artist's tools. Rudimentary as they were, they were sufficient to produce the art that astonishes us today.

The artist's approach to the figures, as seen at Lascaux and at other sites, is naturalistic; he attempts to represent as convincing a pose and action as possible. Each painting reflects the keen observation and extraordinary memory of the hunter-artist, whose accuracy in capturing fleeting poses is hardly surpassed by today's camera (FIGS. 1-1 and 1-5). Yet this observation was selective, the artist seeing and recording only those aspects essential in interpreting the appearance and the character of the animal—its grace or awkwardness, its cunning, dignity, or ferocity. It is almost as if the artist were constructing a pictorial definition of the animal, capturing its very essence.

Any modern interpretation of this cave art must, of course, remain pure speculation. Properties common to all these paintings, however, provide researchers with some fairly definite clues to what they meant to their creators. For instance, the fact that the paintings are never found in those parts of the caves that were inhabited or near daylight rules out any purely decorative purpose. At Font-de-Gaume the first paintings were encountered about seventy yards behind the cave mouth, and in the cave at Niaux the painted animals in the "Salon Noir" are found some 850 tortuous yards from the entrance. The remoteness and difficulty of access of many of these sites and the fact that they appear to have been used for centuries strongly suggest that the prehistoric hunter attributed magical properties to them. And so the paintings themselves most likely had magical meaning to their creators. As Abbé Breuil has suggested, "by confining the animal within the limits of a painting, one subjected it to one's power in the hunting grounds." And, within this context, the artist's aim to be realistic may be explained by his probable conviction that the painting's magical power was directly related to its lifelikeness.

The naturalistic pictures of animals are often accompanied by geometric signs, some of which seem to represent man-made structures, or *tectiforms* (FIG. 1-3), while others consist of checkers, dots, squares, or other arrangements of lines. Several observers have seen a primitive form of writing in these representations of nonliving things, but more likely they, too, had only magical significance. The ones that look like traps or snares, for example, may have been drawn to ensure success in hunting with these devices. In many places there appear representations of human hands, most of them "negative," where the hunter placed his hand against the wall and then painted or blew pigment around it (FIG. 1-4). Occasionally he would dip his hand in paint and then press it against the wall, leaving a "positive" imprint. These, too, may have had magical significance, or may simply have been the "signatures" left by whole generations of visitors to these sacred places, much as the modern tourist leaves some memento of his presence.

The figures are in themselves marvelous approximations of optical fact, but their arrangement upon the cave walls shows little concern for any consistency of placement in

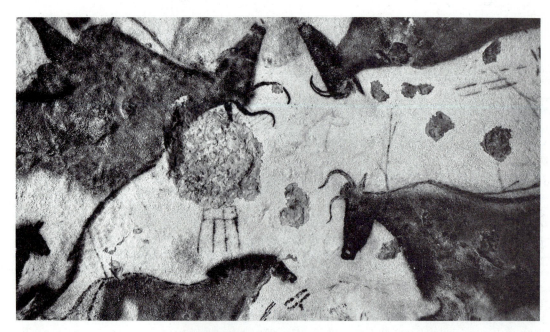

1-3 *Three Cows and One Horse,* ceiling of the Axial Gallery, Lascaux, *c.* 15,000–13,000 B.C. Approx. life-size. Dordogne, France.

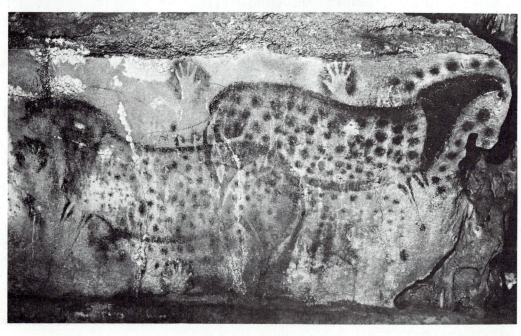

1-4 *Spotted Horses and Negative Hand Imprints,* Pech-Merle, *c.* 15,000–13,000 B.C. 11′ 2″ long. Lot, France.

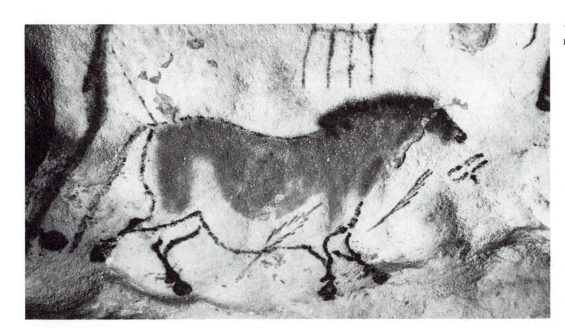

relationship to each other or to the wall space, though this has been claimed. Certainly we find no compositional adjustment to suggest the perspective effect and no notion of separation and enframement. Figures, far from being proportionally related, are often superimposed at random and are of quite different sizes (FIG. 1-1). Generations of artists, working in the same sanctuaries, covered and recovered the crowded walls, though often pains seem to have been taken not to break through the outlines of an earlier figure. It seems that attention to a single figure, the rendering of a single image, in itself fulfilled the purpose of the artist.

The hunter-artist made frequent and skillful use of the naturally irregular surfaces of the walls, of their projections, recessions, fissures, and ridges, to help give the illusion of real presence to his forms. A swelling outward of the wall could be used within the outline of a charging bison to suggest the bulging volume of the beast's body. The spotted horse at Pech-Merle (FIG. 1-4) may have been inspired by a rock formation that resembles a horse's head and neck (on the right of the figure), although the artist's eventual version of the head is much smaller than the formation and highly abstract. Natural forms like those of foliage or clouds, the profile of a mountain, or the shapes of eroded earth and rock can represent for any of us— sometimes quite startlingly—the features of men, animals, or objects. Thus man's first representations may have followed some primal experience of resemblance between a chance configuration of cave wall and the animal he had just been hunting. This might have had for him the effect of an awesome apparition of the very animal, a miraculous and magical reappearance of its vanished life. With the impulse to give the apparition even more presence he could have "finished" the form by cutting an outline

around the relief and continuing it until a silhouette more or less complete and familiar had emerged. The addition of color would enhance the reality of the image.

THE MAGICAL FUNCTION

We have evidence that the hunters in the caves, perhaps in a frenzy stimulated by magical rites and dances, treated the painted animals as if they were alive. Not only was the quarry painted as pierced by arrows, as in the *Chinese Horse* at Lascaux (FIG. 1-5), but hunters may have thrown spears at the images—as sharp gouges in the side of the bison at Niaux (FIG. 1-6) suggest—predestinating and

1-6 *Bison with Superposed Arrows,* Niaux, c. 15,000–13,000 B.C. 50" long. Ariège, France.

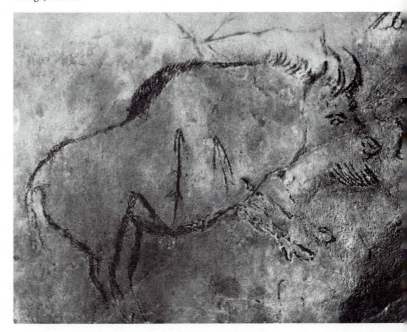

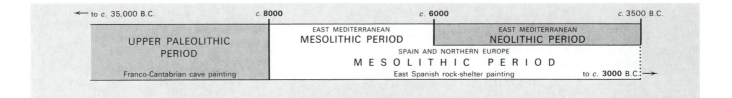

← to c. 35,000 B.C.   c. 8000   c. 6000   c. 3500 B.C.

UPPER PALEOLITHIC
PERIOD

EAST MEDITERRANEAN
MESOLITHIC PERIOD

EAST MEDITERRANEAN
NEOLITHIC PERIOD

SPAIN AND NORTHERN EUROPE
M E S O L I T H I C   P E R I O D

Franco-Cantabrian cave painting   East Spanish rock-shelter painting   to c. 3000 B.C. →

magically commanding the death of the animals. This practice would be analogous to that kind of magic, still cultivated in parts of the world today, that has as a basis the belief that harm can be done to an enemy by abusing an image of him.

This art produced in dark caverns deep in the earth must have had, as most scholars are now convinced, some profound magical functions. Familiar in religious architecture, which had its beginning thousands of years after the era of the caves, are the cavelike spaces of the sanctuary where the most sacred and hidden mysteries are kept and where the god dwells in silence. The sacred has meant the mysterious, and this means in many cases a place of darkness, lit only by fitful light, where, at the culmination of rituals, absolute silence reigns. These features of the sacred environment were already present in the "architecture" of the caves, and the central theme has never been lost despite its myriad variations.

It is significant that the miracle of abstraction—the creation of image and symbol—should have taken place in just such secret and magical caverns. For abstraction is representation, a human device of fundamental power, by which not only art but ultimately science comes into existence, and both art and science are methods for the control of human experience and the mastery of the environment. And that too was the end purpose of the hunter-magician—to control the world of the beasts he hunted. The making of the image was, by itself, a form of magic; by painting an animal, the hunter fixed and controlled its soul within the prison of an outline, and from this initial magic all the rest must follow. Rites before the paintings may have served to improve the hunter's luck. At the same time, prehistoric man must have been anxious to preserve his food supply, and the many representations of pregnant animals (FIG. 1-5) suggest that these cavalcades of painted beasts may also have served magically to assure the survival of the actual herds.

THE REPRESENTATION OF MAN

The figure of man is almost completely excluded from representation among the vivid troops of painted animals. There are at least two notable exceptions. A very puzzling picture at Lascaux (FIG. 1-7) shows a stick-figure man, falling or fallen, before a huge bison that has been disemboweled, probably by the rhinoceros at the left, which slouches away from the scene. The two animals are rendered with all that skilled attention to animal detail we are accustomed to in cave art; the rhinoceros heavy and lumbering, the buffalo tense and bristling with rage, its bowels hanging from it in a heavy coil. But the birdfaced (masked?) man is rendered with the crude and clumsy touch of the unskilled at any time or place. His position is ambiguous. Is he dead or in an ecstatic trance? The meaning of the bird on the staff and of the spear and throw stick is no more obvious. We shall not add here to the already abundant speculation on the meaning of this picture. More important is the question, Why the difference in treatment of the man and the animal figures? Does man in this dawn of magic distinguish himself so much from the beast that he can find no image suitable to self-depiction? Or is he afraid to cast a spell on himself, as he casts it upon the animals, by rendering his image visible?

At Trois Frères in the Pyrenees there is a very strange humanoid creature, masked and wearing the antlers of a reindeer (FIG. 1-8)—the so-called *Sorcerer*. Is this the memory sketch of a shaman or witch-doctor? If so, one can imagine how the fearsome composite apparition—the paws of a bear, tail of a wolf, beard of a man, corporal parts of a lion—could have struck terror into the heart of its audience. The chamber in which the figure appears is crowded with beasts, and Breuil has suggested that the figure may be their god, who has descended into the witch-doctor and filled him with his bestial power. It has also been suggested that this is only a hunter camouflaged to stalk deer, but it would again appear that, for Paleolithic man, mankind simply is not to be counted among the animals; at least his figure must be so disguised—perhaps to avoid magical self-involvement—as to be unrecognizable as a man.

QUALITY

In explaining the great accomplishment of Stone Age man—who pictured the world in order to magically control it—we must not forget that his art is *art*. It is not simply that he made images but that he made them skillfully and beautifully. Ancient and modern art have produced, along with masterpieces, images that are dull, prosaic, and of indifferent quality. The art of the caves is of an extraordinary level of quality. The splendid horse in the Axial Gallery at Lascaux (FIG. 1-5) has been called the *Chinese Horse* because its style strangely resembles that of

Chinese painting of the best period. Not only do the outlines have the elastic strength and fluency that we find in Chinese calligraphy and brushwork, but the tone is so managed as to suggest both the turning under of the belly of the pregnant animal and the change of the color of the coat. At Font-de-Gaume there is a painted reindeer (FIG. 1-9) executed with deft elegance in the contours and remarkable subtlety in the modeling tones. The grace of the antlers is effortlessly translated into an upward-sweeping line that renders the natural shapes with both strength and delicacy. Breuil, while copying the originals, discerned some highly sophisticated pictorial devices that one expects to find only in the art of far later times; for example, the darkening of the forward contour of the left hind leg so as to bring it nearer to the observer than the right leg.

The pictures of cattle at Lascaux and elsewhere (FIG. 1-3) show a convention of representation of the horns that has been called *twisted perspective*, since we see the heads

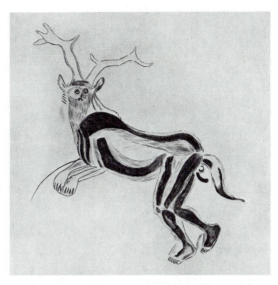

1-8 *Sorcerer*, Trois-Frères, *c.* 13,000–11,000 B.C. 24″ high. Ariège, France.

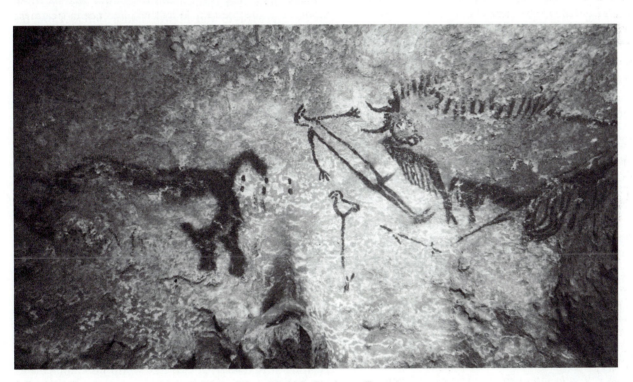

1-7 *Well Scene*, Lascaux, *c.* 15,000–13,000 B.C. Bison 55″ high. Dordogne, France.

in profile but the horns from a different angle. Thus, the approach of the artist is not strictly or consistently optical—that is, organized from a fixed-viewpoint perspective. Rather, the approach is descriptive of the fact that cattle have two horns. Two horns would be part of the concepts "cow" and "bull." In strict optical-perspective profile only one horn would be visible, but to paint the animal in such a way would, as it were, amount to an incomplete definition of it. And for the cave artist this would have been a

defective image, without magic. When we discuss the art of the ancient Near East and Egypt, we shall note again this peculiarity and its significance.

Engravings and Sculpture

The principal bequests of the hunter-artists that can be regarded as fine art are their paintings. However, they have also left us splendid engravings—on stone, ivory, bone,

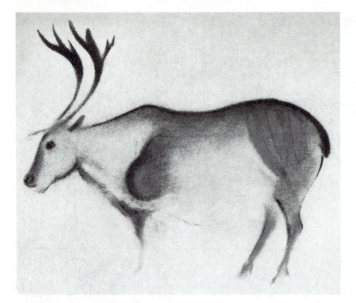

are eroded by weather, we can perceive their characteristics well enough. They are not simply "filled-out" natural rock contours but in parts strongly modeled. The eyes are sharply incised, and, as in the case of the bison incised in reindeer horn (FIG. 1-10), the manes, forelocks, and portions of the head and muzzle have been carefully indicated by hatching.

There are small sculptures in the full round representing the female figure (formerly called Venus figures by archeologists), an exception to the rule of exclusion of the human figure from the cave artist's vocabulary of forms. Perhaps the most famous of these is the *Venus of Willendorf* (FIG. 1-12), a figurine of a woman that is composed of a cluster of almost ball-like shapes. The anatomical exaggeration suggests that this and similar statuettes served as fertility fetishes; the needs for game and human offspring were one in the dangerous life of the hunter. But again the artist's approach to the human figure differs from his approach to animals. He obviously does not aim for that heightened realism so characteristic of his animal representations; facial features, for instance, are seldom indicated in these statuettes, and in some specimens not even the heads are shown. Evidently the artist's aim was not to show the female of his kind but rather the idea of female fecundity; he depicted not woman but fertility.

THE MIDDLE STONE AGE (MESOLITHIC)

Rock-shelter Paintings

As the ice of the Paleolithic period melted in the increasing warmth, the reindeer migrated north, the wooly mammoth and rhinoceros disappeared, and the hunters left their caves. The Ice Age gave way to a transition period known as the Mesolithic, when Europe became climatically, geographically, and biologically much as it is today. During this time there flourished a culture whose art complements that of the caves, from which, indeed, it may partially have originated. Since 1903, diminutive, extraordinarily lively paintings of animals and men in scenes of the hunt, battle, ritual dance, and harvest have been discovered on the stone walls of shallow rock shelters among the barren hills of the eastern coast of Spain (the Spanish Levant). The artists show the same masterful skill in depicting the animal figure as their predecessors of the caves, and it may be that we have here specimens of a lingering tradition or long-persisting habit of vision and representation of animals. But what is strikingly new is the appearance of the human figure, not only singly, but in large, coherent groups, with

and antler, on both flat and curving surfaces—and sculpture. In the *Bison with Turned Head* (FIG. 1-10) we are impressed by the striking vitality and the simplicity with which the formal beauty is expressed—a simplicity and economy of means that distinguishes the great paintings. The head is so turned that it is entirely framed by the massive bulk of the body, and there is a vivid play of curve and countercurve and a surface contrast obtained by the use of decorative hatching to indicate the mane. The artist would have been perfectly familiar with the method of incision of surfaces; incising the outlines of a figure before the tones were introduced was the usual procedure for painting. But the artists of the caves went farther than incision and produced sculpture in deep relief and in the full round. An example of the first is a horse in deep relief (FIG. 1-11) found in the rock shelter of Cap Blanc, not far from Lascaux. The figure is part of a frieze of sculptured horses and bison, some of the figures almost a foot in depth and masterpieces of relief modeling. Though the figures

1-10 *Bison with Turned Head*, La Madeleine, *c.* 11,000–9,000 B.C. Reindeer horn, 4⅛″ high. Dordogne, France. Musée des Antiquités Nationales, St. Germain-en-Laye.

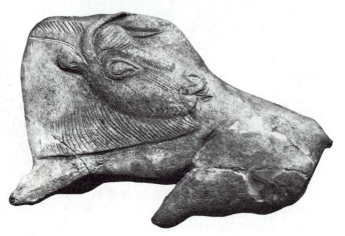

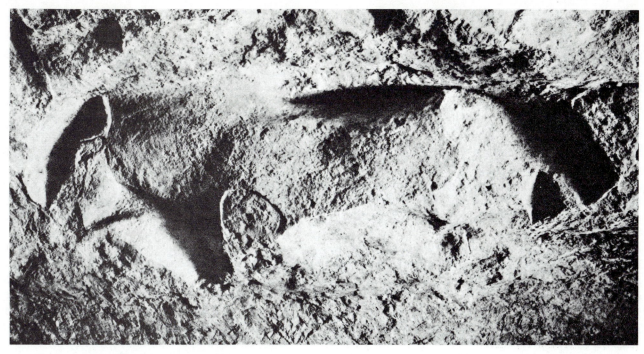

1-11 *Relief Horse*, Cap Blanc, *c.* 13,000–11,000 B.C. 7' long. Dordogne, France.

wide variety of pose, subject, and setting. We have seen that in cave art the human figure almost never appears; the falling or fallen man of the well scene (FIG. 1-7) at Lascaux is quite exceptional. In the rock-shelter paintings the new sentiment for human themes and concerns and the emphasis on action in which man dominates the animal are central. The new vocabulary of forms may have migrated across the Mediterranean from North Africa, where many paintings similar to those in the Spanish Levant have been found. There has been much learned debate about the dating of the whole development, and there is now some agreement that its beginnings were around 8000 B.C. and that the style may have lasted (with many variations) until about 3000 B.C.

Some characteristic features of the rock paintings appear in an energetic group of five warriors (FIG. 1-13) found in the Gasulla gorge. The group, only about nine inches in width, shows a customary tense exaggeration of movement, a rhythmic repetition of basic shape, and in general a sacrifice of naturalistic appearance to narrative and to unity

1-12 *Venus of Willendorf*, *c.* 25,000–20,000 B.C. Stone, 4⅜" high. Naturhistorisches Museum, Vienna. (Cast of original.)

1-13 *Marching Warriors* (ritual dance?), Gasulla gorge, *c.* 8000–3000 B.C. Approx. 9" wide. Castellón, Spain.

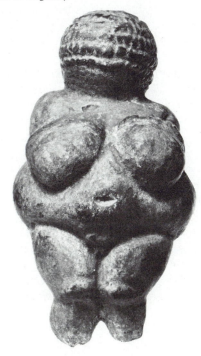

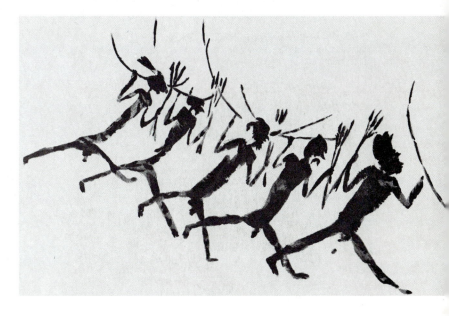

of action. Even so, we can distinguish details that are economically descriptive—bows, arrows, and the feathered headdress of the leader. The widely splayed legs read as a leaping stride, perhaps a march to battle or a ritual dance.

Other such paintings show an even greater uniformity of basic shape, and a nervous, sharp angularity, which suggest the pictograph or—as we have proposed—even the phonetic hieroglyph. And over the millennia the rock painting styles do indeed become more abstract and schematic, more symbol than picture, and it is likely that they record a step in the evolution of the symbolic from the pictorial, an evolution that, in the Near East, culminates in the invention of writing. Later on the liveliness and spontaneity of the rock paintings is lost in the rigid uniformities of almost letterlike shapes repeated as if from a limited stock of signs.

The significance of the rock paintings was probably magical-religious, like the paintings of the caves, though some observers believe them to be no more than pictorial records of memorable events. The paintings are concentrated at particular sites that were used for long periods, while nearby places, better suited for painting, were not used. This suggests that the sites were held sacred, not only by the Mesolithic painters, but by those working well into the historical period. Iberian and Latin inscriptions indicate that supernatural powers were ascribed to some of these holy places as late as the Roman era.

THE NEW STONE AGE (NEOLITHIC)

In Paleolithic art, man, in a supreme feat of intellection, learned to abstract his world by making a picture of it. Thus he sought to control it by capturing and holding its image. In the Neolithic period he made the giant stride toward the actual, concrete control of his environment by settling in fixed abodes and domesticating plants and animals. His food supply assured, he changed from hunter to herdsman, to farmer, and, perhaps as early as 7000 B.C. in the Near East, to townsman. The wandering hunter settled down to organized community living in villages surrounded by cultivated fields. Then began the long evolution toward the incredible technological command of the physical environment that exists today.

Recent research seems to indicate that in several areas of western Europe, local neolithic populations developed, as

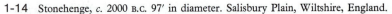

1-14 Stonehenge, c. 2000 B.C. 97′ in diameter. Salisbury Plain, Wiltshire, England.

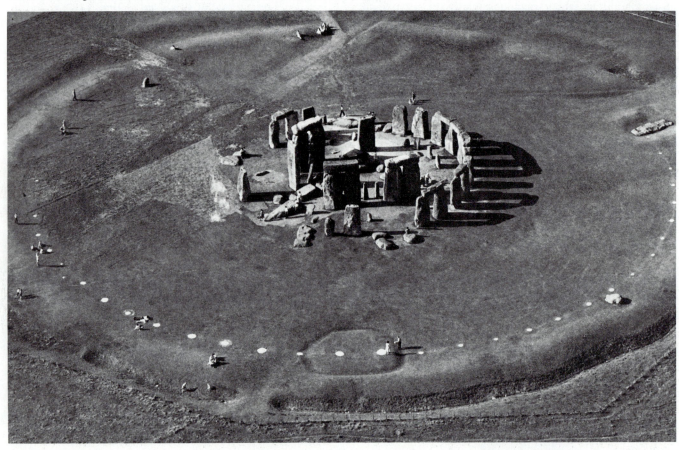

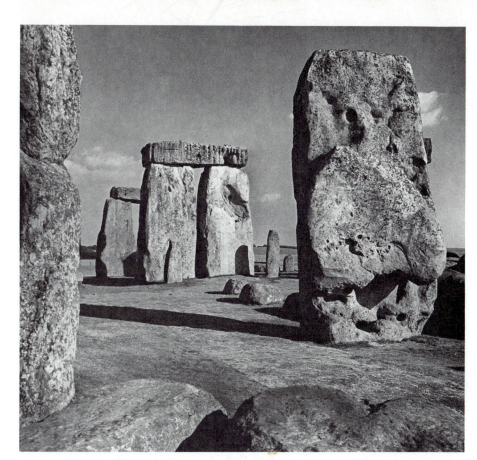

early as 4000 B.C., a monumental architecture consisting of graves and of rows or circles of massive, rough-hewn stones. The very dimensions of the stones, some as high as seventeen feet and weighing tons, have prompted the historian to call them *megaliths* (great stones), and the culture that produced them *megalithic*.

There are several types of megalithic structures. The *dolmen* consists of several great stones set on end, with a large covering slab. Dolmens may be the remains of passage graves from which a covering earth mound has been washed away. The passage grave, the dominant megalithic tomb type—literally thousands exist in France and England—has a corridor lined with large stone slabs leading to a circular chamber often having a *corbeled* vault, in which each of numerous rings of stones projects inward beyond the underlying course, until the rings close at the top. They were frequently built into a hill slope or covered by mounds of earth. At Carnac in Brittany, great single stones, called *menhirs*, set on end, were arranged in parallel rows, some of which run for several miles and consist of thousands of stones. Their purpose was evidently religious and may have had to do with the cult of the dead or the worship of the sun. Sometimes these huge stones were arranged in a circle known as a *cromlech;* among the most imposing cromlechs are those at Avebury and at Stonehenge, in England (FIGS. 1-14 and 1-15). The structure at Avebury is surrounded by a stone bank about four-fifths of a mile in diameter. The remains at Stonehenge are of a complex of rough-cut sarsen stones and smaller "blue-

stones." Outermost was a ring of large monoliths of sarsen stones capped by lintels. Next was a ring of bluestones, which, in turn, encircled a horseshoe (open end facing east) of trilithons—five lintel-topped pairs of the largest sarsens, each of which weighs 45 to 50 tons. Standing apart and to the east is the "heel-stone," which, for a person looking outward from the center of the complex, would have marked the point at which the sun rose at the midsummer solstice.

Stonehenge seems to have been built in several phases around 2000 B.C., according to recently corrected radiocarbon dates. Computer-based calculations have raised something of a controversy, not so much over the date as over the purpose of Stonehenge, which seems to have been a kind of astronomical observatory. The mysterious structure, believed in the Middle Ages to have been the work of the magician Merlin, who spirited it from Ireland, or the work of a race of giants, comes in our own time to be thought of as a remarkably accurate calendar, a testimony to the rapidly developing intellectual powers of man. Even in their ruined condition the monoliths of Stonehenge possess a solemn majesty, created by heroic human effort, physical and intellectual. At Avebury, as at Stonehenge, there is, in the series of concentric circles with connecting curvilinear pathways or avenues, a feeling for order, symmetry, and rhythm that is evidence not only of well-developed and systematized ceremonial rituals, but perhaps also of a maturing geometrical sense born of observation of the apparent movement of the sun and moon.

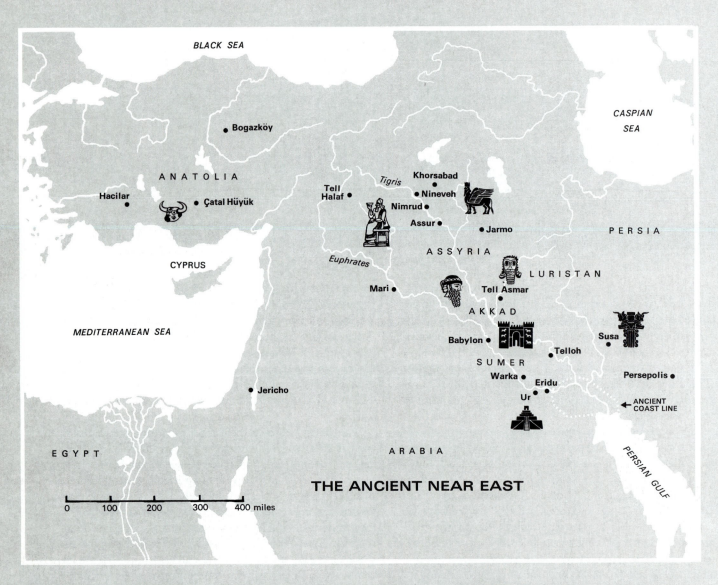

BLACK SEA

• Bogazköy

A N A T O L I A

Hacilar • • Çatal Hüyük

CYPRUS

MEDITERRANEAN SEA

CASPIAN
SEA

Tigris

Tell
Halaf

Khorsabad •
• Nineveh

Nimrud •

Assur •

• Jarmo

PERSIA

A S S Y R I A

Euphrates

Mari •

LURISTAN

Tell Asmar •

A K K A D

Babylon •

Telloh •

S U M E R

Warka • Eridu •

Ur •

Susa •

Persepolis •

← ANCIENT
COAST LINE

EGYPT

• Jericho

ARABIA

THE ANCIENT NEAR EAST

0   100   200   300   400 miles

PERSIAN GULF

chapter two

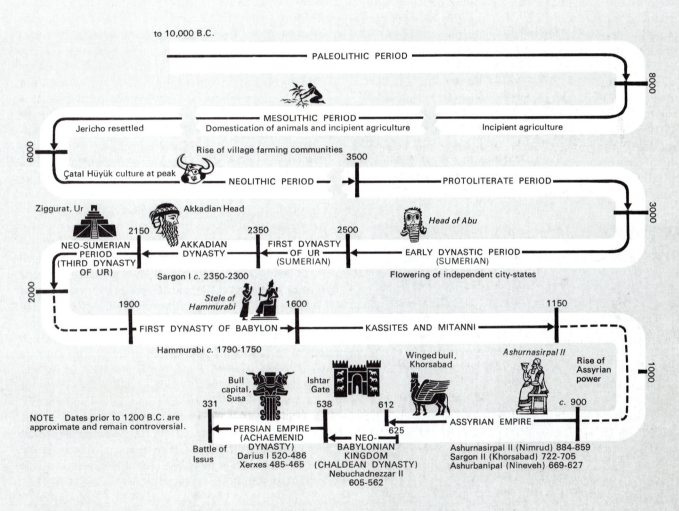

to 10,000 B.C.

PALEOLITHIC PERIOD ——————————— 8000

MESOLITHIC PERIOD
Jericho resettled   Domestication of animals and incipient agriculture   Incipient agriculture

6000   Rise of village farming communities   3500

Çatal Hüyük culture at peak   NEOLITHIC PERIOD   PROTOLITERATE PERIOD

Ziggurat, Ur   Akkadian Head   Head of Abu   3000

2150   2350   2500

NEO-SUMERIAN PERIOD (THIRD DYNASTY OF UR)   AKKADIAN DYNASTY   FIRST DYNASTY OF UR (SUMERIAN)   EARLY DYNASTIC PERIOD (SUMERIAN)

2000   Sargon I c. 2350-2300   Flowering of independent city-states

Stele of Hammurabi

1900   1600   1150

FIRST DYNASTY OF BABYLON   KASSITES AND MITANNI

Hammurabi c. 1790-1750

Winged bull, Khorsabad   *Ashurnasirpal II*   Rise of Assyrian power   1000

Bull capital, Susa   Ishtar Gate

331   538   612   c. 900

NOTE   Dates prior to 1200 B.C. are approximate and remain controversial.

PERSIAN EMPIRE (ACHAEMENID DYNASTY)   625

Battle of Issus   Darius I 520-486   NEO-BABYLONIAN KINGDOM (CHALDEAN DYNASTY)   ASSYRIAN EMPIRE

Xerxes 485-465   Nebuchadnezzar II 605-562   Ashurnasirpal II (Nimrud) 884-859
Sargon II (Khorsabad) 722-705
Ashurbanipal (Nineveh) 669-627

The Ancient Near East

JUST HOW AND WHY the state of human society we call civilization began we are not certain; we are more certain where and when it began. Since the Second World War archeologists have been uncovering the sites in the Near East where the immense transformation began and have pushed back its date as far as 8000 B.C. The onset of civilized life is marked off from all that went before by the development of agriculture. The conventional three-part division of the time preceding recorded history—the Paleolithic, Mesolithic, and Neolithic periods—based on the development of stone implements, is not so basic and decisive as the simpler distinction between an age of food-gathering and an age of food production. In this scheme the Paleolithic period would correspond roughly to the age of food-gathering, with the Mesolithic period, the last phase of that age, marked by intensified food-gathering and the domestication of the dog. The proto-Neolithic would be the period of incipient food production and greater domestication of animals preceding the Neolithic, the period when agriculture and stock-raising become man's major food sources.

According to one view, the area we know today as the Near East—Egypt, Israel, Syria, Iraq, Iran, and Turkey —dried out into desert and semidesert after the last retreat of the glaciers, compelling the inhabitants to move to the fertile alluvial valleys of the Nile in Egypt and the Tigris and Euphrates in Mesopotamia (parts of modern Syria and Iraq). But this view is no longer tenable in light of recent archeological and paleo-environmental findings. The oldest settled communities are found not in the river valleys but in the grassy uplands bordering them. These regions provided the necessary preconditions for the development of agriculture. Species of native plants like wild wheat and barley were plentiful, as were herds of animals—like goats, sheep, and pigs—that could be domesticated; there was also sufficient rain for the raising of crops. It was only after village-farming life was well developed that settlers, attracted by the greater fertility of the soil, moved into the river valleys and deltas. There it was that civilized societies originated—in addition to systematic agriculture—government, law, and formal religion, with such instrumentalities and techniques as writing, measurement and calculation, weaving, metalcraft, and pottery.

For a long time it was thought that these developments occurred concurrently in Egypt and Mesopotamia. But again archeology is forcing a revision of our views. It is becoming clear that Mesopotamia and its neighbors were far ahead of Egypt temporally. Village-farming communities like Jarmo in Iraq and Çatal Hüyük in southern Anatolia (Turkey) date back to the mid-seventh millennium B.C., and the remarkable fortified town of Jericho, before whose walls Joshua appeared thousands of years later, is even older. In Egypt the oldest villages, in the Faiyum district near the Delta, do not seem to have been founded before 4500 B.C., and, furthermore, an urban society like that of Mesopotamia seems never to have developed there. The invention of writing in Mesopotamia preceded that in Egypt by several hundred years, and it may be that the whole development of Egyptian civilization was the result of Mesopotamian influence. Traditionally the history of art in the ancient world begins with Egypt and then passes to Mesopotamia. Archeological studies of Egypt are older, scientific archeology having begun there at the end of the eighteenth century. In addition, the chronology of Egypt is more firmly established, and the general cultural picture is more complete. Nevertheless, in view of the array of new facts presented by the latest archeological investigations, the traditional sequence should be reversed: Mesopotamia and its neighbors should be placed at the beginning of the study of ancient art.

THE BEGINNINGS

Jericho

By 7000 B.C. agriculture was well established in at least three Near Eastern regions: Jordan, Iran, and Turkey (Anatolia). Although no remains of domestic cereal grains have been found that can be dated before 7000 B.C., the advanced state of agriculture at that time presupposes a

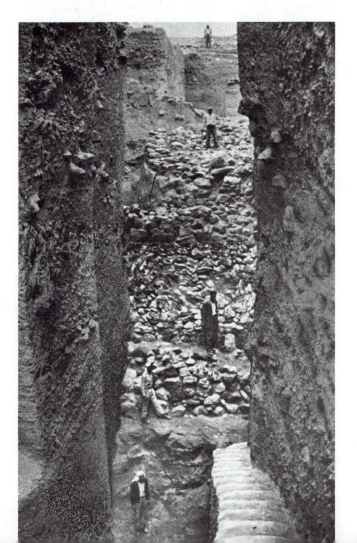

2-1 Proto-Neolithic fortifications, Jericho, 8000–7000 B.C.

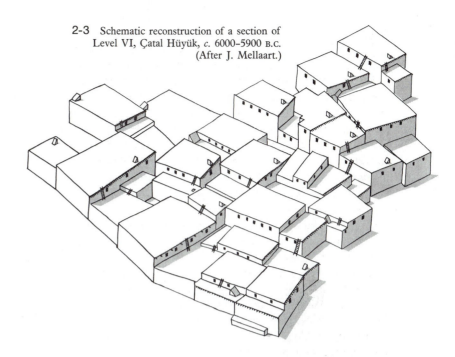

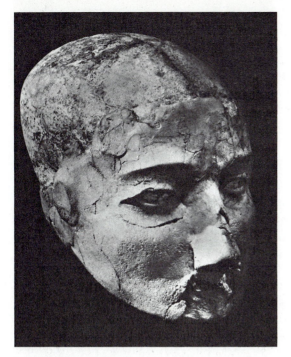

2-2 Human skull, Jericho, 7000–6000 B.C. Features molded in plaster.

long development; indeed, the very existence of a town like Jericho gives strong support to this assumption. The site of Jericho, a plateau in the Jordan river valley with an unfailing spring, was occupied by a small village as early as the ninth millennium B.C. This proto-Neolithic village underwent a spectacular development around 8000 B.C., when a new town was built with houses of mudbrick on round or oval stone foundations. As the town's wealth grew and powerful neighbors established themselves, the need for protection resulted in the first known permanent stone fortifications. By the middle of the eighth millennium B.C. the town, estimated to have had a population of over 2000, had a wide, rock-cut ditch and a five-foot-thick wall surrounding it. Into this wall, which has been preserved to a height of twelve feet, was built a great circular stone tower, thirty feet in height and diameter (FIG. 2-1). Not enough of the site has been excavated to determine whether this tower was solitary, like the keeps in Medieval castles, or one of several similar towers that formed a complete defense system. In either case, a structure like this, built with the aid of only the most primitive kinds of stone tools, was certainly a tremendous technical achievement.

Around 7000 B.C. the site was abandoned by its original inhabitants, but new settlers arrived in the early seventh millennium. They built rectangular mudbrick houses on stone foundations and carefully plastered and painted their floors and walls. Several of the excavated buildings seem to have served as shrines, the plan of one of them being remarkably similar to that of the later Greek megaron (see Chapter Five). These settlers fashioned statuettes of a mother goddess and of animals associated with a fertility cult. Most striking is a group of human skulls on which the

features have been "reconstructed" in plaster (FIG. 2-2). Subtly modeled, the eyes inlaid sea shells, and the hair painted (a painted mustache has been preserved on one specimen), they present a strikingly lifelike appearance. Since the skulls were detached from the bodies before burial and displayed above ground, they may have been regarded as "spirit traps," implying a well-developed belief in survival after the death of the body.

Çatal Hüyük

Perhaps even more remarkable than the Jericho finds are recent discoveries in Anatolia. Excavations at Hacilar and Çatal Hüyük have shown not only that the central Anatolian plateau was the site of a flourishing Neolithic culture between 7000 and 5000 B.C., but that it may well have been the culturally most advanced region of its time. Twelve successive building levels excavated at Çatal Hüyük between 1961 and 1965 have been dated between 6500 and 5700 B.C. On a single site of thirty-two acres (of which only one acre has been explored) it has become possible to retrace, in an unbroken sequence, the evolution of a Neolithic culture over a period of 800 years.

Along with Jericho, Çatal Hüyük has been called "one of man's first essays in the development of town life." The regularity of the town plan suggests that it was built according to some *a priori* plan. A peculiarity of the town is its complete lack of streets, the houses adjoining each other and having access through their roofs (FIG. 2-3). Impractical as such an arrangement may appear today (although it survived in parts of central Anatolia and western Iran), it did offer some advantages. The buildings, being attached, were more stable than free-standing struc-

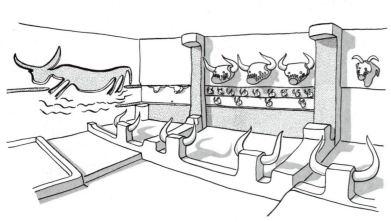

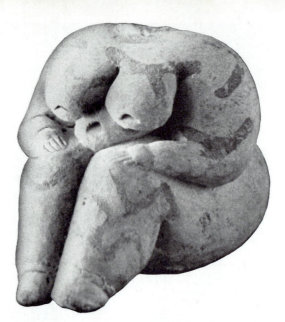

2-4 Reconstruction of a shrine,
Level VI, Çatal Hüyük, c. 5900 B.C.
(After J. Mellaart.)

2-5 *Seated Goddess*,
Çatal Hüyük, c. 5900 B.C.
Baked clay.

tures and, at the limits of the town site, formed a perimeter wall well-suited to defense against human or natural forces. Thus, if an enemy managed to breach the exterior wall, he would find himself not inside the town but inside a single room, with the defenders waiting for him on the roof—a dismal prospect at best.

Here and there the dense building mass is interrupted by an open court, which served as a garbage dump. Liberal amounts of ashes mixed in with the refuse acted as sterilizers, although probably not as deodorants. The houses, varying in size, were of a standard plan and constructed of mudbrick walls strengthened by sturdy timber frames. Walls and floors were plastered and painted, and platforms along walls served for sleep, work, and eating. A great number of shrines have been found intermingled with standard houses. Varying with the different levels, the average ratio is about one shrine for every four houses. This may not hold true for the whole town, only about one thirtieth of which has been excavated.

The shrines (FIG. 2-4) are distinguished from other houses by the greater richness of their interior decoration,

which consisted of wall paintings, plaster reliefs, animal heads, bucrania (bovine skulls), and cult statuettes. Bulls' horns, which adorn most shrines, sometimes in considerable numbers, were set into stylized, remodeled heads of bulls or into benches and pillars and may have been thought to protect the inhabitants and ward off evil. Nothing, however, suggests that the bull, or any other animal, was regarded as a deity. Cult statuettes found at Çatal Hüyük indicate that the people believed their gods to have human form, both male and female. When represented in association with animals—the female deity usually with leopards, the male with a bull—the animals are always shown as subservient.

The statuettes are of stone or baked clay and are quite small, most between two and eight inches high and a few reaching twelve inches. All the female figures, which predominate, seem to represent a mother goddess, but in a great variety of aspects: young, old, in ritual marriage, in pregnancy, giving birth, and as ruler of wild animals. These are described explicitly, and, while the bulbous forms of the headless *Seated Goddess* (FIG. 2-5) may re-

2-6 *Deer Hunt*, detail
of a copy of a wall
painting from
Level III, Çatal Hüyük,
c. 5750 B.C.

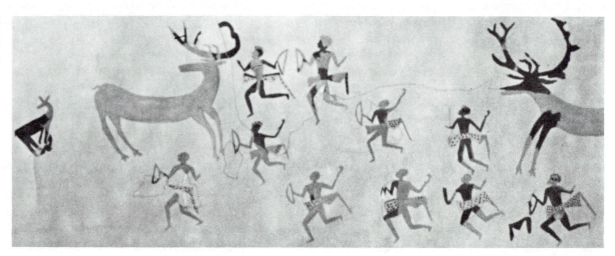

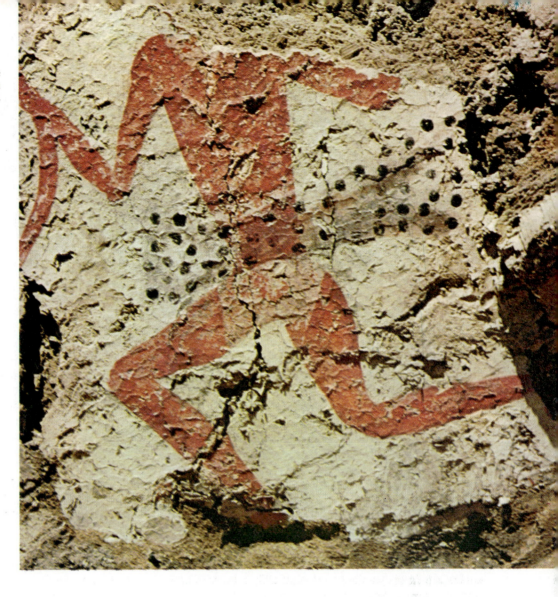

2-7 *Dancing Hunter,* fragment of the wall painting a part of which is shown in copy in FIG. 2-6.

mind us of the *Venus of Willendorf,* the artist's approach toward his subject is quite realistic. Unlike the Paleolithic artist, who tried to represent the abstract concept of fertility, the Neolithic sculptor converts an abstract being (a goddess) into a human figure. The breasts are sensitively modeled, the small hands carefully rendered, and, judging from other examples, it may be safely assumed that the lost head had fairly well described facial features. The figure is painted with crosslike floral patterns that are known also from wall paintings and may here endow the goddess with the specific function of agrarian deity.

Fertility and agricultural symbolism dominate the art of the upper (later) levels of Çatal Hüyük. But hunting also played an important part in the early Neolithic economy, and Paleolithic hunting rituals survived far into the Neolithic period. Numerous crude animal figurines, broken and damaged, have been found at Çatal Hüyük; they may have served as animal surrogates during hunting rites, being buried in pits after having served their purpose. The importance of hunting as a food source (until about 5700 B.C.) is reflected also in wall paintings, in which, in

the older shrines, hunting scenes predominate. In style and concept, the *Deer Hunt* (FIG. 2-6) recalls the rock-shelter paintings of the Spanish Levant, but these figures are more full-bodied and rendered with greater realism. The artist used a full range of pigments, mostly derived from minerals, which he applied with a brush to the white background of dry plaster. A fragment from this hunting scene shows a dancing hunter (FIG. 2-7) dressed in a white loincloth and a leopard skin, holding a bow in one hand, the speed of his movement effectively emphasized by the manner in which the leopard skin whirls around his waist. Once the apparently ritual function of these paintings had been fulfilled, they were covered with a layer of white plaster and later replaced with a new painting of either a similar or a different subject.

In one of the older shrines a painting was uncovered that has been interpreted as a pure landscape. As such it would be unique for thousands of years to come. According to carbon-14 dating, it was painted soon after 6200 B.C. (FIG. 2-8). In the foreground is shown what may be a town with rectangular houses neatly laid out side by side, perhaps

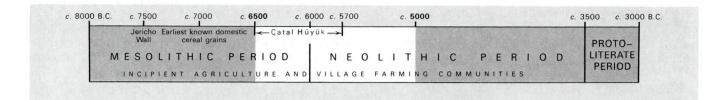
representing Çatal Hüyük; behind it, on a smaller scale, as though far away, appears a mountain with two peaks; dots and lines issuing from the higher of the two cones may represent a volcanic eruption. The mountain has been tentatively identified as the 10,600-foot Hasan Dag, located within view of Çatal Hüyük, and the only twin-peaked volcano (now extinct) in central Anatolia. Since the painting appears on the walls of a shrine, the conjectured volcanic eruption would have had some religious meaning. While the artist might have linked the event with the underworld and witnessed it with fearful awe, his dread might have been mingled with gratitude to a bountiful Mother Earth, for it is believed that Çatal Hüyük derived much of its wealth from trade in obsidian, a vitreous volcanic stone easily chipped into fine cutting edges and highly valued by Neolithic tool- and weapon-makers.

The rich finds at Çatal Hüyük give the impression of a prosperous and well-ordered society that practiced a great variety of arts and crafts. In addition to painting and sculpture, weaving and pottery were well established, and even the art of smelting copper and lead in small quantities was known before 6000 B.C. The society seems conservative in its long retention of Paleolithic traditions and practices, but it was also progressive in its achieving, slowly but relentlessly, a complex, fully food-producing economy. In the arts this development is perhaps mirrored in a de-emphasis of realism in favor of a more abstract symbolism, in the disappearance of hunting scenes, and in a gradual decline in production of statuettes representing

male deities. At the same time representations of the mother goddess increase in number, reflecting perhaps a corresponding change in the importance, if not the social position, of woman. As agriculture took precedence over hunting, female occupations, like the milling of grain, baking, weaving, and the care and feeding of domestic animals, became ever more important. At Çatal Hüyük the change to a fully agrarian economy appears to have been completed by about 5700 B.C. Less than a century later the site was abandoned. A probably related culture at Hacilar, some 200 miles to the west, provides an afterglow. But by about 5000 B.C. the limelight shifts eastward toward the Mesopotamian valley.

SUMER

Some time in the early fourth millennium B.C. in Mesopotamia a critical event took place—the settlement of the great river valleys. It was after this that writing, art, monumental achitecture, and new political forms were introduced in Mesopotamia and Egypt, but with striking differences in function. As Henri Frankfort describes it:

The earliest written documents of Mesopotamia . . . facilitated the administration of large economic units, the temple communities. The earliest Egyptian inscriptions were legends on royal monuments or seal engravings iden-

2-8 *Landscape with Volcanic Eruption (?)*, detail of a copy of a wall painting from Level VII, Çatal Hüyük, c. 6150 B.C.

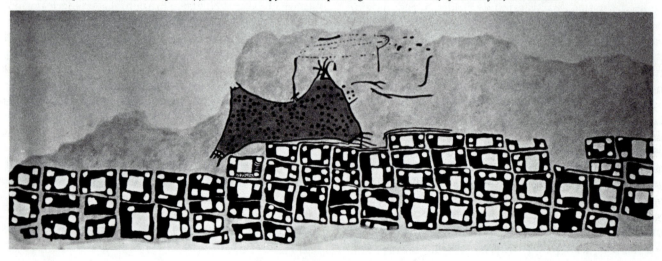

tifying the king's officials. The earliest representations in Mesopotamian art are preponderantly religious; in Egyptian art they celebrate royal achievements and consist of historical subjects. Monumental architecture consists, in Mesopotamia, of temples, in Egypt of royal tombs. The earliest civilized society of Mesopotamia crystallized in separate nuclei, a number of distinct, autonomous cities—clear-cut, self-assertive polities—with the surrounding lands to sustain each one. Egyptian society assumed the form of the single, united, but rural, domain of an absolute monarch.

Thus, not one, but *two* civilizations emerged, each having its own special character. From this time forward world history will be the record of the birth, development, and disappearance of civilizations and the rise and decline within them of peoples, states, and nations. It is with these two mighty, contrasting civilizations bordering the eastern Mediterranean region that the drama of Western mankind truly begins.

In the fertile lower valley of the Tigris and Euphrates man may have found the equivalent of the Garden of Eden celebrated in Genesis and long a part of Mesopotamian tradition. Once he had learned the arts of irrigation and, to a degree, the control of floods, the possibility of creating a great oasis was before him, and he realized it. The turbulence of its history strongly suggests that this land, with its promise of a hitherto unknown life of abundance, was enormously attractive to man.

At the dawn of recorded history the lower Mesopotamian valley was occupied by the Sumerians, whose origin is still one of the great puzzles of ancient history. They were an agricultural people who learned to control floods and built strong-walled towns, such as Uruk, the biblical Erech and the modern Warka, and Lagash, the modern Al-Hiba. After several centuries, Semitic nomad shepherds came from the western desert; they adopted agriculture, absorbed much from Sumerian culture, and built their own cities farther north—Kish, Akkad, Mari, and Babylon. Over the centuries, dominion oscillated between the two peoples, but the Semites produced two of the mightiest kings, Sargon and Hammurabi.

From as early as the Paleolithic caves we have evidence of man's effort to control his environment by picture magic. With the appearance of the Sumerians and the beginning of recorded history the older magic was replaced by a religion of gods, benevolent or malevolent, who personified the forces of nature that often contended destructively with man's hopes and designs. In the fertile valley the fiery heat of summer and the catastrophic floods, droughts, blights, and locusts easily persuaded man that there were powers above and beyond his control, powers that he must somehow placate and win over. Formal religion, a kind of system of transactions between gods and men, may have begun with the Sumerians; and no matter how it has been systematized and diversified since then,

religion has retained its original propitiatory devices of prayer, sacrifice, and ritual, as well as a view of man as imperfect by nature and dependent upon and obligated to some higher being. The religion of the Sumerians and of those who followed them centered about nature gods: Anu, god of the sky; Enlil (Bel), a creator and ruler of earth and "lord of the storm"; Ea (or Enki), lord of the waters (a healing, benevolent god); Nannar (Sin), the moon god; Utu (Shamash), the sun god; and Inanna (associated with the planet Venus), goddess of love and fertility, who, as Ishtar, is later also endowed with the functions of battle goddess.[1]

The City-State and the Ziggurat

Religion, dominating life and investing it with meaning, determined the form of society as well as its expression in architecture and art. The Mesopotamian city-state was under the protection of the god of the city; the king was his representative on earth and the steward of his earthly treasure. The relation of the king to the gods above and to his subjects below may be read in the prayer of an early Sumerian king to the god Enlil of the city of Nippur:

O En-lil, the king of the lands, may Anu to his beloved father speak my prayer; to my life may he add life, and cause the lands to dwell in security; may he give me warriors as many as the grass; the herds of heaven may he watch over; the land with prosperity endow; the good fortune which the gods have given me, may he not change; and may I ever remain the shepherd, who standeth at the head.

The plan of the city reflected this centrality of the god in its life, his temple being its monumental nucleus. The temple was the focus not only of the religion of the city but of its administrative and economic process. It was indeed the domain of the god, who was regarded as a great and rich holder of lands and herds as well as the protector of the city. The whole function of the city was to serve the god as a master, as the function of all men in general was to serve the gods. The vast temple complex, a kind of city within a city, had a multitude of functions. A temple staff of priests and scribes carried on the business of the city, looking after the possessions of the god and of the king. It must have been in such a setting that writing developed into an instrument of precision; the very earliest examples of it have to do with the keeping of accounts and the description of simple transactions, stores, and supplies.

The most prominent part of a temple compound, and indeed the most characteristic structure of the Mesopotamian valley, was the *ziggurat* or temple tower. Neither the origin nor the purpose of these huge, multistoried brick structures is known. They have been interpreted as stair-

[1] Bel and Shamash are Akkadian names; Sin is Babylonian.

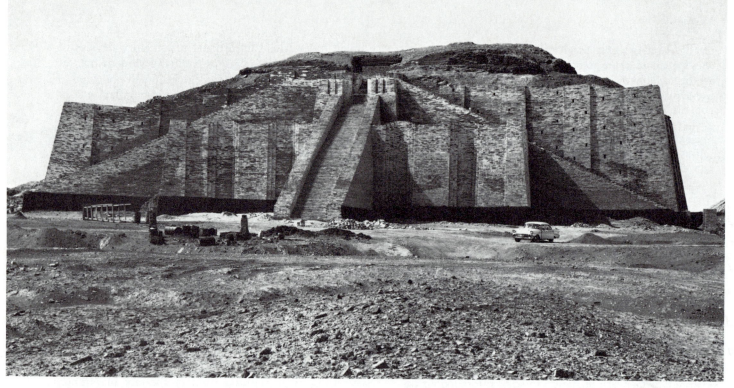

2-9   Ziggurat at Ur, *c.* 2100 B.C.

ways by which the gods of the country mounted to heaven every night. An old Babylonian text (*c.* 1900–1600 B.C.) reads:

> The gods and goddesses of the country—
> Shamash, Sin, Adad and Ishtar—
> have gone home to heaven to sleep.
> They will not give decisions or verdicts [tonight].

It is generally thought that the roof of the shrine (at the top of the ziggurat) was the setting in which priests prayed to the "gods of the night" (the planets and constellations), or prepared a meal for them, or sacrificed a lamb for an omen.

Most of the ruined cities of Sumer—Ur, Warka, Nippur, Larsa, Eridu—are still dominated by their eroded ziggu-

rats. The ziggurat at Ur is a good example, dating from the period called Neo-Sumerian—from the twenty-second to the twenty-first century B.C.—when the builders were pushing for the greatest heights possible (FIGS. 2-9 and 2-10). In one view we see the huge mound of sun-dried brick, truncated and edge-worn by time, weather, and depredation; in the other a conjectural reconstruction. On a massive base, fifty feet high, stand two successively smaller stages, of which presumably the uppermost served as a pedestal for the shrine. Three ramplike stairways of 100 steps each converge toward a tower-flanked gateway from which another flight of steps probably led to the shrine, access to which was forbidden to any but officiating priests. The structure is a solid mass of mudbrick, its lower two stages faced with baked brick laid in bitumen. This facing

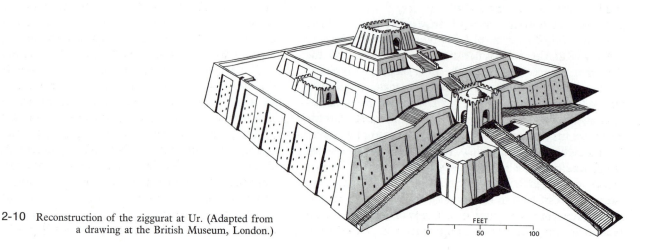

2-10   Reconstruction of the ziggurat at Ur. (Adapted from a drawing at the British Museum, London.)

FEET
0   50   100

has withstood floods and weathering so that the Ziggurat of Ur is the best preserved in southern Mesopotamia. The loftiness of the great ziggurats—especially of the one at Babylon, which was about 270 feet high and intended by its pious builders to reach into heaven—made a profound impression on the ancient Hebrews, who memorialized the latter as the tower of Babel, a monument to the insolent pride of man.

The three great inventions of the Sumerians—a system of gods and god-man relations, the city-state itself, and the art of writing—provided the basis for a new order of human society. In the city-state, consecrated by the presence of the civic deity, men experienced new interrelations with the god and with each other, and these interrelations were formalized and given permanence by being recorded in writing. Life became regularized, and the community assumed functions formerly the individual's, such as defense against man and the caprices of nature. This and the division of labor (specialization), which is encouraged where large numbers of people are concentrated in a coherent community, emancipated the inhabitants from the consuming necessities of daily life so that they could develop and apply skills and talents unthinkable in fluid and unintegrated societies. The relatively fixed character of the city-state also conferred on the community a permanent identity as a city whose king and god were known and present. This sense of identity extended to the individual inhabitant as well, who received his identity from his membership in the community, discovering himself in his interrelations with the city, god, king, and citizens. The new written language may also have contributed to this growing identification, the individual perceiving himself as a name among the names for other things and actions. Thus from the Sumerian creation of stable patterns of life begins that sense of identity, that self-awareness of historical man that will mature and reach its highest development in the civilization of Greece.

Sculpture

We have seen that in the animal paintings of the caves the figure of man almost never appears; he has not come into the field of self-awareness. Though the rock paintings of the Spanish Levant do indeed represent the human figure, they do so only schematically and almost as a kind of picture-writing. Thus we are not prepared for the beautiful female head from Warka (FIG. 2-11). Its ancestry is unknown. Dating from the so-called protoliterate period, when writing first appeared, it is not a complete head but a marble face meant to be attached to a wood backing and wigged, perhaps, in gold. The deep recesses for the eyebrows were filled with colored shell or stone, as were the large eyes. The subject is unknown (goddess, priestess, queen?), but our ignorance of it and of the history of the head does not diminish our appreciation of its exquisite

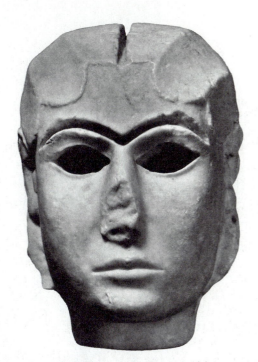

2-11 *Female Head*, Warka, c. 3500–3000 B.C. Alabaster, approx. 8″ high. The Iraq Museum, Baghdad.

refinement of feature and expression, despite the mutilations of time and accident. The soft modeling of the cheeks, the sensitivity of the mouth, the hesitancy of the expression between the sweet and the somber not only render for us a person in herself beguiling and mysterious but suggest a sophistication in the artist beyond our expectation of his time.

One notices at once in the Warka head how disproportionately large the eyes are. This is a trait of a whole group of figures from Tell Asmar (FIGS. 2-12 and 2-13). The reason for this convention, which is not only Sumerian but appears throughout ancient art, can only be guessed. Long before Aristotle asserted that man is distinguished from the animals by being rational and that sight is the most "rational" of the organs of sense, men must have perceived and feared the power of the eye to hold, charm, and hypnotize for ends good or ill. The "evil eye" was feared in the ancient world, as it still is feared. It is a popular belief and a part of folklore that one can learn much about another's intentions and character by "looking him straight in the eye"; and the modern affectation of dark glasses (curiously Sumerian when oversized!) may be both a defense and a badge of attractive mystery. To the ancient artist, the eyes, the "windows of the soul," could have had several associations: Large eyes fixed in unflagging gaze see all, and frontal, binocular vision, distinguishing human from mere animal seeing, represents the all-seeing vigilance and omniscience of the gods and the guarantee of justice. In the conventionalization of the human image, vision understandably becomes a peculiarly human trait—in its lesser physical sense as well as in its greater intellectual, spiritual,

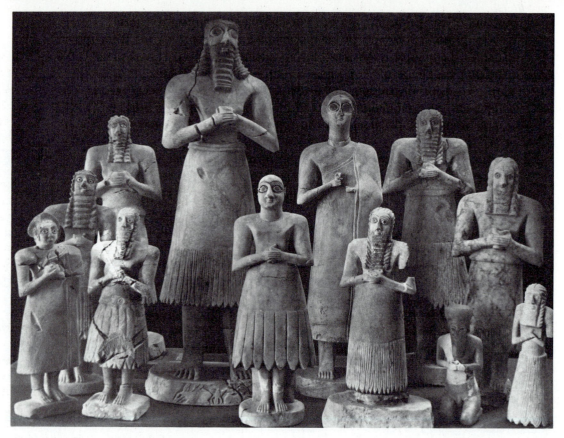

2-12 Statuettes from the Abu Temple, Tell Asmar, *c.* 2700–2600 B.C. Marble, tallest figure approx. 30″ high. The Iraq Museum, Baghdad, and the Oriental Institute, University of Chicago.

and theistic sense. Godlike vision as the foundation of law and justice is evident in the stories of great law-givers of the ancient world like Hammurabi of Babylon, Moses, Lycurgus of Sparta, and Solon of Athens.

Although it may be that none of our speculations entered the mind of the artist of the Tell Asmar figures, some association of vision with supernatural powers seems to be indicated by the fact that the two largest figures, identified as deities by emblems on their bases, also have the largest eyes in relation to their heads. The other statuettes represent worshipers, the larger ones priests, the smaller laymen; with their hands tightly clasped across their chests in the attitude of prayer, their large eyes seem to express reverent awe in the presence of their gods. The purpose of these votive figures was to offer constant prayers to the gods in behalf of their donors, and thus their open-eyed stares may symbolize the eternal wakefulness necessary if they are to fulfill their duty.

CONVENTIONALIZATION

Just as through formal religion and civic life the Sumerians, at the dawn of recorded history, created a new kind of human experience, so through writing and figurative art they found a new way to represent that experience. Writing had been invented by the simplifying of pictures into signs, wedge-shaped (cuneiform) strokes in numerous combinations pressed by a stylus into wet clay tablets. In figurative art, by an analogous process of simplification, the multitude of appearances of things in the optical world was reduced to a few telling traits sufficient to present the human figure and human action. This process of simplification is variously named schematization, stylization, conventionalization, generalization, and formalization. Conventional simplifications of the human figure are universal and not characteristic of ancient art only. Indeed, all artistic styles are conventional in that, in the societies in which

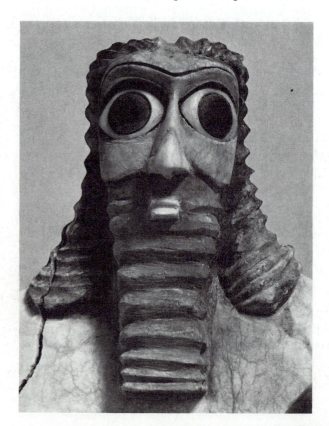

2-13 *Head of the God Abu,* Tell Asmar, *c.* 2700–2600 B.C. Marble. Detail of FIG. 2-12. The Iraq Museum, Baghdad.

they prevail, they are tacitly agreed upon as a comprehensible means of representation. The conventions may be broad or narrow, slow to change or under continual revision, as in our times. In any case, criteria such as fidelity to optical "fact" should not be used in evaluating a style. Although since the 1800s the main trends in modern art have been away from optical "fact," and although today's artists often deliberately disregard photographic "truth," the images they make—such as those seen in comic strips and in commercial art and advertising—are perfectly recognizable to us.

The Sumerians, working out patterns and conventions that regulated the new life that they had in effect devised, also established conventions for the making of the human image. The large eyes of the Warka and Tell Asmar figures are not the only conventionalized details. In the small figures of a shell-inlaid box, the so-called *Standard of Ur* (FIG. 2-14), we find several devices of representation that simplify the narrative, explain the action, and even convey the impression of motion. The panel shown depicts a Sumerian military victory—the advance of the foot soldiers, the charge of the chariots. A second panel (not shown) represents the aftermath of the victorious battle, with lines of prisoners and servants bringing in booty, and the king relaxing, drinking with his nobles, listening to harp and song. The figures are carefully arranged in superimposed strips, each strikingly suggestive of a film or comic strip; and doubtless the purpose is the same—to achieve a continuous narrative effect. They are carefully

spaced, with little overlapping. (Compare this regularized, formal presentation with the casual and haphazard placements of the figure in Paleolithic and Mesolithic art.) Poses are repeated, as in the line of foot soldiers, to suggest large numbers. The horses of the war chariots, the lines of the legs repeated to suggest the other horses of the team and their alignment in space, change from a walk to a gallop as they attack. The figures are essentially in profile, but it is a convention almost universal in the ancient Near East that the eyes—again, very large—are in front view, as are the torsos. The artist indicates the parts of the human body that enter into our concept of what it looks like, and he avoids positions, attitudes, or views that would conceal or obscure the characterizing parts. For example, were the figures in strict profile, an arm and perhaps a leg would be concealed, the body would appear to have only half its breadth, and the eye would not "read" as an eye at all, since it would not have its distinctive flat oval shape, and the pupil, so important in the Tell Asmar figures, would not appear. We could call this approach "conceptual" rather than "optical," since the artist records not the immediate, fleeting aspect of things but rather his concept of the distinguishing and abiding properties of the human body. It is the fundamental forms of things and his knowledge of them, not their accidental appearance, that direct his hand. But this is simply a reflection of the general *formalism* that was imposed at the beginning of the historical period in an effort to create an enduring order. This formalism continued to rule human conduct through his-

2-14 *Scenes of War*, panel from the *Standard of Ur*, c. 2700 B.C. Panel inlaid with shell, lapis lazuli, and red limestone, approx. 8″ × 19″. British Museum, London.

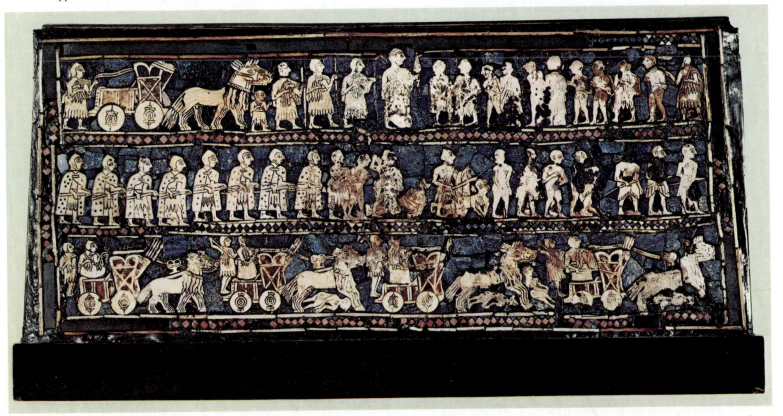

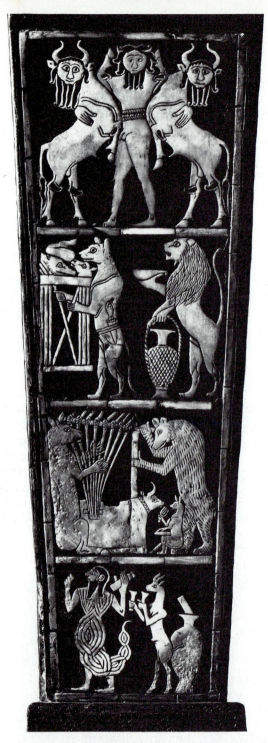

2-15 Soundbox of a harp, Ur, *c.* 2600 B.C. Shell inlay, approx. 12″ high. University Museum, Philadelphia.

tory in thousands of customs, conventions, and ceremonies regarded as sacred and above change. In Greece, many centuries later, Plato conceived the famous philosophy of Forms, claiming that the world of pure form, in which exist the ultimate and unchanging truths of mathematical figures and relationships, is the real world, whereas the world we see, the world of mere appearance, is the realm of the unreal, of illusion, of change, and of death.

THE UNION OF THE FORMAL AND NATURAL

On the inlaid soundbox of a harp from Ur (FIG. 2-15) there are figures representing, in the top register, a Sumerian hero wrestling with two man-headed bulls and, in the lower registers, real and fantastic animals preparing a banquet. The topmost register of the panel presents the figures in heraldic symmetry, and, except that the heads are in front view, they exhibit the conventional formalized pose of the *Standard of Ur.* On the other hand, the figures of the animals in the other registers show the formalism markedly relaxed. The dagger-wearing dog bringing in a laden table, the lion bringing in the wine service, the ass playing the harp, the jackal playing the zither, the bear steadying the harp (or is he dancing?), and the gazelle offering goblets of wine to the scorpion-man—all are seen in more or less true profile. Torsos naturally cut off the view of the far arms, and the near legs obstruct the far legs. Shoulders are properly placed, and features are carefully noted and designated. The heroic human figures have the formality we find in the stylized animals on a coat of arms, but the banquet animals are at ease or seem almost to be burlesquing a stately parade of servants and musicians. Long before the figure of man appears in art we have the naturalistic animal figures of the Paleolithic caves. And for a long time, as if by rule, man is represented with rigid formality, while the animal figure looks and moves much as it would appear to the eye. Our panel shows a delightful Aesop-like scene (the comedy of which may not have been

2-16 Bull's head from the soundbox shown in FIG. 2-15. Gold leaf and lapis lazuli with inlaid eyes, approx. 14″ high. University Museum, Philadelphia.

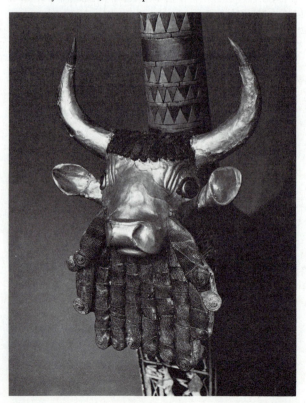

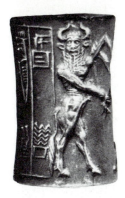
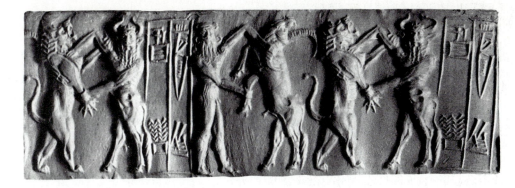

2-17   Cylinder seal and its impression, Ur, *c.* 2700 B.C. Stone, approx. 1½″ high. The Oriental Institute, University of Chicago.

intended) in what is probably a representation of ancient myths. Surely it is a very early specimen of that theme in both literature and art in which animals act as people; thus we pass from the artist of this panel to Aesop's fables, to the Medieval bestiaries, to the zoological creations of Walt Disney.

On the same harp is a splendid bull's head finished in gold leaf and with beard and details in lapis lazuli (FIG. 2-16). (Note where the head is attached to the harp, as it is shown on the third register from the top in FIG. 2-15). The bull, an exemplification of fertility and strength, would naturally become the animal worshiped by early herdsmen, its power invoked against the natural enemies of cattle—drought and predatory beasts. The archaic artist shares with his prehistoric predecessor the genius for rendering with sharp perception the features, almost the personality, of animals. Throughout the ancient Near East and the Mediterranean the bull was revered. In this example, the beard may represent some supernatural amplification of the bull's power. The beard and such humanizing features as the man-heads added to the bulls in the top panel of the soundbox foreshadow the man-headed bulls and lions that appeared much later in Assyria.

The contest of forces natural and supernatural in the Mesopotamians' world is expressed as a struggle between animals and monsters. Such a struggle we find represented in miniature upon a cylinder seal only an inch and a half high (FIG. 2-17), the design cut with exquisite refinement. A seal consisted of a cylindrical piece of stone, usually about an inch or so in height and pierced for the attachment of a cord. Made of various colored stones, both hard and soft, such as rock crystal, agate, carnelian and jasper, lapis lazuli, marble, and alabaster, the seal was decorated with a design in intaglio (incised) so that when it was rolled over soft clay a raised pattern was left. With this device the Sumerian sealed, signed, and identified his letters and documents, which were written on clay tablets. Our illustration shows both the seal and the relief design made from it. A hero fights a bull, and a being—half-man and half-bull—fights a lion. The heraldic attitudes and groupings reflect the formal method of representation, but even in the small area of the seal the skillful artist shows such mastery of animal form that one almost hears the roaring and bellowing of the struggle.

AKKAD

At about 2300 B.C. that loose group of cities we know as Sumer (where the tremendous change from prehistory to civilization had begun) came under the domination of a great ruler, Sargon of Akkad. The Akkadians, though Semitic in origin and speaking a language entirely different from that of Sumer, had assimilated Sumerian culture and under Sargon and his followers introduced a new concept of royal power, its basis unswerving loyalty to the king rather than to the city-state. During the rule of Sargon's grandson, Naram-Sin, governors of cities were called slaves of the king, who, in turn, called himself King of the Four Quarters (of the universe)—in effect, ruler of the earth. A magnificent bronze head of a king from Nineveh (a portrait of Naram-Sin?) embodies this new concept of absolute monarchy (FIG. 2-18). The elaborate coiffure, Sumerian in style, attests the persistence of the tradition of

2-18   *Head of an Akkadian Ruler*, Nineveh, *c.* 2300-2200 B.C. Bronze, approx. 12″ high. The Iraq Museum, Baghdad.

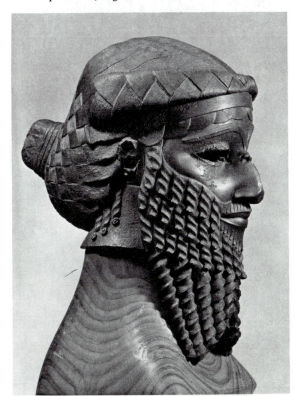

Sumer and serves as crown to the unforgettable face with its expression of majestic serenity. The large eyes, made even larger by the absence of the precious stones once embedded in the sockets, and the emphatic ridgelike brows would seem to go back a long way in tradition, even to the Warka head; the sensitive mouth also recalls that of the earlier work. Here we see to particular advantage that union of the formal with the natural so common in Mesopotamian art. The symmetry of the head and the stylized motifs of the curly locks of hair manage to be consistent with the projection of personality—a strong-minded and

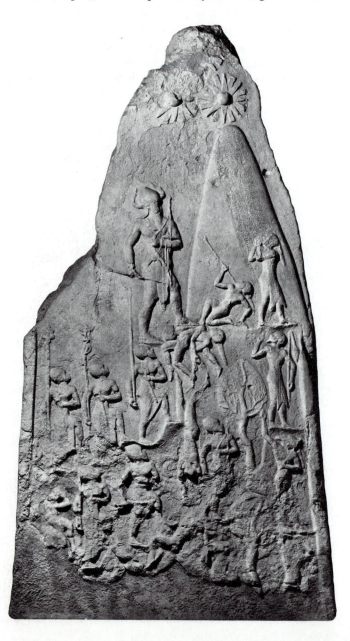

commanding one, yet in a pensive and composed mood, with perhaps just a trace of irony. The age of metals has come, and the piece demonstrates the craftsman's sophisticated skill in casting and in the engraving of details.

The godlike sovereignty claimed by the kings of Akkad may be seen proclaimed in another masterpiece of Akkadian art, the great *Victory Stele of Naram-Sin* (FIG. 2-19). On the stele the warlike grandson of Sargon is represented leading his victorious armies up the slopes of a wooded mountain and through the routed enemy, who are crushed underfoot, fall, flee, die, or beg for mercy. The king stands alone, far taller than his men, treading upon the bodies of two of the fallen enemy. He wears the horned helmet that signifies his deification, and two auspicious astral bodies, representing Shamash and Ishtar, shine upon his triumph. The artist shows an almost startling originality, not only in his ingenious management of the theme, but in the variety of poses and in the setting. The king's troops, a whole army suggested by eight figures marching in two orderly files, carry spears and flying banners as they encounter the shattered enemy (seven figures), one of whom falls headlong down the mountain side. In comparison with the stele figures, those of the *Standard of Ur* seem rather static and formal. The Naram-Sin artist is a daring inventor, and though he adheres to older conventions, especially in the figures of the king and his soldiers (in simultaneous profile and front view), he nevertheless relies upon his own perception to create the first landscape in Near Eastern art since Çatal Hüyük (FIG. 2-8).

The achievements of Akkad were brought to an end by an incursion of barbarous mountaineers, the Guti, who dominated life in central and lower Mesopotamia for about sixty years, when the cities of Sumer, responding to the alien presence, reasserted themselves and established a Neo-Sumerian polity under the kings of Ur. During this age the most conspicuous contribution came from the city of Lagash under its ruler, Gudea. There are about twenty statues of Gudea, and they show him seated or standing, hands tightly clasped, and sometimes wearing a woolen cap; the statue illustrated is characteristic (FIG. 2-20). Gudea, who attributed his good fortune and that of his city to the favor of the gods, zealously looked after the performance of their rites; his statues were numerous so that he could take his (symbolic) place in the temples and there render perpetual service to the benevolent deities. The standing Gudea shown is, like the others, of dolerite, an extremely hard stone that the sculptor works with con-

2-19 *Victory Stele of Naram-Sin,* c. 2300–2200 B.C. Pink sandstone, approx. 6½' high. Louvre, Paris.

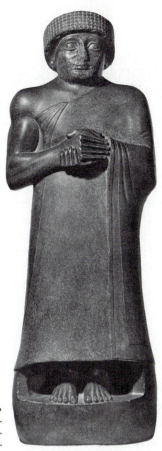

2-20 *Gudea Worshiping*, Telloh, *c.* 2100 B.C. Dolerite, approx. 42″ high. Louvre, Paris.

centralized government that ruled the whole country. Perhaps the most renowned king in Mesopotamian history, Hammurabi was famous for his codification of the confused, conflicting, and often unwritten laws of the Mesopotamian towns. Though not the first to try to bring order out of the chaos, Hammurabi was the first to succeed; echoes of his code are found in the Law of Moses.

The code, beautifully inscribed on a tall, irregularly surfaced black basalt stele, is capped by a relief sculpture of Hammurabi receiving the inspiration for the laws from the flame-shouldered sun god, Shamash (FIG. 2-21). The god is seated on a mountain, indicated by a scale pattern beneath his feet. He holds the symbols of divine power, ring and staff, in a hand stretched toward Hammurabi, represented in a gesture of reverent attention, his hand raised in prayer. We find here again the Mesopotamian artist's instinct for cylindrical volume. Shamash is represented in the familiar convention of combined front and side views, which gives his figure great breadth, while Hammurabi, his servant, is shown in a position closer to profile, by which he occupies far less space. This confrontation between god and man expresses the increasing humanization of natural and supernatural forces, as man, increasingly self-aware, begins (in Babylon) to attribute human form to the gods.

summate skill, making an opportunity out of difficulty. The capped figure stands in the formal frontal pose that descends from the age of Tell Asmar; the great eyes and eyebrow ridges are in the Mesopotamian tradition. One shoulder and arm are bare; the drapery pulls about the torso and under the arm and falls almost vertically from the other arm. The overall contour is simple in the extreme, with no irregular or complex relief. There is a singular unity and compactness to the figure that arises from the artist's conceiving of it as a cylindrical or conical form that resides in the mass of the finely textured stone. The smooth sweep of its contours, the elegance of the profile, and the richness of the polished dolerite all complement each other.

BABYLONIA

Lagash, which had retained its independence during the Guti invasion, became a dependency of Ur during that city's brief resurgence in the late third millennium B.C. For a little over a century the Third Dynasty of Ur ruled over a once-more united realm. Its last king fell before the attacks of foreign invaders, and the following two centuries saw the return of the traditional Mesopotamian political pattern in which several independent city-states existed side by side. One of these was Babylon, until its most powerful king, Hammurabi, was able to reestablish a

2-21 *Stele of Hammurabi* (upper part), Susa, *c.* 1760 B.C. Basalt, entire stele approx. 7′ 4″ high. Louvre, Paris.

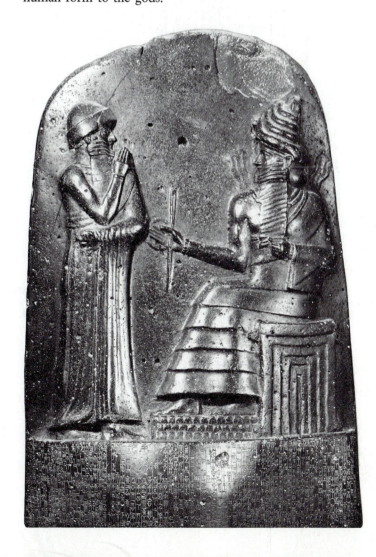

Hammurabi's Babylonian empire was brought down by the Hittites, who, after sacking Babylon around 1595 B.C., retired to Anatolia, seat of Hittite power, leaving Babylonia in the hands of marauding mountaineers, the Kassites. The Hittites, who spoke an Indo-European tongue, developed an art of great power and originality. Their strongly fortified capital, near the modern Turkish village of Bogazköy, was fronted with massive stone gates set between towers (FIG. 2-22). Projecting from the cyclopean stones—so different from the brick of Mesopotamian architecture!—are rugged figures of lions, blunt and brutal in aspect. Whatever the source for the concept of guardian beasts—Mesopotamia, Syria, or Egypt—the Hittite realization of it is original, the figures being strongly bound to and dominated by the architecture, rather than freestanding and in the round.

ASSYRIA

For centuries the Assyrians, the people of northern Mesopotamia, were frustrated in their impulse to power by the kingdoms of the south—Sumer, Akkad, and Babylon—and, on the northwest, by the Mitanni, to whom for a while they were subject. Their opportunity came when their Mitannian overlords were broken by the Hittites and when the weak Kassite kingdom that had succeeded the Babylo-

nian dynasty proved incapable of effective resistance. By about 900 B.C. the Assyrian destiny was already becoming an actuality and for the next three centuries Assyria was the dominant power in the Near East. Assyrian kings became military commanders, and Assyria itself, with its center successively at Calah (the modern Nimrud), Dur-Sharrukin (the modern Khorsabad), and Nineveh, became a garrison state with an imperial structure that extended from the Tigris to the Nile and from the Persian Gulf to Asia Minor. Centuries of unremitting warfare against their neighbors and often rebellious subjects hardened the Assyrians into a cruel and merciless people whose atrocities in warfare were bitterly decried throughout the ancient world. Although they held the restless Babylonian south in thrall, the Assyrians respected the religion and the culture of Sumer-Babylon and were, in fact, dependent on its advanced civilization—as the large library of Ashurbanipal attests. (Discovery of this library in the nineteenth century opened an immense field of knowledge about Assyria.)

Architecture

The unfinished royal citadel of Sargon II of Assyria, built at Khorsabad, reveals in its ambitious plan the confidence of the "great kings" in their all-conquering might (FIG. 2-23). The palace covered some twenty-five acres and had over 200 courtyards and rooms. The city, above which the

2-22 *Lion Gate*, Bogazköy, Anatolia, *c.* 1400 B.C. Lions approx. 7' high.

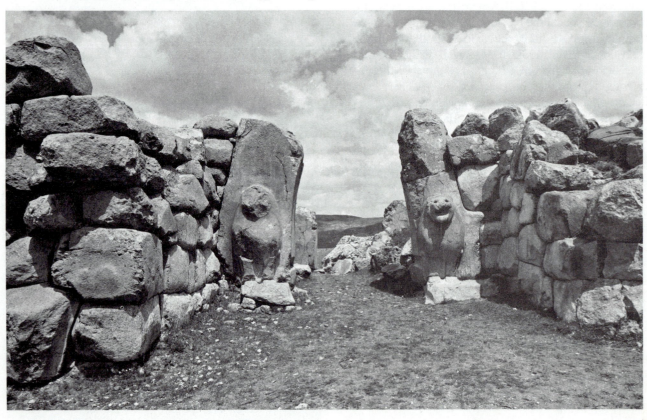

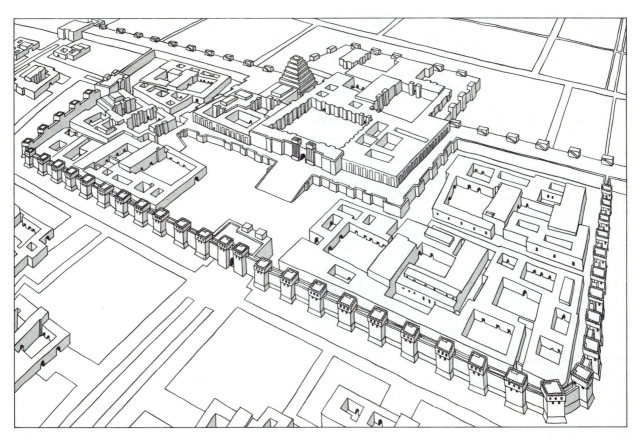

2-23 Reconstruction drawing of the citadel of Sargon II, Khorsabad, *c.* 720 B.C.

citadel-palace stood on a mound fifty feet high, is itself about a square mile in area. The palace may have been elevated solely to raise it above flood level, but its elevation also served to put the king's residence above those of his subjects and midway between them and the gods. Though the builders probably aimed at symmetry, the plan is rambling, embracing an aggregation of rectangular rooms and halls grouped around square courts (FIG. 2-24). The shape of the long, narrow rooms and the massiveness of the side walls suggest that the rooms were covered by brick barrel vaults (see Chapter Six), the most practical roofing method in a region that lacks both timber and good building stone. Behind the main courtyard, each side of which measures 300 feet, were the residential quarters of the king, who received foreign emissaries in state in the long, high, brilliantly painted throne room. Such visitors entered from another large courtyard, passing through the central entrance between huge guardian demons, some thirteen feet in height, and into the presence of enthroned power. Waiting in the court for the audience, visitors had time to meditate upon their own insignificance in comparison with the awesome strength of the king, for the walls of the court were lined with giant figures of the king and his courtiers.

2-24 Plan of the inner precincts of the citadel of Sargon II.

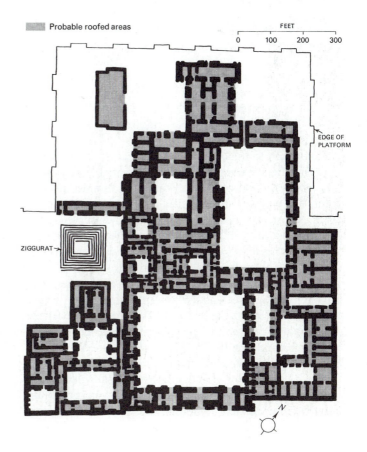

Probable roofed areas

FEET
0   100   200   300

EDGE OF PLATFORM

ZIGGURAT →

N

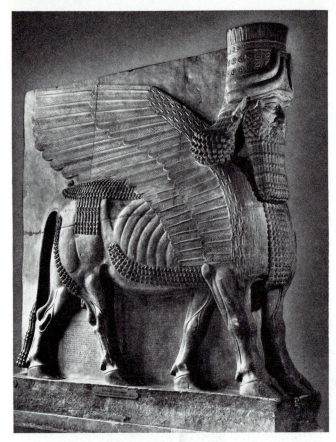

2-25 Winged human-headed bull, Khorsabad, *c.* 720 B.C. Limestone, approx. 13′ 10″ high. Louvre, Paris.

Sargon II regarded his city and palace as an expression of his grandeur, which he viewed as founded upon the submission and enslavement of his enemies. He writes in an inscription: "I built a city with [the labors of] the peoples subdued by my hand, whom Assur, Nabu and Marduk had caused to lay themselves at my feet and bear my yoke at the foot of Mount Musri, above Nineveh." And in another text he proclaims: "Sargon, King of the World, has built a city. Dur Sharrukin he has named it. A peerless palace he has built within it."

In addition to the complex of courtyards, throne room, state chambers, harem, service quarters, and guard rooms making up the palace were the essential temple and ziggurat. The ziggurat at Khorsabad may have had as many as seven stages, of which four have been preserved, each eighteen feet high and each painted a different color. The ascent was made by a continuous ramp spiraling around the building from its base to its summit.

The palace façade consisted of a massive crenelated wall broken by huge rectangular towers flanking an arched doorway. Around the arch and on the towers were friezes of brilliantly colored glazed tiles, the whole effect being sumptuous and grand. Dazzling brilliance seems also to have been part of the royal Assyrian plan to overwhelm the visitor. The doorway was guarded by colossal winged bulls with human heads (FIG. 2-25). These man-headed bulls, derived from age-old composite creatures of Mesopota-

mian art, served to ward off enemies, visible and invisible, and to guard the kings whose traits their faces probably reflect. They are partly in the round and partly in high relief, and they combine the front view at rest with the side view in movement, contriving this combination by the addition of fifth legs. The gigantic size, the bold, vigorous carving, the fine sweep of wings, and the patterning of the surface by the conventional treatment of details produce together a splendor and a stupendous strength that are awesome even today. But we may think of them in all their majesty not so much as guardians of the king as augmentations of his regality. They wear the horned crowns of the god-kings of Akkad and the large-eyed, bearded masks familiar ever since Sumer. The bull and lion bodies of the gate figures, and their eagles' wings, suggest the superhuman strength and fierceness of the king and his swiftness to bring justice or vengeance. The virtues of Assyrian kingship are written large in these hybrid beasts. Ancient art repeatedly testifies to man's persisting fear and admiration of the great beasts that serve as his metaphors for the powers of nature and for the gods themselves.

Relief Sculpture

Although the kings of Assyria had their power depicted in nonhuman forms, they were very much of the world and expected their greatness to be recorded in unmistakably exact and concrete terms. In conformity with his position between his subjects and his gods, every action of the king had importance. Thus, his conquests in battle had the significance of auspicious events, and the same appears to have been thought about his successes in hunting. These two royal activities were recorded in the throne rooms of the earlier palaces; later they were also carved on the walls of what may have been less official rooms. The style of the reliefs, different in the reign of each king who left them, reflects the Assyrian desire for factual reporting, which is also found in the accounts of the campaigns given in bands of inscription that accompany the reliefs.

The history of Assyrian art is mainly the history of relief carving; very little sculpture in the round survives. Even the great winged beasts are thought of as relief sculpture and are locked into their stone slabs, presenting three relief surfaces. To narrate the royal feats pictorially required flat, continuous surfaces upon which could be repeated almost without end the campaigns, sieges, conquests, slaughters, hunts, and even more important, especially in the earlier period, scenes of ritual significance. For the narrative scenes the artists devised a vocabulary of forms that, though conventional, was sharply descriptive. At first, continuity was broken by the edges of the fitted block; in their most developed stage the reliefs extended over the entire wall or walls of a room or corridor.

The astonishing multiplicity of a relief of Ashurnasirpal II at war (FIG. 2-26) compels careful study of the composition if one is to discriminate its details. The king stands in his chariot drawing his bow. He is accompanied by officers, and, in the sky above him, the winged god of Assyria, Ashur, draws his bow and leads him on. The king's team, the reins tight, is passing an enemy chariot already breaking up, its driver thrown down and one horse fallen. Assyrian foot soldiers cut the throats of the enemy wounded. At upper center an Assyrian soldier slays a foe while his comrade tries to save him. Behind them a soldier is lying dead; and, in the upper right, enemy bowmen desperately defend the towers of their city. What is remarkable is the ease with which we read the incidents, though they are not depicted in perspective or in logical sequence. The artist uses the space of his block for a field to be divided as narrative convenience and his own sense of both the factual and the dramatic dictate. The liveliness of individual poses and movements is exceptionally fine and convincing, and

despite the formality that exists in Mesopotamian art side by side with naturalistic details, sophisticated spatial devices appear throughout. One such is the overlapping of figures to suggest greater or lesser distance from the observer; the king's overlapping of his officers is a good example.

The formality of Assyrian art at its most rigid can be seen in another relief of Ashurnasirpal II (FIG. 2-27), in which the king, seated right of center, solemnly raises a ceremonial cup, while the presence of an august personage—at the far left a winged genius who sprinkles holy water—makes the king's act part of a sacred ritual. The slow gestures and stately mien are what we expect of some grave liturgy; we recognize them in religious services today. The cuneiform inscriptions on the flat, thin slabs of relief continue across shallow recesses between the slabs, accentuating the neutrality of the planes and suggesting

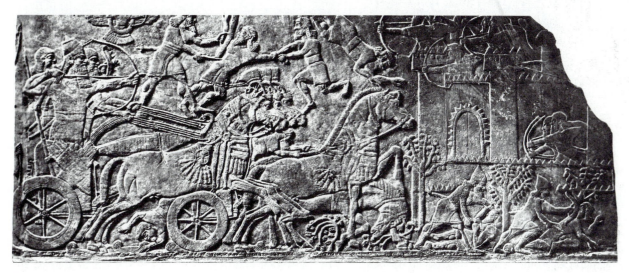

2-26 *Ashurnasirpal II at War*, Nimrud, *c.* 875 B.C. Limestone, approx. 39″ high. British Museum, London.

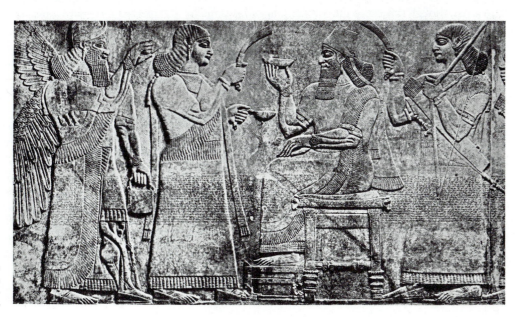

2-27 *Ashurnasirpal II Drinking*, Nimrud, *c.* 875 B.C. Limestone, approx. 7′ 8″ high. British Museum, London.

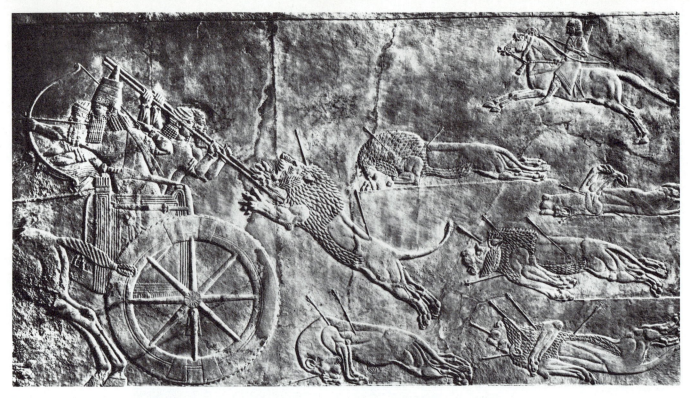

2-28 *Ashurbanipal Hunting Lions,* Nineveh, *c.* 650 B.C. Alabaster, approx. 5′ high. British Museum, London.

that the carving is meant to be not so much a three-dimensional form (that throws shadows) as a report of an event in pictures as well as writing. An interesting Assyrian convention nevertheless makes itself felt—the representation of the human body as thick-set and weighty and the limbs as bulging with muscle, as witness the advanced left leg of the genius and the arms of the king. The calf and forearm muscles are exaggerated, and the veins are like cables, an example of realistic observation converted to a kind of symbol of brute human strength. Also noteworthy is the way in which the profile view of the arms comprises, with the front-view torso, a kind of three-quarter view. The artist, though subject to the conventions of his time, is

experimenting with the problems of representing what his eye sees.

Two centuries later, in a relief from Nineveh showing Ashurbanipal hunting lions (FIG. 2-28), the conventions of the time of Ashurnasirpal II persist, although more realistic elements are introduced. In this relief, lions released from cages in some large, enclosed arena charge the king, who, in his chariot and with his servants protecting his blind sides, shoots down the enraged animals. The king, menaced by the savage spring of a lion at his back, is saved by the quick action of two of his spearmen. Behind his chariot lies a pathetic trail of dead and dying animals pierced by what would appear to be far more arrows than

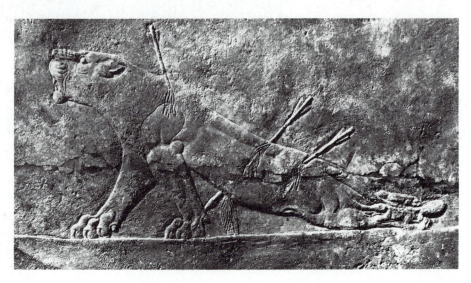

2-29 *Dying Lioness,* Nineveh, *c.* 650 B.C. Limestone, figure approx. 23″ high. British Museum, London.

are needed to kill them. A wounded lioness (FIG. 2-29) drags her hindquarters, paralyzed by arrows that pierce her spine. Blood streams from her wounds—a detail recurring in Assyrian art and revealing the savage character of its patrons. The artist gives a ruthless reading of the straining muscles, the swelling veins, the corrugations of the muzzle, the flattened ears—once more a hard realism under control of the formality of silhouette in low relief. Modern sympathies make of the scene of carnage a kind of heroic tragedy, with the lions as protagonists; but it is unlikely that the artists of the king had any intention other than to aggrandize his image by piling up his kills, by showing the king of men pitting himself against the king of beasts and conquering him.

NEO-BABYLONIA

The Assyrian empire was never very secure, and most of its kings had to fight revolts in large sections of the Near East. The seventh century B.C. saw a steady rise of opposi-

great ziggurat remains. But Herodotus, the ancient Greek traveler and "father of history," has left us, in his brief account of his visit to the temple complex during the fifth century B.C., this description:

> In the one [division of the city] stood the palace of the kings, surrounded by a wall of great strength and size: in the other was the sacred precinct of Zeus-Bel, an enclosure a quarter of a mile square, with gates of solid brass, which was also remaining in my time. In the middle of the precinct there was a tower of solid masonry, a furlong in length and breadth, upon which was raised a second tower, and on that a third, and so on up to eight. The ascent to the top is on the outside, by a path which winds round all the towers. When one is about halfway up, one finds a resting-place and seats, where persons are wont to sit some time on their way to the summit. On the top-most tower there is a spacious temple, and inside the temple stands a couch of unusual size, richly adorned, with a golden table by its side . . . . They also declare that the god comes down in person into this chamber, and sleeps upon the couch, but I do not believe it.

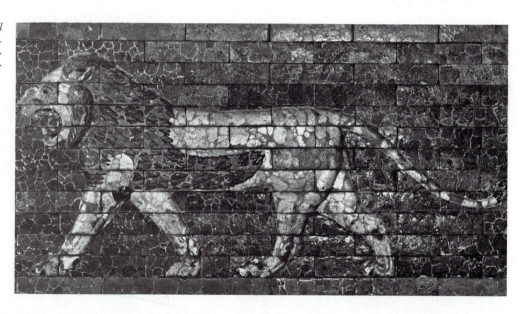

2-30 *Lion from the Processional Way*, Babylon, *c*. 575 B.C. Glazed brick, approx. 41″ high. Louvre, Paris.

tion to Assyrian rule, and, during the last years of Ashurbanipal's reign, the empire began to disintegrate. Under his son and successor it collapsed before the simultaneous onslaught of the Medes from the east and the resurgent Babylonians from the south. Babylon rose once again, and, in a brief renewal (612–538 B.C.), the old southern Mesopotamian culture flourished, especially under the storied King Nebuchadnezzar, whose exploits we read of in the Book of Daniel. Nebuchadnezzar made Babylon a fabulous city once again and its famous "hanging gardens" one of the seven wonders of the ancient world. Of its temple to Bel—the Hebrews' Tower of Babel—only a little of the

A grand approach to the temple complex led down a walled processional way lined with sixty stately figures of lions done in brightly colored glazed bricks (FIG. 2-30). These remarkable beasts, sacred to the goddess Ishtar, are molded in relief and glazed in yellow-brown and red against a ground of turquoise or dark blue. The Babylonian glazes are opaque and hard; possibly each brick was molded and enameled separately. Also, it may be that as a result of this technique these animals, whose vigor is suggested by snarling muzzles, long, nervous tails, and carefully depicted muscles, are more stylized than those of the Assyrian hunting reliefs.

The processional way passed through the monumental, brilliantly glazed Ishtar Gate (FIG. 2-31), the design of which, with its flanking crenelated towers, conforms to the type of gate found in earlier Babylonian and Assyrian architecture. Glazed tiles had been used much earlier, but the surface of the bricks, even of those on which figures appeared, was flat. On the surfaces of the Ishtar Gate, laboriously reassembled, are superposed tiers of figures in profile, the dragon of Marduk and the bull of Adad alternating. Here is the characteristic Mesopotamian formality at its best. The figures make a stately heraldry proclaiming the gods of the temples toward which the Sacred Way leads. The lessons of architectural sculpture from Boghazköy and Khorsabad have been well learned, and the perfect adjustment of figure to wall found in the Ishtar animals has rarely been surpassed; certainly in the history of architecture few more colorful and durable surface ornaments are known.

ACHAEMENID PERSIA

Nebuchadnezzar, Daniel's "King of Kings," boasted: "I caused a mighty wall to circumscribe Babylon . . . so that the enemy who would do evil would not threaten . . . .

2-31   Right: The Ishtar Gate (restored), Babylon, c. 575 B.C. Pergamon Museum, East Berlin.

[and] of the city of Babylon [I] made a fortress." Nevertheless, the handwriting on the wall appeared and the city was taken by Cyrus of Persia (559–529 B.C.), founder of the Achaemenid dynasty, who traced his ancestry back to a mythical King Achaemenes. The impetus of the Persians' expansion carried them far beyond Babylon. Egypt fell to them in 525 B.C. By 480 B.C. the Persian empire extended from the Indus to the Danube, and only the successful resistance of the Greeks in the fifth century prevented it from embracing southeastern Europe as well. The Achaemenid line came to an end with the death of Darius III in 330 B.C., after his defeat in the Battle of Issus and the fall of his empire to Alexander the Great.

Architecture

The most important source of our knowledge of Persian building is the palace at Persepolis (FIG. 2-32), built between 520 and 460 B.C. by Darius I and Xerxes I, successors of Cyrus. Situated on the high plateau to the east of the Mesopotamian river valley, the heavily fortified palace stood on a wide platform overlooking the plain toward the

2-32   Royal Audience Hall and stairway, Persepolis, c. 500 B.C.

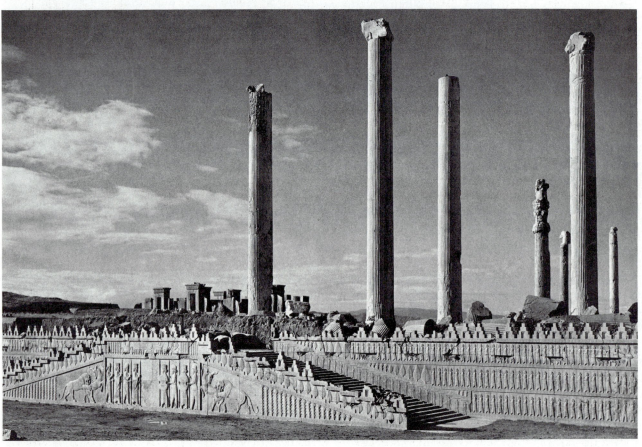

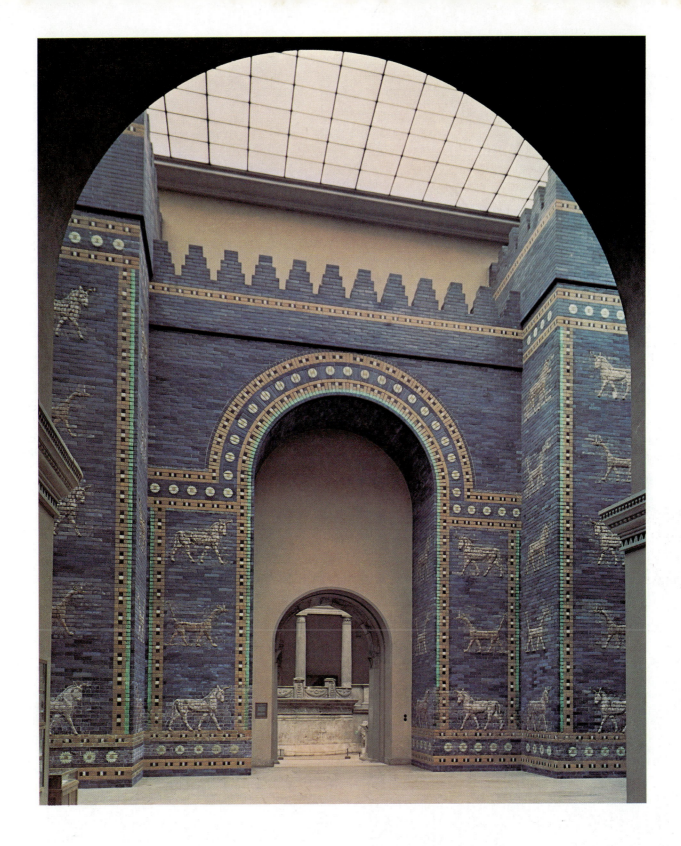

sunset. Although destroyed by Alexander the Great in a gesture symbolizing the destruction of Persian imperial power, its still impressive ruins permit a fairly complete reconstruction of its original appearance.

Unlike the Assyrian palace, which was tightly enfolded around courts (FIG. 2-24), the Persepolis buildings, although axially aligned, were loosely grouped and separated from each other by streets and irregular open spaces (FIG. 2-33). The dominant structure was a vast columned hall, sixty feet high and over 200 feet square. Standing on its own rock-cut podium, which is about ten feet high, this huge audience hall (*apadana*) has been called "one of the noblest

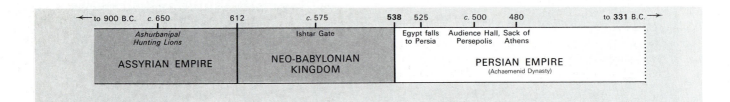
structures of the ancient world." It contained thirty-six forty-foot columns with slender, fluted shafts and capitals composed of the foreparts of bulls or lions arranged to provide a firm cradle for the roof timbers. FIG. 2-34 shows a well-preserved example from the somewhat later palace of Artaxerxes at Susa. These unique capitals are an impressive and decorative Persian invention with no known antecedents or descendants. Unknown also remains the genesis of the square, many-columned hall so characteristic of the Persepolis palace. It has been suggested that it may have been derived from Median architecture, which has remained a blank page in archeologists' books. The Medes were the northern allies, later subjects, of the Persians and are believed to have been the intermediaries through

whom Persian art received a variety of Iranian stylistic elements.

Stone, easily available at the site, was used liberally at Persepolis for platforms, gateways, stairs, and columns; brick was used for the walls, however, and wood for the smaller columns and the roofs. The ruins of the palace at Persepolis (FIG. 2-35) show that stone was used also for door and window frames. The forms are derived from Egyptian architecture, which had impressed Darius, but here the frames are not composed structurally of posts, lintels, and sills but are cut in an arbitrary manner and used as sculptural ornaments. In fact, the entire complex of buildings, and particularly the apadana, seems to have been designed primarily for visual effect; it is a gigantic stage setting for magnificent ceremonials celebrating not only traditional festivals but the greatness of the Persian empire and the power of its king.

Sculpture

The approach to the apadana leads through a monumental gateway flanked by colossal man-headed bulls and thence at right angles toward the elevated great hall, ascent to which is by broad, ceremonial stairways, designed as though for a stage. The walls of the terrace and staircases are decorated with reliefs representing processions of royal guards, Persian and Median nobles and dignitaries, and representatives from the subjected nations bringing tribute and gifts to the king (FIG. 2-36). These reliefs are thought to represent, in a shorthand version, the actual ceremonies that took place at Persepolis during the great New Year festivals. Traces of color found on similar monuments at other Persian sites suggest that, at least in part, these reliefs were colored. Their original effect must have been even greater than it is today as the rows of figures sparkled in a blaze of colors rivaling that presented by the court during the festivals. On the other hand, the present denuded state

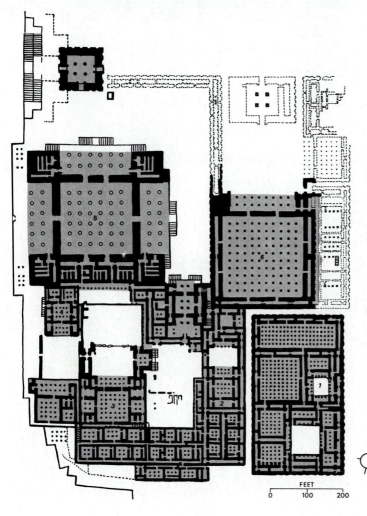

2-33 Plan of the palace complex at Persepolis.

1. Treasury
2. Harem
3. Palace of Xerxes
4. Palace of Darius I
5. Audience hall of Darius I
6. Throne hall of Xerxes
- - - - Partially excavated
     Originally roofed over (speculative)

of the reliefs makes it easier for us to appreciate their highly refined sculptural style. The cutting of the stone, both in the subtly modeled surfaces and the crisply chiseled details, is technically superb. Although they may have been inspired by Assyrian reliefs (FIGS. 2-26, 2-27, and 2-28), these Persian reliefs are strikingly different in style. The forms are more rounded and their projection from the background greater; there is less emphasis on such details as straining sinews and bulging muscles; and, most important perhaps, the figures seem organically more unified, as the torsos are now shown in natural side view and are thus more convincingly related to heads and legs. The supposition that most of these modifications of traditional formal elements are the result of Greek (Ionian) influence becomes almost a certainty when we note how the garments worn by the figures have been stylized in accordance with Greek Archaic practice (see Chapter Five). Despite the modifications, the Persepolis reliefs represent a triumph of Near Eastern formality in art. Their purpose and function, to glorify the king in a manner both decorative and monumental, is fulfilled most successfully.

Craft Art

Love for well-ordered forms enabled the designers to create, on a vast scale, a rich and unified setting for official ceremonials. But the Persians could also work successfully

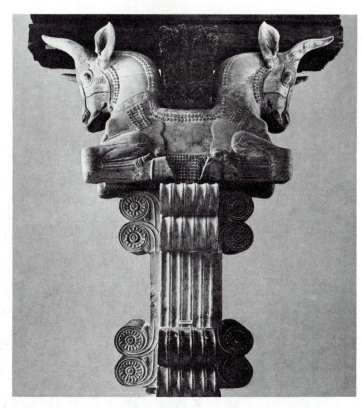

2-34 Bull capital from the Royal Audience Hall of the palace of Artaxerxes II, Susa, *c.* 375 B.C. Gray marble. Louvre, Paris.

2-35 Palace of Darius, Persepolis, *c.* 500 B.C.

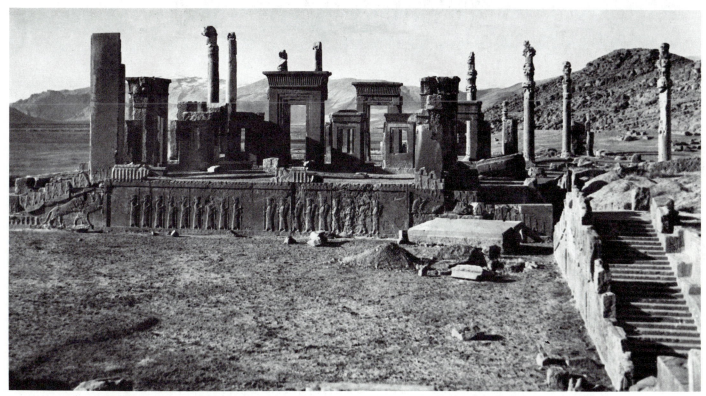

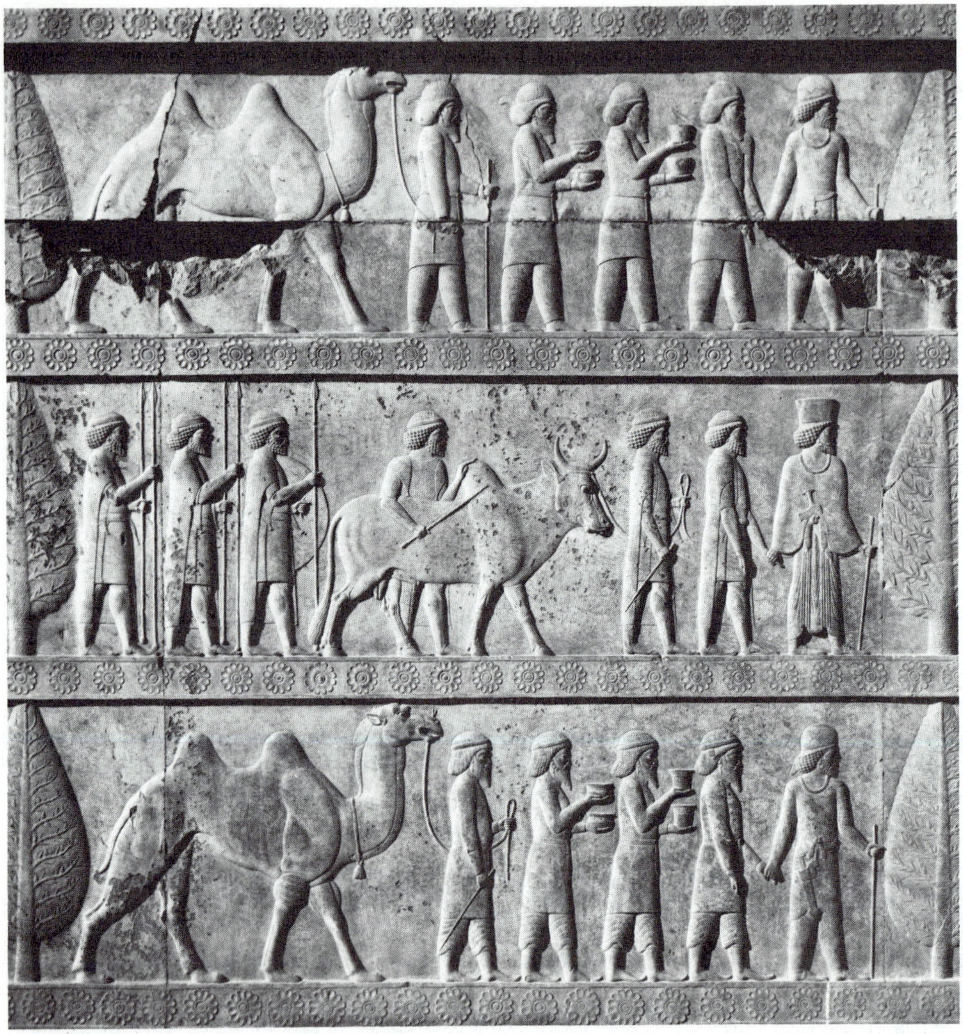

on a much smaller scale. They were excellent goldsmiths and silversmiths; the example shown, a jar handle in the form of a winged ibex (FIG. 2-37), typifies their exquisite and enduring art. Made of silver inlaid with gold, the ibex rears up on a palmette growing from the head of a satyr. The leap of the lithe body rises into the higher leap of the horns, and the suave curves of the wings smooth the motion. All that is needed of truth to nature is here, and none of it intrudes upon the effortless play of fancy.

As with most elements of Persian art, it is not difficult to trace the genesis of this winged ibex. Although the animal's body has regained its organic unity, probably through Mesopotamian influence, its original source of inspiration is to be found among the Luristan bronzes. Luristan, a mountainous region to the east of the Mesopotamian valley, inhabited at different times by Kassites, Medes, and other seminomadic tribes, was the home of a flourishing bronze industry that reached its peak during the eighth and seventh centuries B.C. It produced a variety of portable objects, such as cups, bowls, weapons, bridles, and articles of personal adornment that, collectively, are referred to as nomad's gear. While we do not know by and for whom these objects were made, they form a homogeneous group that is rooted in an old and widespread tradition whose exponents delighted in working with animal forms. This so-called animal style may have originated in the Luristan region; at any rate it spread over much of the ancient world, from the Asiatic steppes to central and western Europe. The Luristan bronzes are characterized by a high degree of abstraction that converts the representations of animals into purely decorative devices. In the handle of the ceremonial cauldron illustrated (FIG. 2-38), the two rearing ibexes make interlocking arcs that echo in linear form the three-dimensional shape of the vessel to which they are attached. Although wingless, their pose, attitude, and purpose leave little room for doubt that they are the forerunners of the Persian ibex. And, incidentally, the source of inspiration for the Persian animal's wings seems to appear in the embossed decoration of the bowl, where the Luristan artist has boldly copied Assyrian winged bulls and sacred emblems (in Assyrian style and technique).

Eclecticism of Achaemenid Art

Thirty years ago, Achaemenid art was called eclectic—that is, derivative and lacking originality. Today, as more knowledge has been accumulated about the earlier periods of art in Iran, much that seemed to have been brought in from the outside can be shown to have had roots also in earlier Iranian periods and to have been accepted in a new form from that source. Thus, the platforms of the palaces at Persepolis are similar to those found in Mesopotamia, but the fact that Persepolis was built on the terrace of a mountain spur may reflect ancient Persian custom. The inhabitants of southwest Iran had rock reliefs carved with lines of marching figures, the monotony of which has been compared with some of the reliefs adorning the stairway façades at Persepolis. On the other hand the guardian figures are of Assyrian origin, the machinelike precision in the carving of details is reminiscent of Assyrian relief sculpture, the columned halls may have been influenced by Egyptian or Median models, and the fluting of columns is derived from Greek (Ionian) practice. And yet, the manner in which these various elements have been combined produces an ensemble that is quite new and different from the art of those nations from which they may derive. A Persian

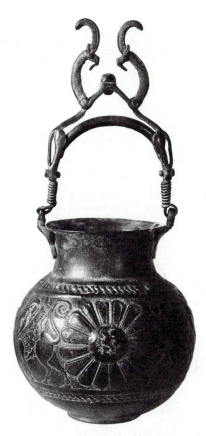

2-38 Ritual cauldron, Luristan, eighth century B.C. Bronze, approx. 12″ high. Cincinnati Art Museum, The Mary Hanna Fund.

column cannot be mistaken for either an Egyptian or a Greek one, and nothing like the Persian apadana has been found in earlier architecture. With all their derivative elements, the architecture and sculpture of Persepolis produce a coherent and majestic impression.

Prior to their conquest of the Near East, the Persians' art had consisted mainly of the small-scale nomad's gear. Their monumental art was created "on the spur of the moment," one might say, when they found themselves masters of the Near East and heirs to its rich culture. To glorify and eternalize their military and political achievements the Persians not only adopted those features of foreign and conquered cultures that seemed to serve this purpose but also brought into the country the artisans who could best realize their ambitious projects. A building inscription at Susa names Ionians, Sardians, Medes, Egyptians, and Babylonians among the workmen who built and decorated the palace. But under the single-minded direction of its Persian masters this mixed crowd with a widely varied cultural and artistic background created a new and coherent style that was perfectly suited to express Persian imperial ambitions. A court style, like that of Louis XIV over two millennia later, it compelled its contributors into a synthesis that was to remain remarkably uniform during the 200-year reign of the Achaemenid dynasty.

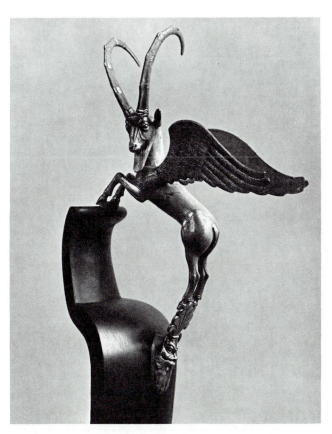

2-37 Jar handle in the form of a winged ibex, Persia, fifth to fourth centuries B.C. Silver inlaid with gold, approx. 10½″ high. Louvre, Paris.

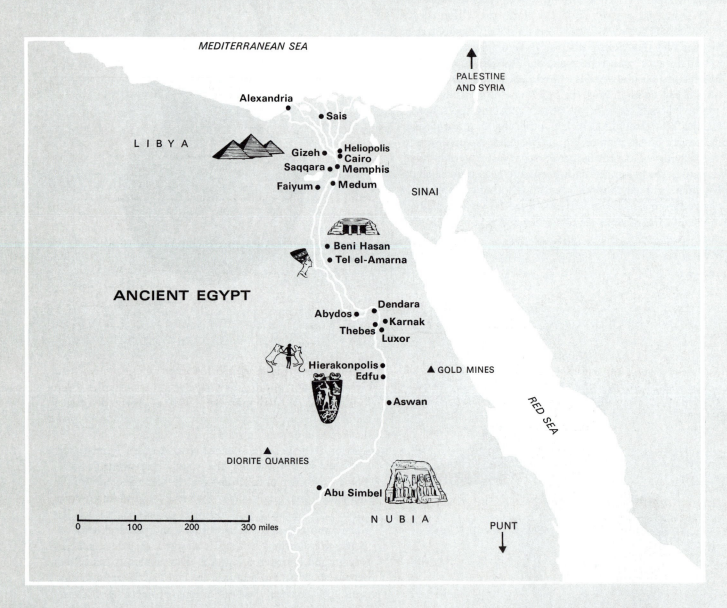

MEDITERRANEAN SEA

PALESTINE
AND SYRIA

Alexandria

Sais

LIBYA

Gizeh
Saqqara
Faiyum

Heliopolis
Cairo
Memphis
Medum

SINAI

Beni Hasan
Tel el-Amarna

ANCIENT EGYPT

Abydos
Thebes

Dendara
Karnak
Luxor

Hierakonpolis
Edfu

▲ GOLD MINES

RED SEA

Aswan

DIORITE QUARRIES

Abu Simbel

0   100   200   300 miles

N U B I A

PUNT

chapter three

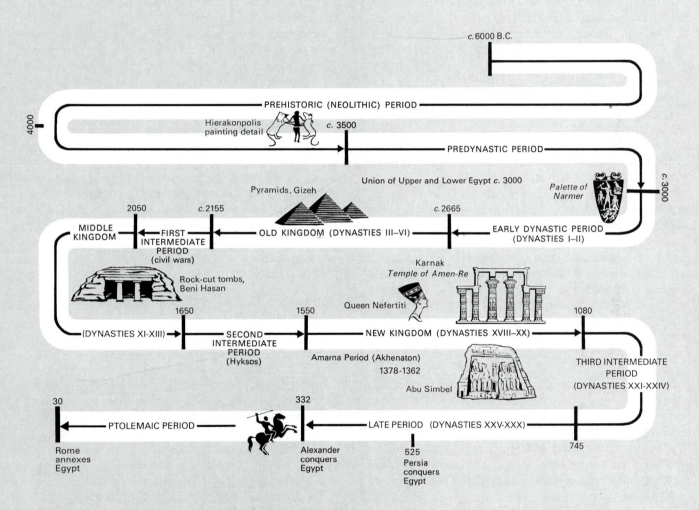

c. 6000 B.C.

PREHISTORIC (NEOLITHIC) PERIOD

4000

Hierakonpolis
painting detail

c. 3500

PREDYNASTIC PERIOD

c. 3000

Union of Upper and Lower Egypt *c.* 3000

Pyramids, Gizeh

Palette of Narmer

2050   *c.* 2155   *c.* 2665

MIDDLE
KINGDOM

FIRST
INTERMEDIATE
PERIOD
(civil wars)

OLD KINGDOM (DYNASTIES III–VI)

EARLY DYNASTIC PERIOD
(DYNASTIES I–II)

Rock-cut tombs,
Beni Hasan

Karnak
Temple of Amen-Re

Queen Nefertiti

1650   1550   1080

(DYNASTIES XI-XIII)

SECOND
INTERMEDIATE
PERIOD
(Hyksos)

Amarna Period (Akhenaton)
1378-1362

Abu Simbel

NEW KINGDOM (DYNASTIES XVIII–XX)

THIRD INTERMEDIATE
PERIOD
(DYNASTIES XXI-XXIV)

30   332

PTOLEMAIC PERIOD

LATE PERIOD   (DYNASTIES XXV-XXX)

745

Rome
annexes
Egypt

Alexander
conquers
Egypt

525
Persia
conquers
Egypt

The Art of Egypt

OVER 2000 YEARS AGO the admiring Herodotus wrote: "Concerning Egypt itself I shall extend my remarks to a great length, because there is no country that possesses so many wonders, nor any that has such a number of works which defy description." He added a little later: "They [the Egyptians] are religious to excess, far beyond any other race of men." Men of discernment, aware of the profusion of monuments left to the world by the ancient Egyptians, have long been in agreement with these observations. While the Egyptians built their dwellings of impermanent materials, they made their tombs (which they believed would preserve their bodies forever), their temples to the immortal gods, and the statues of their equally immortal god-king of imperishable stone. The cliffs of the Libyan and Arabian deserts and the Nile flowing between them could represent, respectively, the timelessness of the Egyptian world and the endless cycles of natural process. Religion and permanence—these are the elements that characterize their solemn and ageless art and express the unchanging order that for the ancient Egyptians was divinely ordained.

Even more than the Tigris and Euphrates, the Nile defined the cultures that lived by virtue of its presence. Originating deep in Africa, the world's longest river descended through many cataracts to sea level in Egypt, where, in annual flood, it deposited rich soil brought thousands of miles from the African hills. Hemmed in by the narrow valley, which even in its widest parts reaches a width of only about twelve miles, the Nile flows through regions that may not have a single drop of rainfall in a decade. Yet, crops grew luxuriantly from the fertilizing silt. Game also abounded then, and the great river that made life possible entered the consciousness of the Egyptians as a god and as a symbol of life.

In predynastic, or prehistoric, and pharaonic times the river held wider sway than it does today. Egypt was a land of marshes dotted with island ridges, and what is now arid desert valley was grassy parkland well suited for grazing cattle and hunting. Amphibious animals swarmed in the marshes and were hunted through tall forests of papyrus and rushes. The fertility of Egypt was proverbial, and, at the end of its history, when Egypt had become a province of the Roman empire, it was the granary of the Mediterranean world.

Before settled communities could be built along the Nile's banks, however, it was necessary to control the annual floods. This was done with dams for diverting flood waters into fields rather than controlling the flow of the river, and the communal effort needed for their construction provided the basis for the growth of an Egyptian civilization, just as the irrigation projects in the Mesopotamian valley had furnished the civilizing impetus for that region a few centuries earlier.

In the Middle Ages, when the history of Egypt was thought of as part of the history of Islam, its ancient reputation as a land of wonders and mystery lived on in more or less fabulous report. Until the later eighteenth century, its undeciphered writing and its exotic monuments were regarded as treasures of occult wisdom locked away from any but those initiated in the mystic arts. Scholars knew something of the history of Egypt from references in the Old Testament, from the unreliable reports of travelers ancient and modern, and from a history of Egypt written in Greek by an Egyptian named Manetho in the second century B.C. Manetho described the succession of pharaohs, dividing them into the still useful groups we call dynasties; but his chronology is very inaccurate and his account untrustworthy.

Scientific history, or at least scientific archeology, had its start when, at the end of the eighteenth century, modern Europe rediscovered Egypt; Egypt became the first subject of archeological exploration, and this was followed by the uncovering of the ancient civilizations of the Tigris and the Euphrates. In 1799, Napoleon Bonaparte, on a military expedition to Egypt, took with him a small troop of scholars, linguists, antiquarians, and artists. The chance discovery of the famed Rosetta Stone, now in the British Museum, gave the eager scholars what they wanted, a key to the till then undeciphered Egyptian hieroglyphic writing. The stone bears an inscription in three sections, one in Greek, which was easily read, one in *demotic* (late Egyptian), and one in formal hieroglyphic. It was at once suspected that the inscription was the same in all three sections and that with the Greek as a key the other two could be deciphered. More than twenty years later, after many false starts, a young linguist, Jean François Champollion, deduced that the hieroglyphs were not simply pictographs but the signs of a once-spoken language—vestiges of which survived in Coptic. Champollion's feat made him a kind of Columbus of the new science of archeology, as well as of that special branch within it, Egyptology. Those who followed Champollion, like Auguste Mariette and Gaston Maspero, sought to build classified collections and to protect Egyptian art from the unscrupulous. Men like Flinders Petrie introduced techniques of excavation, preparing the ground for the development of sound methods for validating knowledge of Egyptian civilization.

Ideally the foundation of archeological knowledge is a reliable chronology. Yet, as the body of archeological evidence enlarges and new scientific methods of dating are developed, the chronology must change to accommodate them. Sometimes what was thought close to certain turns problematical; sometimes what was guesswork or speculation suddenly becomes probable. Because this is more often the case the further back one goes in time, the predynastic beginnings of Egyptian civilization are chronologically vague, as are those of Mesopotamia. Some time

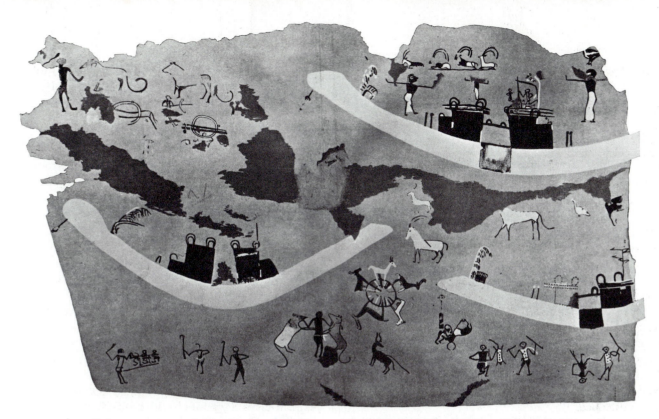

3-1 *Men, Boats, and Animals*, wall painting from a shrine at Hierakonpolis, *c.* 3500 B.C. (After Quibell.)

around 3500 B.C. a people of native African stock may have been exposed to influences from Mesopotamia, or it is possible that, as in Sumer, the sudden cultural development may have been due to an actual incursion of a new people. A wall painting from the late predynastic period, found in a shrine at Hierakonpolis in Upper Egypt (FIG. 3-1), represents men, animals, and boats in a lively, helter-skelter fashion. The boats, symbolic of the journey down the river of life and death, are painted white and seem to carry a cargo of tombs mourned over by women. Also shown are a heraldic grouping of two animals (lions?) on either side of a human figure, many figures of gazelles, and, in the lower right corner, men fighting. The heraldic group, a compositional type usually associated with Mesopotamian art, suggests that by this time influences from Mesopotamia not only had reached Egypt but had already made the thousand-mile journey upstream. The stick-figures and their apparently random arrangement remind one of the Mesolithic rock paintings from the Spanish Levant and North Africa, the style of which flourished also in the central Sahara and may have been another impetus to the development of Egyptian art.

The Hierakonpolis mural is the earliest known representative of that millennia-long tradition of painting that reveals to us the funerary customs of Egypt, so much at the center of Egyptian life. Most paintings are found in tombs and provide the principal archeological evidence for the historical reconstruction of Egyptian civilization. Religion pervaded that civilization. In Herodotus' words, the Egyp-

tian was "religious to excess," and his concern for immortality amounted to near-obsession; his overall preoccupation in this life was to ensure his safety and happiness in the next. To this preoccupation we owe the major part of the monuments the Egyptians left behind them.

The sharp distinction between body and soul, long familiar to Christianity and other later religions, was not made in the religion of the Egyptians. Rather they believed that from birth one was accompanied by a kind of other self, the *ka*, which, upon the death of the fleshly body, could inhabit the corpse and live on. For the ka to live securely, however, the dead body had to remain as nearly intact as possible; to see that it did, the Egyptians developed to a high art the technique of embalming, their success in which is made evident by numerous well-preserved mummies of kings (like Ramses II), princes, and nobles, as well as of some common persons. The first requirement for immortality, mummification, was followed by others: Food and drink had to be provided, as well as clothing, utensils, and all the apparatus of life, so that nothing would be lacking that had been enjoyed on earth. Images of the deceased, sculptured in the round and placed in shallow recesses, guaranteed the permanence of his identity by providing substitute dwelling places for the ka in case the mummy disintegrated. Wall paintings (for the use and delectation of the ka) recorded with great animation and detail the recurring round of human activities, a cycle of "works and days" that changed with the calendar and the seasons. The Egyptians hoped and expected that the images and inventory of life, set up and collected within the protecting, massive stone walls of the tomb, would ensure immortality; but almost from the beginning of the elaborate interments, the thorough plundering of tombs became a profitable occupation. Only one royal burial place remained close to intact, that of King Tutankhamun of the Eighteenth Dynasty; its discovery, in 1924, revealed to a fascinated world the full splendor of a pharaoh's funerary assemblage.

THE EARLY DYNASTIC PERIOD AND THE OLD KINGDOM

Egypt has been known as the Kingdom of the Two Lands, a reference to its very early physical and political division into Upper Egypt and Lower Egypt. The upper land was dry and rocky and rustic in culture; the lower land, opulent, urban, and populous. Even in predynastic times there must have been conflict between the two, for the ancient Egyptians began the history of Egypt, as we do, with the forcible unification of the two lands by a certain Menes.

The "Palette of Narmer"

Menes is thought to be King Narmer, whose image we find on a slate slab from Hierakonpolis (FIG. 3-2). The slab, or palette as it is called, was originally used as a tablet on which eye makeup (to protect the eyes against sun-glare and irritation) was prepared. The *Palette of Narmer* is an elaborate, formalized version of a utilitarian object common in the predynastic period. Its importance is great, not only as a historical document that records the unification of the two Egypts and the beginning of the dynastic pe-

riod, but as a kind of early blueprint of the formula of figure representation that was to rule Egyptian art for some 3000 years. On the palette's back, the king, wearing the high, bowling-pin-shaped crown of Upper Egypt, is about to slay an enemy as a sacrifice. Before him a hawk, symbol of the sky god, Horus, protector of the king, takes into captivity a man-headed hieroglyph for land from which papyrus grows (a symbol for Lower Egypt). Below the king are two fallen enemies and, above, two heads of Hathor, a goddess favorably disposed to Narmer. The other side of the palette shows Narmer wearing the cobra crown of Lower Egypt and reviewing a pile of the beheaded enemy. In both cases it is significant that the king, towering over his own men and the enemy—by virtue of his superior rank—performs his ritual task alone. Historical narrative as we find it in Mesopotamian reliefs (see the *Victory Stele of Naram-Sin,* FIG. 2-19) is not of primary importance in this work; what is important is the concentration upon the king as a deified figure, isolated from all ordinary men and far above them and alone responsible for his triumph. As early as the Narmer palette (about 3000 B.C.) we see evidence of this Egyptian convention of thought, of art, and of state policy—namely, that the kingship is divine, that its prestige is one with the prestige of the gods.

If what belongs to the gods and to nature is unchanging and if the king is divine, then his attributes must be eternal. We have already seen that, in Mesopotamian art, the ever changing natural shapes are formalized into simple poses, attitudes, and actions. The same thing happens in Egypt, even though the instinct for convention leads to a somewhat different style. In the figure of Narmer we find the stereotype of kingly transcendence that, through several slight variations, will be repeated in subsequent representation of all Egyptian dynasts but Akhenaton (see

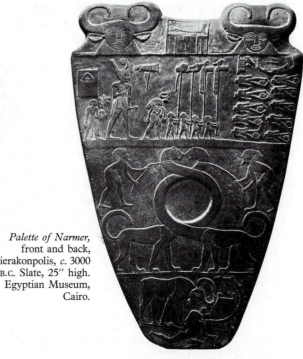
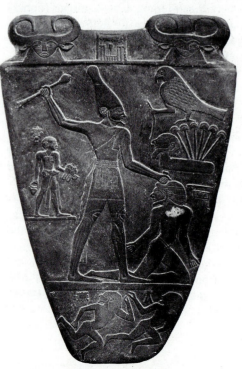

3-2 *Palette of Narmer,* front and back, Hierakonpolis, *c.* 3000 B.C. Slate, 25″ high. Egyptian Museum, Cairo.

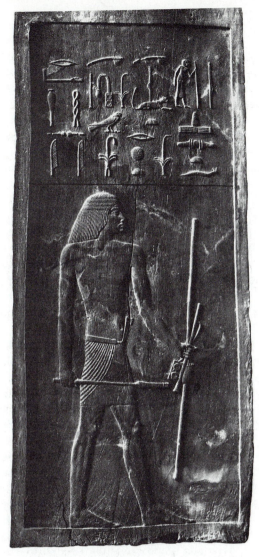

3-3 *Panel of Hesire*, Saqqara, *c.* 2750 B.C. Wood, 45″ high. Egyptian Museum, Cairo.

below) in the fourteenth century. The king is seen in a perspective that combines the profile views of head, legs, and arms with the front views of eye and shoulders. While the proportions of the figure will change, the method of its representation will become a standard for all later Egyptian art. Like a set of primordial commandments, the *Palette of Narmer* sets forth the basic laws that will govern art along the Nile for thousands of years. In the Hierakonpolis painting (FIG. 3-1) figures had been scattered across the wall more or less haphazardly; here a surface has been subdivided into a number of bands, and the pictorial elements have been inserted in a neat and orderly way into their organized setting. The horizontal lines that separate the bands also define the ground that supports the figures—a mode that will persist in hundreds of acres of Egyptian wall paintings and reliefs.

Three centuries later we find the basic conventions of Egyptian figure representation that were fixed in the *Palette of Narmer* refined and systematized on a carved wooden panel representing Hesire, a high official from the

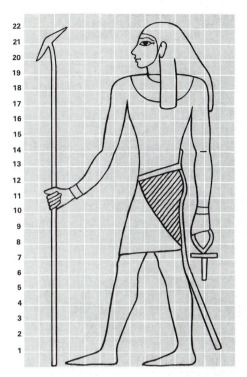

3-4 The "Later Canon" of Egyptian Art. (After Panofsky.)

court of King Zoser (FIG. 3-3). The figure's swelling forms have been modeled with greater subtlety and its proportions have been changed to a broad-shouldered, narrow-hipped ideal; the artist uses the conceptual approach (see Chapter Two, p. 45) rather than the optical, representing what he knows to be true of the object instead of some random view of it and showing its most characteristic parts at right angles to the line of vision. This conceptual approach expresses a feeling for the constant and changeless aspect of things and lends itself to systematic methods of figure construction (FIG. 3-4). Although perhaps not quite so simple as his description of it, the system has been explained by Erwin Panofsky as follows:

> With its more significant lines permanently fixed on specific points of the human body, the Egyptian network [of equal squares] immediately indicates to the painter or sculptor how to organize his figure: he will know from the outset that he must place the ankle on the first horizontal line, the knee on the sixth . . . and so on. . . . It was, for instance, agreed that in a [lunging] figure . . . the length of pace . . . should amount to $10\frac{1}{2}$ units, while this distance in a figure quietly standing was set at $4\frac{1}{2}$ or $5\frac{1}{2}$ units. Without too much exaggeration one could maintain that, when an Egyptian artist familiar with this system of proportion was set the task of representing a standing, sitting, or striding figure, the result was a foregone conclusion once the figure's absolute size was determined.[1]

[1] Erwin Panofsky, *Meaning in the Visual Arts* (Garden City, N.Y.: Doubleday, 1955), pp. 58–61.

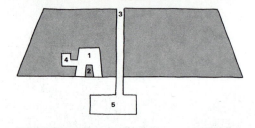

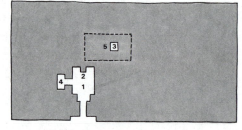

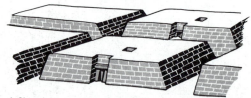

1. Chapel
2. False door
3. Shaft into burial chamber
4. Serdab (chamber for statue of deceased)
5. Burial chamber

3-5 Mastabas, with plan and (at top) schematic section.

In addition to recording an important historical event and to laying down ground rules for the pictorial arts, the *Palette of Narmer* also illustrates several stages in the development of Egyptian writing. The story of Narmer's victories is represented in the different registers with varying degrees of symbolism. Straight pictorial narrative is used to show the king following his standard-bearers in triumphal procession and inspecting the bodies of his slain enemies. This simple picture-writing becomes symbolic when, in a bottom register, the king is shown as a bull breaking down the walls of an enemy fortress. The symbolism becomes more abstract in the pile of decapitated foes: Here each body, its severed head neatly placed between its legs, probably is a numerical symbol representing a specific number of fallen enemies. Finally, in the signs appearing near the heads of the more important figures, pictographs take on phonetic values, as the names of the respective individuals have been written in true hieroglyphs.

Architecture

Similar principles of permanence and regularity appear in the design of the Egyptian tomb, that symbol of the timeless, the silent house of the dead. We find its standard shape in the *mastaba* (FIG. 3-5). The mastaba (Arabic for "bench") is a rectangular brick or stone structure with battered (sloping) sides erected over a subterranean tomb chamber that was connected with the outside by a shaft. The form was probably developed from mounds of earth or stone that covered earlier tombs. It is significant that in Mesopotamia there was relative indifference to the cult of burial and to the permanence of the tomb, while in Egypt such matters are considered to be of the first importance.

About 2610 B.C. the Stepped Pyramid of King Zoser of the Third Dynasty (FIG. 3-6) was raised at Saqqara, the ancient necropolis (city of the dead) of Memphis. Possibly Egypt's oldest stone building, it was the first monumental royal tomb. In form a kind of compromise between the mastaba and the later "true" pyramids at Gizeh, it is in fact a piling of mastabas of diminishing size one upon another, forming a structure resembling the great ziggurats of Mesopotamia. Unlike them, Zoser's pyramid is a tomb, not a temple, and is elevated above the funerary complex arranged around it.

A tomb such as Zoser's had a dual function: to protect the mummified king and his possessions and to symbolize by its gigantic presence his absolute, godlike power. This structure, with its temples (now thought to be a medical shrine), complex of chambered terraces, and great courtyard, was the work of Imhotep, the first artist of recorded history. Grand vizier to King Zoser and a man of legendary powers, he was celebrated in the ancient world not only as an architect but as a wise man, wizard, physician ("the father of medicine"), priest, and scribe—a kind of universal genius who later came to be worshiped as a deity.

At Gizeh, near modern Cairo but across the Nile (the dead were always buried on the side where the sun sets), are three pyramids of pharaohs of the Fourth Dynasty

3-6 Stepped Pyramid of King Zoser, Saqqara, c. 2610 B.C.

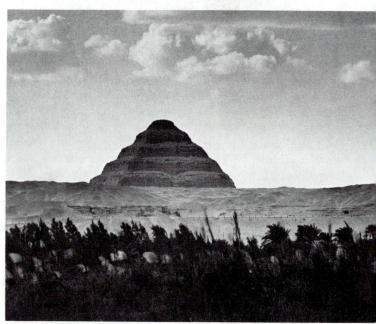

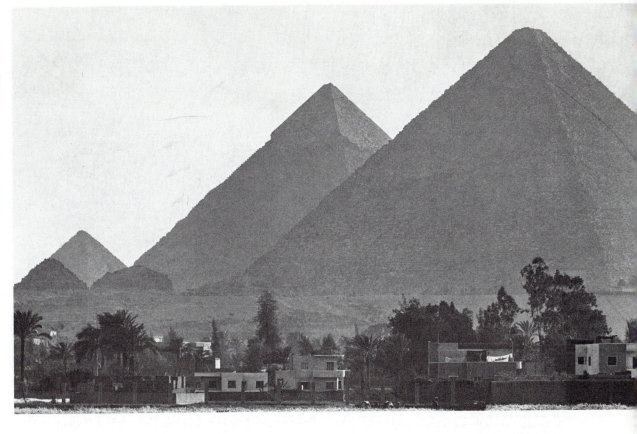

3-7 Great Pyramids of Gizeh: From left, Menkure, *c.* 2460 B.C.; Khafre, *c.* 2500 B.C.; Khufu, *c.* 2530 B.C.

(FIG. 3-7)—Khufu (the Greek Cheops), Khafre (Chephren), and Menkaure (Mykerinus). Built around 2500 B.C., they have been associated with mystery and with "hidden" knowledge and have served as symbols for many things—primeval wisdom, Egypt itself, eternal stability, and the arts of magic. The pyramids of Gizeh represent the culmination of an architectural evolution that began with the mastaba. They did not evolve out of necessity; kings could have gone on indefinitely piling mastabas one upon another to make their weighty tombs. Rather, it has been suggested that when the kings of the Third Dynasty moved their permanent residence to Memphis they came under the influence of nearby Heliopolis. This city was the seat of the powerful cult of Re, the sun god, whose fetish was a pyramidal stone, the *ben-ben*. By the Fourth Dynasty the pharaohs considered themselves the sons of Re and, hence, his incarnation on earth. For the pharaohs, then, it would have been only a step from the belief that the spirit and power of Re resided in the pyramidal *ben-ben* to the belief that their divine spirits and bodies would be similarly preserved within pyramidal tombs.

Is the pyramid form, then, an invention inspired by a religious demand rather than the result of a formal evolution? We need not decide here. Our concern is rather with the remarkable features of the Fourth Dynasty pyramid. Of the three at Gizeh, that of Khufu is the oldest and largest. Except for the galleries and burial chamber it is an almost solid mass of limestone masonry, a stone mountain built on the same principle as the Stepped Pyramid of Zoser, the interior spaces in plan and elevation being relatively tiny, as if crushed out of the scheme by the sheer weight of stone (FIG. 3-8). The limestone was quarried in the eastern Nile cliffs and floated across the river during the seasonal floods. After the masons finished cutting the stones, they marked them with red ink to indicate the place of each in the structure. Then great gangs of laborers dragged them (the wheel was not yet known) up temporary ramps and laid them course upon course. Finally the pyramid was surfaced with a casing of pearly white limestone, cut with such nicety that the eye could scarcely detect the

3-8 Section of the Pyramid of Khufu. (After Hoelscher.)

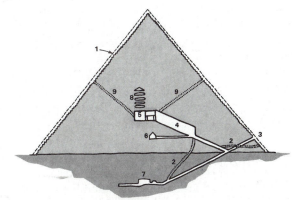

1. Silhouette with original facing stone
2. Thieves' tunnels
3. Entrance
4. Grand gallery
5. King's chamber
6. So-called queen's chamber
7. False tomb chamber
8. Relieving blocks
9. Airshafts?

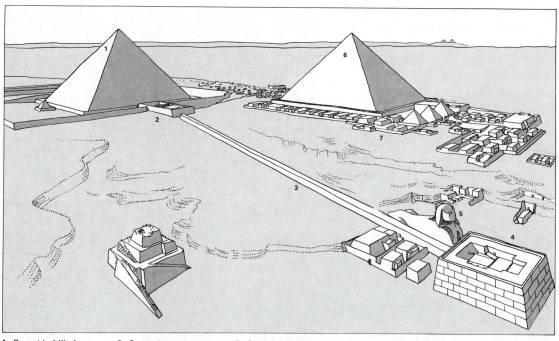

1. Pyramid of Khafre 3. Covered causeway 5. Great Sphinx 7. Pyramids of the royal family and mastabas of nobles
2. Mortuary temple 4. Valley temple 6. Pyramid of Khufu

joints. A few casing stones can still be seen in the cap that covers the Pyramid of Khafre, all that remain after many centuries during which the pyramids were stripped to supply limestone for the Islamic builders of Cairo. The immensity of the Pyramid of Khufu is indicated by some dimensions in round numbers: At the base the length of one side is 775 feet and its area some 13 acres; its present height is 450 feet (originally 480 feet). According to Petrie, the structure contains about 2,300,000 blocks of stone, each of which averages $2\frac{1}{2}$ tons in weight; Napoleon's scholars calculated that the blocks in the three pyramids were enough to build a 1×10-foot wall around France. Yet it is not alone huge size and successful engineering that constitute the art of this structure but its formal design—the proportions and immense dignity so consistent with its funerary and religious function and so well adapted to its geographical setting: The four corners are oriented to the cardinal points of the compass, and the grave and simple mass dominates the flat landscape to the horizon. The ironic outcome of the stupendous effort may be read from the cross section (FIG. 3-8). The dotted lines at the base of the structure indicate the path cut into the pyramid by ancient grave robbers. Unable to locate the carefully sealed and hidden entrance, they started some forty feet above the base and tunneled into the structure until they intercepted the ascending corridor. Many royal tombs were plundered almost as soon as the funeral ceremonies had ended; the very conspicuousness of the pyramid was an invitation to despoilment. The hard lesson was learned by the successors of the Old Kingdom pyramid-builders; they built few pyramids, and those relatively small and inconspicuous.

From the remains around the middle pyramid of Gizeh, that of Khafre, we can reconstruct an entire pyramid complex (FIG. 3-9). This consisted of the pyramid itself, within or below which was the burial chamber; the chapel, adjoining the pyramid on the east side, where offerings were made and ceremonies performed and where were stored cloth, food, and ceremonial vessels; the covered causeway leading down to the valley; and the valley temple, or vestibule of the causeway. Beside the causeway and dominating the temple of Khafre rose the Great Sphinx, carved from a spur of rock to commemorate the pharaoh. The head is often referred to as a portrait of Khafre, although the features are so generalized that little individuality can be discerned. In size it is unique in ancient sculpture.

The valley temple of the Pyramid of Khafre (FIG. 3-10) was built on the post-and-lintel system—upright supports, or posts, with horizontal beams, or lintels, resting on them. Both posts and lintels were huge, rectangular, red-granite monoliths, finely proportioned, skillfully cut and polished, and devoid of decoration. Alabaster slabs covered the floor, and seated statues, the only embellishment of the temple, were ranged along the wall. The interior was lighted by a few slanting rays filtering in from above. Although the Egyptians knew the arch and the vault and had used them occasionally in predynastic tombs, they rarely used them again after about 3000 B.C., the beginning of the dynastic period. Egyptian architects preferred the static forms of the post-and-lintel system, which, if cast into the heavy, massive shapes of the Khafre temple, express perhaps better than any other architectural style the changeless and eternal.

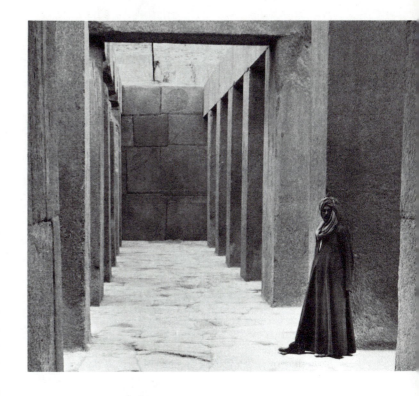

3-10 Middle aisle of the hall of pillars, valley temple of the Pyramid of Khafre, Gizeh, *c.* 2500 B.C.

Sculpture

We have already noted that in the tombs sculpture in the round served the important function of creating an image of the deceased that could serve as an abode for the ka should the mummy be destroyed. For this reason an interest in portrait likenesses developed early in Egypt. Hence, too, permanence of style and material were essential. Though wood, clay, and bronze were used, mostly for images of those not of the royal or noble classes, stone was the primary material: limestone and sandstone from the Nile cliffs, granite from the cataracts of the Upper Nile, and diorite from the desert.

A seated statue of Khafre (FIG. 3-11) was one of a series of similar statues carved for Khafre's valley temple near the Sphinx. These statues, the only organic forms in the geometric severity of the temple structure, with its flat-planed posts and lintels, must have created a striking atmosphere of solemn majesty. Khafre is seated on a throne on the base of which is carved the intertwined lotus and papyrus, symbol of united Egypt. Sheltering his head are the protecting wings of the hawk, symbol of the sun, indicating Khafre's divine status as son of Re. He wears the simple kilt of the Old Kingdom and a linen headdress that covers his forehead and falls in pleated folds over his shoulders. The representation of the king is strongly individualized yet permeated with an imperturbable calm, reflecting the enduring power of the pharaoh and of king-

ship in general. This effect, common to royal statues of the ka, is achieved by devices of form and technique that we can still admire. The figure has great compactness and solidity, with few projecting, breakable parts; the form manifests the purpose—to last for eternity. The body is attached to a back slab, the arms are held close to the torso and thighs, the legs are close together and attached to the

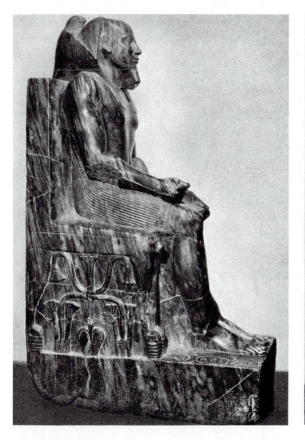
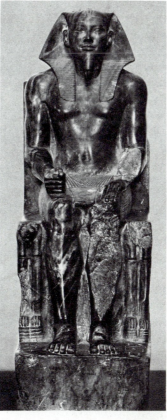

3-11 *Khafre,* side and front, Gizeh, *c.* 2500 B.C. Diorite, 66″ high. Egyptian Museum, Cairo.

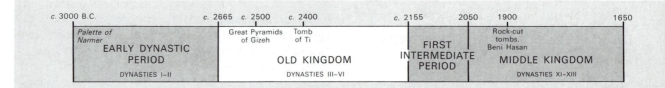

c. 3000 B.C.		c. 2665	c. 2500	c. 2400		c. 2155	2050	1900		1650
	Palette of Narmer		Great Pyramids of Gizeh	Tomb of Ti				Rock-cut tombs, Beni Hasan		
	EARLY DYNASTIC PERIOD			OLD KINGDOM		FIRST INTERMEDIATE PERIOD		MIDDLE KINGDOM		
	DYNASTIES I–II			DYNASTIES III–VI				DYNASTIES XI–XIII		

throne by stone webs. Like Mesopotamian statues, the pose is frontal, rigid, and bisymmetrical. This repeatable scheme arranges the parts of the body so that they are presented in a totally frontal projection or entirely in profile. As Panofsky remarked:

> . . . we can recognize from many unfinished pieces that even in sculpture the final form is always determined by an underlying geometrical plan originally sketched on the surfaces of the block. It is evident that the artist drew four separate designs on the vertical surfaces of the block . . . that he then evolved the figure by working away the surplus mass of stone so that the form was bounded by a system of planes meeting at right angles and connected by slopes . . . . there is a sculptor's working drawing . . . that illustrates the mason-like method of these sculptors even more clearly: as if he were constructing a house, the sculptor drew up plans for his sphinx in frontal elevation, ground plan and profile elevation . . . so that even today the figure could be executed according to plan.[2]

This subtractive method of "working away the surplus . . . stone" accounts for the blocklike look of the standard Egyptian statue, which strongly differs from the Mesopotamian cylindrical or conical shape seen, for example, in the Gudea statues (FIG. 2-20). The hardest stone was used to ensure the permanence of the image—and Egypt, again unlike Mesopotamia, is rich in stone. Even so, the difficulty of working granite and diorite with bronze tools (much of the finishing had to be done by abrasion) made production too expensive for all but the wealthiest.

As the figure was cut to plan, so were its proportions determined beforehand. A canon of ideal proportions, designated as appropriate for the representation of imposing majesty, was accepted and applied quite independently of optical fact. The generalized anatomy persisted in Egyptian statuary even into the Ptolemaic age, when Greek influence might have been expected to shift it toward realism. The Egyptian sculptor seems to have been indifferent to realistic representation of the body, preferring to strive for fidelity to nature in the art of portraiture, at which Egyptians have not been surpassed.

An example of their skill is a so-called reserve (duplicate, or spare) head of a prince of the family of Khufu (FIG. 3-12). Attention is given only to the execution of the face,

[2]Panofsky, *Meaning in the Visual Arts,* pp. 58–59.

which shows the union of the formal with the realistic that gives distinction to so many portait busts of its type. Reserve heads were placed outside the burial chamber and their purpose is not understood. This head displays the extraordinary sensitivity of Old Kingdom portraiture. The personality—sharply intelligent, vivacious, and alert—is read by the sculptor with a penetration and sympathy seldom achieved in the history of sculpture.

In the history of art, especially portraiture, it is almost a rule that formality is relaxed and realism increased where the subject is a person of lesser importance. The famous wood statue of Ka-Aper (or Sheikh el Beled) is a case in point (FIG. 3-13). The work is a lively representation of a man whose function was to serve the king in the spirit world as he had in life. The face is startlingly alive, an effect that is heightened by eyes of rock crystal. The sheikh stands erect in conventional frontal pose, left leg advanced. His paunchy physique lacks the idealized proportions one finds in representations of royalty and nobility; he was,

3-12 Reserve head of a prince, Gizeh, *c.* 2500 B.C. Limestone, life-size. Egyptian Museum, Cairo.

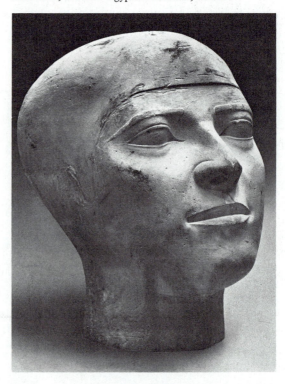

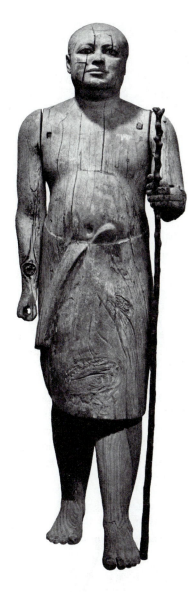

3-13 *Sheikh el Beled,* from his tomb at Saqqara, c. 2400 B.C. Wood, approx. 43″ high. Egyptian Museum, Cairo. (Partially restored.)

ened birds and stalking beasts. Beneath the boats, the water, signified by a pattern of wavy lines, is crowded with hippopotamuses and other aquatic fauna. Ti's men seem frantically busy with their spears, while Ti himself, looming twice their size, stands impassive and aloof in the formal stance that we have seen in the figure of Hesire (FIG. 3-3). The outsize and ideal proportions bespeak Ti's rank, as does the conventional pose, which contrasts with the realistically rendered activity of his diminutive servants and particularly with the precisely observed figures of the birds and animals among the papyrus buds.

A rare and fine example of Old Kingdom painting is the frieze called the *Geese of Medum* (FIG. 3-15). In the prehistoric art of the caves, the rock paintings, and the art of Mesopotamia, we admired the peculiar sensitivity of early artists to the animal figure. They seem to have had empathy with the nonhuman creature, what Keats called negative capability—the power almost to share the being of the animal and to feel as it feels.

3-14 *Hippopotamus Hunt,* tomb of Ti, Saqqara, c. 2400 B.C. Painted limestone relief, approx. 48″ high.

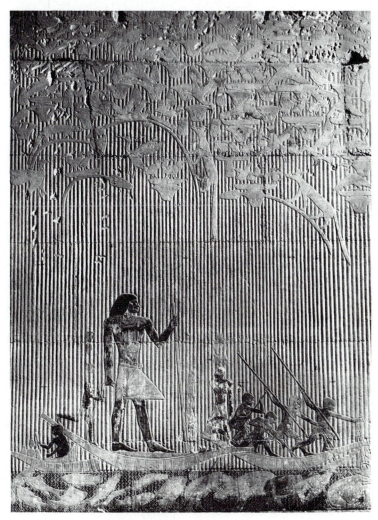

after all, only a minor official. The wood medium permitted the artist to omit the back slab and try a freer pose. Actually, what we see is the wood core that was originally covered with painted plaster, a common procedure when soft or unattractive woods were used.

Painting and Relief

The scenes in painted limestone relief that decorate the walls of the tomb of an Old Kingdom official, Ti, typify the subjects favored by the patrons; most often they are of agriculture and hunting (FIG. 3-14), activities that represent the fundamental human concern with nature and that are associated with the provisioning of the ka in the hereafter. Ti, his men, and his boats move slowly through the marshes, hunting birds and hippopotamuses in a dense growth of towering papyrus. The slender, reedy stems of the plants are delineated with repeated fine grooves that fan out gracefully at the top into a commotion of fright-

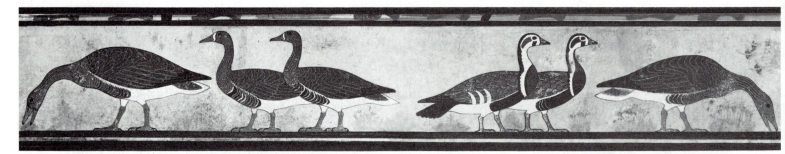

3-15 *Geese of Medum, c.* 2530 B.C. Dry fresco, approx. 18″ high. Egyptian Museum, Cairo.

The *fresco secco* technique used, in which the artist lets the plaster dry before he paints on it, lends itself to slow and meticulous work, encouraging the trained professional to take pains in rendering the image and expressing his exact knowledge of its subject. The delicate, prehensile necks of the geese, the beaks, the suppleness of the bodies, and the animals' characteristic step and carriage are rendered with an exactitude and discernment that would elicit the admiration of an Audubon. The firm, strong execution of the figures is the work of an expert, with superbly trained eye and hand, probably conscious of his power and proud of it. It is probable, too, that religious motives mingled here with esthetic ones, for, after all, once a tomb was sealed no mortal eyes could ever be expected to see the paintings again. It must have been thought that in the darkness and silence the pictures worked their own spell, creating a force that would serve the ka eternally; something of the magic-working of the cave paintings seems to persist here.

The art of the Old Kingdom is the classic art of Egypt in that its conventions, definitively established, remained the basis of subsequent styles of Egyptian art through three millennia.

THE MIDDLE KINGDOM

About 2150 B.C. the power of the pharaohs was challenged by ambitious feudal lords, and for about a century the land was in a state of civil unrest and near-anarchy. Eventually, a Theban ruler, Mentuhotep II, managed to unite Egypt again under the rule of a single king. In the Eleventh, Twelfth, and Thirteenth dynasties that followed (called the Middle Kingdom), art was revived, and a rich and varied literature appeared.

Rock-cut Tombs

Among the most characteristic remains of the Middle Kingdom are the private rock-cut tombs at Beni Hasan (FIG. 3-16). One of the best preserved is the tomb of Khnumhotep, who boasted in an inscription of its elaborateness, saying that its doors were of cedar, seven cubits

(about twenty feet) high. Expressing the characteristic Egyptian attitude toward the last resting place, he added:

> My chief nobility was: I executed a cliff-tomb, for a man should imitate that which his father does. My father made for himself a house of the *ka* in the town of Menofret, of good stone of Ayan, in order to perpetuate his name forever and establish it eternally.

The rock-cut tombs of the Middle Kingdom largely replaced the Old Kingdom mastabas. Hollowed out of the living rock at remote sites these tombs were fronted by a shallow columned portico and contained the fundamental units of Egyptian architecture—portico or vestibule, columned hall, and sacred chamber (FIG. 3-17). The interior of the rock-cut tomb of Amenemhet (FIG. 3-18) shows the hall, the columns of which serve no supporting function, being, like the portico columns, continuous parts of the rock fabric. (Note the broken column in the rear, suspended from the ceiling like a stalactite.) Tomb walls were decorated with paintings and painted reliefs as in former times, and the subjects were much the same.

3-16 Rock-cut tombs, Beni Hasan, *c.* 1900 B.C.

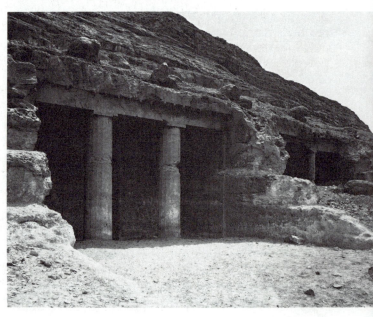

Painting and Sculpture

A painting from the tomb of Khnumhotep (FIG. 3-19) shows servants feeding oryxes (antelopes), the domesticated pets of the Egyptian gentry. The artist here has made a daring attempt to present the shoulders and backs of both human figures in foreshortening. However, working within the rigid framework of convention, he simply joined their front and side views in an unusual combination. As a result

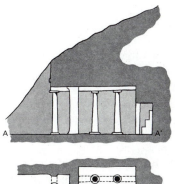

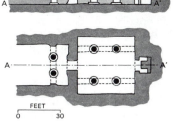

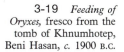

3-17 Plan and section of a rock-cut tomb. (After Sir Banister Fletcher.)

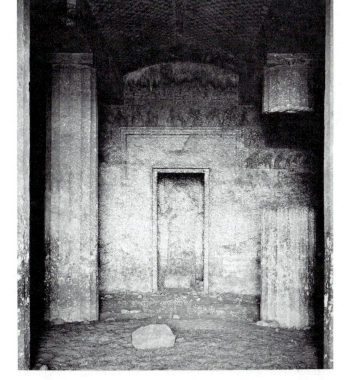

3-18 Interior of the tomb of Amenemhet, Beni Hasan, *c.* 1930 B.C.

3-19 *Feeding of Oryxes,* fresco from the tomb of Khnumhotep, Beni Hasan, *c.* 1900 B.C.

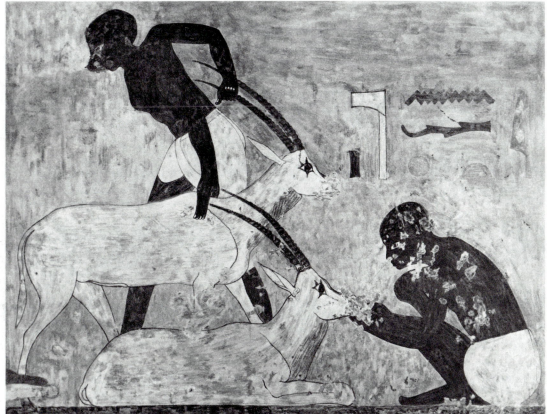

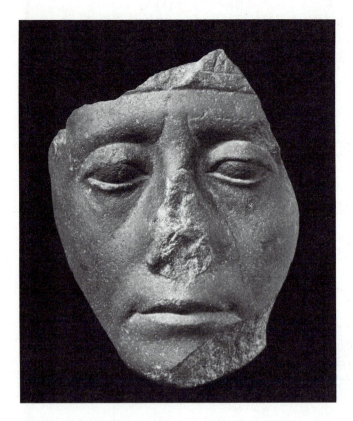

the action reads convincingly enough, but the figures fall short of optical consistency.

In portrait sculpture of the Middle Kingdom a somewhat deepened perception of personality and mood can be noted, as shown in a partially damaged head thought to be of Sesostris III (FIG. 3-20). The head, detail of a sphinx, has a pessimistic expression which reflects, interestingly, the dominant mood of the literature of the Middle Kingdom. The strong mouth, the drooping lines about the nose and eyes, and the shadowy brows show a determined ruler, who had also shared in the cares of the world, sunk in brooding meditation. The portrait is strangely different from the typical realistic and "public" Old Kingdom face, being personal, almost intimate, in its revelation of the mark of anxiety a troubled age might leave on the soul of a king.

THE HYKSOS AND THE NEW KINGDOM

This anxiety may have reflected premonitions of disaster. The Middle Kingdom, like that which had preceded it, disintegrated, and power passed to a line of migrant Semitic Asiatics from the Syrian and Mesopotamian uplands, called the Hyksos, or Shepherd Kings, who brought with them a new and influential culture and that practical instrument, the horse. The invasion and domination of the

Hyksos, traditionally thought to have been a disaster, was latterly reassessed as a seminal influence that kept Egypt in the mainstream of the Bronze Age culture in the eastern Mediterranean. In any event, the innovations introduced by the Hyksos, especially in weapons and the techniques of war, contributed to their own overthrow by native Egyptian kings of the Seventeenth Dynasty. Ahmose I, final conqueror of the Hyksos and first king of the Eighteenth Dynasty, ushered in the New Kingdom (the Empire), the most brilliant period of Egypt's long history. At this time Egypt extended her borders by conquest from the Euphrates in the east deep into Nubia (the Sudan) to the south. Wider foreign contact was afforded by visiting embassies and by new and profitable trade with Asia and the Aegean islands. The booty taken in wars and the tribute exacted from subjected peoples made possible the development of a new capital, Thebes, which became a great and luxurious metropolis with magnificent palaces, tombs, and temples along both banks of the Nile. Thutmose III, who died in the fifty-first year of his reign in the second half of the fifteenth century B.C., was the greatest pharaoh of the New Kingdom, if not of all Egyptian history, and his successors continued the grand traditions he established. The optimistic mood of the new era is recorded in an inscription above the heads of revelers in a painting now in the British Museum:

> The Earth-god has implanted his beauty in every body.
> The Creator has done this with his two hands as balm to his heart.
> The channels are filled with waters anew
> And the land is flooded with his love.

Architecture

If the most impressive monuments of the Old Kingdom are its pyramids, those of the New Kingdom are its grandiose temples. Burial still demanded the elaborate care shown earlier, and, partly following the tradition of the Middle Kingdom, nobles and kings hollowed their burial chambers deep in the cliffs west of the Nile. In the Valley of the Kings, the tombs are rock cut, approached by long corridors extending as deep as 500 feet into the hillside. The entrances to these burial chambers were carefully concealed, and the mortuary temples were built along the banks of the river at some distance from the tombs. The temple, which provided the king with a place for worshiping his patron god and then served as a mortuary chapel after his death, became elaborate and sumptuous, befitting both the king and the god.

The noblest of these royal mortuary temples, at Deir

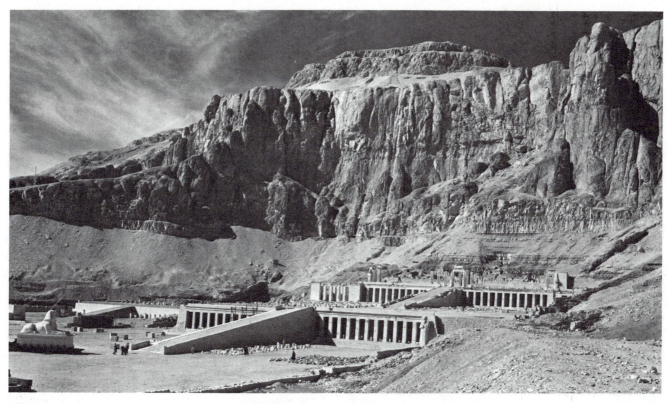

3-21   Mortuary Temple of Queen Hatshepsut, Deir el-Bahari, *c.* 1450 B.C.

el-Bahari, was that of Queen Hatshepsut (FIG. 3-21), who preceded the conquering pharaoh Thutmose III. A princess who became queen when there were no legitimate male heirs, she boasted of having made the "Two Lands to labour with bowed back for her." Built about 1450 B.C. along the lines of the neighboring Middle Kingdom temple of Mentuhotep I, the structure rises from the valley floor in three colonnaded terraces connected by ramps. It is remarkable how visually well suited the structure is to its natural setting. The long horizontals and verticals of the colonnades and their rhythm of light and dark repeat, in man-made symmetry, the pattern of the rocky cliffs above. The pillars of the colonnades, which are either simply rectangular or chamfered (beveled, or flattened at the edges) into sixteen sides, are esthetically proportioned and spaced. Statues in the round, perhaps 200, were intimately associated with the temple architecture. So also was the brightly painted low relief that covered the walls and whose remnants may still be seen. The relief represented Hatshepsut's birth, coronation, and great deeds. In her day the terraces were not the barren places they are now but gardens with frankincense trees and rare plants brought by the queen from an expedition to the faraway "land of Punt" on the Red Sea, an event that figures prominently in the temple's relief decorations.

The immense rock-cut temple of Ramses II, Egypt's last great warrior-pharaoh, who lived a little before the exodus from Egypt under Moses, was built far up the Nile at Abu Simbel. Ramses, proud of his many campaigns to restore the empire, augmented his greatness by placing four colossal images of himself in the temple façade (FIG. 3-22). The whole monument was moved in 1968 to save it from submersion in the new Aswan Dam reservoir. In later

3-22   Temple of Ramses II, Abu Simbel, 1257 B.C. Colossi approx. 60′ high.

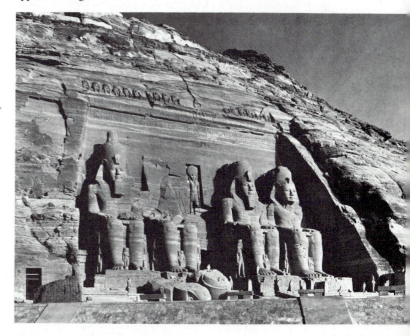

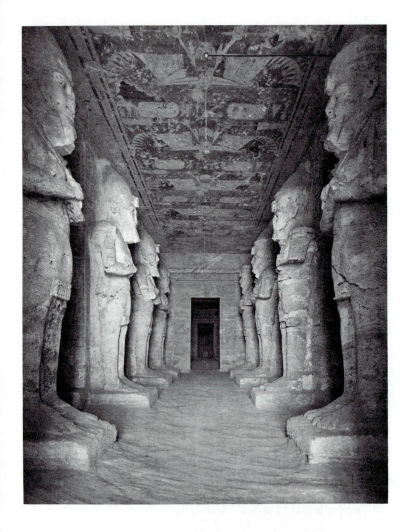

rior also (FIG. 3-23). The giant figures of the king, formed as columns, face each other across the narrow corridor, their exaggerated mass seeming to appropriate the architectural space. The columns are *reserved*—that is, hewn from the living rock—and have no bearing function, in this respect resembling the columns in the tombs at Beni Hasan. The figure-as-column, the *caryatid* form, will appear later in Greek architecture, and its presence at Abu Simbel may be its earliest use.

Distinct from the mortuary temples were the edifices built to honor one or more of the gods and often added to by successive kings until they reached gigantic size as in the temples at Karnak and Luxor (FIGS. 3-27 and 3-28). These temples all had similar plans. A typical pylon temple plan (FIG. 3-24) is bilaterally symmetrical along a single axis that runs from an approaching avenue through a colonnaded court and hall to a dimly lighted sanctuary. The dominating feature of the statuary-lined approach is the façade of the pylon, simple and massive, with sloping walls. The example of a pylon shown in FIG. 3-25 is from the Temple of Horus at Edfu, which was constructed during the Ptolemaic period and is a striking monument to the persistence of Egyptian artistic traditions. Its broad surface is broken by the doorway with its overshadowing cornice, by deep channels to hold great flagstaffs, and by sunken reliefs. Moldings finish its top and sides. Within is an open court colonnaded on three sides, followed by a hall between court and sanctuary, its long axis placed at right angles to that of the entire building complex. This "broad" or hypostyle hall (that is, having a roof supported by columns) is crowded with massive columns and roofed by stone slabs carried on lintels that rest in turn on impost blocks supported by the great capitals. In the hypostyle hall of the Temple of Amen-Re (a variant reading is Imen-Re) at Karnak (FIGS. 3-26 and 3-27) the columns are sixty-six feet high, and the capitals, twenty-two feet in diameter at the top, large enough to hold 100 men. The Egyptians, who did not use cement, depended on the

times, the glories of kings and emperors in periods of conquest and imperial grandeur were also celebrated in huge monuments; gigantism seems characteristic of much of the art of empires that have reached their peaks. Here, Ramses' artists use the principle of augmentation both by size and by repetition. The massive statues lack the refinement of earlier periods, since much is sacrificed to overwhelming size. The grand scale is carried out in the inte-

3-24 Plan of a typical pylon temple.

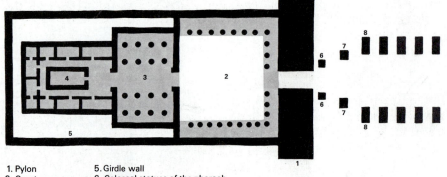

1. Pylon
2. Court
3. Hypostyle hall
4. Sanctuary
5. Girdle wall
6. Colossal statues of the pharaoh
7. Obelisks
8. Avenue of recumbent animals

▨ Probable roofed areas

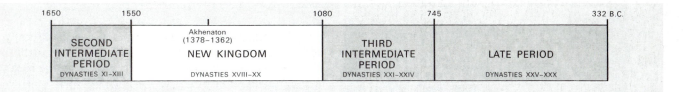

1650	1550	1080	745	332 B.C.

| SECOND INTERMEDIATE PERIOD DYNASTIES XI–XIII | Akhenaton (1378–1362) NEW KINGDOM DYNASTIES XVIII–XX | THIRD INTERMEDIATE PERIOD DYNASTIES XXI–XXIV | LATE PERIOD DYNASTIES XXV–XXX |

weight of the huge stones to hold the columns in place. In many such hypostyle halls the central rows of columns were higher than those at the sides, raising the roof of the central section and creating a clerestory. Openings in this clerestory permitted light to filter into the interior. This method of construction appears in primitive form as early as the Old Kingdom in the valley temple of the Pyramid of Khafre. Evidently an Egyptian invention, it has remained an important architectural feature down to our times and was particularly important in the design of Medieval cathedrals.

The Egyptian temple plan evolved from ritualistic requirements. Only the pharaoh and the priest could enter the sanctuary; a chosen few were admitted to the hypostyle hall; the mass of the people was allowed only as far as the open court, and a high mudbrick wall shut off the site from the outside world. The conservative Egyptians did not deviate from this basic plan for hundreds of years. The corridor axis, which dominates the plan, makes the temple not so much a building as, in Oswald Spengler's phrase, "a path enclosed by mighty masonry." Like the Nile that it almost symbolizes, the corridor may have been an expression of the Egyptian concept of life. Spengler suggests that the Egyptian saw himself moving down a narrow, predestined life-path that ended before the judges of the dead. The whole of Egyptian culture can be regarded as illustrating this theme.

The hypostyle hall at Karnak (FIG. 3-27) shows the smooth-shafted (as opposed to fluted) Egyptian columns with the two basic types of capitals: the bud-shaped and the campaniform, or bell-shaped. Though the columns are structural members, unlike the reserve "columns" of the

3-25 Pylon Temple of Horus, Edfu, *c.* 237–212 B.C.

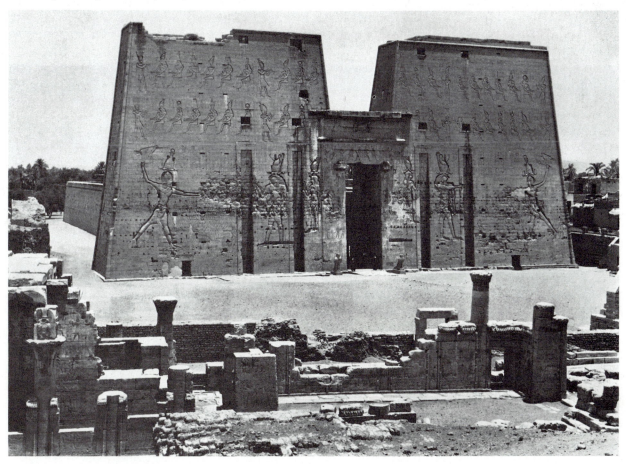

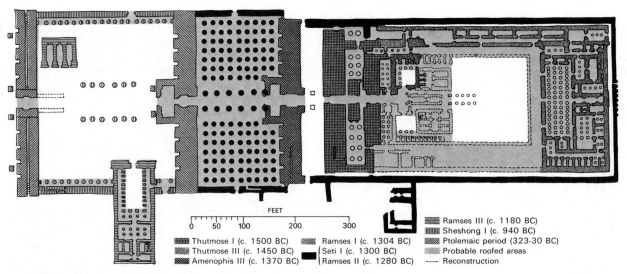

FEET

0   50   100   200   300

▤ Thutmose I (c. 1500 BC)	▨ Ramses I (c. 1304 BC)	▤ Ramses III (c. 1180 BC)
▥ Thutmose III (c. 1450 BC)	■ Seti I (c. 1300 BC)	▦ Sheshong I (c. 940 BC)
▦ Amenophis III (c. 1370 BC)	▏Ramses II (c. 1280 BC)	▨ Ptolemaic period (323-30 BC)
		░ Probable roofed areas
		---- Reconstruction

3-26   Plan of the Temple of Amen-Re, Karnak. (After Sir Banister Fletcher.) Dates in parentheses indicate time of construction.

Middle Kingdom tombs at Beni Hasan and the figure-columns at Abu Simbel, their function as carriers of vertical stress is almost hidden by horizontal bands of relief sculpture and painting, suggesting that the intention of the architects was not to emphasize the functional role of the columns so much as to utilize them as surface for decoration. This contrasts sharply with later Greek practice,

which keeps the vertical lines of the column emphatic and its function clear by freeing the surfaces of the shaft from all ornament.

The courts and colonnades of the Temple of Amen-Mut-Khonsu at Luxor (FIG. 3-28) exhibit the columnar style especially well. The post-and-lintel structure of the temples appears to have had its origin in an early building

3-27   Model of hypostyle hall, Temple of Amen-Re, Karnak, c. 1280 B.C. Metropolitan Museum of Art, New York (bequest of Levi Hale Willard).

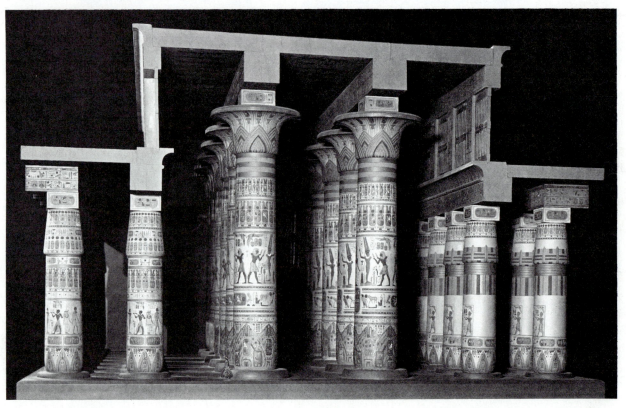

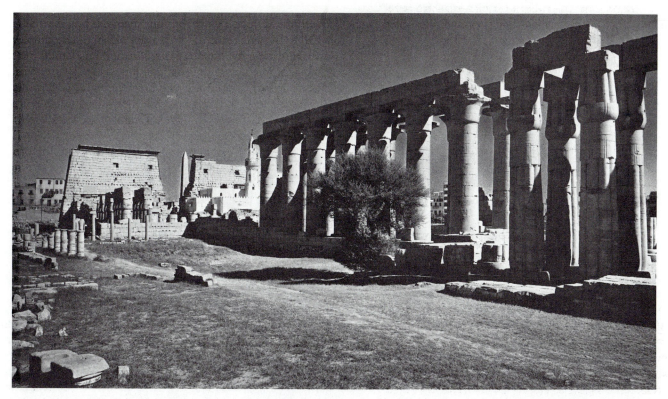

3-28   Court and pylon of Ramses II, *c.* 1280 B.C., and court and colonnade of Amenhotep III, *c.* 1370 B.C. Temple of Amen-Mut-Khonsu, Luxor.

technique that used firmly bound sheaves of reeds and swamp plants as roof supports in adobe structures. Evidence of this origin is seen in the columns themselves, which are carved to resemble lotus or papyrus, with the bud-cluster or bell-shaped capitals. Painted decorations, traces of which can still be seen on the surfaces of the shafts and capitals, emphasized these natural details. In fact, the flora of the Nile valley supplied the basic decorative motifs in all Egyptian art. With respect to a possible Mesopotamian influence, it is important to note that, until the time of Persia, Mesopotamian architecture seldom employed the post-and-lintel system; the column was rarely seen. Moreover, the formalization of plant forms into the rigid profiles of architecture is precisely the same thing as the formalization of human bodies and action that the Egyptians achieved so skillfully in tomb painting and sculpture.

Sculpture and Painting

This radical simplification of form, which preserves in the ka figures the cubic essence of the block, can be seen to advantage in the statue showing Senmut (Queen Hatshepsut's chancellor and the architect of her temple at Deir

el-Bahari) with Princess Nefrua (FIG. 3-29). This curious design, evidently popular in the New Kingdom, concentrates attention upon the portrait head, leaving the "body" a cubic block, which is given over to inscriptions. With

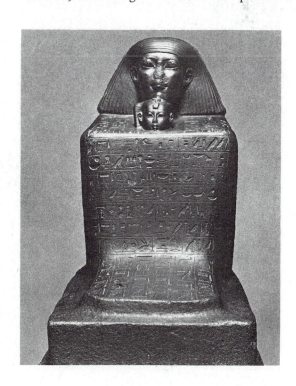

3-29   *Senmut with Princess Nefrua,* block statue, Thebes, *c.* 1450 B.C. Black stone, approx. 40″ high. Staatliche Museen, Berlin.

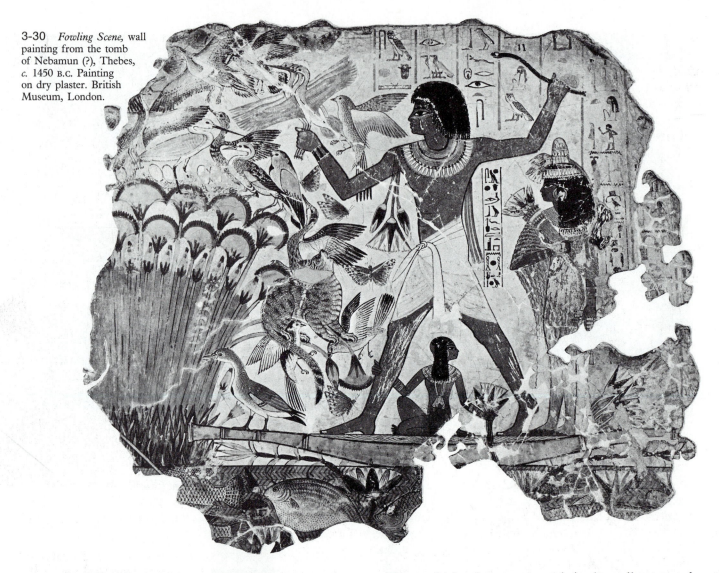

3-30 *Fowling Scene*, wall painting from the tomb of Nebamun (?), Thebes, *c.* 1450 B.C. Painting on dry plaster. British Museum, London.

surfaces turning subtly about smoothly rounded corners, it seems another expression of the Egyptian fondness for volume enclosed by flat, unambiguous planes. The polished stone shape has its own simple beauty.

The persistence of the formulas for projection of an image onto a flat surface can be seen in wall paintings in the tomb of Nebamun (?) at Thebes (FIG. 3-30 and part-opening picture), which dates from the Eighteenth Dynasty. The deceased nobleman is standing in his boat and driving the birds from a papyrus swamp with his throwstick. In his right hand he holds three birds he has caught; a wild cat, on a papyrus stem just in front of him, has caught two more in her claws and is holding the wings of a third in her teeth. His two companions, perhaps his wife and daughter, their figures scaled down in proportion to their rank, are enjoying the lotuses they have gathered. Although the water and the figures are represented by the usual conventions, cat, fish, and birds show a naturalism based upon visual perception like that which we have seen in the *Geese of Medum* (FIG. 3-15).

The tomb chamber, as we see it in the well-preserved New Kingdom tomb of Nakht at Thebes (FIG. 3-31), is similar to the tomb chambers of the Old Kingdom; in the mural the system of registers still preserves the rigid separation of the zones of action. But some innovations of detail appear: here and there a new liveliness and a closer inspection of life. Another fresco fragment from the tomb of Nebamun (FIG. 3-32) shows four ladies watching and apparently participating in a musicale and dance in which two nimble little nude dancing girls perform. The overlapping of the girls' figures, facing in opposite directions, and the rather complicated gyrations of the dance are carefully and accurately observed and executed. Of the four ladies of the audience, two at the left are represented conventionally, but the other two face us in what is a most unusual and very rarely attempted frontal pose. They seem to beat time to the dance; one of them plays the reeds, and the artist takes careful note of the soles of their feet as they sit cross-legged. This informality constitutes a relaxation not only of the stiff rules of representation but of the set

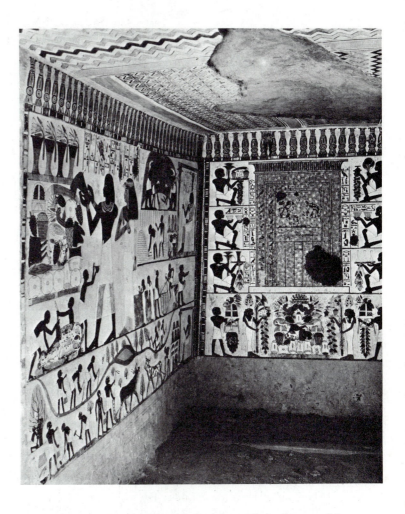

3-31 Tomb of Nakht, Thebes, *c.* 1450 B.C. Fresco on rear wall 55″ x 60″.

themes once thought appropriate for tomb painting. We may also have here the reflection of a more luxurious mode of life in the New Kingdom, and it may have been that the ka now required not only the necessities and comforts in the hereafter but formal entertainment as well.

AKHENATON AND THE AMARNA PERIOD

These small variations of age-old formulas heralded a short but violent upheaval in Egyptian art, the only major break in the continuity of its long tradition. In the fourteenth century B.C. the emperor Amenophis IV (Amenhotep IV), later known as Akhenaton (or Ikhnaton), proclaimed the religion of Aton, the universal and only god of the sun. He thus contested and abolished the native cult of Amen, sacred to Thebes and professed by the mighty priests of such temples as Karnak and Luxor, as well as by the people of Egypt. He blotted out the name of Amen from all inscriptions, and even from his own name and that of his father, Amenophis III. He emptied the great temples, embittered the priests and people, and moved his capital downriver from Thebes to a site now called Tel el-Amarna, where he built his own city and shrines to the religion of Aton.

This action by Amenophis IV—now Akhenaton—though it might savor of the psychotic or of the fanaticism of sudden conversion, was portended by events in the formation and expansion of the power of the great Eighteenth Dynasty. Egyptian might had formed the first world empire. Ruling over Syria and Nubia, bordered by the Hittites, and checking the penetration of the Mitanni, the conquering, imperialist pharaohs had gradually enlarged

3-32 *Musicians and Dancers,* detail of a wall painting from the tomb of Nebamun (?), Thebes, *c.* 1450 B.C. British Museum, London.

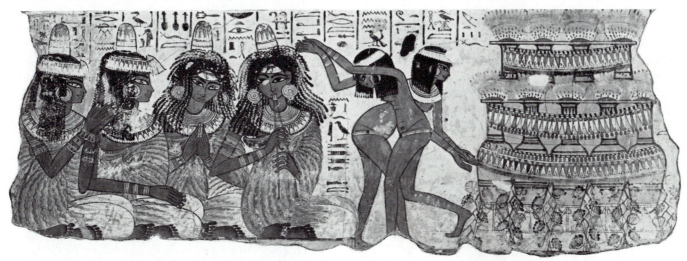

the powers of their old sun god, Amen, to make him not simply god of the Egyptians, but of all men. Even before Egypt had become the main force in the Mediterranean world—before, as James Breasted describes it, "the Egyptian supremacy [was] undisputed from the Greek islands, the coasts of Asia Minor, and the highlands of the Upper Euphrates on the north to the Fourth Cataract of the Nile on the south"—Thutmose I, a founder of the fortunes of the dynasty, could say of the sun god that his kingdom extended as far as "the circuit of the sun." And the military pharaoh, Thutmose III, said of this aggrandized god: "He seeth the whole earth hourly." Thus, Akhenaton was exploiting forces already gathering when he raised the imperialized god of the sun to be the only god of all the earth and proscribed any rival as blasphemous. He appropriated to himself the new and universal god, making himself both the son and prophet, even the sole experient, of Aton. To him alone could the god make revelation. His hymn to Aton survives:

Thou art in my heart.
There is no other that knoweth thee
Save thy son Ikhnaton.
Thou hast made him wise
In thy designs and might.
The world is in thy hand,
Even as thou hast made them . . .
Thou didst establish the world,
And raise them up for thy son,
Who came forth from thy limbs,
The king of Upper and Lower Egypt,
Living in Truth, Lord of Two Lands . . .

Egypt has left us the ingredients, as it were, of the later monotheisms so influential in the world. Akhenaton's brief theocracy seems to have embodied the seeds of later concepts of one god, of an eternal son who is also a king, of a world created by that one god, and of the intimate revelation of that god's spirit to a chosen one.

One of the effects of the new religious philosophy seems to have been a temporary relaxation of the Egyptians' preoccupation with death and the hereafter and a correspondingly greater concern with life on this earth. In art this change is reflected in a different attitude toward the representation of the human figure. Artists aim for a new sense of life and movement, expressed in swelling, curvilinear forms; and their long-fostered naturalistic tendencies, so far confined largely to the representation of animals, are now extended not only to the human figure of the lowly but significantly to royalty also. A colossal statue of Akhenaton (FIG. 3-33), from Karnak, retains the standard

frontal pose; but the strange, epicene body with its curving contours and the long, full-lipped face, heavy-lidded eyes, and dreaming expression, show that the artist has studied his subject with care and rendered it with all the physiognomical and physical irregularities that were part of the king's actual appearance. The predilection for curved lines stresses the softness of the slack, big-hipped body that is a far cry indeed from the heroically proportioned figures of Akhenaton's predecessors. In a daring mixture of naturalism and stylization, the artist has given us an informal and uncompromising portrayal of the king that is charged with both vitality and a psychological complexity that has been called expressionistic.

The famous painted limestone bust of Akhenaton's queen, Nefertiti (FIG. 3-34), exhibits a similar expression of entranced musing and an almost mannered sensitivity and delicacy of curving contour. It may be that the sculptor deliberately alludes to a heavy flower on its slender stalk when he exaggerates the weight of the crowned head and the length of the almost serpentine neck. One thinks of those modern descendants of Queen Nefertiti—the models in the fashion magazines, with their gaunt, swaying frames, masklike, pallid faces, and enormous, shadowed eyes. As

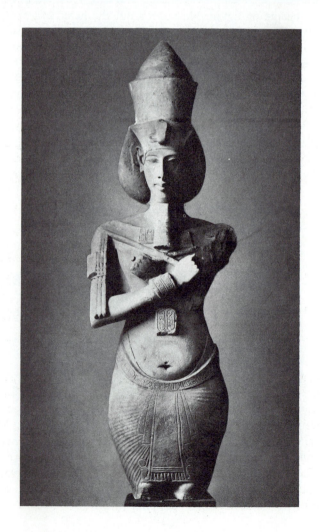

3-33 *Akhenaton*, from a pillar statue in the Temple of Amen-Re, Karnak, *c.* 1375 B.C. Sandstone, approx. 13′ high. Egyptian Museum, Cairo.

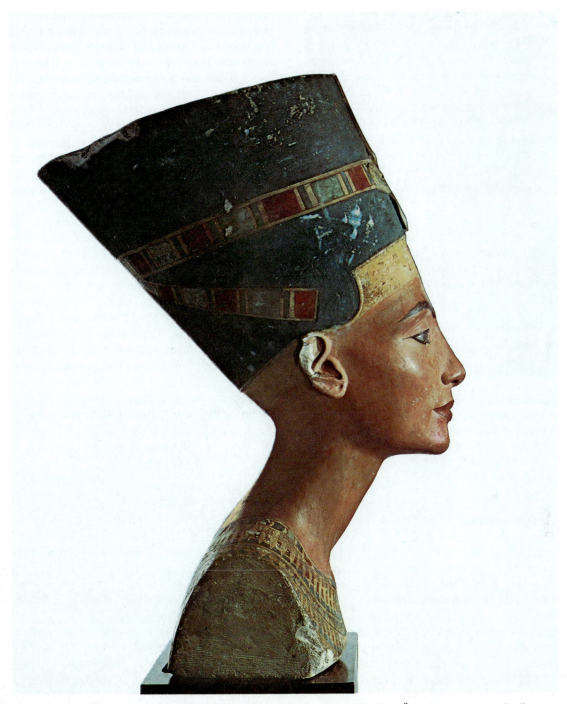

3-34 *Queen Nefertiti*, Tel el-Amarna, *c.* 1360 B.C. Limestone, approx. 20″ high. Ägyptisches Museum, Berlin.

the modern mannerism shapes the living model to its dictates, so the sculptors of Tel el-Amarna may have had some standard of spiritual beauty to which they adjusted the actual likeness of their subjects. Even so, one is made very much aware of the reality of the queen through her contrived mask of beauty, a masterpiece of cosmetic art. The Nefertiti bust is one more example of that elegant blending of the real and the formal that we have noticed so often in the art of the ancient Near East.

During the last three years of his reign Akhenaton's coregent was his half-brother, Smenkhkare. A relief from Tel el-Amarna may show Smenkhkare and his wife Meritaten (FIG. 3-35) in an informal, even intimate, pose that contrasts strongly with the traditional formality in representation of exalted persons. Once-rigid lines have become undulating curves, and the pose of Smenkhkare has no known precedent. The prince leans casually on his staff, one leg at ease, an attitude that presumes knowledge

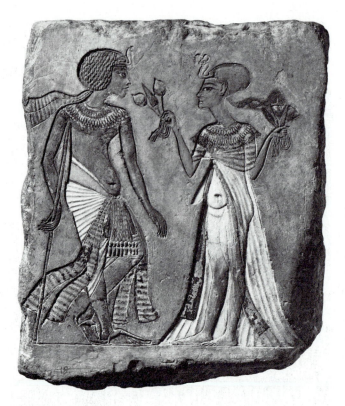

3-35 *King Smenkhkare and Meritaten* (?), Tel el-Amarna, *c.* 1360 B.C. Painted limestone relief, approx. 9½″ high. Staatliche Museen, Berlin.

on the sculptor's part of the flexible shift of body masses, a principle not really grasped until Classical times in Greece. This quite realistic detail accompanies others that are the result of a freer expression of what is observed: details of costume and the departures from the traditional formality, such as the elongated and bulging head of Meritaten and the prominent bellies that characterize figures of the Amarna school. Proportions of figures no longer depend on rank; the princess is depicted in the same scale as her husband on the basis of their natural proportions.

We have seen that there was some slight loosening of the conventions of sculpture and painting even before Akhenaton. But the Amarna style (and a subsequent return to the earlier tradition) marks a break too abrupt and emphatic to let us conclude that the style was simply a local, native flowering. It is at least possible that there was some influence from the Mediterranean world. We know that Egypt had commercial relations with Crete beginning in the predynastic period, and the livelier, less convention-bound art of the Minoans could have proved suggestive and stimulating to the Amarna artists. Although the Cretan palace culture came to an end around 1400 B.C. (see Chapter Four) and Akhenaton did not ascend the Egyptian throne until 1378 (first as coruler with his father), the time lag does not seem too great to preclude such an influence. It may be that some Cretan artists, finding refuge in Egypt,

3-36 Painted chest, tomb of Tutankhamun, Thebes, *c.* 1350 B.C. Approx. 20″ long. Egyptian Museum, Cairo.

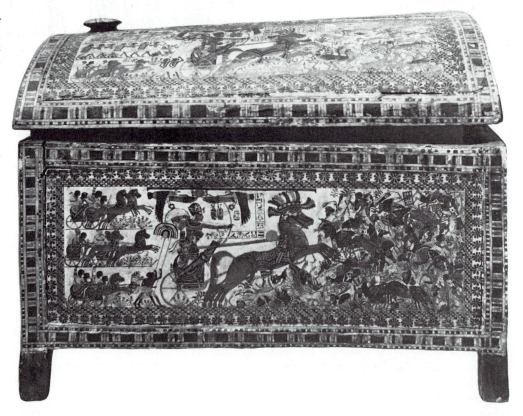

3-37 *Seti I Offering,* Temple of Seti I, Abydos, *c.* 1300 B.C. Painted limestone, Louvre, Paris.

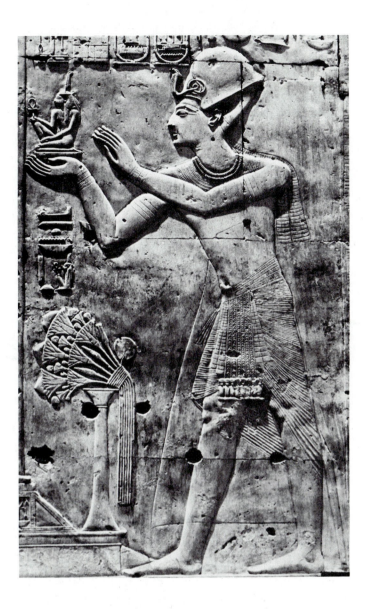

and a sympathetic artist climate under Akhenaton's rule, fertilized the Amarna style.

The survival of the Amarna style is seen in a painted chest of Tutankhamun, the successor to Akhenaton (FIG. 3-36). The lid panel represents the king hunting droves of fleeing animals in the desert while, on the side panel, he rides against the enemies of Egypt. The themes are traditional, but the fluid, curvilinear forms, the dynamic compositions—with their emphasis on movement and action—and the disposition of the hunted animals and enemies who, freed of the conventional ground lines, race wildly across the panel, are features reminiscent not only of the Amarna style but of the lively naturalism of Cretan art.

The pharaohs who followed Akhenaton reestablished the cult and priesthood of Amen, restored the temples and the inscriptions, and returned to the old manner in art. Akhenaton's monuments were wiped out, his heresy anathematized, and his city abandoned. The conservative reaction can be seen in a relief of the pharaoh Seti I (FIG. 3-37). The rigid, flattened shapes repeat the formula of the *Palette of Narmer* (FIG. 3-2) and the static formality of Old Kingdom art. It is as if some fifteen centuries had not passed into history.

For almost a thousand years after the New Kingdom, though Egypt lost the commanding position it once had maintained in the Mediterranean world, the art of its later periods yet showed a power and distinction worthy of that of the classic Old Kingdom and the expansive New Kingdom that followed it.

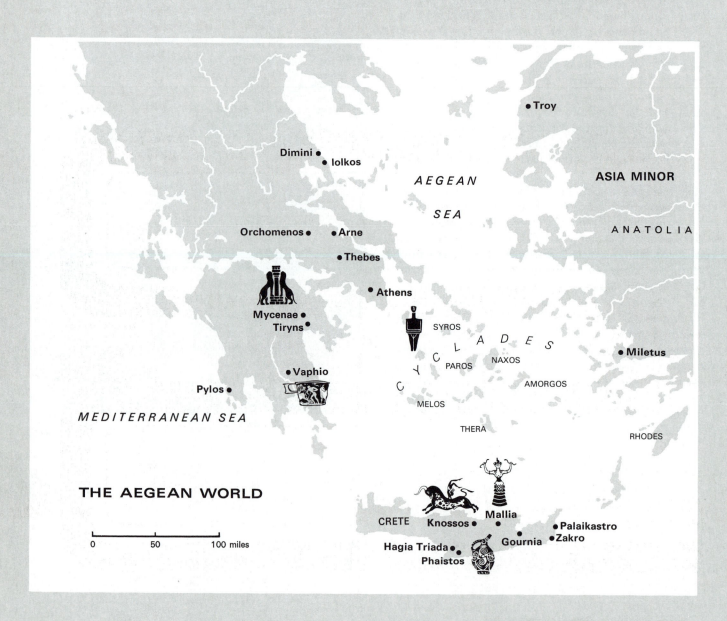

THE AEGEAN WORLD

0   50   100 miles

Troy

Dimini • Iolkos

AEGEAN SEA

ASIA MINOR

ANATOLIA

Orchomenos • Arne

Thebes

Athens

Mycenae •
Tiryns •

SYROS

CYCLADES

PAROS   NAXOS

Miletus

Vaphio

AMORGOS

Pylos •

MELOS

MEDITERRANEAN SEA

THERA

RHODES

CRETE   Knossos •   Mallia

Palaikastro
Zakro

Gournia

Hagia Triada

Phaistos

chapter four

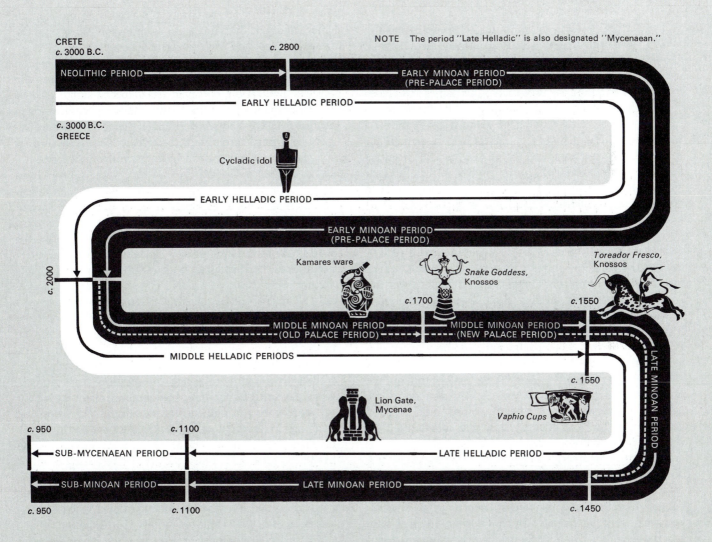

CRETE
c. 3000 B.C.   *c.* 2800   NOTE   The period "Late Helladic" is also designated "Mycenaean."

NEOLITHIC PERIOD   EARLY MINOAN PERIOD
                                                                    (PRE-PALACE PERIOD)

EARLY HELLADIC PERIOD

c. 3000 B.C.
GREECE

Cycladic idol

EARLY HELLADIC PERIOD

EARLY MINOAN PERIOD
(PRE-PALACE PERIOD)

c. 2000

Kamares ware   *Snake Goddess,*   *Toreador Fresco,*
                                      Knossos   Knossos

                              *c.*1700   *c.*1550

MIDDLE MINOAN PERIOD   MIDDLE MINOAN PERIOD
(OLD PALACE PERIOD)   (NEW PALACE PERIOD)

MIDDLE HELLADIC PERIODS

                                                                   c. 1550

Lion Gate,
Mycenae   *Vaphio Cups*

c. 950   *c.*1100

SUB-MYCENAEAN PERIOD   LATE HELLADIC PERIOD

SUB-MINOAN PERIOD   LATE MINOAN PERIOD

c. 950   *c.*1100   *c.* 1450

LATE MINOAN PERIOD

The Art of the Aegean

OMER WROTE of the might and splendor of the Achaean host deployed for war against Troy:

So clan after clan poured out from the ships and huts onto the plain of Scamander, and . . . found their places in the flowery meadows by the river, innumerable as the leaves and blossoms in their season . . . the Locrians . . . the Athenians . . . the citizens of Argos and Tiryns of the Great Walls . . . troops from the great stronghold of Mycenae, from wealthy Corinth . . . from Lacedaemon . . . from Pylos . . . Knossos in Crete, Phaistos . . . and the other troops that had their homes in Crete of the Hundred Towns. . . .

The list goes on and on, outlining the peoples and the geography of the Aegean world in intimate detail. Until about 1870, historians of ancient Greece, though they acknowledged Homer's superb art, discounted him as a historian, attributing the profusion of his names and places to the rich abundance of his imagination. The prehistory of classical Greece remained shadowy and lost—as the historians believed—in an impenetrable world of myth. That they had done less than justice to the truth of Homer's account or, for that matter, to ancient Greek literary sources in general, was proved by a German amateur archeologist, Heinrich Schliemann, who, between 1870 and his death twenty years later, uncovered some of the very cities of the Trojan and Achaean heroes whom Homer celebrates: Troy, Mycenae, Orchomenos, Tiryns. In 1870, at Hissarlik in the northwest corner of Asia Minor, which his knowledge of the *Iliad* had led him to believe was the site of Homer's Troy, he dug into a vast *tell*, or mound, and found there a number of fortified cities built upon the remains of another, together with the evidence of their destruction by fire. Schliemann continued his excavations at Mycenae on the Greek mainland, whence he believed Agamemnon and Achilles had sailed to avenge the capture of Helen, and here his finds were even more startling. Massive fortress-palaces, elaborate tombs, quantities of gold jewelry and ornaments, cups, and inlaid weapons revealed a magnificent preclassical civilization.

But further discoveries were to prove that Mycenae had not been its center. An important Greek legend told of Minos, king of Crete, who had exacted from Athens a tribute of youths and maidens to be fed to the Minotaur—half-bull, half-man—which was housed in a vast labyrinth. Might this legend too be based on historical fact? The lesson of Schliemann's success in pursuing hunches based on careful reading of ancient legends was not lost on his successors. An Englishman, Arthur Evans, had long considered Crete a potentially fertile field for investigation, and Schliemann himself, shortly before his death, had wanted to explore the site of Knossos. In 1900, Evans began work on Crete and a short time later uncovered extensive unfortified palaces of the old sea-kings of Crete, which indeed did resemble labyrinths (FIG. 4-6). His

findings, primarily at Knossos, were augmented by additional excavations there and at Phaistos, Hagia Triada, and other important sites on the southern coast of Crete. In 1962, excavation of another palace was begun on the eastern tip of Crete at Kato Zakro; more recently, in 1966, a queen's burial chamber judged to be about 3400 years old was discovered near Knossos.

MINOAN AND CYCLADIC ART

The civilization of the coasts and islands of the Aegean emerged about the same time as the river-valley civilizations of Egypt and Mesopotamia. Though there was close contact at various times and active exchange of influences, each civilization manifested an originality of its own; the Aegean civilization, however, has a special significance as the forerunner of the first truly European civilization—that of Greece. The sea-dominated geography of the Aegean contrasts sharply with that of the Near East, as does its temperate climate. In the ancient world this made for a busy, commercial seafaring culture, with decentralized authority and a way of life vigorous, vivacious, and pleasure-loving. This is especially true of Crete, the ancient center of Aegean civilization from which radiated its creative forces. As a commercial crossroads for the ancient world, Crete was strategically placed in the east Mediterranean, and her products, both of agriculture and manufacture, were exported widely. The sea provided a natural defense against the frequent and often disruptive invasions that checker the histories of land-bound civilizations like Mesopotamia, and the navies of the sea-kings maintained a prosperous maritime empire that served for the transmission of ideas and influences as well as goods. The controlled accessibility to Crete of impulses from abroad, especially from Egypt and Mesopotamia, may account for the emergence and influence of its culture, which was felt in all of the Aegean area. Modifications of it on the Greek mainland and in the islands of the Cyclades north of Crete have been identified. Thus, the art of Crete itself is called Minoan, after King Minos; that of the mainland, Helladic; and that of the islands, Cycladic. The culture associated with Mycenae on the mainland—the Mycenaean—is classed under Late Helladic (about 1550–1100 B.C.).

The archeological problems confronting investigators of Near Eastern civilizations were much less difficult than those of archeologists working in the Aegean area. Here there survived very few documents like the chronicles and inscriptions of Egypt and Mesopotamia with which to correlate the archeological findings, and there were no "absolute" dates expressible numerically. Evans had to construct a "relative" dating in terms of different periods of ceramic and decorative style from various sites on Crete, in the Cyclades, and at Mycenae. Evans' tripartite division of Minoan art into Early, Middle, and Late Minoan and the further division of each large period into three subperiods are a classic example of a relative chronology, used by the archeologist-historian when he lacks absolute dates. A greater firmness was given the Minoan chronology when points of contact with the chronology of Egyptian art were established. Imported objects of a certain style from the one country were uncovered in datable contexts in the other; in this way, for example, the Middle Minoan period was found to be roughly contemporary with the Middle Kingdom in Egypt.

The two earliest of several scripts found on Crete seem to have been inspired by Egyptian hieroglyphs. Of the later scripts, Linear A and Linear B, only the latter has been deciphered (as late as 1953); it is a pre-Homeric form of Greek. But the tablets inscribed with it represent almost exclusively inventories and tallies of objects and are of little aid in delineating the Minoan culture. For Minoan history, pottery remains have been by far the greatest evidence, since figurative art is relatively scarce and often so fragmentary and diminutive as to preclude building a stylistic continuity upon it. (Potsherds are one of the mainstays of archeology when documentary and monumental evidence is sparse or missing. Broken pots—kitchenware, for example—were often thrown on a garbage heap where, over the years, the perishable materials decayed, leaving only the pottery sherds, which settled into firmly stratified mounds. Careful excavation of such mounds can produce relative chronologies.) Although the sequence of Cretan pottery styles was well established by Evans, some archeologists now feel that his method of dating has become inadequate in view of increased knowledge of the Minoan civilization. A new chronology has been suggested that is based on the construction of the great Cretan palaces. Its relation to the traditional chronology is shown on page 89.

Nevertheless, absolute dates are few, and our knowledge of Minoan history remains vague and provisional. Even the origin of the Cretans is problematical. Some believe that they may have come from Anatolia as early as 6000 B.C., bringing with them a well-developed Neolithic culture, complete with pottery, and that the Bronze Age may have been ushered in by a new wave of immigrants (also from Anatolia?) around the year 2800 B.C.

The Early Minoan Period

The Early Minoan (pre-Palace) period is known to us primarily through pottery and a few scattered pieces of minor sculpture. There is the Mochlos stoneware (named after the site where it was found and apparently copied from Egyptian pieces of the First to Fourth Dynasties), and there are hand-made clay pots decorated with incised geometric patterns.

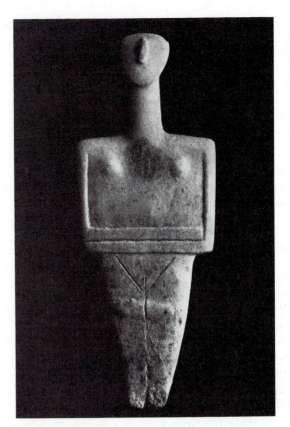

4-1 Cycladic idol, Syros, *c.* 2500–2000 B.C. Marble, 8½″ high.

The most striking and perhaps the most appealing Aegean products of the Early Bronze Age are the numerous marble statuettes from the Cycladic islands. Most of them are representations of nude females with their arms folded across their abdomens. Varying greatly in size (from a few inches in height to life-size), these flat "plank idols" are highly schematized descendants of the Neolithic mother goddess. Their styles are as varied as their sizes and range from figures of almost normal proportions to shapes that resemble violins rather than human figures. The example shown (FIG. 4-1) occupies a middle ground: The organic forms have been converted into geometric shapes (triangles, rectangles, ovals, and cylinders), but the reference to the female figure remains clear, and the manner in which the various stylized parts have been combined has considerable esthetic appeal. Traces of paint found on some specimens show that at least parts of these figures were colored. The eyes were usually painted, and additional color touches were provided by painted necklaces and bracelets.

Occasionally male figures also occur in the Cycladic repertoire. They usually appear as musicians, like the *Lyre Player* (FIG. 4-2), who, wedged between the echoing shapes of chair and lyre, performs a task that seems to have been part of funerary rituals. In the rendering of the figure, the disk-shaped head and the long, tubular neck are in the

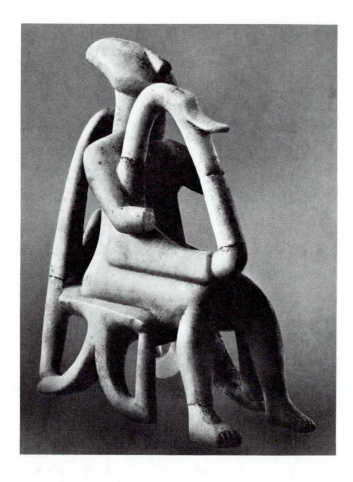

ner walls and subtler shapes and led to the development of a thriving industry. In the so-called eggshell ware, the Minoan potter's art reached a degree of excellence that deserves our highest admiration, if for the delicacy of the ceramic technique alone. But the Cretan artist also developed a style of decoration that complemented the delicate fabric and sophisticated shapes of his pottery. Beginning with relatively simple, curvilinear patterns painted dark on light (FIG. 4-3), he moved toward a fully polychrome style of decoration that found its culmination in the splendid pottery (FIG. 4-4) discovered in the cave at Kamares on the slope of Mount Ida. On a surface swelling robustly with the peculiarly Minoan feel for the vigor and buoyancy of active life we find a lustrous black ground on which is a quasigeometric pattern of creamy white interspersed with yellow and red, forming a colorful and harmonious decoration. As in Egypt, the motifs derive from natural forms; here they are simplified into a play of spirals beautifully adjusted to and integrated with the shape of the vessel.

The Late Minoan Period

Somewhere between 1600 and 1500 B.C. began the period of the new palaces, when the destroyed palaces were rebuilt and the Golden Age of Crete produced the first great Western civilization. The bulk of the surviving archeological material—the evidence of an age of unsurpassed creative energy and precocious artistic achievement—dates from this era, which ended about 1400 B.C.

THE PALACES

The palaces rebuilt for the kings and their retainers were large, comfortable, and handsome, with ample staircases and courtyards for pageants, ceremonies, and games. The largest of them, the palace at Knossos (FIGS. 4-5 and 4-6), was a rambling structure built against the upper slopes and across the top of a low hill rising from a fertile plain. The great rectangular court around which the units of the palace are grouped had been leveled in the time of the old palace, and the manner of the grouping of buildings suggests that it was not preplanned but that several building nuclei grew together, with the court as the major organizing element. A secondary organization of the plan is provided by two long corridors. On the west side of the court a north-south corridor separates official and ceremonial rooms from the magazines, where wine, grain, oil, and honey were stored in large jars (*pithoi*). On the east side of the court, an east-west corridor separates the king's and queen's quarters and reception rooms (south) from the workmen's and servant's quarters (north). At the northwest corner of the entire building complex is the "arena," a theater-like area with steps (seats?) on two sides—a possi-

same style as the plank figures, but the body has gained mass and volume, and the composition has a three-dimensional quality lacking in the plank idols. Although it has not been possible to establish a chronological sequence for these Cycladic figurines, most seem to date from the second half of the third millennium B.C.; the *Lyre Player* is believed to belong to the end of the line and may have been contemporary with the Cretan palaces.

The Middle Minoan Period

The Middle Minoan period is marked by the founding of the old palaces around the year 2000 B.C. Building in Crete emphasized neither tombs, temples, nor fortresses but, instead, palaces for the king and his retainers, around which grew up royal towns. The absence of fortification on Crete is conspicuous in the Aegean world, since fortified sites appear everywhere in the Helladic and Cycladic areas. It attests either to the power of the Cretan navies, to a long-enduring insular peace, or to both. But after only about three centuries, around 1700 B.C., these old palaces were destroyed, probably by one of the frequent earthquakes that ravage this part of the Mediterranean region.

An important technological advance of the beginning of the Old Palace period was the introduction of the potter's wheel, which permitted the throwing of vessels with thin-

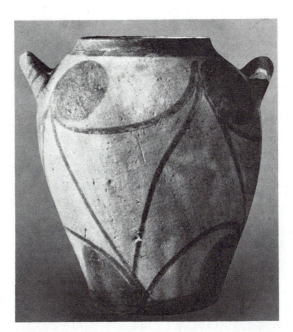

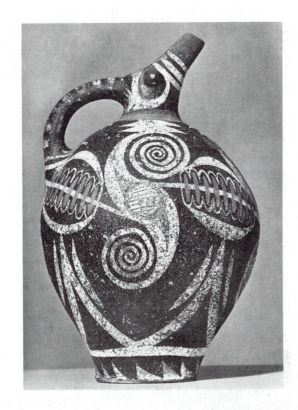

4-3   Small storage jar, Psyra, *c.* 2000–1850 B.C. 11″ high.

4-4   Kamares pitcher, Phaistos, *c.* 1800–1700 B.C. Approx. 10″ high. Archeological Museum, Herakleion.

ble forerunner of the later Greek theater. Its purpose is unknown, but it is a feature that, like the central court, appears in other Cretan palaces. The complexity of the palace's plan came to be associated for the Greeks with the cult of the double axe (*labrys*), celebrated here; thus, perhaps, the Greek myth of the Cretan *labyrinth*. Certainly it was the product of wealth and luxurious tastes and of a love for the convenient. Beneath the palace is a remarkably efficient drainage system of terracotta pipes that must have made Knossos one of the most sanitary cities existing before the twentieth century.

The practical storage system is exhibited in the magazines of the west wing (FIG. 4-7), where some of the pithoi are still in place. Some of the rooms had flat floors; others, like those shown here, had stone-lined pits. The walls were quite thick, as must have been the roofing over these magazines; the masonry may have been covered with earth to keep the interior cool. In most parts of the palace the masonry composing the walls was rough, consisting of unshaped field stones imbedded in mortar; ashlar masonry, made of shaped blocks of stone, was used at building corners and around door and window openings.

4-5   Palace at Knossos, *c.* 1600–1400 B.C. (view from the east).

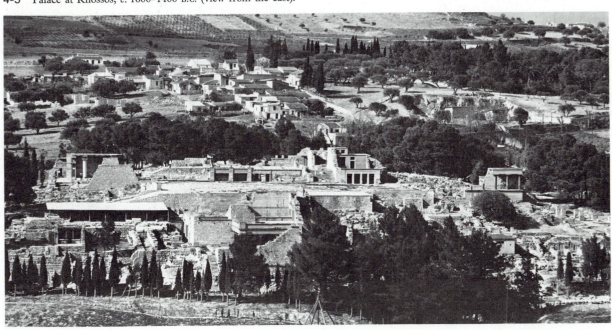

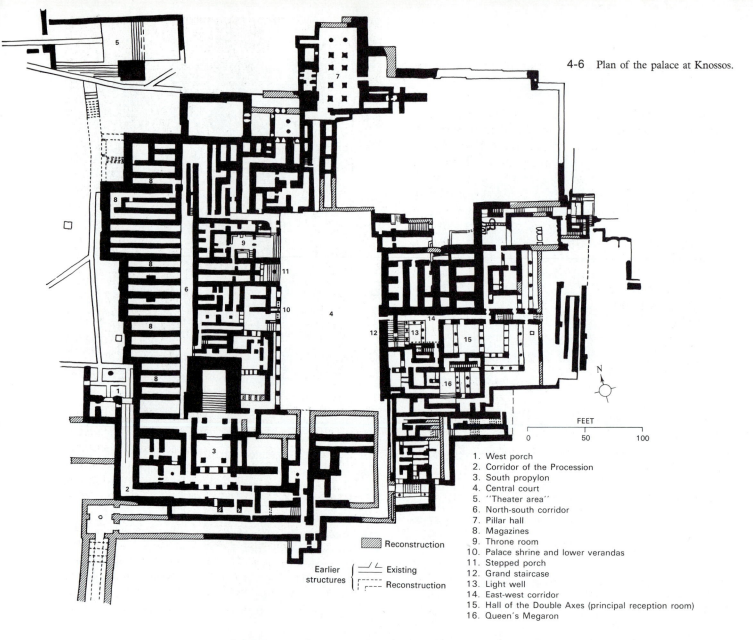

4-6 Plan of the palace at Knossos.

1. West porch
2. Corridor of the Procession
3. South propylon
4. Central court
5. "Theater area"
6. North-south corridor
7. Pillar hall
8. Magazines
9. Throne room
10. Palace shrine and lower verandas
11. Stepped porch
12. Grand staircase
13. Light well
14. East-west corridor
15. Hall of the Double Axes (principal reception room)
16. Queen's Megaron

FEET
0   50   100

▨ Reconstruction

Earlier structures { Existing
                      Reconstruction

4-7 View of the west magazine, palace at Knossos, with large pithoi *in situ*.

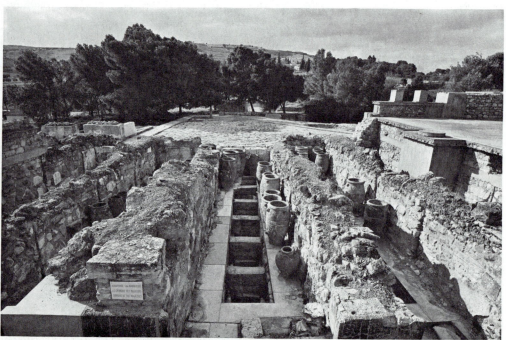

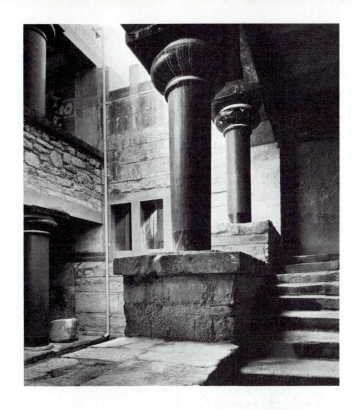

4-8   Reconstruction of a stairwell, palace at Knossos.

The palace had as many as three stories with interior staircases built around light and air wells (FIG. 4-8), which provided necessary illumination and ventilation. Distinguishing features of the Minoan columns, which were originally fashioned of wood but were restored in stone (with, it is now thought, mistakenly bulky proportions), are their bulbous, cushionlike capitals and the manner in which the column shafts taper toward the base. Strong evidence that the column had religious significance for the Cretans is its central position in the Lion Gate at Mycenae (FIG. 4-21) and the fact that the base of a column in one of the lower stories of the palace at Knossos is surrounded by a trough that was used for libations.

PAINTING

A view into the Queen's Megaron, with its pillared hall and light well (FIG. 4-9), shows the typically elaborate wall decoration of the more important rooms at Knossos. Here plastered walls were painted with frescoes, which, together with the red- or blue-shafted columns, must have provided an extraordinarily rich effect. The frescoes depicted many aspects of Cretan life (bullfights, processions, and ceremonies) and of nature (birds, animals, flowers and—as here—marine life with dolphins frolicking among other fauna of the sea).

One of the most memorable figures from the art of Crete is the *Cupbearer* from the procession fresco of the South Propylon at Knossos (FIG. 4-10). It is the only one preserved from a sequence, shown in two registers, that may have contained over 500 figures—if those from the Corridor of the Procession are included. The ceremonial *rhyton*

(vessel for pouring ritual libations) carried by the youth has a typically Minoan shape, found nowhere else except as a Minoan import. And the figure itself is unmistakably Minoan. The youth has long curly hair, wears an elaborately embroidered loincloth with a silver-mounted girdle, and has ornaments on his arms, neck, ankles, and wrist. Although the profile pose with the full-view eye was a familiar convention in Egypt and Mesopotamia, the elegance of the Cretan figure, with its pinched waist, proud, self-confident bearing, and free movement, distinguishes it from all other early figure styles. The angularity of the older styles is typically modified in the curving line that suggests the elasticity of the living and moving being.

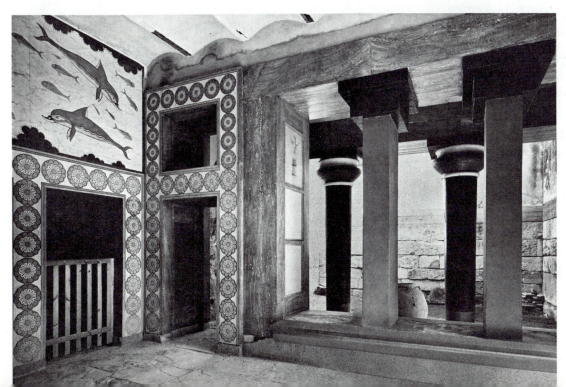

4-9   Reconstruction of the Queen's Megaron, palace at Knossos.

95

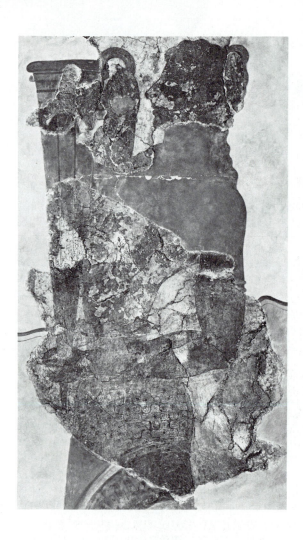

Vivacity and spontaneity characterize the *Toreador Fresco* (FIG. 4-11). Although only fragments of it have been recovered, they are extraordinary in their depiction of vigorous movements of the girls and the young man who is shown in the air, having, perhaps, grasped the bull's horns and somersaulted over its back. We have seen how important the bull is in the Near East, especially in Mesopotamian art. The difference in the Minoan paintings is in the relationship of the bull—it may be that here he is even a god—to human beings. In this fresco, man and beast contest with each other in a dangerous game that takes place in the here and now, the human beings as conspicuous in the action as the bull. In a powerful characterization of the natures of both man and beast, the poise and agility of the toreadors play off against the exploding energy of the bull. (One thinks back to the charging bisons of the Paleolithic caves.) Everywhere within the frame are curving lines, the directional lines of action, and nowhere more conspicuously and vitally than in the electric energy of the line that sweeps from the head of the bull to the whip of his tail.

Because of her cosmetic prettiness—like that of a sophisticated, modern type of womanhood—a girl represented in a fragment of another fresco has been labeled *La Parisienne* (FIG. 4-12). With her conventionally enlarged and front-view eye, her turned-up nose, full red lips, and elaborate coiffure, she is almost disturbingly of our own

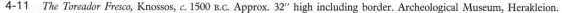

4-11 *The Toreador Fresco*, Knossos, *c.* 1500 B.C. Approx. 32″ high including border. Archeological Museum, Herakleion.

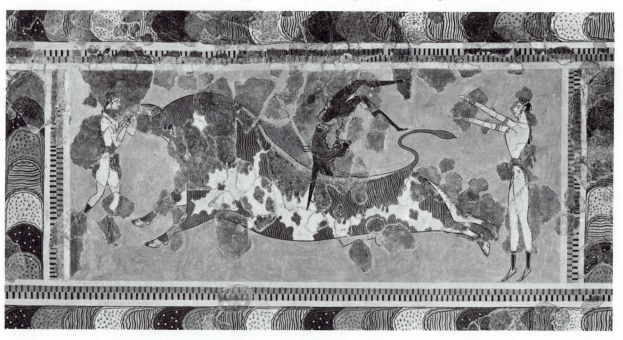

4-12 *La Parisienne,* fragment of a fresco, Knossos, *c.* 1500 B.C. Approx. 10″ high. Archeological Museum, Herakleion.

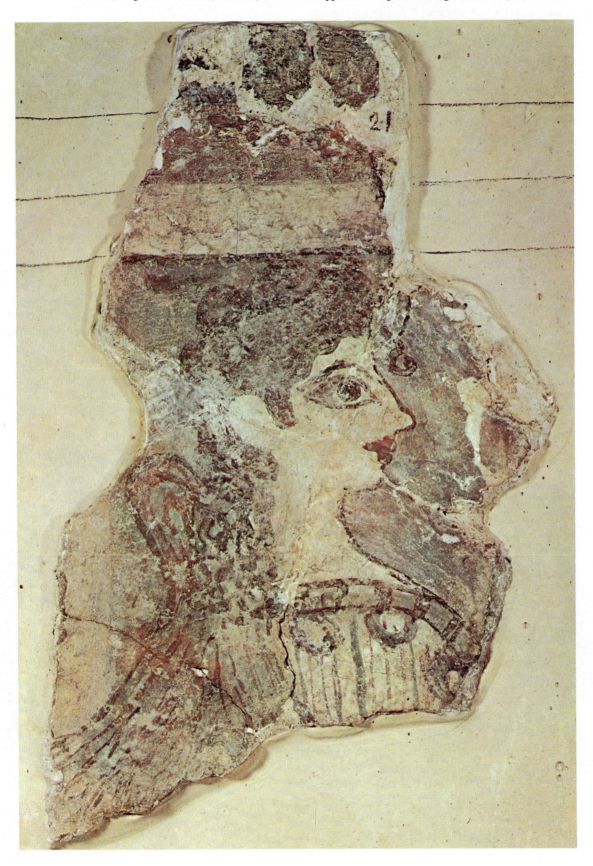

times, especially as we conventionalize her type in popular art. Surely there is nothing quite like this sprightly charm, freshness, and *joie de vivre* in the art of the ancient Near East. The painting method used is appropriate to the lively spirit of the Minoans. Unlike the Egyptians, who painted in the dry fresco technique, the Minoans used a true, or wet, fresco method, which required rapid execution and a skill in getting quick, almost impressionistic effects. If one is to catch an interesting but fugitive aspect of an object or a scene, one must work quickly, even spontaneously, allowing for happy accidents. Thus, because the wet-fresco technique compelled the artist to work rapidly, the spirit of *La Parisienne* is also a product of the resultant verve of his hand, and the simple, light delicacy of the technique matches exactly the vivacity of the subject. It is the Minoan sense of immediate life and the Minoan skill in catching it that strike us as novel in the ancient world and prophetic of great changes in man's outlook on nature.

POTTERY

The Minoan feeling for the dynamics of living nature, revealed in their figurative fresco art, is no less visible in their pottery, among the finest in history. In the Kamares ware (FIG. 4-4) this interest in animate nature does not at once appear; the taste is for abstract spiral forms, scrolls, whorls, and the like. As time went on, the tendency toward naturalism in decoration increased. Motifs were derived from sea life, such as dolphins, seaweed, and octopuses. The tentacles reaching out over the curving surfaces of the *Octopus Jar* from Gournia (FIG. 4-13) embrace the piece and emphasize its elastic volume. This is a masterful realization of the relation between the decoration of the vessel and its shape, always a problem for the ceramist. From the Kamares silhouetting of light abstract forms upon a dark ground, we go, in the *Octopus Jar*, to a silhouetting of dark naturalistic forms upon a light ground. This manner lasts from about 1600 to 1500 B.C., when the fluid, open, and lively naturalistic style becomes increasingly stiff and abstract. This late style can be seen in a three-handled jar of about 1425 B.C. from Knossos (FIG. 4-14). The stalks of its papyrus decoration grow symmetrically, and the flowers turn into stylized scrolls and fans, symmetrically balanced. Wavy bands, simple concentric circles with crosses, and other rudimentary space-fillers occupy the surface rather than adjust to it and embrace it. Such devolution from naturalism to formalism and abstraction can be observed frequently in the history of world art.

An increasing self-awareness, which we have watched slowly evolving in ancient art, requires that man represent himself ever more as he is, in more conditions and situations, with fewer restrictions imposed by tradition. The *Harvester Vase* (FIGS. 4-15 and 4-16), made of steatite (soapstone), gives a sharp new glimpse of man as he is in

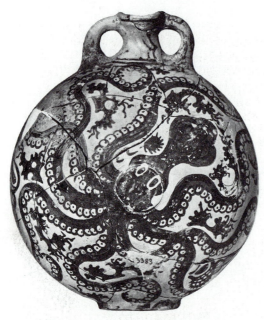

4-13   *The Octopus Jar* (amphora), Gournia, *c.* 1600 B.C. Approx. 8″ high. Archeological Museum, Herakleion.

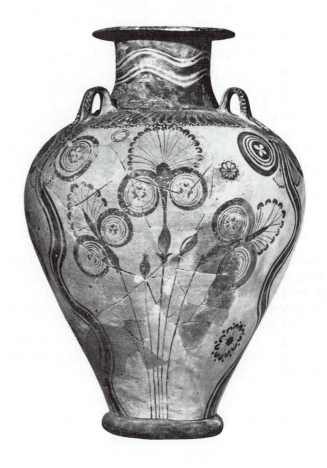

4-14   Three-handled jar with papyrus decoration, Knossos, *c.* 1425 B.C. Approx. 53″ high. Archeological Museum, Herakleion.

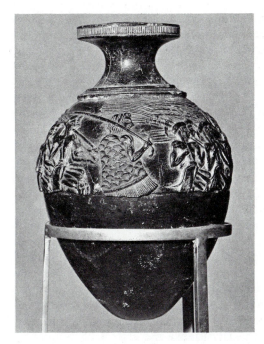

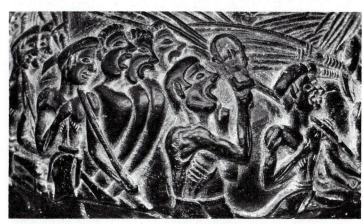

4-15 *The Harvester Vase* (rhyton), Hagia Triada, *c.* 1500 B.C. Steatite, approx. 5″ wide. Archeological Museum, Herakleion. (Lower part is lost.)

4-16 *The Harvester Vase*, detail.

his usual physical context. The egg-shaped rhyton, its lower half missing, shows a riotous crowd of olive-harvesters, singing and shouting. Their forward movement and lusty exuberance are most vividly expressed. The pattern of pitchforks fills the upper part of the band, while the figures below, in higher relief, create a variation in surface. The entire design, like the octopus of the Gournia vase, hugs the shape so tightly that it seems to be an integral part of the wall of the vase. But the figures themselves are depicted with a gusto that matches their mood. They are led by a man who carries a *sistrum*, or rattle, and beats time, while his lungs are so inflated with air that his ribs show. The harvesters' facial expressions are rendered with astonishing exactitude; there are degrees of hilarity and degrees of vocal effort, all marked in the tension or relaxation of facial muscles. This reading of the human face as a vehicle of emotional states is without precedent in ancient art before the Minoans.

SCULPTURE

There is little sculpture in the round in Minoan art, and what there is generally is small; there is no monumental sculpture of gods, kings, and monsters, such as we find in Mesopotamia and Egypt—at least, none has been found. This absence of large-scale sculpture may reflect an absence of a systematic and formal religion—though this is entirely speculation because of our ignorance of Minoan religion. The small figures of "snake goddesses" like the

one shown from Knossos (FIG. 4-17) are hardly more than of talisman or fetish size. They exhibit most of the rigid conventions, including the frontal pose, that we have met in Egypt and Mesopotamia, but the arms have been released from the core of the block and are held forward or aloft. Thus, they are shown to be active and, somehow,

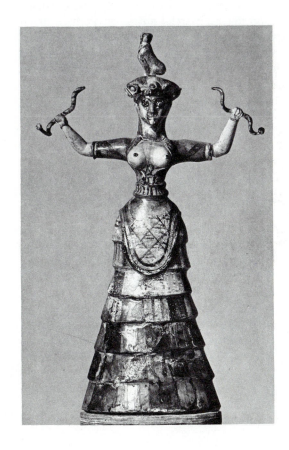

4-17 *Snake Goddess*, Knossos, *c.* 1600 B.C. Faïence, approx. 13½″ high. Archeological Museum, Herakleion.

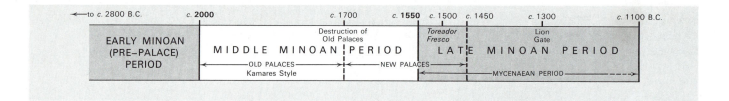

to c. 2800 B.C.   c. 2000   c. 1700   c. 1550   c. 1500   c. 1450   c. 1300   c. 1100 B.C.

EARLY MINOAN (PRE-PALACE) PERIOD   MIDDLE MINOAN PERIOD   Destruction of Old Palaces   Toreador Fresco   Lion Gate   LATE MINOAN PERIOD

OLD PALACES Kamares Style   NEW PALACES   MYCENAEAN PERIOD

seem more alive than their Near Eastern or Egyptian cousins. The Cretans seem to have worshiped a mother goddess sacred to many places and manifest in many forms. Whether or not these miniature figures brandishing snakes are images of her is not certain, but they are clearly identified as Minoan by their costume—the open bodice and flounced skirt worn by Minoan women as we find them depicted many times over. This touch of the real may be another example of man fashioning his gods in his own image.

The circumstances under which the Minoan civilization came to an end are still hotly disputed. One theory, which seems to be gaining adherents, has it that the Cretan palaces were destroyed around 1450 B.C. as the result of a cataclysmic volcanic eruption on the island of Thera, which lies some eighty miles north of Crete, and where important excavations are now in progress. The seismic catastrophe may have caused such a loss of population that the Mycenaeans could move into the island and establish themselves at Knossos without meeting major resistance. From the repaired palace at Knossos they seem to have ruled the island for at least half a century, perhaps much longer. Parts of the palace continued to be occupied until its final destruction around 1200 B.C., this time by the Dorians, but its importance as a cultural center faded soon after 1400, as the focus of Aegean civilization shifted to the Greek mainland.

MYCENAEAN ART

Just as the end of the Minoan, so the origins of Mycenaean culture are still being debated. The primitive Greeks may have moved into the mainland about the time the old palaces were being built in Crete—that is, about the beginning of the second millennium B.C. Doubtless they were influenced by Crete even then, and some believe that for a long time the mainland was a Minoan colony, though the mainlanders developed and held to many cultural features of their own. At any rate, Mycenaean power rose on the mainland in the palmy days of the new palaces on Crete, and by 1500 B.C. a new and splendid culture was flourishing in Greece to which, 700 years later, Homer was to give the epithet "rich in gold." It is possible that the Mycenaeans made close contact in this new era not only with Crete but with Egypt, with which they may have been allied

against the Hittites in the early part of the New Kingdom; and the Mycenaeans' taste for gold, as well as their actual treasure, may have been acquired in the mercenary service of Egypt, which was known in the ancient world for its lavish use of the metal. Thus, the awakening of the Mycenaean world may have been the consequence of a kind of three-way route of influence connecting the mainland, Crete, and Egypt. The destruction of the Cretan palaces left the Mycenaean (mainland) culture supreme, but new waves of migrating proto-Greek peoples, the Dorians, finally submerged the Mycenaean civilization. The steady infiltration of these peoples had already made a fortress architecture necessary (unlike the case in Crete) and by about 1200 B.C. the fortified citadels of the mainland were overwhelmed by the invaders. The heroes and battles of these last centuries of Aegean civilization must have provided the tradition that, hundreds of years later, Homer would immortalize in the first great European epics, the *Iliad* and the *Odyssey*.

Though Mycenae appears to have been the cultural center of the mainland development, the remains of other large citadels have been found at Vaphio, Pylos, Orchomenos, Arne, and (most recently) at Iolkos. The best preserved and most impressive Mycenaean remains are those of the fortified palaces at Tiryns and Mycenae, both built at the beginning of the Late Mycenaean period, about 1400 B.C., and razed (along with the others) between 1250 and 1200 B.C.

Architecture

The Citadel of Tiryns (FIG. 4-18), only ten miles from Mycenae, so that at times they may have been under the same lord, was known by Homer as Tiryns of the Great Walls and by the ancient world as the birthplace of Herakles, the mythic hero of great strength. The ancient sightseer and guidebook-writer, Pausanias, thought the walls of Tiryns quite as spectacular as the pyramids of Egypt. The heavy walls are in sharp contrast with the open Cretan palaces and clearly reveal their defensive character. The buildings within the twenty-foot-thick walls are aligned axially and seem to have been laid out according to a predetermined plan. Unlike the rambling and often confusing layout of the Cretan palaces, the Mycenaean plan is an example of a clear and simple arrangement of the units. The megaron (FIG. 4-19), the three-chambered structure at

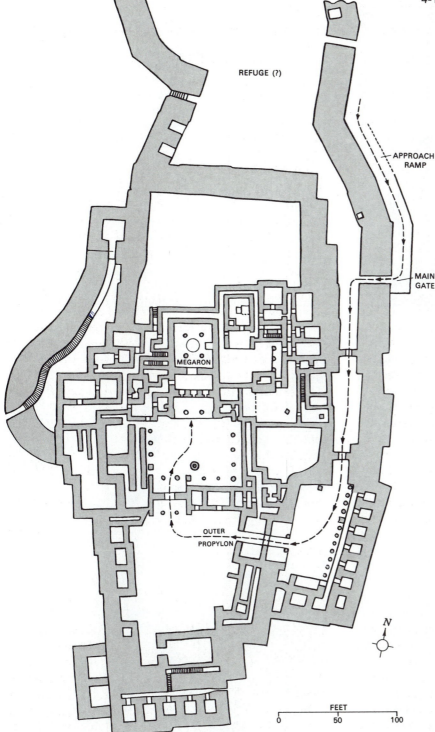

REFUGE (?)

APPROACH RAMP

MAIN GATE

MEGARON

OUTER PROPYLON

N

FEET
0   50   100

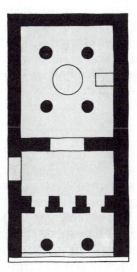

4-19 Plan of the megaron, Tiryns.

the heart of the design and the center of the life of the citadel, embodies the germ of the classical temples of Greece. This fundamental building type does not appear in the palaces of Crete but does appear, surprisingly, at Troy as early as 2000 B.C. A hall of state, the megaron was rectangular, with a central hearth and four columns supporting the roof.

The massive fortification walls at Tiryns and other Mycenaean sites, built of unhewn or roughly dressed stone, were called cyclopean by later Greeks, who imagined them to have been built by that mythical race of giants. Through the walls at intervals run corbeled galleries (FIG. 4-20), which may have been used as part of the defensive structure or as part of a complicated and dra-

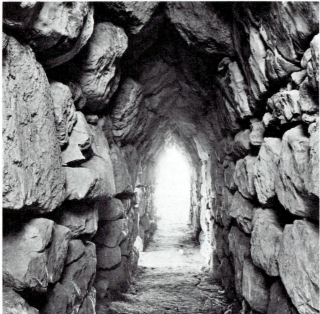

Within the gate and to the right lies the grave circle, an enclosure containing a number of simple shaft graves, stone-lined pits serving as tombs for kings and their families, covered and marked by a stele. Another similar grave circle was recently discovered outside the walls of Mycenae. Both grave circles date from about 1600–1500 B.C. But at this time shaft graves were gradually being replaced by the so-called beehive tombs, of which the best preserved is the remarkable Treasury of Atreus (FIGS. 4-22 and 4-23), misnamed that by Schliemann, who thought it—the most imposing of a group—to be the storehouse for the treasure of Atreus, father of Agamemnon and Menelaus. Built into a hill and approached by a long passage, or *dromos,* the beehive shape of the round tomb chamber, or *tholos,* was achieved by use of corbeled courses of stone laid on a circular base, splendidly cut to the curve of the wall, and ending in a lofty dome, which in this fine example is about forty feet high. This vaulted structure

matic ceremonial path leading, through a porch and vestibule, to the chief room of the palace—the megaron. The corbeled gallery pictured makes use, as its name indicates, of the primitive corbeled arch. The rough appearance of these cyclopean structures is most impressive in its crude monumentality; it possesses an earthy dynamism not found in other, more sophisticated ancient architectural styles.

The sternness of these fortress-palaces was relieved by frescoes, by carvings, and, at Mycenae at least, by monumental architectural sculpture—the Lion Gate (FIG. 4-21). This outer gateway of the stronghold, protected on the left by a wall and on the right by a projecting bastion, is formed of two great monoliths capped with a huge lintel above which the layers of stone form a corbeled arch, leaving a triangular opening that serves to lighten the weight to be carried by the lintel. The triangular space is filled with a slab on which two lions carved in high relief confront each other on either side of a column of the probably sacred Minoan type, resting their forepaws on its base. (This column of the Lion Gate supplies evidence of what the vanished wooden Minoan columns looked like.) Holes near the top of the animals indicate that the heads, now lost, were made of separate pieces of stone or metal. The lions are carved with breadth and vigor, and the whole design admirably fills its triangular space, harmonizing in dignity, strength, and scale with the massive stones that form the walls and gate. We find similar groups in miniature on Cretan seals, and one senses that these lions are not too distant from Mesopotamian heraldic composition.

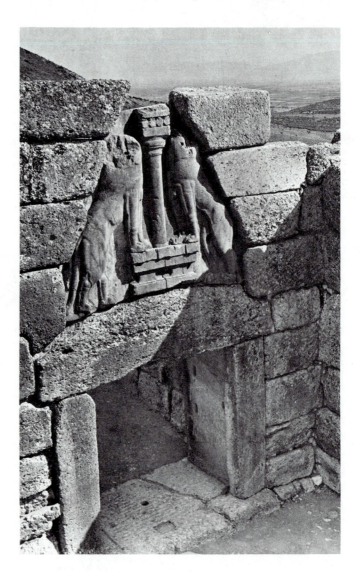

4-21 The Lion Gate, Mycenae, *c.* 1300 B.C. Limestone relief panel, approx. 9½' high.

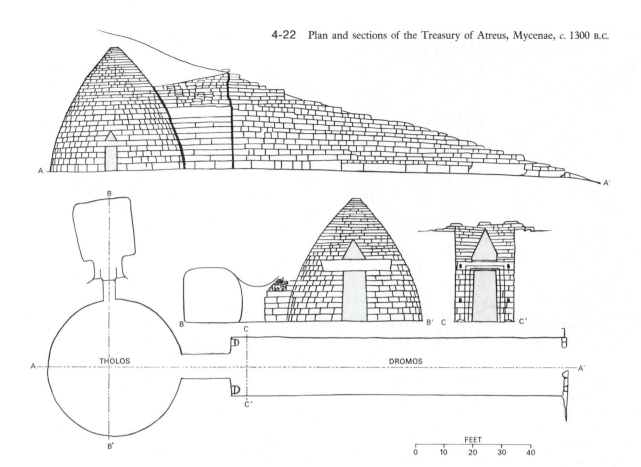

THOLOS

DROMOS

FEET
0   10   20   30   40

without interior supports was the largest unified space in all antiquity until the Roman Pantheon was built 1500 years later.

Pottery, Relief, and Craft Art

Most of the beehive tombs had been thoroughly looted long before their modern rediscovery. On the other hand, rich finds were made in shaft graves at Mycenae. Some bronze daggers, inlaid with gold and silver, found in these graves reveal the influence of the Minoan figure style (FIG. 4-24). On the longest of the three blades illustrated, three hunters with spears, bows, and shields attack a lion that has struck down a fourth hunter, while two other lions flee. The subject is of Mesopotamian derivation, but the costumes are Cretan, and the vigorous, spirited movements of the hunters, the lithe strength and spring of the lions, are of the Minoan taste.

Beaten gold (*repoussé*) masks were found in the shaft graves, attached to the faces of the mummified Mycenaean princes (FIG. 4-25). Powerfully realistic in their record of the features of the deceased, they also testify to the influx

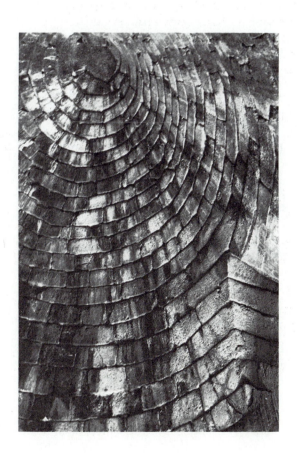

4-23   Interior of the tholos, Treasury of Atreus. Vault approx. 40′ high.

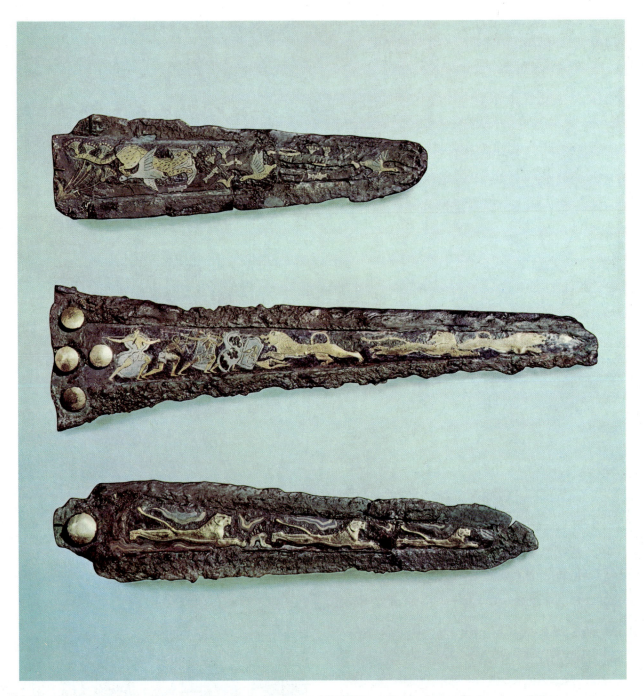

4-24 Inlaid dagger blades from the royal tombs at Mycenae, *c.* 1600–1500 B.C. Bronze, longest blade approx. 9″ long. National Museum, Athens.

of gold from Egypt. This and the elaboration of funeral practices lend strong support to the supposition that the impulse that started this high phase of Mycenaean civilization originated partly in Egypt, partly in Crete.

The golden culture of Mycenae produced such masterpieces as the famous cups from Vaphio (FIG. 4-26). Found in a beehive tomb, these beautiful vessels are still the subject of warm debate among experts who see them as

originating in Crete and those who insist that, despite their undoubted resemblance to Minoan figure style, they are Mycenaean. The cups are a pair, each made of two plates of gold, one of which was worked in *repoussé* for the outside, the other left plain to make a smooth surface for the inside. The plates were fastened together, the handles riveted on, and some of the details then engraved. The subject seems to be Minoan (the men are costumed in the

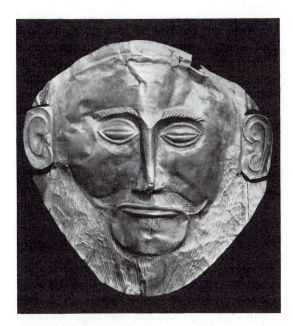

4-25 Funeral mask from the royal tombs of Mycenae, *c.* 1500 B.C. Beaten gold, approx. 12″ high. National Museum, Athens.

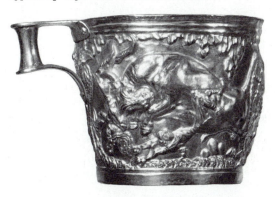

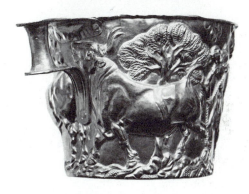

4-26 *The Vaphio Cups,* c. 1500 B.C. Gold with *repoussé* decoration, approx. 3½″ high. National Museum, Athens.

Minoan manner) and related to the bull-leaping ritual; bulls are being trapped and snared, with a cow used as a lure in one case. One cup shows a bull caught in a net. A second bull, charging furiously, impales with its horns a man whose companion falls to one side. A third bull dashes madly from the fracas. The other cup presents a quieter scene. At the right the bull moves toward the cow; in the center he stands beside her; at the left, captured and hobbled, he is bellowing. The three scenes are integrated by the trees and the man, and the whole design is admirably composed to fit the space. In both cups, areas not filled by the animal and human figures contain landscape motifs of trees, rocks, and clouds similar to those in painting. The shallowness of the relief and the conventional treatment of the trees produce a rich play of light and shade together with a variety of textures.

The *Warrior Vase* (FIG. 4-27) represents a file of Mycenaean soldiers strikingly different in costume, physiognomy, and beards from the Cretan types we have seen in Minoan art. This would seem to strengthen the argument of those who regard the Mycenaeans as being of entirely different racial stock from the Minoans and as the indigenous builders of their own civilization. It may be, too, that we are looking here at the last Mycenaean warriors who marched forth to meet the Dorian invaders, under whose onslaught the Mycenaean civilization collapsed after 1200 B.C. The Dorians carried iron weapons, superior to the softer bronze of the Mycenaeans, and their success illustrates the historical commonplace that a superior technology can overcome an otherwise more highly developed civilization. The centuries-long "dark age" that followed the obliteration of Aegean culture, though little survives from it, cannot be considered merely a historical void. New energies were gathering that would form one of the greatest civilizations the world has known, a civilization new, bold, self-confident, and modern.

4-27 *The Warrior Vase,* Mycenae, *c.* 1200 B.C. Approx. 14″ high. National Museum, Athens.

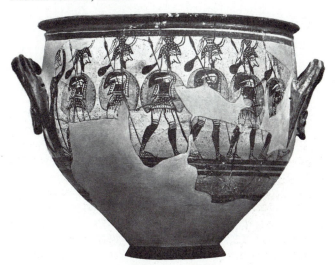

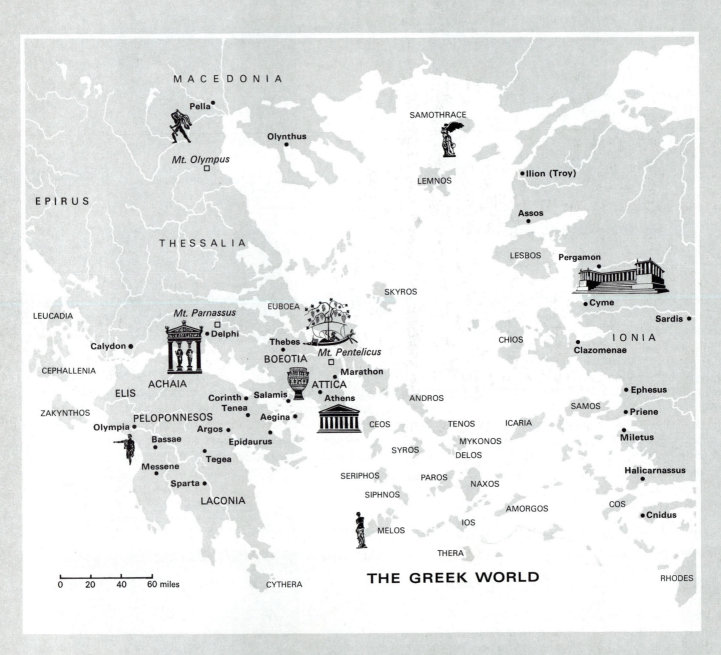

MACEDONIA

Pella

Olynthus

Mt. Olympus

EPIRUS

SAMOTHRACE

LEMNOS

Ilion (Troy)

Assos

THESSALIA

LESBOS

Pergamon

Cyme

Sardis

SKYROS

LEUCADIA

Mt. Parnassus

EUBOEA

CHIOS

IONIA

Calydon

Delphi

Thebes

Mt. Pentelicus

Clazomenae

CEPHALLENIA

BOEOTIA

Marathon

ACHAIA

ATTICA

Ephesus

ELIS

Corinth

Salamis

Athens

ANDROS

SAMOS

Priene

Tenea

ZAKYNTHOS

PELOPONNESOS

Aegina

CEOS

TENOS

ICARIA

Miletus

Olympia

Argos

MYKONOS

Bassae

Epidaurus

SYROS

DELOS

Halicarnassus

Tegea

Messene

PAROS

NAXOS

COS

Sparta

SERIPHOS

Cnidus

LACONIA

SIPHNOS

AMORGOS

MELOS

IOS

0 20 40 60 miles

THE GREEK WORLD

THERA

CYTHERA

RHODES

chapter five

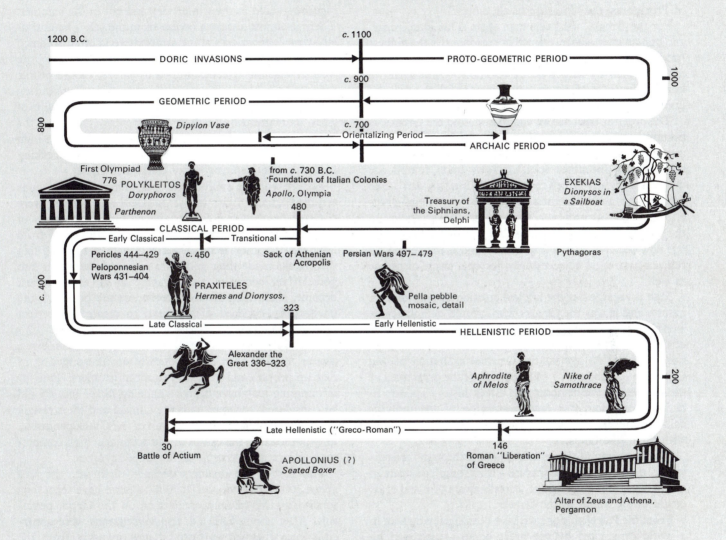

1200 B.C.

c. 1100

DORIC INVASIONS → PROTO-GEOMETRIC PERIOD

1000

c. 900

GEOMETRIC PERIOD

800

Dipylon Vase

c. 700
Orientalizing Period

ARCHAIC PERIOD

First Olympiad
776
POLYKLEITOS
Doryphoros

from *c.* 730 B.C.
Foundation of Italian Colonies

Apollo, Olympia

Parthenon

480

Treasury of
the Siphnians,
Delphi

EXEKIAS
*Dionysos in
a Sailboat*

CLASSICAL PERIOD

Early Classical ← Transitional

Sack of Athenian
Acropolis

Persian Wars 497– 479

Pythagoras

c. 400

Pericles 444–429
Peloponnesian
Wars 431–404

c. 450

PRAXITELES
Hermes and Dionysos,

Pella pebble
mosaic, detail

Late Classical

323

Early Hellenistic

HELLENISTIC PERIOD

Alexander the
Great 336–323

200

*Aphrodite
of Melos*

*Nike of
Samothrace*

Late Hellenistic ("Greco-Roman")

30
Battle of Actium

APOLLONIUS (?)
Seated Boxer

146
Roman "Liberation"
of Greece

Altar of Zeus and Athena,
Pergamon

The Art of Greece

FOR WE ARE LOVERS of the beautiful, yet with simplicity, and we cultivate the mind without loss of manliness. . . . We are the school of Greece." In the fifth century B.C., the Golden Age of Athens, Thucydides has Pericles make this assertion in praise of the Athenians, comparing their open, democratic society with the closed, barracks state of their rivals, the Spartans. But he might be speaking in general of Greek culture as we have received it and of the ideal of humanistic education and life created by that culture. In the humanistic view, man is what matters, and he is, in the words of Protagoras, the "measure of all things."

For the Greeks, what sets man apart is his intelligence, and human intelligence, trained in reasoning, is the highest function nature has created. Moreover, Aristotle assures us that "all men by nature desire to know." And what we know is the order of nature, which is one with the order of human reason.

The order of both nature and reason, said the Greeks, is beautiful and simple, and the beauty of things is one with our knowledge of them; thus, the good life, the achievement of the "beautiful soul," follows upon compliance with that typically Greek command, "Know thyself!" One achieves the good life, then, through an intellectual process; one lives "according to nature"—that is, according to the natural laws of life discoverable by rational man. The self now becomes of first importance, and as man comes to full self-awareness he necessarily becomes aware of nature as well.

Man is regarded as the highest creation of and value in nature, and it was the Greeks who created democracy as well as the natural image of man in art. A late great scholar of Classical Greece, Werner Jaeger, wrote of their exaltation of man: "As against the Oriental exaltation of one God-king . . . and the . . . suppression of the great mass of the people . . . the beginning of Greek history appears to be the beginning of a new conception of the individual. . . . the history of personality in Europe must start with them [the Greeks]."[1]

This honoring of the individual—and through the individual, the laws of human nature—is so completely part of our habit of mind that we are scarcely aware of it and of its origin in the minds of the Greeks.

From the Paleolithic age we have been surveying man in a world dominated by the great beasts—threatened by them, fighting them, dependent upon them (or their embodiment), worshiping them, conceding their might and his own weakness. Now, in Greece, he asserts that his own peculiar power—the power of intelligence—puts him far above the beasts. But the Greek mind is not dryly or pallidly rationalistic; it knows well the forces of the irrational against which reason must struggle constantly. In

fact, Greek art constitutes with Greek culture a compact synthesis of opposites, a harmony between profound passion and rational order. Its clarity and symmetry are not cold but vital; its forms can be rigorous and mathematical, yet full of life.

In marked contrast to Egypt, with its long horizontals of alluvial plain between desert plateaus and seemingly invariable sunshine, Greece is a country of diversified geography and climate. The bays of its deeply indented, rugged coastline make the country half land and half sea; mountain ridges divide it into many small units. The climate is vigorous—cold in the winter, dry and hot in the summer. There is almost always a breeze from the sea. The unusually clear, almost crystalline atmosphere is often softened by a haze. Both sky and sea are brilliant in color. It is little wonder that the Greeks, attuned to nature, should people mountains, woods, streams, sky, and sea with divinities; that they should picture Zeus, the king of this realm of gods, as reigning from their loftiest peak, Olympus; the Muses as dwelling in the deep, cool groves on the long slopes of Parnassus and Cithaeron; and Apollo as speaking from the awe-inspiring rocky clefts of Delphi.

Nature worship evolved into personification. The gods assumed human forms whose grandeur and nobility were not free from human frailty; indeed, unlike the gods of Egypt and Mesopotamia, their only real difference from men was that they were immortal. There is a saying that the Greeks made their gods into men and their men into gods. Man, becoming the measure of all things, must become, if all things in their perfection are beautiful, the unchanging standard of the best; to create the perfect individual became the Greek ideal.

The Greeks, or Hellenes, as they called themselves, appear to have been the product of an intermingling of Aegean peoples and of Indo-European invaders. This intermingling may have been a vitalizing factor that should be considered, together with the climate and the strongly diversified mountain-valley terrain of the Greek peninsula, in hypothesizing the causes of the peculiarly high competitive and creative energy of the Greek peoples.

The first of the invaders began to drift into the area about 2000 B.C., and after 1600 B.C., as we have seen, they formed the Mycenaean civilization on the Greek peninsula. After about 1200 B.C. the Mycenaeans were apparently overwhelmed in turn by new invaders from the north—the Dorians and perhaps the Ionians. The Dorians made the Peloponnesos the center of their power and may have forced the Ionians eastward across the Aegean to the coast of Asia Minor. The origin of the Ionians is still a matter of dispute. Some scholars feel that proto-Ionians lived at Athens during Mycenaean times and that they were displaced during the Doric invasions. Others hold that they developed on the coast of Asia Minor between the eleventh and eighth century B.C. out of a mixed stock of settlers. In either case, the Ionians seem to have been

[1] Werner Jaeger, *Paideia: The Ideals of Greek Culture* (New York: Oxford Univ. Press, 1939), vol. 1, p. xix.

more individualistic than the tribally ordered Dorians, whose most characteristic city became conservative Sparta.

In Ionia, on the east coast of Asia Minor, epics of individual greatness had come to be celebrated by the eighth century B.C., and by the seventh century, the rational philosophers of Miletus had begun to interpret the world in terms of reason rather than religion, beginning that immense transformation of the worship of nature into the science of nature, the science that is still expanding today. Between Ionia and the Peloponnesos lay Attica, and there, in Athens, a conservative tribal order and individualistic striving combined to produce the most fruitful of all the *poleis*, or city-states, of Greece, the one that Thucydides could boast was the "school of Greece."

By the eighth century B.C. the separate Greek-speaking states had held their first ceremonial games in common: the Olympiad of 776 B.C., from which time the historical Greeks calculated their chronology. From then on, despite their chronic rivalries and wars, they regarded themselves as Hellenes, distinct from the surrounding "barbarians," who did not speak Greek. The enterprising Hellenes, greatly aided by their indented coasts and island stepping-stones, became a trading and a colonizing people who enlarged the geographic and cultural boundaries of Hellas. Tribal organizations had evolved into city-states, each an individual unit. Political development differed from state to state, but a kind of pattern emerged in which rule was first by kings, then by nobles, then by tyrants who seized personal power. At last, in Athens, appeared the dynamic balance that was called democracy.

Athens has in many ways become the symbol of Greek culture; many of the finest products of Greek civilization were created by Athenians or by others closely associated with Athens and its traditions. Athens, at the time of its brief flowering after the Persian Wars, was an active business city of about 100,000 people. Above its olive groves and rooftops towered the Acropolis, or higher city, formerly a Mycenaean fortress but in this age crowned with temples rising in bright colors against an intensely blue sky. Under the covered colonnades (*stoas*) that surrounded the city's central marketplace (*agora*), the citizens congregated to discuss the latest political development or a new philosophical idea. Among the Athenians, argument was both a public and a private exercise that went on wherever a few disputants could be assembled. This love of intellectual contest, the vigorous forerunner of science itself, was astonishingly popular, and whether in the house of a rich man or in the marketplace, in the gymnasium, or on the street corner, such discussion was the key to the intense political and intellectual life that developed in the Greek city-state. Bodily exercise also played a large part in education and daily life, and the Athenian aim of a balance of intellectual and physical discipline, an ideal of humanistic education, is expressed in the Latin, *mens sana in corpore sano*, "a sound mind in a sound body."

The tragedies of Aeschylus and Sophocles, played before the eager citizens, presented the individual as having an obligation to the gods, and the rise and fall of his fortunes as a reflection of the contest between blind fate and the new-found power of reason.

The constants of Greek culture were man, nature, and reason, and the Greeks understood goodness to be the harmony of all three. Upon this elementary conviction, new to the world, they built their grand achievements in art, poetry, mathematics, philosophy, logic, history, and science—the heritage upon which the modern Western world was in turn constructed. In discovering man the Greeks discovered and confronted the problem of persistence and change; men pass away, but mankind remains. And although they aspired toward the timeless ideal, the Greeks realized the changes that produce growth and development.

The remains of Greek civilization enable us to reconstruct the development of the Greek style in art. That the Greek style should in fact have *developed* is in itself significant. Development in the art of Egypt, for example, was minimal; the pattern of ritual and of form was not to be broken. Change in Egypt occurred, when it did, *despite* the pattern of the culture as a whole. Of course we must remember that an important factor in the sudden appearance of Greece on the summit of historical eminence was the base on which it rose—the civilizations of Egypt and the Near East, the quality and matter of which the Greeks quite honestly acknowledged borrowing. From these older civilizations they acquired ideas, motifs, conventions, and skills. But from the beginning, the Greeks embraced experiment, even while adopting and holding to the older forms. Development and change were inherent in Greek culture, as conservatism was in Egyptian, and change has recognizable forms, as in the recurring stages of human life from infancy to old age. Greek art displays much more readily discernible stages than the relatively unchanging art of the ancient Near East.

THE GEOMETRIC AND ARCHAIC PERIODS

Pottery serves, as no other artistic medium can, to link the very late Mycenaean (sub-Mycenaean) age with that of historical Greece. For one thing, it has survived. We can trace a continuity from the sub-Mycenaean period into the Classical fifth century B.C. entirely in terms of the figurative decoration of Greek ceramic ware, showing the artist's confrontation with radically new ideas and problems and his equally radical interpretations and solutions. It is appropriate, then, given this continuity and the Greek notion of the development of forms, to begin the study of Greek art with vase paintings that illuminate changes that were

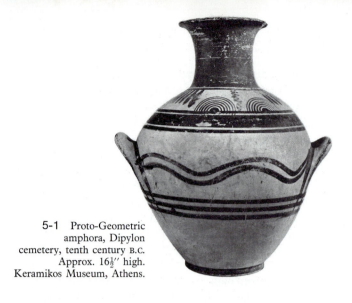

5-1 Proto-Geometric amphora, Dipylon cemetery, tenth century B.C. Approx. 16½" high. Keramikos Museum, Athens.

enumerating his features, which we have seen in the older civilizations, gradually is given up and is replaced by a method of painstaking observation of the pose and motion of the body in life. This did not happen all at once; centuries were involved in the great transformation, and the dated sequence of vases reveals the ordered phases of the change. It is useful to describe these changes at the outset, for, from its earliest appearances on vases, the human figure remains the principal motif of Greek art, as man is central to its thought and interest.

Vase Painting

A Proto-Geometric *amphora* (FIG. 5-1), a two-handled jar for wine or oil, from the tenth century B.C. shows us the formative phase of what is called the Geometric style. Though it borrows the decorative devices of the earlier sub-Mycenaean style, its execution is neater and more painstaking. As the Geometric style develops, the Minoan stock of curvilinear forms is gradually replaced by rectilinear shapes arranged in tight bands that cover more and more of the vessel.

The human figure reappears in the decorative scheme in the period of the culminating Geometric style, specifically in the so-called *Dipylon Vase* (FIG. 5-2), from the eighth century B.C. and named after the Dipylon cemetery in Athens, where it was found. The figures are hardly more than symbols, fashioned of diamond and wedge shapes that fit the severe, regular, geometric characteristics of the banded shapes. The extremely abstract figures are arranged on the shoulders of the vessel, toward which the design builds up from below, the decorative bands generally wider the higher their placement on the body of the vase.

profoundly influential in human history and that take place in a curiously logical order. We have already seen numerous examples of how man represents himself, from the strange, falling stick-figure in the well at Lascaux to the agile Minoans of the Vaphio cups. Now we can review changes in the representation of the human body that are the result not of accidental differences of convention but of carefully accumulated increments of knowledge. These were firmed into a tradition of technical procedure that did not backslide—as was the case in the Egyptian return to old forms after the death of the innovating Akhenaton (see Chapter Three). We can see in the Archaic Greek vases that man for the first time has become the subject of intense analytical study. As the philosopher questions man's nature and purpose, the artist begins to inquire how man looks to others of his kind in the world of optical experience. The old conceptual way of placing him and

5-2 *Dipylon Vase* (Geometric amphora), eighth century B.C. Approx. 59" high. National Museum, Athens.

5-3 Geometric Dipylon krater, Dipylon cemetery, eighth century B.C. Approx. 40½" high. Metropolitan Museum of Art, New York (Rogers Fund).

5-4 *The Blinding of Polyphemos* and *Gorgons* (proto-Attic amphora), Eleusis, c. 675–650 B.C. Approx. 56" high. Museum, Eleusis.

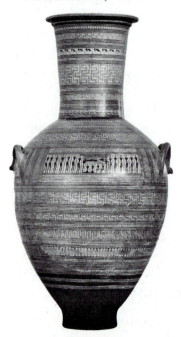

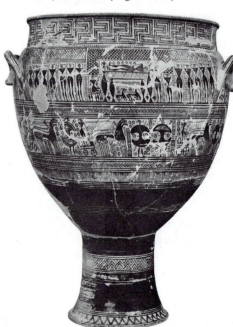

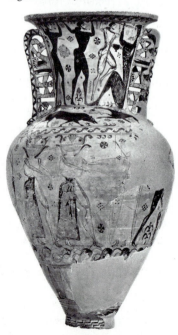

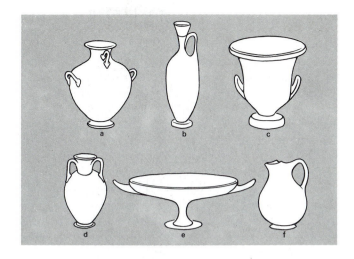

5-5 Greek vase shapes: (a) the *hydria* (from the Greek for "water"), a water jar with three handles, two for lifting and one for carrying; (b) the *lekythos*, an oil flask with a long narrow neck adapted for pouring oil slowly, used chiefly in funeral rites; (c) the *krater* (from the Greek "to mix"), a bowl for mixing wine and water, the usual beverage of the Greeks; (d) the *amphora* (meaning "to carry on both sides," referring to the two handles), a vessel for storing provisions (wine, corn, oil, honey), with an opening large enough to admit a ladle and usually fitted with a cover; (e) the *kylix* (from the Greek "to roll," referring to the vases' being turned on the potter's wheel), chief form of the drinking cup; (f) the *oenochoe* (from the Greek "to pour out wine"), a wine jug, the lip pinched into a trefoil shape to facilitate pouring.

Another type of Greek vase, the *krater,* had a larger body and wider mouth than the amphora. A krater from the Dipylon cemetery (FIG. 5-3), possibly of the same date as the Dipylon vase of FIG. 5-2 or somewhat later, shows a certain loss of refinement as the geometric ornament becomes secondary. The figures represent a funeral procession, with horse-drawn chariots occupied by warriors carrying shields; in the conceptual manner both wheels of each chariot are represented, the horses carefully distinguished, and their legs correct in number. The warriors are standing behind their shields, which are shown in front view. The number of represented figures has increased markedly over that of FIG. 5-2, suggesting that the artist was intrigued with the rediscovery of a subject—the human figure—that had been absent from mainland pottery decoration for over 400 years.

The Geometric period was succeeded by the Orientalizing phase of the Archaic period, a time of marked commercial and colonial expansion that brought the Greeks into closer contact with ancient Eastern civilizations. A consequence of these new relationships was the frequent appearance of Oriental animals and composite monsters on Greek vases, motifs familiar to us from Mesopotamian and Egyptian art: lions, sphinxes, griffins, and centaurs. Stylistically, a vase from Eleusis (FIG. 5-4), typical of the Orientalizing phase, represents a complete and radical break with the orderly Geometric manner. The figurative decor occupies most of the vessel; the arrangement of the motifs is loose, almost casual, and the shapes are mostly curvilinear. It is almost as if the artist were intentionally throwing off the Geometric strait jacket as an awkward restraint upon a new interest—the representation of narrative scenes, some from Homeric legend. On the amphora in FIG. 5-4 where Polyphemos, the one-eyed giant, is being blinded by Odysseus, the human figure—resembling those of the Geometric period, but much more filled out, rounded, and active—now occupies the largest areas of the vessel, and the ornament retreats to the smaller areas in the neck, shoulder, and base. It was in the Geometric period that the Homeric themes were collected in the great epics; the Orientalizing phase marks their diffusion and their achievement of universal popularity in Greece. The illus-

tration of the epics will occupy the surfaces of vases for centuries to come; it might almost seem that this first great reflection of man and his actions, in Greek epic, launched the enterprise of representing him in art.

During the Geometric and Archaic periods, numerous pottery centers developed throughout the Aegean world. They have been divided into two main groups—those of the mainland and those of eastern Greece (the regions east of the mainland). On the mainland the most important centers were Athens in Attica and Corinth in the Peloponnesos, and after 550 B.C. Athens became the principal ceramic center and the largest exporter of vases in the Mediterranean basin. In this brief survey we shall confine ourselves to Athenian wares.

The number of basic Attic vase shapes was limited to six or seven, each subject to four or five variations. The shapes developed out of specific usages and were entirely functional (FIG. 5-5).

The *François Vase* (FIG. 5-6), which was named after its discoverer and is perhaps the finest extant example of an early Archaic krater, with its volute handles and extraordinarily vigorous shape, was found in an Etruscan necropolis. (We are indebted to the Etruscans for their avid collecting of Greek vases, as many of the best-preserved have been found in Etruscan tombs.) It is especially important,

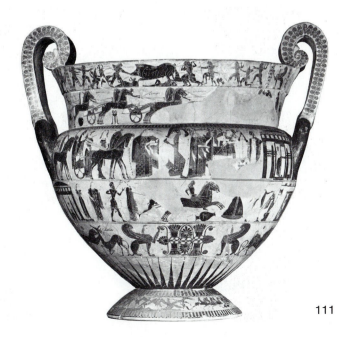

5-6   *The François Vase* (Attic black-figure krater), Chiusi, *c.* 575 B.C. Approx. 26″ high. Museo Archeologico, Florence.

not only for its high quality but for the fact that it is signed by both the potter ("Ergotimos made it") and the painter ("Kleitias drew it"). Signed vases appear for the first time in the early seventh century B.C. and suggest that their makers had pride in their profession and that their art had at least as much prestige, say, as that of the sculptor or wall painter.

The *François Vase* is ornamented with over 200 figures distributed in bands around the vessel. Representing almost the entire Greek pantheon, the figures provide us with one of our first pictorial glimpses of the forms and personages of Greek religion: The subject is the wedding of Peleus, with the gods in attendance. In addition to the scene of the gods and Peleus, father of Achilles, are depictions of the Calydonian boar hunt and the funeral games for Patroklos. On the foot of the vase is an account of an animated battle between cranes and pygmies, above which rays felicitously augment the swelling surface of the krater. The lively scenes are rigidly organized in six bands of varying widths, the widest placed on the vessel's shoulders, a return to the discipline and formality of the Geometric style after the casual and permissive Orientalizing style of the vase from Eleusis (FIG. 5-4).

The *François Vase* is decorated in an early form of the so-called *black-figure* technique, which is shown fully developed and at its best in a *kylix* (drinking cup) by the potter-painter EXEKIAS (FIG. 5-7). Dark figures are silhouetted against the light background of the natural reddish clay. Details are incised into the silhouettes with a sharp, pointed instrument to expose the red beneath; touches of white and purple, particularly on the earlier wares, add color to the dominantly monochrome decoration. Although the black areas are customarily referred to as glazes, it should be pointed out that the black on these Greek pots is neither a pigment nor a glaze but *engobe*, a slip of finely sifted clay that originally is of the same color as the clay of the pot. In the three-phase firing process used by Greek potters, the first (oxidizing) phase turns both pot and slip red; during the second (reducing) phase the oxygen supply into the kiln is shut off and both pot and slip turn black; in the final (reoxidizing) phase the coarser material of the pot reabsorbs oxygen and becomes red again, while the smoother, silica-laden slip does not and remains black. After long experiment, Greek potters developed a velvety, jet-black "glaze" of this kind. The touches of white and purple were used more sparingly, with the result that the figures stood in even stronger contrast against their reddish backgrounds. This superb formal control provides the framework for a wealth of naturalistic detail, some of it strikingly novel.

Exekias' kylix, with a representation of Dionysos sailing over the sea carrying his gifts to mankind and accompanied by sporting dolphins, his boat's mast entwined by a joyful grapevine, introduces a still more spectacular innovation, one that heralds the beginning of a revolution in world art. In his drawing of the boat's sail, Exekias does not show a traditional and conventional symbol that "reads" as a sail, but a sail as a sail would actually look, bellying out and filled with wind. It is an image of the action of wind itself, the wind made palpable as a force, and it must have come from a new awareness of the *physical* presence of nature. This awareness was abroad; it is in the Ionian speculations about the physical constitution of the world, and in the reality-charged poetry of Homer: "But soon an off-shore breeze blew to our liking—a canvas-bellying breeze. . . . The bows went plunging . . . sails cracked and lashed out . . . ."

Though in Homer the gods are still the manipulators of the elements, it is men who feel their effects, who hear the howl of the great winds, smell the brine, and feel the harsh ropes and drenching rain. Man's experience of the world, as well as the world itself, begins to be understood by him in physical terms. Such a profound change in man's awareness of his relation to nature and, in consequence, of his own nature, is one that is bound to make itself felt in art. From Exekias' sail on, Greek art will manifest an increasing comprehension of physical nature as it is apprehended by vision.

Exekias' skill and subtlety also solve to perfection a difficult compositional problem: how to fix the ship within its circular frame. Part of his solution lies in the down-branching weight of the loaded vines, part in the reverse hooklike dolphins, which seem to stitch the composition to its frame.

Around 530 B.C. a new painting technique was invented that reversed the black-figure style by making the background black and leaving the figures reserved in red. The figures of men and animals no longer are dark and earthy, massive against a light ground, but instead are luminous, like light and air, shining forth from the black background. In this new *red-figure* technique the major interior mark-

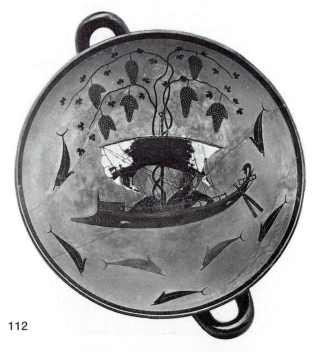

5-7 EXEKIAS, *Dionysos in a Sailboat*, interior of an Attic black-figure kylix, Vulci, c. 550–525 B.C. 12" in diameter. Staatliche Antikensammlugen, Munich.

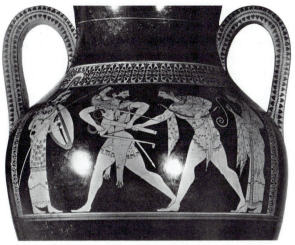

5-8 ANDOKIDES PAINTER, *Herakles and Apollo Struggling for the Tripod*, detail from amphora, *c.* 530 B.C. Outline drawing at right indicates relation to whole vessel. Portion shown approx. 11″ high; whole vessel approx. 23″ high.

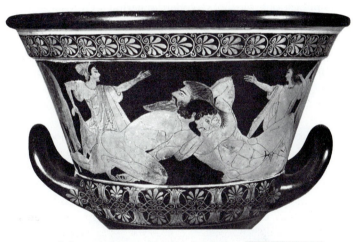

5-9 EUPHRONIOS, *Herakles Strangling Antaios*, detail from krater, Cerveteri, *c.* 510–500 B.C. Outline drawing at right indicates relation to whole vessel. Portion shown approx. 12″ high; whole vessel approx. 19″ high.

PAINTER, who is named for the potter Andokides, several of whose signed vases he decorated. Sometimes called a student of Exekias, the Andokides Painter uses pictorial devices that are rooted in the style of the older master. On an amphora that shows Herakles and Apollo struggling for the tripod (FIG. 5-8) he shows an interest in rich drapery ornaments and textural effects such as are found in the work of his presumed master. His work lacks some of the warmth and sympathy of Exekias' as he is more concerned with exploiting the possibilities of his newly discovered technique. And there he breaks new ground, experimenting with novel and varied effects of color (he liked to use both purple and white) and, in a technique that dispenses with the laborious process of incision, creating new decorative schemes of great elegance.

A krater painted by EUPHRONIOS, one of the most forceful red-figure painters working near the end of the sixth century B.C., shows Herakles strangling the giant Antaios (FIG. 5-9). Euphronios was among the first to devote himself seriously to the study of anatomy and was famous for this in his time. Here he shows two male figures in a complicated wrestling pose, one figure from the side, the other from the front. He attempts such radical experiments as the doubled-under leg of Antaios and the rendering of Antaios' face in white to suggest the pallor of impending death. He makes an effort to describe Herakles' and Antaios' straining, powerful bodies with painstaking attention to the musculature, and though he does not entirely succeed in producing a correct representation, his attempt to apply knowledge gained through observation of bodily action is most significant.

EUTHYMIDES was a contemporary and competitor of Euphronios and, like him, an experimenter. As we can see from his picture of revelers done on an amphora (FIG. 5-10), Euthymides is less concerned with anatomical de-

5-10 EUTHYMIDES, *Revelers*, detail from amphora, Vulci, *c.* 510–500 B.C. Outline drawing at right indicates relation to whole vessel. Portion shown approx. 12″ high; whole vessel approx. 24″ high. Munich, Staatliche Antikensammlungen.

ings were rendered with relief lines applied with a syringe-like instrument that squeezed out the black "glaze" matter evenly and smoothly. Secondary markings, such as those representing hair, muscles, and sometimes even shading, were painted in "dilute glaze" (engobe diluted with water), which could be applied with a fine brush. The style is freer and more facile than the earlier black-figure style, which it largely replaced within twenty years. The artist felt no need to enlarge his limited color scheme, for the polished coppery red against a velvety black created an effect that was rich and elegant. The artist usually credited with the invention of the red-figure technique is the ANDOKIDES

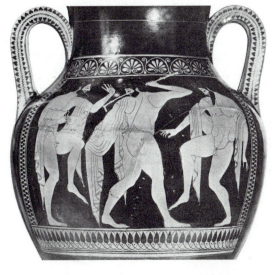

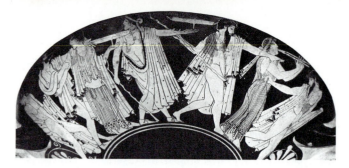

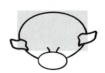

5-11 BRYGOS PAINTER, *Revelers*, detail from kylix, Vulci, *c.* 490 B.C. Outline drawing at right indicates relation to whole vessel. Portion shown approx. 10″ wide; whole vessel approx. 13″ wide. Martin V. Wagner Museen der Universität, Würzburg.

scription than with the problems of foreshortening in the figures and of showing them from different viewpoints. The fairly tipsy dancers, mightily enjoying themselves, are a rather popular subject on late Archaic and early Classical vases, and celebrate the Hellenic sense of the comic that served as counterpoise to its genius for tragic art in the drama. In this case it gives Euthymides an opportunity to present the figures in informal motion and in fairly successful three-quarter back and front views. The turning and twisting of the figures indicate that the artist is beginning to think of them as three-dimensional volumes that have free mobility in a space deeper than the flat, two-dimensional surface of the picture plane—a significant departure from pre-Greek tradition. The maturing self-consciousness of the Greeks is shown not only in their concern for the figures of man but also, of course, in their consciousness of themselves as artists. They sign their names to their work and they are aware that they are doing new and revolutionary things as collaborators and rivals in a common professional enterprise. Euthymides, in an inscription on this amphora (FIG. 5-10), proclaims with naive pride: "Euphronios never did anything like it."

As revolutionary as Euphronios and Euthymides had been, the BRYGOS PAINTER (an anonymous artist who is named after the potter whose vases he decorated) takes a significant step beyond them, around the year 490 B.C. Again the revelers theme, with its gaily swinging movement, gives the experimenting artist his opportunity (FIG. 5-11). For some 2500 years, since the *Palette of Narmer* (FIG. 3-2), painted figures and figures in relief had advanced the *far* leg to show a stride—which, after all, is the best way if the torso is to be shown in front view with minimum distortion of the figure. Euthymides had broken this rule, advancing the near leg of a figure to show it in a three-quarter rear view (FIG. 5-10). But the Brygos Painter, for the first time, presents a striding figure with the near leg advanced and its shoulder turned diagonally toward the observer. (See the two central figures.) The result is the first true *contrapposto* stance that we have. The figure is now understood as an acting unit, not merely an assemblage of parts; the problem of its engineering has been

solved to the extent that it can be represented in convincing movement. This may at first seem to be a small matter, but an apparently superficial detail may be the manifestation of an epoch-making change in the concept of what human beings perceive.

Sculpture

Trends in the development of sculpture in Greece are just as evident as those we have traced in vase painting, though much less sculpture survives. The earliest pieces go back to the beginning of the ninth century B.C. and consist of small-scale representations of animals (horses, oxen, deer, birds) and of human figures in various materials: copper, bronze, lead, ivory, and terra-cotta. Some of these were ornaments on larger objects like vases and bronze tripods; others were separate votive offerings that have been found near ancient sanctuaries. At Olympia they seem to have been manufactured on the spot for sale to visitors to the shrines.

A bronze warrior from the Acropolis of Athens, from the late eighth century B.C. (FIG. 5-12), shows all the clear simplifications of the Geometric period. The figure, a favorite type in Geometric art, is solid cast. (Given the figure's diminutive size, this would be the reasonable casting method, as hollow casting, which was understood, would not have saved much bronze.) The warrior originally held a spear in one raised arm, and a shield in the

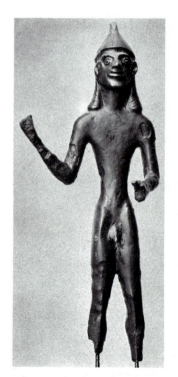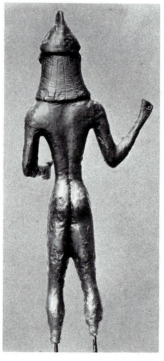

5-12 Geometric bronze warrior, front and back views, Acropolis, Athens, late eighth century B.C. Bronze, approx. 8″ high. National Museum, Athens.

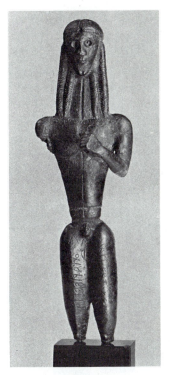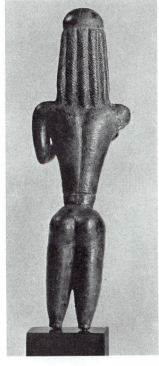

5-13 *Mantiklos "Apollo,"* front and back views, Thebes, *c.* 680 B.C. Bronze, approx. 8″ high. Museum of Fine Arts, Boston (Francis Bartlett Fund).

with a triangular torso, a narrow waist, and bulging thighs; but the forms have gained volume, and the modeling of the pectoral muscles and the description of other anatomical details by means of incised lines show an incipient interest in the structure of the body.

Monumental, freestanding sculpture (life-size or larger) first appeared about 600 B.C., in the earlier stages of the Archaic period. Its rise is contemporary with the Orientalizing phase in vase painting and was probably inspired by foreign sources, most likely Egypt and Mesopotamia, which were in fact the only areas at that time that could show monumental sculpture in abundance. An early example of this monumental, freestanding sculpture is the *Hera* from Samos (FIG. 5-14), which is over six feet tall and has a cylindrical shape that could have been derived only from Mesopotamia (compare FIGS. 2-20 and 2-21). The goddess stands in a frontal pose, feet together, the right arm held tightly to the side, the left bent to the breast and probably originally holding some attribute, or symbol, of authority. She is the goddess as a sheathed column (in origin a tree?), as were the deities of Crete and Mycenae, but here the Greek artist displays his extraordinary sensitivity for surface ornamentation. The stability of the lower portions—where the striations of the *chiton*, or tunic, are placed against the plain surface of the *himation*, a kind of cape—contrasts with the movement in the upper portions, where the himation is drawn in gracefully curving folds around the delicate modeling of the swelling bosom.

other, though both shield and spear are missing in most surviving examples. The rather carefully rendered head and face, with the large eyes and broad grimace, later to become known as the standard "Archaic smile," attest to the fact that this figure is a late specimen of a type whose earlier examples had heads and faces that were little more than shapeless lumps. Moreover, the body forms have become smoother, losing some of their former angularity, as if the artist were trying to rid himself of centuries-old conventions of Geometric figure representation before the new approach—the visual one—could be tried. It is believed that these warrior statuettes were Syrian in inspiration, but a difference important in the evolution of Greek sculpture should be noted: The Greek figures are represented nude, while the Syrian prototypes wear loincloths. As early as this, the Greek instinct for the natural beauty of the human figure, which peculiarly and permanently distinguishes Greek art, is set in contrast with the Near Eastern traditional prejudice against the representation of the nude in sculpture in the round.

Kouros and Kore

A bronze figure of a youth from around 680 B.C. (FIG. 5-13) stands at the beginning of the Archaic period; it is a small forerunner of the later *Kouros* figures (see FIGS. 5-15 and 5-16). The silhouette remains essentially geometric,

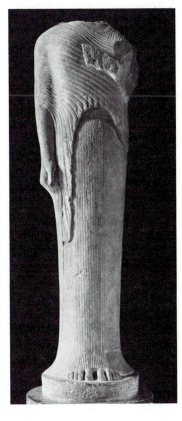

5-14 *Hera* from Samos, *c.* 560 B.C. Marble, approx. 6′ 4″ high. Louvre, Paris.

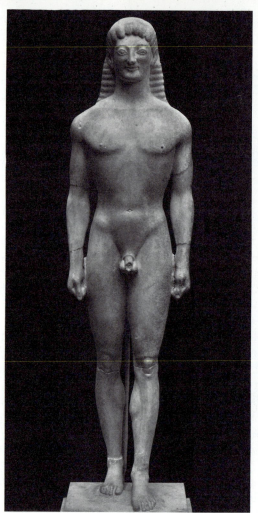

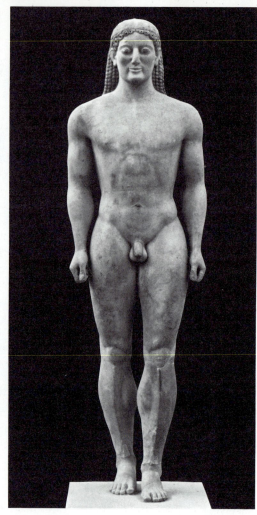

We are reminded of Egyptian statues by the early Kouros figures (FIGS. 5-15 and 5-16). Some of these figures are of youths who are dedicated to a god and are apparently advancing into his presence; others are memorial statues that stand over graves of noblemen. Thus, they are of men, not gods (not, as once thought, "Apollos"), and this is significant, this glorification of men in monumental statues that commemorate their triumph and give them a godlike scale and presence. The Kouroi recall Egyptian statues in the pose (the left foot advanced), in the broad, square shoulders, and in the rigidly frontal and symmetrical design. The Egyptian and Mesopotamian thought of the sculptured human body as a smooth envelope of stone, but the Greek was interested in the structural parts and how they fitted together. The *Kouros* from Tenea (FIG. 5-15) shows us characteristic traits of the type, though the Kouroi differ markedly from each other. Because the figures were freestanding, without the Egyptian stone slab for support, most Kouroi have been found broken at the ankles. Obviously, the Greek sculptor was not aiming for Egyptian permanence so much as for fidelity to appearance, and one of his first steps toward that goal was the liberation of the figure from the original block of stone. On the broad planes of the figure anatomical details are carefully modeled, as in the chest and knee joints. The head is geometrically simplified into flat planes, the eyes large and protruding, and the nose, mouth, ears, and wig all highly stylized attributes of the almost cubic mass of the head. Though still almost provincial Egyptian, the Tenea Kouros is quite un-Egyptian in its nudity and in its more dynamic, half-striding stance. Moreover, this figure is slender and elegant, with the alert, elastic physique of a sprinter. Description of the anatomy by incised line, typical of the earlier models, has been given up, and the torso, thighs, and calves are modeled in the full round with ever closer approximation of anatomical truth.

With the *Kroisos* from Anavysos (FIG. 5-16), we come to the verge of a breakthrough similar to that which we have seen in vase painting. The statue is, according to an inscription on its base, a funerary monument of a youth, Kroisos, who had died a hero's death in battle. Where the anatomy of the Tenea figure is still somewhat generalized, it here becomes specific and accurate. The artist not only understands the structural parts of the figure and their natural relation and how to represent their surfaces by modeling the stone, but he is able to give us what amounts to a *portrait* of the body, a likeness of a particular physique—in this case, that of a muscular wrestler, heavier and more massive than the taut, spare Tenea figure. It is noteworthy that the Greeks begin their monumental sculpture with portraits not of the head but of the body. This "bodiliness" of Greek sculpture persisted for centuries until it became lost in a realism that compelled the sculptor to use illusional devices more appropriate to painting.

What we might think of as companion figures to the Kouroi (youths) are the draped *Korai* (maidens), contemporaneous with the former and manifesting in their own style similar features of concept and design. The *Peplos Kore* (FIG. 5-17), contemporary with the *Kroisos,* is one of numerous figures found on the Acropolis of Athens, where they had been thrown down by the Persians after their sack of the city in 480 B.C. Their purpose is obscure, but they may have been votive figures attending the deities in a kind of permanent and perpetual ritual. In contrast with those of earlier types, the face of this Kore has become more expressively modeled; the chin, cheeks, and corners of the mouth subtly planed. The great eyes, originally with painted lids, may have been intended to have hypnotic power: One thinks back to the ancient head from Warka (FIG. 2-11). The missing left arm was extended, a break from the frontal compression of the arms at the sides in Egyptian statues. The body itself is modeled with a soft smoothness that takes account of the figure beneath the drapery much like the earlier *Hera* from Samos, yet with a great deal more of the anatomically real. Traces of paint may be seen on parts of the figure, for all Greek stone statues were painted, the powder-white of Classical statues being an error of modern interpretation. But the Greeks did not smear their statues garishly with bright colors, indifferent to their place and effect; only the decisive parts, such as eyes, lips, hair, and the edges of drapery, were painted, to provide accents and contrast to the color of the soft marble itself, the latter being waxed and polished. The whole purpose of coloring was to make the statue more lifelike, more convincing as a kind of person confronting the visitor to the shrines of the Acropolis. The remarkable permanence of the color is partly ascribable to the technique of *encaustic,* in which pigment is mixed with wax and applied to the surface while hot. This method was widely used in ancient wall painting and on wood panels as well as in the embellishment of statues.

The preservation of the color of many of the Kore statues is also a result of the Athenians' use of fragments of broken statues and temples as rubble fill in rebuilding the temples and retaining walls of the Acropolis after the Persian destruction. Found in this material by modern archeologists have been works such as the *Kore* from Chios (FIG. 5-18). The figures' luxurious gowns may be evidence that they were made in Ionia, where the wealthy Greek states cultivated the Oriental taste for rich ornamentation in both life and art. Ionian influence was strong in Athens during the Archaic period, and Ionian fashions, featuring the intricately folded, chic chiton, interested not only

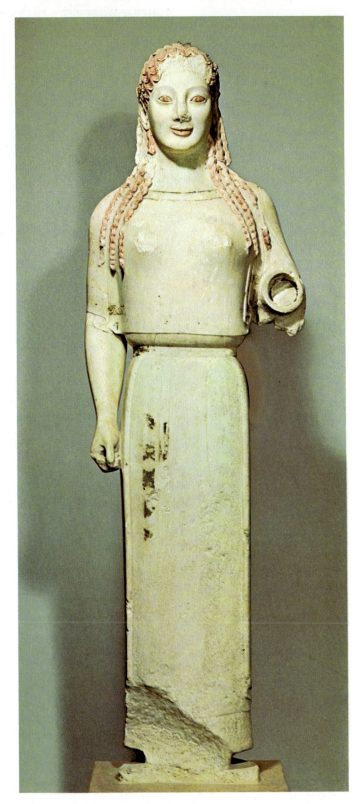

5-17 *Peplos Kore,* Acropolis, Athens, *c.* 530 B.C. Marble, approx. 48″ high. Acropolis Museum, Athens.

women, but sculptors, who found in the representation of delicate texture and fold a peculiarly difficult challenge. For some time they seemed to take delight in working out the complexities of the pleats and folds made by the thin, soft material and were content to let the matter remain one

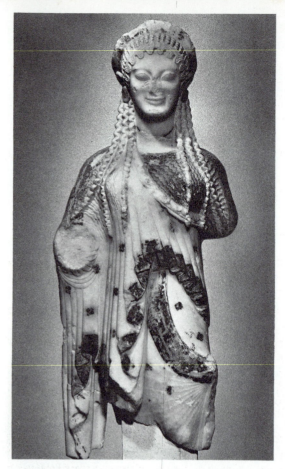

5-18 *Kore* from Chios (?), *c.* 510 B.C. Marble, approx. 21½″ high. Acropolis Museum, Athens.

of decoration rather than structure. Though much must have been learned of the movement of a surface independent of the body beneath it, the Kore figures remain frontal and basically unchanged through a considerable period. Although there are slight changes, the scheme of this example is repeated over and over until the end of the Archaic period. The attractive problem of surface texture appears to have deflected the sculptors of the Kore figures from larger issues.

The larger issues involve not the draped female figure but the nude Kouros type we have been describing; at least, it is there that the break with age-old sculptural traditions takes place. The female nude does not appear in ancient sculpture—with some minor exceptions—until the fourth century B.C. We will see that its appearance in Greek art accompanies changes of a fundamental kind in Greek culture and morals. Why the Greek artist should have represented the male figure nude some 300 years before he represented the female so is not known. He may have found, as any student of the living model in art has found, that the male figure is much more revealing of human structure. He may have had available for observation male models in exercises and at the games; we know that in the Dorian world, of which Sparta was the capital, he would also have been able to observe female models, yet

the male figure had priority. By the time of Plato, nudity in the context of athletics was commonplace in the Greek world, and the prejudice against it could be regarded as barbarous—that is, merely a prejudice of the non-Hellenic Near East. In Plato's *Republic* Socrates remarks:

> Not long ago . . . the Hellenes were of the opinion, which is still generally received among the barbarians, that the sight of a naked man was ridiculous and improper. . . . But experience showed that to let all things be uncovered was far better than to cover them up . . . .

Certainly by about 520 B.C. the male nude must have been familiar enough for the artist to construct from the observation of it a convincingly real image. The establishment of a new convention, the propriety of the nude, implied the setting aside of the 3000-year-old convention of the pre-Greek world that inhibited—probably because nudity was the badge of slavery—the study of the structure of the human body as given to the eye.

In the *Kroisos* figure the independent elements of the body have been sufficiently described. The question must now be: How do the elements work together? From the time of King Narmer, there have been more or less successful approximations of the human figure, the parts enumerated, and the attitudes universally stiff and immobile. What can put these parts into motion? The answer appears in a late Kouros—if we can still call it that—found in the Acropolis rubble and dating from just before the Persian destruction. The statue, which must have been the consequence of a mind deliberating upon what had already been done, is called the *Kritios Boy* (FIG. 5-19), from the name of its presumed sculptor. It is not in action but stands at rest; that is to say, it *really* stands at rest and not merely in a stiff-legged pose or a pose bound to a block. The secret of its new and radical naturalness lies in its artist's knowledge of the principle of *weight-shift,* the shifting of position of the main parts of the body around the vertical but flexible axis of the spine. The shifting of the human body in life never takes place in a rigid, stiff-legged manner; indeed we laugh at, or are in terror of, the science-fiction monster that moves in this ponderous, mechanical way. Rather, when we change place and move, the elastic musculoskeletal structure of our bodies dictates a harmonious, smooth motion of all the elements of the body. Greek artists were the first to grasp this fact, and the artist of the *Kritios Boy* was the first to represent it. The youth turns his head away from the central axis—only very slightly. There is the slightest dip to the shoulders and to the hips, indicating the shift of weight onto the left leg; the right leg is at ease. (One can easily assume this pose and the contrasting flat-footed poses of the earlier Kouros statues.) Once the principle of weight-shift has been realized, all motion of the human figure is possible in the world of representation; not simply in terms of the signs of

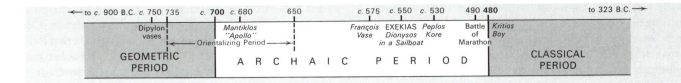

| ← to *c.* 900 B.C. | *c.* 750 | 735 | *c.* **700** | *c.* 680 | 650 | *c.* 575 | *c.* 550 | *c.* 530 | 490 | **480** | to 323 B.C. → |

motion—simple gesture—but in terms of motion of the whole body as we see *and* experience it. After the *Kritios Boy* Greek sculpture rapidly passes through the possibilities of the figure understood as having its own physical principle of motion, a principle revealed to the eye in ordinary optical experience and confirmed by the observer's own physical sense of motion.

So far we have been considering sculpture apart from architecture. But the decoration of buildings, especially temples, with sculpture, both in relief and in the round, offered the Greek sculptor a major opportunity. Since sculpture was applied only to very specific and limited areas of temples, it is necessary first to become acquainted with the basic structure of the various buildings that it adorned.

5-19 *Kritios Boy,* front and side views, Acropolis, Athens, *c.* 480 B.C. Marble, approx. 34″ high. Acropolis Museum, Athens.

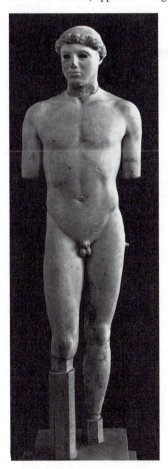
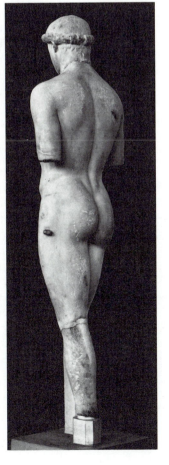

Architecture

Greek architecture and its Roman and Renaissance descendants and hybrids are almost as familiar to us as modern architecture. The "revival" of it by European architects in the late eighteenth century brought about a wide diffusion of its style, and especially official public buildings—court houses, banks, city halls, legislative chambers—designed for impressive formality, imitated the architecture of Classicism, which was fundamentally Greek in inspiration. Although their homes were unpretentious places, they had no monarchs to house royally until Hellenistic times, and they performed state religious rites in the open, the ancient Greeks were industrious builders. Their significant buildings began primarily as simple shrines to protect the statues to their gods. More and more attention was lavished on these, until possibly the belief arose that the qualities of the god were embodied in the structures themselves. Figure sculpture played its part in this program, partly to embellish the protective building, partly to tell something of the deity symbolized within, and partly as a votive offering. But the building was itself also conceived as sculpture, abstract in form and possessing the power of sculpture to evoke human responses. The commanding importance of the sculptured temple, its inspiring function in public life, was emphasized in its elevated site, often on a hill above the city (the *acropolis*). As Aristotle stipulated: "the site should be a spot seen far and wide, which gives due elevation to virtue and towers over the neighborhood." And the reverent awe that must have been attached to the temple and to the genius of its founders echoes in Plato: "Gods and temples are not easily instituted, and to establish them rightly is the work of a mighty intellect."

Although still a matter of ardent debate, one theory holds that the earliest temples were of wood, and that these wooden forms were in time translated into the more permanent materials of limestone and sometimes marble. Marble was expensive, but mountains of it were available: from Hymettos, just east of Athens, with its bluish-white stone; from Pentelicus, northeast of the city, its glittering white stone particularly adapted for carving; and from the islands of the Aegean, Paros in particular, which supplied marble of varying quantities and qualities.

In its plan the Greek temple discloses a close affinity with the Mycenaean megaron and even in its most elaborate form retains the latter structure's basic simplicity (FIG.

5-20): a single or double room (the *naos*) with no windows and one door (two for a double naos) and with (a) a portico with two columns between the extended walls (columns *in antis*), or (b) a colonnade across the front (*prostyle*), or (c) a colonnade across both front and back (*amphiprostyle*), or any of these plans surrounded by (d and e) a single (*peripteral*) or (f) a double (*dipteral*) colonnade. What strikes the eye first in the Greek scheme, after what has been seen of the architecture of the ancient Near East, is its remarkable order, compactness, and symmetry, in contrast, say, to the relative irregularity of the Egyptian temple. The difference lies in the Greeks' sense of proportion and in their effort to achieve ideal forms in terms of regular numerical relations and the rules of geometry.

We can discern in the plans a kind of development from quite simple units to more complex, without, however, any fundamental change in the nature of the units or of their grouping. For Classical Greek architecture, like classical music, has a simple core theme from which is developed a series of complex, but always quite intelligible, variations. And, to change the analogy, the development of the temple scheme is like that other great invention of the Greeks, geometry, where theorems, propositions, and their corollaries are deduced from a simple original set of axioms. The insistence of the Greeks on proportional order guided the experiments with the proportions of temple plans. The earlier, Archaic temples tended to be long and narrow (FIG. 5-20d), with a proportion of the ends to the sides roughly expressible as 1:3. Late Classical and Hellenistic (see below) plans approached, but rarely had a proportion of exactly 1:2, with Classical temples tending to be a little longer than twice the width (FIG. 5-20e) and Hellenistic a little shorter (FIG. 5-20f). Proportion in architecture and sculpture, and harmony in music, were much the same to the Greek mind and indeed reflected and embodied the cosmic order just as did the rationally pursued "good life."

The description of the elevation of a Greek building is in terms of the platform, column, and *entablature;* this combination and relationship of three units is called an order. The three orders developed by Greek builders are differentiated partly by details but chiefly by the relative proportions of the parts. Each order served different purposes and embodied different meanings. The earliest of the Greek architectural orders to be formulated were the *Doric,* of mainland Greece, and the *Ionic,* of Asia Minor and the Aegean islands (FIG. 5-21). The *Corinthian* order followed much later.

The columns, which rest on a platform (*stylobate*), have two or three parts, depending on the order: the *shaft,* which is marked with vertical channels (*fluting*); the *capital;* and (in the Ionic and Corinthian) the *base.* As the shaft rises, its diameter decreases gradually, giving the profile a subtle curve (*entasis*); the top (in the Doric) is marked with one or several horizontal lines (*necking*) that furnish the transition to the capital. The capital has two elements, the lower of which (the *echinus*) varies with the order: In the Doric it is convex and cushionlike; in the Ionic it is small and supports a bolster ending in scroll-like spirals (the *volutes*); and in the Corinthian it is shaped like an inverted bell and is decorated with a design of stylized acanthus leaves. The upper element, present in all orders, is a flat, square block (the *abacus*) that provides the immediate

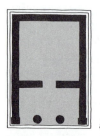
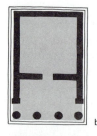
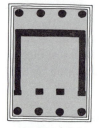

5-20 Six representative plans of the Greek Temple: (a) Treasury of the Athenians at Delphi, a temple *in antis*, in which the portico is formed by the projecting side walls with two columns set between their ends (*antae*); (b) Temple B at Selinus, Sicily, a *prostyle* temple, in which the columns stand in front of the naos and extend to its width; (c) Temple of Athena Nike on the Acropolis at Athens, an *amphiprostyle* temple, in which the prostyle plan has a porch added at the rear; (d) Temple of Hera at Olympia and (e) Temple of Aphaia at Aegina, *peripteral* temples in which a single colonnade surrounds the naos; and (f) Temple of Apollo at Didyma, near Miletus, a *dipteral* temple, in which two colonnades surround the naos. (Drawings are not to scale.)

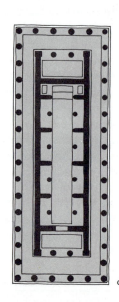
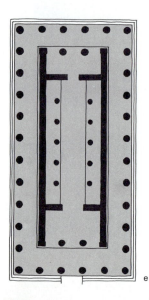
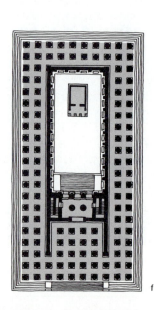

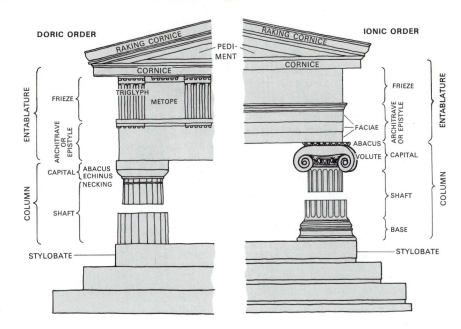

DORIC ORDER
IONIC ORDER

RAKING CORNICE
RAKING CORNICE
PEDI-
MENT
CORNICE
CORNICE
FRIEZE
TRIGLYPH
METOPE
FRIEZE
FACIAE
ENTABLATURE
ARCHITRAVE OR EPISTYLE
ABACUS
ARCHITRAVE OR EPISTYLE
ENTABLATURE
VOLUTE
CAPITAL {ABACUS ECHINUS NECKING
CAPITAL
COLUMN
SHAFT
SHAFT
COLUMN
BASE
STYLOBATE
STYLOBATE

5-21   Doric and Ionic orders. (After Grinnell.)

support for the entablature. The entablature has three parts: the *architrave*, the main weight-bearing and weight-distributing element; the *frieze;* and the *cornice*, a molded horizontal projection. In some buildings, the latter, with two sloping (*raking*) cornices, forms a triangle that enframes the *pediment*. The architrave is usually subdivided into three horizontal bands (*fasciae*) in the Ionic and Corinthian orders. The frieze is subdivided into *triglyphs* and *metopes* in the Doric order and left open in the Ionic to provide a continuous field for reliefs.

The Doric order is massive in appearance, its sturdy columns firmly planted on the stylobate. Compared with the weighty and severe Doric, the Ionic seems light, airy, and much more decorative. Its columns are slenderer and rise from molded bases. While the Doric flutings meet in sharp ridges (*arrises*), the Ionic ridges are flat. The most obvious differences among the three orders are, of course, in the capitals, the Doric severely plain, the Ionic and Corinthian highly ornamental.

In ancient times the Doric and Ionic orders were contrasted as masculine and feminine. The Corinthian order was not developed until the fifth century B.C., when it appeared inside the temple, like a natural form growing in the darkness of the interior. On the exteriors of buildings, however, it was not widely used until Roman times. Since the Renaissance, and until about two generations ago, much of the architecture in the Western world was considered to be in essence the display of the refined beauty of these architectural orders.

According to one theory, many of the parts of the Doric order seem to be translations into stone of an earlier timber architecture. Pausanias, writing in the second century A.D., noted that in the even then ancient Temple of Hera at Olympia (FIG. 5-20d) there was still a wooden column in place; the rest had been replaced by stone columns. It has been inferred, from the varying proportions of these columns, that the wooden columns were replaced at different

times, probably as the wood of the original columns rotted. One feature of the Doric order can be explained best as a translation from the wooden original into stone: the organization of the frieze into triglyphs and metopes. The triglyphs most likely derived from the ends of cross beams that rested on the main horizontal support, the architrave. The metopes would then correspond to the voids between the beam-ends in the original wooden structure.

Sculptural ornament, which played an important part in the design of the temple, was concentrated on the upper part of the building—in the frieze and pediments. It was basically sculpture that was gaily painted in red and blue, with touches of green, yellow, black, and perhaps a little gold, and was applied only to those parts of the building that had no structural function or that suggested a former structural function. This is true particularly of the Doric style, in which decorative sculpture was applied only to the "voids" of the metopes and of the pediment. Ionic builders were less severe in this respect and were willing to decorate the entire frieze and sometimes even the lower drums of columns. Occasionally they replaced their columns with female figures (*caryatids*), something the Doric builder would probably not have done. Using color, the designer could bring out more clearly the relationships of the structural parts, soften the glitter of the stone at specific points, and provide a background to set off the figures. Although it is true that color was used for emphasis and to mitigate what might have seemed too bare a simplicity (in Doric buildings as well as in Ionic), the primary dependence in Greek architecture—as in Greek mathematics, science, and philosophy—was on the setting of clear limits. This thesis had to begin with the axiom that the limits themselves must never be encroached upon, must always contain, and must never be vague. The architectural orders described above were embodiments of codified limits, given plainly to the eye as functioning realities. To the Greek it was

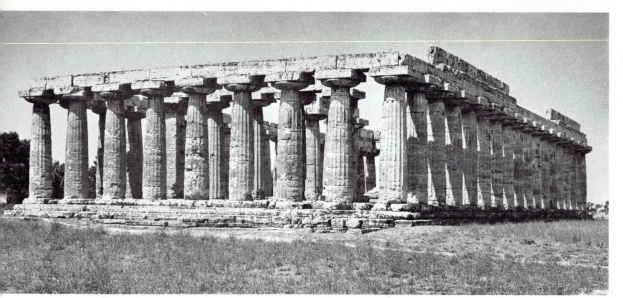

unthinkable to use surfaces in the way that the Egyptian used his gigantic columns—as fields for complicated ornamentation. The very building itself, the Greek temple as given to the eye, must have the clarity of a Euclidean demonstration. This is borne out not only by its plan, elevation, and function-enhancing ornament but also by its "dry-jointed" construction (that is, construction without mortar), which seems evidence that Greek architects looked upon their temples not as "buildings" but as monumental pieces of sculpture.

The placement of the building strengthened its sculptural aspect. Unlike Egyptian temples, Greek temples faced outward. Rites were performed at altars in front of the temple, and the building itself served to house the cult statue and perhaps trophies and treasure. Private cults were frowned upon and public ritual prevailed. Thus it was on the exterior of the building and its surfaces that the architect generally concentrated his efforts to make the temple a

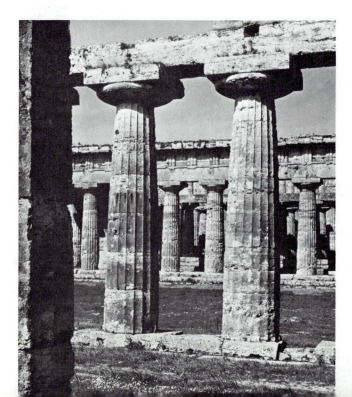

suitable monument to the deity. The studied visual relationships of solids and voids, of light and shade in the colonnades, and the lighter accents of the entablature make a sculptural form out of the rectangular mass of the temple. The history of Greek architecture is the history of the artists' unflagging efforts to express the form of the temple in its most satisfactory—that is to say, what they believed to be perfect—proportions.

The experiment in proportions can be followed rather easily if we begin with the Archaic Doric architecture of the Greek colonies—especially that in Sicily and southern Italy—for it is here that the best-preserved examples of Archaic temples are found. (In examining Greek architecture it is useful to keep in mind the development of the human figure in Greek painting and in sculpture, for the architectural events are not only contemporaneous but reflect a similar concern with proportions.) The "Basilica" at Paestum, south of Naples, dates from about 550 B.C., and is a quite typical example of Archaic Doric style (FIG. 5-22). Called "the Basilica" after a Roman building type that early investigators felt it resembled, it is a peripteral temple with heavy columns of pronounced entasis, closely spaced, with large, bulky, pillowlike capitals, supporting a high and massive entablature that makes the columns seem proportionately squat. These parts of the order will be gradually adjusted until a lighter and taller combination is achieved. There is a structural reason, perhaps, for the heaviness of the design and the narrowness of the spans between the columns. The archaic builders, uncertain of the strength of their materials, may have been providing a broad margin of safety. A detail of the "Basilica" colonnade (FIG. 5-23) shows extreme spread of the cushion capitals and exaggeration of the supporting surface in relation to the spans bridged by the architrave. The columns are built up of separate dry-jointed "drums," fitted with square metal plugs to prevent turning as well as shifting. The whole temple was of this typically Greek construction, the blocks of stone in a horizontal course

5-23 "Basilica" colonnade with view of the Temple of Hera beyond.

being held together by metal cramps, while those of different courses, one above the other, were joined vertically by metal dowels. Through the "Basilica" colonnade one can see the nearby Temple of Hera, which was built eighty to ninety years later and whose columns have proportions strikingly different from those of the "Basilica."

The diagram (FIG. 5-24) showing the evolution in the proportions of the Doric order from Archaic to Classical points up the thesis that Greek art evolves with a certain logic, whether in its figurative forms or its architectural, moving toward a conclusion that is as satisfactory as it is true. Plato, in speaking of the imitative arts, declared that the degree of their truth or rightness is determined by the proportionality of their elements and that if they are to be judged at all they must be judged by the "standard of truth, and by no other whatever." In this diagram we see the architects working toward proportions that could be thought of as "true" and final. Some of the earliest columns (not shown) were extremely slender, under massive capitals. The shafts soon thickened to the shape of the "Basilica" type, as the builders searched for a better relationship between the shaft and the capital. From then on, the forms were constantly refined, the shafts becoming more slender, the entasis subtler, the capitals smaller, and the entablature lighter. The final Classical proportions were considered to be ideal ones beyond which further refinement was impossible.

The Temple of Hera at Paestum (FIG. 5-25) dates from about 460 B.C.; although the forms have been refined, the columns are still massive and closely spaced. This was erected at a time when, on the Greek mainland, the Doric order had already achieved its Classical proportions—as

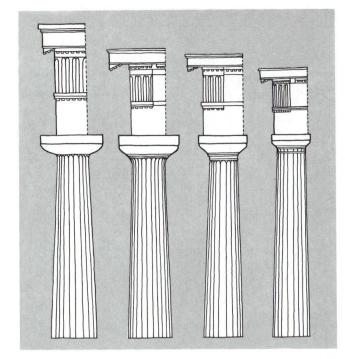

5-24 Evolution of Doric-order proportions, Archaic to Classical. Examples are not drawn to same scale.

early as 490 B.C.—in the Temple of Aphaia at Aegina. There was a considerable time lag between developments on the mainland and their adoption by the colonies in Italy and Sicily, so that the colonial architecture exhibits the usual provincial conservatism characteristic of styles distant from their source of inspiration in the cultural capital. The plan and section of the Temple of Hera (FIG. 5-26) show a noteworthy peculiarity in the support structure of the interior, the columns of which rise higher than the outer, peripteral columns. Each of the two rows of small

5-25 Temple of Hera at Paestum, *c.* 460 B.C.

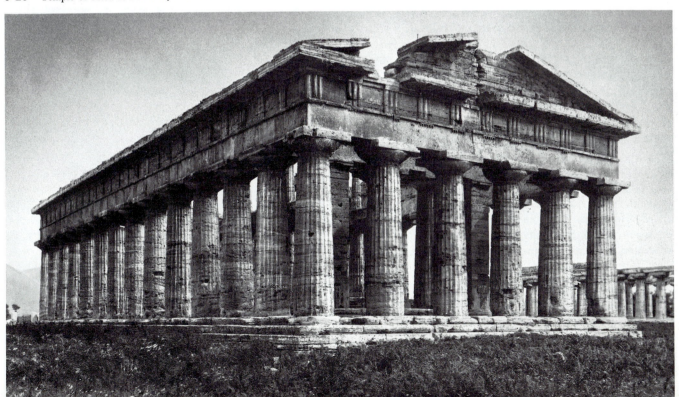

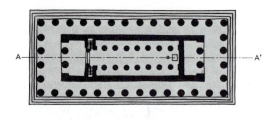

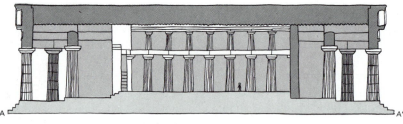

5-26 Reconstruction of the plan and section of the Temple of Hera at Paestum. (After Sir Banister Fletcher.)

FEET
0   50   100

Doric columns that support the roof is made up of two sets of columns, one resting on a stone course that rests on the set of columns below. This was a standard form where Doric columns were used to support the roof, and the reason for this may have been that a single row of large columns, as in the "Basilica," would produce a distortion of scale and look out of proportion and oppressive inside the relatively small naos. Later, the support problem was solved by using Ionic or Corinthian columns in the interior, since they were taller in relation to their diameters than were the Doric ones.

One of the earliest Ionic buildings in Greece is the Treasury of the Siphnians at Delphi, constructed about 530 B.C. (FIG. 5-27). Although it has no Ionic columns, the supporting function being assumed by luxuriously carved caryatids, it has the identifying Ionic feature—the continuous frieze—which here appears as part of a heavy Archaic entablature. The caryatids, with their elaborate costume and very irregular silhouettes, could never fit into a context of Doric architecture, with its severity of line and disdain of ornament.

Architectural Sculpture

We have noted already that decorative sculpture was applied only to those parts of a temple that had no evident structural function—that is, the frieze and the pediment. The caryatids are exceptional, but their use is fairly rare. Ordinarily the weight-carrying columns and the weight-distributing architraves were not decorated, though it may be that war trophies were hung upon the blank Doric architrave. In the Doric order only the metopes bore relief sculpture. It might be argued that the fluting of columns is a form of decoration, but in fact the fluting simply explains and emphasizes the form and function of the column, stressing its verticality. It also exhibits the column's rotundity, for when the sunlight strikes sharply upon the shaft (FIG. 5-23) the fluting throws numerous shadows of graduated width and darkness that lead the eye around the shaft in a series of graded steps, making the effect of

roundness more evident than in the nonfluted column, in which the sunlight creates a single, indistinct line separating the light and dark sides.

The architectural sculptor had a problem similar to that of the vase painter: how to adjust the image to the surface on which it is placed. This is not apparent in the frieze from the Treasury of the Siphnians (FIG. 5-28), for here the sculptor has merely a continuous blank zone to manage and can arrange his figures in a simple file, their heads on the same level, each filling a unit of space of approximately the same dimension. This is a good example of the formalizing effect of architectural line on figurative composition, just as the surface of the ceramic vessel imposed its necessities on the vase painter, making for simplicity and elegance of style. In fact, in the case of the Siphnian figures there is a resemblance stylistically between them and con-

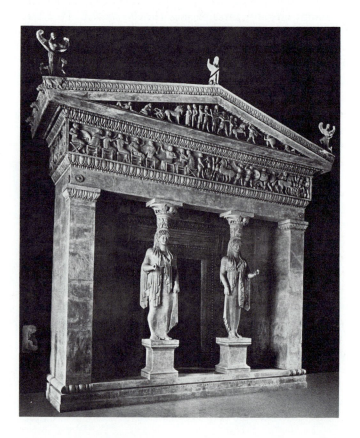

5-27 Treasury of the Siphnians in the Sanctuary of Apollo at Delphi, c. 530 B.C. Museum, Delphi (Façade reconstructed.)

temporary painting like that of the Andokides Painter (FIG. 5-8). But an awkward space like that of the triangular pediment of the Archaic Temple of Artemis (early sixth century B.C.) on the island of Corfu (FIG. 5-29) is more troublesome to manage. The figures are heraldically arranged and bring to mind compositions that go back beyond the Lion Gate at Mycenae to the symmetrical man-beast compositions of Mesopotamia. On the thin panel of stone that fills the space between the cornices of the pediment, the sculptor presents a Gorgon flanked by spotted panthers. The Gorgon, a guardian monster, grimaces hideously, exposing her boar's teeth (her look could turn men to stone) and fulfilling her function as a winged demon to

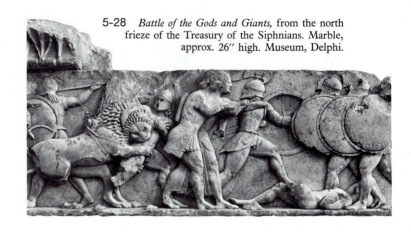

5-28 *Battle of the Gods and Giants,* from the north frieze of the Treasury of the Siphnians. Marble, approx. 26″ high. Museum, Delphi.

5-29 Reconstruction drawing superimposed on a photograph of the remaining fragments of the pediment of the Temple of Artemis at Corfu, *c.* 600–580 B.C.

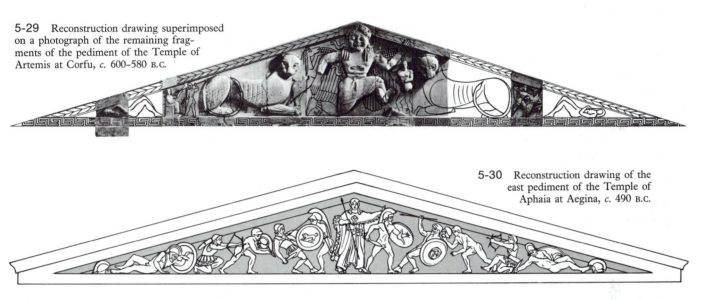

5-30 Reconstruction drawing of the east pediment of the Temple of Aphaia at Aegina, *c.* 490 B.C.

repulse all enemies from the sanctuary of the goddess. To the left and the right of the central Gorgon appear, on a smaller scale, the figures of Chrysoar and Pegasus, those mythological creatures that, according to legend, sprang from the Gorgon's head when she was struck by the sword of Perseus. Still smaller are two groups of figures beyond the panthers: Zeus slaying a giant (on the observer's right) and one of the climactic events of the Trojan War, Neoptolemos killing Priam. In the outer ends of the pediment, recumbent figures represent a fallen Trojan and a dead giant. As pieced together from the surviving fragments, the artist's narrative intention is clear enough, but the odd shape of the surface on which he worked compelled him to distribute his figures somewhat haphazardly around the central ones and to show them on different scales. As time progresses, the Greek artist attempts to fill the space more organically, with figures so grouped that they appear to be of the same size and participating in a unified way in a single event.

Toward the end of the Archaic period Greek sculptors were arriving at a solution to the problem of pedimental composition. In the pedimental sculptures of the Temple of Aphaia at Aegina (FIGS. 5-30 to 5-32) we find that the figures in the different poses, but of the same scale, have been fitted into the difficult triangular space. The figures, heavily cleaned and over-restored in the nineteenth century, probably represent some episode of the Trojan War. Athena, with aegis and spear, stands in the center, with fighting groups on either side. We notice most the freedom of movement and variety of pose. The figures are modeled with great vigor and an understanding of the human physique that, as we have seen in the contemporary vase paintings, reflect a careful observation of nature. The figure of the fallen warrior from the left angle of the pediment (FIG. 5-31) exhibits the daring with which the sculptor tackles the challenging problem of a difficult twisted pose. The bold composition of the turning masses of the body manifests his new confidence in his mastery of the science of representation. The dynamics of muscular tension and relaxation are appreciated and are close to life in their rendering. Mistakes are still made, and the transition from chest to pelvis has not been fully solved in this complex pose. (Note the misplaced navel.) These rather technical considerations should not blind us to the marvel-

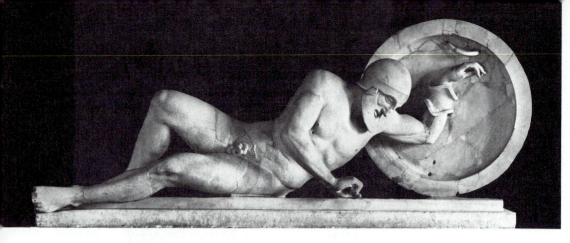

ously expressive power of this figure. The *Fallen Warrior* brings to mind the spare and monumental nobility of Homer's heroes, and particularly the Homeric simile, "darkness came down upon his eyes, and he crashed in the battle like a falling tower."

The figure of the archer Herakles (FIG. 5-32) from the same pediment is another instance of the Greek sculptor's triumph over age-old taboos and difficulties of representation. It is thought that this nimble archer is executing a maneuver hard to perform without long practice but required in the Greek war games and in actual combat. Running forward, he has dropped suddenly almost to one knee, and from this tense position takes aim and fires a flight of arrows in a matter of seconds. Soon he will spring to his feet to run forward again. The practiced strength and poise demanded by such a feat are beautifully caught in the elastic, though momentarily rigid, pose. One might read here the expression of a new spirit in Greek life and art, a spirit buoyant and optimistic as it meets the great challenge of the Persians at Marathon and looks to a future that the old Near Eastern world could never envision and never encompass.

5-32 *Herakles*, from the east pediment of the Temple of Aphaia at Aegina. Marble, approx. 31″ high. Staatliche Antikensammlungen, Munich.

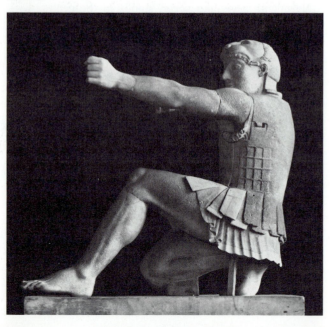

THE FIFTH CENTURY

The Transitional Period

The thirty years or so of the Transitional period constitute the heroic age of the Athenians and of all the Hellenes who joined forces against the invasion of Greece by the Persians. Just as we look back to the age of the American Revolution and of the founding fathers of the republic for our models of heroism and of civic wisdom and virtue, so did the Greeks of the later fifth century revere the men of Marathon, Thermopylae, and Salamis, the battles that daunted and finally turned back the mighty hosts of Asia led by Xerxes. The new world of the Greeks—attributed by them to the Homeric feats of their heroes—turned away from Asia, barbarism, tyranny, and ignorance (it was all the same to the Greeks) to build a Hellenic civilization productive of a new species of mankind. Typical of the time were the views of the great dramatist Aeschylus, who celebrated, in his *Oresteia*, the triumph of reason and law over barbarous crime, blood feud, and mad vengeance. Himself a veteran of Marathon, Aeschylus repudiated in majestic verse all the slavish and inhuman traits of nature that the Greeks at that time of crisis tended to associate with the Persians.

Shortly after Athens was occupied and sacked in 480 B.C., the Greeks won a great naval victory over the Persians at Salamis. This resilient toughness of the Athenians signified a new pride that was to mature into a sense of Hellenic identity so strong that thenceforth the history of European civilization would be distinct from—even though in interaction with—the civilization of Asia. The period of struggle with the Persians, calling repeatedly for courage and endurance, produced in the Hellenes a kind of austere grandeur that is manifested in the art of that period. This quality is rendered in the fine bronze, the *Charioteer of Delphi* (FIG. 5-33). The Greek search for ideal beauty is also fully shown here, as well as the culmination of the long-evolving mastery of the structure of the human figure.

The statue belonged to a group with chariot and horses, probably erected to commemorate the victory of King Polyzalos of Gela at the races in 478 B.C. Because it is life-size, weight, cost, and the tendency of large masses of

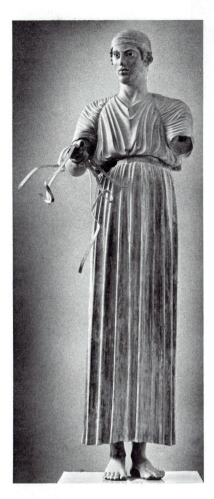

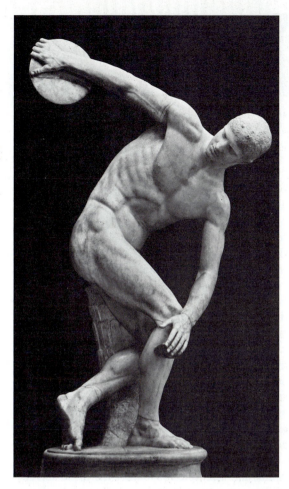

5-33 *Charioteer*, from the
Sanctuary of Apollo at
Delphi, *c.* 470 B.C.
Bronze, approx. 71″ high.
Museum, Delphi.

5-34 MYRON, *Discobolos*,
original *c.* 450 B.C. Roman
copy, marble, life-size.
Museo Nazionale
Romano, Rome.

bronze to distort when cooling would have made a casting in solid bronze impractical, if not impossible. Larger sculptures in bronze were (and are) hollow-cast in the *cire perdue* (lost-wax) method (see Glossary), a process that has been used since Sumerian times and that was introduced into Greece during the sixth century B.C., probably from Egypt.

The *Charioteer* represents a youthful aristocrat who stands firmly on both feet, holding the reins in his outstretched hand. He is dressed in the customary garment of a driver, girdled high and held in at the shoulders and the back to keep it from flapping. The hair is confined by a band tied behind the head. The eyes are made of glass paste and shaded by lashes of hairlike pieces of bronze. We feel the sharp clarity of Archaic work in the figure, especially in the lower part, where the folds of the dress have almost the quality of a fluted column, in the sharp lines of the brow, and in the conventional way in which the hair is worked. But we notice also the skillful modeling of the hand and the feet, and the slight twist of the torso, giving the feeling of an organic structure beneath the drapery. These subtleties are not seen at first and one might mistake the statue for another example of the Archaic formula of rigid frontality. But it is only the formality of the pose, not ignorance of the principle of weight distribution, that determines the tight composure of the figure; it is as "alive" as the pose of a soldier at parade rest. The statue is probably a portrait, yet there are few individualized traits.

This is typical of most works of the Greek Classical period and distinguishes Greek from Egyptian portrait statues, which had a religious function—the preservation of the deceased's likeness meaning the preservation of the ka. Although with the Greeks man comes to complete self-consciousness ("Know thyself!") and although the *figure* of man is idealized, no individual is regarded as being true or perfect or, consequently, an appropriate subject for representation. In the words of Bruno Snell:

> If we want to describe the statues of the fifth century in the words of their age, we should say that they represent beautiful or perfect men, or, to use a phrase employed in the early lyrics for purposes of eulogy: "god-like" men. Even for Plato the norm of judgment still rests with the gods, and not with men.[2]

Thus, the observations made at the beginning of the chapter must be modified: Though with Protagoras "man is the measure," for art the gods are the measure of man, and to achieve the ideal is to achieve the "godlike."

The rapid process of liberation from Archaic limits continues in the renowned *Discobolos* of the sculptor MYRON (FIG. 5-34), from about 450 B.C. As have most freestanding statues by the "Great Masters" of Greek sculpture, this has survived only in Roman marble copies

[2]Bruno Snell, *The Discovery of the Mind: The Greek Origins of European Thought* (New York: Harper & Row, 1960), p. 247.

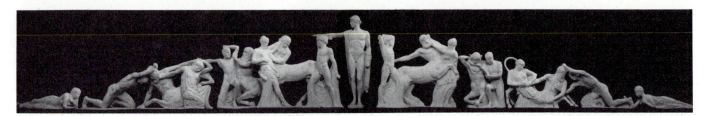

5-35 Reconstruction of the west pediment of the Temple of Zeus at Olympia, 468–460 B.C. Approx. 91' wide.

after the bronze original (see pp. 137–38). Myron's representation of an athlete engaged in the discus throw, still an athletic event in the Olympic games, was revolutionary because of its vigorous and convincing movement; it has been widely reproduced in both the ancient and modern worlds. However, the motion of the *Discobolos* has clearly been restricted to one plane, which means that only two distinct views are possible. The figure, represented at the point between the backward swing and the forward thrust of the arm, becomes by means of certain formal devices an expression of concentrated force. The composition is in terms of two intersecting arcs, creating the impression of a tightly stretched bow a moment before the string's release.

The "severe" early style of the transition finds clearest and most representative expression in the pedimental sculptures of the Temple of Zeus at Olympia (FIG. 5-35). On the west pediment is represented the combat of centaurs and Lapiths at the wedding feast of Peirithous. The centaurs, half beast, had been invited to the celebration but became drunk and attempted to abduct the bride and her maidens. They were prevented from doing so by Peirithous and Theseus, and Apollo, appearing above the combat, approves the heroes' chastisement of this breach of hospitality. The scene symbolizes three things: the Greek victories over the Persians; the sacred truce of Olympia (which outlawed strife within or on the approaches of the consecrated precincts of the temple); and the responsibility of men, who, unlike animals, acknowledge the rule of law.

The grouping of the figures in the Olympia pediments shows considerable improvement over the older Aegina grouping (FIG. 5-30) in the adjustment of the poses to fit the triangular pediment. In the center, Apollo thrusts out his arm amid the tumult (FIG. 5-36). The figure should be compared with the Archaic Kouroi (FIGS. 5-15 and 5-16): From its formality and such lingering archaisms as the tight, decorative treatment of the hair, it seems the last of that great line, although the new understanding of bodily structure shows in the splendid and exact modeling of the athletic physique. The musculature is no longer schematic but swelling with life and power. The transitions from one group of muscles to another are smoothly and subtly made, and this soft flow of planes and contours belies the formal rigidity of the pose.

The face of the *Apollo*, like those of the *Charioteer of Delphi* and the *Discobolos*, is composed in the expressionless mask of regular beauty deemed appropriate to gods and godlike men, despite their action or potential for action. This ideal mask, expressing the conviction of Greek philosophy that reason must be above and in control of the passions, precludes the distortion of the face by any strain of emotion, even in scenes of the most violent action. In the twisted complication of the group of *Hippodameia and the Centaur* (FIG. 5-37), where the bride of Peirithous tries to wrench from her breast the centaur's clutching hand, the girl's face remains serenely neutral. Her predicament is dire, as the artful sculptor dramatically describes it; yet, and significantly, it is only the centaur's face that is distorted, as befits the low creature that it is, surrendering to drunkenness and lust. This distinction between the calm of noble men and the frenzy of the creature abandoned to

5-36 *Apollo*, from the west pediment of the Temple of Zeus at Olympia. Marble, over life-size. Museum, Olympia.

5-37 *Hippodameia and the Centaur*, from the west pediment of the Temple of Zeus at Olympia. Marble, slightly over life-size. Museum, Olympia.

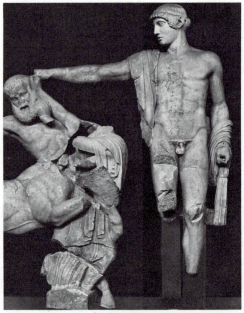

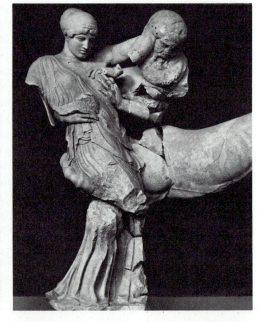

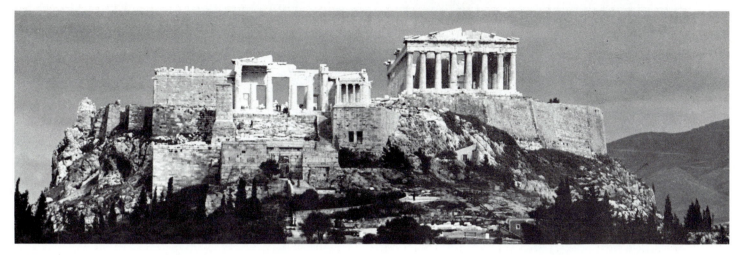

5-38   View (from the west) of the Acropolis today, Athens.

impulse prevails for centuries in Greek art. The Greeks were convinced that overwhelming disaster awaited the man who yielded to the spell cast by the dark god of intoxication and madness, Dionysos; this conviction is reflected in their drama and in their persistent appeal to reason and order, both in art and life. Against Dionysos they attempted to raise the shining figure of Apollo, god of light, beauty, and wisdom. Thus, it was with the pediments of Olympia that the visual arts moved into the realm of philosophy and drama, and it was in the presence of these sculptures that the Greek athletes took their oath at the altar of Zeus before the Olympic games.

The Early Classical Period

The prestige that the Athenians won by their leading role in the repulse of the Persians and by virtue of the powerful fleet they had built in the process made them the dominant political force in the Greek world. They acquired a sea empire disguised as a religious and more or less democratic alliance of city and island states throughout the Aegean. Members of the alliance, which was called the Delian League, had cause enough to complain bitterly that they were more the subjects of Athens than her allies and that she siphoned off a large part of the common treasury (raised as a fund for defense against Persia), for her own uses. Despite chronic warfare within the alliance (and between it and the rival league led by Sparta), Athens, under the leadership of its adroit statesman, Pericles, became an immensely prosperous and proud community. The brief period of her glory under Pericles saw a concentration of human creative energy and a triumph of drama, philosophy, and art such as has been known in no other place or time in all of the Western world.

Disdaining to reassemble the desecrated stones of the Athenian Acropolis after the sack of the city in 480 B.C., the Athenians, led by Pericles, signalized their new power and independence by completely rebuilding the Acropolis, an undertaking that was one of the greatest building projects of antiquity before Roman times. Their success stands

as a rare human achievement against the larger history of human failure. The beauty of the buildings, set upon a towering platform of rock with difficult access (FIGS. 5-38 and 5-39), was recognized and celebrated in ancient times

5-39   Plan of the Acropolis, restored as of 400 B.C.

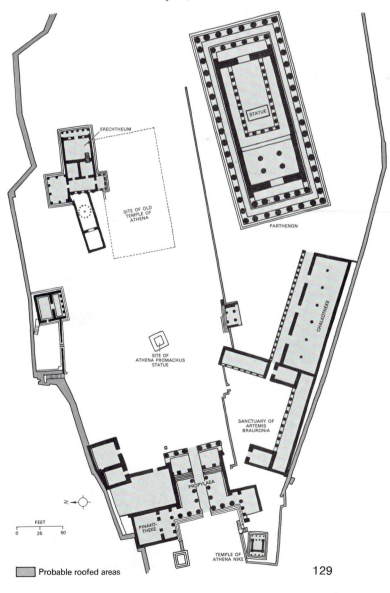

ERECHTHEUM

SITE OF OLD TEMPLE OF ATHENA

STATUE

PARTHENON

CHALKOTHEKE

SITE OF ATHENA PROMACHUS STATUE

SANCTUARY OF ARTEMIS BRAURONIA

PROPYLAEA

PINAKO-THEKE

FEET
0   25   50

TEMPLE OF ATHENA NIKE

Probable roofed areas

129

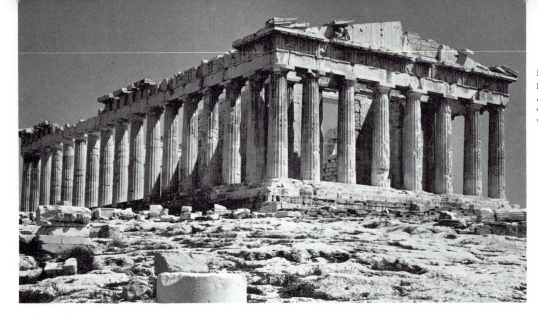

as it is today. Plutarch, writing some 500 years after the rebuilding of the Acropolis, commented:

Pericles' works are especially admired, as having been made quickly, to last long. For every particular piece of his work was immediately, even at that time when it was new, recognized as ancient, because of its beauty and elegance; and yet in its vigor and freshness it looks to this day as if it has just been done. There is a sort of bloom and newness upon those works of his, preserving them from the touch of time . . . .

The late architect Eric Mendelssohn (1887–1953) made almost the same observation when he first visited Athens. Expecting to be depressed by the view of that original source of the academic classicism from which his generation was fighting to free itself, he found himself exclaiming that the Parthenon is "modern," meaning that good architecture is always good, and so, always "modern."

THE PARTHENON

Of the buildings on the Acropolis, the Parthenon (the temple sacred to Athena Parthenos) was the first and the largest to be constructed (FIG. 5-40). Its architects were ICTINOS and CALLICRATES, and its sculptural ornament was produced under the direction of PHIDIAS, friend of Pericles and one of the great sculptors of all time. In plan (FIG. 5-39) the Parthenon is a peripteral temple, its short side slightly less than half the length of its long. Its naos is subdivided into two parts; the larger contained the cult statue of Athena Parthenos in ivory and gold, some forty feet in height, the work of Phidias; the smaller had been designed to serve as treasury of the Delian League, but most of the revenues contributed by the Aegean members were expended upon Pericles' ambitious building projects. The interiors of the two rooms are organized differently. The naos proper had two double rows of small columns for roof support; although long disputed, the purpose of the

rows was, according to some, to provide a second-story gallery from which visitors could view the statue, the foundation of which is still visible. The treasury had four single Ionic columns—one of several Ionic features in the otherwise Doric building, another being the continuous frieze of sculpture that runs around the top of the naos wall on the exterior. Except for these Ionic elements, the Parthenon is the epitome of the classical Doric temple, exhibiting the order at the peak of its refinement.

The building seen today is a partial restoration. Through the centuries the Parthenon has undergone many transformations, having been at one time a Greek temple, at another a Christian church; and then, after the Ottoman conquest of Greece, a Turkish mosque was built inside its naos. In 1687 the naos was being used as an ammunition dump by the Turks, who were then at war with the Venetians. A Venetian rocket scored a direct hit, and the resultant explosion blew out the center of the building. During the past century the colonnades have been reassembled, but the core of the structure remains a ruin.

Despite its dilapidated condition, the Parthenon is probably the most carefully surveyed and measured building in the world. The consequence of this searching study is the revelation that the builders aimed for unsurpassable excellence in every detail; the "refinements" of the structure have become almost a subtopic in the history of Greek architecture. If there is anything we are led to expect from the severe Doric order, it is that its lines must be rigidly and consistently straight and plumb; yet there are few straight structural lines in the Parthenon. The stylobate is convex, so subtly as to be almost imperceptible as a curve; only if one sights along it from one end does the curvature, which is repeated in the entablature, become visible. The columns tilt slightly inward and are not uniformly spaced, standing closer to each other at the corners of the buildings. Moreover, not all the columns are of the same diameter, those at the corners having somewhat greater girth than the rest. The entasis, which gives a kind of muscle-tense elasticity and buoyancy to the profile of the column, has the same subtlety seen in the curvature of the stylobate and the entablature.

These deviations from the mechanical, plumb-line, straight-edged norm are plainly intentional; most have been found in other temples. But interpretations of these refinements do not agree; some feel that they are purely functional, the curvature of the stylobate, for example, facilitating drainage or perhaps anticipating settling of the central part of the building. Others believe that the deviations were intended to offset marginal distortions in the human visual field—optical illusions that might make columns with exactly vertical profiles look pinched and weak. Still other speculation sees the refinements as required by Greek instinct for completeness in the look of the building and for integrity with its surroundings; for example, the downward-tending curve of the stylobate would find its limit in the earth, making a visually stable and strong base for the building's aspect. A reasonable conjecture would be that the Parthenon was intended to be more than a product of engineering logic, that it was to be viewed and appreciated as a great work of sculpture, having the elasticity, resilience, and life of the human figure in statuary. Thus, the particulars would be designed to work in smooth relation to each other and to the whole structure in an organic way in which, of course, the curved line predominates over the straight. The Parthenon columns especially display this in their entasis, appearing to respond to the burden they bear by the seeming swell of their compressed contours, expressing their function not mechanically but organically.

Parts of the building were painted. This painting provided background against which sculpture could be seen clearly and, perhaps more important, delineated the upper parts of the building against the bright sky, so that the temple's basic proportions were crisply shown and could not be misread. Color also ensured that the visible parts of the building would be clearly defined and distinguished one from another.

The insistence upon clarity in argument, which led to the invention of logic by the Greeks, operates just as strongly in the "arguments" of their architectural design. Unfortunately, that early triumph of Greek thought, the syllogism, with its three propositions ending in a logically correct conclusion, cannot quite be matched in the Doric order. As examination of a corner of the Parthenon (FIG. 5-41) will show, Greek architecture was not as "rational" as Greek logic. The Doric frieze was organized according to three inflexible rules: (1) a triglyph must be exactly over the center of each column; (2) a triglyph must be over the center of each intercolumniation; and (3) triglyphs at the corners of the frieze must meet, so that no space is left over. But the architectural "syllogism" is faulty, for the conclusion cannot be harmonized with Proposition I: If the corner triglyphs must meet, they cannot be placed over

the center of the corner column. Though irremediable, this might seem to us a minor flaw, even in a building that aimed at perfection in all details. The Greeks wanted to be sure, and they worked out, in logic, a method for making series of statements conform to a rule for validity. But in Doric architecture, there was something left over, something that did not fit. To the Greeks it must have appeared like the incommensurable "irrational" numbers (such as the square root of two)—a disturbing thing, since it has no limit or definition. (According to a singular and significant Greek legend, the man who first revealed the mystery of the irrationals perished by shipwreck, "for the unspeakable and the formless must be left hidden forever!") In much the same manner as mathematicians and logicians faced with some disturbing contradiction in their results, the architects and artists who aimed at perfection must have found this problem of the corner triglyph a constant irritation and embarrassment. Indeed, it may have contributed to the eventual decline of the Doric order, which began in the fourth century B.C., and to the rise of the Ionic and Corinthian orders, whose continuous friezes eliminate the problem.

The main purpose of the Parthenon, as already noted, was to house the cult statue of Athena Parthenos. Since the image of Athena—for whom the city of Athens was named—was made of ivory and gold, it did not survive centuries of depredation, although it seems to have been in existence as late as the second century A.D. We know the

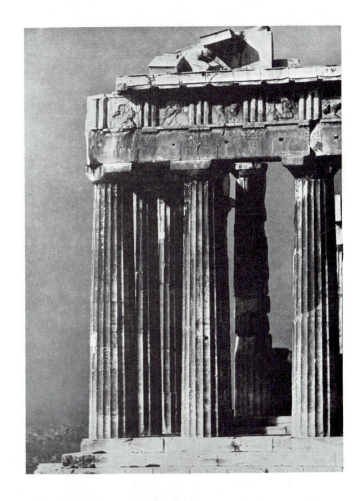

5-41 Southeast corner of the Parthenon.

look of it only from accounts by Pausanias and others and from a few small replicas that differ in detail. Plutarch, in his *Life of Pericles*, tells us that its artist, Phidias, probably the scapegoat in an anti-Pericles plot, was convicted of stealing some of the gold intended for the statue and died in prison (though we know from other sources and recent excavations that he was working on a statue of Zeus at Olympia after he left Athens and that he died in exile). Because work on the colossal cult statue for the naos of the Parthenon must have taken up most of Phidias' time, it is quite likely that he planned and designed the pedimental groups and friezes but left the carving of these architectural sculptures to his students and assistants. Nevertheless, they undoubtedly reflect his style and they are among the most marvelous of all surviving Greek works of sculpture and among the supreme masterworks of all time. The east pedimental group depicted the birth of Athena; the west, her contest with Poseidon for the sponsorship of the city of Athens.

Most of these sculptures are now in the British Museum in London, where they are popularly known as the Elgin marbles. Between 1801 and 1803, while Greece was still under Turkish rule, Lord Elgin, the British ambassador to the Ottoman court at Constantinople, was permitted to dismantle some of the Parthenon sculptures and to ship the best-preserved ones to England. He eventually sold them to the British government, although at a great financial loss to himself. Although he was severely criticized for having "stolen" the treasures of Athens, Lord Elgin's quite civilized motives in saving the statues from almost certain ruin are no longer doubted. During his time there seemed to be no prospect that the statues, surrounded by rubble and neglected for centuries, might one day be salvaged and protected against further damage and decay.

The figure of Dionysos (identified by some as Herakles) from the Parthenon shows the final relaxing of all the limitations of Archaic figurative art. Phidias and his assistants are in full possession of the knowledge of the organic, coordinated human body and render it effortlessly and with entirely convincing consistency in all its parts. This

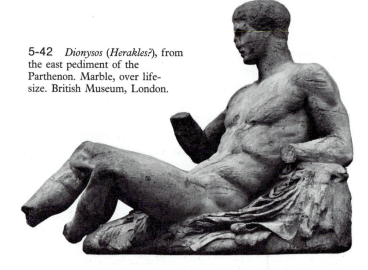

5-42 *Dionysos (Herakles?)*, from the east pediment of the Parthenon. Marble, over life-size. British Museum, London.

fidelity to nature was a revelation even in an age (the nineteenth century) that was at the end of a long tradition of respect for nature in art. The artist Benjamin Robert Haydon, writing in that time, described his reaction to the reclining figure of Dionysos (Herakles?) (FIG. 5-42), which he called Theseus:

> But when I turned to the Theseus, and saw that every form was altered by action or repose—when I saw that the two sides of his back varied, one side stretched from the shoulder blade being pulled forward, and the other being compressed from the shoulder blade being pushed close to the spine, as he rested on his elbow, with the belly flat because the bowels fell into the pelvis as he sat—when I saw in fact the most heroic style of art, combined with all the essential detail of actual life, the thing was done at once and forever. . . . Here were principles which the great Greeks in their finest time established . . . .[3]

These principles seem indeed to be the monumental or heroic style "combined," as Haydon wrote, "with all the essential detail of actual life," the calm grandeur and simplicity of the one being in no way weakened by the precise, dynamic anatomical logic of the other.

[3] In F. H. Taylor, *The Taste of Angels* (Boston: Little, Brown, 1948), p. 502.

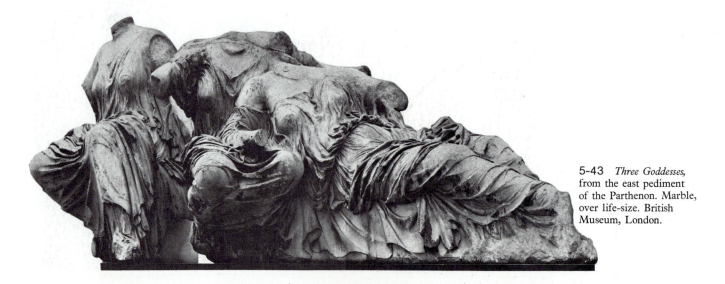

5-43 *Three Goddesses*, from the east pediment of the Parthenon. Marble, over life-size. British Museum, London.

The three goddesses from the east pediment of the Parthenon (FIG. 5-43) show even more than the Dionysos (Herakles?) the reinforcing and complementary actions of the principles of monumentality of scale and simplicity of pose with the "essential detail of actual life." The statues are typically Phidian in style, at once majestic and utterly "real" in the reading of the relaxed forms. In thin and heavy folds, the drapery alternately reveals and conceals the main and the lesser masses of the bodies, at the same time swirling in a compositional tide that subtly unifies the group, the articulation and integration of the bodies producing a wonderful variation of surface and play of light and shade. Not only are the bodies fluidly related to each other, but they are related as well to the draperies, though the latter remain distinct from the bodies materially. The treatment of body and drapery as obviously different stuffs, yet in functional relation to each other, illustrates the thoroughly reasoned laws of appearance that Phidias and his generation had come to know and respect.

The sculptural decorations of the Parthenon are in the pediments (some of the figures of which were just described), on the metopes, and on a continuous Ionic frieze at the top of the external naos wall. Those on the metopes provide an accent of movement, notably by the use of diagonal forms in successive compositions of pairs of struggling interlocking figures done in high relief—centaurs and Lapiths, gods and giants, Greeks and Amazons. The metope illustrated (FIG. 5-44), shows a battle between a Lapith and a centaur, the theme of the Apollo pediment at Olympia (FIG. 5-35). Although some of the metope designs are more successful than others, the figures generally are accommodated with great adroitness to the square spaces, and the whole series displays the ingenuity of the Phidian school in varying the poses and attitudes of the figures and avoiding the monotony that a regularly repeated space could impose. It is interesting also that the fortunes of the contestants are about equally balanced, the Greeks seeming to win or lose as often as their opponents.

The inner Ionic frieze of figures (FIGS. 5-45 and 5-46) was seen from below in reflected light against a colored

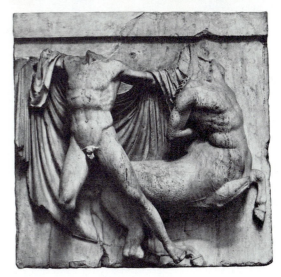

5-44 *Lapith and Centaur,* metope from the Parthenon. Marble, 56″ high. British Museum, London.

5-45 *Horsemen,* from the west frieze of the Parthenon. Marble, approx. 43″ high. British Museum, London.

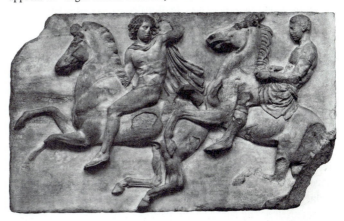

ground. It enriched the plain wall and directed attention toward the entrance to the temple. It may represent the Panathenaic procession, which took place every four years, when the citizens of Athens gathered in the marketplace and carried to the Parthenon the *peplos,* or robe, for the

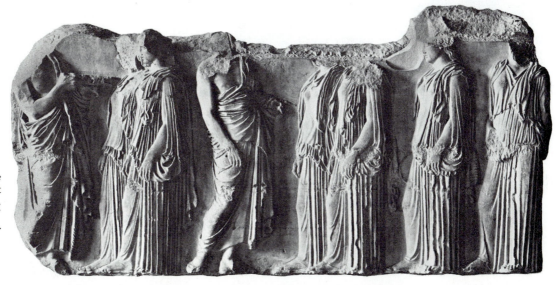

5-46 *Head of the Procession,* from the east frieze of the Parthenon. Marble, approx. 43″ high. Louvre, Paris.

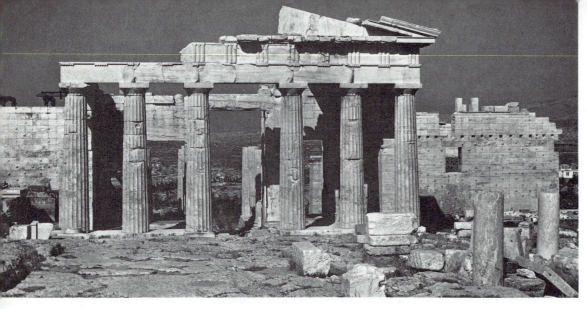

statue of Athena. If so, this is the first known representation of a nonmythological subject in Greek temple reliefs.

The Panathenaic frieze is unique in the ancient world for its careful creation of the impression of the passage of time, albeit a brief fragment of it. The effect is achieved by use of a sequence of figures so posed as to present a gradation of motion—a rudimentary picture of time as an acceleration or deceleration. In order to experience the illusion, the observer must himself be in motion, following the frieze around the colonnade of the temple. In the part of the frieze that decorated the western side of the naos the viewer can see the procession forming: Youths are lacing their sandals and holding or mounting their horses; they are guided by marshals who stand at intervals, and particularly at the corners, to slow movement and guide the horsemen at the turn. In the friezes of the two long sides of the naos the procession moves in parallel lines, a cavalcade

of spirited youths, chariots, elders, jar-carriers, and animals for sacrifice. Seen throughout the procession is that balance of the monumental-simple and the actual, of the tactile and the optical, of the "ideal" and the "real," of the permanent and the momentary that, again, is characteristically Greek and the perfect exemplification of the "inner concord of opposites" that Herakleitos, the philosopher, wrote of in the sixth century B.C. The eye follows the movement of light and shade in the drapery, pausing at any point by shifting focus to the broad areas of planes, with their sharply linear outlines. The movement of the procession becomes slower and more solemn as it nears the eastern side of the naos, when, after turning the corner, it approaches the seated divinities, who appear to be guests of Athena at her great festival. Standing figures—to note one device of the artists—face against the general movement at ever closer intervals, slowing the forward motion of the procession (FIG. 5-46).

OTHER BUILDINGS OF THE ACROPOLIS

To reach the Parthenon, the Panathenaic procession would have wound its way from the lower level of the city of Athens, up the steep slope of the Acropolis, and through the gate called the Propylaea (FIGS. 5-39 and 5-47), another structure of the Periclean project. Built by MNESICLES between 437 and 432 B.C., it was begun immediately upon the completion of the Parthenon but was never finished, partly because of the financial drain of the Peloponnesian War and partly, it is believed, because one of its wings would have trespassed on the sanctuary of Artemis Brauronia. The design is a monumental and subtle elaboration of a gate unit leading through a city wall, the gate hall itself being flanked by buildings containing a library and perhaps the first picture gallery (*pinakotheke*) in history. Here members of the procession could rest in beautiful surroundings after the steep climb and before they passed on to the sacred buildings on the summit. The Propylaea

5-48 Temple of Athena Nike, Acropolis, Athens, 427–424 B.C.

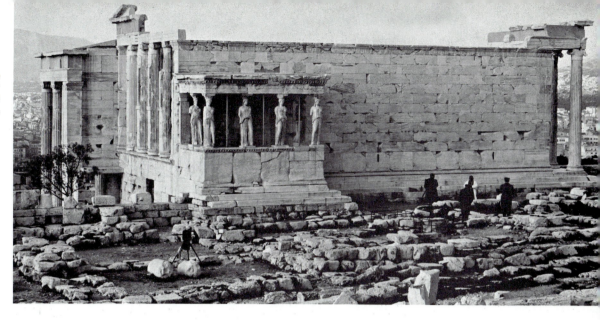

5-49 The Erechtheum, Acropolis, Athens, 421–405 B.C. (view from the south).

shows modifications of Doric regularity in the broadening of the space between the central columns to make the passageway more commodious, and, like the Parthenon, the gateway includes Ionic elements such as the columns lining the corridor and giving greater height where it is needed for the support of the central roof structure.

The beautiful little Ionic Temple of Athena Nike (Athena Victorious), built under the direction of Callicrates between 427 and 424 B.C. (FIGS. 5-20C, 5-39, and 5-48), is the earliest completely Ionic building extant on the Acropolis. Before this time the Ionic order had been used for a whole building in a few treasuries at Olympia and Delphi on the Greek mainland (for example, the Treasury of the Siphnians, FIG. 5-27), and these had been constructed by Aegean islanders, not by Greeks of the mainland. It was through Athens' rule of the islands that it became open to eastern Greek and Ionian influences. The little amphiprostyle temple stands on what used to be a Mycenaean bastion near the Propylaea, to the Doric severity of which this slender, exquisitely proportioned building offers a striking contrast, heightening the effect of both.

Another Ionic building situated on the Acropolis is the Erechtheum (FIGS. 5-39 and 5-49), the last of the Periclean program. Constructed between 421 and 405 B.C., the Erechtheum is most unusual in plan and quite unlike any other Greek temple. It was named after a mythical Athenian hero, Erechtheus, to whom it was in part dedicated. Its many unusual features are due partly to the irregularity of its site and partly to the number of shrines included within it. According to the above-mentioned Pausanias, the Greek geographer and historian of the second century A.D., the Erechtheum stood on the traditional site of the contest between Poseidon and Athena for dominion over Athens, the theme of the sculpture group in the west pediment of the Parthenon. Also at the site were a rock supposed to be at the imprint of Poseidon's trident, the spring of salt water that the stroke of the trident produced, and Athena's olive tree. The asymmetrical arrangement of

the building, which probably was not intended in the original plan, may also reflect an interruption and a "making-do" caused by the impending and final defeat of Athens in the Peloponnesian War, in 404 B.C. Thus, the Erechtheum was not completed as planned, and it can be assumed that the original plan provided for the west face to extend so that the north and south porches would have had their positions in the centers of the long blank walls. In the reconstructed elevations of the east and the west sides (FIG. 5-50) we can observe that on the east the different levels of the friezes are smoothly adjusted, while the west side appears to have been finished hurriedly with a wall to which are attached half-columns, the spaces between which are closed with bronze grilles. These *engaged columns* are rarely used in Classical Greek architecture, though the device is very popular later in Roman architecture. If one approaches the building with some rigid preconception of

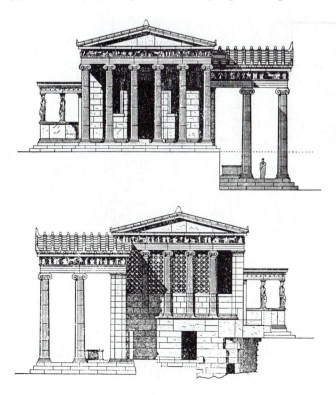

5-50 Reconstructed elevations of the east and west façades of the Erechtheum.

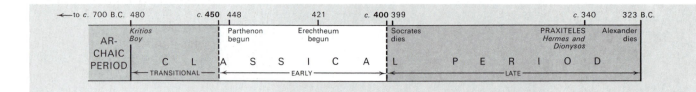

←to c. 700 B.C. 480		c. 450 448		421	c. 400 399			c. 340	323 B.C.
	Kritios Boy		Parthenon begun	Erechtheum begun	Socrates dies			PRAXITELES Hermes and Dionysos	Alexander dies
AR- CHAIC PERIOD	C L	A S	S I	C A	L	P E R	I O	D	
	←— TRANSITIONAL —→		←——— EARLY ———→			←——————— LATE ———————→			

Greek architectural order, its overall effect may be disappointing; however, the orderly asymmetry of the Erechtheum is extremely effective as a complement to the symmetrical unity of the Parthenon, just as the Korai of its Porch of the Maidens complement the Parthenon's Doric columns. Moreover, the carved details of the Erechtheum are without rival in their refined beauty.

SCULPTURE

The Porch of the Maidens, the south porch of the Erechtheum, is so called because its caryatids are its dominating feature (FIG. 5-51). It brings to mind that earlier Ionic caryatid design, the Treasury of the Siphnians (FIG. 5-27), and comparison of the two is useful. Unlike the Siphnian caryatids, those of the south porch of the Erechtheum do not carry a full entablature but one that consists of archi-

5-51   Porch of the Maidens, the Erechtheum.

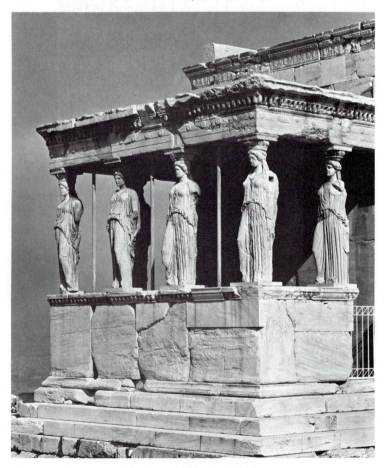

trave and cornice only, the topmost fascia of the architrave being decorated with medallions to simulate the missing frieze. This seems to be a deliberate proportional adjustment undertaken by the sculptors of the Erechtheum figures to avoid the effect seen in the Siphnian caryatids, which look overloaded by the entablature; the sculptors must have been aware that figures graceful in attitude and dimension could scarcely harmonize with a massive architectural superstructure they would be presumed to be supporting. There are technical as well as esthetic reasons for the Erechtheum adjustment: Although the weight of a full entablature was borne by the Siphnian caryatids, in this case the load could have been too great for the necks of the figures, their weakest point; however, esthetic considerations were probably the more persuasive. Thus, again, we find the Classical architect-sculptor balancing in his wonderfully trained judgment the realities of structure with the necessities of ideal beauty. The figures have enough rigidity to suggest the structural columnar and just the degree of flexibility necessary to suggest the living body. The compromise is quite superbly brought off. The corner figures determine the stance by representing the weight as falling on the outer leg. The inner figures repeat this pose so that the legs not carrying the weight, and bent at the knee, do not determine the architectural verticals, nor disturb their natural plumb-line straightness. These figures have all the monumental majesty of those by Phidias on the Parthenon pediments; the pleats and folds of their draperies reveal the quiet power of their bodies, and the very obligation imposed upon them by the architecture serves only to strengthen their noble poise.

The Phidian style dominated Athenian sculpture until the end of the fifth century B.C. Because of the Peloponnesian War fewer large-scale sculptural enterprises were launched, although the style lingered on in smaller works such as the popular grave steles produced in considerable numbers for both local use and export. One of the most harmoniously designed of these is the *Grave Stele of Hegeso* (FIG. 5-52), which was found in the Dipylon cemetery. As was often the case in grave reliefs of the Classical period, the figures are placed in an architectural framework. The deceased is seated on a chair with sweepingly curved back and legs that provides an effective transition from the frozen forms of the architecture to the organic ones of the figures. Hegeso is contemplating a necklace (originally rendered in paint) that she has taken from the box held by her girl servant. The quiet glances of mistress

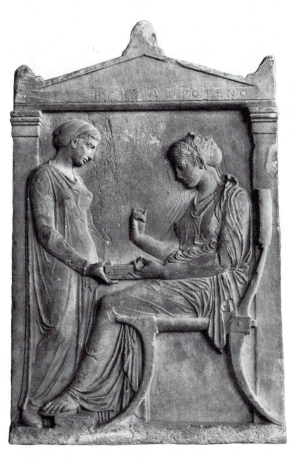

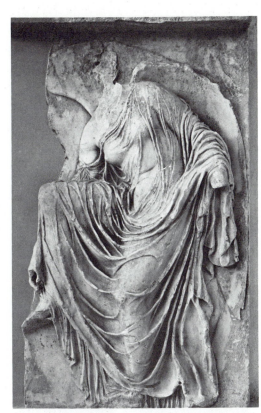

5-52 *Grave Stele of Hegeso*, Dipylon cemetery, *c.* 410–400 B.C. Marble, 59″ high. National Museum, Athens.

5-53 *Nike Fastening Her Sandal*, from the parapet of the Temple of Athena Nike, Acropolis, Athens, *c.* 410 B.C. Marble, approx. 42″ high. Acropolis Museum, Athens.

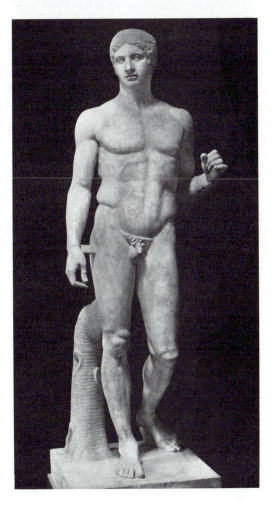

and servant are directed at Hegeso's right hand, which, placed exactly in the center of the panel, is the compositional focal point. Although the stele was carved toward the end of the century, it is devoid of the sentimentality found in many other works of its day; the solemn pathos of the scene links the stele with the grandiose conception of the Parthenon sculptures.

The relief of a Nike fastening her sandal (FIG. 5-53) from a parapet that was constructed around the Temple of Athena Nike about 410 B.C. shows how sculptors, having achieved the Classical perfection of the human form, now exhibit their virtuosity. The function of the concentrically arranged draperies, heavy and clinging to the form as if drenched with water, is to reveal the supple beauty of the young body. The interplay of the intricately moving drapery and the smooth volumes of the body seen in the *Three Goddesses* of the Parthenon (FIG. 5-43) is here refined to make a deliberately transparent veil for the female figure, which now fully emerges from the elaborate costume of the Kore tradition.

In contrast with the Ionian sumptuousness of the Phidian style is a work of the Argive school of southern Greece, the *Doryphoros* (FIG. 5-54) of POLYKLEITOS, a sculptor whose fame rivaled that of Phidias in the ancient world. The work shown here, the original of which is dated 450–440 B.C., is a Roman copy made much later.

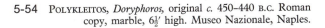

5-54 POLYKLEITOS, *Doryphoros*, original *c.* 450–440 B.C. Roman copy, marble, 6½′ high. Museo Nazionale, Naples.

Almost all extant works of the so-called Great Masters of Greek sculpture are replicas, the originals having disappeared. Originals of Roman copies can be identified through descriptions by ancient authors, especially Pausanias and Pliny the Elder, and occasionally through representations on ancient coins. There are a number of reasons for the disappearance of the originals: In war, statues made of precious materials were often pillaged and bronze statues melted to make weapons or utensils; during the barbarian invasions in the time of the fall of the Roman empire marble statues were used to make lime for mortar. After the Romans conquered Greece, in the second century B.C., they took Greek works of art to Rome to adorn the imperial palaces and the villas of the rich. Numerous copies were made of some statues, reflecting their popularity and fame. Many of the copyists took liberties with the originals; changes were made to conform with popular taste, and very few of the copies even approach the quality and refinement that the originals must have had. When the Romans were copying bronze in marble, they used awkward devices to strengthen weak points—such as a tree trunk placed next to a statue's leg and braces and struts to prevent breakage of the arms, as can be seen in the *Doryphoros.* Nevertheless, the copy of the *Doryphoros* does give evidence of the appearance of the original, and we can compare its blocky solidity and strength with the subtle grace of the Phidian style. Although the unity and equilibrium that pervade the works of Phidias are also in the Polykleitan statue, the origins differ, for while the artists at work on the Parthenon seem to have achieved their results with a deft, spontaneous translation of natural appearances, Polykleitos worked according to a canon of proportions in which he formulated the principles that give rise to unity. Although Polykleitos' own treatise enunciating his canon is lost, Galen, the second century A.D. physician, interprets it as follows in his *Placita Hippocratis et Platonis:*

> . . . [beauty consists] in the proportions, not of the elements, but of the parts, that is to say, of finger to finger, and of all the fingers to the palm and the wrist, and of these to the forearm, and of the forearm to the upper arm, and of all the other parts to each other, as they are set forth in the Canon of Polycleitos.

It was said that in the *Doryphoros* Polykleitos had not simply made a statue but had manifested sculpture itself, and Aristotle uses "sculptor" and "Polykleitos" interchangeably. As the Greeks saw proportion as the central problem in architecture, so did they in sculpture, and they viewed Polykleitos' canon as the embodiment of proportional rationality for sculpture.

In the *Doryphoros,* movement, which began to be expressed successfully in the early fifth century B.C., is disciplined through the use of an imposed system of proportions. The mighty body, with its broad shoulders,

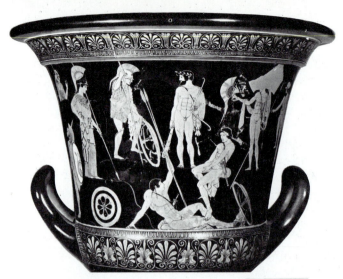

5-55 NIOBID PAINTER, *Argonaut Krater,* Orvieto, Italy, *c.* 455–450 B.C. Outline drawing at right indicates relation to whole vessel. Portion shown approx. 15″ high; whole vessel approx. 21″ high. Louvre, Paris.

thick torso, and muscular limbs, strikes us as the embodiment of the Spartan ideal of the warrior physique, the human equivalent of the Doric order. And, like the Doric order, the figure appeals to the intellect and must be studied long and carefully before it fully reveals itself to the observer. The slow forward walk, the standard Polykleitan pose, stresses the principle of weight-shift—the maneuver that must be made before we can move at all and with which the whole development of the representation of the moving human figure begins. What appears to be a casually natural pose is, in fact, the result of an extremely complex and subtle organization of the various parts of the figure. Note, for instance, how the function of the supporting leg is echoed by the straight-hanging arm to provide the right side of the figure with the columnar stability needed to anchor the dynamically flexed limbs of the left side. If read anatomically, on the other hand, the tensed and relaxed limbs may be seen to oppose each other diagonally (that is, the right arm and the left leg are relaxed, and the tensed supporting leg is opposed by the flexed left arm, which held a spear). Thus, all parts of the figure have been carefully composed to achieve the utmost variety within a compact and stable whole. A most circumspect and subtle artist has combined realism, monumentality, and diversity in a unified design that seems to be beyond the cavil of even the most discriminating critic.

PAINTING

The mural painter POLYGNOTOS enjoyed almost as much fame in antiquity as his contemporaries, Phidias and Polykleitos. Unfortunately, none of his works survive. On the basis of ancient literary sources, it is believed that his style is reflected in the vase decoration of the NIOBID PAINTER, whose *Argonaut Krater* (FIG. 5-55) illustrates a radical break with the traditional decorative style. For over two centuries figures had been arranged isocephalically—that is, with all the heads at one level—in horizontal bands, not only in Greek vase decoration, but also in monumental painting. Evidence for the latter seems to be provided by surviving Etruscan frescoes, which presumably reflect contemporary, or slightly earlier, Greek mural styles (see Chapter Six). On the *Argonaut Krater* the figures have been placed on different levels, and ground lines on which they stand or recline attempt to introduce into painting the illusion of depth, an effect that is thwarted, however, by the uniform size of the figures. We also read that Polygnotos modeled his figures in dark and light, aiming for three-dimensional and sculptural effects. This last feature was not adopted by the Niobid Painter, whose style remains linear and does not reveal what must have been an impressive statuesque quality of Polygnotan figures. Though important as reflecting—dimly, to be sure—the monumental manner of Polygnotos, the Niobid Painter's works also represent the decline of vase painting as the figurative decoration loses contact with the body of the vessel, the earlier cohesion of figure and surface becoming mere adhesion.

Although the work of the Niobid Painter may give some notion of the general compositional schemes of Polygnotos, it tells nothing of his use of color. A pale reflection of it may be found in the so-called white-ground vases of the fifth century B.C. Experiments with the white-ground technique go back to the Andokides Painter, but the method became popular only toward the middle of the fifth century. It is essentially a variation of the red-figure technique, the pot first being covered with a slip of very fine white clay that, when burnished, provided a glossy or matte white surface for drawing in black glaze or dilute brown wash. The range of colors remained severely limited—purple, brown, and several kinds of red—as few colors known to the Greeks could survive the heat of the kiln. Also, the white slip, although highly effective as background for drawing and coloring, was not durable, tending to flake off. Crucial for wares that saw daily use, such as cups and kraters, this impermanence was less so in vessels that had a more limited use, such as funerary *lekythoi* (oil flasks), which were not handled after they had been deposited in the tomb. After mid-century, the white-ground technique was reserved almost exclusively for funerary vases of this type, some of which were even painted in full polychrome *after* the vase had been fired—naturally at an even greater cost in durability.

The example shown in FIG. 5-56 uses the conservative colors that could withstand firing. It shows Hermes handing the infant Dionysos to Papposilenos ("granddad-satyr") and the nymphs in the shady glens of Nysa, where Zeus had sent Dionysos, one of his illegitimate sons, to be raised, safe from the possible wrath of his wife, Hera. The

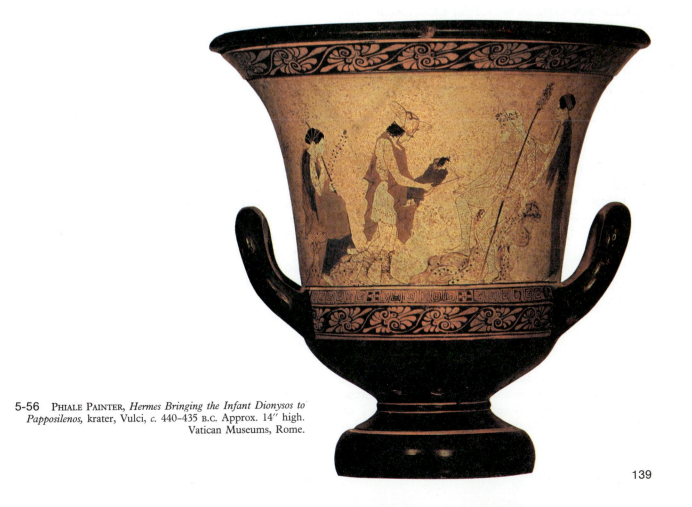

5-56 PHIALE PAINTER, *Hermes Bringing the Infant Dionysos to Papposilenos,* krater, Vulci, *c.* 440–435 B.C. Approx. 14″ high. Vatican Museums, Rome.

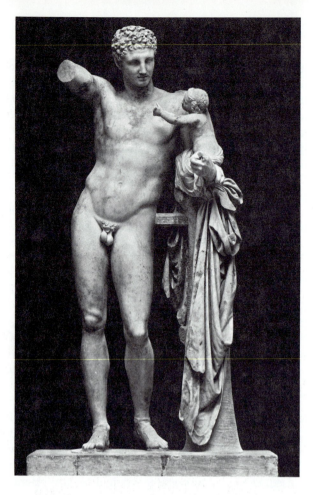

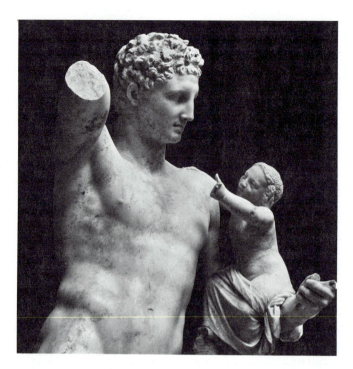

5-57 Left: PRAXITELES, *Hermes and Dionysos*, c. 340 B.C. Marble, approx. 7' high. Museum, Olympia.

5-58 Above: PRAXITELES, *Head of Hermes*, detail of FIG. 5-57.

artist has used reds, brown, purple, and a special snowy white, the last for the flesh of the nymphs and for such details as the hair, beard, and shaggy body of Papposilenos. Despite this rather limited color scheme, the painting's effect is warm and rich; in combination with the compositional devices of the Niobid Painter, it may provide a shadowy idea of the appearance of the famed Polygnotan murals, which had so impressed ancient viewers.

The grandeur of the age of Phidias and Polykleitos, when their styles briefly dominated Greek art, passed with them. What followed, though exquisite and virtuoso, constituted a descent from their heights, becoming elegant, slight, more and more naturalistic, less concerned with lofty themes and majestic forms. The statues of "godlike" men became statues of men of this world.

THE FOURTH CENTURY AND THE HELLENISTIC PERIOD

The Late Classical Period

The disastrous Peloponnesian War, which ended in 404 B.C. with the complete defeat of Athens, left Greece drained of its strength. Sparta and then Thebes took the leadership of Greece, both unsuccessfully. In the latter half

of the fourth century B.C., the Greek states lost their liberty to Philip of Macedon. Athens lost its precedence. The whole structure of life changed; the traditional balance between the city-state and the individual was lost. The serene idealism of the fifth century, born of a simple, robust concept of mind and matter, of man and the state, gave way to chronic civil wars, social and political unrest, skepticism, and cynicism.

The Apollonian command "Know thyself," which Socrates taught as he spoke with the people in their daily gathering places, inevitably changed the Greek point of view to a more individualistic one. Euripides, too, seems to regard the individual as paramount, and his dramas depict a whole spectrum of human passions and crises. Aristophanes, however, ridiculed both Socrates and Euripides for their apparent departures from the good old Classical ways and customs and especially for their emphasis upon the role and value of the individual. During the fourth century B.C. man's intellectual independence was firmly established by Plato—however much he himself regretted the passing of the old ways—whose doctrine of eternal forms such as "virtue," "justice," and "courage" could serve as the rational models upon which the individual could construct his life. Aristotle, perhaps the most versatile of all thinkers, formulated the operations of reason in the science we call logic, converting reason into an instrument applicable to all human experience. Aristotle turned his attention systematically on just about everything that could be of interest to man, and among his fundamental contributions is the outline of the sciences of nature.

Thus, gradually separating himself from the old assurances—the gods, their oracles, and time-honored custom—as prime interpreters of the meaning of life, the Greek carried on his search to know himself and to achieve knowledge of the world and life through observant experience. His dependence upon the city-state lessened, until he boasted with Diogenes: "I am a citizen of the world." Knowing the real, for whatever purpose, becomes the conspicuously Greek faculty and value. In the midst of political disaster, Greece, in the fourth century, enacted a daring drama of human discovery.

SCULPTURE

The humanizing tendency that had been gathering force throughout the fifth century achieved characteristic expression in the sculpture of the fourth century; though themes lose something of the earlier, solemn grandeur and representations of the greater gods give place to those of the lesser, the naturalistic view of the human figure is fully focused. The *Hermes and Dionysos* attributed to Praxiteles (FIGS. 5-57 and 5-58) is a work of such high quality that some authorities insist it must be by Praxiteles himself and not a mere Roman copy. The god is represented standing, with a shift in weight from the left arm (supporting the upper body) to the right leg, so that there is a double distribution of the weight, giving the pose, with its fluid axis, the form of a sinuous, shallow S-curve that becomes a manner with Praxiteles. On his arm Hermes holds the infant Dionysos, who reaches for something (probably a bunch of grapes) Hermes held in his right hand. Hermes is looking off into space with a dreamy expression, half smiling. The whole figure, particularly the head, seems in deep reverie, the god withdrawn in self-admiration. The modeling is deliberately smooth and subtle, producing soft shadows that follow the planes as they flow almost imperceptibly one into another. The delicacy of the features is enhanced by the rough, impressionistic way in which the hair is indicated, and the deep folds of the realistic drapery are sharply contrasted with the flow and gloss of the languidly graceful figure. It needs but a comparative glance at Polykleitos' *Doryphoros* to see how broad a change in artistic attitude and intent took place from the mid-fifth to the mid-fourth century. Majestic strength and rationalizing design are replaced by sensuous languor and an order of beauty appealing more to the eye than the mind. Praxiteles' esthetic of the human nude, slenderer in its proportions, with its emphasis on the exquisitely smooth modeling that reproduces the tones of resilient flesh, naturally led him to become the inventor of the nude female statue. His *Aphrodite of Cnidus* was widely regarded in antiquity as the most beautiful of all statues, the pride of Cnidus, the city that owned it. Its charm can best be understood, not from the inferior Roman copy of it, but from a much later, Hellenistic work, the *Aphrodite of Cyrene* (FIG. 5-59), which at two centuries remove conveys a Praxitelean poetry of sensual beauty. For both the male and female nude, Praxiteles set a new, more personal and naturalistic ideal of physical beauty.

Though Praxiteles' style was greatly admired, and though his theme of the bathing Aphrodite was taken up again and again long after his time, he was not the only influential sculptor in the late Classical period. A fellow Athenian, SCOPAS, is known for a robust and vigorous style more suited to the representation of action and perhaps derived from Polykleitos. A fragmentary head from Tegea in Greece (FIG. 5-60) illustrates Scopas' style and shows a hitherto undepicted tension of facial expression, the features broad and strong, the eyes large, round, and set deeply under knitted brows. As a reflection of inner states through varied facial expressions, this work breaks with the Classical tradition of benign, serene features and prefigures later Hellenistic art, when the depiction of emotion becomes more important to sculpture.

The monumental Tomb of Mausolus, another of the seven wonders of the ancient world, was built for King Mausolus and his queen, Artemisia. Mausolus was king of

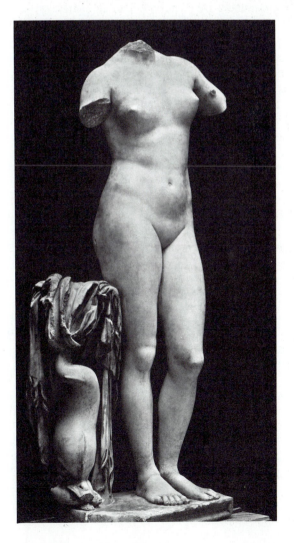

5-59 *Aphrodite of Cyrene*, North Africa, *c.* 100 B.C. Marble, approx. 56″ high. Museo Nazionale Romano, Rome.

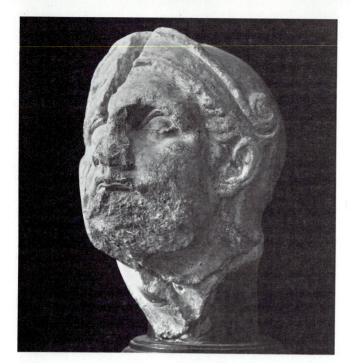

5-60 *Warrior's Head*, from the Temple of Athena Alea at Tegea, *c.* 350 B.C. Marble, approx. 11¾″ high. National Museum, Athens.

sculptor, who is unknown, is particular about the hair— curiously reminiscent of the Archaic—and the dynamics of the drapery. He continues that study of the drapery masses begun in the previous century and is at pains to read them so closely and realistically that he differentiates folds and pleats from the minute creases thin drapery would acquire in use. The colossal monument and the large figures reflect Eastern influence, and already we sense that mingling of East and West that is to compose the Hellenistic styles of the last centuries before Christ.

The most renowned sculptor of the second half of the fourth century B.C. was LYSIPPOS, court sculptor to Alexander the Great. Although Lysippos was very prolific, his work is extant in copies only, including, notably, the *Apoxyomenos* (FIG. 5-62), which represents a young athlete scraping oil and mud from his body before taking his bath. The figure embodies two important innovations of the time, which may be creditable to Lysippos. One was a new canon of proportions, replacing the Polykleitan canon and reflecting a change in taste noticeable in all the arts. The new canon required a more slender, supple, and tall figure, a conception toward which we have already seen Praxiteles moving. This innovation may indeed have been influenced by the second (also foreshadowed in earlier works)—the full realization of the figure as if moving in space, not in the two dimensions of the figures hitherto

Caria, a non-Greek state in southwest Asia Minor, and was in the service of the king of Persia. The colossal portrait-statues of the king (FIG. 5-61) and queen date from about 355 B.C. Presumably they are intended as likenesses; the

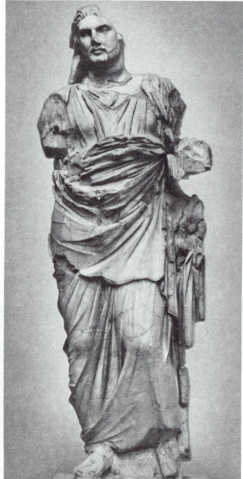

5-61 *Mausolus*, from the mausoleum at Halicarnassus, *c.* 355 B.C. Marble, approx. 9′ 10″ high. British Museum, London.

5-62 LYSIPPOS, *Apoxyomenos*, bronze original *c.* 330 B.C. Roman copy, marble, approx. 6′ 9″ high. Vatican Museums, Rome.

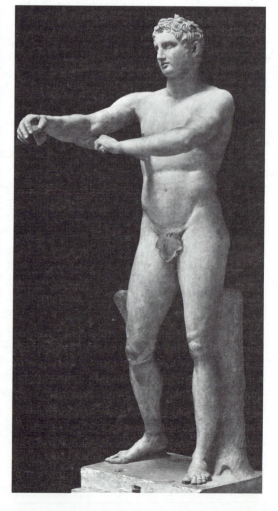

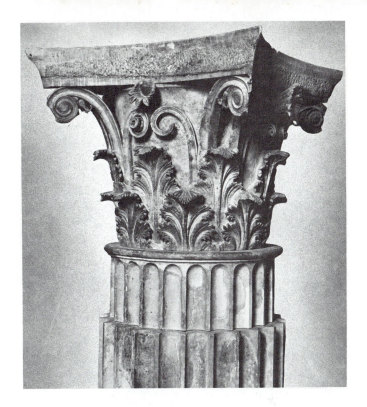

5-63 Corinthian capital from the tholos at Epidaurus, c. 350 B.C. Museum, Epidaurus.

examined (whether Phidian, Polykleitan, or Praxitelean), but in *three* dimensions. Thus, the figure now seems to move in a kind of free spiral through the space around it; it is made to be seen from a variety of angles, and it is related to things in its environment other than itself. The earliest Greek figures had been in a stiff frontal position, with the planes closely related to the stone block from which they had been carved; they were best seen from only one or two positions. Even when the figure was treated less rigidly, so that the torso as well as the arms and legs moved in a curve, it was still seen satisfactorily only from one or two points of view. In this respect an Archaic Kouros (FIG. 5-16) and the *Hermes and Dionysos* of Praxiteles (FIG. 5-57) are more nearly alike than are the *Hermes* and the *Apoxyomenos* of Lysippos. In the latter the arms curve forward, the figure enclosing space in its reach and twisting in it; the small head is thrown into stronger perspective by the large hand interposed between it and the viewer. Lysippos said that he wished to make men the way the eye sees them, allowing thus for accidents of perspective.

As Praxiteles prepared the way for developing optical realism in his subtle surface effects, so Scopas and Lysippos foreshadow Hellenistic themes (see below) demanding force, action, and dramatic emotion. Before the new drama could develop in sculpture, space had to be understood in a new way, not as merely the limit of the body, but as an environment in which the body could act freely, as in nature.

ARCHITECTURE

It is noteworthy that, in its full development of the Corinthian order, the architecture of the fourth century also produced a "body" that offered a complete aspect from any angle. The first Corinthian capital—the order differs from the Ionic only in its capital—had appeared on the inside of the naos of the Temple of Apollo at Bassae, around 450 B.C. It crowned a column that, because it stood as a divider between two parts of the naos, could be seen from all sides. Presumably it was designed for that purpose and provided a much more satisfactory solution than the Ionic capital, which is designed to be seen effectively from two sides only. For Ionic colonnades that turn corners, like those of peripteral structures, special "corner capitals" had to be designed that would look the same on the two sides facing outward. The sharply projecting edge formed by the two meeting volutes never quite satisfied Classical architects, who may also have felt that this solution was achieved only at the expense of the structural logic of the Ionic capital and by a distortion of its functional parts. The problem was solved by the Corinthian capital, which can be seen to equal advantage from all sides. Its original design has been associated with the relief sculptor and metal-worker Callimachos, who may have been at Bassae when the Temple of Apollo was built and of whom the sentimental story was told in antiquity that he was inspired to design the capital when he saw acanthus leaves growing up around a slab-weighted votive basket on the grave of a maiden. Be that as it may, though the Corinthian order appeared in the fifth century B.C., for almost a century it was used on the inside of the temple only. It is uncertain whether this is to be attributed to religious conservatism, which would tend to preserve a feature that had taken on a certain sanctity from its function at the temple's center, or whether experiments with the Ionic were continuing and a Doric tradition persisting. In any event, full emergence of the Corinthian order on a public exterior takes place about the same time as Lysippos' freeing of the sculptured figure from its two-aspect limits.

A capital from the tholos at Epidaurus (FIG. 5-63), where a ring of Corinthian columns stood inside the naos of a Doric structure, illustrates a step along the Corinthian order's elaborative route, which culminates in the characteristic Hellenistic and Roman luxuriance. Here the bell is clothed with carved acanthus leaves and manifests that same increasing attention to the deep and detailed sculpturing of stone surfaces that was noted in sculptured figures.

The monument of Lysicrates (FIG. 5-64), constructed in Athens in 334 B.C., shows the first known use of the Corinthian order on the outside of a building. Significantly, the innovation appears not on a religious but on a commemorative monument. The graceful cylinder to which the Corinthian columns are engaged memorializes the victory of a choric group whose patron was Lysicrates and which had won the prized trophy of the tripod in the wild, dithyrambic contest of song in honor of Dionysos. The

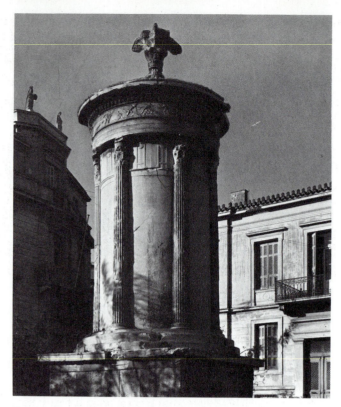

5-64 The monument of Lysicrates, Athens, 334 B.C.

little tholos serves as a base for the monumentalized tripod. Henceforth, the Corinthian order will be more and more in use on the exterior of public buildings, enjoying particular favor among Roman builders. In addition to having solved the vexing problems of both the Doric and Ionic orders—the corner-triglyph and the corner-volute dilemmas—the Corinthian order, with its ornateness, was bound to suit the developing taste for sumptuous elaboration of form and realistic representation that guided artistic effort in the Hellenistic world.

The Hellenistic Period

Philip of Macedon brought the once free Greek city-states into subjection. His son, Alexander the Great, educated in Hellenism, the culture of Greece, by none other than Aristotle, returned the visit the Persians had made to Greece a century and a half before, overthrew their empire, and conquered all the Near East, including Egypt. Greek conquest of this vast area produced a culture and period called Hellenistic, a curious mingling of Western and Eastern ideas, religions, and arts, and a long period of Greek cultural—and partly political—dominance that made her the cosmopolitan heir of Sumer, Babylon, Egypt, Assyria, and Persia. Greedy for the lands their young leader had conquered, his generals asked Alexander on his death bed, "To which one of us do you leave your empire?" In the skeptical manner of the age, but also with more than a tinge of an older irony, he is supposed to have answered, "To the strongest." Although probably apocry-

phal, this exchange points up the near inevitability of what followed—the division of Alexander's far-flung empire among his Greek generals and their subsequent naturalization among the Orientals whom they held subject.

The centers of culture in the Hellenistic period were the court cities of these Greek kings—Antioch in Syria, Alexandria in Egypt, Pergamon in Asia Minor, and others. An international culture united the Hellenistic world, and its language was Greek. Hellenistic princes became enormously rich on the spoils of the East, priding themselves on their libraries, art collections, scientific enterprises, and skills as critics and connoisseurs, as well as on the learned men they could assemble at their courts. The world of the small, austere, and heroic city-state passed away as had the power and prestige of its center, Athens, and a "world" civilization, much like today's, took its place.

SCULPTURE

The tendencies traced thus far all the way from the Archaic period are not interrupted by this change but simply go on to anticipated completions. In sculpture, the "environment" that opened up around the *Apoxyomenos* of Lysippos (FIG. 5-62) is opened still more around the *Nike of Samothrace* (FIG. 5-65). The goddess of victory is here represented as alighting upon the prow of a war galley, triumphant in some conflict among the successors of Alexander in the Greek world around 190 B.C. One of the

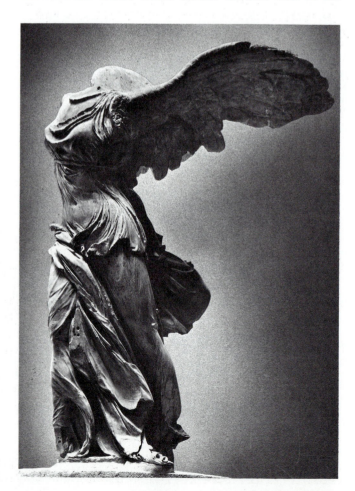

5-65 *Nike of Samothrace, c.* 190 B.C. Marble, approx. 8' high. Louvre, Paris.

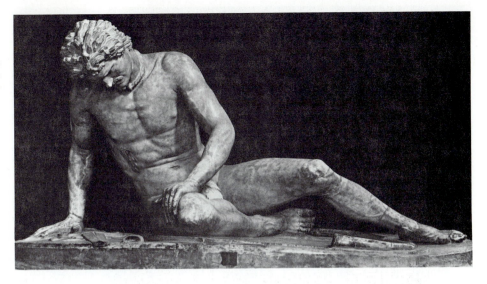

5-66 *Dying Gaul,* bronze original, Pergamon, *c.* 240 B.C. Roman copy, marble, life-size. Museo Capitolino, Rome.

masterpieces of the Hellenistic age, the *Nike,* windswept, her wings still beating, brings strength, weight, and airy grace into an equipoise one would not expect to be achieved in the hard mass of sculptured marble. But it is a fact that the sculptors are here working their stone with a freedom emulative of painters. They achieve shadows and gradations of shadows by variations of surface carving, almost as if they were using heavy as against light brush strokes. The gauzelike stretch of material across the stomach and the waves of drapery around the striding thighs and legs amount not only to an exercise in virtuosity of stonecraft but a successful effort to make stone do what poetry and painting do—that is, render at the same time the visual nuances of the moment and the ongoing essence of action. In the end, the sculptor wants us to sense, from the figure itself, an atmosphere of wind and sea. We recall the billowing sail of Exekias' *Dionysos* (FIG, 5-7), where it all seems to have begun.

The extension of the spatial environment of the figure, so as to suggest a stage upon which it may and does act, appears in sculptures associated with the Hellenistic kingdom of Pergamon and the island republic of Rhodes, from the third through the first century B.C. From a group dedicated by Attalus I of Pergamon (241–197 B.C.) there survives a figure, in Roman copy, of a *Dying Gaul* (FIG.

5-66). The figure is on stage, realistic, and also historical, since it is meant to represent a Gallic casualty in the wars Attalus had just fought with barbarian invaders. Comparison of the *Dying Gaul* and the *Fallen Warrior* from Aegina (FIG. 5-31) shows that, in a little more than two centuries, the principle of uniformity of movement has been well learned. The Gaul, dying from a chest wound that bleeds heavily, slowly loses strength, his weight falling rapidly upon his last support, the trembling right arm; its collapse will be his own. This the observer reads at once from the lines and planes of the body, visually, and with no need of interpretation or filling-out of the meaning. The statue is a triumph of realism. It may mark also the surrender of the interests of sculpture to the stage, where, we know, spectacles of human suffering painted with all realism of detail were sapping the great tradition of drama and diminishing human life in bloody scenes that could only present it as worthless. With the *Dying Gaul* the sculpture of action degenerates into brutal stagecraft. Realism can go no further, even while it triumphs.

A later school of Pergamon exhibits a realism not quite so explicit, yet nonetheless belonging to the Hellenistic taste for tableaux of monumental suffering. A section of the great frieze of the *Battle of Gods and Giants* from the Pergamon Altar of Zeus and Athena (FIGS. 5-67 and 5-68)

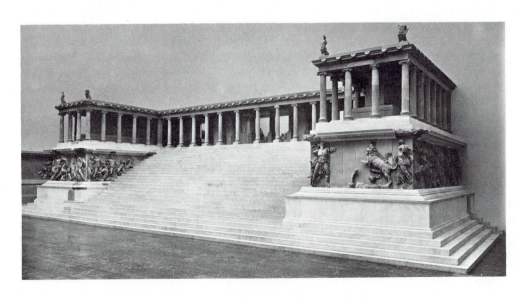

5-67 Altar of Zeus and Athena, Pergamon, *c.* 175 B.C. Staatliche Museen, Antiken-Sammlung, East Berlin. (West front restored.)

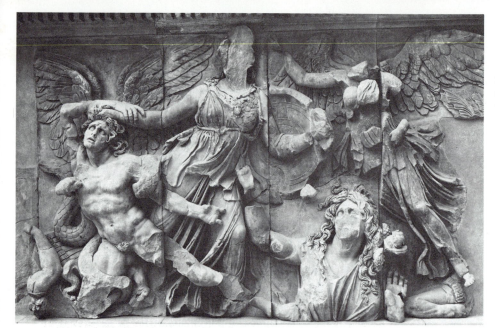

5-68 *Athena Taking Young Alcyoneus by the Hair,*
from the frieze of the Altar of Zeus and Athena.
Marble, 7½' high. Staatliche Museen,
Antiken-Sammlung, East Berlin.

illustrates the highly dramatic kind of figurative sculpture that descended from Scopas and Lysippos. The altar was erected about 175 B.C. by the son and successor of Attalus I to glorify his father's victories. In a representation less factual than the group of dying Gauls, the artists here revert to the traditional Greek approach of presenting historical events in mythological disguise. The suffering and death, the writhing gesticulation, are somewhat formalized, and we do not feel so much that we are in the presence of pain that ordinary men might feel. In the figure of Alcyoneus, the young giant whom Athena takes by the hair (FIG. 5-68), one finds the anguish of the face to be based upon Scopas and the twisting of the figure upon the athleticism of both Scopas and Lysippos. The tragic content is read through the increasingly dramatic style of stonecraft. The Greek revision of the climactic instant is still seen against a neutral background. Now, however, the background is almost obscured by shadows, from which the figures project like bursts of light. All these devices are "baroque" and closely related to those developed in seventeenth-century Europe. The unity of the design is achieved by a fluid, yet binding organization of parts—not unlike that of the figures of the three goddesses of the Parthenon (FIG. 5-43). Indeed, the two major figures of the frieze, Zeus and Athena, are directly inspired by the figures of Poseidon and Athena from the Parthenon pediments; yet this dynamic integration of the whole composition is unlike the carefully studied relationships of *separate* parts seen in the Early Classical period. In such pictorial unity, produced by the movement of light and the contrast of shade, we again recognize the strong influence of painting.

The theme of suffering is so pervasive in the Hellenistic world and its art that it could almost be understood as *the* interpretation of life by men who felt the hopelessness attendant upon the decline of an older, more reasonable system. A late work of Hellenistic sculpture is the *Laocoön* group, a product of a still quite active school of Rhodes (FIG. 5-69). It shows the Trojan priest, Laocoön, and his sons being strangled by sea serpents—some say because of his defiance of Apollo, others because he offended Poseidon (who sided with the Greeks) by warning his Trojan compatriots of the strategy of the Trojan Horse. Whatever his offense, Vergil has described his plight with unsparing realism:

> Laocoön . . . they [the sea serpents] seize and bind in mighty folds; and now, twice encircling his waist, twice winding their scaly backs around his throat, they tower above with head and lofty necks. He the while strains his hands to burst the knots, his fillets steeped in blood and

5-69 *Laocoön* group, early first century B.C. (?) Marble, 8' high. Vatican Museums, Rome. (Partially restored.)

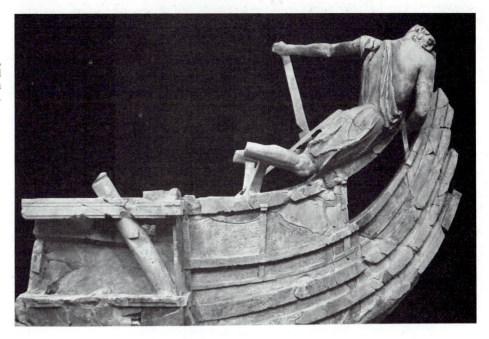

5-70 AGESANDER, ATHANADOROS, and POLYDOROS, *Odysseus' Helmsman Falling*, late second century B.C. (?) Marble, approx. life-size. Sperlonga Museum.

black venom; the while he lifts to heaven hideous cries, like the bellowings of a wounded bull that has fled from the altar and shaken from its neck the ill-aimed axe.

The spectacular torment of Laocoön and his sons is presented with all the devices of rhetorical realism available to artists as well as poets—the tortuous poses, straining muscles, and swelling veins—yet curiously there are lapses from consistent visual fact, as in the—perhaps deliberate—disproportion of the size of the sons in relation to the size of the father, indicating them as *sons*, though they appear simply as small men. The exceedingly popular group was reproduced frequently, sometimes on a colossal scale, and in the eighteenth century the analysis of it by Gotthold Lessing led to his designation of art and poetry as opposed in function and to the foundation of the branch of philosophy called esthetics.

Pliny named ATHANADOROS, AGESANDER, and POLYDOROS —three Rhodians—as the sculptors of the *Laocoön* group. The same three names are inscribed on the stern of a marble ship (FIG. 5-70) that formed part of one of several sculptured groups, fragments of which have been found in a large grotto near the sea at Sperlonga, some eighty miles south of Rome. The cave, adjacent to a large imperial Roman villa built early in the first century A.D., had been used as a kind of dining room. Multifigured sculptured groups appear to have been displayed in two niches and in a round central pool within the grotto. At least some of the sculptures must have been brought from Rhodes and were installed in the grotto around A.D. 29, when the cave was refashioned after a partial collapse.

A definitive interpretation of the scenes is most difficult, since the groups were found only in fragments, the figures evidently having been smashed to make lime or out of religious fanaticism. Three scenes from the *Odyssey* seem to have been represented: the blinding of Polyphemos (among the finds are the legs of a colossus that must have

stood nearly twenty feet high), Scylla attacking Odysseus' ship, and a sinking ship. FIGURE 5-70 shows the terrified helmsman falling from the stern of the sinking vessel. The dramatic group may have been placed—strikingly— against the dark, stalactite-covered walls of the cave. Probably the finest of the fragments is the head of Odysseus (FIG. 5-71) from another group. Less convulsed and emotional than Laocoön's head, it nevertheless reflects strikingly the horrifying situation and the fear of impending death. The effect is produced—without the use of grimaces or the exaggerated eyes and anguished mouth of Laocoön—by the wind-tossed, whirling hair and beard that frame the face of the Homeric hero. While the dating of the Sperlonga sculptures remains a matter of ardent debate, it is felt that they must be earlier than the *Laocoön*,

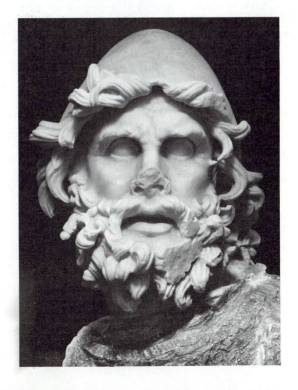

5-71 AGESANDER, ATHANADOROS, and POLYDOROS, *Head of Odysseus*, late second century B.C. (?) Marble, life-size. Sperlonga Museum.

147

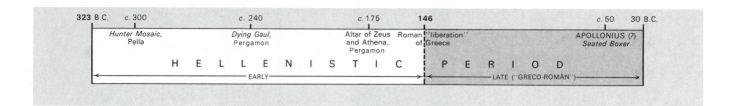

323 B.C.	c. 300		c. 240		c. 175	146		c. 50	30 B.C.

Hunter Mosaic, Pella   *Dying Gaul,* Pergamon   *Altar of Zeus and Athena,* Pergamon   Roman "liberation" of Greece   APOLLONIUS (?) *Seated Boxer*

H E L L E N I S T I C   P E R I O D

←————— EARLY —————→   ←————— LATE ("GRECO-ROMAN") —————→

as they show the expressive power of the Rhodian sculptors at its height, before it succumbed to the theatrical exhibitionism that marks the latter group.

Side by side with the drama of suffering, Hellenistic sculpture continued the tradition of ideal, Praxitelean beauty, as in the *Aphrodite of Cyrene* (FIG. 5-59) already referred to. Another Hellenistic descendant of this Praxitelean line is the *Aphrodite of Melos* (FIG. 5-72), the famed *Venus de Milo.* Here, as in the former, the ideal is taken out of the hypersensible world of reasoned proportions and made into an apparition of living flesh—like the coming alive of Pygmalion's statue of Galatea. The feeling for stone as stone has quite surrendered to the ambition of making stone look as though it were the soft, warm substance of the human body. Such effects as these can be obtained only by an artist with brilliant technical facility working in the conviction that the business of the artist is to produce from stone a vision of beauty, faithful to optical reality, yet so modified as to make the keenest appeal to the senses as a flawless manifestation of the human form.

Faithfulness to optical fact can also lead the sculptor to represent, with unflattering explicitness, the opposite of beauty, as in the *Old Market Woman* (FIG. 5-73). The bent, hobbling creature is offered to the viewer as an object of contempt, pity, or disgust, depending upon his temperament.

The disparity in subject of these two works reflects the wide scope of theme and the visual curiosity of Hellenistic sculptors. The sculptor aims to move the observer in terms of the theme of his work. He wishes, moreover, for recognition by the observer of those traits in the statue that the observer knows in life, so that a large part of the response to the statue comes from the observer's familiarity with its model or type in the context of his own experience. Thus, while the Classical sculptor generally showed young adults at the height of their physical development, the Hellenistic artist expanded his subject matter to include not only the very old but also the very young. It seems unlikely that a fifth-century B.C. sculptor would have imagined that a boy strangling a goose (FIG. 5-74) could be a subject worthy of

5-72 *Aphrodite of Melos, c.* 150–100 B.C. Marble, approx. 6′ 10″ high. Louvre, Paris.

5-73 *Old Market Woman,* second century B.C. Marble, 49½″ high. Metropolitan Museum of Art, New York (Rogers Fund).

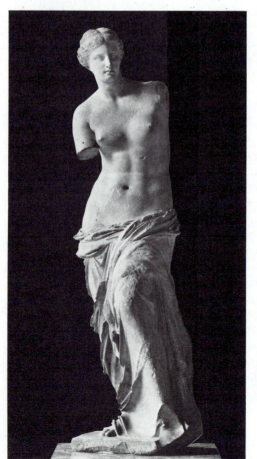

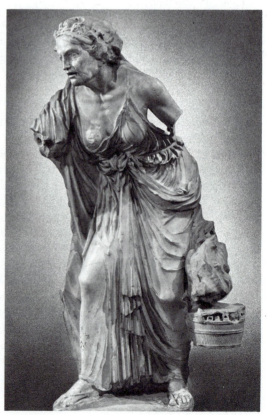

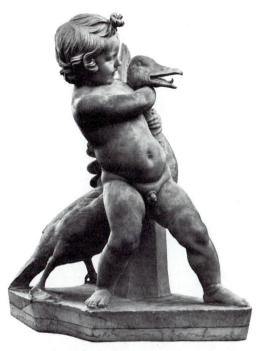

5-74 BOETHOS, *Boy Strangling a Goose*, second century B.C. Marble, approx. 33″ high. Staatliche Antikensammlungen, Munich.

representation. The sculpture may strike us as somewhat unpleasant, with its sadistic overtones, but doubtless it was intended to be "cute" and to elicit fond smiles as well as praise of the artist, BOETHOS, for his ingenuity in inventing a curious subject. And it must be admitted that Boethos has succeeded, from the formal point of view, in converting a trivial subject into a remarkably effective work of art. The swirling forms have been contained in a compact, pyramidal composition that is at once complex and unified and in which the voids, like the solids, have been carefully studied and used as functioning parts of the whole.

The *Seated Boxer* (FIG. 5-75), a very late Hellenistic work (perhaps more properly referred to as Greco-Roman, since it dates about a century after the absorption of Greece into the Roman empire), shows a heavily battered veteran of the arena resting, perhaps beaten and listening to the berating of his manager. The boxer is a man of huge physique, but his smashed face, broken nose, and deep scars tell the gist of his story. The sculptor appeals not to our intellect but to our emotions as he strives to evoke compassion for the battered hulk of a once mighty fighter. Story, realism, and human interest become the Hellenistic artist's interest at the end of the development of Greek sculpture, which thus ran, in a few centuries, a spectrum of possibilities and realizations from the *Apollo* of Olympia to a brutish boxer past his prime. This should in no sense be construed as a decline of artistic quality or a failure of spiritual force. Hellenistic art is to be appreciated within the whole history of art for its thematic variety, its virtu-

osity of technique, its power and passion in expressing the drama of human life. Its strength is felt throughout the development of Roman art, which, in many ways, is the extension of it.

ARCHITECTURE

The greater variety, complexity, and sophistication of Hellenistic culture called for an architecture on an imperial scale and of wide diversity—far beyond what the Classical city-state could ever require. Building activity shifted from the old centers on the Greek mainland to the opulent cities of the Hellenistic monarchs in Asia Minor, sites more central to the Hellenistic world. Great scale and ingenious development of interior space, the latter peculiarly a feature of Hellenistic architecture, are shown in the oracular Temple of Apollo at Didyma (the Didymaion) near Miletus, the old Ionian city on the west coast of Asia Minor (FIGS. 5-20f and 5-76). This dipteral Ionic temple is raised upon a seven-stepped base some thirteen feet above the level of the large naos, which was intentionally left open to the sky (*hypaethral*). The temple is 167 by 358 feet, the great columns over sixty-four feet high. The deep and column-filled pronaos precedes an antechamber from which oracles may have been delivered. Entrance to the temple's interior was not through this room, which has a threshold some five feet high, but through two lateral barrel-vaulted tunnels sloping down toward the inner court, which was planted with bay trees in honor of

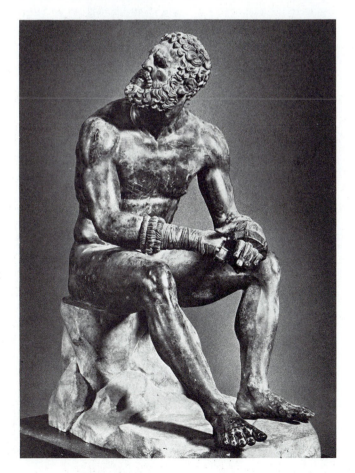

5-75 APOLLONIUS (?), *Seated Boxer*, c. 50 B.C. Bronze, approx. 50″ high. Found in Rome. Museo Nazionale Romano, Rome.

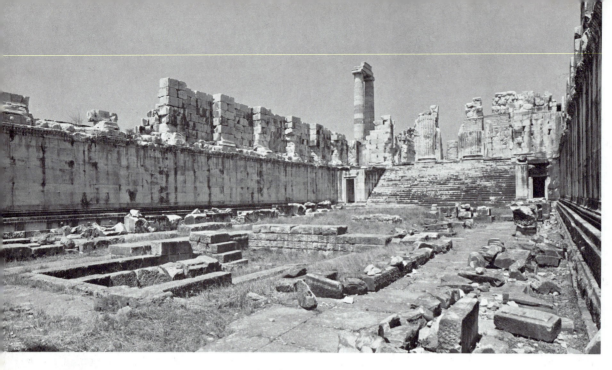

Apollo. In the back of this court stood a small prostyle shrine that protected the cult statue, the foundations of which may be seen in the illustration. On the opposite end of the court a stairway some fifty feet wide rose majestically toward three portals leading into the oracular room, which, approachable from both front and back, was the focal point of the entire design. This complex spatial planning of large interiors leads directly into later Roman practice and marks a sharp departure from Classical Greek architecture, which stressed the exterior of the building almost as a work of sculpture, and left the interior relatively undeveloped.

Another example of dexterous planning of uncovered space is the theater at Epidaurus, which Pausanias declared to be the best in Greece (FIGS. 5-77 and 5-78). Although the building (about 350 B.C.) is late Classical rather than Hellenistic, it is already highly sophisticated and has all the functioning units and formal arrangement of later theaters. The slightly more than semicircular auditorium is built into the side of a hill, and the diameter of its projected circle is 387 feet. Staircase aisles, laid out on radii projected from the center of the circular *orchestra*, where the plays were performed, separate blocks of stone benches, which themselves are separated into two tiers by a broad corridor. The orchestra, the *proscenium*, and the *skene* are arranged for maximum convenience of view of the performance and of preparations of the actors. The *parodos* (passageway between stage and seats) on each side is wide enough to permit rapid exit. This careful thinking-out of the plan for the convenience of an audience marks, as do the New Comedy plays acted at this time, increasing concern for individual views and responses.

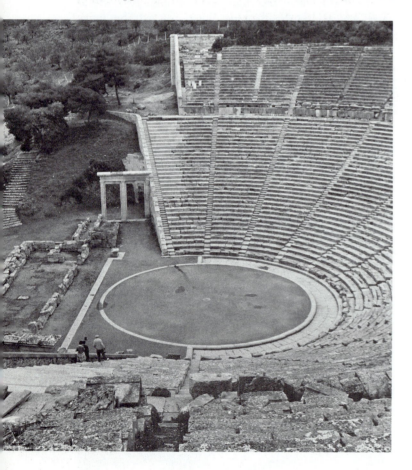

The thoughtful adaptation of space to serve human uses, rather than, as in ancient times, to honor gods and to satisfy the whims of kings, is part of Greek humanism's contribution to history. The Hellenistic Greeks also broadened their conception of architectural design to take in whole cities. The regular street patterns of the gridiron

5-77 View of the theater at Epidaurus, *c.* 350 B.C.

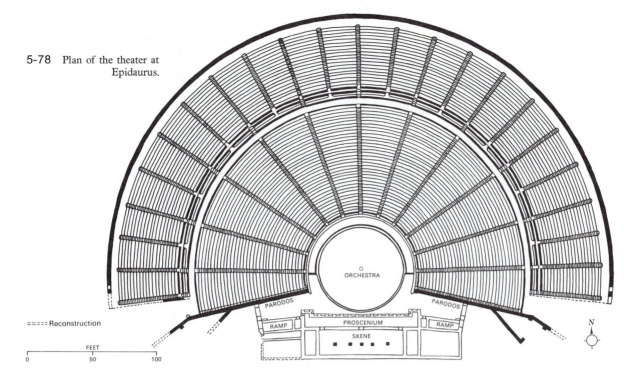

5-78 Plan of the theater at Epidaurus.

ORCHESTRA

PARODOS   PARODOS
RAMP   PROSCENIUM   RAMP
SKENE

N

===== Reconstruction

FEET
0   50   100

type, which go back to the Archaic period in Greece were systematized during the fifth century B.C. by HIPPODAMOS, a Milesian architect, whose name has been linked with the rectangular plans of Hellenistic urban foundations.[4] The Hippodamian scheme, as illustrated by Priene (FIG. 5-79), consists of a close-meshed network of streets that intersect at right angles, without any particular axial emphasis that might suggest dominant traffic patterns. Here the plan has

[4]Knowledge of ancient urbanism is rather scanty, since archeologists generally prefer to investigate limited sites, and it is rarely economically feasible for them to uncover and trace miles of city streets. The fragmentary evidence shows, however, that cities with regular, usually rectangular street plans existed in both ancient Egypt and Mesopotamia.

been superimposed upon an irregular, sloping site without regard to the nature of the terrain. Only the defensive walls on the city's perimeter closely follow the topographical contours, with the result that walls and street plan are unrelated. On the other hand, the system is neat and orderly and, by making few distinctions of either a social or economic nature, essentially democratic.

The major ordering principles of so-called Hippodamian plans were the rectangle and relationships among rectangles. The agora was centrally located and thus easily accessible to all citizens. It was partially surrounded by long, roofed, colonnaded stoas which housed markets and offices and were the architectural expression of the public

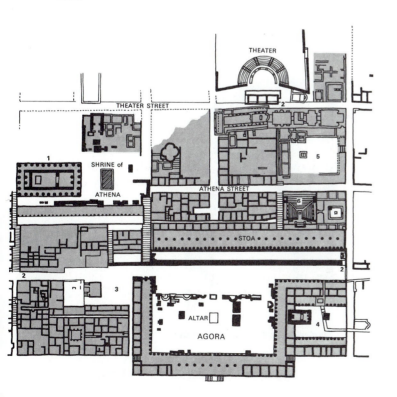

THEATER
THEATER STREET
SHRINE of ATHENA
1
ATHENA STREET
2
5
6
STOA
3
ALTAR
AGORA
4
2

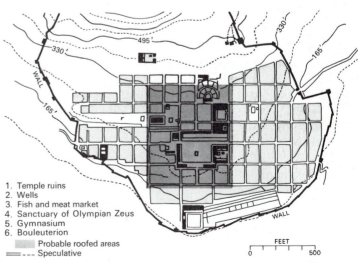

1. Temple ruins
2. Wells
3. Fish and meat market
4. Sanctuary of Olympian Zeus
5. Gymnasium
6. Bouleuterion

Probable roofed areas
---- Speculative

WALL
330
495
165
330
165
WALL

FEET
0   500

5-79 Priene, fourth century B.C. Above: Simplified ground plan. Darker-toned rectangle indicates area shown in detail at left.

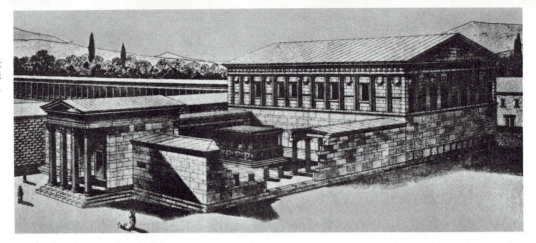

5-80 Bouleuterion at Miletus, late third century B.C.

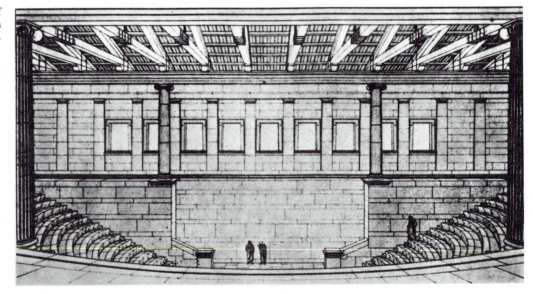

5-81 Reconstruction of council chamber in bouleuterion at Miletus.

life of the city. Here its business and politics, its administration and its gossip went on, and it is from the fact that they taught their rational moral discipline in a stoa that the philosophy of the Stoics takes its name.

As important as the stoa for the life of the civic organism (and forming part of the agora) was the *bouleuterion*. As meeting place of the city council, it required a large roofed and enclosed space in which lines of sight were uninterrupted and acoustics were good. Efforts to fulfill these requirements came to fruition in the late third century B.C. in a new building type, an impressive example of which is the bouleuterion of Miletus (FIGS. 5-80 and 5-81). Here the architectural problems were solved by incorporating a curved, theater-like auditorium of steeply rising tiers of seats into a rectilinear masonry shell with a timber roof supported by four columns ingeniously placed so as not to obstruct the audience's view of the rostrum.

It is at this point in the history of architecture that we can speak of domestic building as such and discover the look of a human dwelling capable of being called a house (FIG. 5-82). Typically, the lot on which the Hellenistic house stood was enclosed by a wall to shut out the dirt and noise of the narrow street. A single door opened into an

office, or service quarters, from which a covered passage led to the main unit through a courtyard into which opened roofed chambers. Wealthier residents had, in addition to the forecourt (similar to the Roman *atrium*) a colonnaded garden, the *peristyle*.

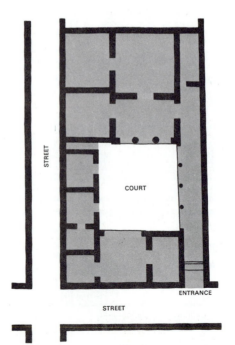

5-82 Plan of House XXXIII, Priene. (Partially restored.)

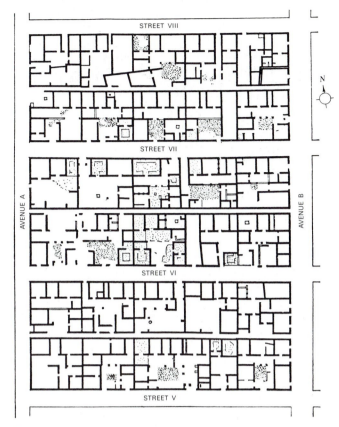

5-83   Plan of residential blocks at Olynthos, late fifth century B.C.

The residential requirements of ordinary people without means were recognized and occasionally satisfied in Classical and Hellenistic Greece with planned housing projects. Such a development was one built in a suburb of Olynthos in the late fifth century B.C. Here groups of ten houses were arranged in rectangular blocks of about 300 by 120 feet, neatly fitted together in a Hippodamian grid pattern (FIG. 5-83). Though the individual houses varied in plan, one feature common to all was a spacious central courtyard with verandahs. Residential grouping of this sort may look forward to the Roman *insula*, an even more integrated scheme not unlike that of a modern apartment house (p. 186). On a small scale the Priene and Olynthos houses reflect the general interest in designing convenient interior spaces, as well as the growing concern for utility and convenience in the daily life of the ordinary individual.

Priene was a provincial town, and its houses were relatively unpretentious. It was in the capitals of the Hellenistic kingdoms—at Alexandria in Egypt, Pergamon in Asia Minor, and Pella in Macedonia—that life unfolded its richest and most sumptuous aspects. Here the kings and their retainers surrounded themselves with luxury that became proverbial, and their way of life set a standard that was to be surpassed only by the Roman emperors in later antiquity.

The great urbanized citadel of the Attalid kings at Pergamon was a wonder of the ancient world and, even in its present ruined state, still commands our admiration. Beau-

tifully accommodated to its dramatic, mountainous site, the city proper was linked with the acropolis, some 800 feet above it, by an agora, a gymnasium, and the Sanctuary of Demeter, which were sited on intermediate levels. On the acropolis stood the fortress-palace of the rulers and, grouped around a theater, the temples and sanctuaries like the Altar of Zeus and Athena noted above (FIGS. 5-67 and 5-68). It was here that Pergamon achieved its greatest splendor in a most sophisticated and dynamic grouping of architectural masses (FIGS. 5-84 and 5-85). The deployment of the structures for maximum visibility along flexible axes is a free departure from the symmetric regularity of the Hippodamian scheme and must have produced, at a distance, a faceted effect like that of a great gem, reflecting in its brilliance the wealth and power of the Pergamene dynasty. We have already seen the sculptural celebration of Pergamon's victories over the Gauls, and it is noteworthy that the Attalid kings were known in Hellenistic times as patrons of culture and art quite as much as for their statecraft and their prowess in war.

MOSAICS

Among the most lasting symbols of Hellenistic luxury were the floor mosaics with which the wealthy residents of these court cities embellished their houses. Mosaic as an art form had a rather prosaic and utilitarian beginning. (The Sumerian custom of covering walls with baked clay cones and the technique of shell inlay, as found in the *Standard of Ur,* FIG. 2-14, were not long-lived.) In the Mediterranean region the mosaic technique seems to have been invented primarily for the purpose of developing a flooring that was both inexpensive and durable. Originally, small pebbles collected from beaches and riverbanks were set into a thick coat of cement. It was soon discovered, however, that the stones could be arranged in decorative

5-84   Model of the acropolis, Pergamon. Staatliche Museen, Antiken-Sammlung, East Berlin.

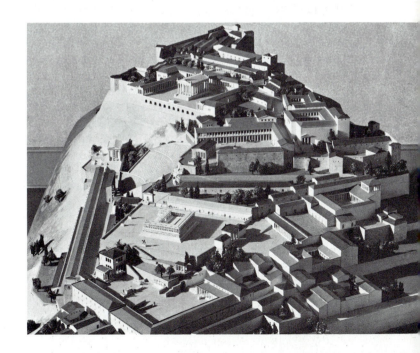

5-85 Plan of the acropolis, Pergamon.

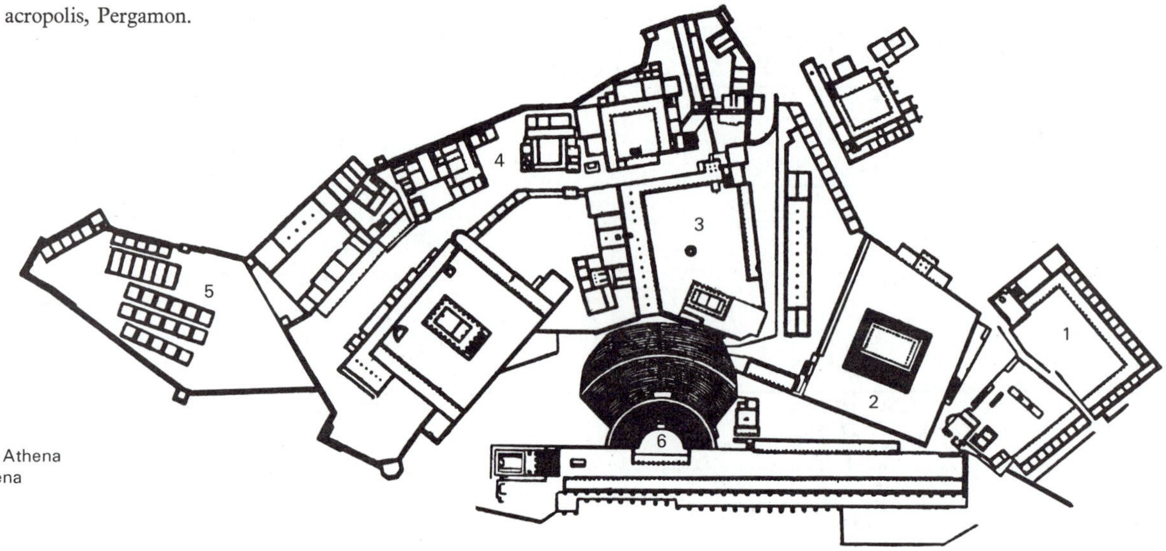

1. Upper agora
2. Altar of Zeus and Athena
3. Sanctuary of Athena
4. Palaces
5. Arsenal
6. Theater

patterns. At first these were quite simple and confined to geometric shapes; examples of this type that date back to the eighth century B.C. have been found at Gordium in Asia Minor. Eventually the stones were arranged to form more complex pictorial designs, and by the fourth century B.C. the technique had been developed to the point where mythological subjects could be represented on a large scale and with a rich variety of colors.

The most famous of these fourth-century pebble mosaics were found at Olynthos, which was destroyed by Philip of Macedon in 348 B.C., and at Pella, the Macedonian capital under King Archelaus around 400 B.C. Although almost forgotten until the late 1950s (excavations there were begun in 1957), it was at Pella that Alexander was born, that Aristotle taught, and that Euripides died. Under Alexander, Pella became virtually the capital of the world, as he ruled his vast empire from there. Although little has been preserved of the buildings' superstructures, furniture, or other works of art, the uncovered floor mosaics give ample evidence of the luxury and beauty of Pella's houses. A detail from one of several well-preserved pebble mosaics shows an almost life-sized figure from a scene representing a lion hunt (FIG. 5-86). The stones that have been arranged to form the picture are neither hewn nor shaped but natural pebbles. A variety of colors has been used to produce a polychrome effect, but the chief pictorial impact is derived from a strong dark and light contrast. Some outlines and interior markings are defined with thin strips of lead, a refinement that increases the clarity of the design but which was to enjoy no lasting favor.

Because they were cheap and durable, pebble mosaics remained popular through Roman times; in fact, they are still used for decorative pavements in Mediterranean countries. However, the desire for ever greater pictorial realism led to the simple but revolutionary practice of cutting stones to desired shapes so they could be fitted together more closely. At first these shaped stones, or *tesserae*, which permitted more precise description of detail, were used together with pebbles in limited areas that were felt to require greater definition. Perhaps originating in Hellenistic Sicily, "true" mosaics, composed entirely of cut stones, were designed at Pergamon and Delos by the second century B.C., and the technique had been perfected to include colored glass (*smalto*) for strong colors, such as pure blue, red, and green, that are rarely found in natural materials. One of the most durable of the artistic media, mosaic was highly refined and popular in Roman times and became one of the chief vehicles for pictorial expression of early Christian and Byzantine artists.

While Alexander and his successors were Hellenizing the East, a power was rising in the western Mediterranean that in its own way would, like Greece, greatly determine the history of Europe and the Europeanized world. In one fateful year, 146 B.C., that power—Rome—sacked the Greek city of Corinth and destroyed an old enemy, Carthage, absorbing the small Greek states into the Roman province of Achaia and constructing around the ruins of Carthage the province of Africa. Thus, in a double stroke, Rome took under its aegis the culture of Greece and brought to an end in the Mediterranean West the ancient Near Eastern civilization that had continued to flourish in the old Phoenician sea-empire. Although this constituted another step in the Westernizing of the ancient world, it did not mean a blocking of the channels of commercial and intellectual intercourse with the East. For what Rome adopted from Greece it passed on to the Medieval and modern worlds in a form much transformed by the Oriental message of Christianity. If Greece is peculiarly the inventor of the European spirit, Rome is its propagator and amplifier.

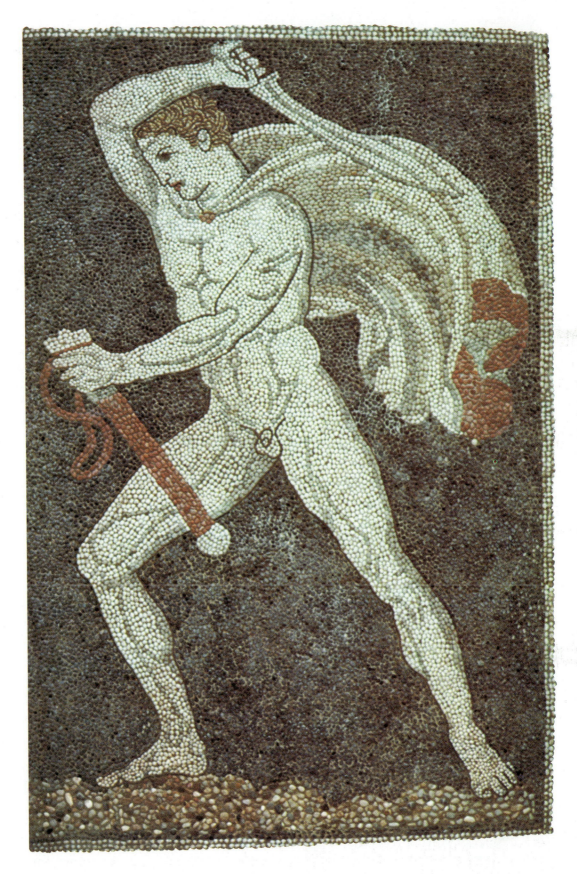

5-86 *Hunter,* detail of the *Lion Hunt* mosaic, Pella, *c.* 300 B.C.
Pebble mosaic, approx. 66″ high.

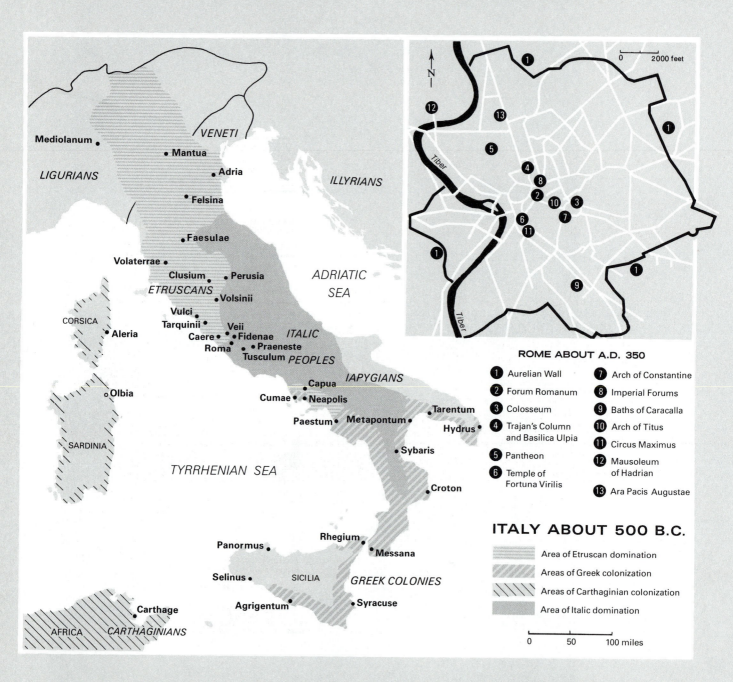

ROME ABOUT A.D. 350

①	Aurelian Wall	⑦	Arch of Constantine
②	Forum Romanum	⑧	Imperial Forums
③	Colosseum	⑨	Baths of Caracalla
④	Trajan's Column and Basilica Ulpia	⑩	Arch of Titus
⑤	Pantheon	⑪	Circus Maximus
⑥	Temple of Fortuna Virilis	⑫	Mausoleum of Hadrian
		⑬	Ara Pacis Augustae

ITALY ABOUT 500 B.C.

Area of Etruscan domination
Areas of Greek colonization
Areas of Carthaginian colonization
Area of Italic domination

0   50   100 miles

chapter six

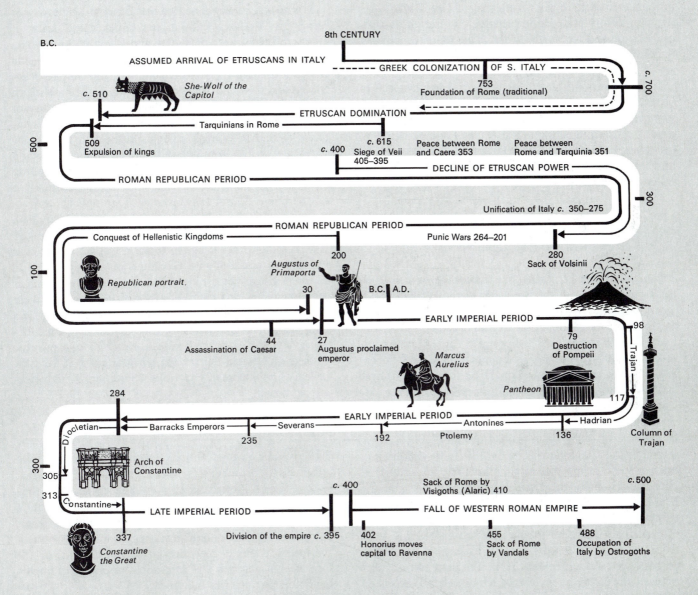

B.C.

8th CENTURY

ASSUMED ARRIVAL OF ETRUSCANS IN ITALY

‑‑‑‑‑ GREEK COLONIZATION OF S. ITALY ‑‑‑‑‑

753
Foundation of Rome (traditional)

c. 700

c. 510
She-Wolf of the Capitol

ETRUSCAN DOMINATION

Tarquinians in Rome

500

509
Expulsion of kings

c. 400

c. 615
Siege of Veii
405–395

Peace between Rome and Caere 353

Peace between Rome and Tarquinia 351

ROMAN REPUBLICAN PERIOD

DECLINE OF ETRUSCAN POWER

300

Unification of Italy c. 350–275

ROMAN REPUBLICAN PERIOD

Conquest of Hellenistic Kingdoms

Punic Wars 264–201

280
Sack of Volsinii

100

Republican portrait.

Augustus of Primaporta

200

30

B.C. A.D.

44
Assassination of Caesar

27
Augustus proclaimed emperor

EARLY IMPERIAL PERIOD

79
Destruction of Pompeii

98

Trajan

Marcus Aurelius

Pantheon

117

284

EARLY IMPERIAL PERIOD

Column of Trajan

Diocletian

Barracks Emperors

Severans

Antonines

Hadrian

235

192

Ptolemy

136

300

305

Arch of Constantine

313

Constantine

LATE IMPERIAL PERIOD

c. 400

Sack of Rome by Visigoths (Alaric) 410

FALL OF WESTERN ROMAN EMPIRE

c. 500

337
Constantine the Great

Division of the empire c. 395

402
Honorius moves capital to Ravenna

455
Sack of Rome by Vandals

488
Occupation of Italy by Ostrogoths

Etruscan and Roman Art

THE PEOPLE of Italy, while touched at an early date by the radiance of Greece, had deep and tenacious qualities of their own. Etruscan (or Etrurian) and Roman art, like any other, must be recognized as a synthesis of influences from outside sources and of elements indigenous to the country. Roman art, the immediate heir of all earlier Mediterranean cultures, was in many ways a synthesis of the arts of antiquity, in a manner quite distinct from that of Greek art. Rome was also deeply involved in bringing civilization to western Europe and to North Africa. The art of Rome was, therefore, in later times often regarded as the symbol of the art of antiquity.

In terms of political development, the early histories of Greece and Italy are roughly parallel, but the vigorous advance in Greece after the Persian Wars of the fifth century B.C., culminating in the Age of Pericles, found no counterpart in Italy, where culture was retarded by the bitter struggles among competing Italic peoples and between them and the Etruscans.

THE ETRUSCANS

The origin of the Etruscans, like that of the Mycenaeans, has long been one of the mysteries of the ancient world. Their language, though written in a Greek-derived script and extant in inscriptions that are still obscure, is unrelated to the Indo-European linguistic family. Ancient historians, as fascinated by the puzzle as are modern scholars, generally felt that the Etruscans emigrated from Asia Minor, and Herodotus, the "father of history," specifically declares that they came from Lydia. This tradition has persisted, and since the Etruscan culture emerges as distinct from those of other Italic peoples around 700 B.C., their arrival in Italy has long been put at the eighth century B.C. Such a view seems too simple, however, and does not explain adequately the evident connections between the Etruscan and earlier Italic cultures. Some modern scholars feel that the Etruscans are the direct descendants of very old pre-Indo-European people who had moved into Italy from the north. But this theory, in turn, cannot fully account for certain elements of the Etruscan culture, particularly the elaborate burial cult, which seems to be linked with Oriental customs.

A compromise theory points out that Herodotus gives no dates and that the migration he refers to could well have occurred during the period of the great Mediterranean shake-up and shifting of peoples that occurred around 1200 B.C. and caused the collapse of the Mycenaean civilization. At that time, immigrants from Asia Minor could have settled in Italy, mingled with the native population, and produced the culture of the so-called Villanovans, who, in turn, may have been the direct predecessors of the

Etruscans. The changes that produced the Etruscan culture proper would then have to be explained in terms of increasing exposure to foreign influences—first Oriental and then Greek—brought about by expanding commerce and trade. In this connection it is noteworthy that the Etruscans enjoyed high repute as skilled seafarers (or disrepute as pirates) in antiquity and that they emerged into the light of history during the so-called Orientalizing period.

It is now generally conceded that Etruscan art developed largely as a consequence of the Greek colonization of southern Italy during the eighth and seventh centuries B.C. Although responsible for halting further Greek expansion northward along the Tyrrhenian coast, and despite deep-rooted distrust and antagonism toward their southern neighbors, the Etruscans—without relinquishing any of their native characteristics—eagerly absorbed Greek influences. Using the Greek colonial cities as a model, the Etruscans shifted from village life to an urban civilization and established themselves in strongly fortified hilltop cities. By the sixth century B.C. they controlled most of northern and central Italy from such strongholds as Tarquinii (modern Tarquinia), Caere (modern Cerveteri), Veii, Perusia (modern Perugia), and Volsinii (modern Orvieto). But these cities never united to form a state, and so it is improper to speak of an Etruscan nation or kingdom. The cities coexisted, flourishing or fading independently and at different times, and any semblance of unity among them was based primarily upon common linguistic ties and religious beliefs and practices. This lack of political cohesion eventually made the Etruscans relatively easy prey for Roman aggression. During the ten-year siege of Veii, for instance, no Etruscan city came to the aid of its beleaguered cousin.

Architecture

Little is known of Etruscan architecture. Their cities were either razed or rebuilt by the Romans, and those that survived were located on sites so well chosen that they continue to be inhabited to this day, making excavation impossible. Scattered remnants suggest that the Etruscans, at least during their later history, made considerable use of the masonry arch, a structural device not favored by the Greeks[1] but one that was to become of profound importance for later Roman building.

The early Etruscan house is known to us chiefly through clay models that served as cinerary urns, and from tomb chambers in which domestic interiors were re-created. To judge from the interior of the fifth-century B.C. Tomb of the Reliefs (FIG. 6-3), an originally simple rectangular structure with sloping roof grew progressively more elaborate, reaching its climactic development in the *atrium*

---

[1]However, a masonry vaulted corridor from 320 B.C. was recently excavated at Nemea.

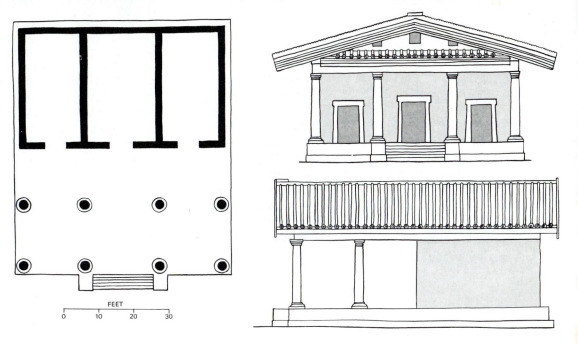

6-1 Plan and elevations of an Etruscan temple. (After Vitruvius.)

FEET
0   10   20   30

houses of Pompeii and Herculaneum. Invention showed itself in the development of the atrium, a high, square or rectangular central hall that was lighted through a large opening in the roof and around which the other rooms were symmetrically arranged. This atrium was the focus of family life and the shrine for the *lares* and *penates,* the household gods. The ancient sacred hearth of Mediterranean family religion found an appropriate achitectural expression in the noble atrium, which gave to Italic domestic architecture an importance and dignity beyond that developed by the Greeks.

Our knowledge of the Etruscan temple is based upon a few preserved foundations and a description given by the ancient Roman authority on architecture, Vitruvius (FIG. 6-1). It may very possibly have had its origins in Greece. Its plan, for example, closely resembles the Greek prostyle plan (FIG. 5-19b). Yet the Etruscan adaptation, in typical fashion, developed its own characteristics. Resting on a high base (*podium*) with steps at one end only, it was constructed mostly of wood and sun-dried brick in a post-and-lintel system and had a heavy wooden superstructure richly decorated with brightly painted terra-cotta reliefs. The Etruscan emphasis on a highly ornate façade, with relatively spare treatment of the sides and rear, concentrated attention upon the entrance porch. There was an axial organization quite different from that of the Greek temple. Behind the sunlit pavilion of the porch, the shrine, divided into three cellae of equal size, formed dark cavelike spaces. The temple was not meant to be seen as a sculptural mass from the outside and from all directions, like the Greek temple, but was intended instead to function primarily as an interior space. It was a place of shelter, protected by the wide overhang of its roof.

It is in the remains of their elaborate burial grounds that the Etruscans reveal themselves with the greatest clarity. In a rich array of wall paintings and painted reliefs with which they decorated the interiors of their tombs, they recount their zestful lives, their banquets, and their dances, which, in their suppleness and verve, seem partly Ionian and partly barbarian. They tell us both of their athletic contests and of their wars. Their rise and fall from power is reflected in a gradual change from optimism to pessimism and in the choice of ever more morbid and bloodthirsty subjects as their political fortunes declined. Although the Etruscans' reputation for cruel and unrestrained behavior is based largely upon the testimony of the ancient Greeks and Romans, who were their enemies, elements in their tomb paintings indicate that their society had many aspects that were in fact violent and extravagant. Indeed, these qualities may have played a decisive role in the formation of an energetic and creative culture that was to contribute to the rise to world rulership of their Roman successors.

The Etruscans built their cemeteries at some distance from their cities. Hundreds of tombs arranged in orderly manner along a network of streets produce the effect of veritable cities of the dead (*necropolises*). The tombs varied according to region and local custom. In the northern part of Etruria they were usually constructed above ground, while in the south they were often excavated from the live rock, particularly in areas where tufa soil facilitated digging. Tufa, primarily strongly compressed volcanic ash, is easily excavated and hardens to a concretelike consistency on exposure to the atmosphere. Tufa can also be cut into durable building blocks that require no firing; it was used extensively by the Etruscans and Romans, and a minor tufa brick industry flourishes in Italy today.

A characteristic Etruscan tomb type is the *tumulus,* a round structure that has been partially excavated and covered with earth (FIG. 6-2). This form was favored in Cerveteri and, in view of its domical shape, seems to carry on an ancient Mediterranean tradition. The majority of

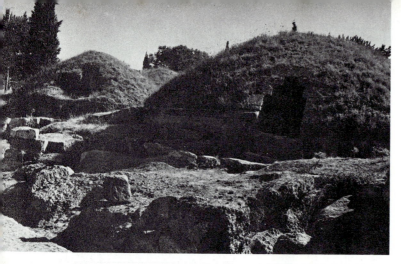

6-2   Necropolis at Caere (Cerveteri), fifth to fourth centuries B.C.

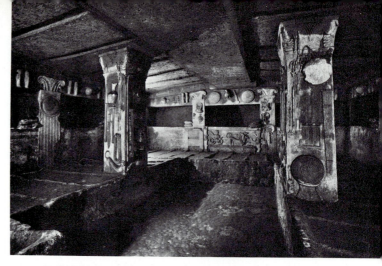

6-3   Tomb of the Reliefs, Caere (Cerveteri), fifth to fourth centuries B.C.

Etruscan tomb interiors, however, including those of the tumuli, are rectangular and reproduce the rooms of domestic architecture. A striking example is the Tomb of the Reliefs (FIG. 6-3), a large underground chamber in Cerveteri, in which massive piers with pseudo-Ionic (Aeolic) capitals support a slanting beamed ceiling. The piers are *reserved*—that is, formed by cutting away the live tufa until the remaining rock has the shape of a column, as in the Egyptian rock-cut tombs at Beni Hasan (FIG. 3-16). This, like most Etruscan tombs, was designed for multiple burials, the final resting place of an entire family and its servants. Sarcophagi, cinerary urns, and other tomb furnishings were placed in niches and on the benchlike pro-

jection at the base of the walls. Decoration in the Tomb of the Reliefs consists of painted plaster reliefs representing weapons, tools, and kitchen utensils, and displays a generous inventory of Etruscan objects of daily use.

Painting

Unlike the Caerans, the Tarquinians adorned the walls of their subterranean tomb chambers with colorful and lively murals. Although the subjects of tomb painting in Etruria are sometimes drawn from Greek legend, they are more often concerned with scenes of banquet and revel, as in the Tomb of the Leopards in Tarquinia (FIG. 6-4). This small

6-4   *Revelers,* detail of a wall painting from the Tomb of the Leopards, Tarquinia, *c.* 470 B.C. Approx. 42″ × 76″.

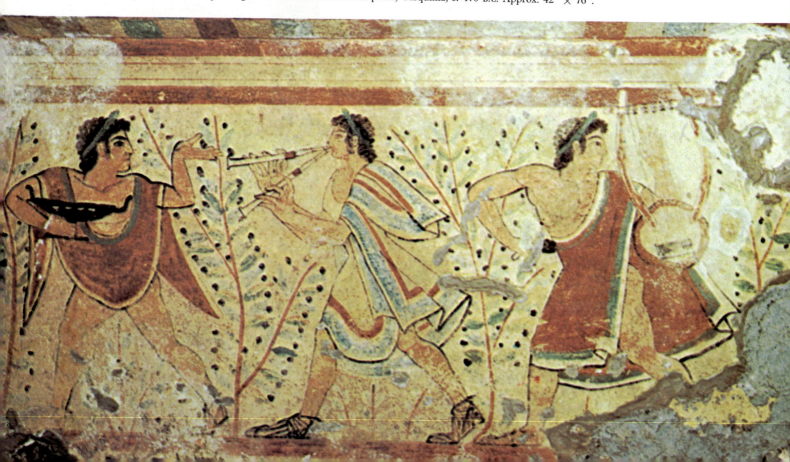

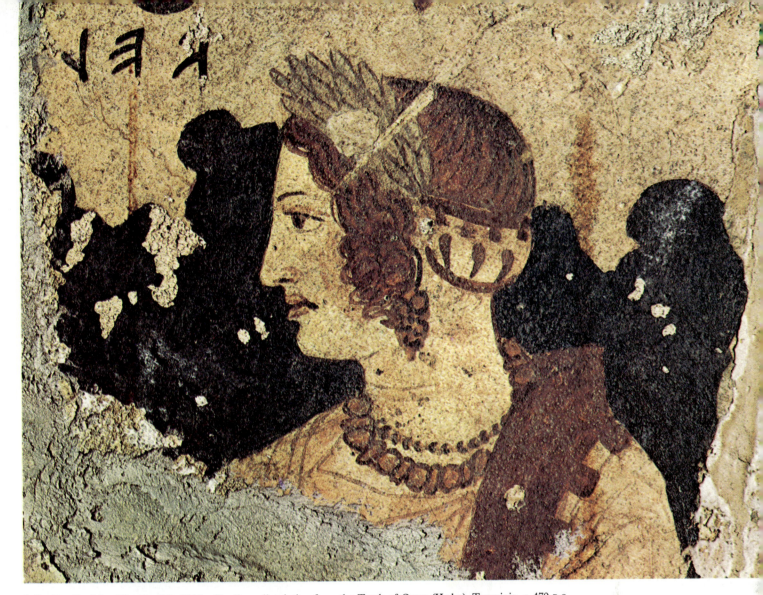

6-5   Detail of the *Woman of the Velcha Family,* wall painting from the Tomb of Orcus (Hades), Tarquinia, *c.* 470 B.C.

chamber tomb is decorated in the manner favored in Tarquinia during the fifth century B.C.: a banquet scene on the wall opposite the entrance and groups of dancers and musicians on the side walls. These wonderfully vital pictures express especially well the peculiarly life-affirming exuberance that fills Etruscan art as it must have filled Etruscan existence. Three young men, one clad only in a light scarf, the other two in the elegant *chlamys* (cloak), seem to be hurrying through a grove of graceful little laurel trees, the leader carrying a cup of wine and beckoning, the others playing the double flute and the seven-stringed lyre. They seem already to be dancing, facing rhythmically in opposite directions as if performing some circling step. The gestures have a kind of choreographic exaggeration, especially those of the enlarged hands and fingers of the flutist, which hold and touch the instrument with such sureness and delicacy. It is rare in the painting of the ancient world that spirited movement is portrayed so convincingly, and it would be difficult to find from that

time so fitting a monument to the beauty of youth, springtime, music, and the dance. The picture is a kind of fresco painting on a thin slip applied to the living rock wall or on a stucco paste made from the rock. The color—blacks, blues, blue-greens, and ocher-reds—still retain much of their original freshness and harmonize easily and naturally with the creamy yellow ground.

But the later Etruscans seem to have surrendered their native, joyous vigor for a quiet, classicizing formalism like that in the *Woman of the Velcha Family,* from a chamber in the Tomb of Orcus (Hades) in Tarquinia (FIG. 6-5). The composed, even reflective, expression of this splendidly painted head suits the somber theme that is its context— the sufferings of the dead in Hades in the midst of the menacing demons of the underworld. The earlier Etruscan euphoria has disappeared, extinguished by the more cosmopolitan religions of the Hellenistic world, which stressed not the last happiness of the funeral revels but the sadness of man's fate.

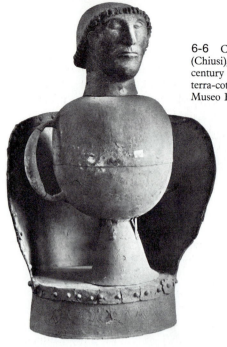

6-6 Canopic urn from Clusium (Chiusi), second half of the seventh century B.C. Hammered bronze with terra-cotta head, approx. 33″ high. Museo Etrusco, Chiusi.

Sculpture

The Etruscan tombs yield a notable furniture of sculptured objects in both clay and bronze, materials that the Etruscans apparently preferred, though numerous stone sarcophagi survive. The forms are modeled rather than carved, modeling being a technique that would be congenial to the impetuous temperament and fluid style characteristic of the Etruscans. Funerary urns and sarcophagi with recumbent portrait figures present some of the best examples of Etruscan sculpture. A canopic (cinerary) urn (FIG. 6-6) from Clusium (modern Chiusi) has a terra-cotta head as a lid, the whole set in a bronze model of a chair; the head is obviously intended as a portrait likeness of the deceased whose ashes are here contained. The strongly rounded form of the urn has a crude vitality that is carried into the head, with its blunt, aggressive features and massive neck. The accent upon the individuality of the deceased is specifically Etruscan and is seen to fullest advantage in the reclining effigies of a man and his wife on the lid of a sarcophagus from Cerveteri (FIG. 6-7). The work is a kind of throwing into three dimensions and a formalizing of the animated banquet scenes painted on Etruscan tomb walls to satisfy the demands of some cult ritual of the dead, the details of which are unknown. But there is nothing here of the solemn or the macabre, and the Etruscan instinct for the lifelike is preserved. The figures shown are relaxed and genial—much in contrast with the funerary formality of Egyptian statues—and the Archaic features of style, though present, produce no stiffness or awkwardness.

The *Apollo* from Veii (FIG. 6-8), an acroterion figure from the ridgepole of an Etruscan temple, is evidence that, like the Greeks, the Etruscans made use of architectural sculpture. But the Greek Archaic elements, though immediately evident, are superficial; the awkward, lurching vigor of the powerful figure is a forceful example of Etrus-

6-8 *Apollo* from Veii, *c.* 510 B.C. Terra-cotta, approx. 70″ high. Museo Nazionale di Villa Giulia, Rome.

6-7 Sarcophagus from Caere (Cerveteri), *c.* 520 B.C. Terra-cotta, approx. 6′ 7″ long. Museo Nazionale di Villa Giulia, Rome.

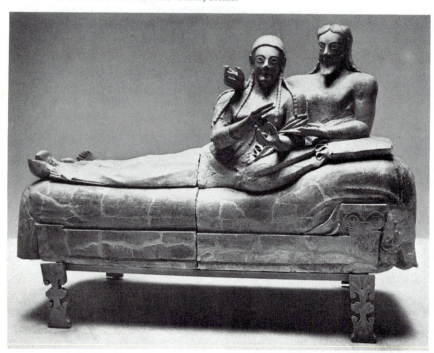

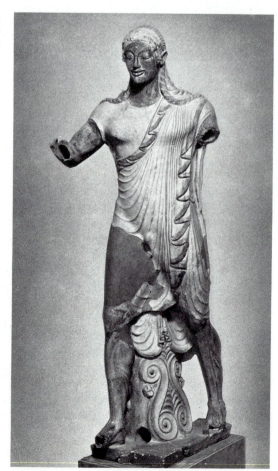

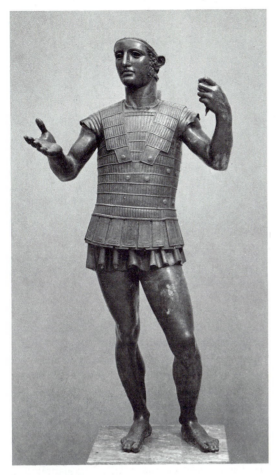

6-9 *Mars* from Todi, early fourth century B.C. Bronze, approx. 56″ high. Vatican Museums, Rome.

ponent in Etruscan art, but the animal force, the huge, swelling contours, and the plunging motion are anything but Ionian and little enough mainland Greek. The *Apollo* from Veii, given its architectural function, naturally differs from the painted Etruscan forms we have seen; yet it has in common with them the peculiarly Etruscan strength, energy, and excitement.

The absorption of Greek influences by the Etruscans continued during the height of the latter's power—when they were sending their own art commodities throughout the Mediterranean, including Greece—and through the centuries of their decline. The so-called *Mars* from Todi exemplifies Etruscan interpretation of the Greek Classical style (FIG. 6-9) in the beginning of the fourth century B.C. The figure, dressed in more or less contemporary military garb, executes a peculiar movement of the whole body, involving sideways and contrary directions of head, torso, arms, and legs, without seeming to move from his position. The sculptor may have been exaggerating the Polykleitan weight-shift stance, but there is a kind of agility to it, quite unlike the balanced weight-and-poise of the Polykleitan type. We find again, as in the much earlier *Apollo* from Veii, that an Etruscan interpretation of prevailing Greek style brings out the native quality of energy, whether in the blunt drive of the *Apollo* or in the almost sprightly stance of the *Mars*.

One of the most famous animals in the history of world art, the *She-Wolf of the Capitol* (FIG. 6-10), owes her fame not simply to her antiquity and her magnificence as a work of art, but to the fact that for centuries she has been the totem of the city of Rome. Ancient legend tells us that the founding heroes of Rome, Romulus and Remus, being abandoned as infants, were suckled by a she-wolf. The cult of Romulus and Remus was as old as the fourth century B.C., and we know that a statue of a she-wolf was dedicated on the Capitoline Hill in Rome in 296 B.C. We do *not* know whether the present statue of the she-wolf on the Capitoline Hill is the original (the suckling infants were made in

can clay-modeling techniques and the use to which the confident, quick-conceiving, and quick-executing sculptor could put them. In contrast with, say, the serene majesty of the *Apollo* at Olympia (FIG. 5-36), this one moves like a dangerous giant. His overpowering physical presence reflects small concern for the Greek preoccupation with harmonious proportions or idealized humanity. The Ionian elaboration of the drapery lines bespeaks the Eastern com-

6-10 *She-Wolf of the Capitol,* c. 500 B.C. Bronze, approx. 33½″ high. Museo Capitolino, Rome.

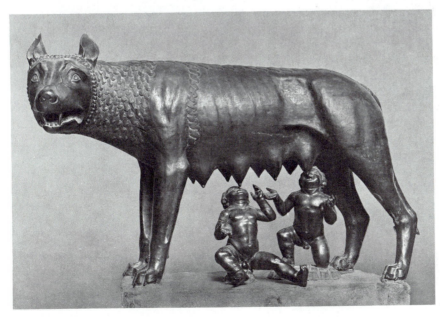

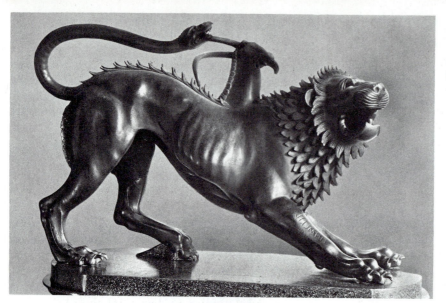

6-11 *Chimera*, Arezzo, fifth to fourth centuries B.C. Bronze, approx. $31\frac{1}{2}''$ high. Museo Archeologico, Florence.

the Renaissance); its dating has been hotly debated, but its Etruscan origin is now widely accepted. The vitality we have noted in the human figure of Etruscan art is here concentrated in the tense, watchful animal body, with its spare flanks, gaunt ribs, and taut and powerful legs. The lowering neck and head, the alert ears, glaring eyes, and ferocious muzzle render the psychic vibrations of the fierce and, at the same time, protecting beast; the incised lines along the neck give us its rising hackles as it watches danger approach. Not even the great animal reliefs of Assyria can match, much less surpass, this profound reading of animal temper.

Somewhat later we have the splendid *Chimera* from Arezzo (FIG. 6-11), a bronze monster with a rough-maned lion's head, a serpent's tail (restored in the Renaissance by Benvenuto Cellini), and a second head—that of a goat—whose right horn is seized by the serpent. Although the *Chimera* bears the wounds inflicted by the hero Bellerophon, who hunted and slew it, it is not merely illustrative of the event; rather, the figure almost certainly has some further demonic significance. The Etruscans, much of whose art is associated with mortuary ritual, had a well-developed demonology, an aggregation of demonic types that plague the dead in the underworld. Unlike the Greeks, who preferred to humanize their demons, the Etruscans, with their roots partly in Asia, employed their customary expressive force to represent them as dreadful animal hybrids. The precedents for the monster types go back to the sphinxes of Egypt and the winged, man-headed bulls of Mesopotamia, as well as to the ornamental animal bronzes of Luristan and the associated animal-heraldic style of much of the metalwork of central Asia. It may be that these traditions lingered in the Etruscan spirit, and the manifestation of them in such powerful form as the *Chimera*—so anti-Greek and so Asiatic—attests most firmly to the Eastern component in Etruscan culture. By the time of the Middle Ages, a whole population of monsters swarmed through the art of the West.

Also assimilated from the East and passed on by the Etruscans to the Romans was the practice of divination, whereby the future, as a product of arcane forces (personified as gods or demons) was thought to be predictable to some degree. On the assumption that all nature constituted a universe of affinities, prediction—the art of the priesthood—was based on the state of the viscera of sacrificed animals (especially the liver), the flight of flocks of birds, and unseasonable and unusual events. The engraved back of a bronze mirror (FIG. 6-12)—exquisitely wrought, with all the refinement for which the Etruscan craft arts were celebrated—represents a winged figure labeled Calchas, a priest in Homer's *Iliad*, divining from a liver that he holds in his hand and upon which he muses. The figure is a kind of miniature emblem for that world of benign and malign forces that surrounded ancient men and which they tried to approach or fend off by prophecy, sacrifice, oracle, omen, spell, incantation. Greek rationalism made little headway

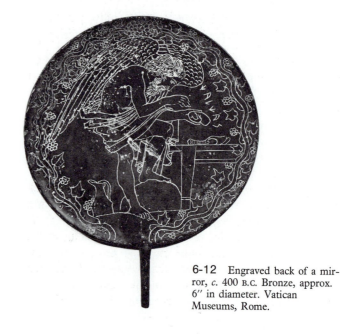

6-12 Engraved back of a mirror, *c.* 400 B.C. Bronze, approx. 6″ in diameter. Vatican Museums, Rome.

against the ancient world's overwhelming faith in the magical manipulation of nature.

Closely related to the delicately incised, Classical mirrors of the fourth century B.C., like the Calchas one, are the bronze cists of Praeneste (modern Palestrina), which doubtless echo the styles of the great Greek masters of mural painting—Polygnotos, Euphranor, and others. Etruscan bronze vessels and mirrors with incised mythological scenes were famous and highly prized objects in Greece. Perhaps the outstanding member of this type is the so-called *Ficoroni Cist* of NOVIUS PLAUTIUS (FIG. 6-13). Most significantly, the artist, Novius Plautius, is not Etruscan; he signed his work in Latin and made it in Rome. He has made a skillful adaptation of a frieze of Greek figures, faithfully taking over the idealized naturalism of the Late Classical period. Naturalistic innovations appear: figures seen entirely from behind or in three-quarter rear view, complicated seated poses, figures on several levels rather than rigidly attached to a single groundline, details of landscape, and a kind of approximate perspective space. The artist represents in his work the passing of the Etruscan genius and the acceptance of the irresistible influence of Greece. Yet something of the Etruscan sense for the real will persist through the formal Classicism of Greece, which, in turn, will partly direct the course of the art of Rome; and this earlier Etruscan sense will sharpen into the characteristic Roman taste for the factual in art as in human affairs.

THE ROMANS

The Roman power that succeeded and replaced the Etruscan and Greek colonial powers on the Appenine peninsula compelled the contesting peoples of Italy into a Roman state and, eventually, the peoples of western Europe, the Mediterranean shores, North Africa, and the Near East into a Roman empire. The rise and triumph of Rome, and the awesome spectacles of its decline and fall, make, in the stately words of the great historian of it, Edward Gibbon, "a revolution which will ever be remembered, and is still felt, by the nations of the earth." From the Tigris and Euphrates to the borders of Scotland stretched a single government under whose energetic and efficient—if sometimes ruthless and brutal—rule lived people of innumerable races, creeds, tongues, traditions, and cultures: Britons, Gauls, Spaniards, Germans, Africans, Egyptians, Greeks, Syrians, Arabs, to name only a very few. If the Greek genius, as we review it, shines most brightly in art, science, philosophy, history, and—in general—the things of the intellect and imagination, the Roman genius shines in the realm of worldly action—in law and in government. Roman monuments of art and architecture are distributed throughout the world that the Romans governed and are the most conspicuous and numerous of all the remains of

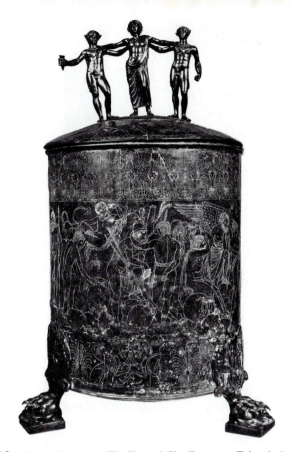

6-13 NOVIUS PLAUTIUS, *The Ficoroni Cist*, Praeneste (Palestrina), late fourth century B.C. Bronze, approx. 21″ high. Museo Nazionale di Villa Giulia, Rome.

ancient civilizations we have so far studied. But Roman monuments of a kind also survive in our concepts of law and government, in our calendar, in our festivals, rituals, languages, and religions, in the nomenclature of many of the sciences, and, for our special interest here, in the concept of art as worthy of historical study and criticism.

The main energies of Rome were devoted to conquest and administration, conquest opening the way for the spread of Roman civilization. Roman cities sprang up not only all around the Mediterranean basin but also as far north as the Danube, the Rhine, and the Thames. Each city was a center for the propagation of Roman government, language, and customs and was closely connected with the city of Rome itself by a well-planned system of roads and harbors. Rome about A.D. 200 was the capital of the greatest empire the world had known, an empire efficiently organized with 50,000 miles of sea routes and expertly engineered highways safe for travel and commerce. Rome itself was both cosmopolitan and splendid. The size, power, and complexity of the empire called for an impressive capital, and while the practical demands arising from the administration of a great empire required high engineering skill for the construction of bridges, roads, sewers, and aqueducts, the imperial ideal called also for public buildings that would express the dignity and diversity of the state. Roman art takes its character in large part from the imperial role the Roman state was required to play.

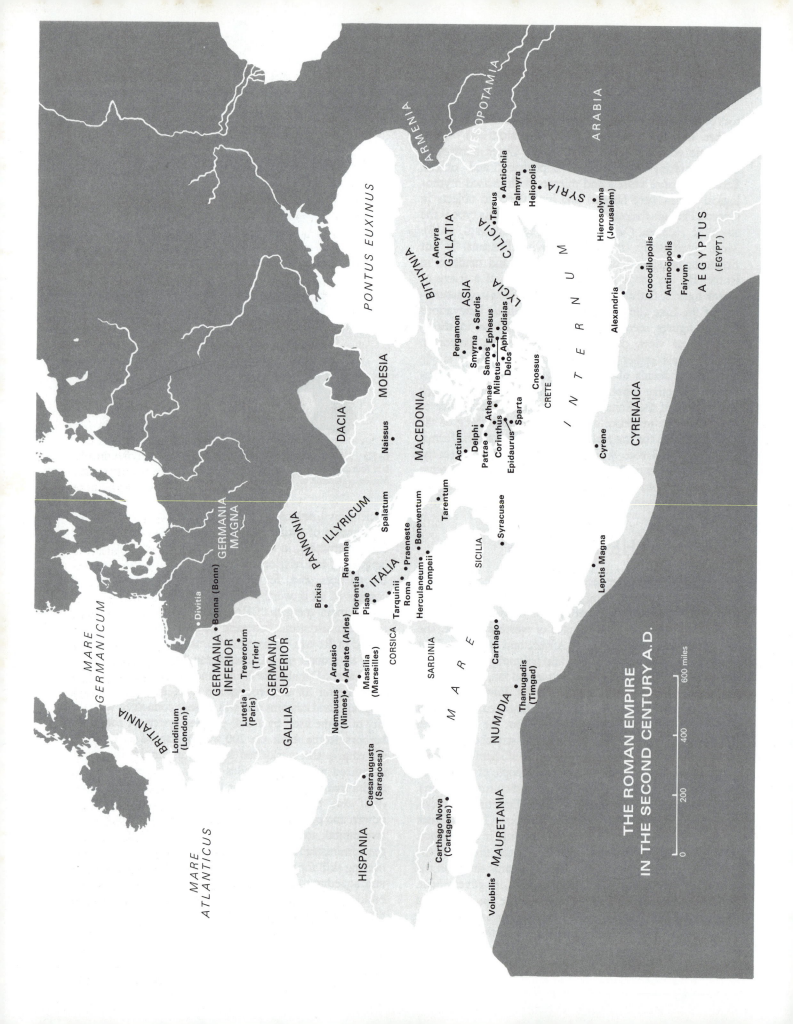

MARE GERMANICUM

MARE ATLANTICUS

BRITANNIA

Londinium (London)

GERMANIA MAGNA

Divitia

Bonna (Bonn)

GERMANIA INFERIOR

Treverorum (Trier)

GERMANIA SUPERIOR

GALLIA

Lutetia (Paris)

Nemausus (Nîmes)

Arausio

Arelate (Arles)

Massilia (Marseilles)

Caesaraugusta (Saragossa)

HISPANIA

Carthago Nova (Cartagena)

CORSICA

SARDINIA

MAURETANIA

Volubilis

NUMIDIA

Thamugadis (Timgad)

Carthago

PANNONIA

ILLYRICUM

Spalatum

Brixia

Florentia

Pisae

Ravenna

Tarquinii

Roma

Praeneste

ITALIA

Herculaneum

Pompeii

Beneventum

Tarentum

SICILIA

Syracusae

MARE

DACIA

MOESIA

Naissus

MACEDONIA

Actium

Delphi

Patrae

Athenae

Corinthus

Epidaurus

Sparta

Cnossus

CRETE

PONTUS EUXINUS

BITHYNIA

Ancyra

GALATIA

ARMENIA

Pergamon

ASIA

Smyrna

Sardis

Samos

Ephesus

Miletus

Aphrodisias

Delos

LYCIA

CILICIA

Tarsus

MESOPOTAMIA

Antiochia

Palmyra

Heliopolis

SYRIA

ARABIA

Hierosolyma (Jerusalem)

INTERNUM

Crocodilopolis

Antinoöpolis

Faiyum

AEGYPTUS (EGYPT)

Alexandria

Cyrene

CYRENAICA

Leptis Magna

THE ROMAN EMPIRE IN THE SECOND CENTURY A.D.

0   200   400   600 miles

| ← to c. 700 B.C. | c. 510 | c. 470 | | c. 300 | | 146 | c. 80 | 27 B.C. | | A.D. 70 | 118 | | A.D. 284 |

to c. 700 B.C. c. 510 c. 470   c. 300   146   c. 80   27 B.C.   A.D. 70   118   A.D. 284

Apollo of Veii | Revelers, Tomb of the Leopards | Woman of the Velcha Family, Tomb of Orcus | Conquest of Greece | Sanctuary of Fortuna Primigenia | Colosseum begun | Pantheon begun

ETRUSCAN DOMI-NATION | ROMAN REPUBLICAN PERIOD | B.C. A.D. | EARLY IMPERIAL PERIOD

Although early under both Etruscan and Greek influence, Roman art came to have its own quite distinctive characteristics. The Romans, almost from the beginning of their rise, had been fully aware of Greek art, but it was only in the later Republican and Augustan ages that Hellenism became a conscious fashion. "Conquered Greece," wrote Horace, "led her proud conqueror captive." Shiploads of Greek marbles and bronzes were brought to Rome by generals and provincial governors to adorn their mansions, and, when the supply was exhausted, copies were made or Greek artists were employed to create new works. Fashionable art for a time became to a large extent mere copying of Greek works. Finally a deeper assimilation took place, and the art of Imperial Rome emerged, a product of its richly varied heritage and its unique genius.

This art-historical view of Roman art is comparatively new. Until about 1900 the scholars saw Roman art as merely decadent Greek art, unoriginal and inferior. It is true that, drawing as it necessarily does upon what went before, it does not have the degree of originality that distinguishes the great styles of Egypt, Mesopotamia, Greece, and even Etruria. Yet it is more than a mere "propagator and preserver of the classical heritage"; it is the "first comprehensive stage of western European art." While it makes use of Classical forms, it expresses non-Classical concepts. It combines an interest in individual personality with one in such abstract concepts as "law," "state," and "civilization." The vast body of the material of Roman art—found on three continents, with much of it still not evaluated and with much more still underground—suggests methods almost of mass production, in which the anonymous artist (almost no names survive, in contrast with those of writers and poets) becomes the servant of his patron—private or public, wealthy connoisseur or the Roman state. Nevertheless, in the collective as well as in the individual case, Roman art survives as an imposing style taking its own course from the days of the late republic.

The Republican Period

The Roman republic was founded after the last of the (possibly Etruscan) kings had been driven out. From the fifth century B.C. to the collapse of the republic and the assassination of Julius Caesar in 44 B.C., the external business of Rome was expansion abroad and the consolidation of imperial power in the Western world. In a succession of wars, the most harrowing and dangerous of which were the wars with Carthage, the Romans developed their peculiar qualities of character: disciplined valor, tenacity, practicality, obedience to authority, and a pitiless realism in recognizing the facts of power. Yet the constitutional structure of the republic, adequate to a limited city-state, could not begin to meet the requirements of empire. Internal quarrels between classes—the patricians and the plebeians—were inflamed by dispute over disposition of the enormous wealth won abroad. When successful armies led by popular generals intervened in the politics of the republic, civil war began. Lasting almost a hundred years, during which dictators like Marius, Sulla, Caesar, and Pompey ruled, the war exhausted the state and destroyed its constitution. When the great-nephew of Julius Caesar, Octavian, finally found himself alone at the head of the Roman world (when he called himself Augustus), the republic was little more than a pious, ritualized memory.

It is in this period of the crisis of the republic, even while Greek influence became increasingly strong, that Roman art began to emerge as an entity distinguishable from the late Hellenistic style. In 146 B.C., when Greece was absorbed into the Roman empire as the province of Achaia, a sculptural style came into being that we call Greco-Roman, the term an admission that the two styles cannot be readily separated from each other. Much of the original sculpture of the period was produced by Greek immigrant artists—for instance, the *Seated Boxer* (FIG. 5-75). But the growing Roman fascination with individual traits of personality is apparent in portrait sculpture, a field in which the Romans made one of their most original contributions (the others being architecture and landscape painting) and in which they achieved a quite typical, uncompromising, and often unflattering realism. However, the Hellenizing idealism that is found balancing this hard Roman realism in the last days of the republic bears witness to the peculiar dualism in the Roman attitude toward the defeated Greeks—admiration for their art and grace and contempt for their "unmanly" cleverness and for their lack of skill in managing their own affairs as a people. Cicero described this Roman ambiguity of sentiment and scored the Greeks on their un-Roman insincerity in terms a little like those of nineteenth-century American travelers commenting on the French.

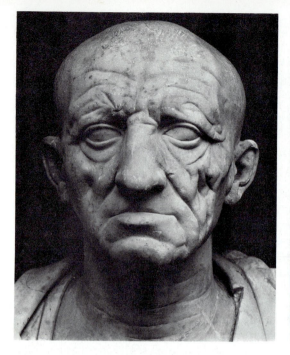

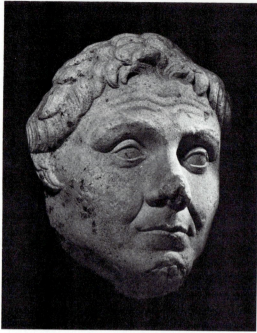

6-14 *Head of a Roman, c.* 80 B.C.
Marble, life-size.
Palazzo Torlonia, Rome.

6-15 *Pompey the Great, c.* 55 B.C.
Marble, life-size.
Frank E. Brown Collection, Rome.

I grant them literature, I grant them a knowledge of many arts, I do not deny the charm of their speech, the keenness of their intellects, the richness of their diction; finally, if they make other claims, I do not deny them. But truth and honor in giving testimony that nation has never cherished. . . . Greeks never trouble to prove what they say but only make a display of themselves by talking.

But it was the idealism of Greek art that again and again captivated the Romans. Greek statues in great profusion stood in the Roman forums and in both public and private buildings; villas and baths were museums of Greek sculpture—whether originals, copies, or adaptations to suit Roman taste. We read of 285 bronze and 30 marble statues brought from Corinth in 146 B.C., after the barbarous sack of that city, and of 500 bronzes brought from Delphi by Nero; when the stockpile of originals ran low, the demand for Greek sculpture was satisfied by copies made after Greek works.

PORTRAIT SCULPTURE

But even while under the spell of Hellenism, Roman portraitists produced works that have no parallel in Greek art. During the Hellenistic period, the quality of generalization that had distinguished earlier portraits had already given way to a style that was more particularizing and descriptive. The Roman's desire for literalness, together with his custom of keeping in his house, always before his eyes, the *imagines* (death masks, usually of wax) of his ancestors, influenced the sculptor to accentuate individual traits still further. Also operative was the Etruscan influence, which, with its expressionistic realism, persisted in Late Republican portraiture. The *Head of a Roman* (FIG. 6-14), for example, is striking by virtue of its "character," at once

alive and masklike. But the character may simply be accidental, the result of the artist's painstaking report of each rise and fall, each bulge and fold, of the facial surface, executed as if he were proceeding like a map-maker, concerned not to miss the slightest detail of surface change. The artist apparently tries neither to idealize the subject—that is, to improve him in conformity with an ideal, as in Greek practice—nor to interpret his personality. The blunt and bald record of his features, the kind given by a life mask or death mask, is quite enough. Thus, this "verism," a kind of superrealism, is the artist's objective, and it is determined not so much by esthetic motives as by religious convention. The habit of mind that demands faithful records of this kind is familiar to us in our curiosity about the fidelity of photographs of our forebears.

A quite different approach to the portrait subject can be seen in a bust of Pompey the Great (FIG. 6-15). A sculptor confronting a powerful and famous man may be conscious of the need for a method different from mere recording; he may want to idealize but also to personalize—that is, interpret the subject's personality. We, coming 2000 years after Pompey, bring to our scanning of him far more knowledge of the man than we could ever bring to the contemplation of a portrait of an unknown Roman. Pompey was first the partner and then the rival of Julius Caesar in the devastating civil war that wrecked the Roman republic in the first century B.C. We know of him as a great general, successful in war and—almost—the proprietor of all the Eastern world held by Rome. We know of him also as a political incompetent and as an ambitious man of the middle class who allowed himself to be made the dupe of the extremists of the Senatorial party. We know of him as hopelessly irresolute, disappointing even his closest friends because he was unable to make up his mind. We know that he lost to Caesar the bloody battle of Pharsalus, after which he was ignominiously assassinated by one of his own men. Yet he was a good man who refused to enrich himself by plunder of the provinces, a practice from which most of his contemporaries did not refrain. Cicero wrote of Pompey to a friend: "I knew him as a man honest, grave, and high-minded."

Thus, Pompey is a complex of traits played upon by the accidents of history; yet what kind of man of only slightly more than good talent could have bested Caesar? Knowing what we do about Pompey's strength and weakness, his triumphs and ultimate failure, we naturally approach his portrait bust as we might approach a bust of Washington or Lafayette—with curiosity about the individual man and his history. In the same way, it is likely that the artist of the bust, though different from us in his cultural responses, would still have cared to make a likeness that would be more than a mere facial record. This is evident in the work, which has none of the rigidity of the death mask and possesses a subtly modeled surface over which the light plays softly. The modeling is obviously contrived to suggest rather than to describe. The strong lines of the broad head and the somewhat flat surfaces of the face are softened by a curiously ambiguous expression. Would we be wrong to read in it self-doubt mingled with affectation or bluster under an official mask of power? At any rate, the very fact that we are tempted to such interpretation testifies to the sophisticated artist's power to make us thoughtful before his image of a great and unfortunate man.

ARCHITECTURE

Striking as is the manifestation of Roman originality in its naturalistic portraiture, it is even more so in its architecture. During the Republican period the Roman identity is first and most fully expressed in architecture and city-planning. Unlike the religious architecture of the civilizations (including the Greek) that preceded it, the Roman temple was not a particularly inventive or conspicuous type. Rather it was upon imposing and utilitarian civic structures and plans that the Roman builders concentrated, though of course they also built temples, which were modeled upon schemes in which Greek and Etruscan elements were blended in unique fashion. The Temple of Fortuna Virilis in Rome (FIG. 6-16), dating from the late second century B.C., looks at first glance like an Ionic peripteral temple. It consists of a large cella located behind a deep porch (see FIG. 6-1). But the building stands on a high podium which may be of Etruscan origin, and the cella occupies its entire width. This means that only the porch columns are freestanding, while those along the exterior walls of the cella are engaged, being purely decorative and having no supporting function. Seen from a distance, they give the illusion of being freestanding; hence the designation "pseudoperipteral" for this type of construction. A favorite with Roman builders, this temple

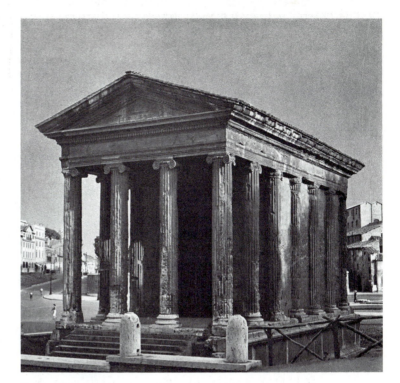

6-16 Temple of Fortuna Virilis, Rome, late second century B.C.

type has survived in many examples, most of them larger than the one shown and employing the Corinthian order.

The same superficial resemblance to Greek architecture appears in the Temple of the Sibyl at Tivoli (FIG. 6-17). Built in the early first century B.C., it looks at first like a Corinthian tholos. However, like the Fortuna Virilis, it stands upon a podium, ascent to which is by means of a single flight of stairs that leads to the entrance of the cella. This arrangement introduces an axial alignment that is not found in Greek tholoi and that serves to lessen the isola-

6-17 Temple of the Sibyl, Tivoli, early first century B.C.

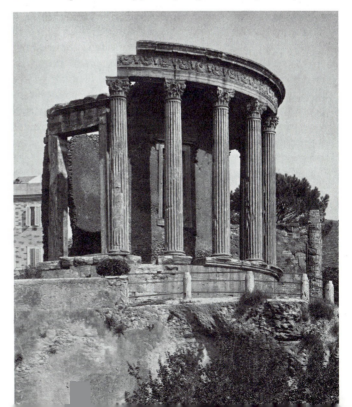

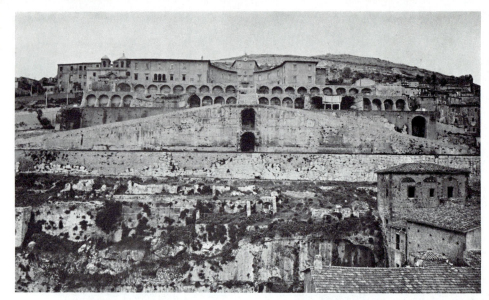

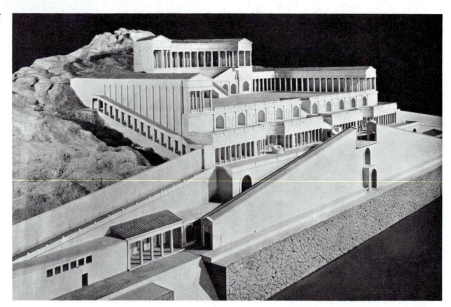

tion of the building from its surroundings, diminishing somewhat the independent sculptural aspect so prized by the Greeks. A closer examination of the Temple of the Sibyl reveals other "un-Greek" features: The columns are monolithic—all of a piece—and not built up in the drum sections that were usual with the Greeks; the Romans preferred to use the monolithic column, often on great scale, wherever possible. The frieze is embellished not with figure sculpture, as would be the case in Greece, but with a favorite Roman decorative motif—garlands held up by *bucrania* (ox skulls), probably symbolic of fertility and of the alternation of death and resurrection; this motif is rhythmically repeated around the whole frieze. Finally, and also in contrast with Greek practice, the cella wall is built not of cut stone but of concrete into which blocks of tufa have been set in an ornamental pattern.

These significant departures from the Greek model are seen even more clearly in the Sanctuary at Praeneste (FIGS.

6-18 and 6-19), which was dedicated to Fortuna (Fate) and built under the first Roman dictator of the republic, Sulla, around 80 B.C., at a site where oracular lots had long been cast. The great size of the sanctuary reflects the growing taste for colossal Hellenistic designs during the Late Republican period. Seven terraces rising against the hillside are placed with rigid axial symmetry. The top terrace carried a semicircular double colonnade that contained the sanctuary proper, probably in the form of a small round temple. Although something of it had been studied, we have full knowledge of the great temple only by an accident of war: Palestrina, modern successor of the Medieval town that had been built over Praeneste, was bombed during World War II, and clearing of the resultant ruins disclosed the impressive remains of the Roman buildings. It was seen that the Roman builders had converted an entire hillside into a man-made design in a symbolic and ostentatious display of power and dominion. This assertive

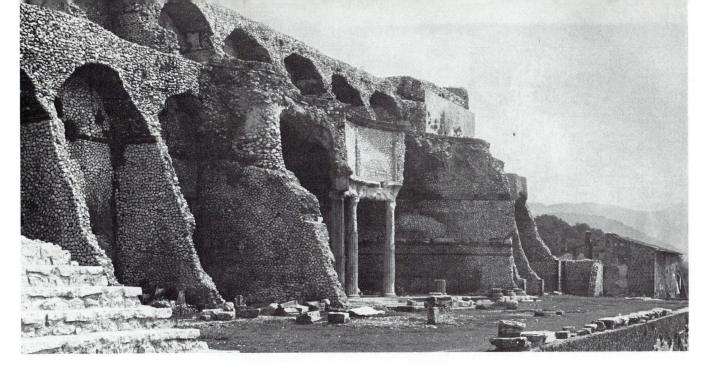

6-20　Detail of the Sanctuary of Fortuna Primigenia.

subjection of nature to man's will and rational order is the first full-blown manifestation of the Roman imperial spirit and contrasts with the more restrained Greek bent, which crowns a chosen hill with sacred buildings rather than transforms the hill itself into architecture.

The substructures for the terraces (FIG. 6-20) were built in concrete (*opus concretum*), and it is here that we can find in grand scale the use of that favorite Roman building material, developed in the second century B.C. and applied for centuries wherever the necessary ingredients were available. Concrete (of generally inferior quality) had been used in the Near East, chiefly for the building of fortification walls, but its combination with the arch and the vault, as here at Praeneste, was revolutionary. As perfected during the Early Imperial period, concrete vaulting permitted Roman builders to cover, without interior supports, spaces of a scale never dreamt of before. Its use enabled the Roman architect to think of architecture in terms radically different from those of earlier builders—as an architecture of space rather than of sheer mass, as was the case in the Egyptian pyramid or the Mesopotamian ziggurat or even the lighter but still space-encumbering post-and-lintel systems of the Greeks. (See discussion of the Roman Pantheon, pp. 190–92.) Roman concrete, a mixture of lime-mortar, water, and volcanic dust found in limited areas, chiefly in central Italy, was poured over rubble that had been laid in courses between forms. Once solidified, this rubble concrete was cohesive and strong, though rough in appearance; but it was the custom to face the rough surfaces with marble slabs, plaster, or ornamental brick or stone work. In Praeneste, the concrete is faced with small, flat, irregularly shaped stones that produce a figuration called *opus incertum*.

In the eighteenth century the imagination of Europe was excited by the discovery of the buried cities of Pompeii and Herculaneum, which had been overwhelmed by an eruption of Mount Vesuvius in A.D. 79. Their discovery, prior to the first archeological expeditions to Egypt, fascinated Europe and provided the initial impetus for modern archeological curiosity. What made the discoveries—new ones are still being made in the excavations of both cities—of such poignant human interest, as well as so infinitely valuable for scientific history, was that they revealed to modern eyes, in almost perfect preservation and detail, the everyday communal life of these times and places past. Pompeii, a prosperous city of about 20,000, had been stopped dead in the very motion of everyday life and had been preserved intact in volcanic ashes, invisible and forgotten for some 1600 years. The remains of the city permit us to reconstruct the Roman way of life during the Early Imperial period with a completeness far beyond that achieved at any other archeological site. The fullness of its record, its appeal to our sense of the dramatic and terrible accidents of life, and its usefulness for describing the architectural and artistic environment of quite ordinary men in an ancient city warrant considerable attention.

Though destroyed during the Early Imperial period, the city and most of its architectural monuments date from the Republican period. The plan of Pompeii, as seen in the parts excavated so far (FIG. 6-21), is not that of the ideal *castrum* type, but rather the irregular plan of a *grown* city, one that was subjected at various periods to revisions and regularizing. The Roman castrum type of city plan, based on the layout of a military camp, was used in the outlying, frontier, colonial regions and had its major development during the Early Imperial period (see FIG. 6-43), although an early form of it was used at Ostia in the fourth century

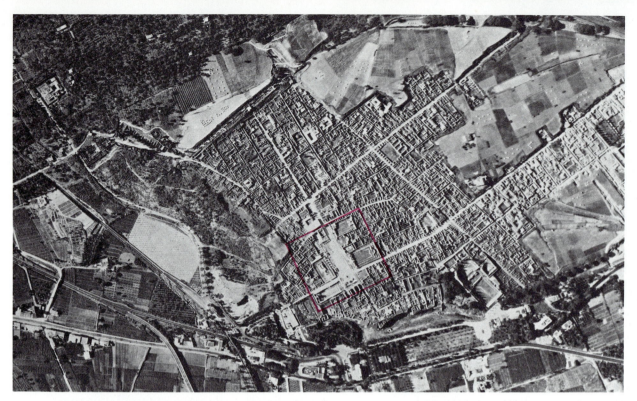

6-21 Aerial view of the excavated portion of Pompeii. Area enclosed by red rectangle near center of photograph is shown in FIG. 6-22.

6-22 Plan of the forum of Pompeii. Area diagrammed is indicated in FIG. 6-21 by red rectangle inscribed near center of photograph.

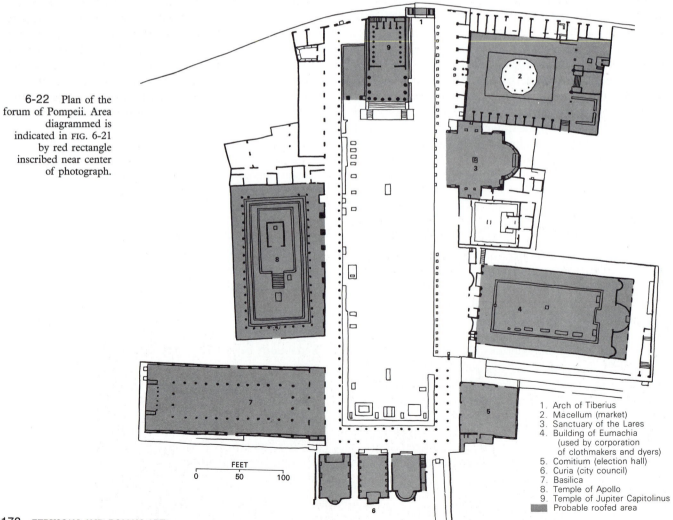

1. Arch of Tiberius
2. Macellum (market)
3. Sanctuary of the Lares
4. Building of Eumachia
   (used by corporation
   of clothmakers and dyers)
5. Comitium (election hall)
6. Curia (city council)
7. Basilica
8. Temple of Apollo
9. Temple of Jupiter Capitolinus
■ Probable roofed area

FEET
0   50   100

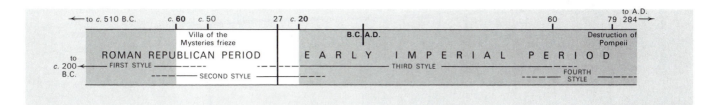

to A.D.

←to c. 510 B.C.   c. **60**   c. 50   27 c. **20**   B.C.|A.D.   60   79 284→

Villa of the   Destruction of
Mysteries frieze   Pompeii

to   ROMAN REPUBLICAN PERIOD   E A R L Y   I M P E R I A L   P E R I O D
c. 200← —FIRST STYLE———— ———— ——————————THIRD STYLE——————————
B.C.   ————SECOND STYLE————   ————   FOURTH
                                                          STYLE

B.C. Pompeii, which started as a small, unplanned settlement in the vicinity of the Greek colony of Neapolis (modern Naples), was founded in the sixth century B.C. by the Oscans, early local rivals of the Romans. It was seized in 425 B.C. by the Samnites—also rivals of the Romans—who fortified and replanned it under the influence of expanding Greek concepts of rational urban planning. But the Greek grid system could not be rigidly applied without tearing down most of the city; as a result, the main organizing features—the north-south and east-west thoroughfares—do not intersect at right angles, and the blocks between them are irregular. The city was conquered by Sulla in the eighties and refounded as a Roman colony in 80 B.C. In A.D. 62 it was partially destroyed by an earthquake; it had not yet been entirely rebuilt by the time of its final destruction seventeen years later. Pompeii has been especially valuable to the historian of Roman architecture since many building types that later become standard are found there in their early, if not earliest, examples; these include the oldest amphitheater extant and the earliest known public baths.

Next to the Roman Forum, from whose design it differs significantly, the forum of Pompeii (FIGS. 6-22 and 6-23) is the most important example of an early Roman civic center. The Pompeian forum is a rectangular court, in the proportion $3\frac{1}{2}$:1, that is unified by and the boundaries of which are defined by continuous colonnades around three sides. The other type of plan, represented by the Roman Forum, is bordered by more monumental, but individual and disconnected, structures. Like most Roman forums, that of Pompeii is set apart from the major traffic arteries, and vehicles could not enter it. Its long, north-south axis is dominated by the Capitolium, a large temple set on a high podium and dedicated to the three gods who protected Rome and her colonies. Several smaller temples flank the long sides of the forum. At the south end stands the triple hall of the Curia (city council), representing civic authority, and the Basilica, the seat of law and business. (This basilica, dating back to about 100 B.C., is an early example of one of the most important and influential classes of Roman buildings, the one from which the basic form of the Christian church building will derive.) Thus, the forum combines the functions of a religious, commercial, and administrative civic center and is the heart of the town. In the same way, it is a kind of imperial center in miniature, and this combination of functions, as architecturally expressed in the Roman Forum, will come to represent the central concerns and focus of the whole Roman empire.

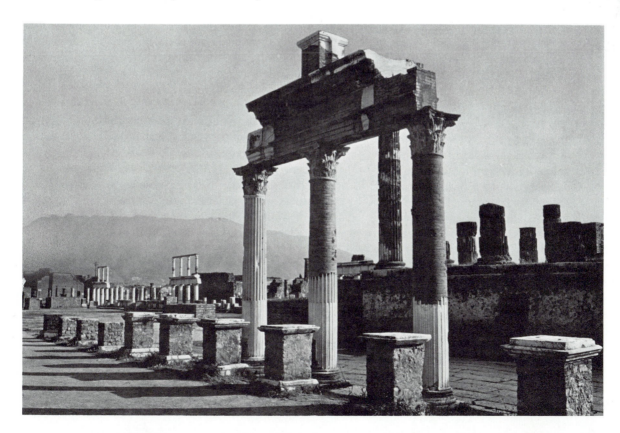

6-23 Forum of Pompeii.

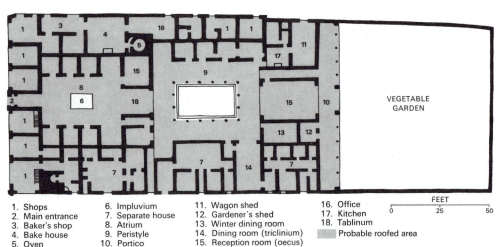

1. Shops
2. Main entrance
3. Baker's shop
4. Bake house
5. Oven
6. Impluvium
7. Separate house
8. Atrium
9. Peristyle
10. Portico
11. Wagon shed
12. Gardener's shed
13. Winter dining room
14. Dining room (triclinium)
15. Reception room (oecus)
16. Office
17. Kitchen
18. Tablinum

Probable roofed area

FEET
0   25   50

One would not expect the formality of a civic center to be found in the streets that surround it. These would be less monumental and regular, and their spaces less ample—even narrow and cramped. The streets had heavy flagstone pavements with flanking sidewalks. Stepping stones for pedestrians crossing the street were so spaced as to be straddled by the wheels of vehicles. Most intersections had continuously flowing public fountains. The problem of human convenience in an urban society, though not dealt with on the enormous scale that it is today, was worked out in Pompeii with an efficiency we can believe suited the needs of the people. The town had its commercial sections, like that of the Via dell' Abbondanza, where the streets were flanked by rows of small shops, offices, taverns, bakeries, and where we can still see many painted advertisements on the walls. Here and there the rows of shops were interrupted by a gateway leading into a private residence, which spread out in the back of the shops and was entirely enclosed and isolated from them and from the noise and dust of the street.

The private house is probably the most precious and best-preserved record of urban life to come from Pompeii. The town houses of the well-to-do, like the House of Pansa (FIG. 6-24), an atrium type, protected in Pompeii and Herculaneum by the volcanic ash and lava in which they were buried, are extraordinarily well preserved, with their mural decorations still fresh and sometimes with their equipment and household utensils intact. Such a house stood flush with the sidewalk. Through a narrow door one entered a vestibule that led into the atrium. The latter had an opening in the center of the roof (the *impluvium*) and a depression in the floor below it to collect rainwater. Along the sides were small rooms; at the end, where the atrium extended the full width of the building, were two wings, *alae*. Behind the atrium was the *tablinum*, in which family archives and statues were kept. The tablinum could be shut off or could afford a passage to the peristyle, a large colonnaded court of Hellenistic origin. This court con-

tained fountains and a garden, around which were arranged the family's private apartments. At the back there was sometimes a vegetable garden or orchard. Along the outer sides of the house and opening onto the street were the shops. Thus the house faced inward, depending upon its courts for light and air. As in the Etruscan atrium, units were symmetrically arranged on a long axis that reached back from the street and, when opened through its entire length, afforded a charming vista of open court, gardens, fountains, statues, colored marbles, mosaics, and brightly painted walls. Some of the largest of these atrium houses in Pompeii rivaled, if they did not surpass, the palaces of Hellenistic kings; the House of the Faun, in which the Alexander mosaic (FIG. 6-37) served as a floor ornament, covered almost 30,000 square feet. Of course, these houses, popular particularly in the region around Mount Vesuvius, were the homes of patricians and rich merchants; artisans, craftsmen, and shopkeepers lived in much more modest quarters, the latter often in single rooms in back of or above their shops.

In their fullest development, in the late Roman republic, the elaborate, skillfully planned houses of the great combine an older Italic nucleus with features of the Hellenistic house and represent the highest achievements of domestic architecture in antiquity. That domestic architecture had a prominent place in Roman civilization was manifest in every part of the empire. The character of Roman domestic religion, which exhibited a traditional Italic feeling for the home, family, and hearth as sacred, helps explain the careful elaboration of the domestic architecture.

PAINTING AND MOSAIC

The interiorizing design, with its open and independent arrangement of units, guaranteed complete privacy. Because of the small number of doors and windows, it also offered considerable stretches of wall space suitable for

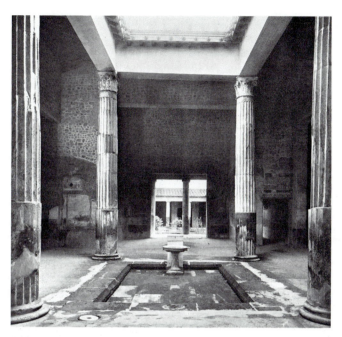

6-25 Atrium of the House of the Silver Wedding, Pompeii, second century B.C.

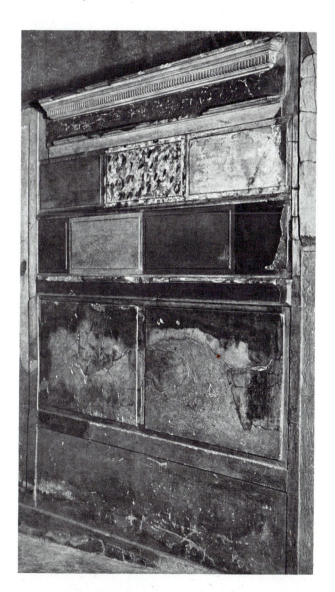

decoration, as the atrium of the House of the Silver Wedding in Pompeii (FIG. 6-25) clearly shows. The decoration commonly used varied between types that emphasized the wall as a barrier and others that visually opened the wall and enhanced the space of the room. The colors were sometimes delicate greens and tans, sometimes striking reds and black (to throw the panels or figures into relief), and there was rich creamy white in the borders. The Romans obtained a certain brilliance of surface by a careful preparation of the wall. After the plaster, which was specially compounded with marble dust, was laid on in several layers, it was beaten with a smooth trowel until it became very dense; it was then polished to a marblelike finish.

The progression from flat to spatial wall decoration in Pompeii and Herculaneum has been divided, somewhat arbitrarily, into four successive but overlapping styles. The first style (about 200–60 B.C.), called *incrustation*, divided the wall into bright polychrome panels of solid colors with occasional schematically rendered textural contrasts (FIG. 6-26). This style is a continuation of Hellenistic practice, and examples of it have been found in houses at Priene and on the island of Delos. A wall painting from a villa in Boscoreale, near Pompeii (FIG. 6-27), shows the second, or

6-26 First-style ("incrustation") wall painting from a Samnite house, Herculaneum, second century B.C.

6-27 Second-style ("architectural") wall painting from the cubiculum of the Villa Boscoreale, near Pompeii, first century B.C. Metropolitan Museum of Art, New York.

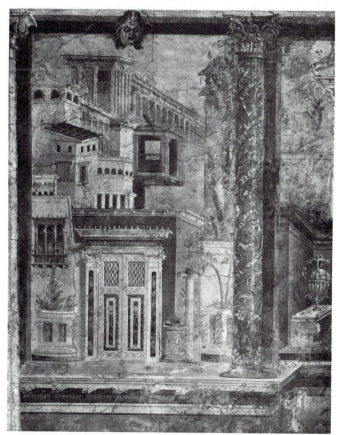

architectural, style (about 60–20 B.C.), in which the decoration is no longer restricted to a single visual plane. The space of the room is made to look as if it extended beyond the room itself by the representation of architectural forms in a visually convincing but not really systematic perspective. Columns, pilasters, and window frames painted on the wall served as enframements of distant views of cities and landscape. In the *herringbone perspective* used, the orthogonals, or lines of perspective projection, do not converge on a single vanishing point on the horizon (as in Renaissance perspective); rather, there tend to be *several* vanishing points (with associated orthogonals) distributed on an axis that runs vertically through the center of the panel. Though not consistently employed, this method does give a rather convincing illusion of objects receding in space.

A second-style mural in the Villa of the Mysteries, near Pompeii (about 50 B.C.), displays painted figures that are among the finest to have come down to us from the ancient world (FIG. 6-28). While other rooms in the villa are decorated in a style very similar to the pure architectural style of the villa in Boscoreale, the second-style illusionism here is confined to a painted ledge that looks like a shallow extension of the room proper and which affords the figures a kind of narrow supporting stage. The figures, set against a red-paneled background, in the style of a relief, are part of a large composition that once circled the walls of the room, which may have doubled as a banqueting room and as a place for the celebration of the rites of some mystery cult, perhaps that of Dionysos. The meaning of these scenes is in dispute; we may, however, be fairly certain that this group represents the initiation of a young novice into the cult. Whipped by a winged genius or deity, she crouches for solace in the lap of a solicitous older woman while a splendidly painted nude dances in Bacchic frenzy. The mystery cults, which are discussed below in connection with Christianity, made their way into the Roman empire in increasing numbers and variety from the Hellenized East. All included mysteries that were never to be divulged by the initiate, and which, when understood after painful introduction into the secret rites, would afford salvation through mystical union with a deity. The pictured ceremony from the Villa of the Mysteries is not only a work of art of high order, but a most important record of one aspect of the gradual religious transformation of the Roman world by the westward migration of Oriental spiritualism. As always with Roman paintings of quality, the question arises, Is it original Roman or derivative from a Greek Hellenistic original in some temple now lost? No decisive answer can be given.

The question arises again, and more insistently, when we look at the second-style *Odyssey Landscapes* (FIG. 6-29) from a house on the Esquiline Hill in Rome. In these landscapes, dating from the late first century B.C. and now in the Vatican, the painted columns divide the otherwise continuous stretch of landscape into eight compartments in which are represented scenes from the Homeric epic. The shimmering landscapes extend the space of the room and almost absorb the subordinated, rapidly sketched figures by their luminosity. At the same time the landscapes seem to be brought into the room almost magically. The flickering play of color and light and especially the shaded edges of the solids give a stagelike presence, as of easily shifted props, that suggests distance and isolated action. The second style, though "architectural," here exhibits its versatility, for the sole purpose of the rigid frames is to create the illusion of open and unconstrained landscape. Therefore, if it could be established that the conception of an "all-encompassing" space in works like the *Odyssey Landscapes* is original with Rome, then a solid Roman contribution to the history of art could be acknowledged.

The architectural quality of the second style fades toward the end, and the triumph of the illusionism we see coming forward in the *Odyssey Landscapes* may be seen in the detail of a wall painting from the House of Livia in Primaporta, near Rome, made toward the end of the first century B.C. (FIG. 6-30). The extension of the space of the room—with its complementary effect, the bringing of the landscape into the room—creates the image of a garden just outside the limit of the wall. (This is a curious anticipation of the widely popular "picture window" of recent modern architecture in which one enjoys a "view" by fixing it within a frame, at the same time thinking of the garden as continuous with the room.) Here "deep" perspectives and distant views are not desired, but rather the intimacy and freshness of natural beauty easily within contact. In the second style, as it develops, the "view" comes ever closer, until one may think that it is one's own garden, free of any human intrusion, enclosed and isolated by the painted limits of the fence and by the back-stopping of the foliage itself, which occupies a plane close to the viewer and shuts out distance.

The passing of the wall from the state in which it is a framed view into nature to that in which it merely supports smaller framed views takes place in the third, or *ornate,* style (about 20 B.C.–A.D. 60), during the time of the early empire. Simulated architecture disappears, as the wall is now subdivided into a number of panels by means of vertical and horizontal bands that may be filled with vine scrolls or other decorative designs (FIG. 6-31). The flat nature of the wall is here reaffirmed, and illusionism is confined to the pictures set into and emphasized by the decoratively patterned framework. At times whimsical and capricious, this style is characterized by delicate forms and colors, graceful elegance, and a deliberate rejection of the monumental constructions of the second style.

The fourth Pompeian wall style, called the *intricate,* dates from around A.D. 60 to A.D. 79 and may be seen to good advantage in the Ixion Room from the House of the Vetii (FIG. 6-32). Here, the painters, under the influence of contemporary Roman theatrical design, returned to the use

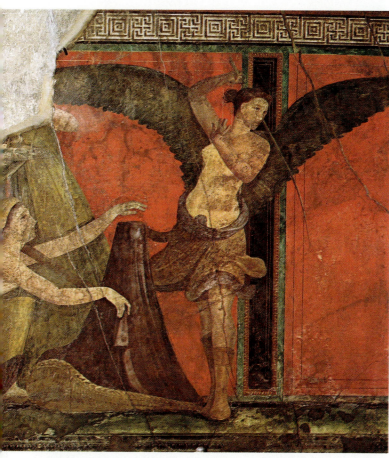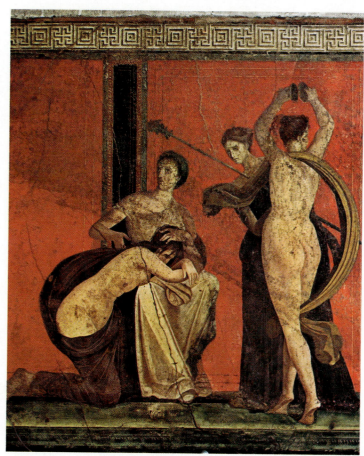

6-28 Details of a frieze from the Villa of the Mysteries, Pompeii, *c.* 50 B.C. Second-style ("architectural") wall painting. Figures approx. 54–60″ high.

6-29 *Ulysses in the Land of the Lestrygonians,* part of the *Odyssey Landscapes,* second-style ("architectural") wall painting from a house in Rome, late first century B.C. Approx. 60″ high. Vatican Library, Rome.

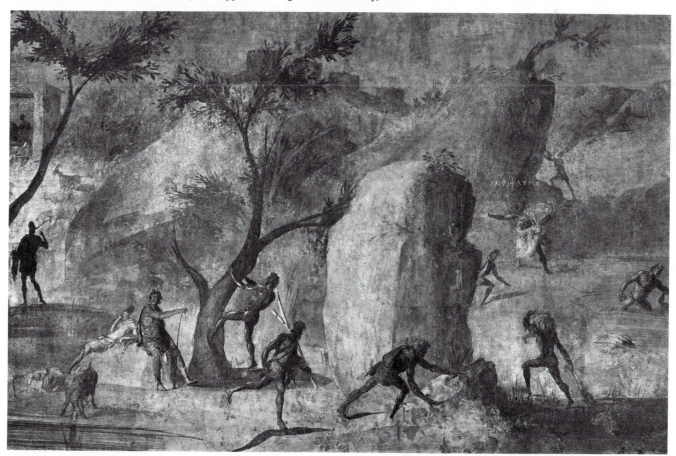

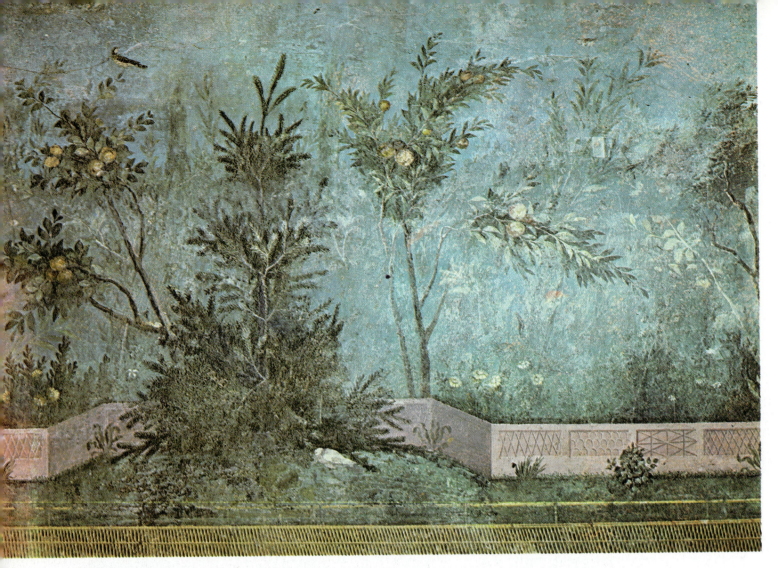

6-30 *Garden Scene*, detail of a wall painting from the House of Livia, Primaporta, late first century B.C. Portion shown approx. 9′ wide. Museo Nazionale Romano, Rome.

of architectural frames and open vistas. An aerial perspective, however, rather than a linear one, is created by areas of color flooded with light and atmosphere. It unites the wall in a complex way, incorporating all the lessons of previous experiments in optical illusion. In fact the fourth style is a kind of résumé of its predecessors: The incrustation manner appears along the lower walls, and architectural panels are set into the ornate third-style wall articulation, which is also reflected in the individual picture panels. Though the aerial perspective produces a certain unifying effect, there is no single point of view from which the designs can be taken in or from which they can be related; obviously it is intended that we pass the pictures as we do in a gallery, stopping at each one, aware that it need have no relation in subject or style to its neighbor.

The small panels show a great variety of subject matter, ranging from still life to genre, from mythology to landscape. A still life with peaches and a carafe, from Herculaneum (FIG. 6-33), about A.D. 50, demonstrates that the Roman painter sought illusionistic effects in depicting small objects quite as much as in depicting architectural forms and landscape spaces. Here his method involves light and shade with scrupulous attention to contour shadows and to highlights; doubtless he worked directly from an arrangement he made himself, the fruit, the stem and leaves, and the translucent jar being set out on shelves to give the illusion of the casual, almost accidental, relation of objects in a cupboard. But the picture is exact in neither drawing nor perspective, and the light and shade are approximate. Still, the illusion the painter contrives here marks the point of furthest advance made by the ancients in the technique of representation. He seems here to have an inkling that the look of things is a function of light, and he strives to paint *light* as he strives to paint the touchable *object* that reflects and absorbs it. It is interesting that painters like Paul Cézanne—often called the founder of modern art—in discarding the systematic organizing devices of perspective and chiaroscuro (light and dark), produce distortions and irregularities in painted objects that resemble those of this ancient still life.

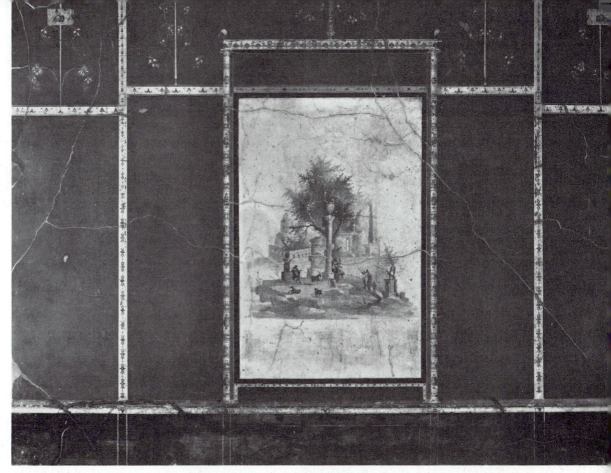

6-31 Third-style ("ornate") wall painting from a villa at Boscotrecase, near Pompeii, early first century A.D. Museo Nazionale, Naples.

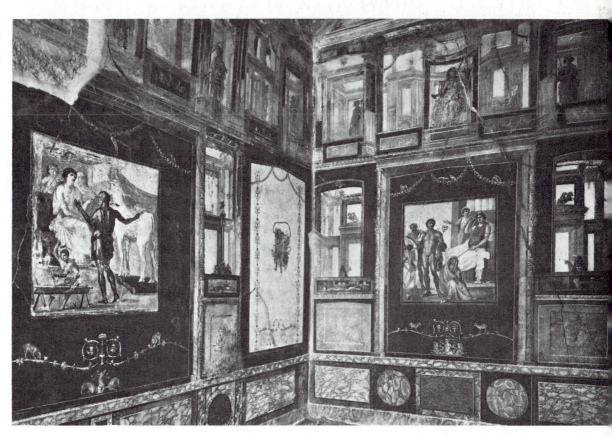

6-32 Fourth-style ("intricate") wall painting from the Ixion Room, House of the Vetii, Pompeii, first century A.D.

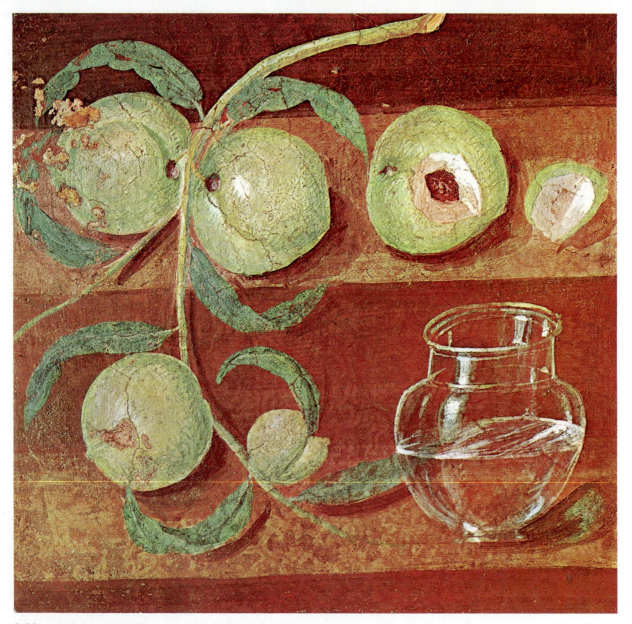

6-33 *Still Life with Peaches,* wall painting transferred to panel, Herculaneum, *c.* A.D. 50. Approx. 14″ × 13½″. Museo Nazionale, Naples.

A painting from the House of the Dioscuri in Pompeii (FIG. 6-34) offers evidence of the high degree of skillful illusionism achieved by the painters of the fourth style. The subject may be a scene from mythology or a genre scene. A woman seated before a stone building and a small hut receives a cup from a bowing man—or does she extend the cup to him? It is difficult to decide. Whatever the interpretation, the brush technique is a deft impressionism, the strokes firm and practiced; and the painter is entirely sure of the poses and the relationship of the figures in space. The problems of figural attitude, anatomy, movement, and proportion, which we have seen confronting the ancient artist for millennia, seem now to have their familiar solutions, so that the artist of this work proceeds easily and confidently, his brush quickly expressive of his knowledge.

That the style of the Dioscuri painting was contemporaneous with other quite different styles is apparent from a painting from Herculaneum representing Herakles finding the infant Telephos in Arcadia (FIG. 6-35). The subject indicates that the picture was copied from some Hellenistic original—or originals, for the artist proceeds as if he were lifting figures from different sources and arranging them with little relation to one another. Thus, the personification of Arcadia, the large seated figure, is not in proportion to Herakles, nor is the treatment the same: The statuesque Arcadia has the pale, hard modeling we associate with sculpture, while the play of light and highlight upon the supple surfaces of the Herakles figure is closely related to the effects we expect in pictorial illusionism, though the technique is by no means the free "painterly" one we see in the Dioscuri work. All the figures are precisely modeled,

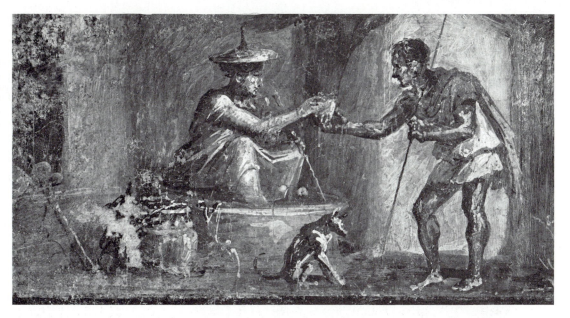

6-34 Genre scene (?), detail of a wall painting transferred to panel, from the House of the Dioscuri, Pompeii, first century A.D. Entire painting approx. 15" × 17". Museo Nazionale, Naples.

with firm outlines. The artist is concerned chiefly with the solid volumes of the bodies and not with light or with the space the whole group occupies; each figure is contained, as it were, by its own particular space, the space it "fits." The depiction of space as an enveloping and unifying factor in pictorial design may not be characteristic in Greek art, and this picture, as we have said, copies a Greek model. On the other hand, the special Roman contribution to painting may be precisely the representation of space as *surrounding* the whole group of objects and figures in any given composition and not merely coming between them.

It still seems to be a general tendency to deny any originality to Roman paintings and to insist that they are direct copies of or closely inspired by Hellenistic originals. No doubt, many Roman paintings do appear to be direct copies—for example, the *Herakles and Telephos* just discussed and the Alexander mosaic shown in FIG. 6-37. In fact, many paintings were probably done by transplanted Greek artists, and we might even grant that the Greek-derived style was the dominant one. But the Roman *landscape* seems to represent a radically different approach, particularly in its expression of a concept of space that is simply not evident in Greek art, and all attempts to derive Roman landscape painting from Hellenistic Greece lead us into extremely tenuous speculation based on unknown (or nonexistent) Greek prototypes. All extant Greek works show the Greek artist thinking in terms of solid volumes, like those of human figures—as in the *Herakles* painting—and confining space to a mere separating function rather than an all-containing one. Thus, it might be much simpler to credit the Romans with the development of a new concept in painting—namely, the projection of an enveloping, unifying volume of space on a flat surface. This refinement of abstraction—where space, filled with air and light, is actually represented as just as real as the objects it surrounds and contains—would complete the long development of representation that begins with the silhouettes of early Egypt and Mesopotamia and even

earlier. At any rate, many now accept the view that the architectural illusionism of the second style is a Roman development and that this illusionism was a step in the transition to the spaces depicted in the smaller landscape panels (FIG. 6-36). For an artist thinking of the wall surface as a kind of extension of the space of the room (as in architectural illusionism), the next step would be to take a segment of the wall and convert it, windowlike, into a small block of framed space that extends "through" the wall and contains its little universe of depicted objects.

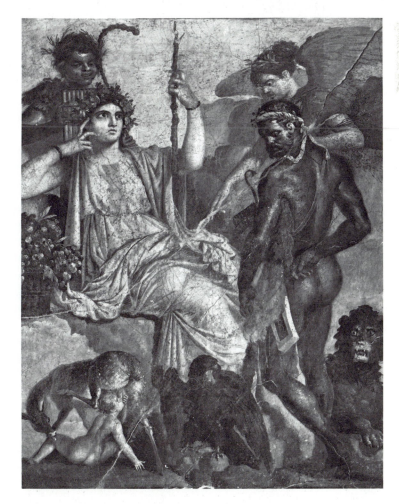

6-35 *Herakles and Telephos*, wall painting, Herculaneum, *c.* A.D. 70. Approx. 7' 2" × 6' 2". Museo Nazionale, Naples.

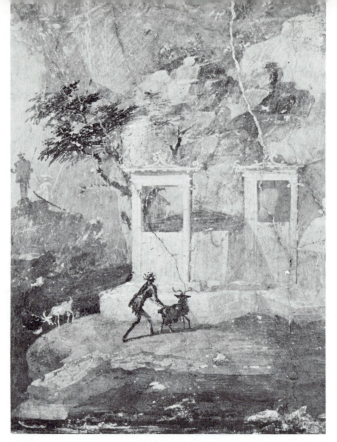

6-36 *Pastoral Scene,* detail, wall painting transferred to panel, Pompeii, first century A.D. Approx. 20″ high. Museo Nazionale, Naples.

spective but used (effectively, if unsystematically) the diminution of figures and objects and particularly atmospheric perspective, with its hazed and sketchy outlines, the shift from local color toward blue, and the blurring of distant contours (compare FIG. 6-29).

The love of country life and the idealizing of nature—what we may call the Arcadian spirit—prevails in these landscapes. Characteristically, they contain shepherds, goats, fauns, little temples, garlanded columns, copses of trees, and other accessories, which from their mood—part religious, part idyllic—have been called sacral-idyllic scenes (FIGS. 6-31 and 6-36). The Arcadian spirit of the time speaks in the formal, pastoral poetry of Vergil, and in one of his odes Horace, proclaiming the satisfactions afforded the city man by his villa in the countryside, where life is beautiful, simple, and natural in contrast with the urban greed for gold and power, asks, "Why should I change my Sabine dale for splendor full of trouble?"

The attitude that celebrates the virtues of rustic life must be very closely associated with an original Roman development in architecture. Many Arcadian landscapes have been found in *villas*—country houses developed by the Romans when congestion in the cities became severe, as it did in Pompeii during the first century B.C. The villas were never located very far from town (one might call them suburban), and their wealthy owners could enjoy the advantages of city life and the quiet of the countryside. The very spaciousness of the landscape around the villa came to be the subject matter of the wall paintings we have been examining. The modern desire to escape the tensions of the city and to return to nature is ancient in its architectural and pictorial expression, not to mention its appearance in literature. We will encounter this Arcadianism

In any case, the artist of the fourth style, chiefly interested in representing space, makes the objects as small as possible and unifies the whole composition, as we have seen, with light and atmosphere. Of course, recession in depth is suggested, not accurately projected. As noted above, the Romans had no system of mathematical per-

6-37 *The Battle of Issus,* from the House of the Faun, Pompeii, *c.* 80 B.C. Mosaic, approx. 8′ 10″ × 16′ 9″. Museo Nazionale, Naples.

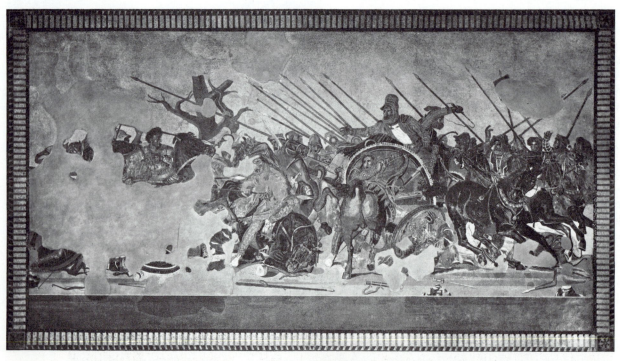

again and again in the history of the West—in the Renaissance and in the nineteenth and twentieth centuries, when urban pressures strain human nerves.

The floors as well as the walls of Roman buildings were ornamented, usually in mosaics. Mosaic had its beginnings in the ancient Near East (see Chapter Five, pp. 153–55). It was used by the Greeks in place of carpets, often in geometric patterns. The Romans continued the practice and, from the first century A.D. on, even applied mosaic to walls. A striking aspect of Roman mosaics is the attempt frequently made in them to copy not only the subject matter of painting but also the painter's technique in modeling, shading and the like. This was possible only if extremely small tesserae (the bits of glass or stone composing the mosaic) were used, as, for example, in the famous Alexander mosaic from the House of the Faun in Pompeii (FIG. 6-37), which is likely a copy of a Hellenistic original and perhaps should be thought of as more Hellenistic than Roman. The mosaic, which represents the rout of Darius and his army by Alexander the Great at the battle of Issus, has those qualities of Greek style we have noted: the essentially sculpturesque emphasis upon the solid forms, space defined by the forms themselves, and no attempt to show an enveloping space. Nevertheless, a remarkable taste for fidelity to appearance is shown in the details of action. The horses plunge into and out of the picture at the most daring angles, and the human figures are posed in such variety of descriptive attitude as to convince us the artist was pursuing an ultimate realism. In keeping with this is the high degree of tonal smoothness that was achieved by the setting-in of tesserae so small that some fifty separate bits were used to describe a single eye perhaps $1\frac{1}{2}$ inches wide. The Romans appear to have developed a taste for

this kind of minute workmanship, and the technical quality of mosaics must have been judged by the size of the tesserae used—the smaller the better. Since, after all, the mosaics were seen at a distance of only five or six feet (one walked on them), such a criterion seems natural enough. The standard changes during the Early Christian period, when mosaics were placed high on church walls and apse vaults, making such minute differences scarcely noticeable and such a painstaking technique meaningless.

The vast range of subjects represented in mosaics is comparable to that of Roman painting. Themes from classical mythology vied in popularity with historical subjects (FIG. 6-37) or with topical ones such as genre aspects of rural existence and scenes from the popular theater, gladiatorial battles, chariot races, or hunting.

Stylistically the development was toward simplification of the extremely complex and detailed work such as that in the Alexander mosaic (FIG. 6-37). Tesserae tend to become larger, the designs flatter and less illusionistic. From mid-first century A.D. on, human figures and animal forms appear in black silhouette on white ground, prefacing the black and white mosaics that became the favorite floor decorations in Italy during the second and third centuries A.D. They were popular especially in bathing establishments, and a masterpiece of this type was found in the Baths of Neptune at Ostia (FIG. 6-38). Here, appropriately enough, marine divinities, accompanied by nereids and tritons, are carried across the waters by dolphins and horses with fishtail bodies. The fluid, dynamic design is based on a repetition of curvilinear forms that evokes the movement of the sea.

At the same time, polychrome mosaics moved up the walls, at first to decorate grottoes and fountains, but even-

6-38 Floor mosaic from the Baths of Neptune, Ostia, second century A.D.

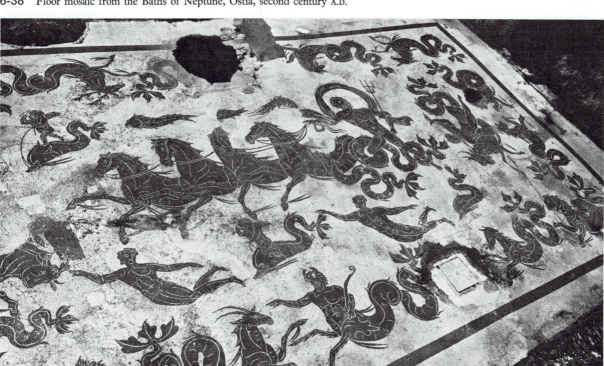

tually covering entire walls, as in the example shown in FIG. 6-39. Less exposed to wear, as from sandaled feet, wall mosaics permitted the use of relatively fragile materials, such as glass paste (*smalto*) and enamel for stronger coloristic effects than were possible with colored stone or marble tesserae. The brilliant blue of our example, due largely to the liberal use of smalto, contributes also to the rich tonality in the modeling of the figures, which recalls the glassy surfaces we have seen in the Herakles from the Herakles and Telephos group (FIG. 6-35).

Painting, with all its advanced illusionistic devices, remains the standard for mosaic representation. What was achieved by way of subtle, pictorial effect can be seen equally in mural painting and in the smaller scale of the painted panel. We may judge the quality of panel painting by a portrait from Faiyum in Egypt, some sixty miles south of modern Cairo (FIG. 6-40). In Greek and Roman times Faiyum was a busy, populous province, and its cemeteries have yielded some 600 portraits painted on wood and attached to the mummy cases of the deceased.

The making of such portraits must have been a regional custom, as very few have been found elsewhere; they supply for us our largest gallery of ordinary people of the vast Roman imperial world when it was at the height of its power. While some Pompeian wall frescoes give us hints as to what Greek murals may have looked like, the Faiyum portraits give us the best idea we have of Hellenistic Greek painting techniques. Most of the portraits are done in the encaustic technique (pigments in hot wax—see p. 117), but *tempera* (pigments in egg yolk) was used occasionally. Easel painting, upon small, portable panels, had been highly esteemed in Greece, where the encaustic technique had a long tradition. Polygnotos had worked in it in Classical times and, as mentioned earlier, it had been used for the architectural decoration of buildings like the Parthenon. The example here shows the very highest level of craftsmanship—refined brushwork, soft and delicate modeling, and the subtlest possible reading of a sensitive subject. The Faiyum portraits were probably painted from living persons, and in this instance we have the meeting of

6-39 Wall mosaic in the House of Neptune and Amphitrite, Herculaneum, *c.* A.D. 70.

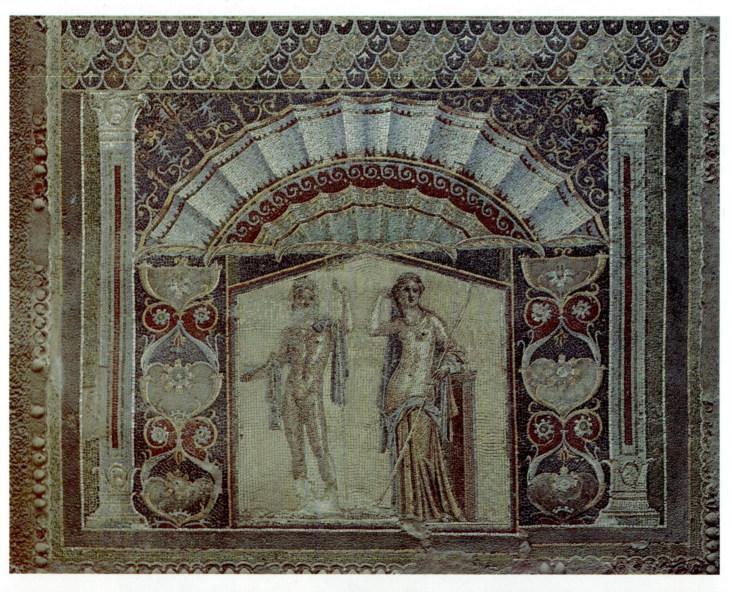

an unusually perceptive artist with a subject whose personality would try his whole skill to render. The composure, the emphasized thoughtful eyes, the Hellenizing hairstyle, are familiar in the portraits made during the time of the Stoic emperor Marcus Aurelius (about A.D. 160) and in the portraits of the emperor himself. The calm demeanor of the subject, the gaze that "sees the world steadily and sees it whole," evokes the philosophy of the emperor himself as set forth in his *Meditations*. As earlier we confronted the bust of Pompey, familiar with his history, so it is an aid to us in meeting this image from the age of the Antonines to read the philosophic emperor as we read the painted features of our subject:

> Every moment think steadily as a Roman and a man to do what you have in hand with perfect and simple dignity. . . . do every act of your life as if it were the last, laying aside all carelessness and passionate aversion from the commands of reason, and all hypocrisy, and self-love, and discontent with the destiny which has been given to you.

Our history has taken us beyond the period of the republic into that of the empire in order to show how Rome carried the ancient world's representation of landscape and of human individuality—begun in Mesopotamia and Egypt—to its fullest expression.

The Early Empire

When Octavian Caesar, the great-nephew and heir of Julius Caesar, routed the forces of Antony and Cleopatra at Actium in 31 B.C., he brought to an end some ninety long years of destructive civil war that had shattered the Roman republic. Though Octavian believed and proclaimed himself the restorer of the republic and the protector of its constitution and traditions, he became in fact the first emperor of Rome and to all intents and purposes ruled as emperor, taking the venerable name "Augustus," which was bestowed upon him by a grateful Senate. The peace that began with Augustus has been called the Pax Romana, for, under the auspices of a long line of emperors, peace prevailed within the Roman world for 150 years, a record in world history.

Augustus, determined to establish his authority unshakably, kept command of the military and financial resources of the empire in his own hands and deliberately set out to build a new and magnificent Rome in order to give a splendid image to the imperial reality. As they carried the boundaries of the empire further in all directions, the Julio-Claudian emperors, Augustus' successors in the first century A.D., continued his policy of glorifying by architecture, art, and a vast variety of public works the visible aspect of empire, sometimes to an extravagant degree. In the second century the empire—under Trajan, Hadrian,

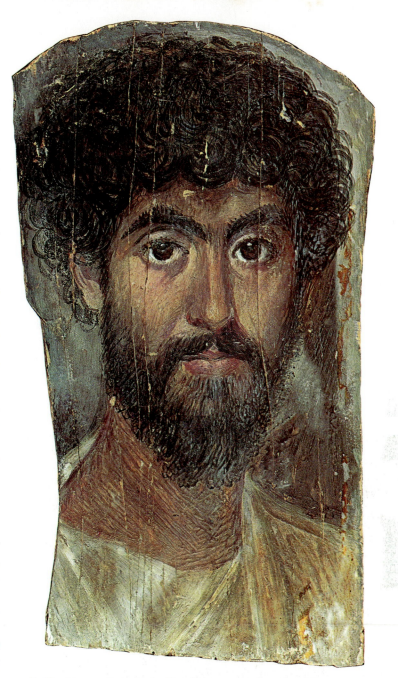

6-40   *Mummy Portrait of a Man,* Faiyum, second century A.D. Encaustic painting on wood panel, approx. 13¾″ × 8″. Albright-Knox Art Gallery, Buffalo (Charles Clifton Fund).

and the Antonines—reached its greatest geographical extent and the summit of its power (see map, p. 166); the might and influence of Rome was unchallenged in the Western world, though there was always the pressure of the new, Germanic peoples on its northern borders, of the Berbers in the south, and of the Parthians and resurgent Persians on the east. These pressures increased in the third century, and, combined with the decline of imperial authority within the empire, disintegration of the economic and administrative structure, and military anarchy, almost brought the empire to collapse. In A.D. 285 it was restored by the last pagan emperor, the capable Diocletian, under whom took place the savage persecution of a sect called the Christians. Within a generation the triumph of this sect was to mark a major turning point in the history of the world.

ARCHITECTURE AND PUBLIC WORKS

The grandiose imperial designs of the early empire are of course reflected in its architecture, perhaps most conspicuously there. The relatively stable conditions produced by the Pax Romana made possible the Romanization of the provinces, and urbanism—the planning and building of cities—played in this process a principal role. The rapid growth of population, especially city population, we have mentioned above as a reason for the escape to the suburban villa. The pressure of population in the city itself made the sprawling atrium house—wasteful of space—obsolete. In Rome, a population of close to one million had to be housed in multistory apartment blocks (*insulae*). Some 45,000 of these—built to the maximum legal height of five stories (sixty to seventy feet high)—accommodated almost 90 percent of Rome's population. Most of the almost 50,000 inhabitants of Ostia, the port city of Rome, were housed in such apartment houses, some of which have been preserved to the level of the third story. Most were built of brick-faced concrete. The ground floors were occupied by shops, above which were the apartments, accessible by individual staircases. Many of the apartments were substantially more spacious than are most of ours today, the suites sometimes containing as many as twelve rooms, arranged on two levels. A reconstruction of an Ostian insula (FIG. 6-41) shows the apartment blocks built around a central court; some of the larger of these courts may have been landscaped and contained a small shrine. Apparently, many apartments had balconies, still a standard feature of modern Italian apartment houses. Only deluxe apartments had private toilets; others were served by community latrines, usually on the ground floor. The insulae had no private baths, but public baths were conveniently located throughout the various quarters of the city and were equipped with highly developed heating systems, which private houses and apartments lacked. (This is still true of

parts of modern Italy.) The crowded conditions encouraged rent-gouging and jerry-building. Deficiency in materials was often compounded by bad design, such as a foundation area too small in relation to the height of a building—the latter a means of maximal exploitation of the limited space available. The poet Juvenal wryly complains about the poorly constructed city buildings:

> . . . we inhabit a city propped up for the most part by slats: for that is how the landlord patches up the crack in the old wall, bidding the inmates sleep at ease under the ruin that hangs above their heads.

To an extent greater than is commonly known, the convenience of the ancient Roman of ordinary and less than ordinary means depended on facilities provided by the state—by authority imperial, provincial, or municipal. Millions of individuals depended upon the government for food distribution, water supply and sanitation, recreation and entertainment, and roads and bridges, not to mention the protection afforded by police and fire-fighters. The administration of these services in the great days of the empire was efficient even by our standards, given of course the limitations we would expect from a less highly developed technology and communication system. Second only to food distribution, an adequate water supply for the populations of the overcrowded cities was the most imperative need. The Romans methodically developed water-supply systems as part of urban planning. The city of Rome began to build aqueducts for itself as early as the fourth century B.C., and Roman aqueducts or their ruins still stand in many former Roman cities, both in Italy and in the provinces. Water was carried from the source to the city by gravity flow, requiring the building of channels with a continuous gradual decline over distances often exceeding fifty miles; we can appreciate even in modern terms what an outstanding achievement of surveying and engineering this represents. The Pont du Gard near Nîmes (FIG. 6-42), in southern France, is one of the most impressive specimens of Roman engineering skill. Each large arch spans some eighty-two feet and is constructed of unce-

6-41 Reconstruction of an insula, Ostia.

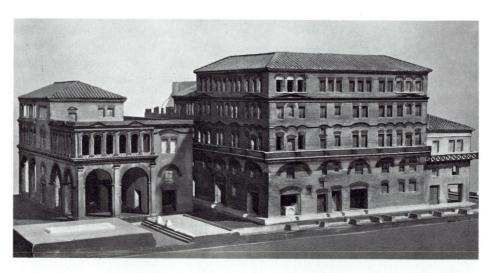

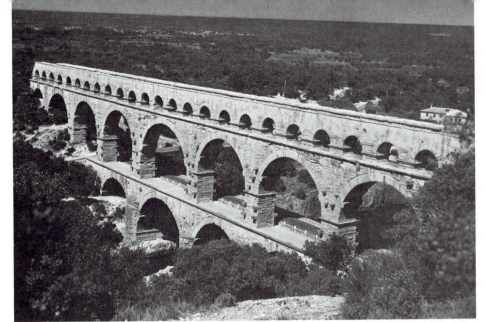

6-42 Pont du Gard, near Nîmes, southern France, first century B.C.

mented blocks weighing up to two tons each. The quickening rhythm of the small top arches (which carry the channel), placed in groups of threes over the larger arches, manifests the Roman engineer's sense for the esthetic as well as the practical. The finished aqueduct carried water to Nîmes over a distance of some thirty miles and provided each inhabitant with about 100 gallons a day. Services like this, and the awesome structures through which they were provided, could not help but impress upon the diverse peoples who had come under the rule of Rome the advan-

tages of compliance with such practical power and the benefits that could come from Romanization.

If the construction of aqueducts could show the value of homage to Rome, how much more the erection of a whole city! At Timgad (Thamugadi) in North Africa (FIG. 6-43) the Romans built a city, around A.D. 100, that lasted until its destruction by the Arabs in the sixth century A.D. Built along a major military road 100 miles from the sea, it was probably planned to house a military garrison to keep local tribes in check. But this primary function was soon ex-

6-43 Plan of Timgad (Thamugadi, Algeria), founded c. A.D. 100.

1. Forum
2. Theater
3. Library
4. House of Januarius, baptistry
5. East bath
6. North bath
7. Small baths
8. Temple of Ceres

0   100   200   300   400   500 FEET

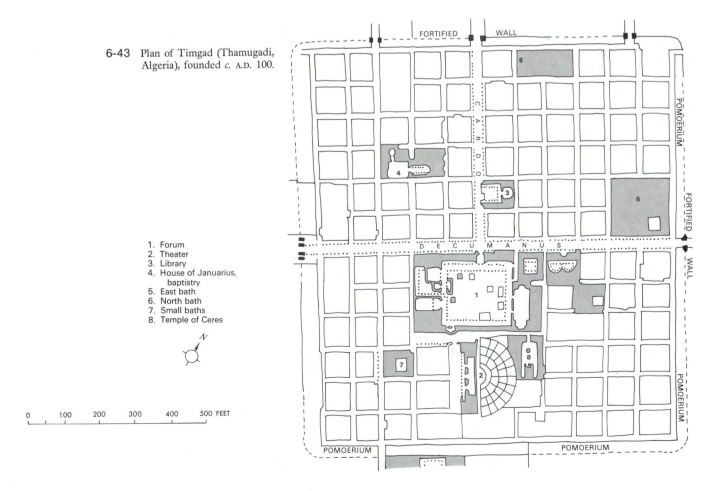

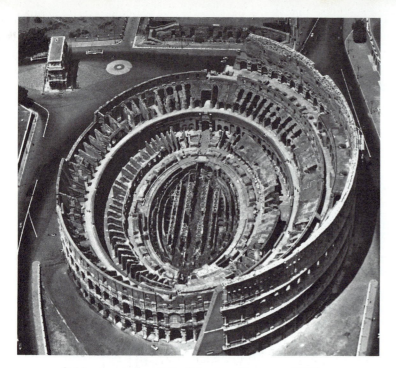

6-44 Aerial view of the Colosseum, Rome, A.D. 70–82.

panded, and no costs were spared to make this little provincial town into an attractive focal point for the local inhabitants. Here the empire was a physical presence to the Africans, the city representative of the authority of the emperor and the civilization of Rome. Like many other

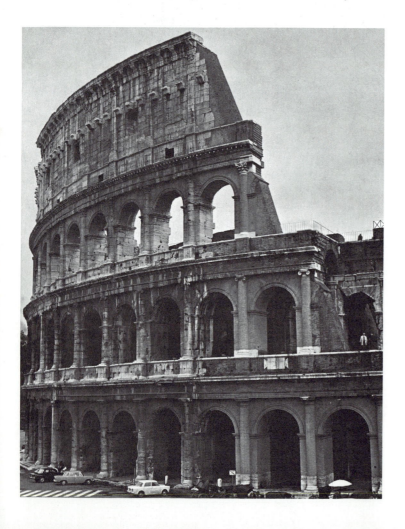

colonial settlements, Timgad served as a key to the process of Romanization. The town was planned with great precision, its design probably based on the layout of the Roman military encampment, the *castrum*. (The question of precedence remains unresolved: The castrum may have been based on the layout of the Roman colonial city.) The typical provincial Roman city has the form of a square divided into equal quarters by two main arteries crossing at right angles, the *cardo* being the north-south axis, the *decumanus* the east-west; the forum is located near this crossing. The quarters are subdivided into square blocks, and the forum and public buildings like the theater, baths, and library occupy areas that are multiples of these blocks. At Timgad monumental gates led into the city, the streets of which were colonnaded. The city covered some thirty acres, and its original population of 2000 soon grew to 15,000. The whole plan was essentially a modification of the Hippodamian scheme (see p. 153) but more rigidly ordered and systematized, with the forum set off from the main traffic pattern. The fact that most of these colonial settlements were laid out in the same manner—whether in North Africa, the Near East, or England—expresses more concretely than any building type or other construction project the unity and centralized power of the Roman empire at its height.

The architectural images of Rome set up in the far reaches of the empire had their even more monumental equivalents in the capital itself. When all roads did indeed lead to Rome, they could find their symbolic terminus in such stupendous works as the Colosseum (FIGS. 6-44 and 6-45), which for modern men still represents Rome as does no other building. So closely was it identified in the past with the city and the empire that an aphorism out of the early Middle Ages went: While the Colosseum stands, Rome stands; when the Colosseum falls, Rome falls; and when Rome, the world!

The Flavian Amphitheater, popularly renamed the Colosseum, after a now lost colossal statue of Nero that stood nearby, was begun by Vespasian, first in the Flavian line of emperors. It was dedicated in A.D. 80 by his successor, Titus, who had employed on the building of it prisoners from the Jewish Wars (see FIGS. 6-59 and 6-60). The building type is an invention of the Romans, who expanded the "theater" into an "amphitheater," which is essentially two facing theaters enclosing an oval space, the arena. The Roman Colosseum is the largest of its type, but most major cities in the empire had an amphitheater. Some, like that at Verona, are still being used today for theatrical performances or games. The Colosseum was originally meant for the staging of lavish spectacles, battles between animals and gladiators in various combinations. The mythic beast-men struggles we saw represented in Mesopotamian art here came to bloody reality. The extravagantly inhuman shows cost thousands of lives, among them those of many Christians, and the Colosseum has

6-45 Outer wall of the Colosseum.

never quite outlived its infamy. The emperors competed with each other over who could produce the most elaborate spectacles. For the opening performance in A.D. 80 the arena was flooded and a complete naval battle, with over 3000 participants, was duplicated.

The oval arena of the Colosseum (FIG. 6-44) is surrounded by steeply rising rows of seats, which had a capacity of over 50,000 spectators. Its substructure consists of a complex system of radial and concentric corridors covered by concrete vaults that rise to support the upper rows of seats. Originally, tall poles around the top of the structure supported ropes on which awnings could be spread to provide shade for the spectators. The basements below the arena proper contained animal cages, barracks for gladiators, and machinery for raising and lowering stage settings as well as the animal and human combatants. A great deal of technical ingenuity involving lifting tackle was employed to suddenly hurl hungry beasts from their dark dens into the violent light of the arena.

Roman ingenuity in the management of architectural space to fit a complex function may be observed even in the exterior of the Colosseum—namely, the arcuated entrance-exit openings that must have permitted rapid filling and emptying of the vast interior space. The relation of these openings to the tiers of seats within was very carefully thought out and, in essence, may be observed in the modern football stadium. The Colosseum exemplifies the Roman talent for matching public and private convenience within large-scale service structures that require the enclosure and the spanning of great spaces.

The exterior of the building (FIG. 6-45), with its numerous functional openings, consists of ashlar masonry in which dry-jointed blocks were held together by metal cramps and dowels, as in Greek architecture. Its present pock-marked appearance (as if it had been blasted by large shrapnel) is due to the fact that the metal fittings were pried from the joints during the Middle Ages, when metal was very hard to come by. With these jointing units gone, vibrations from modern traffic have been shifting the stones, and the entire structure is in danger of collapse. The exterior walls are 161 feet high, and each of the three stories shows the characteristic combination of the Roman arch and vault construction with one of the ornamentally enclosing Greek orders. This setup, in which an arch is enframed by two engaged columns that carry a lintel, appears in triumphal arches and other Roman buildings, and, revived in the Italian Renaissance, has a long, illustrious history in Classical architecture. For the moment it is necessary only to note that although this exterior feature serves no structural purpose, it does have an esthetic function, that of integrating the units of the surface by rhythmic horizontal and vertical repetition of the enframed arch. Although the arrangement of the orders finds no correspondence of a functional sort in the interior of the Colosseum, the rule of the arrangement is strict, following the

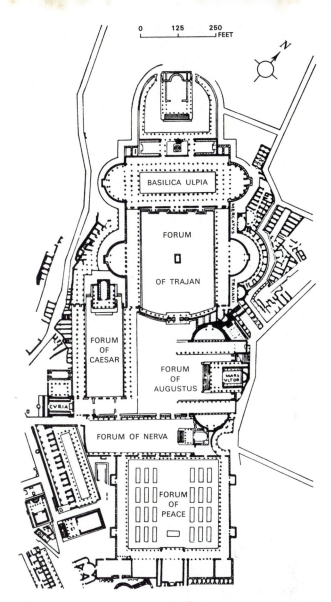

6-46 Plan of the imperial forums in Rome.

standard Roman vertical sequence for multistoried buildings: Doric-Ionic-Corinthian, from the ground floor up. This sequence is based on the proportions of the orders, with the Doric, appearing to be the strongest, taken to be capable of supporting the greatest load.

The imperial forums of the emperors rivaled the Colosseum as majestic expressions of the imperial ideal. These forums were erected not so much as fundamental civic units of direct service to the people as ostentatious glorifications of imperial power. They stood witness to the "piety, might, good fortune, magnanimity and happiness"—as their triumphal inscriptions so often proclaimed—of the successive emperors who built them. They were not planned as a unit, but each forum was added to another, their unity being achieved by strict axial alignment (FIG. 6-46). Most consist of large colonnaded courts, with some of them designed to set off a temple dedicated to the god who was the special protector of the

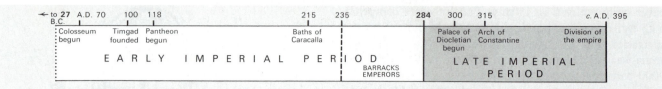

	to **27**	A.D. 70	100	118		215	235		**284**	300	315		c. A.D. 395
	B.C.	Colosseum begun	Timgad founded	Pantheon begun		Baths of Caracalla			Palace of Diocletian begun	Arch of Constantine		Division of the empire	

E A R L Y I M P E R I A L P E R I O D

BARRACKS EMPERORS

L A T E   I M P E R I A L
P E R I O D

emperor. The demands of impressive scale and great, sweeping vistas led sometimes to massive transformation of whole neighborhoods. The building of the Forum of Trajan required the rebuilding of a market district and the modification of an entire hillside.

Dominating the Forum of Trajan was the huge Basilica Ulpia of about A.D. 112 (FIG. 6-47). A larger version of the basilica in Pompeii, it was of a type that was perhaps the most characteristic of those developed by the Romans. The basilica was a public hall designed to accommodate large numbers of people on various kinds of business. It was the locale of stock exchanges, law courts, business offices, and administrative bureaus and must have provided a center for civic services analogous to those of multiple-building municipal centers today. Later, the Christians adapted the basilica (but more especially its subtype, the palace audience hall) to religious purposes, modifying it into the typical Christian church building. In plan the basilica was rectangular, with two or more semicircular *apses*. In the Basilica Ulpia one of the apses contained the Shrine of

Liberty, where slaves were set free; the other may possibly have served in ceremonies of the emperor's cult. The entrance was on one of the long sides, an orientation that was changed by the Christians. The building was vast— 426 by 138 feet; illumination for this great interior space was afforded by clerestory windows provided by elevation of the timber-roofed nave above the colonnaded aisles. In the Basilica Ulpia we once again encounter the Romans' instinctive feeling for broad, uninterrupted architectural spaces enclosed for the convenience of human transaction. Despite an imposing exterior, the interior space is what counts here, and though it is a colonnaded space, its effect is not like that of the externally perceived Greek temple but rather like a dipteral Greek temple inverted: It is to be experienced from within, not from without.

One of the best preserved of all Roman monuments and one of the most renowned and influential buildings in the history of architecture is the Pantheon (FIGS. 6-48 to 6-50), built about A.D. 125, in which the effect of interior space is quite overwhelming, especially since its exterior scarcely

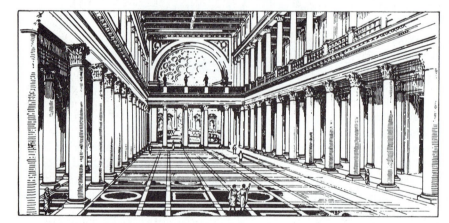

6-47 Reconstruction and plan of the Basilica Ulpia, Rome, *c.* A.D. 112. (After Sir Banister Fletcher.)

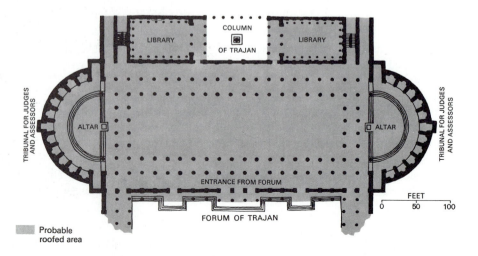

Probable roofed area

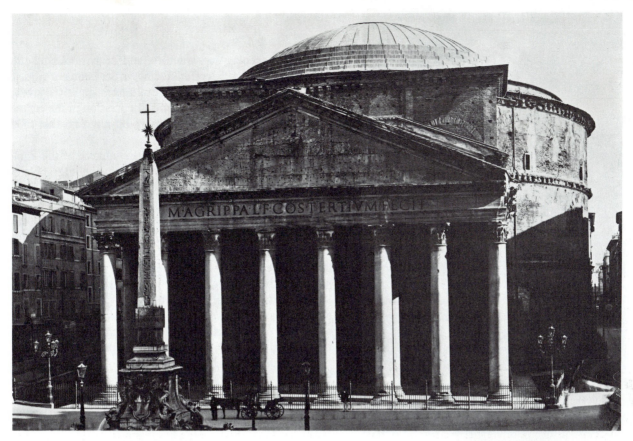

6-48 The Pantheon, Rome, A.D. 118–25.

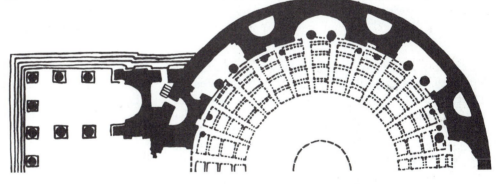

6-49 Section and half-plan of the Pantheon. (Plan is symmetrical.)

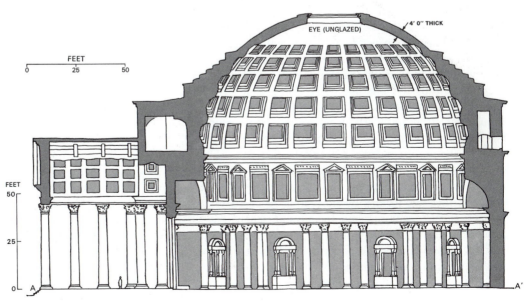

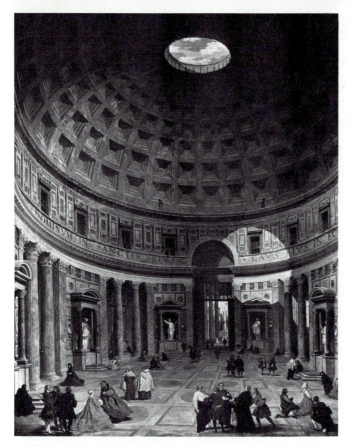

6-50 *Interior of the Pantheon*, painting by Giovanni Pannini, *c.* 1750. National Gallery of Art, Washington, D.C. (Samuel H. Kress Collection).

suggests it. It is a domed rotunda fronted with a rectangular portico. The original effect must have been different, for the building was only partly freestanding, its back and one of its sides hidden by older structures. Moreover, the portico was partly embraced by a no-longer-extant colonnaded court. Built in the time of Hadrian, it may have been conceived by that versatile ruler.

The structure is of monumental simplicity and great scale. The circular interior is covered by a hemispherical dome 144 feet in diameter, the summit of the dome being the same distance from the floor. The design is thus based upon the intersection of two circles, one horizontal, the other vertical, imaginable as sections of a globe of space inscribed within the building. The dome is a shell of concrete that gradually thickens toward the base in order to augment structural strength where it is most needed. The center of the dome is dramatically pierced by a round opening (the *oculus*, or "eye") 30 feet in diameter, which, left unglazed and open to the sky, is the only source of light for the interior. Supporting the dome are piers of immense thickness formed by alternating rectangular and rounded niches, each covered by a vault that channels pressures exerted by the weight of the dome into solid masonry. The dome is coffered for the multiple purpose of making a handsome geometric foil of squares within the vast circle, of reducing the weight and mass of the dome

without weakening its structure, and of symbolizing the starry heavens, each coffer having in its center a gilded bronze rosette. The floor of the building is slightly convex, and drains are cut into the shallow depression in the center (directly under the oculus) to carry off any rain that falls through the opening far above.

Giovanni Pannini's painting of the interior of the Pantheon (FIG. 6-50) exhibits better than any photograph the unity and scale of the design, the simplicity of its relationships, and its breathtaking grandeur. It almost records the experience one has on first entering this tremendous, shaped space, a feeling not of the weight of the enclosing masses, but of the palpable presence of space itself, for the architecture here displayed is first of all an architecture of space. In the architectures so far studied, the form of the space enclosed is determined by the placement of the solids, which do not so much shape it as interrupt it. The solids are so prominent in Egyptian and Mesopotamian architecture that it is the solids we *see;* space is only "negative," simply *happening* between the solids. We think of this as an architecture of mass. Greek architecture, also primarily concerned with masses and their relations, and with the shaping of the solid units, is designated as skeletal or sculptural architecture. It is the Roman architects who initially conceive architecture in terms of units of space that can be shaped by enclosures. The interior of the Pantheon, in keeping with this interest, is a single, unified, self-sufficient whole, uninterrupted by supporting solids; it is a whole that encloses the visitor without imprisoning him, a small cosmos that opens through the oculus to the drifting clouds, the blue sky, the sun, universal nature, and the gods. To escape from the noise and torrid heat of a Roman summer day into the sudden cool and calm immensity of the Pantheon is an experience almost impossible to describe and one that should be promised oneself. Above all, it is an *architectural* experience.

It should not be forgotten that Roman inventiveness in the construction of great interior spaces depended upon engineering knowledge of the properties of solids and of the statics of inert masses. The arch, the vault, and the dome were structural units appropriated and developed by the Romans with skill unsurpassed in the ancient world and not often since. Basically the problem as the Romans met it was this: how to enclose and roof over a vast space and how to give this space proper illumination while still keeping it open and free of the necessary roof supports. (Compare this approach with that embodied in the hypostyle halls of Egypt, as shown in FIG. 3-27.)

The simplest vault used by the Romans was the *barrel vault* (FIG. 6-51a)—in essence, a deep arch that forms a half-cylindrical roof over an oblong space, the edges of the half-cylinder resting directly upon the side walls, which must be either thick enough to support the weight or reinforced by buttresses. This vault can be made of concrete by use of a temporary wooden form (known as

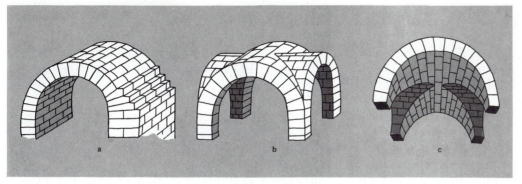

6-51 Roman vaulting systems: (a) barrel vault; (b) cross-barrel vault seen from above; (c) cross-barrel vault seen from below. Actual Roman vaulting was made of concrete, not the cut stone shown here.

centering) that is the size and shape of the finished vault and that holds the fluid concrete until it hardens. The vaulting of the central hall of the Thermae (Baths) of Caracalla (FIG. 6-52) and of the Basilica of Constantine (FIG. 6-76) was made by having the main barrel vault intersected at right angles at regular intervals by other barrel vaults, thus obtaining what is known as the *cross-barrel vault* (FIG. 6-51b and c). If the height of the intersecting and main barrel vaults is the same, the result is a *groin vault,* the line of intersection being called the groin. (Groin lines can be seen readily in FIG. 6-52.) Besides being lighter in appearance than the barrel vault, the cross, or groin, vault requires less buttressing: In the barrel vault the thrust—that is, the downward and outward forces exerted by the vault, like those of the arch—is along the entire length of the wall, requiring a corresponding buttressing; in the groin vault it is exerted only along the lines of intersection (the groins), and heavy buttressing is needed only at those points where they meet their vertical supports (the walls or piers). Thus, the interior can be kept free of load-carrying walls, and more light can be admitted through the use of clerestory windows located in the free space where buttressing is not needed (in effect, the ends of the cross vaults). Buttressing can be provided by heavy walls perpendicular to the main wall and pierced by arches, which thus form side aisles to the main hall (FIG. 6-77), and by short wall sections above the aisle roofs that channel part of the vaults' thrust into the outside vaults.

All this was elementary to the builders of the gigantic Baths of Caracalla (FIGS. 6-52 and 6-53), dating from about A.D. 215. The enclosure of great spaces by vaulting was at this time common practice. Although nothing of the covering is left, the baths reveal traces of the vaults that sprang up from the thick walls to heights of up to 140 feet; under them, spread out in unending variety, were spaces designed for the intellectual as well as physical recreation of thousands of leisured Romans—all at the expense of the state. Just the central buildings of the huge complex, in which the emperors hoped to keep an unruly and indigent populace preoccupied with pleasure, covered an area

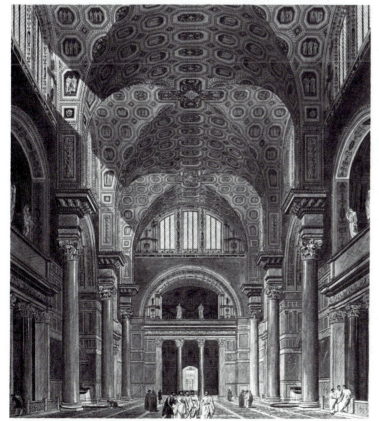

6-52 Central Hall of the Baths of Caracalla, Rome, *c.* A.D. 215. (Restoration drawing by G. Abel Blonet.)

6-53 Plan of the Baths of Caracalla. (After Sir Banister Fletcher.)

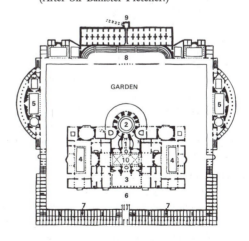

1. Tepidarium
2. Calidarium
3. Frigidarium, with swimming pool
4. Open peristyles
5. Lecture rooms and libraries
6. Promenade
7. Shops
8. Stadium
9. Aqueduct and reservoirs
10. Central Hall

roughly 240 by 120 yards; and the baths, which were the center of interest as well as the architectural center of the design, had a capacity of 1600 bathers. The functions of various parts of the complex are still matters of controversy. The design was symmetrical along a central axis occupied by pools that were filled with water of different temperatures: the *frigidarium*, the cold-water pool; the *tepidarium*, the central room containing smaller warm-water pools; and the *calidarium*, a circular hot-water pool in a domed rotunda. The central buildings also contained steam baths, dressing rooms, lounges, lecture halls, and *palaestrae* (exercise rooms). This whole core complex was surrounded by landscaped gardens bordered by secondary buildings that housed shops, restaurants, libraries, gymnasiums, and (perhaps) a stadium. The long side of the entire complex measured almost one-quarter of a mile. Beneath it all was a subterranean world of corridors (some wide enough to accommodate vehicles), storerooms, and heating chambers populated by slaves and stokers, for the halls and the water were heated by a system in which hot air was circulated through tubes and hollow bricks beneath the floors, in the walls, and sometimes in the vaults. The water was plentifully supplied by an individual aqueduct.

This enormous dedication of human ingenuity in the service of human ease! For a negligible admission fee one could lounge for a whole day at the baths in surroundings of the greatest magnificence. In fact, the baths were so lavish, ornate, and luxurious that moralists of the time complained of their wasteful ostentation. Seneca, comparing his degenerate times with those of the heroic Scipio, who bathed in austerely simple surroundings, complained:

> But who in these days could bear to bathe in such a fashion? We think ourselves poor and mean if our walls are not resplendent with large and costly mirrors; if our marbles from Alexandria are not set off by mosaics of Numidian stone, if their borders are not faced over on all sides with difficult patterns, arranged in many colours like paintings; if our vaulted ceilings are not buried in glass; if our swimming pools are not lined with Thasian marble, once a rare and wonderful sight in any temple. . . . What a vast number of statues, of columns that support nothing, but are built for decoration, merely in order to spend money! And what masses of water that fall crashing from level to level! We have become so luxurious that we will have nothing but precious stones to walk upon.

The baths were of course not merely that, but social centers in which one could spend the whole day "sweetly doing nothing." And the baths were cultural centers as well, with their libraries, and with their profusion of magnificent statues. A large number of the abovementioned Roman copies after Greek originals were found in public baths, and a few of the most important in the Baths of Caracalla. To the Romans, baths of this type were a natural and indispensable part of civilization.

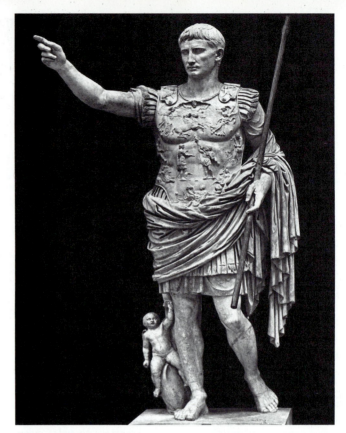

6-54 *Augustus of Primaporta*, c. 20 B.C. Marble, 6′ 8″ high. Vatican Museums, Rome.

SCULPTURE AND MONUMENTAL RELIEF

Sculpture in the empire begins under the influence of Augustan Rome's admiration of Hellenic culture and of the emperor's apparent determination to base a cultural renewal of Rome on it. That the Hellenized glorification of the empire was politically motivated is doubtless true; we have seen in architecture how building was molded to the end of manifesting the imperial authority. But the imperial motivation had the esthetic consequence that work of the highest quality in all the arts was produced bearing the seal, as it were, of the Hellenic spirit. The *Augustus of Primaporta* (FIG. 6-54), about 20 B.C., no less than the *Aeneid* of Vergil, is an example of the sedate, idealizing manner we recognize as "Augustan." The statue, which once stood in front of the imperial villa in Primaporta, about ten miles north of Rome, represents Augustus proclaiming a diplomatic victory to the people. The work is of the highest quality and is very likely by a Greek artist. At first glance it might appear to be in the realistic mode of Republican statues, but at the second we find it strongly idealized, made according to Polykleitan proportions and even reminiscent of the *Doryphoros* (FIG. 5-53), especially the walking pose. The reliefs on the emperor's breast plate are Roman in subject and refer to contemporaneous events—at least in the central theme: A Parthian returns a Roman standard to a Roman soldier. But these historical references are enframed by mythological and allegorical figures representing the sky god, the earth goddess, and the

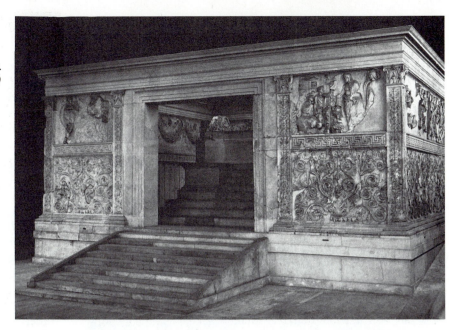

6-55 Ara Pacis Augustae, Rome, 13-9 B.C. Marble, approx. 35' wide. (Cornice restored.)

pacified provinces of Spain and Gaul. Together the figures symbolize blessings of the new Golden Age expected to come with the Augustan peace. They also place side by side the idealizing and realistic tendencies in Roman art that will alternate and intermingle throughout imperial times.

The tendencies mingle in the sculptured figures of the Ara Pacis Augustae (Altar of the Augustan Peace) yet remain distinguishable (FIG. 6-55). Completed and dedicated in January, 9 B.C., to commemorate pacification of Spain and Gaul in 13 B.C., the altar can stand as a monument to the pacification of the whole empire in the Augustan years following the establishment of the new government in 27 B.C. The actual altar is raised upon an interior platform that is surrounded by a nearly square enclosure, 39 by 35½ feet. The exterior and interior surfaces of the enclosing walls are decorated with reliefs. On the interior walls are garlands suspended from bucrania (compare the frieze of the Temple of the Sibyl at Tivoli, FIG. 6-17). The exterior walls have a lower zone of a

delicately carved, decorative acanthus leaf pattern arranged in spiral designs. The upper zone depicts a procession of men, women, and children and, on separate panels, allegorical subjects. The wall surfaces are framed by florid Corinthian pilasters in a composition reminiscent of the second style of Pompeian wall painting.

The *Tellus Relief* (FIG. 6-56) represents the ancient Roman earth mother, Tellus, flanked by personifications of the elements, their draperies blowing about them, seated in a fertile landscape against clouds simulated in low relief. Although we have come to think of the interest in the illusion of landscape as Roman, the poses, the style of the draperies, and the lateral placement of the figures in a single plane attest the Greek influence. The whole tableau celebrates the Augustan peace as the source of a new bounty of nature and the new richness and fertility of earth as the foundation of Roman wealth and power.

The *Procession* (FIG. 6-57) on the Ara Pacis, led by the emperor himself, almost certainly was intended to represent the actual solemnities when the altar was dedicated.

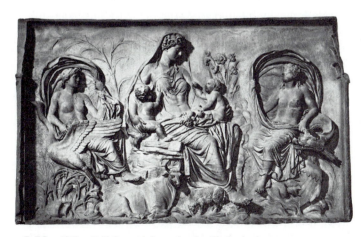

6-56 *Tellus Relief,* panel from the Ara Pacis Augustae.

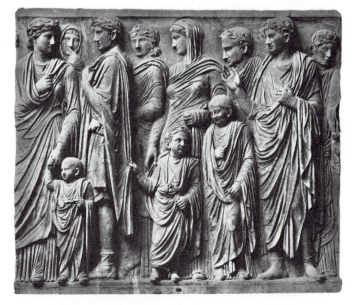

6-57 *Procession,* portion of the frieze of the Ara Pacis Augustae. Marble, approx. 63″ high.

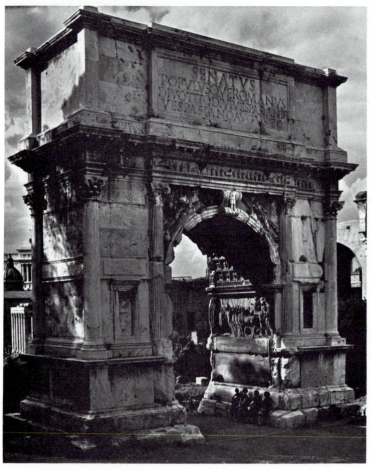

6-58   Arch of Titus, Rome, A.D. 81.

The historical particularity of the frieze is characteristic of the Roman feeling for the factual, especially as we have seen it expressed in the portrait bust, in a pragmatic architecture, and to a degree in landscape painting. This contrasts with the Greek practice of disguising historical events in the mythological, as in the great frieze of Pergamon, where a historical war between Greeks and Gauls becomes a struggle between gods and giants. In some respects the Roman feeling for narrative bound to actual events resembles more the Assyrian approach than the Greek. Yet the style of the figures of the procession is Hellenizing, and may be directly inspired by the Panathenaic frieze of the Parthenon (FIGS. 5-45 and 5-46). In the Ara Pacis the procession moves in several files. Differences in distance are signified by differences in degree of relief—the nearer the figure, the higher the relief. There is studied differentiation of individual persons; the heads are moderately idealized portraits; and there are "human interest" touches—for example, the clinging, restless children quieted by the adults. The overall demeanor is solemn, as befits the occasion, and we get the impression of a quiet concourse of participants behaving as they think proper to a quasireligious ceremony. The draperies, the

quiet dignity, the ordered deployment within a shallow plane of space echo the older Classical style, and the Ara Pacis, with its blend of real and ideal, signifies the Augustan style and that of the empire in general.

The memorializing of actual events in monumental form finds striking expression in the imperial triumphal arch, one of the most popular types of commemorative monuments. Essentially, the triumphal arch is an ornamental version of a city gate moved to the center of the city to permit entry of triumphal processions into the forum. The Arch of Titus (FIG. 6-58), dated A.D. 81, is located at a point where the Via Sacra enters the Roman Forum. As a building type the triumphal arch exerted considerable influence on the architecture of the Renaissance. Closely related to the Colosseum arch order, it consists of a single arch flanked by massive piers to which the Corinthian order has been attached decoratively. Its typical superstructure, the *attic*, bears the commemorative inscription. Occasionally the flanking piers are also pierced by arches, producing a triple arch like that of Constantine (FIG. 6-80). The walls of the passageway of the Arch of Titus are decorated with relief panels representing the triumphal return of Titus from the conquest of Jerusalem at the end of the Jewish Wars (A.D. 66–70). In later arches the sculptural decor is moved to the outside surfaces of the structure as in the Arch of Constantine.

One of the archway reliefs shows soldiers of the Roman army carrying spoils from the temple in Jerusalem, including the seven-branched candelabrum from the Holy of Holies (FIG. 6-59). The panel is much damaged. Beam holes in the upper part date from the Middle Ages, when the family of the Frangipani converted the arch into a private fortress and built a second story into the vault— only one of many examples of later indifference to the esthetic and historic value that recent times have discovered in the ruins of Rome. But enough remains to show that spatial effects aimed at in the Ara Pacis reach full development here. The illusion of movement is complete and convincing. The marching files press forward from the left background into the center foreground and disappear through the obliquely placed arch in the right background. The energy and swing of the column suggest a rapid marching cadence and the chant of triumph. The carving is extremely deep. The heads of the forward figures have been broken off, probably because they stood vulnerably free from the block, emphasizing their different placement in space from the heads in low relief, which are intact. The deep relief produces dramatically strong shadows, the light and shade quickening the movement and strikingly suggesting the "momentary flash of a passing parade." The work brings to mind the experiments with light and space in Imperial painting and architecture.

Across the archway is represented the *Triumph of Titus* (FIG. 6-60), which has a slower pace, without the thrusting movement of the marching soldiers carrying the spoils

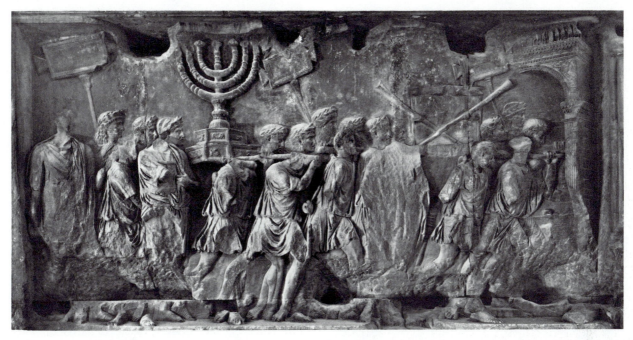

6-59   *Spoils from the Temple in Jerusalem,* relief from the Arch of Titus. Marble, approx, 7′ high.

from the temple and without the spatial experiments found there. The numerous layers of figures create an illusion of depth, and a bold attempt at representing the overlapping horses turning into the way, drawing the chariot of Titus, persuades us that the sculptor's intentions are alike in both panels. The close correspondence between the event as shown in the panels and a description of it by Josephus (contemporaneous Jewish soldier, statesman, and historian) points up the Roman bent for the factual:

> Most of the spoils that were carried were heaped up indiscriminately, but more prominent than all the rest were those captured in the Temple at Jerusalem—a golden table weighing several hundredweight, and a lampstand similarly made of gold. . . . The central shaft was fixed to a base, and from it extended slender branches placed like the prongs of a trident, and with the end of each one forged into a lamp: these numbered seven, signifying the honour paid to that number by the Jews. After these was carried the Jewish Law, the last of the spoils. Next came a large group carrying images of Victory, all fashioned of ivory and gold. Behind them drove Vespasian first with Titus behind him: Domitian rode alongside, magnificently adorned himself, and with his horse a splendid sight.

6-60   *Triumph of Titus,* relief from the Arch of Titus. Marble, approx. 7′ 10″ high.

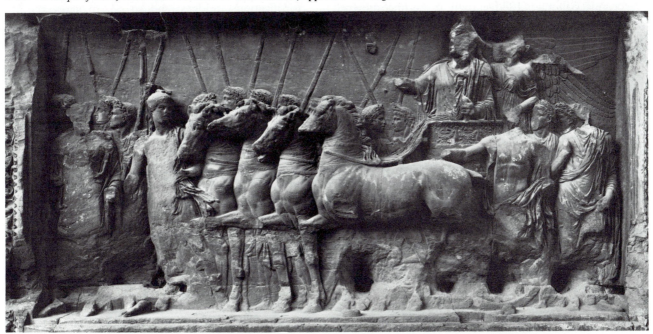

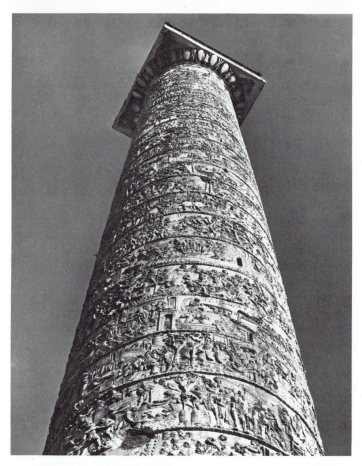

6-61 Column of Trajan, Rome, A.D. 113.

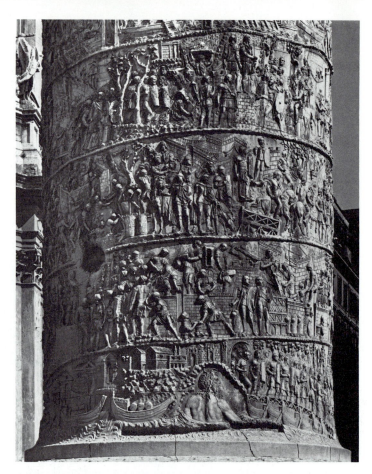

6-62 Detail of the two lowest bands of the Column of Trajan. Marble, bands approx. 36″ high.

The Column of Trajan, another kind of commemorative monument, dating from A.D. 113, stood in his forum before the temple of the Trajanic deities (FIGS. 6-61 and 6-62). The column, perhaps the work of Trajan's favorite architect and military engineer, APOLLODORUS of Damascus, was often copied: As late as the nineteenth century, in commemoration of the victories of Napoleon, a column inspired by it was set up in the Place Vendôme in Paris. The original column is 128 feet high. It was once crowned by a statue of Trajan, which was lost in the Middle Ages and replaced by a statue of St. Peter in the sixteenth century. The square base served as Trajan's mausoleum, and his ashes were deposited there in a golden urn in A.D. 117. The column records Trajan's two successful campaigns against the Dacians, as a result of which the Roman dominion was extended across the Danube into what is now Hungary and Rumania. Under Trajan the limits of the empire reached their greatest expansion. The marble reliefs, in a 625-foot band that winds the height of the column, represent a continuous record of the campaigns, told in 150 separate episodes with literally thousands of figures. The band increases in width as it moves toward the top of the column (from thirty-six inches to fifty inches) for better visibility from the ground. But recognition of the upper subjects must have been a problem, although the column originally stood in a small courtyard surrounded by two-story buildings, from the upper story or roofs of which the topmost reliefs may have been recognizable.

The carving is of relatively low relief in order to reduce shadows to a minimum, since they would tend to impair the legibility of the work. This low relief constitutes a significant reduction in illusionistic depth. The sculptured narrative puts much emphasis on military architecture, fortifications, bridges, and so on, to show the Roman technical superiority over the barbarian foe. At the bottom appears a pontoon bridge built across the Danube, with the river god looking on in amazement at the achievement. On the fourth circuit of the column Trajan is shown speaking to his troops. The emperor's figure is seen many times throughout the narrative, appearing as a kind of major motif. The story of the campaigns is told throughout with objectivity; the enemy is not belittled and the Roman victories are hard won. But only about a quarter of the reliefs show battle scenes. Much of the balance represents what Rome thought to be her mission—bringing civilization to the benighted. Towns are built, crops harvested, rituals performed, and imperial speeches given. In short, the reliefs of the column are not only an exaltation of Trajan, but a hymn to *romanitas*.

The Column of Trajan reliefs embody some features of great importance for the art of the Middle Ages. We have indicated one of them above, a flattening of relief, and have shown the functional reason for it—better visibility. But the sacrifice of the strong illusionism of the Arch of Titus reliefs, even of those of the Ara Pacis, may have another reason: a desire for completeness of narrative description that requires that a great number of actions be shown in a limited space. Thus *narrative* fact rather than *visual* fact is required, and truth to appearance ("illusionism," "realism"), to greater or less degree, can be sacrificed. A very singular and important sacrifice is made in the Column of Trajan compositions, and that is in the representation of space. In the Ara Pacis and the Arch of Titus the figures are represented as standing and moving on the same groundline, at the eye level of a presumed observer who occupies an imagined place on the same line; thus, all the heads are approximately on the same level. But the figures of the Column of Trajan are placed in rows one above the other, a device altogether different from the approximate perspective of illusionism. From a perspective viewpoint the figures and architecture are entirely haphazard in their arrangement; from the point of view of narrative they occur where the story demands. Often relative proportions are sacrificed: Soldiers are represented as large as the walls they attack, or, though not represented in this illustration, cavalrymen are as large as or larger than their horses. We can say that conventions of Medieval art already appear in the sculptures of the Column of Trajan.

These features were not immediately adopted. They appear in the somewhat later Column of Marcus Aurelius; but in a relief of Marcus Aurelius sacrificing (FIG. 6-63),

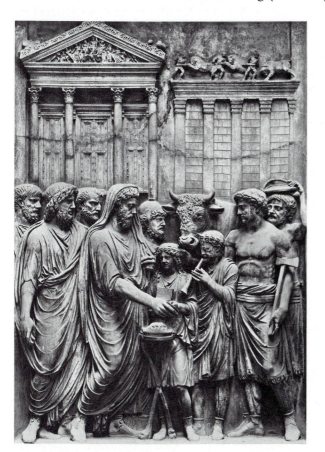

one of three panels surviving from a triumphal arch dedicated to that emperor and carved about A.D. 180, the older illusionism persists, though not to the degree that we find it in the Arch of Titus. In this relief the procession was cut up into panels (each a part of a larger whole to be imagined by the viewer), since the narrative requirements are not so demanding. There is much of Hellenic Classicism in the poses of the figures and in their draperies. (The drapery of the figure at the left is an echo of the *Nike* on the balustrade of the Temple of Athena Nike on the Acropolis, shown in FIG. 5-53.) Hadrian, Antoninus Pius, and Marcus Aurelius were all Hellenophiles, and it is in their reigns that perhaps the last powerful influence of Classical Greece was felt in Roman art. The figures in the relief are cut to ideal proportions, but a considerable Roman realism appears in the details and in such illusionistic devices as the perspective of the background architecture and the varying depth of relief to show distance. The bland composure of the faces of the Ara Pacis does not appear; the times have changed, the end of the Golden Age has come. A kind of brooding solemnity prevails as the grave philosopher-emperor—the sculptor gives us a portrait likeness—prepares the sacrifice that may produce omens of a troubled future for the empire.

PORTRAIT SCULPTURE

Two portrait busts from Republican times have already shown us the Roman aptitude for and skill in this art, an expression of the now familiar Roman instinct for the factual. It is scarcely an accident that the historical reliefs just discussed have portrait figures in them. Literally thousands of portrait busts have been found from the times of the republic and of the empire, and the best are evidence of the important contribution of the Romans to portrait art. Two tendencies of style determine the production of portrait sculpture—the verism of the republic, and the Hellenizing idealism of the empire; in the later period the tendencies alternate and sometimes converge. It is significant that members of the lower social classes generally are portrayed realistically in all periods, while official portraits (of the ruling class, that is) tend to shift between realism and idealism, depending in part upon the general style of the period, the preference of the sitters, or the artist's own interest in the psychological probing of personality.

A portrait of the emperor Augustus (FIG. 6-64), a detail of the Primaporta figure (FIG. 6-54), which can be profitably compared with earlier portraits from the republic (FIGS. 6-14 and 6-15), is very subtly idealized without any apparent loss of likeness. The hair, adhering closely to the skull, is reminiscent of fifth-century B.C. Greek style and reflects Augustus' Classical taste prevailing over Hellenistic realism. We have met the Classicism of the Augustan age in the Ara Pacis and have pointed out that Vergil's *Aeneid*, deliberately imitating Homer and commissioned by Au-

6-63 *Marcus Aurelius Sacrificing,* from an arch of Marcus Aurelius, late second century A.D. Marble, approx. 10½' high. Palazzo dei Conservatori, Rome.

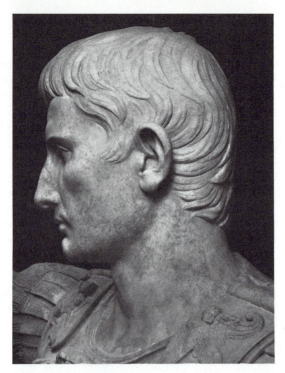

6-64   *Head of Augustus,* detail of FIG. 6-54.

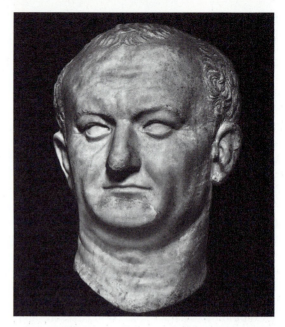

6-66   *Vespasian, c.* A.D. 75. Marble, life-size. Museo
Nazionale Romano, Rome.

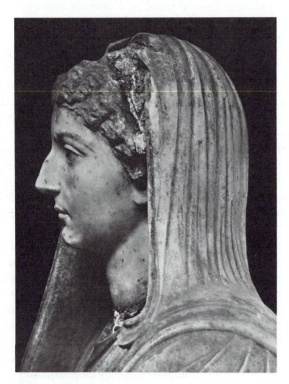

6-65   *Livia,* wife of Augustus, *c.* A.D. 20. Marble, head
approx. 15″ high. Antiquario, Pompeii.

gustus himself, reveals in its form the same Classical spirit.
Livia, the second wife of Augustus and mother of the
emperor Tiberius, is shown in a portrait bust as the shrewd
and tough, yet tactful and elegant woman she is believed to
have been (FIG. 6-65). There is the same Augustan idealization and the same retention of the likeness. The lifelike

quality is enhanced by effective use of color, much of
which is preserved in the hair, eyes, and lips.

The emperor Vespasian, succeeding Nero, the last of the
Julio-Claudian line, which had begun with Augustus,
reigned from A.D. 69 to 79. His portrait bust (FIG. 6-66)
forcefully reveals the veteran general who had fought
successfully in all parts of the empire. Vespasian was a man
of simple origin and simple tastes who desired to return to
republican simplicity after Nero's extravagant misrule. He
was a good administrator—honest, shrewd, and earthily
humorous, all of which qualities speak from his portrait.
The artist has attempted no flattery; quite possibly Vespasian himself discouraged him from idealizing overmuch,
for he preferred to have the blunt, rugged aspect of the
soldier. From the portrait we can understand the active
man whose care was restoration of the empire and who is
reported to have said on his deathbed: "An emperor should
die standing." The portrait, while a little subtler in characterization, is almost republican in its directness.

The bust of a lady from the Flavian period (FIG. 6-
67)—embracing the reigns of Vespasian and his sons, Titus
and Domitian—is a departure from the usually rather stern
portraits of Roman women. It is a rare masterpiece in its
inimitable union of sensitive beauty, noble elegance, and
lucid intelligence. The elaborate coiffure stands in striking
textural contrast to the delicate, softly modeled features,
and the technique and effort to reproduce the luminosity
and glow of actual flesh recalls the art of Praxiteles. This
truly regal work, exemplar of Roman portrait art at its
height, can be instructively compared with the head of
Queen Nefertiti (FIG. 3-34), done in the subtle Amarna
style of Egypt.

Great persons of ambivalent qualities are particularly
interesting to us, and this makes their portraits—such as

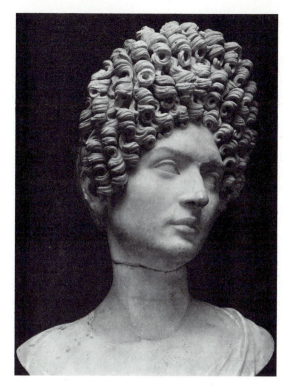

6-67 *Portrait of a Lady,* c. A.D. 90. Marble, life-size. Museo Capitolino, Rome.

that of Pompey (FIG. 6-15)—more interesting perhaps than those of persons of more uniform character. This quality of ambivalence was especially true of the emperor Hadrian (FIG. 6-68). We can approach his portrait informed by the account given of his personality by an ancient biographer. Hadrian, beyond all the other emperors a lover of Greek art and culture and himself a skillful artist and architect, poet, scholar, and writer, is thus described:

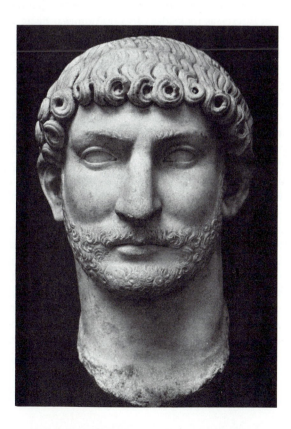

He was grave and gay, affable and dignified, cruel and gentle, mean and generous, eager for fame yet not vain, impulsive and cautious, secretive and open. He hated eminent qualities in others, but gathered round him the most distinguished men of the state; at one time affectionate towards his friends, at another he mistrusted and put them to death. In fact he was only consistent in his inconsistency [*semper in omnibus varius*]. Although he endeavored to win the popular favor, he was more feared than loved. A man of unnatural passions and grossly superstitious, he was an ardent lover of nature. But, with all his faults, he devoted himself so indefatigably to the service of the state, that the period of his reign could be characterized as a "golden age."

We might bring also to the contemplation of his portrait the poem, long famous, that he wrote at the end of his life:

> Charming, fleeting, little soul,
> My body's guest and comrade,
> Where now will you go
> Naked, pallid, unmoving
> Never again to play?

In this portrait Hadrian affects the Greek coiffure, in form much like the early Classical ringlets of the *Apollo* from the Temple of Zeus at Olympia (FIG. 5-36). He adopts also the Greek beard, abandoning the age-old tradition of the clean-shaven face. (This may have been inspired by portraits of Pericles.) In any event, from now on most Roman emperors will be presented bearded. The head is idealized, but with restraint, the features a little regularized and retouched, perhaps, but not so as to interfere with the likeness. A certain ambiguity and inscrutability shadows the face. But, when we know a little of him, we are prepared for this.

The last emperor of the great imperial line that had included Trajan and Hadrian was the Stoic Marcus Aurelius. We have touched on his philosophy in looking at the Faiyum portrait of a man from his time, a man whose serenely gentle and reflective face manifests the emperor's philosophy. A great equestrian bronze portrait statue of Marcus Aurelius (FIG. 6-69) has survived from the ancient world, unique in that it *did* survive, for there are no other examples of what must have been a statue type popular with the Roman emperors. (Medieval Christians probably melted the statues down for their bronze and because they were impious images from the pagan, demonic world of the Caesars. It is thought that the Christians mistakenly took the *Marcus Aurelius* statue for that of the first pro-Christian emperor, Constantine, and that that is why it escaped destruction.) The emperor, whom we have seen earlier in his role of head priest, *pontifex maximus,* with his toga drawn over his head (FIG. 6-63), is portrayed here exercising his office as commander of the legions, perhaps

6-68 *Hadrian,* c. A.D. 120. Marble, approx. 16″ high. Museo Ostiense, Ostia.

passing before the people. His gesture here, magisterial, benignly authoritative, much like a later papal blessing, conveys at once the awesome and universal significance of the Roman *imperium,* the almost godlike presiding of the emperor over the whole world. Yet, at closer view, we see the same features as in the sacrifice panel—those of a man calmly aloof, meditative, a little resigned. The magnificent, high-stepping charger, the war horse mettlesome and impatient with the tameness of the parade, breathes hotly through dilated nostrils. This superb bronze was the inspiration and sometimes the despair of the sculptors of the Renaissance. It stands today on the Capitoline Hill, the authentic ancient centerpiece of Michelangelo's great architectural design (see Chapter Thirteen), representing as does no other single object the lost authority of empire.

After Marcus Aurelius the downward course of the empire became precipitous, though not at once; Septimius Severus held it level for a while. His son Caracalla (FIG. 6-70), under whom the great baths named after him went toward completion, was a brutal man, murderer of his own brother. He reigned briefly between A.D. 211 and 217, and his murder grieved no one. Gibbon writes of him:

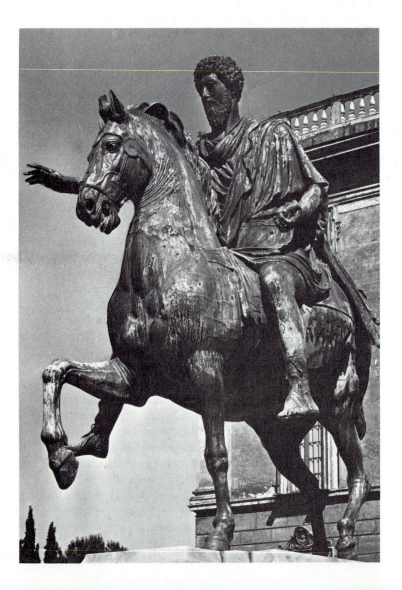

"Caracalla was the common enemy of mankind." To render his violent traits, the sculptor had to return to realism. We find a burly, suspicious, almost snarling man, more a cut-throat than an emperor, a man who could scarcely be more the opposite of Marcus Aurelius. Significantly for what was to follow—the military anarchy of the third century, when the "barrack emperors" were set up (and pulled down) by the army—Caracalla pursued the tyrant's rule that if one has the loyalty of the army, one need not consider the people. His soldiers, however, were not wary enough to protect him from the dagger of an assassin, and his death was the model death of the tyrant, in form repeated again and again throughout the terrible third century. "Such," writes Gibbon, "was the end of a monster who disgraced human nature." Yet Michelangelo was later to base his noble bust of Brutus on this bust of Caracalla.

Internal unrest combined with attacks on frontiers by the new Sassanian line of Persian kings in the east and German tribes in the north brought the empire to the verge of collapse. In the space of fifty years some twenty of the barrack emperors were exalted and then assassinated by factions of the army. This created anguish and foreboding throughout the empire, curiously reflected in numerous portraits like that of one of the barrack emperors himself, Philip the Arab (FIG. 6-71). Philip became emperor after having his predecessor, Gordianus, executed. In considering his portrait it will be useful to know something of the close of his career. An adventurer himself, he knew that he was surrounded by adventurers—especially in the army—who were ready to follow his example. Faced with a revolt, Philip appointed a brave and intelligent aristocrat, Decius, to put it down and to calm the army. The army accepted Decius as its leader on condition that he agree to depose Philip or be put to death himself. Decius then led the best of the army against Philip, who was slain; Decius became emperor. The portrait thus shows the face of a man who knows he is utterly without security. Fear, distrust, suspicion work the face into a mask of guilt and anxiety. The brow is furrowed. The deep-set eyes shift sideways. The eye pupils are carved, an innovation that focuses on the psychic state. The hair is cropped short, the beard stubbly. The short, nervous chisel strokes adapt to the nervous mood. (In the works of later sculptors they will become increasingly abrupt and schematic, leading to the geometric patterning of the fourth century.) But it is the face, with its terrible tensions, that was rarely seen before in the history of art. From the Archaic masks we come at last, in the third century A.D., to a face so "modern" in what it reflects of trouble that we experience a shock of recognition. Both the ideal and the real in Roman sculpture are now replaced by something new—expression—wherein the artist is concerned first of all with expressing an emotional state—either his subject's or his own, and perhaps both.

6-69 Equestrian statue of Marcus Aurelius, *c.* A.D. 165. Bronze, over life-size. Capitoline Hill, Rome.

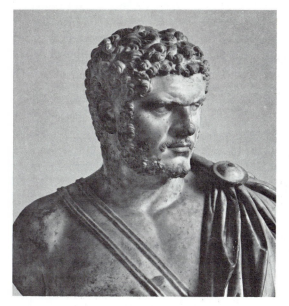

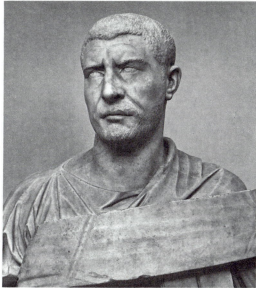

The Late Empire

The anarchy of the third century—when at one time as many as eighteen claimants struggled for the throne and it seemed as if the empire would be divided into a number of small, weak states—was brought to an end by a vigorous leader, Diocletian, in A.D. 285. Diocletian saw the impossibility of ruling the vast empire alone, what with the continual German and Persian attacks in the north and east and countless revolts in the provinces. He restored the political order by dividing authority among four persons, the *tetrarchs,* including himself as prime mover. Diocletian appointed a coruler called, like himself, "augustus," and each of the two "augusti" then adopted an assistant of slightly lower rank, the "caesar." One augustus and one caesar ruled in the east, and the other pair in the west. Though political control was restored, a fatal precedent was set: the division of authority within the empire.

Under Constantine, who did away with Diocletian's system and ruled alone, the practice was begun of dividing the empire, like personal property, among the emperor's sons—a crippling, divisive custom that was to last into the Middle Ages. Even more divisive was Constantine's founding of a city named after him (Constantinople, now Istanbul, on the site of the ancient Greek city of Byzantium), which led inevitably to the decline of the city of Rome and the shift of imperial emphasis to the east. Byzantium gives its name to the later civilization of the eastern Roman empire.

After the reign of Theodosius, at the end of the fourth century, the empire was irreparably divided, though the emperors of the east, at Constantinople, continued for centuries to claim the west. These claims were in vain, for in the fifth century the barbarians took power in the West—the Ostrogoths in Italy, the Vandals in Africa, the Visigoths in Spain, the Franks and Burgundians in Gaul, the Angles and Saxons in Britain. These Romano-Germanic petty kingdoms succeeded to the once centralized and almost universal power of Rome and became the predecessors of the nations of modern Europe. The eastern half of the empire lived on as the Byzantine empire for a thousand years, until the conquest of Constantinople by the Turks in 1453.

ARCHITECTURE

Developments in architecture powerfully express the ebbing authority of the Roman empire. In the days of Augustus and Trajan the "walls" of the empire had been the might of the legions on its remotest borders; behind the bulwark of the legions a great empire could rest secure. But late in the third century the emperor Aurelian was forced by circumstances to girdle the city of Rome itself with walls, turning it into a fortress; Rome became what it had been at the start, a walled city, now dwindling into the ghost of an empire. Aurelian's insecurity was shared by Diocletian, who, unlike Tiberius in the first century A.D., could not afford to retire to the undefended paradise of Capri but had built for his retirement a well-fortified palace on the Dalmatian coast at Spalato (modern Split, in Yugoslavia), about A.D. 300 (FIGS. 6-72 and 6-73). The complex, covering about ten acres, is laid out like a Roman colonial city. The plan is almost identical with that of Timgad (FIG. 6-43), although its military aspects, such as the fortified walls and tower-flanked gates, are even more dominant on the relatively small scale of a palace. Such a fusion of military with imperial palace architecture strikingly reflects the changed life style of the late imperial period, when increased centralization and standardization infused all levels of Roman society, private and official alike, with militaristic thinking. In architecture, such

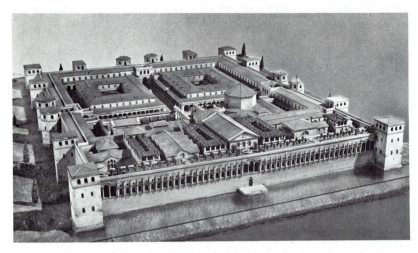

6-72 Palace of Diocletian, Spalato (Split), A.D. 300–05.
(Reconstruction by E. Hebrard.)

6-73 Plan of the palace of Diocletian.
Original Roman masonery
is shown in solid black.

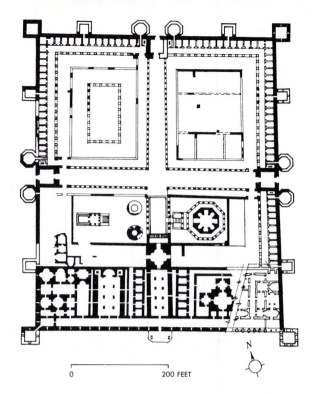

0   200 FEET

N

standards of military behavior as obedience and subordination are reflected in symmetry, axiality, and unity of direction, all shown in the plan of Spalato.

The broad, columned street leading toward the palace constitutes a ceremonial axis that dominates the layout. All other architectural features are symmetrically arranged around this avenue, which leads into a large columned court that fronts the entrance of the palace proper (FIG. 6-74). Designed as a three-bay classical portico, this façade is marked by an unusual and quite unclassical feature: Over the central bay the entablature arches upward into the triangular face of the pediment. Formally the purpose of this "broken pediment" undoubtedly was to stress the central axis of the design. Symbolically it became the "gable of glorification" under which the emperor appeared before those gathered in the peristyle court.

6-74 Peristyle court,
palace of Diocletian.

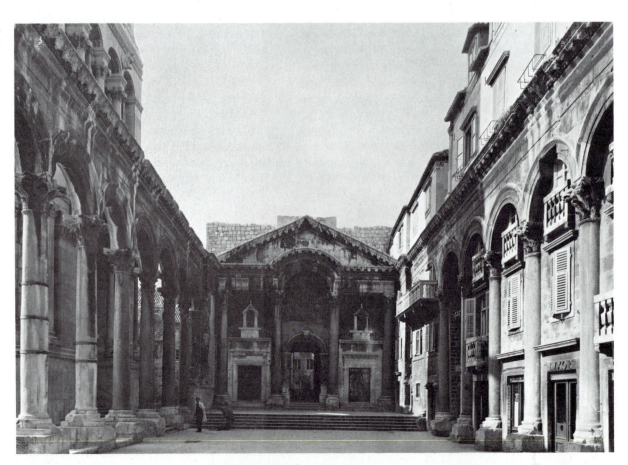

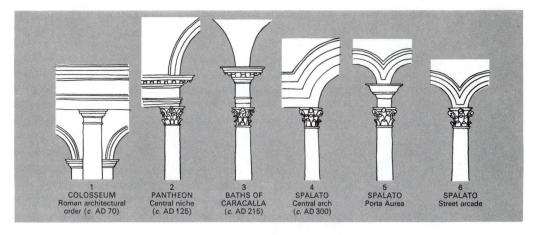

| 1
COLOSSEUM
Roman architectural
order (*c.* AD 70) | 2
PANTHEON
Central niche
(*c.* AD 125) | 3
BATHS OF
CARACALLA
(*c.* AD 215) | 4
SPALATO
Central arch
(*c.* AD 300) | 5
SPALATO
Porta Aurea | 6
SPALATO
Street arcade |

The feature of the broken pediment had appeared earlier, mostly in the eastern provinces of the empire—for example, in the façade of the great temples at Baalbek, in Syria. It is, to repeat, an un-Classical device—hardly imaginable in a building like the Parthenon—and represents a transitional stage between the Classical, column-supported, horizontal entablature and the springing of arches directly from column capitals, as is the case in the flanking colonnades of this same peristyle. The process of change from the *trabeated* (post-and-lintel) architecture of Greco-Roman antiquity (and earlier) to the *arcuated* (arch-column) architecture of the Middle Ages begins in the first century A.D., and we see it here in the arcade of Spalato in its perfected form and on a grand scale. It is interesting to observe its gradual emergence from the Roman arch order (FIG. 6-75) and the Roman architect's reluctance to give up the conventional three-part division of the entablature even when it had become only a block-like fragment, as in the capital from the Baths of Caracalla. Later, Byzantine architects will retain the entablature-block, but will rid it of the old Classical features, geometrizing it into a flat-sided, trapezoidal "impost" block (FIG. 7-33).

Although the center of empire was moved by Constantine to his new city on the site of ancient Byzantium, he completed some important building projects prior to leaving Rome. One of these was the vast basilica begun between 306 and 310 by Maxentius, rival of Constantine, and finished by Constantine after 313 (FIGS. 6-76 and 6-77). All that remains of the building are three barrel-vaulted bays of the north aisle, with brick-faced concrete walls twenty feet thick supporting the coffered vaults. The interior, like that of the Baths of Caracalla, was richly marbled and stuccoed. The ruins are most impressive by virtue of their

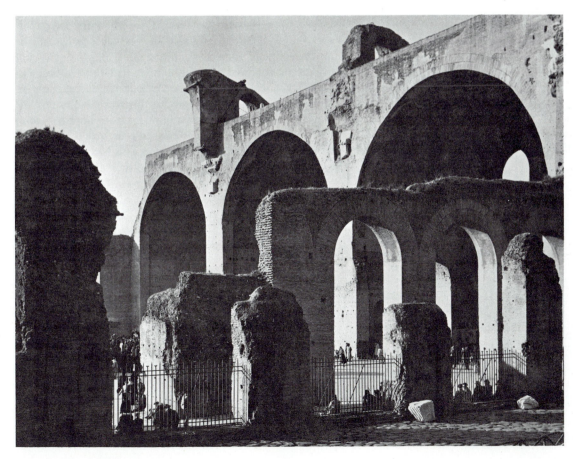

6-76 Basilica of Constantine, Rome, *c.* A.D. 310–20.

205

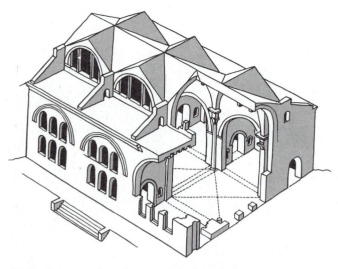

6-77 Reconstruction of the Basilica of Constantine.

size and mass yet represent only a small part of the original structure, which measured 300 by 215 feet and had a groin-vaulted central nave rising 114 feet. The reconstruction (FIG. 6-77) shows groin vaults (over the central nave) that permitted lighting of the interior through the ends of the cross vaults, which were left open in a manner similar to clerestory construction. Buttresses reinforce the vault (where the groins join vertical supports) and channel part of the pressures exerted by the weight of the vault across the aisles and into the outside walls. Remains of the

6-78 *Constantine the Great, c.* A.D. 330. Marble, approx. 8½' high. Palazzo dei Conservatori, Rome.

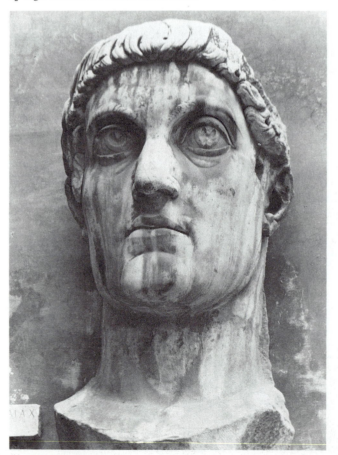

springing of the central vault and of buttresses can be seen in FIG. 6-76. This late great building of the ancient world is a monument to the ingenuity of Roman architects. Exemplar of an architecture of space, it is designed on a grand, imperial scale—spacious, fully illuminated, uninterrupted by rows of vertical supports, and constructed of a highly malleable, versatile, fireproof material. In this it fulfills the requirements of architecture in periods of high civilization; not until Hagia Sophia will they be so artfully fulfilled again.

SCULPTURE AND MONUMENTAL RELIEF

In the western apse of the Basilica of Constantine was a colossal statue of the emperor, a seated figure some thirty feet high, the head of which has been preserved (FIG. 6-78). The figure was composed of a brick core, a wooden torso covered with bronze, and head and limbs of marble. The head alone is 8½ feet high and weighs over eight tons. The characteristics of the earlier busts we have described, in which the real and the ideal alternate or blend, are here no longer dominant. Rather we have the onset of traits familiar in the earlier, Archaic period: simplification of detail, with a regularizing of the features and a flattening that make of the face a rigid mask uncompromisingly frontal in aspect.[2] The eyes become enormously large in proportion to the rest of the features, though in the Constantine head they still turn slightly to the side and upward as in certain third-century portraits like that of Philip the Arab (FIG. 6-71). Those unchanging qualities of the permanent form, which we have seen in Egypt and Mesopotamia—particularly in the representation of kings—once more make their appearance. The personality of the emperor is lost in the immense image of eternal authority. It is his authority, not his personality or his psychic state, that the sculptor exhibits. The colossal size, the Archaic rigidities, the eyes directed at no thing or person of this world—all combine to make a formula of overwhelming power appropriate to the exalted position of Constantine as absolute despot, which, by the early fourth century, he had certainly become. It is not surprising that the first of the Christian emperors, in authority the European equivalent of a Ramses II, should be embodied in colossal form like the giant statues of the Egyptian king at Luxor and (formerly) Abu Simbel.

[2] The living emperor himself, on formal occasions may have in appearance approximated a statue. H. P. L'Orange quotes the ancient writer Ammianus Marcellinus describing Constantius II, a successor to Constantine, on his entry into Rome: "He looked so stiffly ahead as if he had an iron band around his neck and he turned his face neither to the right nor the left, he was not as a living person, but as an image." L'Orange adds: "This hieratic emperor style, which as divine majesty (*divina maiestas*) in the same way leaves its mark upon palace, image and living reality, can furthermore be traced through Byzantium all the way down to the Holy Russian Empire. (*Art Forms and Civic Life in the Late Roman Empire* [Princeton: Princeton Univ. Press, 1965], pp. 124–25.)

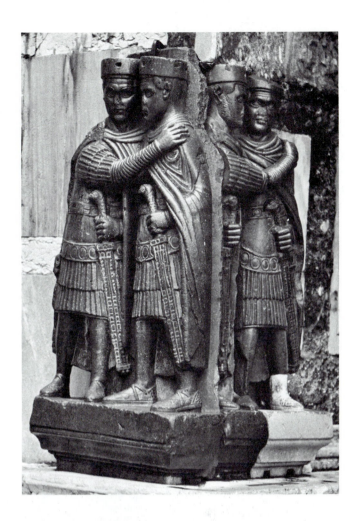

6-79 *The Tetrarchs, c.* A.D. 305. Porphyry, approx. 51" high. Piazza San Marco, Venice.

The profound changes in style that occur at an accelerated pace in the fourth century, introducing the epoch of Medieval art, can be seen in the group called the *Tetrarchs,* dating from about A.D. 305 (FIG. 6-79). Although it is an earlier work than the portrait of Constantine, it reflects much more strongly the trend toward Archaism. Carved from porphyry in one of the eastern provinces (perhaps Egypt), the group represents the four co-rulers of the empire: Diocletian and Maximian (the augusti) and Galerius and Constantius "Chlorus," father of Constantine (the caesars). They embrace each other to symbolize their hoped-for but not realized serenity and concord. They seem, even as they embrace, to be huddled in fear and foreboding, facing some impending disaster, in an expression of the already noted prevalent anxiety of the age. Classical features have disappeared; the figures are ill proportioned, with large heads on squat bodies, giving them a gnomelike appearance. The drapery is schematic, the bodies shapeless. Seven hundred years of Greek and Roman idealism and naturalism here terminate. No portrait likenesses are tried; the masklike faces are the same face in quadruplicate. Individuality and personality already belong to the past.

The waning creative power and technical skill of Rome in the west can be seen in the Arch of Constantine (A.D. 312–15) in the city of Rome (FIG. 6-80). It is the last

6-80 Arch of Constantine, Rome, A.D. 312-15.

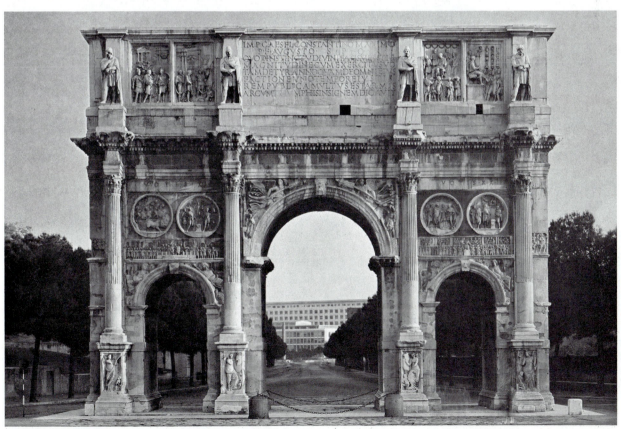

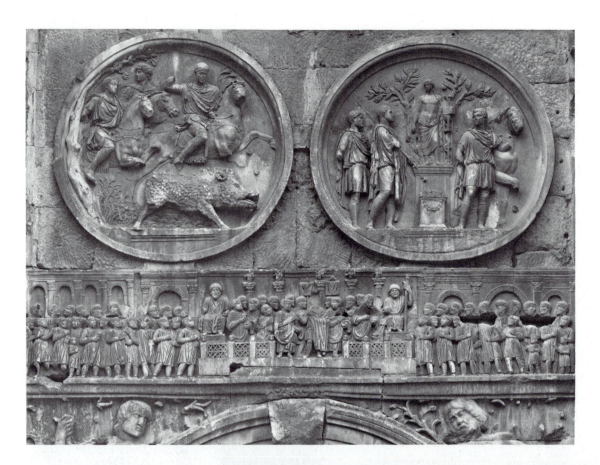

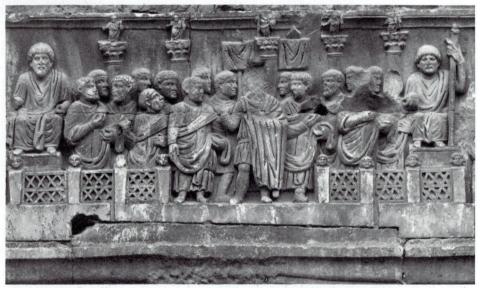

6-81   Above: Reliefs from the Arch of Constantine: medallions, A.D. 117–38; frieze, early fourth century A.D. Marble, frieze approx. 40" high.

6-82   Right: Detail of the frieze shown in FIG. 6-81.

great triumphal arch preserved in the declining city. Dedicated to Constantine by the now figurehead Senate, it commemorates the victory over his rival Maxentius, a victory which made him the absolute monarch of the Roman empire. But the occasion produced no corresponding stimulus for the imagination of his builders. The de-

sign of the arch is copied from that of the earlier Arch of Septimius Severus, of the early third century, and most of its decorative sculpture is taken from the monuments of rulers like Trajan, Hadrian, and Marcus Aurelius.

Beneath two Hadrianic medallions are reliefs belonging to Constantine's own period (FIGS. 6-81 and 6-82), which give us an opportunity to estimate the degree of change from the style of the Early Imperial age to a new style that it is not inappropriate to call Medieval. Constantine, surrounded by his entourage, stands at the center of a rostrum, addressing the people. His central position corresponds here to the frontality of his colossal statue and expresses a new, rigid formality of composition that will more and more depend upon fixed positions of figures rather than representation of action. The figures are nonclassical in their lack of proportionality; in this respect they are like the *Tetrarchs.* Moreover, they do not move on any principle of classical-naturalistic movement but rather with the mechanical and repeated stances and gestures of puppets. The relief is flattened back into the block, the forms no longer fully modeled, the details incised. The lines of figures are superposed (a device seen in the Column of Trajan); the spatial arrangement is, as noted, not casual, but a careful head-counting lineup. The gestures are few and, like the uniform heads, reproduced again and again. We have not so much a historical narrative of action as the labeling of an event frozen into a tableau; thus, the ordered groups could quickly be read and labeled as "crowd," "emperor," "servants of the emperor," the artist desiring to include all the essential participants without the ambiguity that can accompany description of particulars. The latter have been reduced to the absolute minimum, their place having been taken by formal placement and repetition of attitude and gesture.

We began the story of Roman art with two sculptured portraits that define in different ways the Roman bent for realism. We can end that story with two portraits stamped on Roman coins (FIG. 6-83), portraits of emperors whose reigns are separated by two centuries—Hadrian (A.D. 117–138) and the emperor Maximin Daia (A.D. 308–314), tetrarch of the East, in the tetrarchy with Constantine, Licinius, and Galerius at the time of the first Edict of Toleration of the Christians. We have described the portrait and character of Hadrian (p. 201), and in this bronze medallion we have a sensitive, classicizing, naturalistic report of the great emperor's features. This classical naturalism contrasts with the almost startling abstraction of the features portrayed on the gold coin of Maximin Daia, which convey through both sharp and blunt simplifications of form the awesome strength of late imperial authority. Two centuries have transformed the image of the emperor as a particular man into an image of the emperor as the mask of power. Individual traits are suppressed in the force of the idea and the idea of force. The idea, not the thing, will henceforth dominate in art.

The Archaizing of Greek and Roman figurative art in the Constantinian reliefs, the *Tetrarchs,* and the coin portrait of Maximin Daia reflects a transformation in the way the peoples of the late Roman world interpret the structure of appearance. Underlying this change in interpretation is a mighty spiritual change—the assimilation of Christianity into Greco-Roman civilization, a phenomenon so far-reaching in its influence as to separate the psychologies of two millennia, that of Greece-Rome and that of Medieval Christianity.

6-83 Top: medallion of Hadrian (second century A.D.). Bronze, 1.6″ in diameter. Bottom: gold coin with portrait of Maximin Daia (A.D. 308–314). Gold, 0.8″ in diameter. Both Museo Nazionale, Rome.

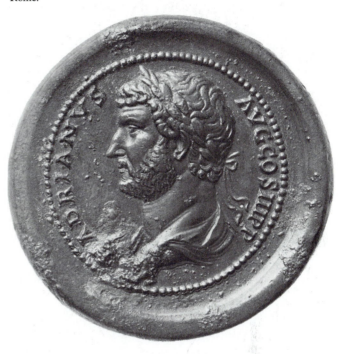

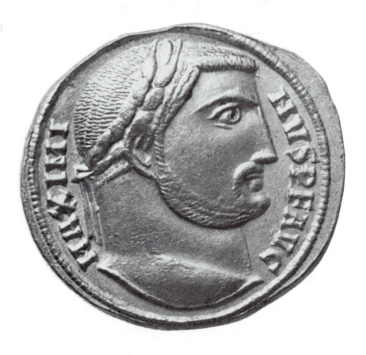

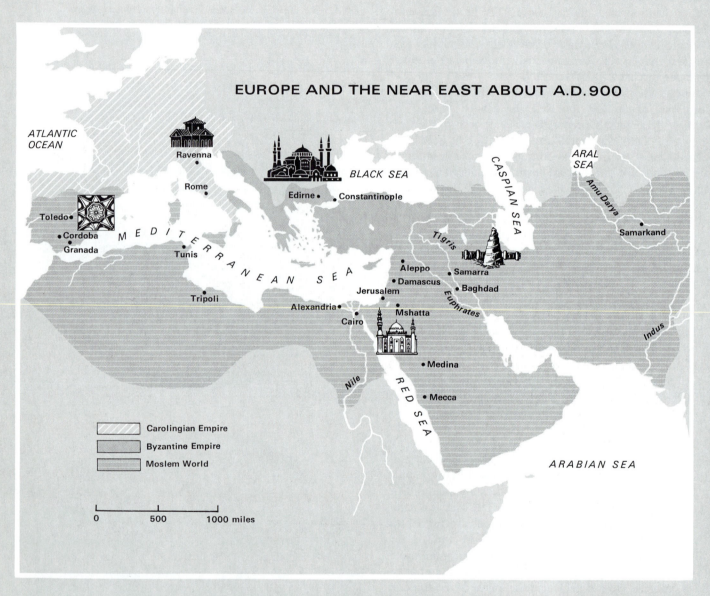

EUROPE AND THE NEAR EAST ABOUT A.D. 900

ATLANTIC
OCEAN

Ravenna

Rome

BLACK SEA

CASPIAN SEA

ARAL
SEA

Edirne • Constantinople

Amu Darya

Toledo •

• Cordoba

• Granada

Tigris

M E D I T E R R A N E A N   S E A

Samarkand

Tunis

Aleppo

Samarra

Damascus

Baghdad

Jerusalem

Euphrates

Tripoli

Alexandria

Mshatta

Cairo

Indus

Nile

Medina

RED SEA

Mecca

ARABIAN SEA

Carolingian Empire
Byzantine Empire
Moslem World

0   500   1000 miles

chapter seven

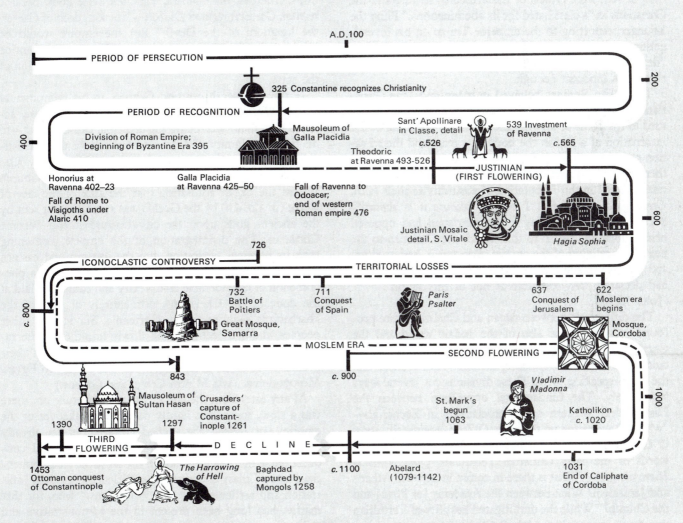

A.D.100

PERIOD OF PERSECUTION

200

325 Constantine recognizes Christianity

PERIOD OF RECOGNITION

400

Division of Roman Empire;
beginning of Byzantine Era 395

Mausoleum of
Galla Placidia

Sant' Apollinare
in Classe, detail

539 Investment
of Ravenna

Theodoric
at Ravenna 493–526

c.526

c.565

Honorius at
Ravenna 402–23

Galla Placidia
at Ravenna 425–50

JUSTINIAN
(FIRST FLOWERING)

Fall of Rome to
Visigoths under
Alaric 410

Fall of Ravenna to
Odoacer;
end of western
Roman empire 476

600

Justinian Mosaic
detail, S. Vitale

Hagia Sophia

726

ICONOCLASTIC CONTROVERSY

TERRITORIAL LOSSES

c. 800

732
Battle of
Poitiers

711
Conquest
of Spain

Paris
Psalter

637
Conquest of
Jerusalem

622
Moslem era
begins

Great Mosque,
Samarra

MOSLEM ERA

SECOND FLOWERING

Mosque,
Cordoba

1000

843

c. 900

Vladimir
Madonna

Mausoleum of
Sultan Hasan

Crusaders'
capture of
Constant-
inople 1261

St. Mark's
begun
1063

Katholikon
c. 1020

1390

1297

THIRD
FLOWERING

D E C L I N E

1453
Ottoman conquest
of Constantinople

The Harrowing
of Hell

Baghdad
captured by
Mongols 1258

c. 1100

Abelard
(1079-1142)

1031
End of Caliphate
of Cordoba

Early Christian, Byzantine, and Islamic Art

CHRISTIANITY, like many Eastern cults, was a peculiarly persuasive religion of salvation. Its immense success in making converts among the teeming populations of the great imperial cities brought it to the attention of the Roman authorities. Because Christians refused to acknowledge the state religion, which was the cult of the emperor, and because they refused to participate in its rather perfunctory rites, they were regarded as politically subversive and were bitterly persecuted. Tacitus, reflecting the attitudes of his time, regarded the Christians as believers in a degenerate doctrine and practitioners of obscene and perverse rites that, he felt, were typical of Eastern cults; he refers to the Christians as "a class hated for its abominations." Pliny the Younger, reporting to the emperor Trajan on his investigation of Christian beliefs, writes that he has found only a "depraved and extravagant superstition," though Christian ritual was innocent enough.

The pagan Romans believed in many gods, the Christians in one. The educated pagan must have thought absurd to the point of insanity the Christian doctrines of the incarnation of a god in the body of a man, and the salvation or redemption of all mankind through the death and then the resurrection of the god-man Christ. The Christians exulted in this imputation of absurdity to their faith; *Credo quia absurdum* ("I believe *because* it is absurd") became their slogan. Pagan and Christian had opposed orientations: the pagan to this world, the Christian to the next. The religion of the empire, *Romanitas*, had its ritual and practice in the fact of imperial dominion; but Christ had declared "My kingdom is not of this world . . . ." (John 18:36).

The differences between pagan and Christian were profound, as were those also of the Judaic world and the Christian church. Further differences would divide the cultures of the Greek-speaking eastern Mediterranean and the Latin-speaking West. These divisions cut several ways and deeply. The fundamental opposition between the Eastern and Western spirit proclaimed in Zechariah—"when I have raised up thy sons, O Zion, against thy sons, O Greece . . ." (9:13)—rings angrily once again in the words of the early Christian Tertullian: *Quid Athenae Hierosolymis!*—"What is there in common between Athens and Jerusalem? What between the Academy [of Plato] and the Church?" While the unmitigated hostility of Tertullian was by no means shared by all Christians, an antagonism between the ancient Semitic East and the Hellenic world that had for a while conquered it was inevitable and could not be suppressed.

Greek naturalism and rationalism had become integral to the western Roman world; yet, at the same time, they had become changed through contact with the old civilizations of the Middle East. Although the mystery cults, with their suspiciously secret rites, their savior gods, their redemptive messages and occult sciences, their solar and fertility myths, drew heavily upon Egypt, Babylon, Persia, and even India, they borrowed a good deal of the intellectual apparatus of Hellenic philosophy, mysticizing it and making of it a kind of magical formulary and a *gnosis*, the privileged knowledge of only an initiated few.

Although Christianity, based as it was on Jewish teaching and tradition, differed radically from many of the crude cults with which Romans like Tacitus confused it, it joined with those cults in the long, vast historical reaction against the Hellenized West—both its world view and that material manifestation of it, the increasingly oppressive Roman empire. To Christians, the empire, with its exactions, cruelties, materialism, wars, and false gods, became *regnum Caesaris regnum Diaboli*—"the kingdom of Caesar, the kingdom of the Devil." But the empire would be inherited by the Christians in A.D. 325 when Constantine recognized Christianity and made it the official religion of the state.

In the eighteenth century, Gibbon, in his monumental history, *The Decline and Fall of the Roman Empire*, accused Christianity of being the principal cause of that—to his times—calamity. We do not now believe that Christianity had that role, but as early as the fifth century A.D., Augustine wrote his *City of God* to defend the Church against the pagan accusation that the sack of the city of Rome (in A.D. 410 by the Goths) was a punishment sent by the ancient gods upon the city because it had become Christian. The disintegration of the empire, beginning with its nominal separation into the western and eastern empires toward the end of the third century, was a phenomenon of considerable complexity and cannot be laid at the door of the Christians, nor entirely at that of the "barbarians"—those Celtic, Germanic, Slavic, and other peoples who had been pressing slowly into the Mediterranean world for thousands of years. (We have met their predecessors in the great migrations that disturbed Egypt, Mesopotamia, Asia Minor, Crete, and Greece.)

At any rate, from the end of the third century on, there was a slow, sometimes hardly perceptible takeover of the empire, not indeed the unified empire, but its already fragmented remains. The spiritual and ideological conquest made by the Christians in the politically consequential form of mass conversion paralleled the gradual infiltration and settlement by the "barbarians," who, for that matter, had long been present in the administrative and military structure as well as in recognized possession of imperial territories. The subsequent actions of these "barbarians," Christianized and in control of the western empire by the end of the fifth century, make up the history of the Middle Ages in the west. The eastern empire, actually but not officially severed from the western by the beginning of the fifth century, goes its own continuous way as the Byzantine empire, reverting to its Greek language and traditions, which, to be sure, had become much "Orientalized." The Byzantine world was a kind of protraction of the life of the late empire and the Early Christian culture that filled it. With a quite Oriental conservatism, which reminds us somewhat of the ancient Near Eastern civilizations, the Byzantine empire remains Greek, orthodox, unchanging for a thousand years, preserving the forms of its origin, oblivious to and isolated from the new.

In the seventh century, Islam, a new spiritual force, erupted from Arabia and swept across the Near East and the southern Mediterranean world with amazing speed. Islam created a new civilization that rivaled Christianity and would have far-ranging influence in medieval Europe. Arabic translations of Aristotle and other Greek writers of antiquity were eagerly studied by Christian scholars of the twelfth and thirteenth centuries; Arabic love lyrics and poetic descriptions of nature inspired the early French troubadours; Arab scholars laid the foundations of arithmetic and algebra as they are still taught in our schools, and their contributions to astronomy, medicine, and the natural sciences have made a lasting impression in the Western world. While Islamic art may not properly fall within the scope of Western art in the more limited sense, it nevertheless deserves our attention at this point in our survey, particularly since its early monuments share with those of Early Christian and Byzantine art derivation from earlier Near Eastern and Mediterranean artistic traditions. Most early monuments of Islamic art thus belong to the succession of late Roman, early Byzantine, and Iranian art, although different social and religious needs soon transformed similar prototypes into forms quite different from those they were to take in the Christian world.

EARLY CHRISTIAN ART

The style we call Early Christian we could as accurately call Late Roman, or, as art-historical usage has it, Late Antique. Christian works are distinguished from pagan only by subject, not by style. After all, the Christians of the time were as much "Roman" as the pagans; they were trained in the same crafts, were brought up in the same environment, and spoke the same language. The Christian church itself, both in its organization and its philosophy, owed much to the Greco-Roman structure of life; and Early Christian art shows simple transformation of pagan themes into Christian and the freest kind of borrowing of pagan motifs and manners. Hybrid forms are produced throughout the Christianized late empire in the greatest profusion and with the greatest intermingling of regional styles, making it almost impossible to recognize any one style—or even half a dozen—that could definitely be called Early Christian or that could serve as an exclusive exemplar of what we mean by Early Christian.

What happens in the plastic arts is a kind of "denaturing" of Greco-Roman naturalism, something we have seen beginning as early as the Column of Trajan and well advanced in the reliefs from the Arch of Constantine, the sculpture group *The Tetrarchs,* and the coin portrait of Maximin Daia. Archaizing modes supervene upon the old naturalism, and things come to look less and less like the Greco-Roman prototypes from which ultimately they derive. This denaturing process, variously influenced by barbarian styles, continues well into the western Medieval period. It should by no means be thought merely the negation of the Greco-Roman style, or a clumsy botching of it by men who had lost the sense of it and the necessary manual skill. Rather it is the product of an entirely new world view—one that inevitably brings about the transformation of the naturalistic, classical tradition. Early Christian art shows that transformation in process—already well-begun in the late third century, while the Roman empire was still intact.

The Early Christian era divides conveniently into the Period of Persecution—from the establishment of the earliest communities, in the first century A.D.—and the Period of Recognition—from A.D. 325, when Constantine established Christianity as the official religion of the Roman empire, until about A.D. 500, when the western provinces of the empire had come under the sway of barbarian princes. (Some authorities would extend the period of Early Christian art to the eighth century A.D., when it is terminated in the East by the Iconoclastic Controversy.) In the earlier period, as we have seen, the Christians were, in the Roman view, a troublesome, even dangerous, sect that needed to be curbed. During this time it is likely that the Christians, shrinking from the kind of attention public shrines might attract, worshiped in the private houses of their wealthier communicants, perhaps the elaborate atrium houses of the type we have seen in Pompeii (see p. 174). It is quite possible that the atrium forecourt of the later public churches, the basilicas, derived from their liturgical relation to the earlier atrium of the private house.

The Catacombs

The most significant monuments of the Period of Persecution are the least conspicuous of all the monuments of Rome; they are entirely underground. The catacombs, so called, are vast networks of galleries and chambers beneath Rome and other cities, designed as cemeteries for the burial of the Christian dead, many of them sainted martyrs. From the second through the fourth century the catacombs were in constant use, and it is estimated that as many as four million bodies were accommodated in the Roman catacombs alone. In times of persecution they could have served as places of concealment for fugitives; evidence of this function survives in blocked and cut-off staircases, secret embrasures and passages, and concealed entrances and exits. Doubtless the Christian mysteries

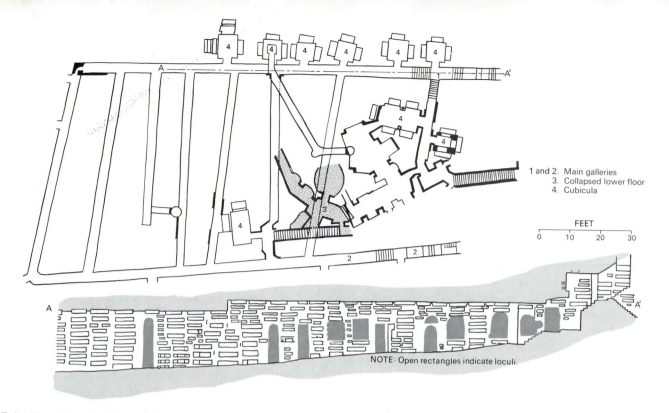

1 and 2. Main galleries
3. Collapsed lower floor
4. Cubicula

FEET
0   10   20   30

NOTE: Open rectangles indicate loculi.

7-1   Plan of the catacomb of Callixtus, Rome, second century A.D., and section through main gallery of oldest region.

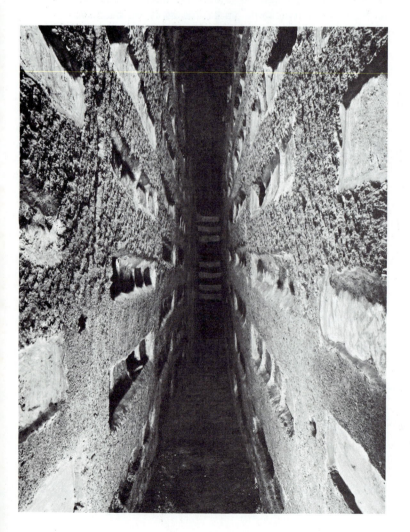

must have been enacted here, although the principal function of the catacombs was mortuary.

In Rome the catacombs were tunneled out of the granular tufa stratum, the convenient properties of which had been exploited earlier by the Etruscan necropolis-builders (see p. 159). After a plot of ground had been selected for the cemetery (Christians were not prevented by Roman law from owning property), a gallery three to four feet wide was dug around its perimeter at a convenient level below the surface (FIG. 7-1). In the walls of these galleries, embrasures were opened parallel to the gallery axis to receive the bodies of the dead; these openings, called *loculi*, were one above the other, like shelves (FIG. 7-2). Often, small rooms, called *cubicula*, were constructed in the walls to serve as mortuary chapels, and these were variously vaulted. When the original perimeter galleries were full of *loculi* and *cubicula*, other galleries would be cut at right angles to them, the process continuing as long as lateral space permitted. Then lower levels would be dug and connected by staircases, some systems going as deep as five levels. When adjacent burial areas belonged to members of the same Christian confraternity, or by gift or purchase fell into the same hands, communications were opened between the respective cemeteries, which thus spread laterally and gradually acquired a vast extent. After Christianity received official sanction, the catacombs fell into disuse except as holy places, monuments to the great martyrs, which were visited by the pious.

7-2   Gallery and loculi of the catacomb of Pamphilius, Rome, third century A.D.

Many cubicula were decorated with frescoes that were Late Antique (pagan) in manner and even in subject, the latter interpreted by the Christians to conform with their own beliefs. The geometric patterning of a ceiling in the catacomb of Saints Pietro and Marcellino in Rome (FIG. 7-3) becomes akin to the Dome of Heaven (the large circle), which has been inscribed with the basic symbol of the Christian faith, the cross. The cross-arms terminate in lunettes in which are represented the key episodes from the Old Testament story of Jonah, who is thrown from his ship on the left, emerges from the whale on the right, and, safe on land on the bottom, contemplates the miracle of his salvation and the mercy of God. (Jonah, an often-painted figure in Early Christian art, was honored as a prefiguration of Christ, who rose from death as Jonah had been delivered from the belly of the whale.) The compartments between these lunettes are occupied by *orans* figures, members of the Christian community with arms raised in the attitude of prayer, a priestly gesture still made in the ritual of the Roman Catholic mass and likely of great antiquity. The central medallion shows the figure of Christ as the Good Shepherd whose powers of salvation are underscored by his juxtaposition with the story of Jonah. As a theme, the Good Shepherd can be traced back through Greek Archaic to Egyptian art, but here it becomes the symbol for the loyal protector of the Christian flock who said to his disciples, "Feed my lambs, feed my sheep." It is noteworthy that in the catacombs, during the Period of Persecution, Christ was almost invariably represented either as the Good Shepherd or as a teacher. Only later, when Christianity became the official state religion of the Roman empire, did Christ take on imperial attributes such as the halo, the purple robe, the throne, and others denoting rulership.

The style of the catacomb painters is most often the quick, sketchy impressionism we have seen in earlier Roman painting of the last Pompeian period, and the execution ranges from good to inferior, most often the latter. We must take into account that the catacombs were very unpromising places for the art of the mural decorator. The air was spoiled by decomposing corpses, the humidity was excessive and the lighting, provided largely by oil lamps, was entirely unfit for elaborate compositions and painstaking execution. For ceiling designs and those on arches and lunettes the painter was required to assume awkward and tiring poses, and it is no wonder that he proceeded hastily and that often his results were poor.

Architecture

Although some ceremonies were held in the catacombs, it is likely that regular services were held in private houses that were rearranged and partitioned off to make "community" houses, or in simple columned halls. The latter have not survived intact, having been destroyed in the last great persecutions under Diocletian; the remains of one, a kind of rudimentary basilica, dating from A.D. 311, have been found beneath the cathedral of Aquileia. When Christianity achieved imperial sanction under Constantine, there was suddenly the urgent need to set up buildings that

7-3 Painted ceiling from the catacomb of Saints Pietro and Marcellino, Rome, fourth century A.D.

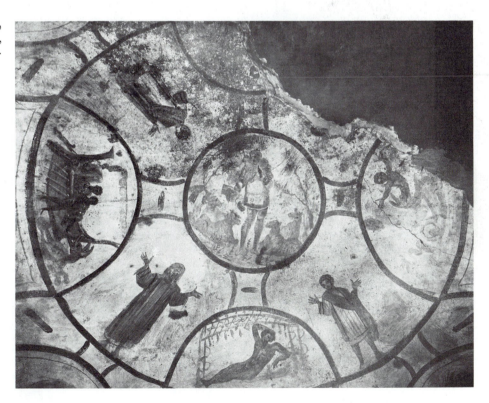

c.A.D. 250	306	325 c.333	c. 350	c. 395	410	c.425	493	c. 526
"Ludovisi Battle Sarcophagus"	Constantine becomes emperor	Old St. Peter's	Santa Costanza, Rome	Division of the empire	Fall of Rome	Mausoleum of Galla Placidia begun	Theodoric at Ravenna	

PERIOD OF PERSECUTION   PERIOD OF RECOGNITION

would meet the requirements of the Christian liturgy and would help aggrandize the Christian cult. All the architectural ingredients were present: the atrium house, the catacomb chapel, the Roman basilica, and the imperial audience hall. How these combined into the masterful composition that was one of the first Christian church buildings of the new age, old St. Peter's in Rome (FIGS. 7-4 and 7-6), we do not know; discussion about the origins of the Christian basilica has not ended. Begun in 333, St. Peter's is probably the most important design in the history of church architecture. Its wide influence was augmented by the belief that it stood where Peter, first of the apostles, had been buried. Its extraordinary dimensions are difficult to realize from the old drawings; the nave was as long, as high, and twice as wide as the nave of a great Gothic cathedral. Its interior was "one of the most spacious, most imposing, and most harmonious . . . ever built, imperially rich in its marbles and mosaics, grandiose yet forthright and large in the best Roman sense of the word."[1]

[1] Kenneth Conant, *Early Medieval Church Architecture* (Baltimore: Johns Hopkins Press, 1942), p. 6.

The plan of St. Peter's (FIG. 7-4) shows a rectangular building entered from the street through a gateway building, the *propylaea,* that leads into an open, colonnaded court, the atrium; that part of the colonnade joined to the façade functions as an entrance hall, the *narthex.* The body of the church consists of the nave, low side aisles, apse, and transverse aisle, or *transept,* which is placed between the nave and the apse and projects slightly beyond the walls of the nave and aisles. This fundamental arrangement was used in subsequent Christian architecture, though it would be wrong to think that there is some rigid, standardized basilican design; for instance, the transept, an occasional feature of churches in the city of Rome, is often lacking in other churches, especially in the smaller ones.

The cross section shows a great columned hall that obviously relates to such Roman secular basilicas as the Basilica Ulpia in the Forum of Trajan (FIG. 6-47). Unlike the slightly earlier Basilica of Constantine, St. Peter's was not vaulted, but timber roofed, as were, traditionally, most Roman basilicas (the vaulted Basilica of Constantine being an exception). The pagan basilica's lateral entrance is moved to the short side of the Christian church. Only one of the multiple apses is retained, and that is placed opposite and at a dramatic distance from the entrance. Evenly spaced columns no longer surround but flank the central nave. All these modifications of the pagan basilica make for

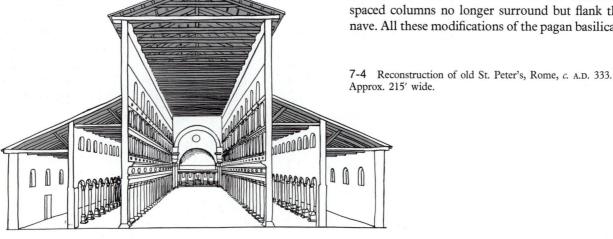

7-4 Reconstruction of old St. Peter's, Rome, c. A.D. 333. Approx. 215' wide.

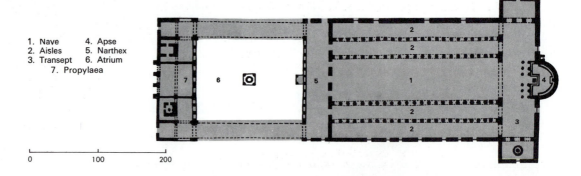

1. Nave   4. Apse
2. Aisles   5. Narthex
3. Transept   6. Atrium
      7. Propylaea

0   100   200

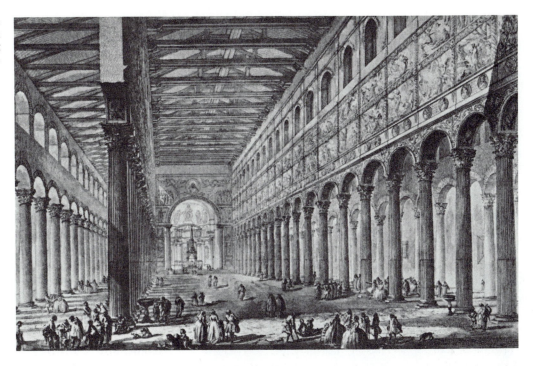

7-5 Interior, St. Paul's Outside the Walls, Rome, late fourth century, in an etching by Piranesi.

a sweeping perspective that converges on the shrine as the focus of the whole design and the place of the principal mystery of the Christian faith.

The old church of St. Peter no longer stands, and it is from an eighteenth-century print of its slightly later stylistic associate, St. Paul's (FIG. 7-5), that we can get some idea of what it looked like, some idea of its great space, scale, and majesty. The "spiritualizing" of the secular Roman design is expressed not only in the realignment of the building's axis (so as to focus one's whole experience on the ritual climax of the design) but in its extreme simplicity of structure and the lightness of its bearing walls and columns. Roman mass—huge walls and ponderous weight, sculptured surfaces in relief and recess, and whole populations of statuary—has been lightened, rarefied, smoothed; we could say it has been "dematerialized" to suit the new orientation toward a spiritual rather than a physical world.

The bird's-eye view of St. Peter's in reconstruction (FIG. 7-6), though partly conjectural, shows the very Roman stepped podium, which we have seen before in the Temple of Fortuna Virilis (FIG. 6-16) and which has Etruscan predecessors; a propylaea and forum-become-atrium are other elements with not only Roman but ancient antecedents. We believe that the exterior was, like that of Christian basilicas in general, unadorned, the whole decorative enterprise being reserved for the interior. It is as if the building imitated the ideal Christian, with grave and plain exterior and a soul glowing and beautiful within.

The rectangular basilican church design was long the favorite of the western Christian world. But the Early Christians also adopted another classical building type— the central-plan, a round or polygonal domed structure; this was later favored in the east, where Byzantine architects developed it to monumental proportions and amplified its theme in numerous ingenious variations. In the west the central-plan building type was used generally for structures adjacent to the main basilicas, like mausoleums, baptistries, and private chapels. A highly refined example of this central-plan design is Santa Costanza in Rome (FIGS. 7-7 to 7-9). Built in the mid-fourth century, it early served as the mausoleum of Constantia, daughter of the emperor Constantine. Its antecedents can be traced to the beehive tombs of the Mycenaeans, although its direct

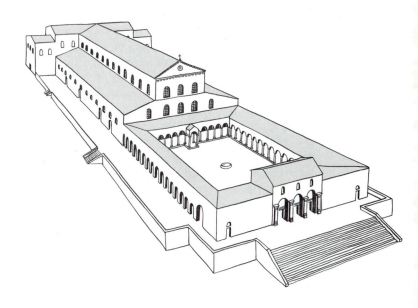

7-6 Conjectural reconstruction of old St. Peter's. (After K. J. Conant.)

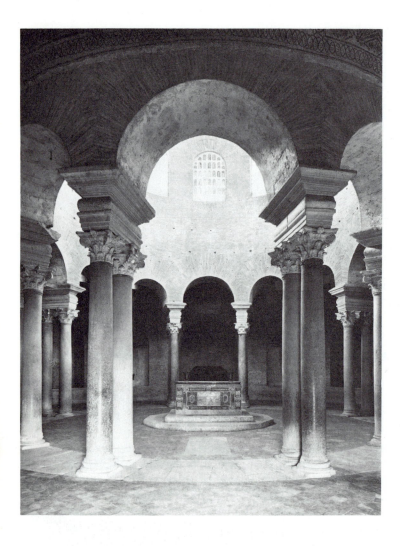

design in the apparently diverse basilicas of the fourth and early fifth centuries. It might also partly explain how such apparently contradictory and opposed designs as the long church and the central church could be imagined as working together in meeting the requirements of Christian belief and ritual. Given centuries of tradition, it would have been perfectly natural for Constantine to memorialize the place of Jesus' death and burial by a traditional type of monument, the domed rotunda, as he did in the Church of the Holy Sepulchre in Jerusalem. At the same time the existing basilica scheme might have been seen as offering the space needed for the congregations of pilgrims coming to the holiest place in Christendom. For several centuries then, the architectural problem—though never explicitly stated—was how to integrate the long plan and the central plan.

Mosaic and Painting

As the church-building enterprise under Constantine and his successors was designed to meet the urgent ceremonial needs of Christianity, now suddenly become official and public, so wholesale programs of decoration for the churches were also called for. To advertise the new faith in all its diverse aspects—its dogma, scriptural narrative, and symbolism—and to instruct and edify the believer, acres of wall in dozens of new churches had to be filled in a style and medium that would most effectively carry the message. Brilliantly ornamental mosaics—with sparkling tesserae of reflective glass, rather than the opaque marble tesserae that had been preferred by the Romans—became the standard vehicle of expression almost at once. Mosaics were particularly suited to the flat, thin-walled surfaces of the new basilicas, becoming a durable, tangible part of the wall, a kind of architectural tapestry. The light flooding through the clerestories was caught in vibrant reflection by the mosaics, which produced abrupt effects and contrasts and sharp concentrations of color that could focus attention on the central, most relevant features of a composition. Mosaic, worked in the Early Christian manner, is not intended for the subtle changes of tone that a naturalistic painter's approach would require; although, as we have seen in the Roman mosaics, tonality is well within the mosaicist's reach. But in mosaic, color is placed, not blended; and bright, hard, glittering texture, set within a rigorously simplified pattern, becomes the rule. As noted earlier, for mosaics placed high on the wall, far above the observer's head, the painstaking use of tiny tesserae, seen in Roman floor mosaics, becomes meaningless. Early Christian mosaics, designed to be seen from a distance, employ larger stones; the surfaces are left uneven so that the tesserae's projecting edges can catch and reflect the light, and the

inspiration may have been the Pantheon, or the pool-enclosing rotunda of some public baths, like those of Caracalla. The Pantheon's mass, however, has been metamorphosed, as with the mutation of the pagan into the Early Christian basilica. In Santa Costanza the circle of paired columns that carries the domed cylinder is well free of the external walls, free enough to leave space for a barrel-vaulted corridor, or *ambulatory*. In fact, it is as if the basilican wall-arcade has been bent around a circle, the ambulatory corresponding to the basilican aisles and, like them, equipped with a high, ample clerestory. The exuberant naturalism of the luxurious mosaics in the vault of the ambulatory (FIG. 7-9) suggests a lingering influence of the pagan spirit.

All the important buildings of the fourth century, including Santa Costanza and the great longitudinal basilicas, are closely associated with Constantine and his immediate relatives, for it was through their patronage and supervision and as an expression of the new ideal of the Christian *imperium* that these buildings came to be. This close relationship of the Constantinians with Constantinian architecture may help to explain a certain consistency of

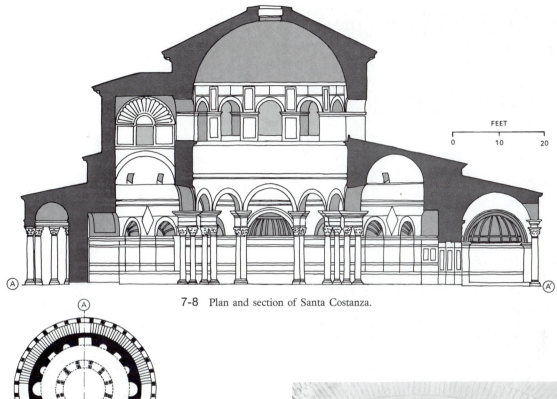

7-8 Plan and section of Santa Costanza.

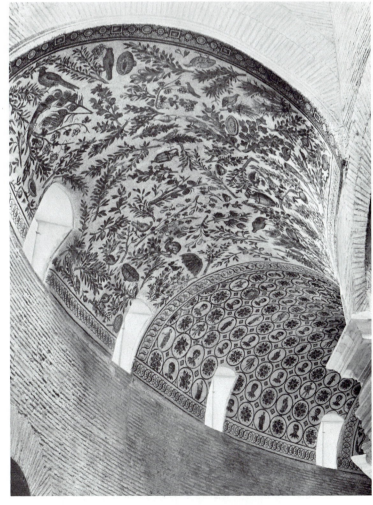

designs are simple, for optimum legibility. Through several centuries, in the service of Christian theology, mosaic was the medium of some of the supreme masterpieces of world art.

Content and style find their medium; the content of Christian doctrine took centuries to fashion, and for a long time even the proper manner of representing the founder of Christianity was in question. When Christianity became official, Jesus' status changed. In early works he is shown as teacher and philosopher; in later works his image becomes imperialized as the ruler of heaven and earth. In the fourth and fifth centuries there was hesitation about how he should be represented, and variant types of images were produced. After some crucial theological questions on Jesus' nature were resolved, a more or less standard formula for his depiction emerged.

In the minds of simple Christians only recently converted, Jesus could be easily identified with the familiar deities of the Mediterranean world, especially Helios

7-9 Detail of mosaics in the vault of the ambulatory, Santa Costanza.

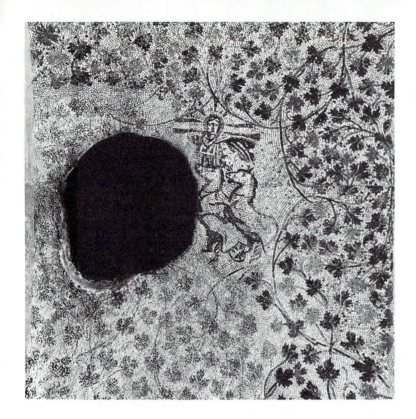

horses of the sun-chariot through the heavens—a conception far more grandiose than that of the Good Shepherd.

The style, or styles, of Christian art emerged as a transmutation of Greco-Roman art; for the mosaicists, the point of departure was Roman illusionism. This can be seen in the apse mosaic of the church of Santa Pudenziana in Rome, dated about A.D. 410, the earliest surviving example in a succession of monumental apse mosaics extending through the history of Christian art (FIG. 7-11). Though drastically restored in the nineteenth century (almost the whole of the right half has suffered), enough remains to show the persistence of Roman forms and the assimilation of Roman imperial attributes to the image of Christ. On an emperor's throne, Christ, clad in imperial purple and gold, sits within the Heavenly Jerusalem and presides over the Church Triumphant. He is flanked on either side by ascending ranks of apostles deployed like a Roman emperor's entourage of senators. Above them on either side of the throne are two women, the personifications of the Church of the Gentiles (New Testament) and the Church of the Synagogue (Old Testament). Above and behind the head of Christ is the jeweled cross that Constantine raised on the site of Christ's crucifixion. Within the gold-streaked, blue sky there hover the four symbolic creatures of the visions of Ezekiel and the Book of Revelation, represent-

(Apollo), the sun god, or his romanized eastern aspect, Sol Invictus (the Unconquered Sun). The late third-century vault mosaic of a small Christian mausoleum in a pagan cemetery, excavated underneath St. Peter's in Rome in the 1940s (FIG. 7-10), shows Jesus as Apollo, driving the

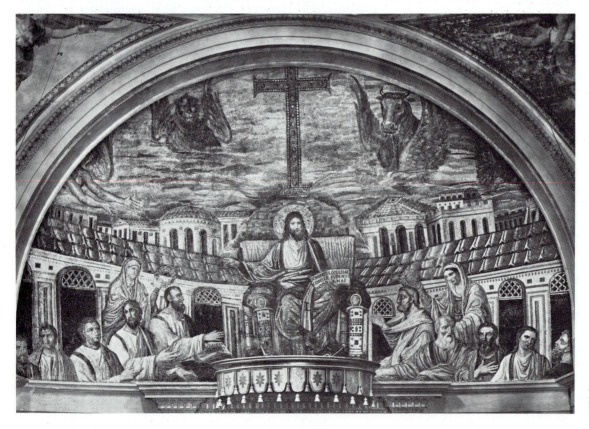

7-11 *Christ Enthroned in Majesty, with Saints,* apse mosaic, Santa Pudenziana, Rome, A.D. 402-17.

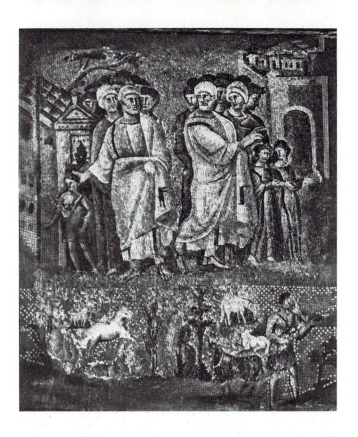

7-12 *The Parting of Lot and Abraham,* mosaic from Santa Maria Maggiore, Rome, *c.* A.D. 430.

ing the Four Evangelists: the winged Man of St. Matthew (partly obscured by the arch), the Lion of St. Mark, the Ox of St. Luke, and—also partly obscured—the Eagle of St. John. (This is an early appearance of these symbols, which we shall find commonly represented later, and throughout Medieval art; see, for example, FIG. 7-28.) The background recalls the kind of perspective illusionism and naturalistic depiction of architectural forms found in Pompeian wall paintings, and the buildings may reflect to some degree those actually in Jerusalem at that time.

As in Santa Pudenziana, so in the great mosaic cycle in Santa Maria Maggiore in Rome, also dating from the early fifth century, we can witness the union of the old naturalism and the new symbolism. The panel representing the parting of Lot and Abraham (FIG. 7-12) tells its story (Gen. 13:5-13) succinctly: Agreeing to disagree, Lot leads his family and flocks to the right, toward the city of Sodom, while Abraham moves toward a building on the left (the church?). Lot's is the evil choice, and the instrumentalities of the evil, his two daughters, are represented in front of him, while the figure of the yet unborn Isaac, the instrument of good, stands before his father, Abraham. The cleavage of the two groups is emphatic, and each is represented by a shorthand device one could call a "head-cluster," which will have a long history in Christian art. The figures turn from each other in a kind of sharp dialogue of glance and gesture and we recognize here a moving away from the flexibility of naturalism toward the significant gesture and that primary method of Medieval representation, *pantomime,* which simplifies all significance into body attitude and gesture. The wide eyes turned in their sockets, the broad gestures of enlarged hands, the opposed movements of the groups, remind us of some silent, expressive chorus that comments only by gesture upon the action of the drama. Thus, the complex action of Roman art stiffens into the art of simplified motion or dumb show, which has great power to communicate without ambiguity and which, in the whole course of Medieval art, will produce the richest kind of variety. Also foreshadowing the character of later Christian art is the fact that the figures of the panel have been moved to the foreground and that the artist takes no great pains to describe either space or landscape setting; background town and building are symbolic rather than descriptive. But within this relatively abstract setting, the figures themselves loom with massive solidity. They cast shadows and are modeled in dark and light to give them that three-dimensional appearance that testifies to the artist's heritage of Roman pictorial illusionism. It will require another century and much modification under non-Hellenized Eastern influence before he will be able to think of his figures entirely as symbols rather than plastic bodies.

The Illuminated Manuscript

Santa Maria Maggiore is an early and outstanding example of the complementarity of the new basilican architecture and the new, detailed mosaics and paintings designed for them. But the earlier art of the catacombs could not have provided the resources for narratives as elaborate as those of Santa Maria Maggiore; catacomb painting was much too narrow in scope of subject and much too rudimentary in style and technique. Rather, the church decorators must have drawn upon a long tradition of pictures in manuscripts going back to pharaonic Egypt and highly developed by the Hellenistic Greeks of Alexandria; thousands of texts must have been available to the Constantinian artists, richly illustrated with themes—Hebrew, Greek, and Christian, and combinations of all three. We know that Constantine summoned numerous savants and literati of Alexandria and that he established a library where they gave instruction; we know also that he was a generous donor of manuscripts to the Church. Hence, it is no wonder that Constantinople became a center of traditional and Christian learning that was transmitted by the copying and recopying of manuscripts through the centuries. The dissemination of manuscripts, as well as their preservation, was greatly aided by an important invention in the early Imperial period. The long manuscript scroll (*rotulus*) used by Egyptians, Greeks, and Romans and made of the fragile papyrus was superseded by the *codex,* which was made much like the modern book, of separate pages bound together at one side and having a cover. Papyrus was replaced by much more durable *vellum* (veal skin) and

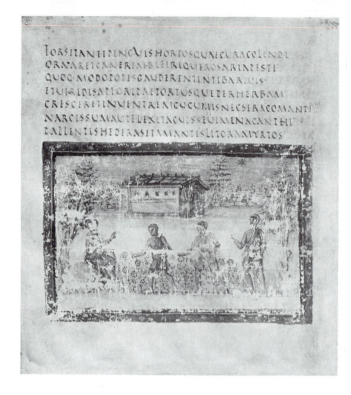

IORSIIANTIIPINQVISHORTOSQVAECVRACOLENDI
ORNARETCANEREBPIBLIARIQVEROSABIMESTI
QVOQMODOPOTISGAVDERENTIINTIBARIVIS
ETVIRIDISATIORLATIORTOSQVLTERHERBNAI
CRESCIREIINVENTAENICOCVMISNECSERACOMANTI
NARCISSVMAVTIILEXITACVISSEVIMINACANTHI
LALLENTISHEDERASITAMANTISLITORAMYRTOS

7-13 Miniature from the *Vatican Vergil*, early fifth century A.D. Approx. 12″ × 12½″. Vatican Library, Rome.

significance only slightly less than that of the text from which it drew its authority. The passage from the scroll to the codex—that is, from continuous narrative to a series of individual pictures—can be seen in two manuscripts of different date, the later still reflecting the scroll procedure. The *Vatican Vergil* (FIG. 7-13), from the early fifth century and the oldest painted manuscript known, is pagan in content, representing a scene from Vergil's *Georgics,* in which a seated farmer, at the left, instructs two of his slaves in the art of husbandry, while Vergil, at the right, listens and records the instructions. (One remembers the Roman idealization of country life and nature.) The style is Late Antique and reminiscent of Pompeian landscapes. The quick, impressionistic touches that suggest space and atmosphere, the foreshortened villa in the background, the small, active figures in their wide, spacious setting—all these are familiar features of Roman illusionistic painting. We saw the heavy black frame isolating a single episode in the late Pompeian styles; it contrasts with the form of the *Vienna Genesis* (FIG. 7-14), which uses the continuity of a frieze, or in this case a scroll. The episode from Genesis represents Joseph receiving his brothers (who do not recognize him) in Egypt, where he has become the Pharaoh's chief administrator. They have come from Israel destitute and starving and, forgetting their cruelty to him, Joseph permits them to gather food. Overcome with emotion, he has withdrawn behind a screen to weep. Three distinct episodes are represented, with Joseph in two of them. The picture might almost have been cut out of a continuous

parchment (lamb skin), which provided better surfaces for painting than did papyrus. These changes in the durability, reproduction, and format of texts greatly improved the possibility that the records of ancient civilization could survive long centuries of neglect, even if not in great number.

The sacred texts were copied as faithfully as possible, and so were the pictures in them. After the great fathers of the Eastern Church recommended the didactic use of pictures in churches and books, the picture came to have a

7-14 *Joseph Recognizes His Brothers,* from the *Vienna Genesis,* early sixth century A.D. Approx. 4″ × 7½″. Österreichische National-bibliothek, Vienna.

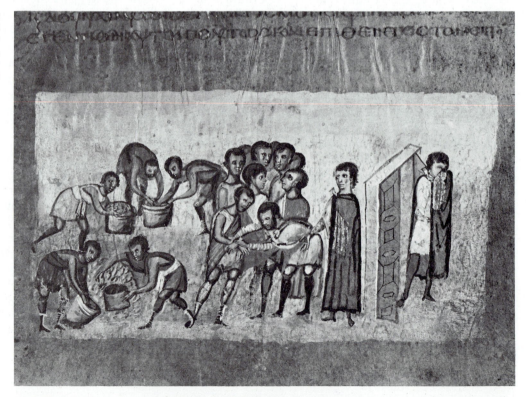

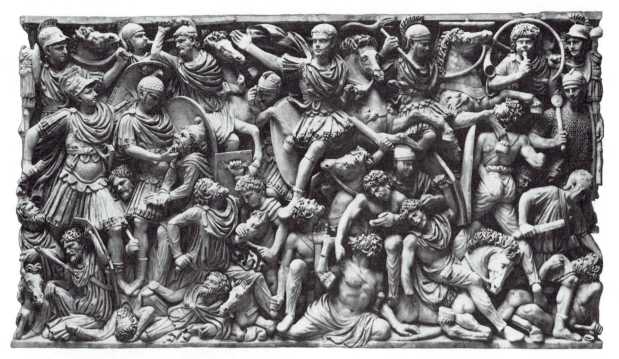

7-15 *Battle Between Romans and Barbarians,* front panel of the so-called *Ludovisi Battle Sarcophagus,* third century A.D. Marble, approx. 56″ high. Museo Nazionale, Rome.

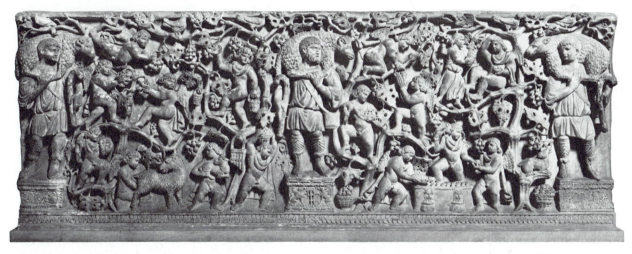

7-16 *The Good Shepherd Sarcophagus,* from the catacomb of Praetextus, Rome, late fourth century A.D. Museo del Laterano, Rome.

scroll, for it seems as if it should continue to the left and right. (Although this is not the case here, pictures often *were* cut out of scrolls and fixed to the pages of a codex.) The figures are the reduced Hellenistic types, acting in a neutral space entirely without landscape and performing in the silhouetted, pantomimic way that presents the story with all possible economy. While the figures retain only a narrative importance, the page itself becomes sumptuous, a rich purple ground lettered in silver. The luxuriousness of ornament that will be more and more typical of sacred books absorbs the human figure or relegates it to a secondary function. What will come to count above all are the spiritual beauty of the text and the material beauty of the vehicle that serves and intensifies it. The luster of holy objects—"sages standing in God's holy fire"—becomes the intent and being of Byzantine art.

Sculpture and Craft Art

The transformations that take place in architecture in the period of early Christianity—whereby the multipurpose pagan basilica is adapted to the single purpose of Christian ritual, and the heavy materiality of Roman buildings is "dematerialized" in the screenlike thinness and lightness of Christian structure—is paralleled in the sculpture of the time. We have seen anticipations of the change as early as the second century in the Column of Trajan (FIG. 6-61), and we have seen the change almost complete in early fourth-century reliefs of the Arch of Constantine (FIGS. 6-81 and 6-82). A third-century relief on the so-called *Ludovisi Battle Sarcophagus* (FIG. 7-15) should be interpolated between them. This work, still quite pagan in theme and spirit, represents a struggle between Romans and barbarians and is most instructive as an illustration of the "flattened relief" and the "piled-up" perspective so characteristic of the denaturing of Greco-Roman naturalism and the emerging Medieval style. While a strong descriptive realism persists in details of physiognomy, dress, action, gesture, and accessories, pattern has taken over from figure composition. The writhing figures are all within the same plane; at the same time the "foreground" figures (those at the base of the pattern) are relatively small, while the "background" figures at the top of the pattern are the largest. This *reverse perspective* strengthens the surface into a dense mass with no illusion of space beyond (behind) it. Carving has less and less a role, and quick effects of light and dark are had by gouging, punching, and drilling the surface. As yet the formal placing of the figures that we find in the Arch of Constantine has not appeared; but of course the subject does not call for that, and the sarcophagus composition represents more the dissolution of the style of the Trajanic reliefs than the advent of Constantinian formalism. But the patterning and constriction of surface, the sacrifice of realism of space and proportion, are all present and share the characteristics of Early Christian art.

Toward the end of the fourth century we find the flattening and patterning process well advanced. The *Good Shepherd Sarcophagus* (FIG. 7-16) has a thick, spaceless surface that is perforated rather than carved, producing a kind of hard lacing of flat darks and lights. This sarcophagus is interesting, too, for what it reveals of Christian adaptation of pagan material. We have seen that the Good Shepherd theme appears in pre-Christian times and that the Christians take it to signify Christ. Here the motif appears three times, possibly in an allusion to the Trinity. Around the Good Shepherd twines a grapevine heavy with grapes and through which climb busy cupids bringing in the harvest. Three cupids crush the grapes in a wine press, and their wine, once sacred to Bacchus, has now become symbolic of the blood of Christ; the cupids themselves, once associated with love and erotic passion (Cupid is the son of Venus), are forerunners of Christian cherubs. Thus, a purely pagan theme with orgiastic overtones is transmuted by Christian intention into a symbol of redemption through the blood of Christ. The figure style, with its stumpy proportions, frontalizing pose, and stereotyping of action, had its predecessor in the reliefs on the Arch of Constantine and is common (with many variations) to a great number of sarcophagi from the fourth, fifth, and sixth centuries.

Despite the great changes in sculpture during the second half of the third century the classical tradition is by no means extinguished, even though there seems to be an almost deliberate turning away from Greco-Roman art to something archaic, abstract, and bluntly expressive, as in the group of figures called the *Tetrarchs,* the Arch of

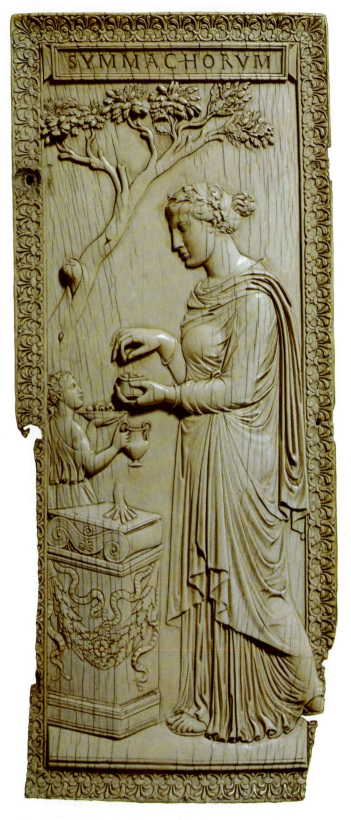

7-17 *Priestess Celebrating the Rites of Bacchus,* leaf of an ivory diptych of the Nicomachi and the Symmachi, *c.* A.D. 380–400, 11¾″ × 5½″. Victoria and Albert Museum, London.

Constantine, and the coin portrait of Maximin Daia. The tradition lives on through the Middle Ages, if not with always entirely discernible continuity, yet in intermittent revivals, renovations, and restorations, however they may be called. It exists commingled with, or side-by-side and in contrast with, the opposing, nonclassicizing Medieval styles. The end of the Medieval world will be signalized by the rise of classical art to dominance in the Renaissance. It has been recently observed that the greatest achievement of Early Christian art from the third to the seventh century is to have "preserved, in the face of vast and cataclysmic changes, basic and essential elements of the Greco-Roman heritage."[2] As we follow the course of stylistic change through the history of western art, especially in the Middle Ages, the strength of the classical tradition in its dialogue with competing strains and tendencies of style should always be kept in mind.

Monumental sculpture begins its decline in the fourth century and does not recover its place in the history of art until the twelfth. The Christian tended to be suspicious of the freestanding statue, linking it with the false gods of the pagans. In his *Apologia*, Justin Martyr, a second-century ecclesiast mindful of the First Commandment admonition to shun graven images, accuses the pagans of worshiping statues as gods. But the Greco-Roman experience was still a living part of the Mediterranean mentality and, at least in the west, the Semitic ban on images in sacred places was not likely to be adopted. The reasoning of the fathers of the early Church—that the use of pictures and statues could be justified on the grounds that they instructed the illiterate in the mysteries and stories of the faith—was later supplemented by the theological argument that since Jesus was "made flesh and dwelt among us," he had a human nature and human likeness that could be represented in art.

In any event, during the Early Christian and Byzantine periods, sculpture dwindled to craft art and small work—sarcophagus reliefs, commemorative ivory panels, metalwork, church furniture and accessories, book covers and the like. Yet, in this great reduction of the scope of the medium, works of exquisite craftsmanship could still be produced that reflected, even in Christian times, the persistence of pagan, classical ideals of beauty. An ivory plaque (FIG. 7-17), produced probably in Rome toward the end of the fourth century, exhibits srikingly the endurance of classical form. The ivory, one of a pair of leaves of a diptych, commemorates the marriage of members of two powerful Roman families of the senatorial class, the Nicomachi and the Symmachi, who remained pagan during this first triumphal period when the emperor Theodosius decreed Christianity as the only legally recognized religion of the empire. They seem consciously here to reaffirm their

faith in the old pagan gods; certainly they favor the esthetic ideals of the classical past, much as we find them realized in such works as the Parthenon frieze (FIG. 5-46) and the Ara Pacis Augustae (FIG. 6-55). The illustration represents a pagan priestess celebrating the rites of Bacchus and Jupiter; its companion piece shows a priestess honoring Ceres and Cybele. Here the priestess prepares a libation at an altar where burns the sacred fire. The precise yet fluent and graceful line, the easy, gliding pose, and the mood of spiritual serenity bespeak an artist practicing within a still vital classical tradition, for which idealized human beauty is central. That tradition was probably deliberately sustained by the great senatorial magnates of Rome, who resisted the empire-wide imposition of the Christian faith in the later fourth century.

A later work, carved in the eastern empire, perhaps in Constantinople, offers still further evidence of the persistence of classical form, though there are subtle deviations from its rules. It is an ivory leaf from a diptych dating from the early sixth century and depicting St. Michael the Archangel (FIG. 7-18). The prototype of the *St. Michael* must have been a pagan Victory; the flowing classical and still naturalistic drapery, the delicately incised wings, and the facial type and coiffure are of the pre-Christian tradition. But there are significant divergences from it, even so—misinterpretations or misreadings of the rules of naturalistic representation. Subtle ambiguities in the relation of the figure to its architectural setting appear in such details as the placing of the scepter and the hovering of the feet above the stair without real relation to it. These matters have, of course, little to do with the striking beauty of the form; they simply indicate the course that stylistic change is taking, as the Greco-Roman world fades into history and the Medieval era begins.

We find that change almost completed in the *Diptych of Anastasius* (FIG. 7-19), which represents the emperor Anastasius I, as consul, about to throw down the *mappa* (handkerchief), the signal for the games to start. Though the diptych, dated A.D. 517, is about contemporary with the *St. Michael* ivory, the mutation of classical naturalism is much further advanced (a reminder that the process does not proceed evenly along the same historical front or at the same tempo). The figure of the emperor in both panels is elevated above the lively scenes taking place in the arena. He is enthroned in rigid frontality, making a static, suspended gesture, entirely symbolic, the abstraction of his consular authority. His features are masklike, and his quasidivine status is announced by a halo. The halo, a shell form, would originally have been an architectural feature, part of the pediment of the niche; here—in an excellent example of a misreading of a prototype—it has migrated to its place behind the emperor's head. The details of the architecture are confused and have lost their original architectural significance, and the flattening and patterning

[2]Ernst Kitzinger, *Byzantine Art in the Making* (Cambridge, Mass.: Harvard Univ. Press, 1977), p. 126.

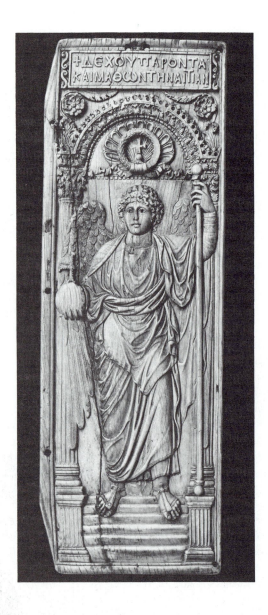

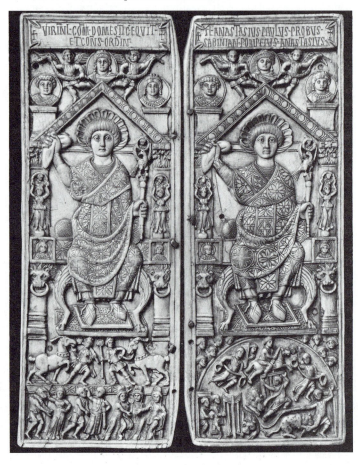

of the surface is as we have seen it developing earlier. The work is entirely ornamental and symbolic; the living man is lost in the concept—in this case, the concept of supreme and suprahuman authority. One hundred years after the *Diptych of Anastasius,* the *Sarcophagus of Archbishop Theodore* (FIG. 7-20) is not only ornamented with entirely symbolic forms, but the human figure is dismissed altogether. Peacocks, symbolic of eternity, flank a *chi-rho* monogram (XP are the first two letters of "Christ" in Greek). The XP is supplemented in the monogram with the alpha (A) and the omega (Ω), the first and last letters of the Greek alphabet, representing the words of Christ: "I am the Beginning and the End." The fruiting vines behind the peacocks represent, as we have seen, the source of the redeeming blood of Christ. Set within wreaths on the lid of the tomb, the *chi-rho* monogram appears three times; it had already served as the *labarum* carried upon the standards of the Imperial Christian army. Thus, the hope of the

deceased archbishop and the guarantee of his salvation are expressed entirely in symbol: eternity; redemption through the blood of Christ, who stands at the beginning and the end of time; and the triumph of Christianity. The accidents and irregularities of figural representation, the busyness of narrative, are replaced by timeless signs of salvation and immortality.

BYZANTINE ART

The transition from Early Christian to Byzantine art is neither abrupt nor definite and, in fact, defies accurate definition. The almost contemporary diptychs of St. Michael (FIG. 7-18) and of Anastasius (FIG. 7-19) are both products of eastern carvers and might well be classified as Byzantine works. Yet the *St. Michael* is still firmly

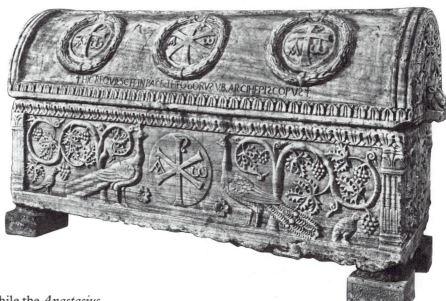

7-20 *Sarcophagus of Archbishop Theodore*, seventh century A.D. Marble. Sant' Apollinare in Classe, Ravenna.

rooted in the Greco-Roman tradition, while the *Anastasius* panels show the Medieval stress on the event rather than its appearance. In this latter approach, essentially Near Eastern or Semitic, forms evolved into decorative symbols placed before a shallow, often neutral background that makes little if any allusion to optical space.

One point of departure for the abstract, symbolic Eastern Christian art may be a mural painting from Dura-Europos, a small garrison town on the west bank of the Euphrates in the heart of ancient Mesopotamia and on the very edge of the Roman empire (FIG. 7-21). It dates from the second to third century A.D., the time of the Roman occupation. The detail shown here may depict an attendant and priests of a forgotten pagan cult of Parthia or Palmyra (modern Tadmor). The figures stand with formal frontality in front of (within?) an architectural background. Their drapery is rendered by line, not tone, and their gestures are slow, ceremonial, and grave. Each figure is in itself a single vertical design entity, isolated from its neighbor. The bodies are hovering, weightless, their feet in ambiguous relation to the ground and to the architectural setting, reminding us of the *St. Michael* ivory carved centuries later. Although the meaning of the enacted ceremony is lost to us, it must have been represented with utmost clarity to initiates, who could read the depicted symbols and gestures like a pictorial script, a script that moved laterally across the surface of the printed wall unobstructed by perspective and other illusionistic devices.

As Christian dogma developed, this form of symbolic interpretation of reality was more and more favored, and a flat, decorative, abstract "Byzantine" style, rooted in such Near Eastern works as the Dura-Europos murals, began to dominate Christian art. And, although Western illusionism, was tenacious and enjoyed repeated revivals, the transition was more or less complete by the middle of the sixth century. It can be conveniently observed in the monuments of a single city, Ravenna.

7-21 *Priests with Attendant*, detail of a mural from the Temple of the Palmyrene Gods, Dura-Europos, second to third centuries A.D.

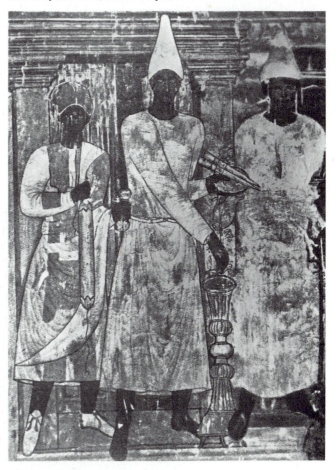

Ravenna

Early in the fifth century, when the Visigoths, under their king, Alaric, threatened to overrun Italy, Emperor Honorius moved the capital of his crumbling empire to Ravenna, an ancient Roman harbor on Italy's Adriatic coast, some eighty miles south of Venice. There, in a city surrounded by swamps and thus easily defended, his imperial authority survived the fall of Rome to Alaric in 410. Honorius died in 423, and the reins of government were taken over by his half-sister, Galla Placidia, whose biography reads like an outrageously exaggerated adventure story. Galla Placidia died in 450, some twenty-five years before the last of her weak successors was deposed. In 476 Ravenna fell to Odoacer and eventually, in 493, it was chosen by Theodoric, the Goths' greatest king, to be the capital of his Ostrogothic kingdom, which encompassed much of the Balkans and all of Italy. During the short history of his unfortunate successors the importance of the city declined. But in 539 the Byzantine general Belisarius conquered Ravenna for his emperor, Justinian, and led the city into the third and most important stage of its history. Reunited with the (eastern) "empire," Ravenna remained the "sacred fortress" of Byzantium, its foothold in Italy for 200 years, until its conquest successively by the Lombards and the Franks. It enjoyed its greatest cultural and economic prosperity during the reign of Justinian, at a time when the "eternal city" of Rome was threatened with complete extinction by repeated sieges, conquests, and sackings.

The seat of Byzantine dominion in Italy, ruled by Byzantine governors, or *exarchs,* Ravenna and its culture became an extension of Constantinople, and its art, more than that of the Byzantine capital (where relatively little has survived outside of architecture), clearly reveals the transition from Early Christian to Byzantine style.

The climactic points of Ravenna's history are closely linked with the personages of Galla Placidia, Theodoric, and Justinian. All left their stamp on the city with monuments that have survived to our day (one might say miraculously, since the city was heavily bombed in the Second World War) and that make Ravenna one of the most complete repositories of fifth- and sixth-century mosaics in Italy. The monuments of Ravenna, particularly the Justinianic ones, represent ideas that ultimately will determine the forms of culture, and certainly art, of the Middle Ages.

Galla Placidia's own mausoleum (the identity of which has recently been questioned) is a rather small cruciform structure with a dome-covered crossing (FIGS. 7-22 and 7-23). Built shortly after 425, it was originally attached to the narthex of the now greatly altered basilican palace church of Santa Croce. Although its plan is that of a Latin cross, the cross-arms are very short and appear to be little more than apsidal extensions of a square. Thus, all emphasis is placed on the tall, dome-covered crossing, and the building becomes, in effect, a central-plan structure. On the other hand, this small, unassuming building also represents one of the earliest successful fusions of the two basic early church plans, the longitudinal and the central, and introduces us, on a small scale, to a building type that will have a long history in Christian architecture—the basilican plan with a domed crossing.

The mausoleum's plain, unadorned brick shell encloses one of the richest mosaic ensembles in Early Christian art.

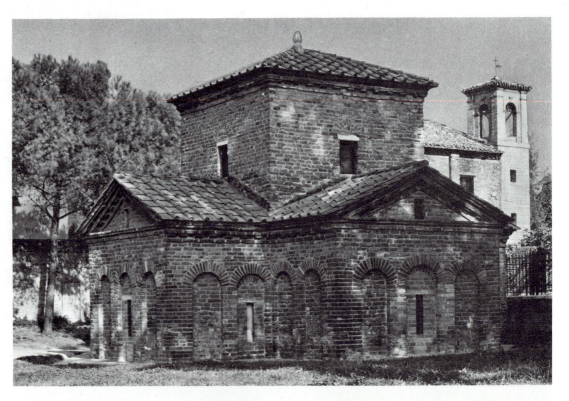

7-22 Mausoleum of Galla Placidia, Ravenna, A.D. 425–50.

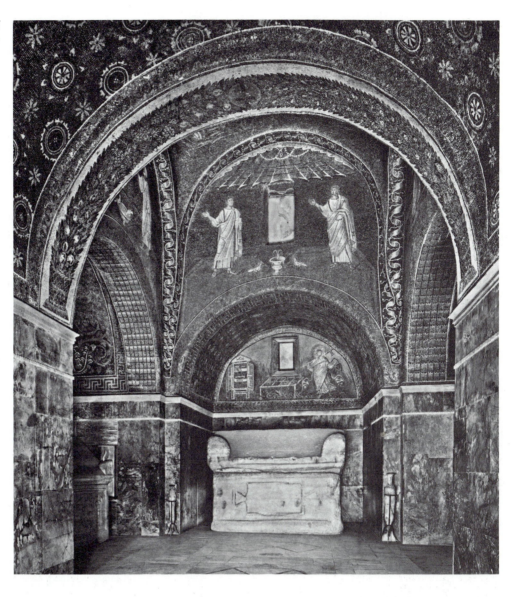

7-23 Interior of the mausoleum of Galla Placidia.

Every square inch of the interior surfaces above the marble-faced walls is covered with mosaic decor: the barrel vaults of nave and cross-arms with garlands and decorative medallions reminiscent of snowflakes on a dark blue ground; the dome with a large golden cross against a star-studded sky; other surfaces with representations of saints and apostles; and the lunette above the entrance with a representation of Christ as the Good Shepherd (FIG. 7-24). We have seen earlier versions of the Good Shepherd, but none so regal as this. Jesus no longer carries a lamb on his shoulders but is seated among his flock in splendid isolation, haloed and robed in gold and purple. To his left and right the sheep are evenly distributed in groups of three. But their arrangement is rather loose and informal (compare FIG. 7-26), and they have been placed in a carefully described landscape that extends from foreground to background and is covered by a blue sky. All forms are tonally rendered; they have three-dimensional bulk, cast

shadows, and are disposed in depth. In short, the panel is replete with devices of Roman illusionism and its creator still has roots deep in the Hellenic tradition. Some fifty years later his successors will work in a much more abstract and formal manner.

Around 504, shortly after he settled in Ravenna, Theodoric ordered the construction of his own palace church, a three-aisled basilica dedicated to the Savior. In the ninth century, the relics of Apollinaris were transferred to this church, which was rededicated and has been known since as Sant' Apollinare Nuovo. The rich mosaic decorations of the interior nave walls (FIG. 7-25) are arranged in three zones, of which the upper two date from the time of Theodoric. Between the clerestory windows are represented Old Testament patriarchs and prophets, and above them scenes from the life of Christ alternate with decorative panels. The lowest zone originally bore subjects of either Arian or political character. Although Christians,

Theodoric and his Goths were Arians—followers of the teachings of Bishop Arius—a sect declared heretical by the Orthodox Church. After the Byzantine conquest of Ravenna, Bishop Agnellus ordered all mosaics that bore reference to Theodoric or to Arianism removed and replaced with the present procession of orthodox saints, male on one side, female on the other. Since Agnellus had no quarrel with the subjects on the upper two levels, they were left intact, and our example, which shows the miracle of the loaves and the fishes (FIG. 7-26), must date from about 500. It well illustrates the stylistic change that has occurred since the decoration of Galla Placidia's mausoleum. Jesus, beardless and in the imperial dress of gold and purple, faces directly toward us as he directs his disciples to distribute the miraculously augmented supply of bread and fish to the great crowd to which he has preached. The artist makes no attempt to supply details to the event. Rather he emphasizes the sacramental character of it, the spiritual fact that Jesus, outstanding in the group, is performing a miracle by the power of God. The fact of the miracle takes it out of the world of time and of incident, for what is important in this scene is the presence of almighty power, which requires nothing but an unchanging presentation in terms of formal, unchanging aspect. The story is told with the bare minimum of figures necessary to make its meaning explicit, and these figures have been aligned laterally, moved close to the foreground, and placed in a shallow picture box that is cut off by a golden screen close behind the back of the figures. The landscape setting, which was so explicitly described by the artist who worked for Galla Placidia, is here merely suggested by a few rocks and bushes that enclose the figure group like parentheses. That former reference to the physical world, the blue sky, is now replaced by a neutral gold, which is to be the standard background color from now on. Remnants of the former illusionism are to be found only in the handling of the individual figures, which still cast shadows and retain some of their former volume. But the shadows of the drapery folds have already narrowed into bars and will soon disappear.

The Ravenna epoch closes with the church of Sant' Apollinare in Classe where, in the great apse mosaic, the Byzantine style reaches full maturity. Here, until the ninth century (when it was transferred to Ravenna, as described above), rested the body of St. Apollinaris, who suffered his martyrdom in Classe, Ravenna's port city. The building itself (FIG. 7-27) is of the Early Christian type, a three-aisled basilica with a plan quite similar to that of Theodoric's palace church in Ravenna. The peculiar design of the apse, which combines a semicircular interior with a polygonal exterior, is typical for Ravenna churches and is probably of Byzantine origin. As usual for the period, the outside of the building is plain and unadorned. (The cylindrical bell tower, or *campanile*, is of later date.) The interior decoration in this case is confined to the triumphal

arch and the apse behind it. Of these mosaics the one decorating the semivault above the apse (FIG. 7-28) was probably completed by 549, when the church was dedicated. It shows, against a gold ground, a large blue medallion with a jeweled cross, symbol of the transfigured Jesus, and may refer to the cross Constantine set up on the hill of Calvary to commemorate the martyrdom of Christ. We have seen it at Santa Pudenziana in Rome (FIG. 7-11). Just above, there is the hand of God. On either side in the clouds appear the figures of Moses and Elijah, who had appeared before Christ during his transfiguration; below these two figures are three sheep, the three disciples who accompanied Christ to the foot of the Mount of the Transfiguration. Beneath, in the midst of green fields with trees, flowers, and birds, stands with uplifted arms the patron saint of the church, Apollinaris, accompanied by twelve sheep representing perhaps the Christian congregation under the protection of St. Apollinaris and forming, as they march in regular file across the apse, a wonderfully decorative base. On the face of the triumphal arch above are represented in the rainbow-streaked heavens the image of Christ in a medallion and the Signs of the Evangelists. The twelve lambs are the twelve apostles, issuing from the cities of Bethlehem and Jerusalem. The iconographical program is completed by the two palms of Paradise in the narrow spandrels of the arch and by the two archangels below them.

Comparison with the Galla Placidia mosaic (FIG. 7-24) shows how the style and the artist's approach to his subject have changed during the course of a century. In each case we are looking at a human figure and some sheep in a landscape. But now, in the mid-sixth century, the artist no longer tries to re-create a segment of the physical world but tells his story in terms of flat symbols, lined up side by side. All overlapping is carefully avoided in what must have been an intentional effort to omit all reference to the three-dimensional space of the material world and physical reality. Shapes have lost their volume to become flat silhouettes into which details have been inscribed with lines. The effect is that of an extremely rich flat tapestry design that tells its story directly and explicitly without illusionistic devices. The Byzantine style becomes the ideal vehicle for the conveyance of the extremely complex symbolism of the fully developed Christian dogma. Our apse mosaic, for example, has much more meaning than first meets the eye. The transfiguration of Christ—here into the image of the cross—symbolizes his own death, with its redeeming consequences, but also the death of his martyrs—in this case, St. Apollinaris. The lamb is also a symbol of martyrdom and is appropriately used to represent the martyred apostles. The whole scene expands above the altar, where the sacrament of the Eucharist is celebrated, the miraculous recurrence of the supreme redemptive and transfigurative act. The very altars of Christian churches, where the mystery of the Eucharist takes

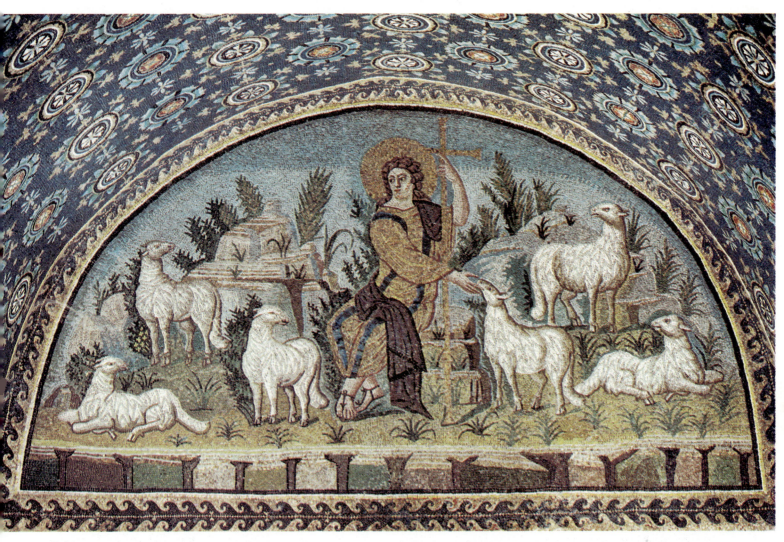

7-24 *Christ as the Good Shepherd,* mosaic from the entrance wall of the mausoleum of Galla Placidia, Ravenna, A.D. 425–50.

7-25 The nave of Sant' Apollinare Nuovo, Ravenna, *c.* A.D. 504.

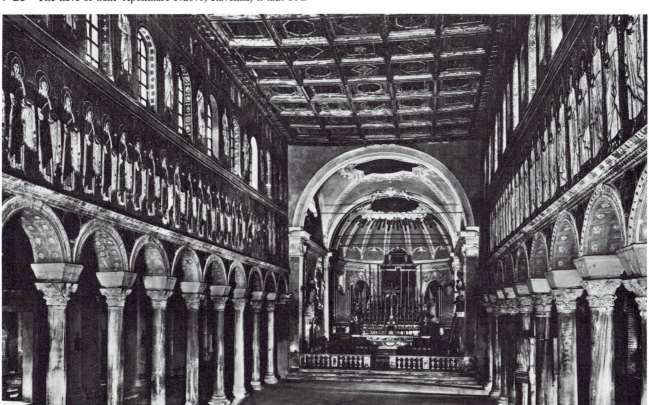

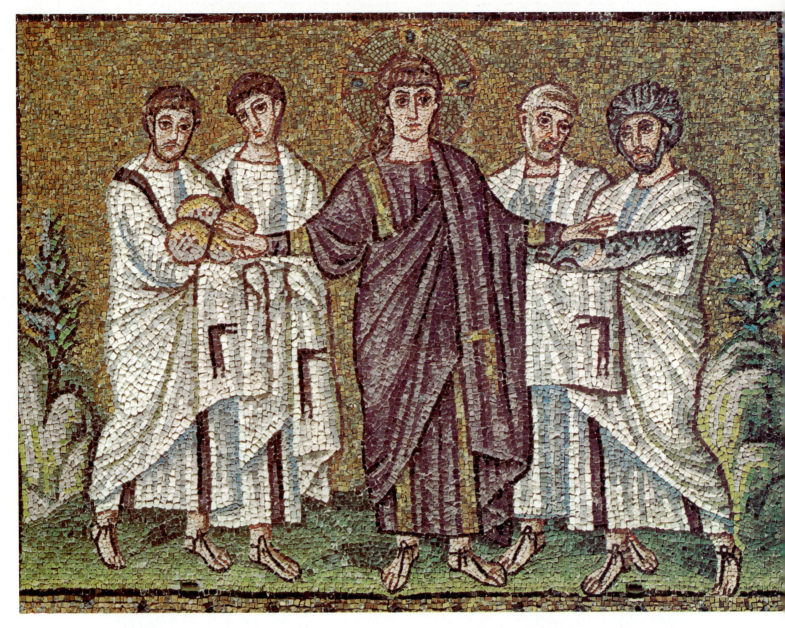

7-26 *The Miracle of the Loaves and the Fishes,* mosaic from the nave wall of Sant' Apollinare Nuovo, Ravenna, *c.* A.D. 504.

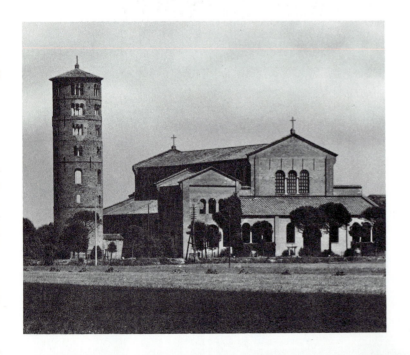

place, were from early times sanctified by the bones and relics of martyrs; thus the mystery and the martyrdom were joined in one concept—namely, that the death of the martyr, in imitation of Christ, is a triumph over death that leads to eternal life. The images above the altar present a kind of inspiring vision to the eyes of the believers, for the way of the martyr is open to them, and the reward of eternal life is within their reach. The organization of the symbolism and of the images is hieratic, and the graphic message must have come to the faithful with overwhelming force. Looming above their eyes is the apparition of a great mystery ordered in such a way as to make perfectly simple and clear the "whole duty of man" seeking salvation. That the anonymous artists working under the direction of the priests expended every device of their craft to render the idea explicit is plain enough; believing men could read it as easily as an inscription. The martyr's

7-27 Sant' Apollinare in Classe, Ravenna, *c.* A.D. 533–49.

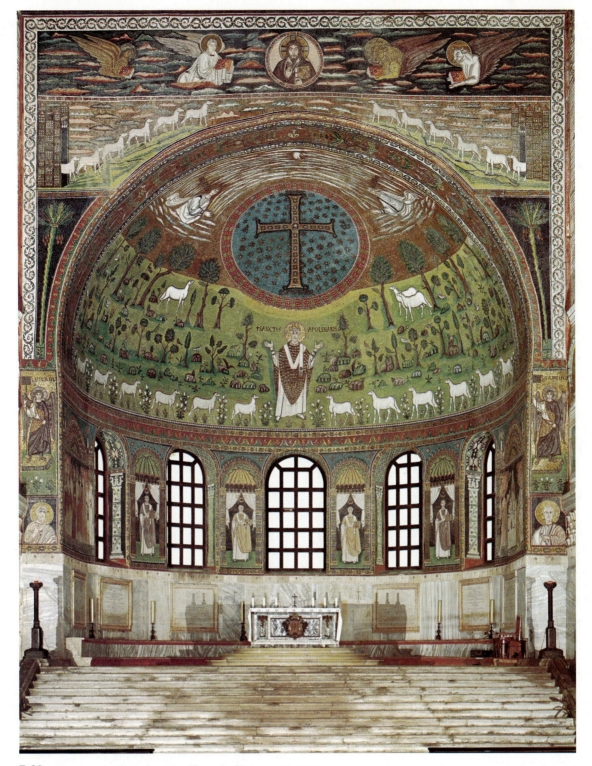

7-28 Apse mosaics from Sant' Apollinare in Classe, *c.* A.D. 549.

glorification beneath the cross inscribed in the starry heavens presented in one great tableau the eternal meaning of Christian life in terms of its deepest mystery.

The Byzantine style, born of the Orientalizing of Hellenistic naturalism, appears in monumental grandeur and ornamental splendor in the mosaics of San Vitale (FIG. 7-29), which, in the high quality they share with the beautiful building itself, symbolize the achievements of the age of the emperor Justinian and are worthy representatives of the First Byzantine Golden Age. Begun shortly after Theodoric's death and dedicated by Bishop Maximianus in 547, San Vitale (FIG. 7-30) shares with the other Ravenna churches its plain exterior (slightly marred by a Renaissance portal) and the polygonal apse. But beyond that it is an entirely different building (FIG. 7-31). The structure is centrally planned and consists of two concentric octagons

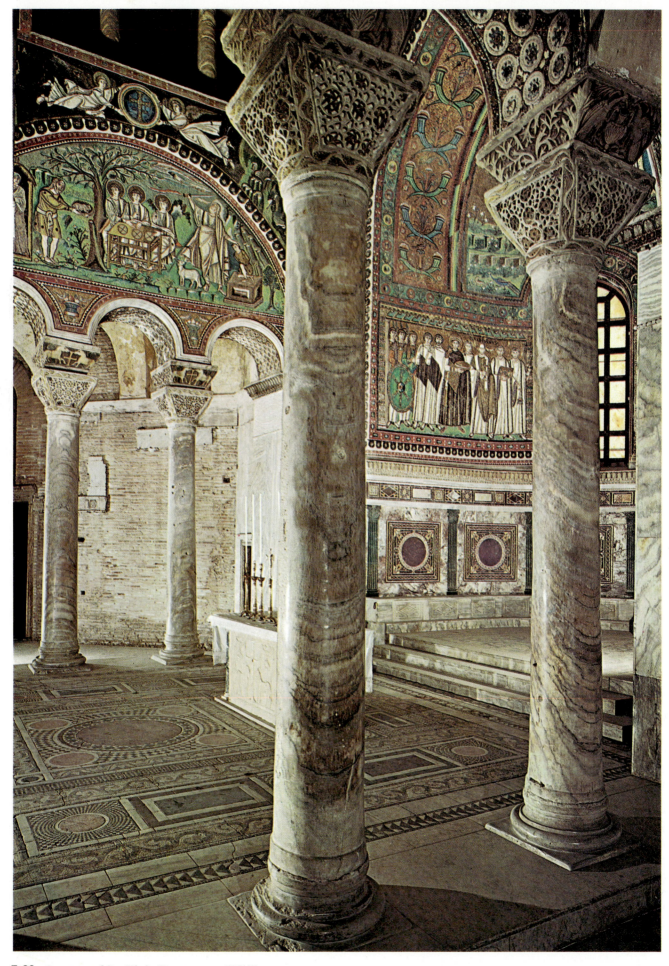

7-29   Sanctuary of San Vitale, Ravenna, A.D. 526–47.

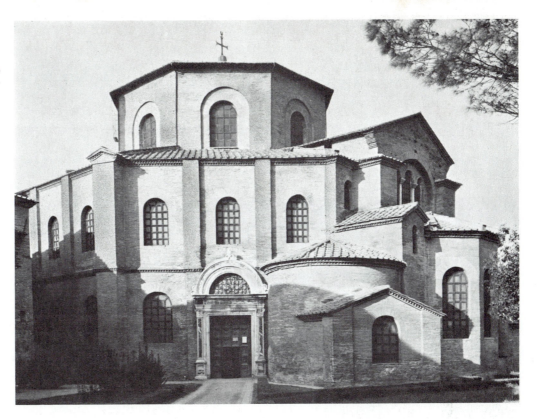

7-30 San Vitale, Ravenna, A.D. 526–47.

of which the dome-covered inner one rises above the surrounding one to provide the interior with clerestory lighting. The central space is defined by eight large piers that alternate with curved, columned niches, pushing outward into the surrounding ambulatory and creating, on the plan, an intricate, multifoliate design. These niches effect a close integration between inner and outer spaces that otherwise would simply have existed side by side as independent units. A cross-vaulted sanctuary preceding the apse interrupts the ambulatory and provides the plan with some axial stability. This effect is weakened, however, by the unsymmetrical placement of the narthex, the odd angle of which has never been fully explained. (The no-longer-extant atrium may have paralleled a street that ran in that direction; it has also been suggested that the angle of the narthex might have been intended to force the visitor to the church to reorient himself as he enters the complex arrangement of the main space, and, thereby, to experience the transition from the material world outside into the spiritual world of the Church.) As shown in FIG. 7-32, the ambulatory has been provided with a second story, the so-called gallery, which was reserved for women and is a typical feature of Byzantine churches. Probably also of Byzantine origin are the so-called impost blocks, which have been inserted between the simply profiled but richly patterned column capitals and the springing of the arches (FIG. 7-33). Resembling an inverted, truncated pyramid, these impost blocks appear in most Ravenna churches (compare FIG. 7-25) and may be highly abstracted reflections of entablature segments that had been inserted between column and arch by Late Roman architects (compare FIG. 6-75).

7-31 Plan of San Vitale.

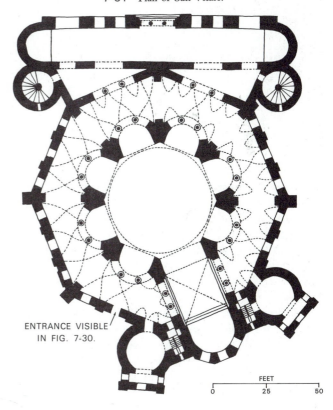

ENTRANCE VISIBLE IN FIG. 7-30.

FEET
0   25   50

The sum of San Vitale's intricate plan and elevation produces an effect of great complexity. Walking through the building, one is struck by the rich diversity of ever changing perspectives. Arches looping over arches, curving and flattened spaces, and shapes of wall and vault seem

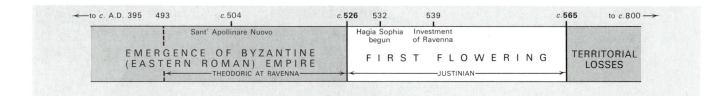
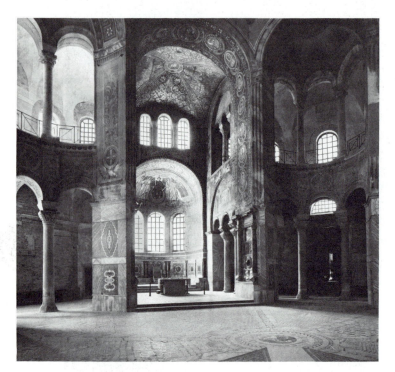

7-32 Interior of San Vitale.

7-33 Capital from San Vitale.

composition, a theme of which is the holy ratification of the emperor's right to Ravenna and to the whole of the western empire of which it was now the principal city. The apse mosaics are portrait groups representing Justinian on one wall and his empress, Theodora, on the other (FIGS. 7-34 and 7-35). The monarchs are accompanied by their retinues in a depiction of the offertory procession, that part of the liturgy when the bread and wine of the Eucharist are brought forward and presented. Justinian, represented as a priest-king, carries a vessel containing the bread, and Theodora the golden cup with the wine. Images and symbols covering the entire sanctuary express the single idea of man's redemption by Christ and the reenactment of it in the Eucharist. Moses, Melchizedek, Abraham, and Abel are represented as prefigurations of Christ and also as priestly leaders of the faithful whose offerings to God were declared acceptable to Heaven. In the representation of the Second Coming (FIG. 7-36), Christ, seated on the orb of the world, with the four rivers of Paradise beneath him and rainbow-hued clouds above, extends a golden wreath of victory to Vitalis, the patron saint of the church, who is here introduced by an angel. At Christ's left another angel introduces Bishop Ecclesius, in whose time the founda-

to change constantly with the viewer's position. Light filtered through alabaster-paned windows plays over the glittering mosaics and glowing marbles that cover the building's complex surfaces, producing an effect of sumptuousness that is not Western but Oriental. And, indeed, the inspiration for this design is to be found in Byzantium rather than Rome. In Constantinople, some ten years before the completion of San Vitale at Ravenna, a church had been dedicated to the saints Sergius and Bacchus that looks like a rough preparatory sketch for the later church in which the suggestions of the earlier plan may be seen developed to their full potential.

Slightly earlier than those of Sant' Apollinare in Classe, but of higher quality, the mosaics that decorate the sanctuary of San Vitale, like the building itself, must be regarded as one of the climactic achievements of Byzantine art. Completed less than a decade after the surrender of Ravenna by the Goths, the decorations of apse and forechoir proclaim the triumph of Justinian and of the Orthodox faith. The multiple panels of the sanctuary form a unified

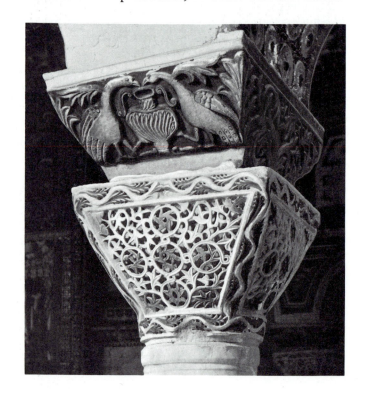

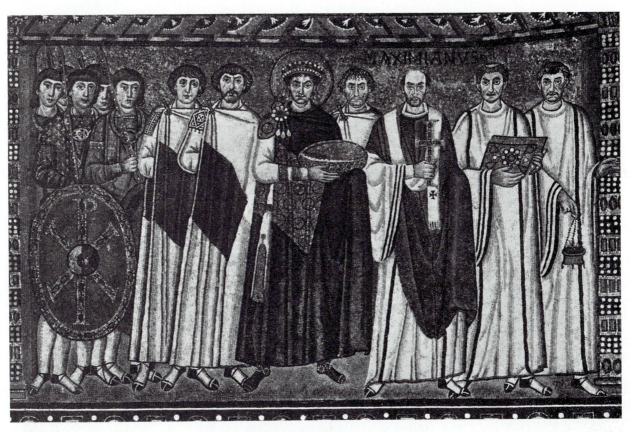

7-34 *Justinian and Attendants, c.* A.D. 547, apse mosaic from San Vitale.

7-35 *Theodora and Attendants, c.* A.D. 547, apse mosaic from San Vitale.

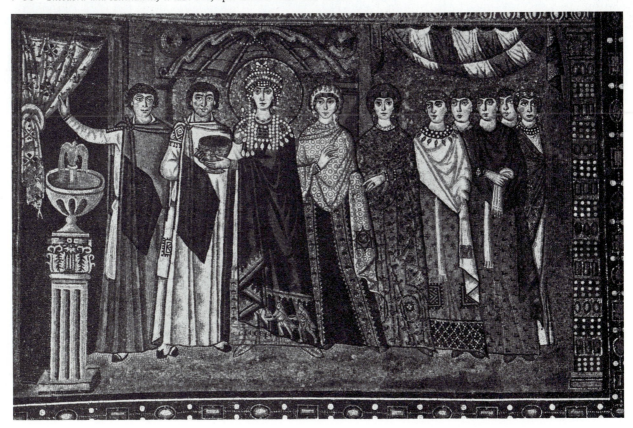

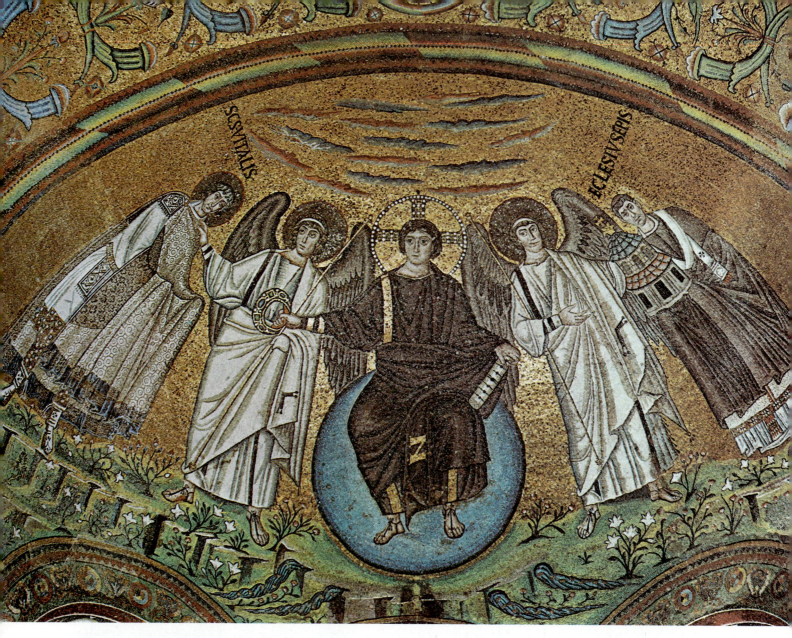

7-36 *Christ Between Angels and Saints* (*The Second Coming*), apse mosaic from San Vitale.

tions of the church were laid, and who carries a model of it. The arrangement recalls Christ's prophecy of the last days of the world: "And then shall they see the Son of man coming in the clouds with great power and glory. And then shall he send his angels, and shall gather together his elect from the four winds, from the uttermost part of heaven" (Mark 13:26–27). It appears that Justinian's offering is also acceptable, for the wreath extended to St. Vitalis is also extended to him where he stands in a dependent mosaic (FIGS. 7-29, 7-34, and 7-37). Thus, his rule is confirmed and sanctified by these rites in which, as is so typical of such expressions of the Byzantine imperial ideal, the political and the religious are one:

In the atmosphere of Byzantium, the Christian emperor appeared as a Christ-like high priest and . . . the principles of his administration seemed to be symbolized in the litur-

gical rite. In the offertory procession he appeared like the priest-king Melchizedek, "bringing forth bread and wine" on behalf of his people, to propitiate God.[3]

The laws of the Church and the laws of the state, united in the laws of God, are manifest in the person of the emperor and in his God-given right. The pagan emperors had been deified; it could not have been difficult, given that tradition, to accept the deification of the Christian emperor. Justinian is distinguished from his dignitaries not only by his wearing of the imperial purple, but by the halo, a device emanating from ancient Persia and originally signifying the descent of the honored one from the sun—and hence his godlike origin and status.

[3] Otto von Simson, *Sacred Fortress: Byzantine Art and Statecraft in Ravenna* (Chicago: Univ. of Chicago Press, 1948), p. 35.

The etiquette and protocol of the imperial court fuse here with the ritual of the liturgy of the Church. The positions of the figures are all-important, since they express the formula of precedence and the orders of rank. Justinian is exactly at center. At his left is Bishop Maximianus, the architect of his ecclesiastical-political policy and the one responsible for the completion of San Vitale and its consecration in 547. The bishop's importance is stressed by the label giving his name, the only identifying inscription in the composition. Between Justinian and Maximianus is Julius Argentarius, the principal benefactor of the church. The figures are in three groups—the emperor and his staff (standing for the imperial administration), the clergy, and the army, who bear a shield with the *chi-rho* monogram seen on the *Sarcophagus of Archbishop Theodore* (FIG. 7-19). Each group has a leader, one of whose feet precedes (by overlapping) the feet of those who follow. There is a curious ambiguity in the positions of Justinian and Maximianus; though the emperor appears to be slightly behind the bishop, the sacred vessel he carries overlaps the bishop's arm. Thus, symbolized by place and gesture, the imperial and churchly powers are in balance. The paten carried by Justinian, the cross carried by Maximianus, and the book and censer carried by his attendant clerics produce a movement that modifies strikingly the rigid formality. There is no indication of a background; the observer is expected to understand the procession as taking place in this very sanctuary, where the emperor will appear forever as participant in the sacred rites and proprietor of this royal church, the very symbol of his rule of the western empire. The portraits of the empress Theodora and her entourage, on the other hand, are represented within a definite architecture, perhaps the narthex of San Vitale. The empress stands in state beneath an imperial canopy, waiting to follow the emperor's procession and to pass through the curtained doorway to which she is beckoned by an attendant. The fact that she is outside the sanctuary and only about to proceed attests that in the ceremonial protocol her rank is not quite that of her consort—even though the representation of the Three Magi on the border of her robe recalls their offerings to the infant Christ and makes an allusive connection between Theodora and the Virgin Mary.

The figure style shows the maturing of conventions of representation that go back to Dura-Europos and earlier. Tall, spare, angular, and elegant, the figures have lost the rather squat proportions characteristic of much Early Christian work. The gorgeous draperies fall straight, stiff, and thin from the narrow shoulders; the organic body has dematerialized, and, except for the heads, we have a procession of solemn spirits gliding noiselessly in the presence of the sacrament. Byzantine style will preserve this hieratic mood for centuries, no matter how many individual variations will occur within its conventions.

One can hardly talk of Byzantine art without using the term "hieratic." Christianity, originating as a mystery cult, kept mystery as its center; one might say that the priest becomes a specialist in mystery. The priestly supernaturalism that disparages matter and material values prevails throughout the Christian Middle Ages, especially in orthodox Byzantium, and it is that hieratic supernaturalism that determines the look of Byzantine figurative art—an art without solid bodies or cast shadows, with blank, golden spaces, with the perspective of paradise, which is nowhere and everywhere.

The portraits in San Vitale are individualized despite the prevailing formality (FIG. 7-37); however, this is true only of the principals, those of the lesser personages on the outskirts of the groups being more uniform. There can be little doubt that in these portrait groups, which memorialize the dedicatory ceremony, it was intended that close likenesses be made of those centrally involved—the emperor and empress and the high officials of church and state. Since pagan times, the image of the deified emperor in public and sacred places has been tantamount to his actual presence, for the image and the reality were taken to be essentially one. The setting up of the image of the emperor was "an act which furnished the occasion for the declaration of submission on the part of the people";[4] and those who gazed on the images must have known that they owed them absolute reverence: "In these awe-inspiring images the sovereigns, though far away in Byzantium, had actually set foot on the soil of Italy."[5]

Thus the symbol, the image, and what they represent are most often one and the same. Just as the image of Justinian or Theodora or a saint is venerated as if it were the person, so are a cross, relics, and mementos. Even vessels associated with holy rites come to be venerated as real presences of sacred powers that can cure not only spiritually but physically. To the believer, this communion of reality between objects and what they represent is logical enough; if the body of Christ is reproducible through the ritual of the Eucharist, then representations of all holy things ought to be just as real as what they represent. Symbols, images, narratives, sacramental objects—the furniture and accessories of ritual—can all be venerable and spiritually potent in themselves; this is like the magic of the Paleolithic caves, where the hunter-artists believed they summoned and controlled their animal quarry by the miracle of representation.

In Ravenna a powerful statecraft under the management of Justinian and Maximianus had been able to combine in a group of monuments the full force of Christian belief and political authority. In the process there was made a model of religious art, sacramental-magical in its power,

[4] Von Simson, *Sacred Fortress*, p. 28.
[5] Ibid., p.39.

that could work in the service both of the Church and the sanctified imperial state; this model, image, or ideal unity of the spiritual and temporal would strongly influence the Middle Ages in both east and west. The hieratic style of Byzantium, matured and exemplified in Ravenna, will remain as both the standard and the point of departure for the content and form of the art of the Middle Ages.

Constantinople

Ravenna, the city that had become the successor to Rome as imperial capital in Italy, and then, as the so-called Exarchate, the beachhead of Byzantium in the Germanized

west, finally passed from Byzantine control. The images of Justinian and Theodora in San Vitale, proclaiming that the empire was still whole, were powerless to make it so. But the east remained firmly in the hands of successions of emperors for a thousand years, and Constantinople became the magnificent citadel of Byzantine civilization whence streamed its influence to all points of the compass. At the time the imperial presence in Ravenna was being symbolized in architecture and art, the vast church of Santa Sophia, or more properly Hagia Sophia, Church of the Holy Wisdom, was being built for Justinian in Constantinople by the architects ANTHEMIUS of Tralles and ISIDORUS of Miletus between 532 and 537. The church remains

7-37 *Justinian and Maximianus,* detail of an apse mosaic (FIG. 7-34) from San Vitale.

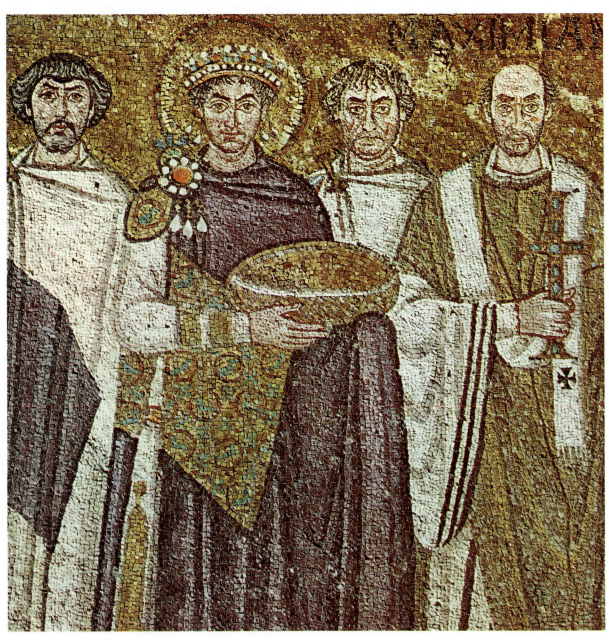

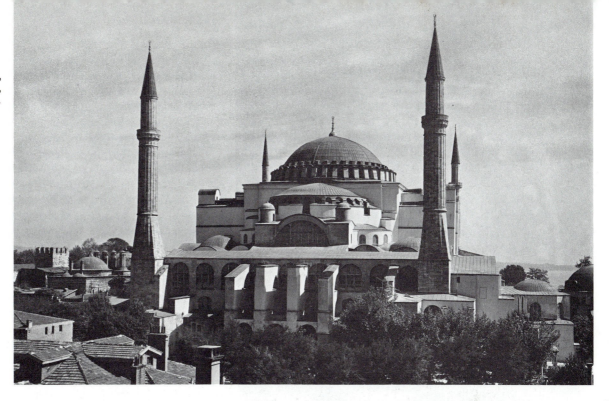

7-38 Hagia Sophia, Constantinople, A.D. 532–37.

today one of the supreme achievements in the history of world architecture (FIGS. 7-38 to 7-41). Its dimensions alone, formidable for any structure not made of steel, would attract attention. In plan it is about 240 by 270 feet; the dome is 108 feet in diameter, its crown some 180 feet above the pavement. It rivals in scale the great buildings seen so far in pagan and Christian Rome—the Pantheon, the Baths of Caracalla, the Basilica of Constantine. In exterior view the great dome dominates the structure; but the external aspects of the building are much changed from their original appearance—by huge buttresses added to the original design and by four towering Turkish minarets added after the Ottoman conquest of 1453, when Hagia Sophia became an Islamic mosque. The building was secularized in the twentieth century and is now a museum.

The characteristic Byzantine plainness and unpretentiousness of exterior, which in this case also disguises the great scale, scarcely prepares us for the interior of the building (FIG. 7-38). One encounters first the huge narthex with its many entrances, and then the open, tremendous space above, where the soaring dome, canopylike, rides on a halo of light provided by windows in the dome's base. The impression made on the people of the time, an impression not lost on us, is given in the words of the poet Paulus, an usher at the court of Justinian:

About the center of the church, by the eastern and western half-circles, stand four mighty piers of stone, and from them spring great arches like the bow of Iris, four in all; and, as they rise slowly in the air, each separates from the other . . . and the spaces between them are filled with

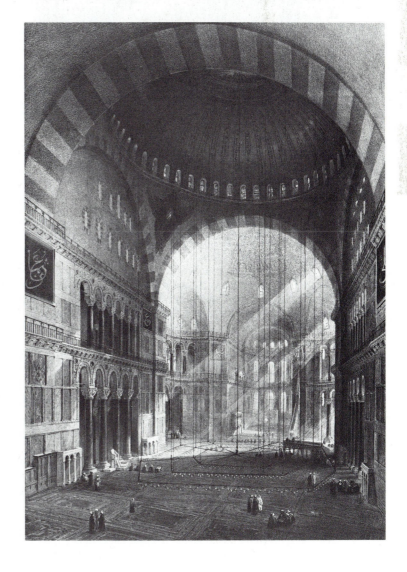

7-39 *Interior of Hagia Sophia,* engraving from *Aya Sophia* by Chevalier Fossati, London, 1852.

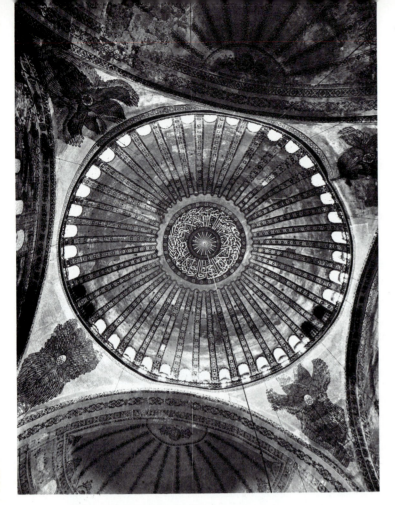

7-40 Vaults of Hagia Sophia.

arches whose planes bound a square. By transferring the weight to piers rather than to the wall itself, pendentive construction makes possible a lofty, unobstructed interior space such as is particularly evident in Hagia Sophia. In our view of the interior the arches that bound two of the great pendentives supporting the central dome can be seen converging on their massive piers. The domes of earlier central-type buildings, like the Pantheon, Santa Costanza, or even San Vitale, had sprung from the circular or polygonal bases of a continuous wall or arcade. The pendentive system is a dynamic solution to the problem of setting a round dome over a square or rectangle. It made possible the union of the central structure and the long basilican type. Hagia Sophia, in its successful fusion of the types, becomes a domed basilica, a uniquely successful conclusion to several centuries of experiment in Christian church architecture. However, the thrusts of its pendentive construction make other elements necessary: huge wall piers to north and south, and, east and west, half-domes whose thrusts descend in turn into still smaller domes (FIG. 7-40) covering columned niches that give a curving flow to the design, reminiscent of San Vitale. And, as in San Vitale, the wandering space, the diverse vistas, the screenlike, ornamented surfaces, mask the lines of structure. The arcades of the nave and galleries have no real structural function; like the walls they pierce they are only part of a fragile "fill" between the great piers. Structurally, though Hagia Sophia may seem Roman in its great scale and majesty, it does not have Roman organization of its masses. The very fact that what appears to be wall in Hagia Sophia is actually a concealed (and barely adequate) pier indicates that Roman monumentality was sought after as an *effect* and not derived directly from Roman building principles.

What struck early visitors to Hagia Sophia, and many generations of them since, was the quality of light within it and the effect it had upon one's spirit. The forty windows at the base of the dome gave the peculiar illusion that the dome rested upon the light that flooded through them, so that an observer of the time thought that it looked as if the dome were suspended by a "gold chain from Heaven." Procopius, the historian of the age of Justinian, wrote: "One would declare that the place were not illuminated from the outside by the sun, but that the radiance originated from within, such is the abundance of light which is shed about this shrine." Paulus, whom we have already quoted, observed: "the vaulting is covered over with many little squares of gold, from which the rays stream down and strike the eyes so that men can scarcely bear to look." We thus have a vastness of space shot through with light and a central dome that *appears* to be supported by the light it admits. Light is the mystic element, light that glitters in the mosaics, that shines forth from the marbles, that pervades and defines spaces that in themselves seem to escape definition; light becomes the agent that seems to

wondrous skill, for curved walls touch the arches on either side and spread over until they all unite above them. . . . The base of the dome is strongly fixed upon the great arches . . . while above, the dome covers the church like the radiant heavens. . . . Who shall describe the fields of marble gathered on the pavement and lofty walls of the church? Fresh green from Carystus, and many-colored Phrygian stone of rose and white, or deep red and silver; porphyry powdered with bright spots; emerald-green from Sparta, and Iassian marble with waving veins of blood-red and white; streaked red stone from Lydia, and crocus-colored marble from the hills of the Moors, and Celtic stone, like milk poured out on glittering black; the precious onyx like as if gold were shining through it, and the fresh green from the land of Atrax, in mingled contrast of shining surfaces . . . .[6]

The dome rests upon four *pendentives*. In pendentive construction (FIG. 7-44)—developed, apparently after many years of experiment, by builders in the Near East and *the* contribution of Byzantium to architectural engineering—a dome rests upon what is in effect a second and larger dome from which have been omitted the top portion and four segments around the rim—the latter forming four

[6]In W. R. Lethaby, "Santa Sophia, Constantinople," *Architectural Review,* April 1905, p. 12.

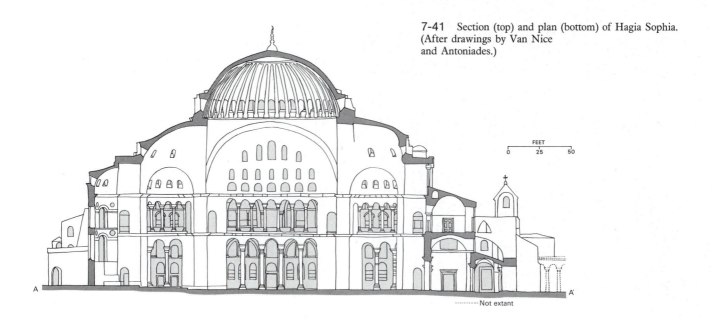

7-41 Section (top) and plan (bottom) of Hagia Sophia. (After drawings by Van Nice and Antoniades.)

FEET
0   25   50

------ Not extant

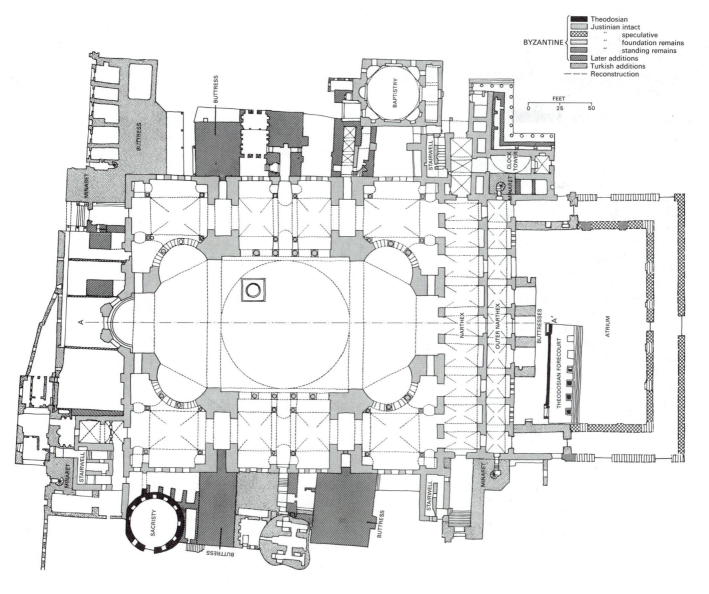

BYZANTINE	Theodosian
	Justinian intact
	" speculative
	" foundation remains
	" standing remains
	Later additions
	Turkish additions
	Reconstruction

FEET
0   25   50

BAPTISTRY

BUTTRESS

BUTTRESS

MINARET

STAIRWELL

CLOCK TOWER

MINARET

NARTHEX

OUTER NARTHEX

BUTTRESSES

A'

THEODOSIAN FORECOURT

ATRIUM

A

STAIRWELL

MINARET

SACRISTY

BUTTRESS

BUTTRESS

STAIRWELL

MINARET

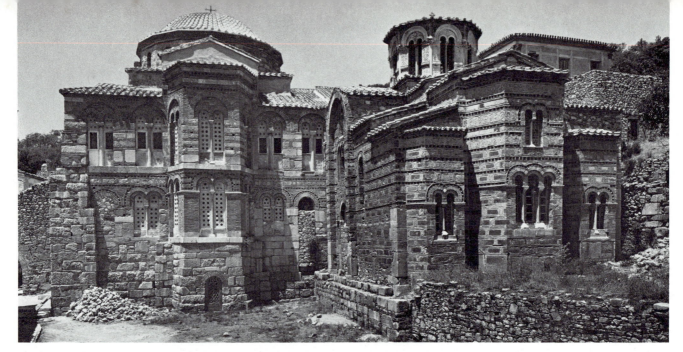

7-42 Monastery churches at Hosios Loukas, Phocis, Greece: Church of the Katholikon, c. 1020 (left), and Church of the Theotokos, c. 1040 (right).

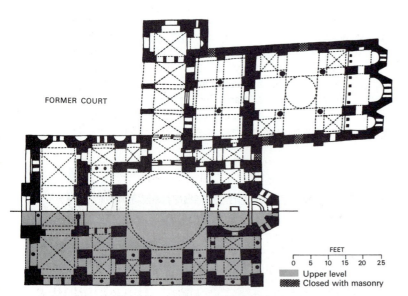

FORMER COURT

FEET
0   5   10   15   20   25

□ Upper level
▨ Closed with masonry

7-43 Plans of the Church of the Katholikon (bottom) and the Church of the Theotokos (top).

dissolve material substance and transform it into an abstract, spiritual vision. At Hagia Sophia, the intricate logic of Greek theology, the ambitious scale of Rome, the vaulting tradition of the Near East, and the mysticism of Eastern Christianity are combined to create a monument that is at once a summation of antiquity and a positive assertion of the triumph of Christian faith.

Hagia Sophia was a unique hybrid, uniting the western basilican with the eastern central plan in a design without successors, for after it the east forsook the long church for a thousand years or more, developing the central plan, while in the west the basilican plan was consciously revived in Carolingian times.

LATER BYZANTINE ART

Between the tenth and the twelfth century there occurred, under the auspices of the Macedonian dynasty, what has been called the Second Flowering or Second Byzantine Golden Age, when Byzantine culture reencountered its Hellenistic sources and accommodated them to the styles inherited from the Age of Justinian, the time of the *First Flowering.*

Architecture

In architecture a brilliant series of variations on the domed central theme appeared. From the exterior the typical later Byzantine church building is a domed cube (less often some rectangular form having other than a square as its basis), the dome rising above the square on a kind of cylinder or drum. The churches are small, vertical, high-shouldered, and, unlike earlier Byzantine buildings, have exterior wall surfaces with ornament in relief. In the Church of the Theotokos (FIG. 7-42 and 7-43), about 1040, at Hosios Loukas in Greece, one can see the form of a domed cross with four equal-length, vaulted cross-arms (the "Greek Cross"). Around this unit, and by the duplicating of it, Byzantine architectural design developed bewilderingly involved spaces. The adjacent, larger Church of the Katholikon (FIGS. 7-42 and 7-43) uses a dome over an octagon inscribed within a square, the octagon formed by *squinches*—arches, corbeling, or lintels that bridge the corners of the square (FIG. 7-44). This arrangement represents a subtle extension of the older schemes such as Santa Costanza's circular plan, San Vitale's octagonal, and Hagia Sophia's dome on pendentives rising from a square. The

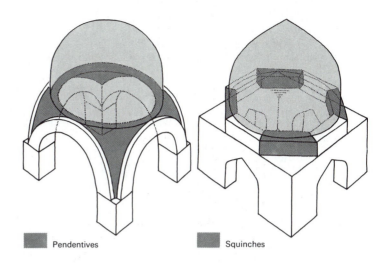

Pendentives   Squinches

complex core of the Katholikon lies within two rectangles, the outermost being the exterior walls. Thus, in plan, from the center out there is a circle-octagon-square-oblong series whose parts exhibit a remarkably intricate interrelationship.

The interior elevation of the Katholikon reflects its involved plan (FIG. 7-45). Like earlier Byzantine buildings it creates a mystery out of space, surface, and light and dark. High and narrow, it forces our gaze to rise and revolve: "The overall spatial effect is overwhelmingly beautiful in its complex interplay of higher and lower elements, of core and ancillary spaces, of clear, dim, and dark zones of lighting."[7] Middle and Late Byzantine architecture thus seems to aim for complex interior spaces that issue into multiple domes in the upper levels; these, in exterior view, produce spectacular combinations of round forms that shifting perspectives develop dramatically. The splendid Church of Holy Apostles, built in the time of Justinian and now no longer in existence, is reflected in plan in St. Mark's in Venice, which reproduces it (FIGS. 7-46 to 7-48). The original structure of St. Mark's, dating from the eleventh century, is disguised on its lower levels by Romanesque and Gothic additions. But in plan, or from an air view, the domes, grouped along a cross of equal arms (the Greek Cross again) make the Byzantine origins at once evident. The inner masonry shells are covered with swelling, wooden, helmetlike forms sheathed in gilded copper; these not only protect the inner domes but make an exuberant composition appropriate to this great community church of the proud Venetian republic. Venice was, like Ravenna some eighty miles to the south, under strong Byzantine influence, despite the independence it had won early in the Middle Ages and preserved for centuries. The interior of St. Mark's is, like its plan, Byzantine in effect, though its great Justinianic scale and intricate syncopation of domed bays are modified slightly by western Romanesque elements. Certainly its light effects and its rich cycles of mosaics are entirely Byzantine.

Byzantine influence was wide-ranging, not only in Italy but in the Slavic lands and in the regions of the east where Islam had expanded. Byzantium brought its script, its religion, and much of its culture to Russia. The "holy" Russia before the revolution of 1917 was largely Byzantine in its traditions—one might even say, in its mood. Russian architecture, magnificently developed in the Middle Ages, is a brilliant provincial variation on Byzantine themes.

The ecclesiastical architecture of medieval Russia was at first strongly under the influence of Constantinople, if not actually produced by Greeks. The church of St. Dmitri at Vladimir (FIG. 7-49) is built on the typical plan of a square

[7] Richard Krautheimer, *Early Christian and Byzantine Architecture* (Baltimore: Penguin, 1965), p. 244.

enclosing a Greek cross and crowned with a single dome on a high drum. The church is of stone, which is rare in Russia, where brick, stucco, and wood are the usual materials. Wall spaces, which have few openings, are decorated here with moldings. Some of these, rising unbroken from the ground to the roof, divide the wall into panels; others, much shorter, form blind arcadings. The surface within the arcadings is elaborately carved in low reliefs that are peculiarly well-adapted to stone and, in subject matter and form, are close to Sassanian (Persian) and other western Asiatic carvings. The whole composition of St. Dmitri is a masterpiece of simplicity and compactness, with a classic,

7-45 Interior of the Church of the Katholikon (view facing east).

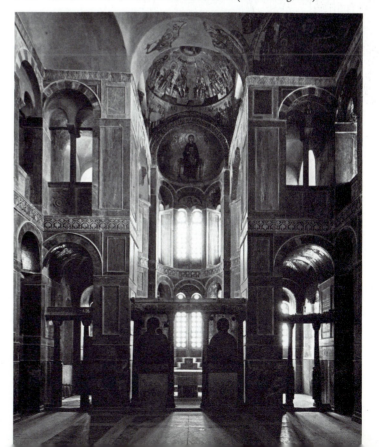

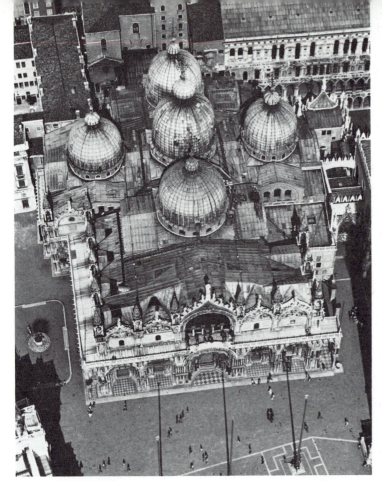

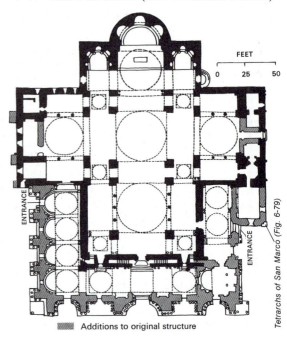

Additions to original structure

monumental dignity. Later structures will develop a colorful complexity of plan and elevation. In Moscow, within the walls of the Kremlin, stands the Cathedral of the Annunciation (FIG. 7-50), dating from the later fifteenth century. The domed-cross plan of Byzantium here receives a most spirited expansion. The cathedral is built on a square plan with eastern apses; its helmetlike domes, now greatly multiplied, rise in a kind of triumphant crescendo to the climax of the central unit, which is crowned with the typical Russian bulbous "onion" or "beet" dome. The bright metal caps, peaked with crosses like miniature masts, reflect the moody Russian skies and proclaim, as if in architectural polyphony, the glory of the Orthodox faith.

Painting and Sculpture

While architecture enjoyed a fairly continuous development throughout the Byzantine period, that of the representational arts (painting and sculpture) suffered a severe setback during the eighth and ninth centuries, when they became the subject of a violent controversy. The Iconoclastic Controversy over the propriety of religious imagery, which raged for more than 100 years (730–843), began with the temporary victory of the image-destroyers (iconoclasts), who interpreted the biblical ban against graven images literally. In 730 an imperial edict banned

religious imagery throughout the Byzantine empire, and artists were either forced to migrate to the west, where the edict was unenforceable, or, if they chose to remain in Byzantium, to turn their talents to secular subject matter, which was not affected by the ban.

Migrant Byzantine painters worked in Italy in a classicizing style and with religious subject matter. Although little remains of their work, examples can be found in Rome—especially in Santa Maria Antiqua—where a succession of Greek popes in the eighth century provided an atmosphere encouraging to the forbidden culture and art of Iconoclastic Byzantium. At Castelseprio in northern Italy there are remarkable murals of uncertain date, but likely of the late seventh or early eighth century (FIG. 7-51), which are without doubt the art of a gifted Byzantine painter whose deft hand and fluent, sweeping style show the enduring illusionistic classicism born in Hellenistic times and destined to recur often in the centuries after the First Golden Age. This naturalistic manner could exist side by side with the austere and abstract style seen at Ravenna or could merge with it. When the ban against religious images was lifted in 843 A.D., and religious painting was again encouraged in Byzantium, a manner emerged that was a subtle blend of the pictorial, classicizing Hellenistic and the later, more abstract and formalistic Byzantine style.

An eleventh-century crucifixion scene on the wall of the monastery church at Daphne in Greece (FIG. 7-52) shows

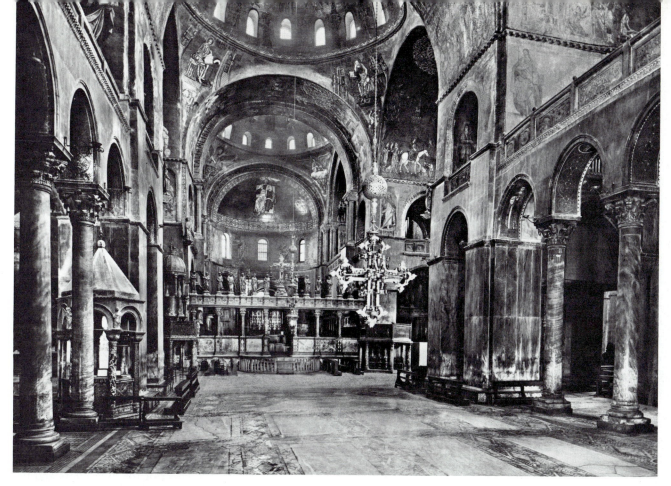

7-48   Interior of St. Mark's (view facing east).

7-49   St. Dmitri at Vladimir, 1194–97.

7-50   Cathedral of the Annunciation, Moscow, 1482–90.

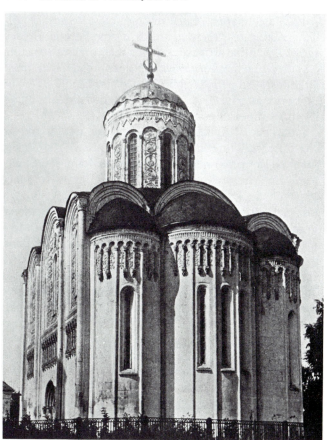

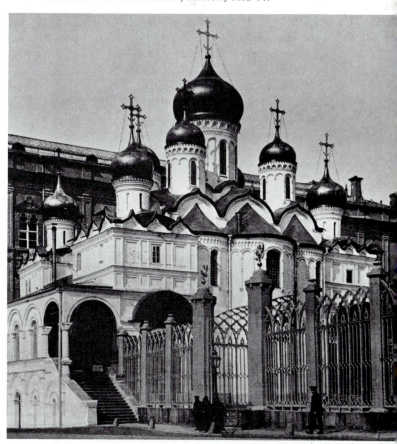

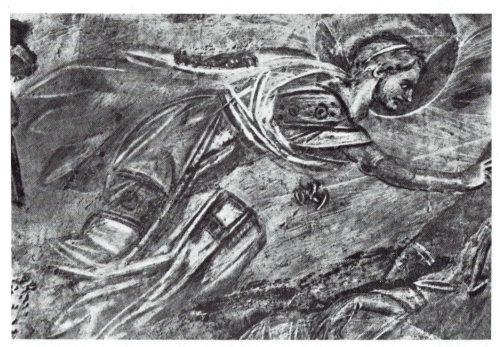

the simplicity, dignity, and grace of classicism fully assimilated by the Byzantine artist in a perfect synthesis with Byzantine piety and pathos. Christ is represented on the cross, flanked by the Virgin and St. John. A skull at the foot of the cross indicates Golgotha, the "place of skulls." Nothing is needed to complete the tableau. In quiet sorrow and resignation, the Virgin and St. John point to Christ as if to indicate the meaning of the cross. Symmetry and closed space produce an effect of the motionless and unchanging aspect of the deepest mystery of the Christian religion; and the timeless presence is, as it were, beheld in unbroken silence. The picture is not a narrative of the historical event of the Crucifixion but a devotional object, a thing sacramental in itself, to be viewed by the monks in silent contemplation of the mystery of the Sacrifice. Although elongated, these figures from the Second Golden Age of Byzantine art have regained their organic structure to a surprising degree, particularly as compared with those of the Justinian period (compare FIGS. 7-34 and 7-35). The style is a masterful adaptation of classical statuesque qualities to the linear Byzantine style.

Variations of Byzantine style appear widely in the twelfth century throughout the Balkan world (Yugoslavia, Bulgaria, Romania) and in Venice, South Italy, and Sicily, where there were Mediterranean powers eager to adopt Byzantine art and culture. At Nerezi, in Macedonia (Yugoslavia), there are paintings of astonishing emotional power, contrasting dramatically with the almost stern formalism and hieraticism of the Daphne mosaic. The *Lamentation* (FIG. 7-53), from the last third of the twelfth century, is a tableau of passionate grief, the friends of Christ in attitudes and with expressions and gestures of quite human bereavement. The artist has striven above all to make his realization of the theme utterly convincing. His stirring staging of the subject looks forward to the art of thirteenth-century (Gothic) Italy, when the reception of this mode of emotional realism will carry all before it into

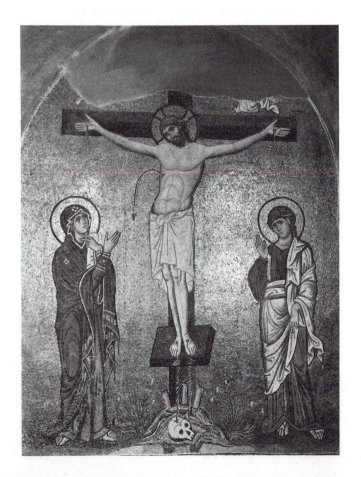

7-52 *The Crucifixion*, mosaic from the monastery church at Daphne, Greece, eleventh century.

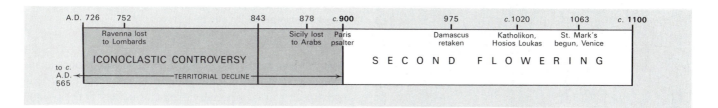

A.D. 726	752	843	878	c. 900	975	c. 1020	1063	c. 1100
	Ravenna lost to Lombards		Sicily lost to Arabs	Paris psalter	Damascus retaken	Katholikon, Hosios Loukas	St. Mark's begun, Venice	

to c. A.D. 565 ← ICONOCLASTIC CONTROVERSY — TERRITORIAL DECLINE → SECOND FLOWERING

the Italian "proto-Renaissance" and the art of Giotto (compare FIG. 11-14).

In the art of the Second Golden Age, particularly in its latter phase, there is a kind of dialogue between the formal, symbolic, hieratic style of the Daphne mosaic, and the intense, emotional, active style of the Nerezi murals, the choice of alternative depending upon site and ecclesiastical, political, and artistic intentions. An example of the hieratic style accommodated to a monumental site is the apse mosaic of the royal church of Monreale in Sicily (FIG. 7-54), part of a total program of ecclesiastical-artistic aggrandizement of and by Roger, the great Norman king of Sicily, who imported the splendor of Byzantium to glorify his reign. Christ, as "Pantocrator," judge of the world, looms menacingly in the vault of the apse, a colossal image of kingly power and authority, whether spiritual or temporal. (The king would believe his own sovereign power came directly from the divine.) Below Christ in rank and dignity are ranged symmetrically the enthroned Virgin and saints. Here Byzantine formality manifests the very image of heavenly and earthly power, the former explicitly, the latter by association. From Sicily, from Venice, from the Byzantine Balkans, the art of Byzantium finds its way into the West, stimulating and influencing the art of the periods we call Romanesque and Gothic.

From the last great period, the Third Golden Age of Byzantine art, we have a late example of vigorous, expressive action, related to the drama of the Nerezi painting but with a heightened naturalism that parallels developments in contemporaneous Italian art, and may even lead them in sophistication. A recently uncovered fresco in the vault of a side chapel of the Mosque of the Ka'riye in Istanbul (built in 1320 and originally the Church of the Blessed Savior of the Chora) represents, although inscribed *Anastasis* ("Resurrection"), the harrowing of hell (FIG. 7-55). Christ, after his death upon the cross, descends into hell, tramples Satan, and rescues Adam and Eve, while other worthies of the Old Testament stand by awaiting their liberation. The movement of the central figures is highly dramatic. The white-robed, aureole-surrounded figure of Christ is laden with energy as he literally tears the parents of mankind from their tombs. The dynamic postures of the figures are reinforced by swirling draperies, agitated by the winds of a supramaterial force. But we also notice that, here and there, the carefully and precisely drawn drapery folds tend to take on a life of their own, as the Late Byzantine artist often shows delight in creating linear patterns for their own sake. These abstract, decorative, linear patterns tend to obscure the fact that, in its late stages, Byzantine art becomes increasingly realistic.

While the characteristics of Byzantine painting were developed in large-scale mural decorations, it was through miniatures in manuscripts and through small panel paintings, more popularly known as *icons*, that the elements of the style were spread abroad. A fine example of the former is a page from a book of the Psalms of David, the so-called

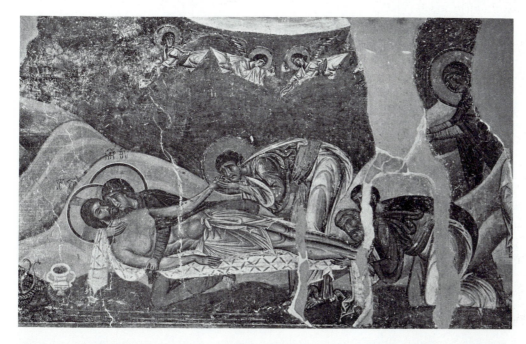

7-53 *Lamentation over the Dead Christ*, wall painting, Nerezi, Yugoslavia, 1164.

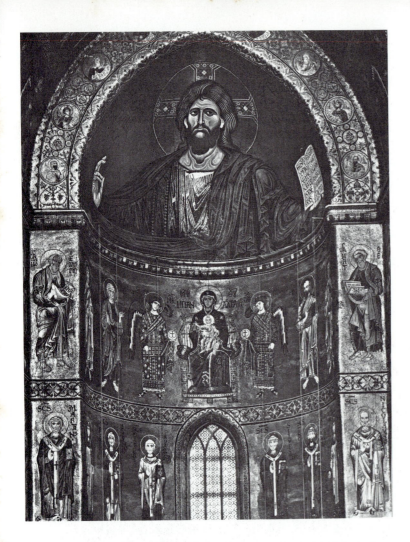

natural that, in art, inspiration should be drawn once again from the Hellenistic naturalism of the pre-Christian Mediterranean world, especially Alexandria. David, the psalmist, is represented seated with his harp in a flowering, Arcadian landscape recalling those of Pompeian murals. He is accompanied by an allegorical figure of Melody and surrounded by sheep, goats, and his faithful dog. Echo ("Spring"?) peers from behind a trophied column, and a reclining male figure points to an inscription that identifies him as representing the mountains of Bethlehem. None of these allegorical figures appears in the Bible; they are the stock population of Alexandrian and Pompeian landscape. Apparently the artist had before him a work from Late Antiquity or perhaps earlier, which he partly translated into Later Byzantine pictorial idiom. In the figure of Melody we find some incongruity between the earlier and later style. Her pose as well as her head and torso are quite Hellenistic; Hellenistic too is the light, impressionistic touch of the brush, but the drapery enwrapping the legs is a pattern of hard line. Byzantine illuminations like this will again and again exert their influence on Western painting in the Romanesque and Early Gothic periods.

A most characteristic type of Byzantine painting was the devotional panel bearing the portrait of a saint, the icon. The icon's origins were of great antiquity, deriving from the kind of painted Roman portrait we have already seen in the Faiyum type (FIG. 6-40) and the mosaic portrait medallions conspicuous in Byzantine churches, like that of Christ in the triumphal arch of Sant' Apollinare in Classe (FIG. 7-28). An example of the icon is the famous *Vladimir Madonna* (FIG. 7-57), which was probably painted by an artist in Byzantium in the twelfth century, exported to

Paris Psalter (FIG. 7-56), which reasserts the artistic values of the classical past with astonishing authority. It is believed to date from the early tenth century, a time of enthusiastic and careful study of the language of ancient Greece as well as its literature, a time when the classics were regarded with humanistic reverence. It was only

7-55 *The Harrowing of Hell,* fresco from the Mosque of the Ka'riye, Istanbul, c. 1310–20.

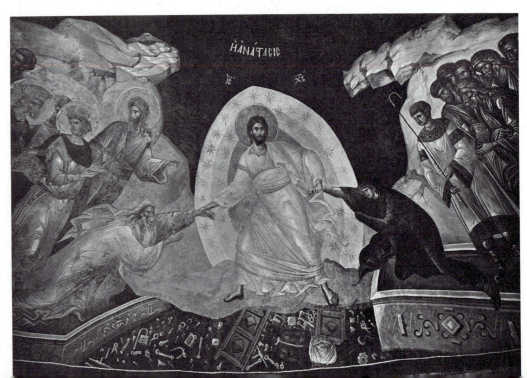

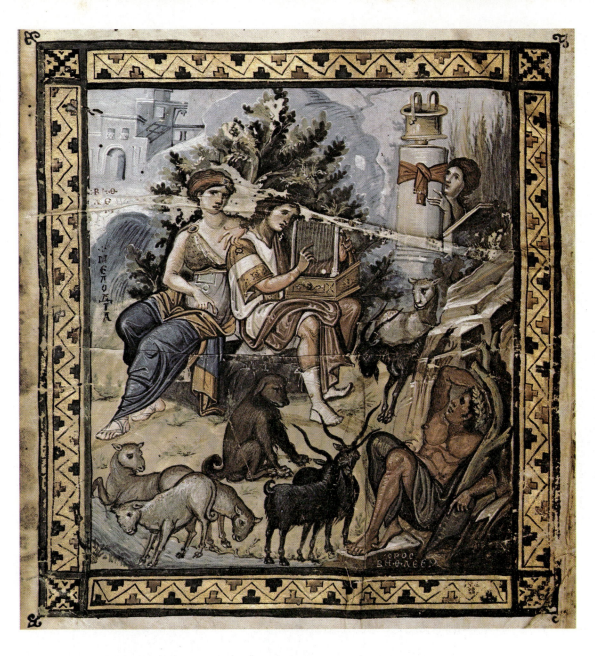

7-56 *David Composing the Psalms,* page from the so-called *Paris Psalter, c.* 900. Approx. 15″ × 11″. Bibliothèque Nationale, Paris.

Vladimir, and then taken to Moscow in 1395 to protect that city from the Mongols. As these icons were quickly blackened by incense and the smoke from devotional candles burned before them, they were frequently repainted, often by inferior artists. In our panel, only the faces show the original surface, but the painting retains its Byzantine characteristics in the typical configuration of the Madonna's face, with its long, straight nose and tiny mouth, and in the decorative sweep of the unbroken contour that encloses the two figures and creates a flat silhouette against a golden background. The deep pathos of the Madonna's expression shows an interest in depicting emotion that will flow into the art of Russia and the West.

In Russia, icon painting flourished for centuries, extending the life of the style well beyond the collapse of the Byzantine Empire in 1453. The development of the iconostasis—the large icon-bearing screen that shuts off the sanctuary from the rest of the church—into an elaborate structure with more than five tiers had an important effect on icon painting. The purpose of these paintings was to enable the worshiper to read pictorially. Clear pictorial legibility in wavering candlelight and through clouds of incense required strong pattern, firm lines, and intense color. Hence the relatively sober hues of the early Byzantine paintings gave way to the more characteristically Russian colors, intense and contrasting. It was under a renewed Byzantine impulse, after the waning of the Mongol domination, and through the requirements of the iconostasis (just then coming to its highest development), that Russian painting reached a climax in the work of ANDREI RUBLËV (*c.* 1370-1430). His monumental *Old Testament Trinity* (FIG. 7-58) is a work of great spiritual power as well as an unsurpassed example of subtle line in union with intensely vivid color. About a table are seated the three angels who appeared to Abraham near the oaks of Mamre (Gen. 18:2-15). (The angels are interpreted in Christian

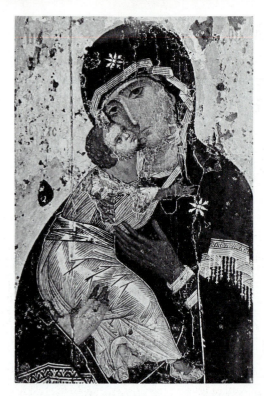

thought as a prefiguration of the Holy Trinity after the incarnation of Christ.) The figures, each framed with a halo and sweeping wings, are suavely, languorously poised within an implicit circle, each in its way appearing rapt in meditation upon the mystery of the Trinity. The tranquil demeanor of each figure is set off by the light, linear play of the draperies. Forms are defined by color, with areas frequently intensified by the juxtaposition of a complementary hue. The intense blue and green folds of the cloak of the central figure, for example, stand out starkly against the deep red robe and the gilded orange of the wings. In the figure on the left the highlights of the orange cloak are an opalescent blue-green. The color harmonics, it has been noted, are Oriental in their unmodulated saturation, brilliance, and purity. In Russian painting the Byzantine tradition was enlivened and enriched by a feeling and touch not Byzantine but native—or, rather, the fusion of the two; the same can be said of Russian architecture.

We should not forget, in considering the rich ecclesiastical art of Byzantium and Russia, the indispensable part

7-57 *The Vladimir Madonna,* twelfth century. Original dimensions of panel approx. $30\frac{1}{2}'' \times 21''$. State Historical Museum, Moscow.

7-58 ANDREI RUBLËV, *The Old Testament Trinity Prefiguring the Incarnation, c.* 1410. Painted panel, $56'' \times 45''$. Tretyakov Gallery, Moscow.

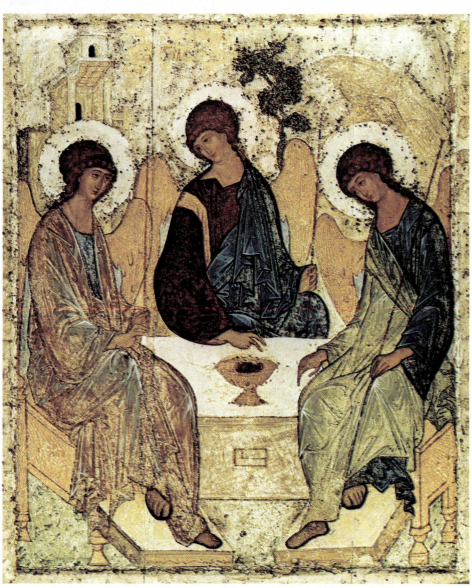

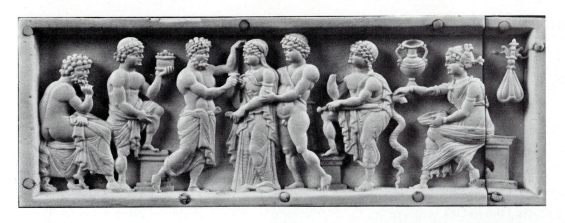

7-59 *The Sacrifice of Iphigenia*, panel from the Veroli Casket, tenth or eleventh century. Ivory; whole casket, 4½" × 16". Victoria and Albert Museum, London.

7-60 *Christ Enthroned with Saints*, the Harbaville Triptych, *c.* 950. Ivory, central panel 9½" × 5½", side panels 8½" × 2¾". Louvre, Paris.

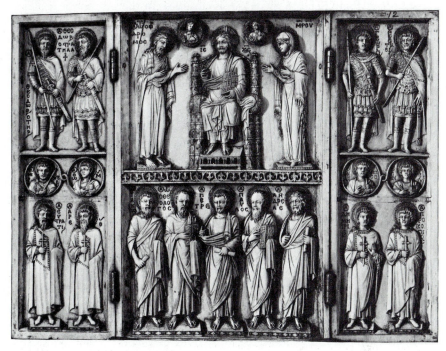

played by other arts in the ensemble of a church interior: the carvings and rich metalwork of the iconostasis; the finely wrought jeweled halos and other ornaments on the icons; the candlesticks and candelabra, the miters and ecclesiastical robes stiff with gold, embroidery, and jewels; the illuminated books bound in gold or ivory inlaid with jewels and enamels; the crosses, croziers, sacred vessels, and processional banners. Each contributed with its great richness of texture and color to the total effect. In the life of orthodox Byzantium, to produce this effect was to honor God and his vicar the emperor.

Although carved ornament continued to be used in Byzantine churches, monumental stone sculpture was never encouraged to the degree that it was in western Europe. Life-size figures in the round apparently offended the East Christians. Their uneasiness with them was underlined by the Iconoclastic Controversy; they early associated statues with pagan idols, whereas painted images, particularly with the stylistic conventions that developed, could create forms less directly identifiable with natural ones. The Byzantine sculptor was called on, however, to

carve small statues and reliefs, particularly in ivory, to be used for devotional purposes primarily, though there are also secular themes. These were used in the adornment of books, caskets, portable plaques, and venerable images in much the same manner as the painted icons.

From the Second Golden Age we have a panel from a small work in ivory, the *Veroli Casket* (FIG. 7-59), which testifies to the persistence of classical form and content in Byzantine art, and to their strong revival in the tenth century. This panel represents a scene at the end of Euripides' play, *Iphigenia in Aulis*, where Iphigenia, at center, is about to be sacrificed. The characters are all identifiable, and the human types, the poses, costumes, and accessories are all from classical antiquity, though the stunting of the proportions—perhaps partly a consequence of the diminutive space—and bulbous modeling show the figures at a considerable distance in time and style from their prototypes in the Greco-Roman world.

From about the same time, the *Harbaville Triptych*, a portable shrine with hinged panels (FIG. 7-60), manifests in its figures the hieratic formality and solemnity we have learned to associate with Byzantine art and which we have seen as standard in the mosaics of Ravenna. A softer, more fluent technique, and the looser stance of the figures, mitigates the hard austerity of the customary frontal pose. This may also result from the influential, classicizing spirit of the Second Golden Age. Originating in a workshop associated with the imperial palace in Constantinople, the triptych marshals Christ and the saints in such a way as to align the powers of church and state, of God and emperor. Christ is enthroned between St. John and the Virgin in the upper central zone. Beneath them are six apostles. In the wings are soldier saints like George and Theodore, and bishop saints like Demetrius and Procopius. Between the levels are portraits of other saints. We have in effect a miniature, sculptured iconostasis, with the sacred personages placed in their celestial ranks of authority, like officials ranked in the imperial hierarchy.

Portable works like icons and ivories found their way to distant lands as royal gifts, as items of trade, or as plunder, so that the rich and potent religious art of Byzantium became known throughout Europe. Everywhere it had directing influence and, as we have seen, nowhere more than in Russia. For the medieval West the art of Byzantium was to inspire through its steady influence a return to principles of classical humanism and naturalism long implicit in it.

ISLAMIC ART

In 622 Mohammed fled from Mecca to Medinet-en-Nabi ("City of the Prophet," now Medina). From this flight, known as the Hegira, Islam dates its era.[8]

During the century that followed, the new faith spread with unprecedented speed from Arabia, where it was first espoused, through the Middle East to the Indus Valley and westward across North Africa to the Atlantic Ocean. By 640 Syria, Palestine, and Iraq had been conquered by Arab warriors in the name of Islam. In 642 the Byzantine army abandoned Alexandria, marking the Moslem conquest of Lower Egypt. In 651 Iran was conquered; by 710 all of North Africa had been overrun, and a Moslem army crossed the straits of Gibraltar into Spain. A victory at Jerez de la Frontera in 711 seemed to open all western Europe to the Mohammedans. By 732 they had advanced north to Poitiers in France, where an army of Franks under Charles Martel, the grandfather of Charlemagne, opposed them successfully. Although they continued to conduct raids in France, they were unable to extend their control beyond the Pyrenees. But in Spain the great Cali-

phate of Cordoba flourished until 1031 and, indeed, it was not until 1492, when Granada fell to Ferdinand and Isabella, that Islamic influence and power in the West came to a close. In the East the Indus River had been reached by 751, and only in Anatolia was stubborn Byzantine resistance able to slow the Moslem advance. But relentless Moslem pressure against the shrinking Byzantine Empire eventually caused its collapse in 1453, when the Ottoman Turks conquered Constantinople.

The early lightning successes of Islam were due largely to the zeal and military prowess of Arab warriors who set out to conquer the earth for Allah and who burst upon the Near Eastern and Mediterranean worlds when Persian and Byzantine military power was at a low ebb. But the fact that these initial conquests had effects that endured for centuries can be explained only by the nature of the Islamic faith and its appeal to millions of converts.

Many of the features of the Islamic faith are derived from the Judeo-Christian tradition. Its sacred scripture is the Koran, the collection of Mohammed's revelations ordered to be gathered by the caliph Othman (644-56) and unchanged to the present day. Its basic teachings and ethics are similar to those of the Bible, and the Old Testament prophets as well as Jesus are counted among the predecessors of Mohammed. On the other hand, every Moslem believes he has direct and equal access to God without need for complex ritual or an intervening priesthood. Furthermore, a new social order, quite different from the Christian one, was established by Mohammed in that he took charge of the temporal as well as the spiritual affairs of his community. This practice of uniting religious and political leadership in the hands of a single ruler was continued after Mohammed's death by his successors, the caliphs, who based their claims to authority on their descent from the families of the Prophet or those of his early followers.

Architecture and Architectural Ornament

During the early centuries of Islamic history, the political and cultural center of the Moslem world was the Fertile Crescent (Palestine, Syria, Iraq), that melting pot of East and West strewn with impressive ruins of earlier cultures that became one of the fountainheads of the development of Islamic art. The vast territories conquered by the Arabs were ruled by governors, originally sent out from Damascus or Baghdad, who eventually gained relative independence by setting up dynasties in various territories and provinces—the Umayyads in Syria (661-749) and in Spain (756-1031), the Abbasids in Iraq (749-1258, largely nominal after 945), the Fatimids in Tunisia and Egypt (909-1171), and so on. Despite the Koran's strictures against sumptuousness and license, the caliphs were not averse to surrounding themselves with luxuries commensurate with

[8] Islam, "exclusive worship of the one God (Allah)" was Mohammed's name for his new religion. Mohammedan, Muhammadan, Muslim, Moslem—all refer to the same faith.

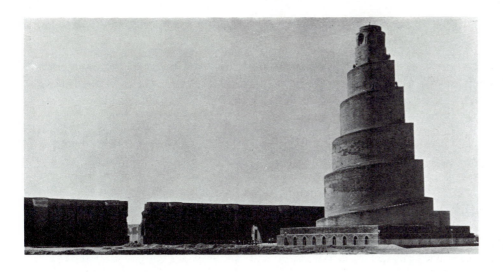

their enormous wealth and power. This duality is expressed by the two major architectural forms developed during the early Islamic period: the mosque and the palace.

Moslem religious architecture is closely related to Moslem prayer, the performance of which is an obligation laid down in the Koran for all Moslems. Prayer as a private act requires neither liturgical ceremony nor a special locale; only the *qiblah*—the direction (toward Mecca) in which the prayer is addressed—is important. But prayer also became a communal act for which a simple ritual was established by the first Moslem community. Once a week the community convened—probably in the Prophet's house, the main feature of which was a large, square court with two *zullahs,* or shaded areas, along the north and south sides. These zullahs consisted of thatched roofs carried by rows of palm trunks; the southern one, wider and supported by a double row of trunks, indicated the qiblah. During these communal gatherings, the *imam,* or leader of collective worship, standing on a pulpit known as *minbar,* near the qiblah wall, pronounces the *khutbah,* which is both a sermon and an act of allegiance of the community to its leader. The minbar thus represents secular authority even as it serves its function in worship. The requirements of this ritual were satisfied by the hypostyle mosque, the origin of which is still in dispute, but one of whose prototypes may well have been the Prophet's house in Medina. Once the Moslems had firmly established themselves in their conquered territories, they began to build on a large scale, impelled perhaps by a desire to create visible symbols of their power that would surpass those of their non-Islamic predecessors in size and splendor; the great size of some of the early mosques, however, may also be explained by the fact that they were intended to contain the entire Moslem population of a given city.

The Great Mosque of Samarra on the Tigris River (FIGS. 7-61 and 62), built between 848 and 852 but now ruined, is the largest mosque of the Islamic world, measuring 800 by 520 feet. Over half its ten-acre area was covered by a wooden roof carried by 464 supports ar-

ranged in aisles around the open central court and leading toward the qiblah wall, the importance of which was emphasized by the greater number of aisles on its side. In the center of the qiblah wall is a niche, the *mihrab,* which became a standard feature in all later mosques. Its origin, purpose, and meaning are still matters of debate; Oleg Grabar feels that it may originally have honored the place where the Prophet stood in his house at Medina when he led the communal prayers. If the mihrab has this symbolic function, it is unusual, since one of the characteristics of early Islamic art is its concerted avoidance of symbols. In this respect, early Islamic art offers a striking contrast to medieval Christian art; the avoidance of religious symbolism, in fact, may reflect conscious rejection of Christian customs and practices.

On the north side of the Great Mosque of Samarra stands a single, large minaret from which a *muezzin* called the faithful to prayer. Although its shape is reminiscent of the ancient ziggurats of Mesopotamia, it was probably inspired not by them but by a certain kind of spiral tower of unknown purpose found in Sassanian Iran. More numerous were minarets that were square in plan and derived from the towers of Early Christian churches in the Near East. Cylindrical minarets, from which evolved the slender needles that are so characteristic of later mosques, became popular only in the eleventh century.

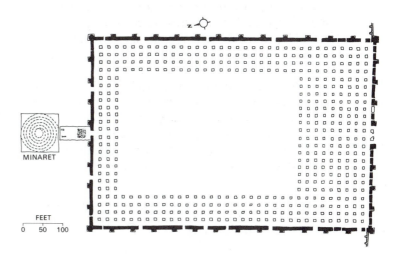

7-62 Plan of the Great Mosque, Samarra.

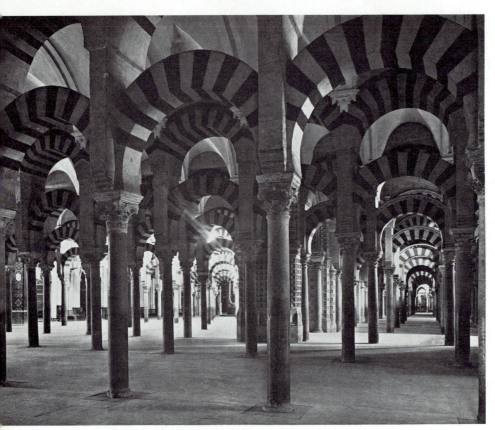

7-63 Interior, mosque at Cordoba, Spain, eighth to tenth centuries.

7-64 Plan of the mosque at Cordoba.

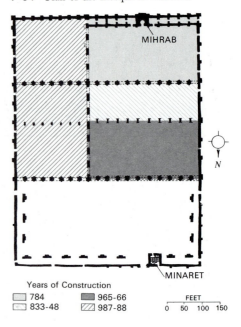

Years of Construction

☐ 784   ■ 965-66

▨ 833-48   ▥ 987-88

FEET
0 50 100 150

The early Moslem hypostyle system, as illustrated by the Samarra mosque, was diffused and, except for the orientation of the building and the position of the qiblah wall, lacked architectural focus and direction. On the other hand, it was a flexible system that permitted enlargement and addition with minimum effort. Its main element was the single support, either a column or a pier, which could

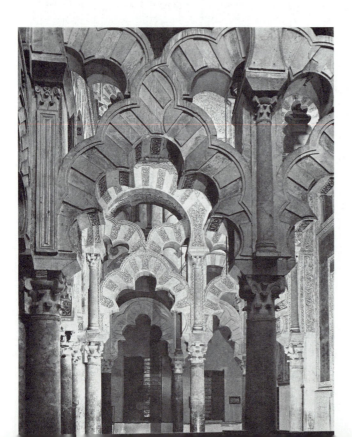

be multiplied at will and in any desired direction. A striking illustration of the flexibility of this system is the mosque of Cordoba (FIGS. 7-63 and 7-64), which was begun in 784 and enlarged several times during the ninth and tenth centuries. The additions followed the original style and arrangement of columns and arches, and the builders were able to maintain a striking stylistic unity for the entire building. The 36 piers and 514 columns are topped by a unique system of double-tiered arches that carried a wooden roof, now replaced by vaults. The lower arches are horseshoe-shaped, a form perhaps adapted from earlier Near Eastern architecture or of local Spanish origin and now closely associated with Moslem architecture. Visually these arches seem to billow out like sails blown by the wind, and they contribute greatly to the light and airy effect of the mosque's interior.

In areas the builders wished to emphasize, like that near the mihrab (FIG. 7-65), the arches become highly decorative, multilobed shapes. Other early Islamic experiments with arch forms had led to the pointed arch, which, however, was not used to cover variable spaces, as in Gothic buildings. Early Islamic buildings had wooden roofs, and the experiments with arch forms were motivated less by structural necessity, than by a desire to create rich and varied visual effects. The same desire for decorative effect seems to have inspired the design of the dome that covers the area in front of the mihrab (FIG. 7-66), one of four domes built during the tenth century to stress the axis leading to the mihrab. Here the large ribs that subdivide

7-65 Mihrab, mosque at Cordoba.

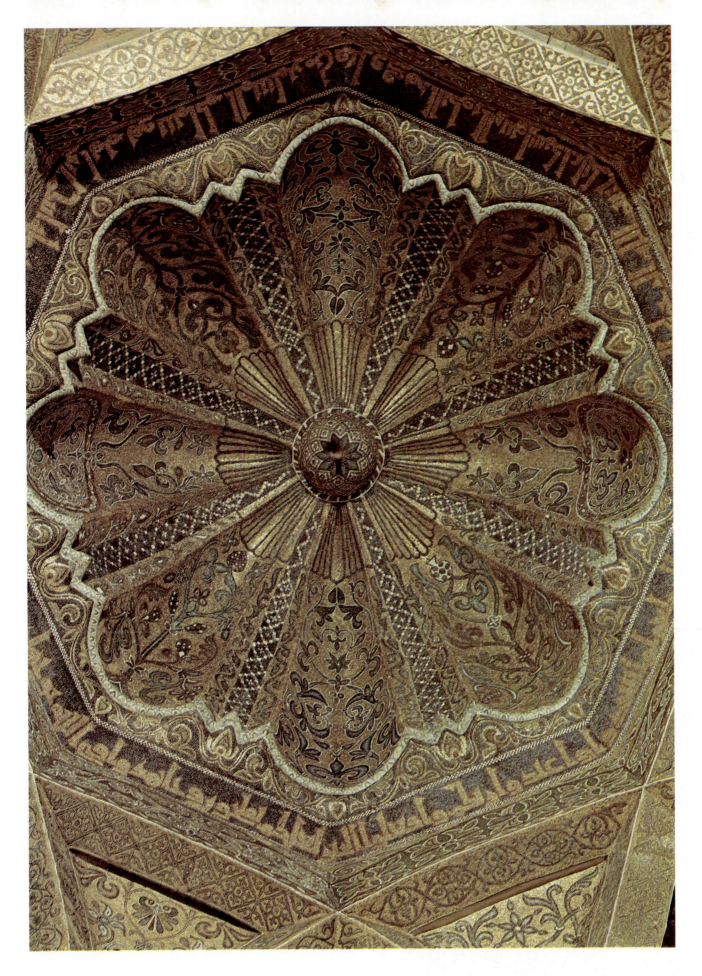

7-66 Dome before mihrab, mosque at Cordoba.

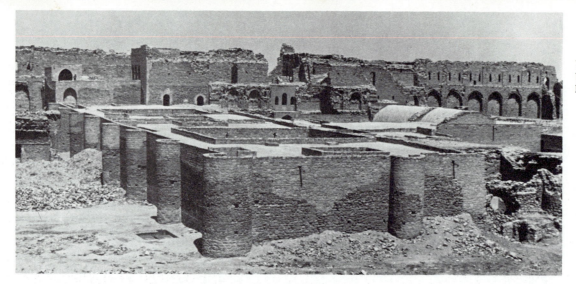

7-67 Palace at Ukhaydir, Iraq, late eighth century.

the hemispherical surface of the dome into a number of smaller sections are primarily ornamental. Only in the hands of Gothic builders, centuries later, were ribs in combination with the pointed arch to become fundamental structural ingredients of a new and revolutionary architectural vocabulary.

Of the early palaces there are only scattered remains, and they are of limited historical importance, serving primarily to illustrate the way of life of Moslem aristocrats and to provide us with some notion of the decorative styles of early Islamic art. Even the purpose of these early palaces is not quite certain. They were built both in cities and in the open country. The rural palaces, which are the better investigated, seem to have had a function similar to that of Roman villas. That they reflect an Islamic taste for life in the desert seems too simple an explanation, although a desire to avoid plague-infested cities may well have been at least a partial motivation of their builders. But these rural palaces probably also served as nuclei for the agricultural development of conquered territories; and they may also have been symbols of authority over conquered and inherited lands, as well as expressions of the newly acquired wealth of their owners.

One of the better preserved of these early Moslem palaces is that of Ukhaydir in Iraq (FIGS. 7-67 and 68), built in the second half of the eighth century. Rather larger than most, the palace here is a separate entity within a fortified enclosure. From the outside the high, tower-studded walls look much like those of the Great Mosque of Samarra (FIG. 7-61). This similarity illustrates a flexibility that is characteristic of early Islamic monuments, as relatively minor changes could convert them from one purpose to another. Differences between a mosque, a palace, or a caravanserai were rarely evident from the exterior; the structures tended to share a rather grim, fortified look that belied their military inefficiency. The high walls may have offered safety from marauding nomadic tribes but, more important to the builders, they may also have fulfilled abstract considerations, like the promise of seclusion for a mosque or, for a palace, privacy for the prince and the symbolic assertion of his power over newly conquered territories.

The plan of the palace at Ukhaydir expresses its dual residential and official function. An elaborate entrance complex, consisting of a monumentalized gate and a Great Hall between two small domed rooms, leads onto the large central court beyond which is a reception hall surrounded

FEET

0   50   100

Well

GREAT HALL

MOSQUE

N

7-68 Plan of the palace at Ukhaydir.

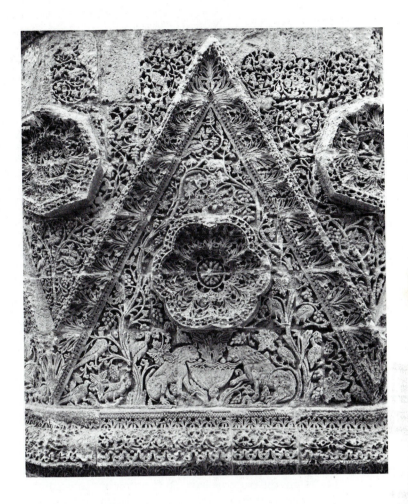

by satellite rooms. Flanking this ceremonial axis are four smaller courts, all with three rooms on each of two sides. These grouped rooms appear to be self-contained and probably served as family living units or guest houses. To the right of the entrance hall is a standard feature of these early palaces—a mosque, here incorporated into the main building complex, though sometimes standing by itself. Most palaces also were provided with fairly elaborate bathing facilities, whose technical features, such as heating systems, were taken over from the Roman tradition of baths. (The baths at Ukhaydir, only recently discovered near the mosque, are not shown on the plan.) Just as in classical antiquity, these baths probably served more than merely hygienic purposes. Large halls frequently attached to them seem to have been used as places of entertainment. Thus a characteristic amenity of classical urban culture that died out in the Christian world survived in medieval Islamic culture.

The decoration of the Ukhaydir palace seems to have been rather sparse and confined to simply molded stucco and occasional decorative brickwork. In this respect, finds made in the western palaces in Syria and Palestine (modern Israel and Jordan) have been much richer. At Mshatta, an unfinished palace in the Jordanian desert, for instance, gate and façade were decorated by a wide, richly carved stone frieze (FIGS. 7-69 and 70). Its design, arrangement, and relation to its carrier serve well to illustrate the major characteristics of early Islamic decoration.

A long band, almost fifteen feet high, is decorated with a series of triangles of the same size framed by an elaborately carved molding. Each triangle contains a large rosette that projects from a field densely covered with curvilinear vegetal designs; no two of the triangles are treated the same way, and into some of them, as in the example shown, figures of animals are introduced. The sources of the various design elements are easily identified as late Classical, early Byzantine, and Sassanian Persian, but their combination and arrangement are typically Islamic.

Most of the design elements of Islamic ornament are based on plant motifs, which are sometimes intermingled with symbolic geometric figures and with human and animal shapes. But the natural forms often become so stylized that they are lost in the purely decorative tracery

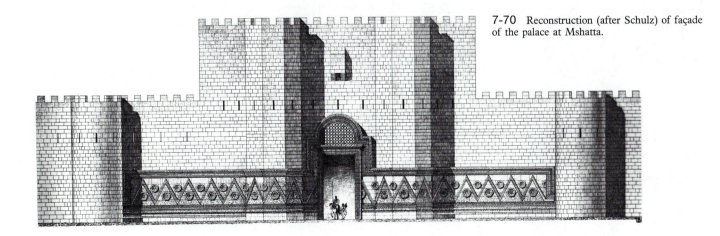

7-70 Reconstruction (after Schulz) of façade of the palace at Mshatta.

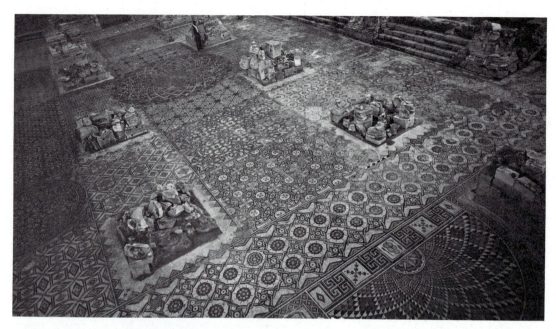

7-71 Floor mosaic, palace at Khirbat al-Mafjar, Jordan, second quarter of eighth century.

of the tendrils, leaves, and stalks. These arabesques form a pattern that will cover an entire surface, be it that of a small utensil or the wall of a building. (This *horror vacui* is similar to tendencies in barbarian art, although other aspects of Islamic design distinguish it from the abstract barbarian patterns.) The relationship of one form to another in the Islamic is more important than the totality of the design: the patterns have no function but to decorate. This system offers a potential for unlimited growth, as it permits extension of the designs in any desired direction.

Most characteristic, perhaps, is the design's independence of its carrier, since neither its size (within limits) nor its forms are dictated by anything but the design itself. This arbitrariness imparts a certain quality of impermanence to Islamic design, a quality that, it has been said, may reflect the Moslem taste for readily movable furnishings, such as rugs and hangings.

Stone carving was only one of several techniques used for architectural decoration. Floor mosaics and wall paintings continued a long Mediterranean tradition. In later

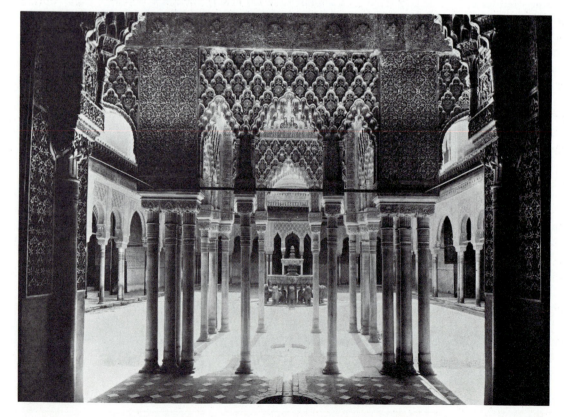

7-72 Court of the Lions, the Alhambra, Granada, Spain, 1354–91.

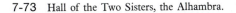

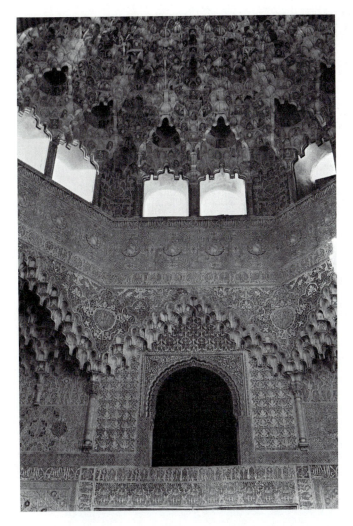

periods colored tile became increasingly important. A magnificent example of a floor mosaic was found in the bath of the palace at Khirbat al-Mafjar near Jericho in Jordan (FIG. 7-71). Set into square and rectangular fields covered with a rich variety of floral and geometric patterns are medallions with extremely intricate abstract designs, some of them creating the illusion of a downward projection of the dome or half-dome under which they were placed. Particularly popular were stucco reliefs, a method of decoration that was known, but not common, in pre-Islamic Iran and Iraq. Cheap, flexible, and effective, the basic material—wet plaster—was particularly adaptable to the execution of the freely flowing line that distinguishes Islamic ornament, and it became a favorite technique.

Some of the very richest examples of stucco decoration are found in the Alhambra palace in Granada, Spain, the last Moslem stronghold in western Europe in the Middle Ages. In the Court of the Lions and the rooms around it (FIGS. 7-72 and 73) stucco decoration runs the gamut of the medium's possibilities and creates an exuberant atmosphere of elegant fantasy that seems to be the visible counterpart of the visions of the more ornate Moslem poets.

The court itself (FIG. 7-72), proportioned according to the Golden Mean, is framed by rhythmically spaced single, double, and triple columns with slender, reedlike shafts that carry richly decorated block-capitals and stilted arches of complex shape. All surfaces above the columns are covered by colored stucco moldings that seem aimed at denying the solidity of the stone structure that supports them. The resulting buoyant, airy, almost floating appearance of the building is enhanced by the "stalactite" decorations that break up the structural appearance of the arches, transforming them into near-organic forms.

This same tendency to disguise architectural forms is shown even more vividly in the Hall of the Two Sisters (FIG. 7-73), which adjoins the Court of the Lions. Here, all surfaces are covered by a polychromed lacework of stucco and tile in which an almost limitless variety of designs is held together by symmetry and rhythmic order. The overall effect of the incredibly rich decoration is that of tapestries suspended from walls and dome, the "stalactites" resembling pendant tassels. In this hall, the Moorish (North African and Spanish) style, heralded in the Mosque of Cordoba (FIG. 7-64), has reached its ultimate refinement. Its influence on Spanish art remained strong throughout the Middle Ages and well into the Renaissance, and traces of it may be observed in the art of the Hispanic colonies of America.

A very different architectural concept is expressed in the Madrasah and Mausoleum of Sultan Hasan in Cairo (FIGS. 7-74 and 7-75). The madrasah, a combined school and mosque, was a building type developed in Iran and brought westward by the advancing Selçuk Turks during the eleventh century. It shares with the hypostyle mosque the open central court but replaces the early Islamic forests of columns with austere masses of brick and stone. The court is now surrounded by four vaulted halls, the one on the qiblah side larger than the other three. Crowded into the angles formed by these halls are the various apartments, offices, and schoolrooms of the Moslem educational institution. Decoration of the main building is confined to moldings around the wall openings and a frieze below the crenellated roofline. These serve to accentuate, rather than disguise, the geometric clarity of the massive structure, which presents a striking contrast to the filigreed elegance of the contemporary Alhambra.

Attached to the qiblah side of the madrasah is the mausoleum, which is a simple cubical structure covered by a dome. Mausoleums—central-plan domed structures—were adopted either from Iran or from the Antique vocabulary of the Mediterranean, as they had not been a part of the original inventory of Islamic architecture. They were built either as memorials to Holy Men, or for the secular function of commemorating Islamic rulers. By the tenth century the building type was well established in Iran, whence

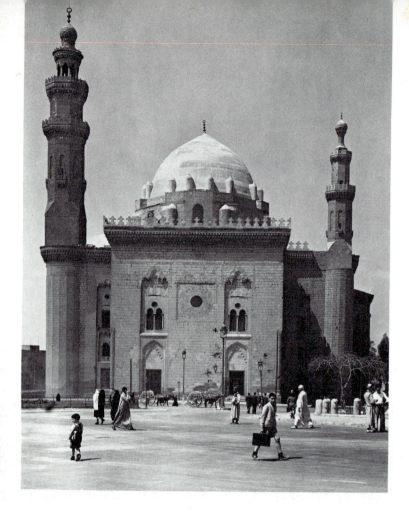

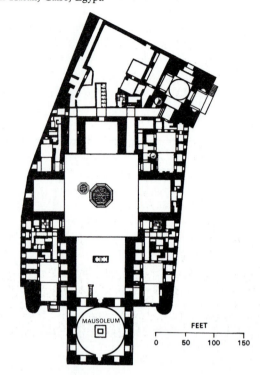

7-74 Madrasah and attached mausoleum of Sultan Hasan, Cairo, Egypt, 1356–63.

7-75 Plan of the Madrasah and mausoleum of Sultan Hasan, Cairo, Egypt.

MAUSOLEUM

FEET
0   50   100   150

7-76 Taj Mahal, Agra, India, 1632–54.

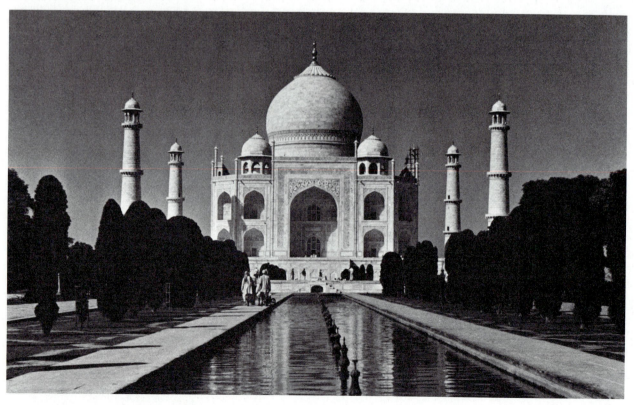

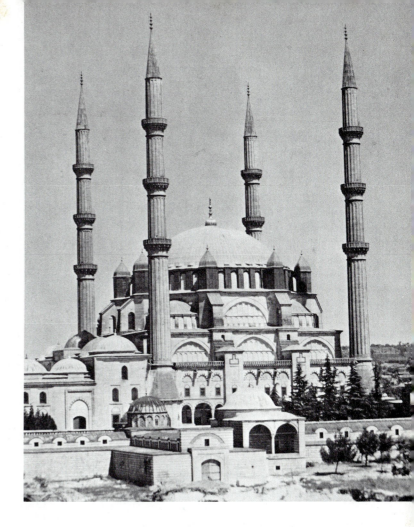

it spread both east and west; it became especially popular in Egypt, which, of course, had its own age-old tradition of large-scale funerary monuments.

The most famous of all Islamic mausoleums is the fabled Taj Mahal at Agra (FIG. 7-76), which was built by one of the Moslem rulers in India, Shah Jahan, as a memorial to his wife, Mumtaz Mahal. The basic shape of the monument is that of the Cairo mausoleum, but modifications and refinements have converted the massive, cubical structure into an almost weightless vision of cream-colored marble that seems to float magically above the tree-lined reflecting pools. The interplay of shadowy voids with gleaming marble walls that seem paper-thin creates an impression of translucency, and elimination of the Cairo structure's heavy, projecting cornice (which separated the blocky base of the earlier building from its dome) ties all the elements together. The result is a sweeping upward movement toward the climactic, balloon-shaped dome. Carefully related minarets and corner pavilions introduce, and at the same time stabilize, this soaring central theme. While the entire monument recalls the fragile elegance of the Alhambra, it far surpasses the latter in subtle sophistication and represents one of the high-water marks of Moslem architecture.

OTTOMAN ARCHITECTURE

A related, yet different Islamic architecture was developed by the Ottoman Turks. The Turkic people, of central Asian origin, had been converted to Islam during the ninth and tenth centuries. They moved into Iran and the Near East in the eleventh century and, by 1055, the Selçuk Turks had built an imposing, though short-lived empire that stretched from India to western Anatolia. It crumbled under the onslaught of the Mongols under Jenghis Khan in the 1240s. After its fall a number of local dynasties established themselves in Anatolia, among them the Ottomans, founded by Osman I (1290–1326). Under his successors the Ottoman state rapidly expanded over vast areas of Asia, Europe, and North Africa to become, by the middle of the fifteenth century, one of the great world powers.

Ottoman art, like Islamic art in general, expressed itself primarily in terms of architecture. But while other Moslem countries had adopted the hypostyle mosque as their standard religious structure (FIGS. 7-61 to 7-67), Ottoman builders developed a new type of mosque whose core was a square prayer hall covered by a dome. In fact, the dome-covered square, which had been a dominant form in Sassanian Iran, became the nucleus of all Ottoman architecture. The combination, in addition to its appealing geometric clarity, was permeated with religious symbolism. To the Ottomans, a circle set into a square signified Heaven, with the circle, which has neither beginning nor end, symbolizing eternity, and the square the four corners of the universe. At first used singly, the domed units came to be used in multiples—a turning point in Ottoman architecture, since it drew in its wake the desire to create unity of space and form out of conglomerate aggregates. The resultant Ottoman style is geometric and formalist, rather than ornamental.

When the Ottoman Turks conquered Constantinople (which they renamed Istanbul) in 1453, their architectural code was firmly established. Although impressed by Hagia Sophia (FIGS. 7-38 to 7-41) which, in some respects, conformed to their own ideals, Ottoman builders were not overwhelmed by it. Direct influence of Hagia Sophia was not felt until about 1500, when a second half-dome, opposite the mihrab, was used for the first time.[9] But the processional way of Hagia Sophia's interior never satisfied Ottoman builders, and Anatolian development moved instead toward the centralized quatrefoil mosque. First examples of this clover-leaf plan, an ideal of Ottoman mosque design, were built in the 1520s—to be eclipsed only by the works of the most famous of Ottoman architects, SINAN THE GREAT (c. 1491–1588), called Koça ("the

[9]They had already adopted (from Byzantine architecture) the half-dome-covered apsidal projection for the mihrab, and also pendentive construction, although they preferred the Selçuk method of supporting domes with squinches or series of corbels (FIG. 7-44).

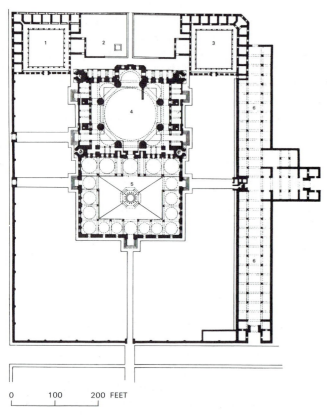

7-78 Plan of Selimiye complex, Edirne.

0   100   200 FEET

7-79 Interior, Mosque of Selim II, Edirne.

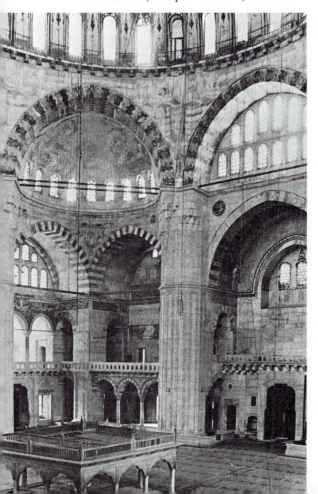

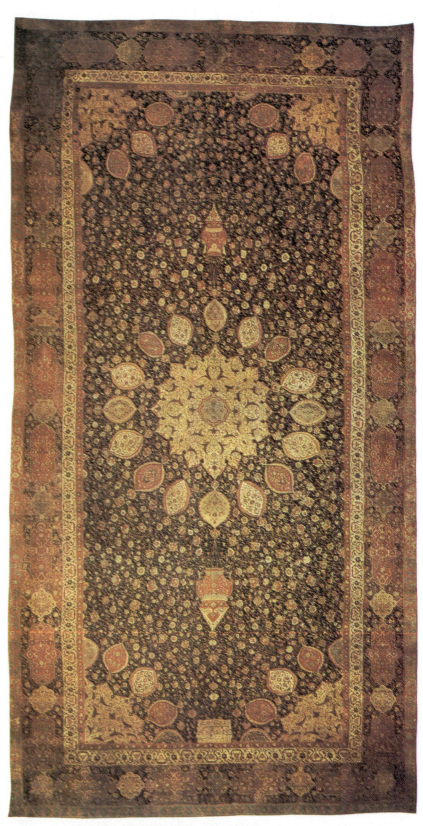

7-80 Carpet from the tomb-mosque of Shah Tahmasp at Ardebil, Iran, 1540. Approx. $34\frac{1}{2}' \times 17\frac{1}{2}'$. Victoria and Albert Museum, London.

architect"). A contemporary of Michelangelo and with equal pretensions to immortality, Sinan carried Ottoman architecture to the height of its classical period. By his time, the use of the basic domed unit was universal. It could be enlarged or contracted as needed, and almost any number of units could be used together. Thus the typical Ottoman building of Sinan's time was an assembly of parts, usually erected with an extravagant margin of structural safety. Measures and forms had been standardized, and design and engineering methods tended to be conservative, with little room given to experimentation. But despite such strictures, which might have been stifling to a lesser architect, Sinan constantly searched for solutions to the problems of unifying the additive elements and of creating a monumental, centralized space with ideal proportions.

In his early buildings Sinan experimented with the clover-leaf plan, as well as with that of Hagia Sophia. In the mosque of Süleyman I in Istanbul he flanked the central unit, in which the main dome is abutted by two half-domes north and south, with dome-covered aisles. But where Hagia Sophia isolates the lateral aisles, Sinan, by reducing interior obstructions to a minimum, made every effort to combine them with the central area and to make central and flanking spaces flow into each other through wide and lofty arcades.

Sinan's efforts to overcome the limitations of a segmented interior found their ultimate expression in the Selimiye Cami at Edirne (FIGS. 7-77 to 7-79), where he created a structure that fully expresses "the earthly squareness of the gathering place of the faithful under the canopy of eternity" and where, at the same time, the mihrab is visible from almost any spot in the building. It is said that the mosque was built for Selim II at Edirne (which had been the capital of the Ottoman empire from 1367 to 1472) because the Sultan could find no adequate space for it in Istanbul. Its massive dome, effectively set off by four slender, pencil-shaped minarets (over 200 feet high), dominates the city's skyline. Grouped around the mosque are various dependencies. (Most important mosques had numerous annexes, including libraries and schools, hospices, baths, soup kitchens for the poor, markets, and hospitals, as well as a cemetery containing the mausoleum for the sultan responsible for the building of the mosque. These utilitarian buildings were grouped around the mosque and axially aligned with it if possible; more generally they were adjusted to their natural site and linked with the central building by plantings of shrubs and trees.)

The mosque is preceded by a rectangular court that covers an area equal to that of the building. This *avlu* (a courtyard forming a summer extension of the mosque) is surrounded by porticoes formed by domed squares. Behind it the building rises majestically to its climactic dome, which equals that of Hagia Sophia in width. But it is the organization of the interior space of this mosque that reveals the genius of its builder. The mihrab has been recessed into an apse-like alcove deep enough to permit illumination from three sides, which makes the brilliantly colored tile panels of its lower walls sparkle as though with their own glowing light. The plan of the main hall is an ingenious fusion of an octagon with the symbolic dome-covered square. The octagon, formed by the eight massive dome supports, is pierced by the four half-dome-covered corners of the square. The result is a fluid interpenetration of several geometric volumes that represents the culminating solution to Sinan's lifelong search for a monumental, unified interior space. The square "singing gallery," a platform for the muezzins which at first may seem like a distracting piece of furniture, punctuates the central space. It restates the basic squareness of the prayer hall and provides an anchoring focus to a design that might seem diffuse without it. Placed under the center of the dome, it marks "the navel of the mosque."

Sinan's building elegantly resolves complicated laws of statics. The Islamic tendency to disguise the structural function of architectural elements (as for instance in the Alhambra, FIGS. 7-72 and 7-73) is minimized and confined to a honeycomb treatment of squinches and to "stalactite" capitals, a form of decoration that was popular from the twelfth century onward. Sinan's forms are clear and legible, like mathematical equations, height, width, and masses being related to each other in a simple but effective ratio of 1:2. The building is generally regarded as the climax of Ottoman architecture. Sinan himself proudly proclaimed it his masterpiece and, indeed, it encloses one of the most impressive domed spaces ever built.

Object Art and Textiles

The furnishings of the palaces as well as the mosques reflected a love of rich and sumptuous effects. Metal, wood, glass, and ivory were artfully worked into a great variety of objects for use in mosque or home. Basins (often huge), ewers, jewel cases, writing boxes were made of bronze or brass, chased and inlaid with silver; enameled glass was used with striking effect in mosque lamps; richly decorated ceramics of high quality were produced in large numbers. Islamic potters, experimenting with different methods of polychrome painting of their wares, developed luster painting, a new and original technique that gives a metallic shine to a surface. Their designs used the motifs found in architectural decoration. This ready adaptability of motifs to various scales as well as to various techniques again illustrates both the flexibility of Islamic design and its relative independence from its carrier.

The most prestigious and highly valued objects of all were textiles, which, in the Islamic world, served more than purely utilitarian or decorative purposes. Produced by imperial factories, they were used not only in homes, palaces, and mosques, but served also as gifts, rewards, and signs of political favor.

The Moslem weavers adopted and developed the textile traditions of Sassanian Iran and the Mediterranean region, the latter best known through Coptic textiles from Egypt. The art spread across the Islamic world and, by the tenth century, Moslem textiles were famous and widely exported. The art of carpet-making was developed to a particularly high degree in Iran, where the need for protection against the winter cold made carpets indispensable both in the shepherd's tent and in the prince's palace. In houses and palaces built of stone, brick, plaster, and glazed tile, carpets also provided a contrasting texture as floor and divan coverings and wall hangings.

The carpet woven for the tomb-mosque of Shah Tahmasp at Ardebil (FIG. 7-80) is a large example of the medallion type and bears a design of effectively massed large elements surrounded and enhanced by a wealth of subordinated details. The field of rich blue is covered with leaves and flowers (chiefly peonies, a Chinese influence) attached to a framework of delicate stems that weave a spiral design over the whole field. Great royal carpets like the Ardebil are products of the joint effort of a group of weavers who probably were attached to the court. Pile weaving is a slow process at best, and, since a carpet like the Ardebil often has more than 300 knots to the square inch, a skilled weaver working alone would probably have needed more than twenty years to complete it.

Since the Ardebil carpet was made for a mosque, its decoration excludes human and animal figures, although other carpets from Ardebil show that the Koran's strictures against the representation of man and animal were not taken as seriously in secular art. The ban against the worship of idols, however, had practically eliminated the image of man from Islamic religious art, and even in early secular art it appeared only occasionally in secluded parts of palaces as part of royal imagery. For this reason also, large sculpture in the round and mural or panel painting, as developed in Europe and in the Far East, was rather rare in early Islamic art. Contributing to this lack of interest in monumental plastic art may have been the predilections of the people that made up the Moslem world; many of them—Arabs, Turks, Persians, and Mongols—were nomads, who traditionally preferred small, movable objects (the so-called "nomad's gear") to large-scale works of art. And so, perhaps, it should not be surprising that, when painting did develop in later times, it was mainly on the small scale of book illumination.

The Art of the Book

The Arabs had no pictorial tradition of their own, and it seems possible that their interest in book illumination developed almost accidentally, as a by-product of their practice of translating and copying illustrated Greek scientific texts. In some of the earliest Islamic illuminated manuscripts, only a few dating earlier than about A.D. 1200, the illustrations seem to have been drawn by the scribes who copied the texts. Whatever its origins (often Christian and Mediterranean, but also local Iranian and Buddhist), by 1200 an art of book illustration had developed, mostly in Iraq and Iran.

The Persian rulers were lovers of fine books and maintained at their courts not only skilled calligraphers, but also some of the most famous artists of their day. The secular books of the Timurids and the Safavids were illustrated by a whole galaxy of painters. Famous among them were BIHZAD (c. 1440-1536), AQA MIRAK, and SULTAN MUHAMMAD, court painters of Tahmasp (1524-1576), a great art patron. Although the rulers were Moslems, orthodox Islamic restrictions regarding depiction of the human figure were rather liberally interpreted by them and did not affect their secular arts, so that, within the framework of illustrating specific stories, the gay scenes of their life of pleasure—the hunt, the feast, music, and romance—and battle scenes fill the pages of their books. In them we feel the luxury, the splendor, and the fleeting happiness of Omar.

In *Laila and Majnun* (FIG. 7-81) the painter Aqa Mirak illustrates one of Nizami's romantic poems. The scene represents a school, apparently in a mosque, and deals less with the pleasures than with some of the more earnest aspects of life. Seated on a rug is a turbaned *molla*, or teacher, rod in hand, listening to a youth reading; around him are other youths studying, all seated on their knees and heels or with one knee raised, the customary sitting postures of the East. Here and there are crosslegged bookrests. In the foreground one boy is pulling his companion's ear, and at the left, near the large water jar, two are playing ball. In the middle distance are the lovers Laila and Majnun, each obviously aware of the other's presence. Although the figures are drawn expressively with delicate, flowing lines, they are flat, with no shading and with but a hint of perspective; the tiles in the court and the rugs on the floor appear to be hanging vertically. The painting is conceived from a point of view concerned not with natural appearance but with pattern and vivid color. To this end the tones are kept bright and clear. The decorative quality of the miniature is emphasized by the broad margins of the page, which are tinted and flecked with gold.

In its general appearance the miniature is much more closely related to the Ardebil carpet than to any European painting or, for that matter, to Chinese painting, by which it was certainly influenced. It falls within the general framework of the Islamic decorative style, which, despite early religious restrictions and the constraints that derive from a limited formal vocabulary, became one of the richest and most harmonious decorative styles in the world.

7-81 *Laila and Majnun in Love at School,* miniature from a manuscript of the Khamsa of Nizami, 1524-25. Colors and gilt on paper. Metropolitan Museum of Art, New York.

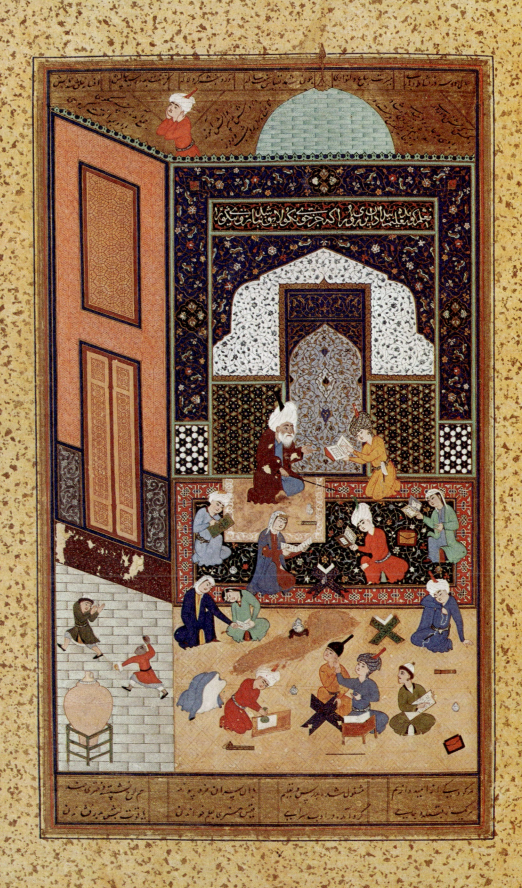

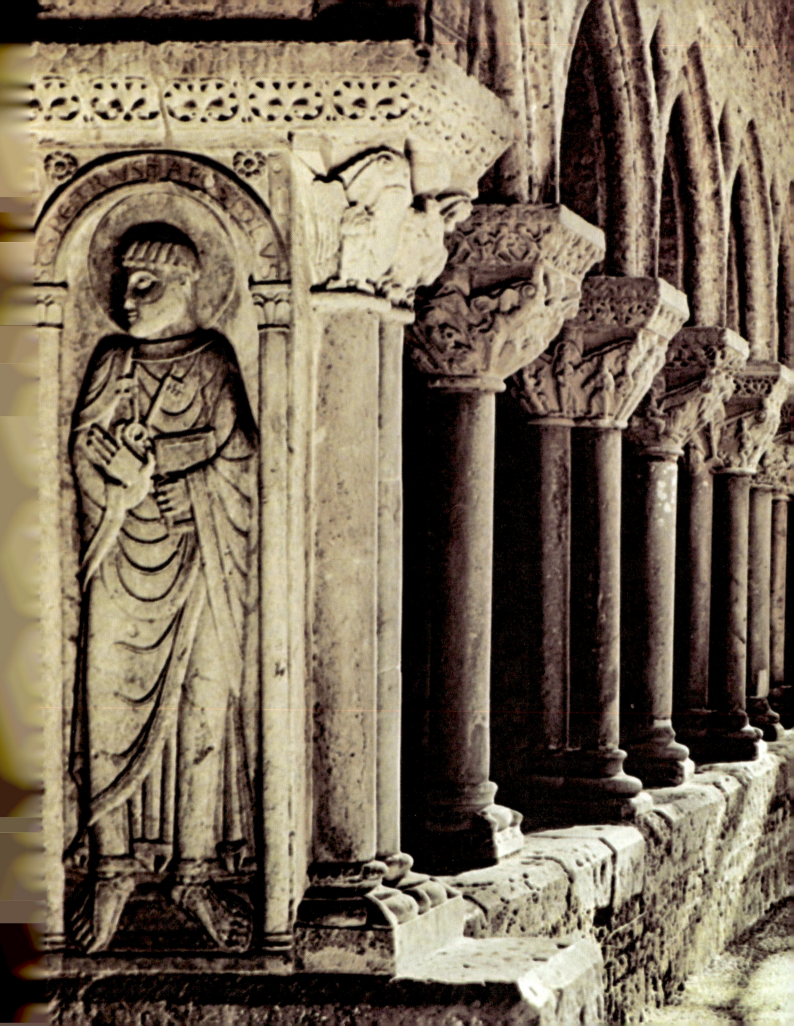

part two
The Middle Ages

The poets of the Augustan age were singing the glories of "eternal Rome" while Jesus of Nazareth, obscure founder of the religion that was to transform the city of man into the city of God, was born and died. Within three centuries Christianity had become the official cult of the dying empire and the faith of the new peoples, the barbarians, who were to inherit its remains. While Byzantium, eastern remnant of the Christianized Roman empire, maintained a continuous sovereignty, the empire in the west disintegrated. What had been the imperial provinces broke up into contesting barbarian kingdoms—those of the Franks, Burgundians, Visigoths, Anglo-Saxons, Lombards, and others. Historians have called the ensuing epoch, the thousand years from about 400 to 1400, the Middle Ages or the Dark Ages. For centuries it was thought that this interval between the passing of the Roman empire and the rebirth of its civilization in the Renaissance was rough and uncivilized—in a word, "barbarous"; that between the ancient and the modern world life was empty, cruel, and "dark," simply a blank between (in the "middle" of) two great civilizations. Even today the word "medieval" is often used disparagingly.

But since the late eighteenth century, historians have been thoroughly revising this view, and with it the belief, long held, that Medieval art was crude and primitive. The same romantic enthusiasm for past civilizations that motivated the archeological revolution of Schliemann's time, and the consequent recovery of the ancient past, sent scholars in quest of the meaning of Medieval culture, the meaning of monuments that existed in great number, and, in this case, aboveground and visible. Although we now see these centuries with very different eyes, perceiving their innovation and their greatness, the names "Middle Ages" and "Medieval" continue to be used, simply for convenience.

Medieval civilization represents an interrelation of Christianity, Greco-Roman tradition, and the new, energetic spirit of the Celtic-Germanic peoples—the barbarians, as the Greeks and the Romans had called them. Christianity, firmly established, constituted a unifying force even in the midst of anarchy and chronic warfare. It mitigated the harsh passions of rough warriors. It kept alive learning and knowledge of the useful arts. Though itself often corrupted, it was just as often reformed. By the thirteenth century, when the Church was at the height of its power, western Europe had evolved as a great and original civilization, one that was constantly stimulated by influences from the Greco-Roman past and from Byzantium and the world of Islam but ever reworking those influences in novel ways. The Christian Church, with its monopoly on education, also preserved and handed on aspects of the Roman culture not directly related to religion: the Latin language, Roman law, Roman administrative organization and practice, the idea and ideal of the Roman empire—all elements used by the Church but, as the Renaissance would show, susceptible of entirely secular application.

Though the spirit of Christianity was oriented toward the world of the supernatural and though its learning was centered in theology, which regarded questions about the nature of the physical world both irrelevant to salvation and irreverent in intention, by the thirteenth century there was stirring, even within the Church, a new curiosity about man's natural environment that could not be entirely stifled by the prevailing religious disposition. In a thirteenth-century summation of Medieval knowledge—the influential encyclopedia called the *Speculum Majus* (*Great Mirror*)—Vincent of Beauvais, a Dominican monk, included the "Mirror of Nature," a comprehensive compilation of lore about natural things. By no means an objective or scientific analysis of nature in the modern sense, it was rather a descriptive record of the appearances of things as the reflection of God's glory and beneficence. Within the Medieval setting, notwithstanding its thoroughly religious view of nature, a different impulse was being felt, a secular and intellectual curiosity about the world that was to mature into modern science.

In addition, the period produced technological advances that pointed to consequences far beyond anything the ancient world had known. The invention and development of tools and mechanisms that extended man's powers over his environment and facilitated manufacture was encouraged not least by the new dignity that the Church's condemnation of slavery conferred on manual labor and skills. The free craftsman—not, as in the ancient world, the slave—was the Medieval agent of production; organized in guilds, he constituted the firm foundation of Medieval urban economy. Thriving towns, populated by free men, provided a stimulus for commerce and industry, and new towns were founded and flourished. Most of the prosperous European cities of today were established or underwent renovation at about the twelfth century; indeed, Florence, mother city of the modern world, had early laid the foundations of its wealth and, by the fifteenth century, had the spirit and the means to lead Europe into the bold, creative age of discovery we call the Renaissance.

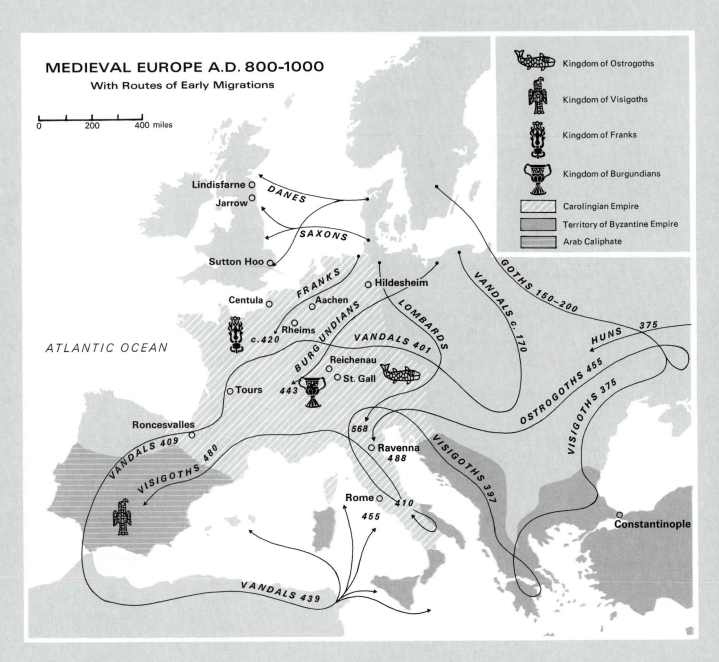

MEDIEVAL EUROPE A.D. 800-1000
With Routes of Early Migrations

0   200   400 miles

Kingdom of Ostrogoths

Kingdom of Visigoths

Kingdom of Franks

Kingdom of Burgundians

Carolingian Empire

Territory of Byzantine Empire

Arab Caliphate

Lindisfarne

DANES

Jarrow

SAXONS

Sutton Hoo

FRANKS

Centula

Aachen

Hildesheim

ATLANTIC OCEAN

Rheims

c. 420

BURGUNDIANS

LOMBARDS

VANDALS 401

GOTHS 150~200

VANDALS c. 170

HUNS

375

Reichenau

St. Gall

OSTROGOTHS 455

Tours

443

568

VISIGOTHS 375

Roncesvalles

Ravenna
488

VANDALS 409

VISIGOTHS 480

VISIGOTHS 397

Rome

410

455

Constantinople

VANDALS 439

chapter eight

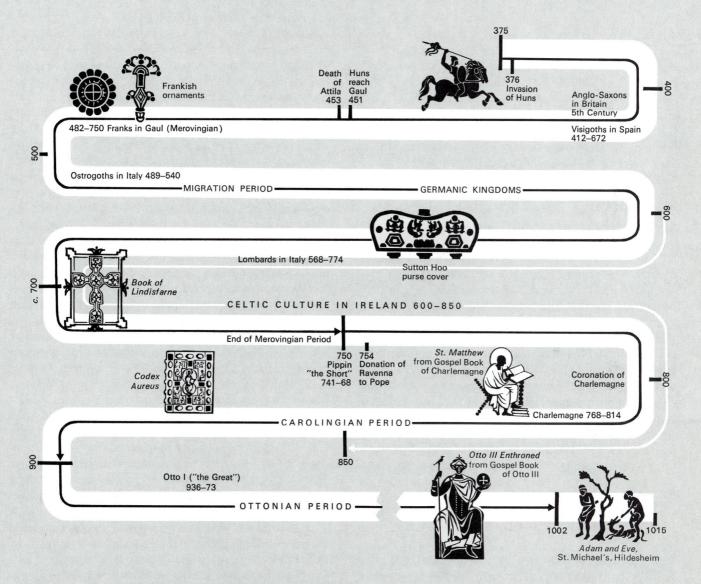

375

376
Invasion
of Huns

Death
of
Attila
453

Huns
reach
Gaul
451

Frankish
ornaments

Anglo-Saxons
in Britain
5th Century

400

482–750 Franks in Gaul (Merovingian)

Visigoths in Spain
412–672

500

Ostrogoths in Italy 489–540

————— MIGRATION PERIOD ————— ————— GERMANIC KINGDOMS —————

600

Lombards in Italy 568–774

Sutton Hoo
purse cover

*Book of
Lindisfarne*

c. 700

CELTIC CULTURE IN IRELAND 600–850

End of Merovingian Period

*Codex
Aureus*

750
Pippin
"the Short"
741–68

754
Donation of
Ravenna
to Pope

St. Matthew
from Gospel Book
of Charlemagne

Coronation of
Charlemagne

800

————— CAROLINGIAN PERIOD —————

Charlemagne 768–814

900

850

Otto III Enthroned
from Gospel Book
of Otto III

Otto I ("the Great")
936–73

————— OTTONIAN PERIOD —————

1002

1015

Adam and Eve,
St. Michael's, Hildesheim

Early Medieval Art

For thousands of years waves of migrating people moved slowly across the great Eurasian steppes down into the Mediterranean world; we have met them as the Achaeans and Dorians of Mycenaean times, and again as the Gauls, who invaded Asia Minor and were defeated by Attalus I of Pergamon in the third century B.C.

In the second century A.D. the Goths moved southward from the Baltic region and settled on the north shore of the Black Sea, subjugating the Scythians and Sarmatians who had inhabited the area for some eight centuries. On their march, the Goths had met and defeated the Vandals, pushing them toward central Europe and setting in motion one of the longest and most infamous migratory treks in history, one that was to end only in the fifth century with the establishment of a Vandal kingdom in North Africa. The Goths themselves split into two groups in the early fourth century—the Ostrogoths (eastern Goths), who remained in Sarmatia, and the Visigoths (western Goths), who moved on into the Danube river basin.

For centuries these migratory movements had been checked by Roman military might along the Rhine and Danube rivers. Despite constant friction with them since the first century B.C., the Romans had been able to contain the barbarians along their northern frontiers. In the fourth century, however, the eruption of the Huns from the east pressed those tribes and nations against the Roman boundaries, which Rome found more and more difficult to defend. In A.D. 376 the Roman emperor Valens allowed the Visigoths, hard-pressed by the Huns, who had already conquered their Ostrogothic cousins, to settle west of the Danube. Maltreated by Roman officials, the Visigoths revolted two years later and, in a battle near Adrianople, killed the emperor and nearly two-thirds of his army. After this, Rome offered little resistance to the different barbarian nations, who crossed into western Europe almost at will. It is the following four centuries of ethnic upheavals in Europe that we refer to as the Migration period.

THE MIGRATION PERIOD

As the name of the period implies, the invasions of Roman territory by barbarian tribes were in reality migrations of ethnic groups seeking not to overthrow the Roman empire, for which they often had great admiration, but a place where they could settle peacefully. However, they were seldom allowed to do so, as other tribes and nations would press in behind them and force them to move on. The Visigoths, for example, who moved in and out of Italy and formed a kingdom in southern France, were forced southward into Spain under pressure from the Franks, who had crossed the lower Rhine and established themselves in northern France. The Huns themselves, the force that triggered this chain reaction of ethnic dislocations, reached France and Italy in mid-fifth century, and only the death of their great leader, Attila, in 453 prevented them from consolidating their vast conquests. As Hunnish power waned, the Ostrogoths shook off their yoke, moved first to Pannonia (junction of modern Hungary, Austria, and Yugoslavia) and then to Italy, where, under Theodoric, they established their kingdom only to have it fall less than a century later to the Lombards.

During this time of upheaval, strife, fear, and uncertainty, the Church, benefiting from the prestige of such early leaders as Augustine and Gregory the Great, constituted the only central authority, political as well as spiritual; the popes had in effect succeeded the Roman emperors. It was at this time that the foundations for the later authority of the Church were firmly established. In this connection, we should bear in mind that most of the barbarian tribes entering the Roman empire were already Christian, although of the Arian creed, which had been condemned as heretical by the Orthodox Church. In its contest with the eastern Orthodox Church for leadership in Christendom, papal Rome was strengthened when the Frankish king, Clovis, was converted to Catholicism. During his reign (481–511) the Franks gained control over the Burgundians (who had moved from the Baltic area into the region around Lake Geneva in the early fifth century), the Visigoths, and other groups in the area now France. With the recognition of the pope in Rome by this Frankish kingdom and with the success (in the sixth century) of Augustine's mission to England, where he became the first archbishop of Canterbury, Catholicism and the authority of Rome became firmly established in western Europe.

Accounts of the barbarian character vary. Tacitus, pointing up a moral for his Roman contemporaries, praises their courage, good looks, moral purity, fidelity, and good treatment of women but finds them guilty of drunkenness and wanting in perspicacity in matters of money. We can get a better picture of the Germanic character from their epics, songs, and sagas, which show a somber pessimism built upon a fundamental belief in fate, in the inevitable. Their heroes, like Siegfried and Beowulf, struggle against a pagan world of dreadful monsters. Fierce joy in battle alternates with bragging and carousing; and narratives of stoic valor, with expressions of despair. Interpersonal loyalty, which became the basis of feudal ties and feudal law, is glorified in their poetry, as in this fragment of an Anglo-Saxon epic describing the last stand of a band of Saxons against the Danes:

Remember the times when we spoke over our mead, when we raised up our boasts along the benches, heroes in the hall in anticipation of a hard fight! Now let us see who is brave. . . . Byrhtivold spoke up, an old retainer . . . he taught his warriors their duty: "Mind shall be the harder, heart the keener, courage the greater as our strength grows less."

The imagination of these wandering people teemed with fantastic creatures of all sorts. Their belief that the deep, dark forests of the north virtually swarmed with zoomorphic and demonic populations was widely shared by the nomadic hunters of all tribes. Dragons, like Siegfried's Fafnir and Beowulf's Grendel, symbolize the mysterious and threatening universe of fierce forces that the later Medieval world will picture as the devils and demons of hell. Medieval man, long after he ceased his wandering and despite Christianization, remained more than half pagan; his terrors were bound up with his tribal experience and the memory of fiend-filled forests and pagan rites. (Charlemagne, in suppressing the Saxons, decreed against human sacrifice.) Against this background, it is not surprising to find that the Germanic tribes readily adopted an art form that, although foreign, was ideally suited to their imagination—the Eastern "animal style" already encountered in Mesopotamian art.

Craft Art

The original art of the Germanic peoples was abstract, decorative, and geometric and ignored the world of organic nature. It was confined to the decoration of small, portable objects—weapons or items of personal adornment such as bracelets, pendants, and belt buckles. Most characteristic, perhaps, and produced in considerable numbers by almost all tribes, was the *fibula*, a decorative pin usually used to fasten garments (FIG. 8-1). The fibulae were made of bronze, silver, or gold and were profusely decorated, often with inlaid precious or semiprecious stones. The entire surface of objects is covered with decorative patterns, reflecting the *horror vacui* so common in the art of primitive cultures. But we also note that the decorative patterns are carefully adjusted to the basic shape of the object they adorn and that they describe and amplify its form and structure, becoming an organic part of the object itself.

This highly disciplined, abstract, and functional type of decorative design was wedded to the animal style during the early centuries of the Medieval era. Probably of prehistoric origin, the animal style had reasserted itself in the Luristan bronzes (FIG. 2-38) of the ninth and eighth centuries B.C. and was a dominant element of the artistic repertoire of the Scythians, who passed it on to their Gothic overlords in the third century A.D. From that time on, the Goths became the main transmitters of this style, which was readily adopted by many of the other Germanic tribes. But its application was severely controlled by the native Germanic sense of order and design. Abstracted to the point of absolute integration with dominantly geometric patterns, the zoomorphic elements frequently become almost unrecognizable, and one must often examine a fibula (FIG. 8-1) carefully to discover that it terminates in an animal head.

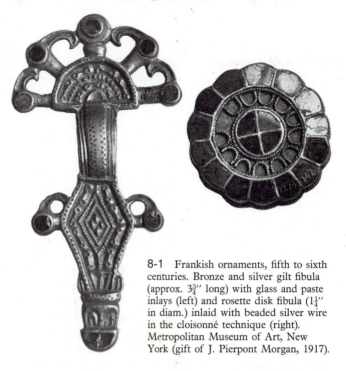

8-1 Frankish ornaments, fifth to sixth centuries. Bronze and silver gilt fibula (approx. $3\frac{3}{4}''$ long) with glass and paste inlays (left) and rosette disk fibula ($1\frac{1}{4}''$ in diam.) inlaid with beaded silver wire in the cloisonné technique (right). Metropolitan Museum of Art, New York (gift of J. Pierpont Morgan, 1917).

The art of the Germanic people was expressed primarily in metalcraft. One of their preferred methods of decoration was *cloisonné*, a technique that may be of Byzantine and, ultimately, of Near Eastern origin. In this technique, used in the circular ornament shown in FIG. 8-1, small metal strips (the *cloisons*), usually of gold, are soldered edge-up to a metal background. An enamel paste (to be subsequently fired) or semiprecious stones, such as garnets, or pieces of colored glass, are placed in the compartments thus formed. The edges of the cloisons remain visible on the surface and are an important part of the design. This cloisonné personal gear was highly prized and handed down from generation to generation. Dispersion of some of the princely hoards at an early date would account for discovery of identical techniques and designs in widely divergent areas. Certainly cloisonné ware must have been given to vassals as gifts and tokens of gratitude; everywhere in barbarian poetry the name for the prince and lord is "treasure-giver." Other collections or "treasures" must have been accumulated over time, which could explain the different forms present in the magnificent discovery made at Sutton Hoo in Suffolk, England, one piece from which is shown in FIG. 8-2.

Excavated in 1939, the Sutton Hoo site is now associated with the ship burial of the East Anglian king Anna, who died in 654. The purse lid shown is by no means the best of the pieces found, fine as it is. There are four symmetrically arranged groups of figures: The end groups consist of a man standing between two beasts, he frontal, they in profile, a heraldic type of grouping that goes back to ancient Mesopotamia (FIG. 2-15), though of course with variation. The two center groups represent eagles attacking ducks, again a familiar predatory motif that both Mesopotamian and Egyptian art yield us. The animal figures are adjusted to each other with the cunning design we associate with the whole animal style through centuries; for example, the convex beaks of the eagles fit against the concave beaks of the ducks. The two figures fit together so snugly that they seem at first to be a single dense, abstract design; this is true also of the man-animals motif. Above these figures are three geometric designs, the outer ones clear and linear in style, the central one showing an interlace pattern, the interlacements turning into writhing animal figures. Interlacement was known outside the barbarian world but was seldom used in combination with animal figures. It has been suggested that the barbarian fondness for the interlace pattern came from the quite familiar experience of interlacing leather thongs. In any event, the interlace, with its possibilities for great complexity, had natural attraction for the adroit jeweler.

Metalcraft and its vocabulary of interlace patterns and other motifs, beautifully integrated with the animal form, is without doubt *the* art of the Early Middle Ages in the West. Interest in it was so great that the colorful effects of jewelry designs were imitated in the painted decorations of manuscripts, in stone sculpture, in the masonry of the early churches, and in sculpture in wood. A striking example of the last is an animal head from another ship burial, one found near Oseberg in Norway (FIG. 8-3) that dates from the early ninth century. The Oseberg animal head expresses, as do few monuments of its age, the animal fierceness, the untamed, pagan energy of the merciless northern sea-rovers who harassed the Christian-German settlements of western Europe from the late ninth until the eleventh century. It brings together in one composition a strikingly real description of the muzzle of a snarling animal, its eyes protruding in predatory excitement, with a vigorously carved passage of interlacements in areas that would bear a lesser burden of expression—the neck and the space between the flaring nostrils and the grimacing mouth. It is thus a powerfully expressive example of the union of the two fundamental motifs of barbarian art, the animal form and the interlace.

Illumination

When we remember that barbarian art was essentially one of small portable objects, part of the collection of accessories and instruments that made up the nomad's gear, it is not surprising that monumental art—whether architecture, painting, or sculpture—is not to be found in what the migrating peoples have left. The masterpieces of barbarian art, which show the meeting of its decorative tradition with those of the art of the Mediterranean world, are illuminations in liturgical books, for with Christianization of the barbarians, the book became an important vehicle of their art. These books were easily transportable, and we can follow the movements of some of them from place to place, since their styles, copied in or copying other books, are traceable in sequences of influence.

The complicated interchanges of influences recorded in manuscript illumination from the sixth to the eleventh century are the consequence not only of the restless migration of the new people, but also of the missionary activities of the Church as it sought to stabilize the wandering groups and to establish its authority. Foremost in this activity from the sixth century to the time of Charlemagne was the monastically organized Church of Ireland. Monasticism, a system by which communities of persons lived away from the world and dedicated themselves to the spiritual life, was instituted in the eastern Christian world by Basil in the fourth century and in the west by Benedict in the sixth century. The Celts of Ireland, converted to Christianity in the fifth century, adopted eastern rather than western monasticism and were not firmly connected to the Roman rule or to the papacy. Their independence was strengthened by their historical good luck: They were not invaded by the Germanic migrants. While western Europe from about 400 to 750 sank gradually into conflict, confusion, and ignorance, Ireland experienced a golden age. Irish monks, filled with missionary zeal, founded monastic establishments in the British islands—at Iona, off the west coast of Scotland, and at Lindisfarne, on the Northumbrian (northeastern) coast of Anglo-Saxon England. From these foundations, which became great centers of learning for both Scotland and England, Irish monks, filled with a "wonderful spirit of missionary enterprise," journeyed through Europe, founding great monasteries in Italy, Switzerland, Germany, and France and making the names of "Scot" (the old term for "Irish") and "Ireland" familiar in all western Christendom. The spread of Irish-Christian influence was countered by the Church of Rome, which felt that the Irish, long isolated from Roman Christianity, were tainted by heresy and separatism. The right hand of the papacy in this action was the Anglo-Saxon Winfred, or, as he is known to history, St. Boniface, Apostle to the Germans.

This encounter between Irish and Germanic Christianity is curiously reflected in the mingling of design elements in the illuminated pages of gospel books produced in Ireland and England between the seventh and ninth centuries. These "Hiberno-Saxon" manuscripts combine Irish and Anglo-Saxon motifs, sharing essentially, but by no means in all details, the same style. An ornamental page—only one of several from a gospel book, the *Book of Lindisfarne*—is an exquisite example of Hiberno-Saxon art at its best (FIG. 8-4). Here the craft of intricate ornamental patterning, developed through centuries, is manifested in a tightly compacted design. Serpentine interlacements of fantastic animals devour each other, curling over and returning upon their writhing, elastic shapes. The rhythm of expanding and contracting forms gives a most vivid effect of motion and change, a palpable rippling as in the surface of a rapids. The inscribed cross, a variation upon the stone Celtic crosses familiar in Ireland, regularizes the rhythms

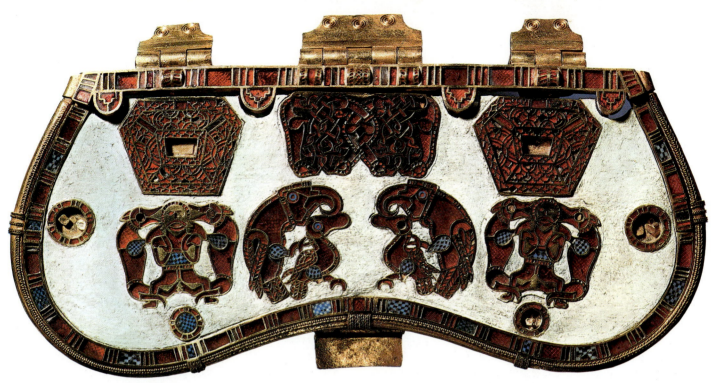

8-2 Purse cover from the Sutton Hoo ship burial, c. 655. Gold and enamel, 7½″ long. British Museum, London.

of the serpentines and, perhaps by contrast with its heavy immobility, seems to heighten the effect of motion. The motifs are placed in detailed symmetries, with inversions, reversals, and repetitions that must be closely studied with the magnifying glass if one would appreciate not so much their variety as their mazelike complexity. The zoomorphic forms are intermingled with clusters and knots of line, and the whole design pulses and vibrates like an electromagnetic energy field. The color is rich yet cool, the entire spectrum being embraced but in hues of low intensity. Shape and color are so adroitly adjusted that a smooth and perfectly even surface is achieved, a balance between

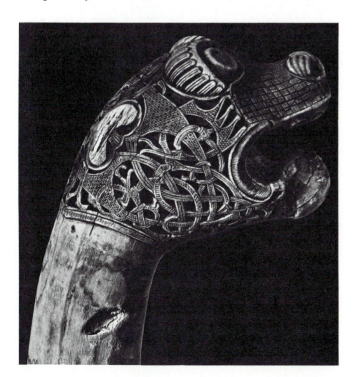

an overall, steady harmony of key (color) with maximum motion of figure and line. The discipline of touch is that of a master familiar with long-established conventions; yet neither the discipline nor the convention stiffens the supple lines that tirelessly and endlessly thread and convolute their way through the design. This joy at working in the small on infinitely complex and painstaking projects—this goldsmith's, jeweler's, and weaver's craft—will live in Northern art throughout the Middle Ages in architectural detail, ivory carving, illumination, stained-glass work, and, ultimately, in panel painting. The instinct and taste for intricacy and precision, propagated in the art of the wandering Celt-Germans, will broaden beyond art into technology and the making of machines. Modern historians make much of Medieval technological invention, declaring that it innovated well beyond Greek and Roman achievement and pointed the way to the technological revolutions of modern times.

The barbarian craft remained, but the Hiberno-Saxon ornamental style, with its gorgeous essays in interlacements, was fated to be replaced by the Mediterranean styles descended from Early Christian and Late Antique art. Political realities hastened its demise. Irish Christianity lost its influence in Anglo-Saxon England and on the continent; the adherents to the rule of Benedict, the Benedictine order of monks, who wholeheartedly followed the papacy and the Roman version of Christianity, gained the upper hand in power and influence, and though the Irish

8-3 Animal head from the Oseberg ship burial, c. 825. Wood, approx. 5″ high. University Museum of National Antiquities, Oslo, Norway.

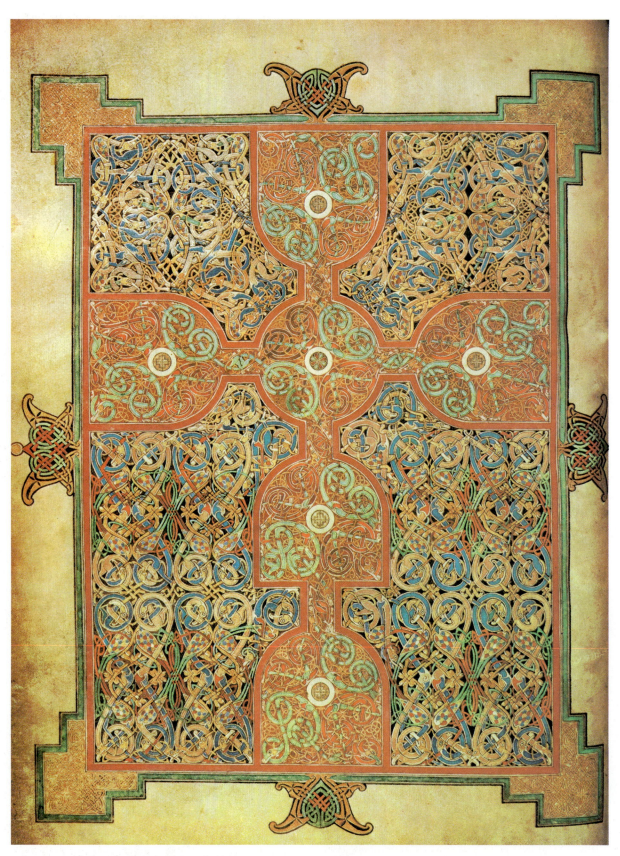

8-4 Ornamental page from the *Book of Lindisfarne*, Lindisfarne, late seventh century. Illumination, approx. 13″ × 10″. British Library, London.

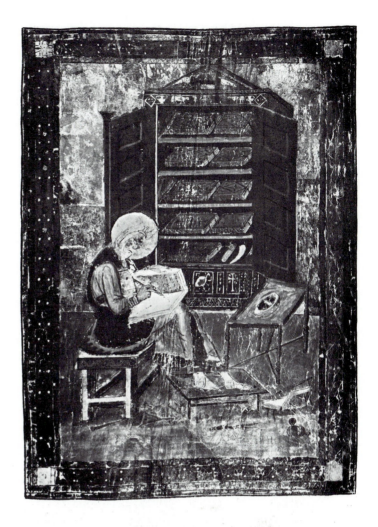

Church held out for some time, eventually it accepted the Roman form. Even while Hiberno-Saxon art prevailed in Ireland, Scotland, and Northumbria, other monastic foundations in England were copying Mediterranean prototypes. Naturally, the ascendancy of the Roman Church would be expressed in manuscripts from the Mediterranean area, and wherever the Roman orthodoxy was accepted an orthodox style of manuscript illumination had to follow. The contrast between the two very different styles is particularly striking in juxtaposition. The *Ezra* of the Codex Amiatinus (FIG. 8-5) was copied from an Italian manuscript, the Codex Grandior of Cassiodorus, early in the eighth century by an illuminator with Italian training in some Anglo-Saxon monastery, probably Jarrow. The same original must have been seen and "translated" a few years earlier by an artist trained in the abstract Hiberno-Saxon manner; his version appears as the St. Matthew figure in the *Book of Lindisfarne* (FIG. 8-6). The *Ezra* of the Codex Amiatinus, as well as the architectural environment, is closely linked with the pictorial illusionism of Late Antiquity. The style is essentially that of the brush, the color, though here and there in flat planes, blended smoothly to model the figure and give gradual transitions from light to dark. This procedure must have been continued in the Mediterranean world throughout the Early Middle Ages, despite the formalizing into line that we have seen taking place in mosaics. But the Hiberno-Saxon artist of the *Lindisfarne Matthew,* trained in the use of hard, evenly stressed line, apparently knows nothing of the illusionistic, pictorial technique, nor, for that matter, of the representation of the human figure. Though he carefully takes over the pose, he interprets the form in terms of line exclusively, "abstracting" the unfamiliar tonal scheme of his model into a patterned figure not unlike what we see in the King, Queen, and Jack of a deck of cards. The soft folds of drapery in the *Ezra* become in the *St. Matthew* a series of sharp, curving lines regularly spaced. There is no modeling, no light and shade. The long training in the peculiar linear style of barbarian art made it necessary for the *Lindisfarne* artist to convert the strange Mediterranean forms into the linear idiom familiar to him; he finds before him a tonal *picture* and makes of it a linear *pattern.*

The Medieval artist did not go to nature for his model but to a prototype—another image, a statue or a picture in a book. His copy might be one in a long line of copies, and in some cases we can trace these copies back to a lost original, inferring its former existence. The Medieval practice of copying pictures is of course closely related to the copying of books, especially sacred books like the Scriptures and the books used in the liturgy. The Medieval scribe or illuminator (before the thirteenth century, most

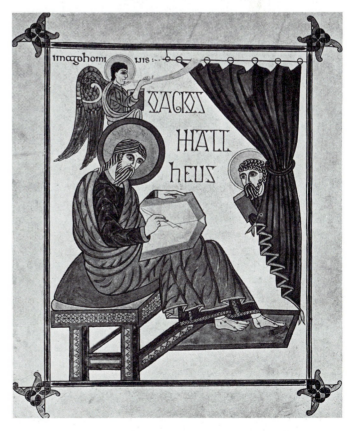

8-6 *St. Matthew,* from the *Book of Lindisfarne,* Lindisfarne, late seventh century. Approx. 11″ × 9″. British Library, London.

often a monk) could have reasoned that just as the text of a holy book must be copied faithfully if the copy is also to be holy, so must the pictures be rendered faithfully. Of course, in the process of copying, mistakes are made; and, while scholars seek to purge the book of these textual "corruptions," "mistakes" in the copying of pictures yield new pictorial styles, or represent the confluence of different styles, as in the relationship of the Codex Amiatinus and the *Book of Lindisfarne*. In any event, one should realize that the style of Medieval images, whether in sculpture or painting, was the result of copying from sources thought to have sacred authority, and not from the imitation of natural models. Thus, one learned what was true from authorities who declared the truth—the Scriptures and the fathers of the Church—and one painted "true" pictures or sculpted "true" statues from authoritative images. To question authority on one's own, to investigate "nature" on one's own, would be to question God's truth as revealed and interpreted. This would be blasphemy and heresy. It would be wrong, however, to leave the impression that dependence upon authority in art is characteristic solely of the Middle Ages. In the Renaissance and since—and certainly today—new styles gain sudden authority and win widespread reverence and imitation, even if for reasons different from those operative in the Middle Ages.

THE CAROLINGIAN PERIOD

The late eighth and the early ninth centuries saw the remarkable historical phenomenon now called Charlemagne's renovation, an energetic, brilliant emulation of the art and culture, not to say the political ideals, of Christian Rome. Out of the confusions attendant upon the migrations and settlement of the barbarians, Charlemagne's immediate forerunners built by force and political acumen a Frankish empire that contained or controlled a large part of western Europe. Charlemagne, wishing, like Constantine, whom he consciously imitated, to create a unified Christendom as a visible empire, was crowned by the pope in Rome in A.D. 800 as head of the restored empire; the new entity became the Holy Roman Empire, which, waxing and waning over a thousand years and with many hiatuses, existed as a force in central Europe until its extinction by Napoleon in 1806.

Charlemagne was a sincere admirer of learning and the arts, and in order that his empire should be as splendid as that of Rome (he thought of himself as successor to the Caesars) he invited to his court at Aachen the best minds and the finest craftsmen of western Europe and of the Byzantine East. Though himself unlettered and scarcely able to write, he could speak Latin fluently and loved the discourses he frequently held with the learned men he gathered around him. He must also have admired the splendid works created in the scriptorium of the school he had established in his palace. One of his dearest projects had been the recovery of the true text of the Bible, which, through centuries of miscopying by ignorant scribes, had become almost hopelessly corrupt. Part of the great project, undertaken by the renowned scholar Alcuin of York at the new monastery at Tours, was the correction of the actual script used, which, in the hands of the scribes, had become almost unreadable. The Carolingian rehabilitation of the inherited Latin script produced a clear, precise system of letters; the letters on this page are descended from the alphabet renovated by the scribes of Tours.

Painting and Illumination

Charlemagne, his successors, and the scholars under their patronage imported whole libraries from Italy and Byzantium. The painted illustrations in these books must have astonished northern painters, some of whom had been trained in the Hiberno-Saxon pattern-making manner, others in the weak and inept Frankish styles of the seventh and eighth centuries. Here suddenly they were confronted with a sophisticated realism that somehow had survived from the Late Antique amidst all the denaturing tendencies that followed. The famous *Coronation Gospels* (the *Gospel Book of Charlemagne*), formerly in the Imperial Treasury in Vienna, may have been a favorite of Charlemagne himself: An old tradition records that it was found on the knees of the dead emperor when, in the year 1000, Otto III had

8-7 *St. Matthew*, from the *Gospel Book of Charlemagne, c.* 800–10. Approx. 9″ × 6¾″. Kunsthistorisches Museum, Vienna.

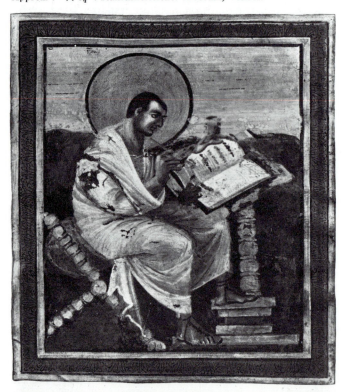

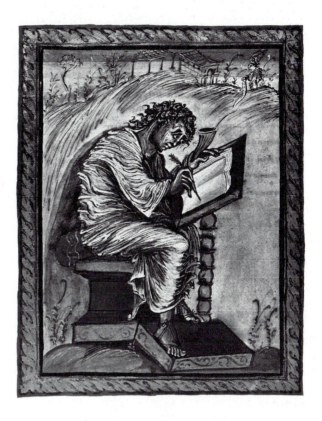

the imperial tomb at Aachen opened. The picture of St. Matthew composing his gospel (FIG. 8-7) descends from ancient depictions in sculpture and painting of an inspired philosopher or poet seated and writing; its technique is of the same antiquity—deft, illusionistic brushwork that easily and accurately defines the masses of the drapery as they wrap and enfold the body beneath. The acanthus of the frame of the "picture window" recalls the fourth Pompeian style, the landscape background is thoroughly classicizing, and the whole composition seems utterly out of place in the north in the ninth century. How were the native artists to receive this new influence, so alien to what they had known and so strong as to make their own practice suddenly obsolete?

The style evident in the *Coronation Gospels* was by no means the only one that appeared suddenly in the Carolingian world; a wide variety of styles in all stages of change from antique prototypes were distributed through the court schools and the monasteries—a bewildering array, one can believe, for the natives, who now attempted their appropriation by copying them as accurately as possible. Thus, Carolingian painting is extremely diverse and uneven, and classification becomes a difficult matter of ascertaining prototypes and the descendants of prototypes. If the *Coronation Gospels* painting is by a Frank, rather than an Italian or a Byzantine, it is an amazing feat of approximation, since, except for the Jarrow copyist, there is nothing to prepare the way for it in the Hiberno-Saxon or Frankish West. Another *St. Matthew,* in a gospel book made for Archbishop Ebbo of Reims (FIG. 8-8), may be an interpretation of a prototype very similar to that used by the *Coronation Gospels* master, for it resembles it in pose and in brushwork technique. But there the resemblance stops: The classical calm and solidity have been replaced by an energy that amounts to frenzy, and the frail saint almost leaps under its impulse. His hair stands on end, the folds of his drapery writhe and vibrate, the landscape behind him rears up alive. He appears in frantic haste to take down what his inspiration, the tiny angel in the upper right hand corner, dictates. All fidelity to bodily proportions or structure is forsaken in the artist's effort to concentrate on the act of writing; the head, hands, inkhorn, pen, and book are the focus of the composition. This contrasts strongly with the settled pose of the *Matthew* of the *Coronation Gospels* with its even stress so that no part of the composition starts out at us to seize our attention. The native power of expression is unmistakable and will become one of the important distinguishing traits of Late Medieval art. Just as the painter of the *Lindisfarne Matthew* transformed the *Ezra* portrait in the Codex Amiatinus (FIGS. 8-3 and 8-4) into something original and strong,

translating its classicizing manner into his own Hiberno-Saxon idiom, so the Ebbo artist translated his classical prototype into a Carolingian vernacular that left little classical substance. The four pictures should be carefully studied and compared.

Narrative illustration, so richly developed in Early Christian and Byzantine art, was revived by the Carolingians, and many fully illuminated books—some, large Bibles—were produced. One of the most extraordinary and enjoyable of all Medieval manuscripts is the famous *Utrecht Psalter,* written at Hautvilliers near Reims, France, about 830. The text, in three columns, reproduces the Psalms of David and is profusely illustrated by pen-and-ink drawings in the margins. The example shown in FIG. 8-9 depicts figures acting out Psalm 150, in which the psalmist exhorts us to praise the name of God in song and with timbrel, trumpet, and organ. The style shows a vivid animation of much the same kind as the *St. Matthew* of the *Ebbo Gospels* and may have been produced in the same school. The bodies are tense, shoulders hunched, heads thrust forward. The spontaneity of their actions and the rapid, sketchy technique with which they are rendered have the same nervous vitality as the figure in the *Ebbo Gospels.* From details of the figures, their dress and accessories, scholars feel certain that the artist was following one or more manuscripts done some 400 years earlier; but his interest in simple human emotions and actions, the pantomimic skill in the variety and descriptiveness of gesture, are essentially Medieval characteristics, though

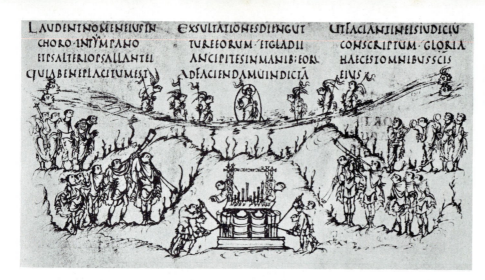

they begin in Early Christian art. Note, for example, how the two musicians playing the pipe organ shout at their helpers to pump air more strenuously. It is this candid observation of man, often in his unguarded moments, that is to lend both truth and charm to the art of the Late Middle Ages.

Craft Art

To our knowledge there was little or no monumental sculpture in the Carolingian age. The traditional taste for sumptuously wrought and portable metal objects, which produced the barbarian works we have seen, persisted under Charlemagne and his successors and produced numerous precious and beautiful works like the book cover of the Codex Aureus of St. Emmeram (FIG. 8-10). Dating from the second half of the ninth century, it probably originated at either the St. Denis or Reims court of Charles the Bald, a grandson of Charlemagne. Its golden surface is set with pearls and precious jewels. Within the inscribed, squared cross, Christ appears in an attitude not far removed from that in the apse mosaic of San Vitale (FIG. 7-36), an example of the persistence of types and attitudes from Early Christian art into subsequent periods. Round him are seated the Four Evangelists, and there are four scenes from the life of Christ. In general, manuscript illumination provides the generative prototypes for ivory and metal work. Here the style of the figures echoes that of the *Ebbo Gospels* and the *Utrecht Psalter,* though it is modified by influences from other Carolingian schools. There is no trace of the intricate interlace patterns of Hiberno-Saxon art, though the complex and delicate floral filigree clustering about the border jewels and enamels recalls them and makes a foil for the classicizing figure style. At the centers of the Carolingian renovation the translated, classicizing style of Italy prevails, in keeping with the tastes and aspiration of the great Frankish emperor who fixed his admiring gaze upon the culture of the south.

Architecture

In his eagerness to reestablish the imperial past, Charlemagne also encouraged the revival of Roman building techniques, and in architecture, as in sculpture and painting, innovations made in the reinterpretation of earlier Roman-Christian sources became fundamental for Medieval designs. Perhaps "importation" is more appropriate here than "revival," since the Mediterranean tradition of stonemasonry could never have been more than an admirable curiosity to northern builders. Although northern Europe was dotted with Roman colonial towns that contained many large and impressive stone structures, the Germanic tribes had always relied upon their vast forests to supply them with building materials; northern architecture was a timber architecture and continued to be so well into the Middle Ages. The typical north European dwelling was a timber-frame structure (FIG. 8-11) that, in its essentials, has survived into our time. Its basic structural unit is the *bay,* which is constructed of four posts placed at the corners of a rectangle and interconnected and braced against each other with horizontal or oblique members. Such a unit is self-supporting; it can be roofed, and, depending upon the desired size of the building, it can be multiplied at will. Thus, the interior of such a structure is characterized by a repetition of identical units that move in orderly progression down the length of the building. The plan of such a building is related to the size and proportions of one of its bays in that the bay is the module, or basic unit of measurement, and the structure a multiple of that unit.

Charlemagne's adoption of southern building principles for the construction of his palaces and churches was epoch-making for the subsequent development of the architecture of northern Europe. For his models he went to Rome and Ravenna, one the former heart of the Roman empire that he wanted to revive, the other the long-term western outpost of Byzantine might and splendor that he wanted to emulate in his own capital at Aachen. Ravenna fell to the Lombards in 751 but was wrested from them

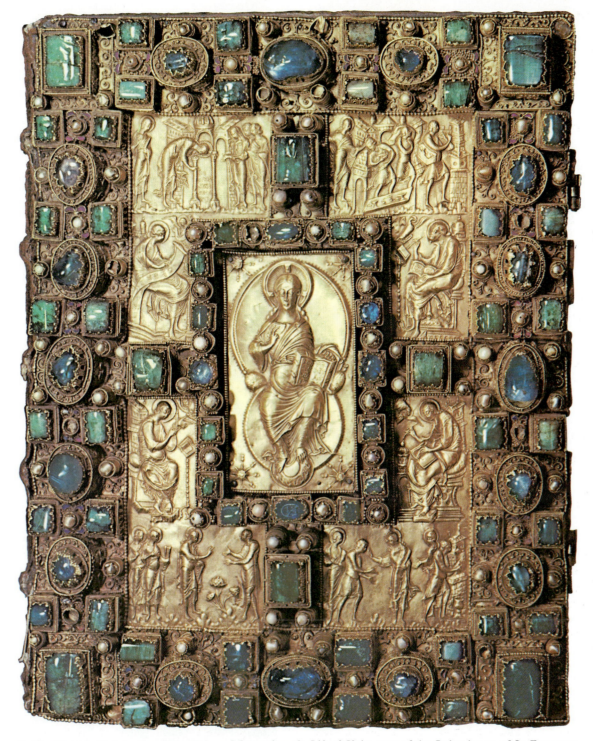

8-10 *Christ in Majesty, Four Evangelists, and Scenes from the Life of Christ,* cover of the Codex Aureus of St. Emmeram, *c.* 870. Gold set with pearls and precious stones, 17″ × 13″. Bayerische Staatsbibliothek, Munich.

only a few years later by the Frankish king, Pippin the Short, founder of the Carolingian Dynasty and father of Charlemagne. Pippin donated the former Byzantine exarchate to the pope and thus founded the papacy's temporal power, which was to last until the late nineteenth century. In 789 Charlemagne visited Ravenna, and historians have long thought that he chose one of its churches as the model for the chapel of his own palace at Aachen. But although its plan (FIG. 8-12) shows a resemblance to San

Vitale's (FIG. 7-31), recent study disproves a direct relation between the two buildings. The Aachen plan is simpler, for the apselike extensions reaching from the central octagon into the ambulatory have been omitted, so that the two main units stand in greater independence of one another. This solution may lack the subtle sophistication of the Byzantine building but gains in geometric clarity. A view of the interior of the Palatine Chapel (FIG. 8-13) shows that the "floating" quality of San Vitale has been converted into

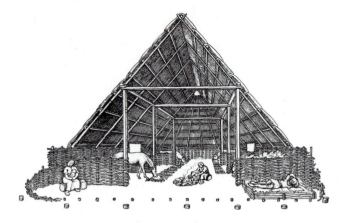

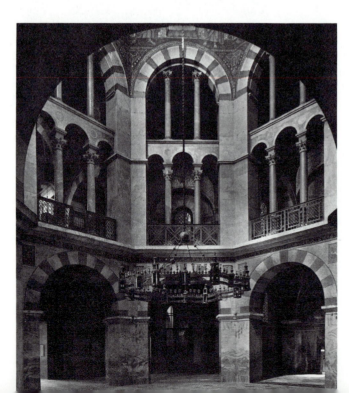

blunt massiveness and stiffened into solid geometrical form. The conversion of a complex and subtle Byzantine prototype into a building that expresses robust strength and clear structural articulation foreshadows the architecture of the eleventh and twelfth centuries and the style we call Romanesque.

It was, however, the basilican, not the central plan, that was to provide the basis for and determine the development of Romanesque architecture. Although several churches of the basilican type were built in northern Europe during the reign of Charlemagne, none has survived; nevertheless it is possible to reconstruct the appearance of some of them with fair accuracy. Some appear to have followed their Early Christian examples quite closely, as the abbey church of Fulda (begun in 802), which derives directly from Old St. Peter's and other Roman basilicas with transepts. But in other instances, Carolingian builders subjected the basilica plan to some very significant modifications, converting it into a much more complex organism.

The study of a most fascinating Carolingian document, the ideal plan for a monastery at St. Gall, Switzerland (FIG. 8-14), may give some insight into the motivations of the Carolingian planner. The monasteries, as we have seen, were of central importance in the revival of learning.

8-11 Conjectural reconstruction of an Iron Age house upon foundations excavated at Ezinge, Holland. (After W. Horn.)

Monasticism held that the most perfect Christian life should be led in seclusion, removed from the temptations of ordinary life. In 526, Benedict had adapted the earlier regulations to the needs of western Europe. This "Benedictine Rule," which won out over Irish monasticism and which demanded among other things vows of poverty, chastity, and obedience, provided the basic organization for most western monasteries. Daily life was rigidly controlled and each monastic community was self-sufficient. About 819 a schematic plan for such a community was copied from a lost original—probably designed by the abbot of Reichenau—and sent to the abbot of St. Gall as a guide in his planned rebuilding of that monastery. Near the center, dominating everything, was the abbey church, with the cloister (not unlike the early colonnaded atrium) at one side. Around the cloister were grouped the most essential buildings: chapter house (meeting room), dormitory, refectory, kitchen, and storage rooms. Other buildings—including an infirmary, school, guest house, bakery, brewery, and workshops—were grouped around this central core of church and cloister. That the scheme may have been meant to be more than an ideal and actually to have been built is indicated by Walter Horn's recent discovery that the original plan must have been laid out on a modular base of $2\frac{1}{2}$ feet and that parts or multiples of this module have been used consistently throughout the plan. Therefore, the width of the nave, indicated on the plan as forty feet, would equal sixteen $2\frac{1}{2}$-foot modules; the length of the monks' beds, $2\frac{1}{2}$ modules (6 feet, 3 inches); and the width of the paths in the vegetable garden, $1\frac{1}{4}$ modules.

Although the church is essentially a three-aisled basilica, it has features not found in any Early Christian churches.

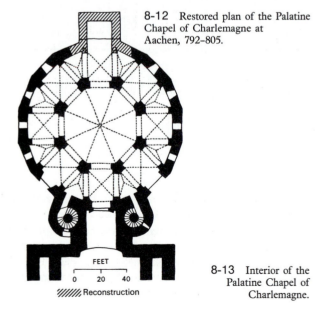

8-12 Restored plan of the Palatine Chapel of Charlemagne at Aachen, 792–805.

FEET
0   20   40
///// Reconstruction

8-13 Interior of the Palatine Chapel of Charlemagne.

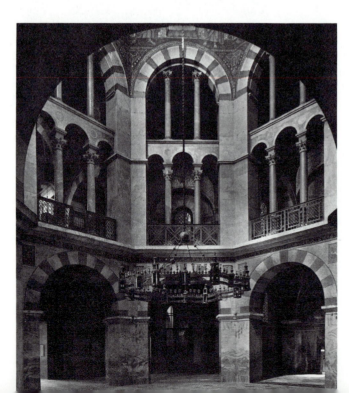

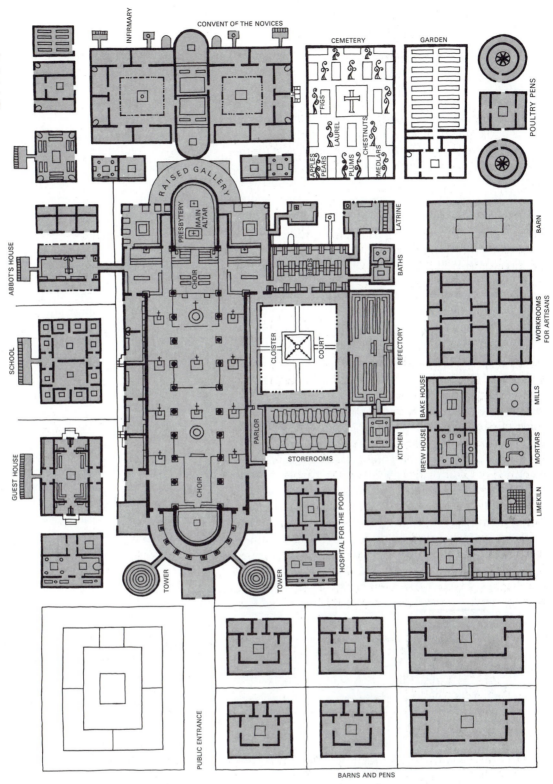

8-14 Schematic plan for a monastery at St. Gall, Switzerland, c. 819. (Redrawn after a ninth-century manuscript.)

The following labels appear on the plan:

INFIRMARY · CONVENT OF THE NOVICES · CEMETERY · GARDEN · POULTRY PENS · FIGS · LAUREL · APPLES · PEARS · PLUMS · CHESTNUTS · MEDLARS · RAISED GALLERY · PRESBYTERY · MAIN ALTAR · LATRINE · BARN · BEDS · BATHS · ABBOT'S HOUSE · CHOIR · CLOISTER · COURT · REFECTORY · WORKROOMS FOR ARTISANS · SCHOOL · BAKE HOUSE · MILLS · PARLOR · KITCHEN · BREW HOUSE · MORTARS · GUEST HOUSE · STOREROOMS · CHOIR · HOSPITAL FOR THE POOR · LIMEKILN · TOWER · TOWER · PUBLIC ENTRANCE · BARNS AND PENS

Most immediately noticeable, perhaps, is the addition of a second apse on the west end of the building. The origin and purpose of this feature have never been satisfactorily explained, but it remains a characteristic regional element of German churches to the eleventh century. Not quite as evident, but much more important for the subsequent development of church architecture in the north, is the fact that the transept has the same width as the nave. Early Christian builders had not been concerned with the proportional relationships among the various portions of their buildings, which they assembled only in accordance with the dictates of liturgical needs. On the St. Gall plan, however, the various parts of the building have been related to each other in a geometric scheme that ties them together into a tight and cohesive unit. Equalizing the widths of nave and transept automatically makes the area in which they cross (the *crossing*) a square. This feature is shared by most Carolingian churches. But the St. Gall planner has also taken the subsequent steps that become fundamental for the development of Romanesque architecture: He has used the crossing square as the unit of measurement for the remainder of the church plan. The arms of the transept are equal to one crossing square; there is one square between transept and apse; and the nave is 4½ crossing squares long. The fact that the aisles are half as wide as the nave integrates all parts of the church in a plan that is clear, rational, lucid, and extremely orderly.

The St. Gall plan reflects a Medieval way of thinking and is important for Romanesque art and architecture. As a guide for the builder of an abbey, it expresses the authority of the Benedictine Rule and serves as a kind of prototype. In the interest of clarity and orderliness the "rule" is worked out with systematic care. There is balancing of units and a kind of division and subdivision of the site. (This parallels the Medieval invention of that most con-

venient device, the division of books into chapters and subchapters.) The neat "squaring" that characterizes the scheme will especially dominate Romanesque architectural design together with the principle of the balance of clearly defined, simple units. The eagerness of the Medieval mind to explain the Christian faith in terms of an orderly, rationalistic philosophy built upon carefully distinguished propositions and well-planned arguments finds visual expression in the plan of St. Gall.

Although the rebuilding project for St. Gall was not consummated, the church of St. Riquier at Centula in northeast France gives some idea of what the St. Gall church would have looked like (FIG. 8-15). A monastery church like that of St. Gall, the now-destroyed St. Riquier was built toward the very end of the eighth century and therefore predates the St. Gall plan by approximately twenty years. The illustration, taken from a seventeenth-century copy of a much older drawing, shows a feature not indicated on the plan of St. Gall but most likely common to all Carolingian churches—multiple, integrated towers. The St. Gall plan shows only two towers on the west side of the church, but they stand apart from it in the manner of the Italian campaniles. If we assume a tower above the crossing, the silhouette of St. Gall would have shown three towers rising above the nave. St. Riquier had six towers (not all are shown in the illustration) built directly onto or rising from the building proper. As large, vertical, cubic and cylindrical masses, these towers rose above the horizontal roofline, balancing each other in two groups of three at each end of the basilican nave. Round stair towers on the west end provided access to the upper stories of the so-called *westwork* (entrance structure) and to the big, spired tower that balanced the similar one above the eastern crossing. Such grouping of three towers at the west, quite characteristic of churches built in the regions dominated by the Carolingians and their successors in German lands, probably foreshadows, in rudimentary form, the two-tower façades that were to become an almost universal standard in Late Romanesque and Gothic architecture. The towered westwork contained on the second floor a complete chapel flanked by aisles—a small upper church that could be used for parish services, the main floor of the building being reserved for the use of the clergy. (One must remember that this was a monastery church.) A gallery opened upon the main nave, and from it, on occasion, the emperor and his entourage could watch and participate in the service below. The plan of St. Riquier, as reconstructed (FIG. 8-16), shows an emphatic handling of the crossing square, which has been set apart from the rest of the building by massive arches. The dimensions of the square have been used once for the fore-choir, and again for the westwork chapel. But beyond that, the plan is not as fully developed as that of St. Gall. The aisles are only one third the width of the nave, the transept arms are about two thirds the

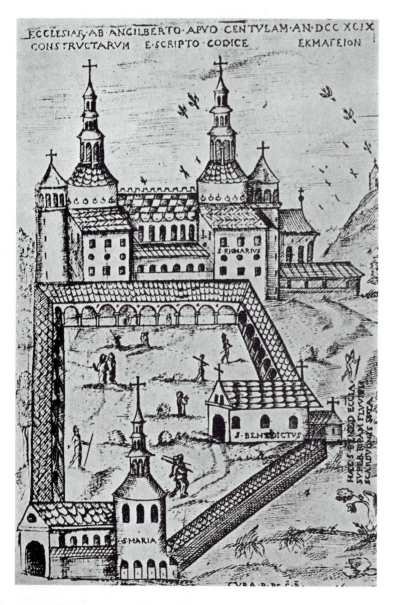

8-15 Monastery church of St. Riquier at Centula, France, *c.* 800. Engraving made in 1612 after a destroyed eleventh-century miniature.

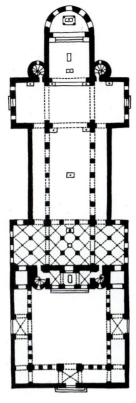

8-16 Plan of St. Riquier (reconstructed).

crossing square, and the length of the nave has not been related to either the crossing square or any other components of the building's plan. However, the St. Riquier design, particularly the silhouette with its multiple integrated towers, was highly influential, especially in Germany.

THE OTTONIAN PERIOD

Charlemagne's empire survived him by less than thirty years. Under his three grandsons, Charles the Bald, Lothar, and Louis the German, the Carolingian empire was partitioned by 843 into a western, a central, and an eastern area, very roughly foreshadowing the later sections France, Lorraine, and the Germanies. Intensified incursions of the Vikings in the west helped bring about the collapse of the Carolingians and the suspension of their great cultural effort. The breakup of the empire into weak kingdoms, ineffectual against the invasions, brought a time of darkness and confusion perhaps even deeper than the seventh and eighth centuries. The scourge of the Vikings in the west was complemented by invasions of the Magyars in the east and by the plundering and piracy of the Saracen corsairs in the Mediterranean. Only in the mid-tenth century did the eastern part of the former empire consolidate under the rule of a new Saxon line of German emperors called, after the names of the three most illustrious members of the family, the Ottonians. The three Ottos made headway against the invaders from the east, remained free from Viking depredations, and were able to found an empire that, nominally at least, became the successor to Charlemagne's Holy Roman Empire. The culture and tradition of the Carolingian period were not only preserved but advanced and enriched. The Church, which had become corrupt and disorganized, recovered in the tenth century under the influence of a great monastic reform encouraged and sanctioned by the Ottonians, who also cemented ties with Italy and the papacy. When the last of the Ottonian line, Henry II, died in the early eleventh century, the pagan marauders had become Christianized and settled, the monastic reforms had been highly successful, and there were signs of a cultural renewal that was destined soon to produce greater monuments than had been known since ancient Rome.

Architecture

Ottonian architects followed the direction of their Carolingian predecessors. St. Michael's, the abbey church at Hildesheim (FIG. 8-17) built between 1001 and 1031, retains the tower groupings and the westwork of St. Riquier, as well as its massive, blank walls. But the addition of a second transept and apse result in a better balancing of east and west units. The plan and section of St. Michael's (FIG. 8-18) clearly show the east and west centers of gravity, the nave being merely a hall that connects them. Lateral entrances leading into the aisles from north and south are additional factors making for an almost complete loss of the traditional basilican orientation toward the east. More refined and precise than St. Riquier, the marked-off crossing squares have now been used as a module for the dimensions of the nave, which is three crossing squares long and one square wide. This fact is emphasized visually by the placement of heavy piers at the corners of each square. These piers alternate with pairs of columns as wall supports and the resultant "alternate-support system" will become a standard feature of many of the Romanesque churches in northern Europe. Contrary to one view, the alternate-support system is not related to the development of Romanesque systems of vaulting. It made its first appearance in timber-roofed structures of the tenth century (such as St. Cyriakus at Gernrode, begun in 961) and appears to be the logical outcome of the Carolingian suggestion that the length of a building could be a multiple of the crossing square. Thus, the suitability of the alternate-support system to some Romanesque vaulting systems is only incidental; it seems to have been adopted not as a structural but as an esthetic device that furnishes visual proof of the geometrical organization of the building's plan. It has been suggested that the alternate-support system is an importation from the Eastern Empire, perhaps from Thessalonica (modern Saloniki). If so, it seems to have been adopted enthusiastically by northern architects who, it has been lately proposed, may have seen it as an ideal means of converting unbroken basilican interiors into

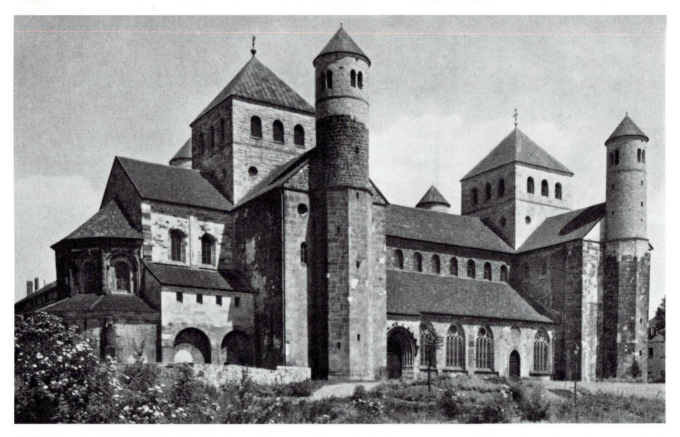

8-17 Abbey church of St. Michael at Hildesheim, Germany, *c.* 1001–1031. (Restored.)

8-18 Plan and section of St. Michael's.

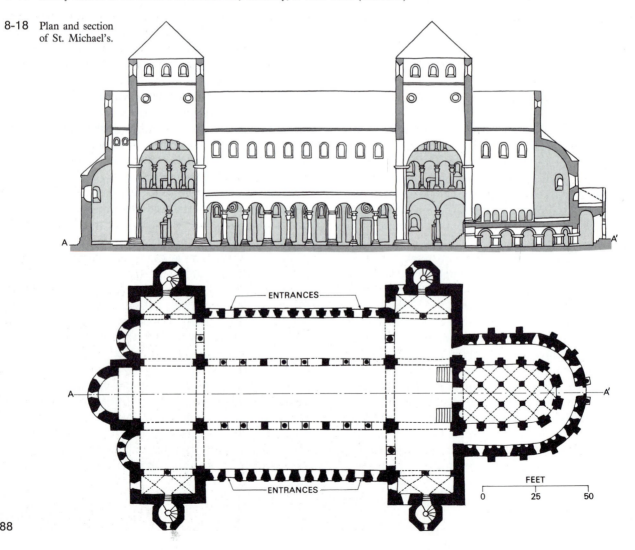

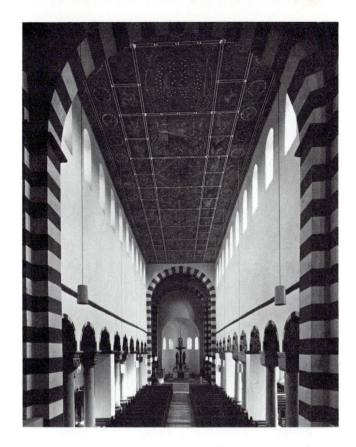

the modular units to which they were accustomed in their native timber architecture (see p. 282).

A view of the interior of St. Michael's (FIG. 8-19) shows the a-b-b-a rhythm of the alternating light and heavy wall supports. It shows as well that this rhythm is not yet reflected in the upper nave walls, that in fact it has not yet been carried further than the actual supports themselves. Although its proportions have changed—it has become much taller in relation to its width than a Roman basilica—the nave retains the continuous and unbroken appearance of its Early Christian predecessors. Only when the geometric organization of the church plan is fully reflected in the elevation of the nave walls and the interior space takes on the appearance of being composed of a number of vertical segments do we see a fully developed Romanesque interior.

Sculpture

St. Michael's is an important and highly refined transitional monument that fills a gap between the Carolingian and Romanesque styles. Its builder, Bishop Bernward, who made Hildesheim a center of learning, was not only skilled in affairs of state, but an eager scholar, a lover of the arts, and, according to his biographer, an expert craftsman and bronze-caster. His stay in Rome in 1001 as guest of the emperor, Otto III, whom he had tutored and whose friend he was, must have acquainted him with monuments like the Column of Trajan, which may have influenced the great column-like paschal candlestick he set up in St. Michael's; and the wooden doors of an Early Christian church, Santa Sabina, may have inspired the remarkable bronze doors he had cast for his splendid church. The doors were cast in a single piece, the first of their kind since ancient Rome. Carolingian sculpture, like most sculpture since antiquity, had been small art in ivory and metal; the St. Michael's doors anticipate the coming rein-

statement of large-scale sculpture in the Romanesque period. The style of the figures on the doors derives from Carolingian manuscript illumination but has an expressive strength of its own—once again a case of the form derived from a prototype becoming something new and firmly itself (FIG. 8-20). God is accusing Adam and Eve after their fall from grace. As he lays upon them the curse of mortality, the primal condemnation, he jabs his finger with the force of his whole body, the force concentrating in the gesture, the psychic focus of the whole composition. The frightened pair crouch not only to hide their shame but to escape the lightning bolt of the divine wrath. Each passes the blame, Adam pointing backward to Eve, Eve pointing downward to the deceitful serpent. The setting, the starkly

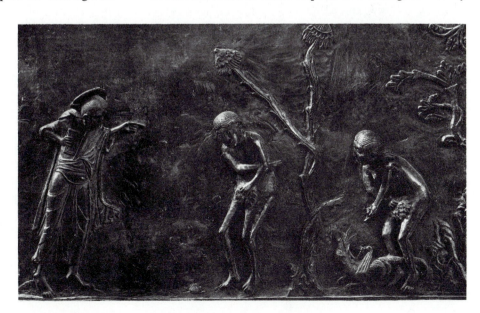

8-20 BISHOP BERNWARD, *Adam and Eve Reproached by the Lord,* 1015, from the bronze doors of St. Michael's. Approx. 23″ × 43″.

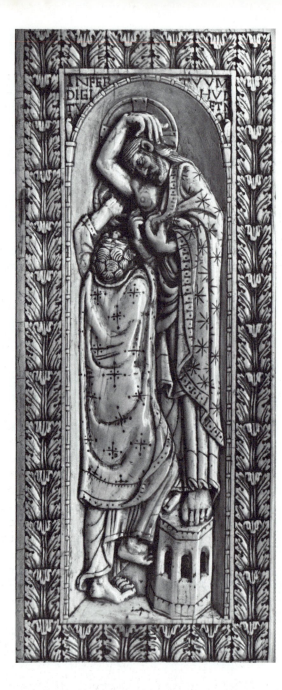

Thomas, who demands to feel the bodily wounds of the master he has seen crucified. In the panel he explores the wound in Christ's side in a kind of climbing, aggressive curiosity. Christ, his right arm raised to reveal his side, bends over Thomas in an attitude that wonderfully combines gentleness, benign affection, protectiveness, and sorrow. The figures are represented entirely in the context of emotion; the concentration on the single act of Christ's revelation to the doubter, the emotional vibrations that accompany the doubt, and the ensuing conversion of Thomas determine every line of the rendering. We are not aware of the presence here of the influence of a prototype; we seem to have before us an original work of great power.

Painting and Illumination

It must be assumed that by Ottonian times artists had become familiar enough with the Carolingian figurative modes to work with considerable independence, developing a functional, vernacular style of their own. A supreme example of this is an illumination in the *Lectionary of Henry II* (FIG. 8-22), in which an angel announces to the shepherds the birth of Christ. The angel has just alighted upon a hill, his wings still beating, and the wind of his landing agitates his draperies. He looms immense above the startled and terrified shepherds, filling the sky, and bends upon them a fierce and menacing glance as he extends his hand in the gesture of authority and instruction. Emphasized more than the message itself is the power and majesty of God's authority. The electric force of God's violent pointing in the Hildesheim doors is seen again here with the same pantomimic impact. Although the figure style may ultimately stem from the Carolingian school at Tours, the painters of the scriptorium of Reichenau (an island in Lake Constance in Switzerland) who produced the *Lectionary* have made of their received ideas something fresh and powerful; there is a new sureness in the touch that is epitomized by the way the draperies are rendered in a hard, firm line, the planes partitioned in sharp, often heavily modeled shapes. We saw this in Middle and Late Byzantine art, and indeed there was close connection between the Ottonian and Byzantine spheres. Yet, for the most part, the Ottonian artists went their own way, for Ottonian painting was produced for the court and for the great monasteries, for learned princes, abbots, and bishops, and thus had an aristocratic audience that could appreciate independent and sophisticated variations on inherited themes. While an illumination like the *Annunciation to the Shepherds* could by no means be called classical, there is a sculpturesque clarity about it, a strong, relief-like projection

flat ground, throws into relief the gestures and attitudes of rage, accusation, guilt, and fear; once again the story is given with all the simplicity and impact of skilled pantomime.

We have seen how the instinct for pantomimic pose and gesture guides the representations and narratives of Medieval art from the very beginning. Such pantomime, emphasized by telling exaggeration, appears in an ivory carving that surely is among the masterpieces of the art of the Middle Ages (FIG. 8-21). Only nine by four inches, the panel carries a composition of two intertwined figures beautifully adjusted to the space. The theme is that of the persuasion of Doubting Thomas when, after the Resurrection, Christ appears to his sorrowing disciples. All believe that he is truly Christ and truly risen except the skeptical

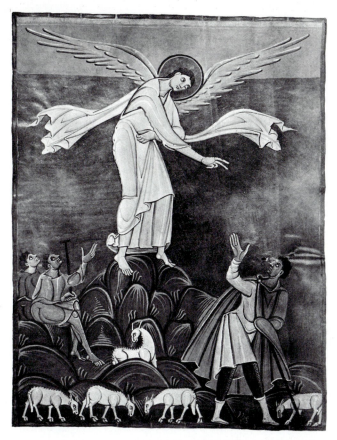

8-22 *The Annunciation to the Shepherds*, from the *Lectionary of Henry II*, 1002-1014. Approx. 13″ × 17″. Bayerische Staatsbibliothek, Munich.

and silhouette, that suggests not a hesitating approximation of misunderstood prototypes from antiquity but a confident, if unconscious, catching of the antique spirit. At the same time, the powerful means of expression of the *Annunciation* miniature imply an intensification of Christian spirituality, perhaps related to the broad monastic reforms of the tenth and eleventh centuries. With that force of expression goes a significantly new manner of fashioning the human figure in art, one that is not slavishly dependent upon prototypes, even while prototypes are exchanged and studied. Ottonian figurative art reveals a translation of prototypal material into a kind of ready idiom of forms and a native way of drawing. Although there are exceptions, for the most part Ottonian figures will have lost the old realism of the *Coronation Gospels* (FIG. 8-7), inherited from the antique, and will move with an abrupt, hinged, jerky movement not "according to nature" but nevertheless with sharp and descriptive expressiveness. This new manner will be passed on to the figurative artists of the Romanesque period. As the western European spoken and written languages emerge from the polyglot Latin-Germanic of the early centuries into the vernacular tongues we recognize today, so figurative art gradually develops out of the same kind of mixture of Latin, Germanic, and Celtic elements into a new, strong, and self-sufficient vernacular of representation.

A picture from the *Gospel Book of Otto III*, representing the emperor himself (FIG. 8-23), sums up much of what went before and points to what is coming. The emperor is represented enthroned under a canopy (the *baldachin*), holding the scepter and cross-inscribed orb that represent his universal authority. He is flanked by the clergy and the barons—the Church and the State—both aligned in his support. Stylistically remote, the picture still has a clear political resemblance to the Justinianic mosaic in San Vitale. It was the vestigial imperial ideal, awakened in the Frankish Charlemagne and preserved for a while by his Ottonian successors in Germany, that had given some partial unity to western Europe while the barbarians were settling down. This imperial ideal, salvaged from ancient Rome and bolstered by the experience of Byzantium, would survive long enough to give an example of order and of law to the barbarians; to this extent, ancient Rome lived on to the millennium. But native princes in England, France, Spain, Italy, and eastern Europe would aspire to a sovereignty outside the imperial Carolingian and Ottonian hegemony; staking their claims, they make the history of the Medieval power contests that lead to the formation of the states of Europe as we know them. In the illumination, Otto, sitting between the rival Church and State, represents the very model of the Medieval predicament that will divide Europe for centuries. The controversy of the Holy Roman Emperors with the popes will bring the German successors of the Ottonians to bitter defeat in the thirteenth century; and with that defeat, the authority of ancient Rome will come to an end. The Romanesque period that is to follow will in fact deny the imperial spirit that had prevailed for centuries. A new age is about to begin, and Rome, an august memory, will cease to be the deciding influence.

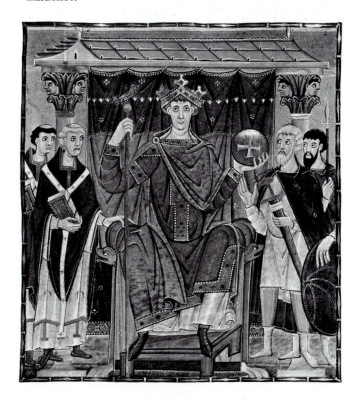

8-23 *Otto III Enthroned Receiving the Homage of Four Parts of the Empire* (with nobility and clergy), from *Gospel Book of Otto III*, 997-1000. Approx. 10″ × 14″. Bayerische Staatsbibliothek, Munich.

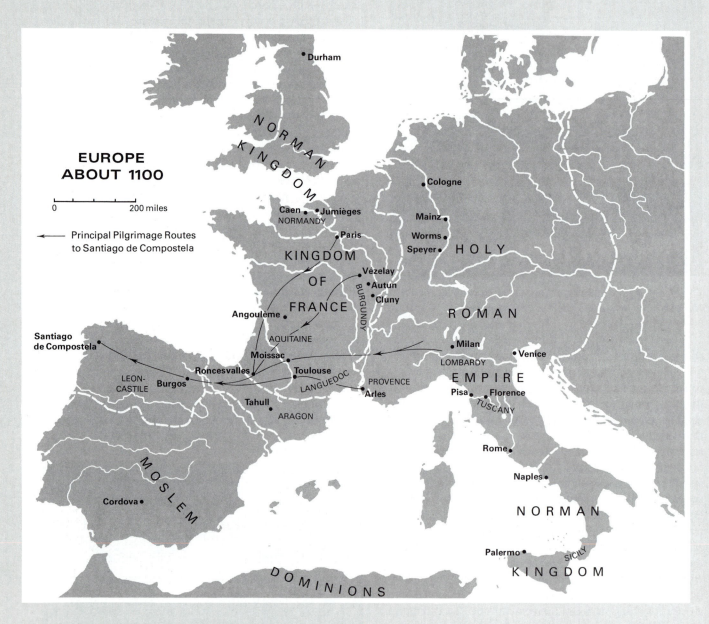

EUROPE
ABOUT 1100

0 ————— 200 miles

⟵ Principal Pilgrimage Routes
to Santiago de Compostela

Durham

NORMAN
KINGDOM

Cologne

Caen • Jumièges
NORMANDY

Mainz

Paris

Worms

Speyer

HOLY

KINGDOM

OF

FRANCE

Vézelay
Autun
Cluny

BURGUNDY

ROMAN

Angoulême

AQUITAINE

Milan

Venice

Santiago
de Compostela

Moissac

LOMBARDY

EMPIRE

Roncesvalles

Toulouse

PROVENCE

LEON-
CASTILE

Burgos

LANGUEDOC

Arles

Pisa

Florence

TUSCANY

Tahull

ARAGON

Rome

MOSLEM

Naples

Cordova •

MOSLEM

NORMAN

Palermo •

SICILY

DOMINIONS

KINGDOM

chapter nine

292

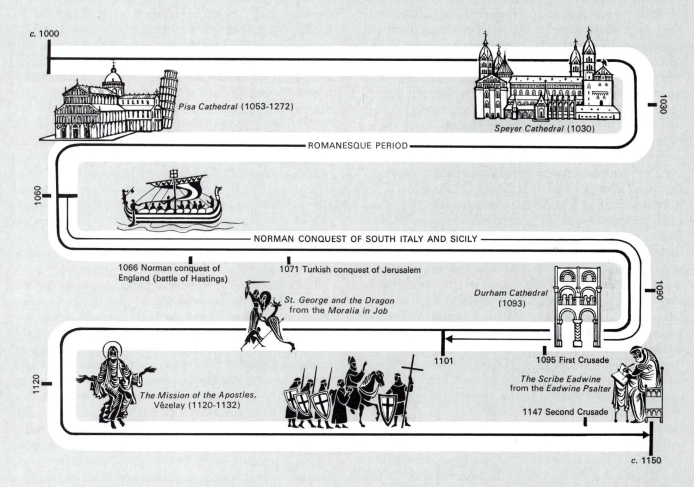

c. 1000

Pisa Cathedral (1053-1272)

Speyer Cathedral (1030)

1030

ROMANESQUE PERIOD

1060

NORMAN CONQUEST OF SOUTH ITALY AND SICILY

1066 Norman conquest of
England (battle of Hastings)

1071 Turkish conquest of Jerusalem

St. George and the Dragon
from the Moralia in Job

Durham Cathedral
(1093)

1090

1101

1095 First Crusade

The Scribe Eadwine
from the Eadwine Psalter

1120

The Mission of the Apostles,
Vézelay (1120-1132)

1147 Second Crusade

c. 1150

Romanesque Art

THE MID-ELEVENTH CENTURY marks a turning point in European history; Europe *as* Europe begins to emerge. The past was a boiling confusion of barbarian movements coalescing into settlements that aggregated into "empires" like the Carolingian and Ottonian, which had their spiritual and political roots in the memory of the Roman *imperium.* Now, although a Latin culture and tradition persist and are still accepted with reverence, the Medieval people are not so retrospective; they have new experiences and take new directions.

After the disintegration of the Carolingian state, when the successors to the imperializing Ottonians had begun to limit their concerns to Italy and the German duchies, numerous feudal political entities—petty and great, within and without the outlines of the old Frankish and Saxon "empires"—pursued their own interests and developed in their own ways. Two institutions gave them a certain coherence—the Christian Church and feudalism. If the descendants of the barbarians had anything in common, it was their Christianity above all else. Feudalism, which had its origins both in barbarian custom (see Chapter Eight) and in late Roman institutions, preserved a stability, but it was a stability of a local kind, being naturally antagonistic to broad, centralized government.

Essentially, feudalism was an economic system involving a complicated series of interpersonal relations, obligations, and services based on land tenure: One held a piece of land, a *fief,* and paid for it not in money but in service, often military. Feudal obligation led downward from a lord to his vassal to the lower orders of society and ultimately to the serf, who was bound to the land and to the unquestioning service of the lord. The lords or nobles held fiefs in various ways from each other or from an overlord, such as a king. Inevitably many of them became large landowners and so powerful that they ignored their obligations and defied their king. Their time was spent in petty wars to protect or to increase the extent of their holdings. The *château fort,* or castle, surrounded by walls and moats, was the symbol and seat of feudal authority; today the moldering ruins of these castles in the countrysides of Europe recall the modern visitor to an age when government was always visible, singular, personal, and absolute.

The Romanesque baron or knight, still in the heroic tradition of the Germanic hero, was loyal, defiant, and proud. However, being a Christian, he was without the deep barbarian fatalism of the earlier Saxons and Norse and hoped not only for immortal honor in battle (won as much by the power of religious faith as by his own strength and courage), but for life eternal in heaven. This was the mood—the psychological "set"—of the aristocratic, warring magnates who led the crusades and maintained the feudal system.

Monasticism, which reached its peak at the same time as feudalism, provided seclusion from the world, an assurance of salvation, and almost the only means of receiving an education. The history of monasticism, which, as we have seen, began in the Early Middle Ages, is essentially a series of reform movements. Since gifts and bequests to them were potent means of assuring salvation, monasteries grew wealthy. With wealth came luxury and laxness and recurrent reforms to combat them. The reforms led to the formation of new monastic orders. The two great Romanesque orders were the Cluniac and the Cistercian. The former, which especially fostered the arts, was founded early in the tenth century and had its main abbey at Cluny near Mâcon in France. Encouraged by the Ottonian emperors, it owed allegiance only to the pope in Rome and formed, with the vast number of its priories scattered all over Europe, a centrally organized administration in sharp contrast to the decentralizing tendencies of feudalism. The Cluniac reform, based on a liberal interpretation of St. Benedict's original rule, stressed intellectual pursuits, the study of music, and the cultivation of the other arts. The wealth and the vastness of the resources of the Cluniac order soon provoked still another reform, one that emphasized self-denial and the virtues of manual labor and gave rise to the Cistercian order, which also grew rapidly.

Thus, with feudalism and monasticism triumphant and replacing the emperors, the barons and the monastery clergy—the latter often themselves feudal lords—played a peculiarly cooperative role, and the feudal stratification of society into strictly separated classes was given religious sanction. Notwithstanding this cooperation, however, the chief conflict of the time was between the popes and the feudal principals not over the justice or injustice of the feudal system but over the question, Who is the supreme feudal lord; who is king?

There was great movement of population in the endless pilgrimages to innumerable shrines and in the Crusades (the first two of which belong to this period), which saw treks of thousands of people from western Europe to the Holy Land. The pilgrimage was a principal feature of Medieval Christian life. Travel to the distant shrine of a saint, whose spiritually powerful relics could there be venerated, was commonly enjoined as a penitential act upon which the salvation of the pilgrim depended; of such shrines, that of St. James (Santiago) at Compostela in Spain was the most famous in the West, outside of Rome itself. Travel, extremely dangerous in those turbulent times, became the duty and the hope of thousands. The Crusades were a militant expansion of the pilgrimages. Crusader and pilgrim were bound by similar vows and hoped not only to expiate sin and win salvation, but to glorify God and extend the power of the Church. Most important of the immediate results of the Crusades were the establishment of the Church as a leader of the people and the reopening of commerce with the great trading centers in the Near East.

Pisan ships carried the crusading barons to the Holy Land and brought back their bones. The Pisans prospered, as did the burghers of the towns that the barons left behind them and to whom they had given charters of liberty in return for financing their campaigns. Thus, the Crusades created subcurrents of independence: The towns got their charters, and a middle class of merchants and craftsmen grew up to countervail the power of feudal barons and the great monasteries. A growing city culture was quick to receive new impulses from abroad. The lines of commerce, often the arteries of ideas, conveyed new learning to Europe. The Crusades, destructive as they were, effected a new insight into Greek science and philosophy through contact with Islam, which had assimilated Greek culture much earlier. Within a century, the relatively limited knowledge possessed by the Carolingians and Ottonians was expanded to an enormous store. It was from this store that men would draw the materials and inspirations for renaissance after renaissance until, in the sixteenth century, a distinction would come to be made between pagan and Christian antiquity. Within this context of an emerging world, unique though shadowed with a tremendous past, the art called Romanesque appeared in the eleventh and twelfth centuries. It is a confident art, one that does not hesitate among alternatives and is sure even in the midst of its own changes.

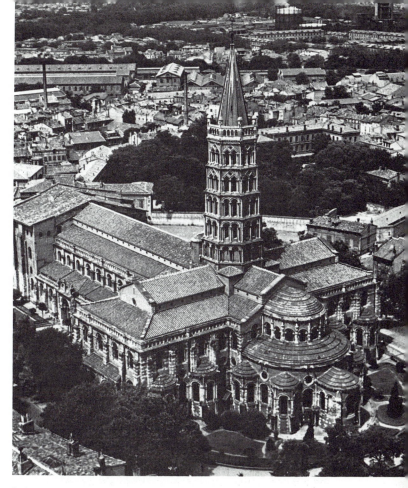

9-1   Aerial view of St. Sernin, Toulouse, c. 1080-1120.

ARCHITECTURE

"Romanesque" is a term first used in the nineteenth century to designate buildings whose round arches and blunt, heavy walls were supposed to bear some resemblance to ancient Roman architecture, just as the developing "Romance" languages were related to Latin. Although the Romanesque style varies widely and embraces numerous provincial differences within its two-century span, architectural historians now regard it as complete within itself and not as the imperfect antecedent of Gothic. Thus, despite its variety, Romanesque architecture is readily recognizable as such. An aerial view of the church of St. Sernin at Toulouse in the south of France (FIG. 9-1) shows certain features that appear in Romanesque buildings no matter how their arrangement differs. There is an overall blocky appearance, a grouping of large, simple, easily definable geometrical masses—rectangles, cubes, cylinders, and half-cylinders. The main masses are subdivided by enframing buttresses or colonnettes. Exterior wall surfaces, which had been plain and unadorned through the Ottonian period, now reflect the interior organization of the structure. This enlivening of formerly blank wall surfaces foreshadows the structural translucency that was to typify Gothic architecture.

The new demands of a people with religious as well as commercial reasons to travel shaped the new architecture. The building impulse, which became almost a Medieval

obsession, was noted by an eleventh-century monk, Raoul Glaber, who wrote:

> . . . there occurred, throughout the world, especially in Italy and Gaul, a rebuilding of church basilicas. Notwithstanding the greater number were already well established and not in the least in need, nevertheless each Christian people strove against the others to erect nobler ones. It was as if the whole earth, having cast off the old . . . were clothing itself everywhere in the white robe of the church.[1]

Glaber does not mention that a contributing cause of this eleventh-century building "obsession" may have been the widely felt relief and thanksgiving that the millennium— 1000 A.D.—did not bring an end to the world, as had been feared.

Great building efforts were provoked not only by the pilgrimages and the Crusades and the needs of growing cities, but by the fact (notably in Italy and France) that hundreds of churches had been destroyed during the depredations of the Northmen and the Magyars. Architects of the time seemed to see their fundamental problem in terms of providing a building that would have space for the circulation of its congregations and visitors and would be

[1] In E. G. Holt, ed., *Literary Sources of Art History* (Princeton: Princeton Univ. Press, 1947), p.3.

solid, fireproof, well lighted, and acoustically suitable. These, of course, are the necessities of any great civic or religious architecture, as we saw in ancient Rome, but in this case fireproofing must have been foremost in the builders' minds, for the wooden roofs of the pre-Romanesque churches of Italy, France, and elsewhere had burned fiercely and totally when set aflame by the marauders from north, east, and south in the ninth and tenth centuries. The memory was fresh in the victims' minds; the new churches would have to be covered with cut stone, and the structural problems arising from this need for a solid masonry were to help determine the "look" of Romanesque architecture.

Languedoc-Burgundy

St. Sernin was one of the churches constructed in the Cluniac-Burgundian style, which met the requirement for a stone ceiling by the use of a semicircular barrel vault above which was a timber-roofed loft. These churches dominated much of southern France and were closely related to those built along the pilgrimage road to Santiago de Compostela in northwest Spain. The plan of St. Sernin (FIG. 9-2) is of extreme regularity and geometric precision. The crossing square, flanked by massive piers and marked off by heavy arches, has been used as the module for the entire body of the church. In this *square schematism* each nave bay measures exactly one half and each square in the aisles one quarter of a crossing square, and so on throughout the building. The first suggestion of such a planning scheme is seen almost three centuries earlier in the St. Gall plan. Although St. Sernin is neither the earliest nor the only (perhaps not even the ideal) solution, it does represent a crisply rational and highly refined realization of the germ

of an idea first seen in Carolingian designs. A view of the interior (FIG. 9-3) shows that this geometric floor plan is fully reflected in the nave walls, which are articulated by half-columns that rise from the corners of each bay to the springing of the vault and are continued across the nave as transverse arches. Ever since Early Christian times, basilican interiors had been framed by long, flat walls between arcades and clerestories that enclosed a single, horizontal, unbroken volume of space. Now the aspect of the nave is radically changed so that it seems to be composed of numerous, identical, vertical volumes of space that have been placed one behind the other, marching down the length of the building in orderly procession. This segmentation of St. Sernin's interior space corresponds with and renders visual the geometric organization of the building's plan, and as noted above, is also reflected in the articulation of the building's exterior walls. The result is a structure in which all parts have been integrated to a degree unknown in earlier Christian architecture.

The grand scale of St. Sernin at Toulouse is frequent in Romanesque churches. The popularity of pilgrimages and of the cult of relics brought great crowds even to relatively isolated places, and large congregations were common at the shrines along the great pilgrimage routes and in the reawakening cities. Additional space was provided by increasing the length of the nave, by doubling the side aisles, and by building, over the inner aisle, upper galleries, or *tribunes*, the latter for overflow crowds on special occasions. Circulation was complicated, though, since the monks' choir often occupied a good portion of the nave. The extension of the aisles around the eastern end to make an ambulatory facilitated circulation, and the opening of the ambulatory (and often the transepts) into separate chapels (as at St. Sernin) provided more space for worshipers and for liturgical processions. Not all Romanesque churches were as large as St. Sernin, however, nor did every one have an ambulatory with radiating chapels, but such chapels are typical Romanesque features, especially when treated as separate units projecting from the mass of the building.

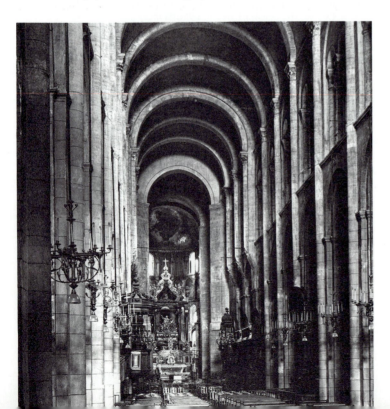

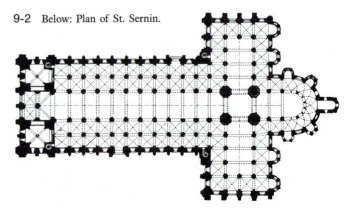

9-2 Below: Plan of St. Sernin.

9-3 Left: The nave of St. Sernin.

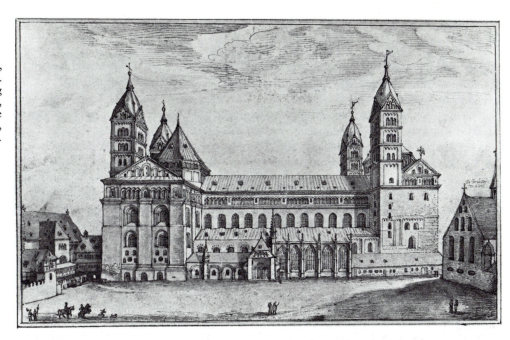

9-4 Speyer Cathedral, Germany, begun 1030. Pen-and-ink drawing by Wenzel Hollar, *c.* 1620. Graphische Sammlung Albertina, Vienna.

The continuous, cut-stone barrel (or tunnel) vaults at St. Sernin (FIG. 9-3) put constant pressure along the entire length of the supporting masonry. If, as in most instances, including St. Sernin (FIG. 9-2), the nave was flanked by side aisles, the main vaults rested on arcades, the main thrust being carried to the thick outer walls by the vaults that were over the aisles. In larger churches the tribune galleries and their vaults (in cross section, often a quadrant, embracing a 90-degree arc), were an integral part of the structure, buttressing the high vaults over the nave. The wall-vault system at St. Sernin is successful in its supporting function; its great scale provides ample space, and its squaring-off into cleanly marked bays, as well as the relief of wall and pier, are thoroughly Romanesque. But the system fails in one critical requirement—that of lighting: Because of the great thrust exerted by the barrel vault a clerestory was difficult to construct, and windows cut into the haunch of the vault would make it unstable. A more complex and efficient type of vaulting was needed; one might say that, structurally, the central problem of Romanesque architecture was the development of a masonry vault system that admitted light.

Romanesque architectural ingenuity in working toward this end had numerous experimental consequences that appear as a rich variety of substyles. We have already mentioned that one of the apparently confusing features of Romanesque architecture is the great variety of regional and local building styles, a variety that makes classification, coordination, and interpretation still very difficult for scholars. Ten or more types may be identified in France alone, each with its distinctive system of vaulting and its varying solutions to the lighting of the interior.

Among the numerous experimental solutions, the groin vault turned out to be the most efficient and flexible. The groin vault had been widely used by Roman builders, who saw that its concentration of thrusts at four supporting points would allow clerestory fenestration. The great Roman vaults were made possible by an intricate system of brick-and-tile relieving arches as well as by the use of concrete, which could be poured into forms and which solidified into a homogeneous mass. The technique of mixing concrete did not survive into the Middle Ages, however, and the technical problems of building groin vaults of cut stone and heavy rubble, which had very little cohesive quality, limited their use to the covering of small areas. But during the eleventh century, Romanesque masons, using cut stone joined by mortar, developed a groin vault of monumental dimensions, which, while still using heavy buttressing walls, eventually evolved into a self-sufficient skeletal support system.

Germany-Lombardy

The progress of vaulting craft can best be seen in two regions, Germany-Lombardy and Normandy-England. The cathedral of Speyer in the German Rhineland (FIG. 9-4) was begun in 1030 as a timber-roofed structure. When it was rebuilt by the emperor Henry IV between 1082 and 1106, it was covered with groin vaults. It thus may be one of the earliest fully vaulted Romanesque churches in Europe. Its exterior preserves the Ottonian tradition of balanced groups of towers east and west but adds to it a rich articulation of wall surfaces. A great many of the decorative features, such as the arcades under the eaves, the stepped arcade gallery under the gable, and the moldings marking the stages of the towers, may be of Lombard origin. So may be the inspiration for the groin vaults covering the aisles, since groin-vaulting on a small scale had been used by Lombard builders throughout the Early Middle Ages. The large groin vaults covering the nave (FIG. 9-6), however, probably the achievement of German masons, represent one of the most daring and successful vaulting enterprises of the time. (The nave is 45 feet wide, and the crowns of the vaults 107 feet high.) The plan (FIG.

9-5) shows that the west apse and the Ottonian lateral entrances have been given up, that the entrance has been moved back to the west end, and that the processional axis leading to the sanctuary has been reestablished. The marked-off crossing, covered by an octagonal dome, has obviously been used as the module for the arrangement of the building's east end. Since the nave bays are not square, use of the crossing as a unit is not so obvious. In fact, however, the length of the nave is almost exactly four times the crossing square, and every third wall-support marks off an area in the nave the size of the crossing; the aisles are half the width of the nave. Although the plan has some irregularities and has not been worked out as neatly and precisely as that of St. Sernin, the builders' intention to apply the square schematism is quite clear. Curiously, the alternate-support system, which is now carried all the way up into the vaults (FIG. 9-6), seems to be unrelated to the geometric facts of the plan. This discrepancy may be explained by the fact that the original building of 1030 was a timber-roofed structure and that the walls were articulated by a series of identical shafts that rose to enframe the clerestory windows (FIG. 9-7). The alternate-support sys-

tem was introduced in the 1080s (when the building was vaulted) perhaps partially to strengthen the piers at the corners of the large vaults and to provide bases for the springing of the transverse arches across the nave. That every other support was chosen to anchor a nave vault may simply have been because the walls were not as stable as the massive piers that carry the crossing dome, so that it would be safer to reduce each area to be vaulted by one third. The resultant bay arrangement, in which a large unit in the nave is flanked by two small units in each aisle, becomes almost standard in northern Romanesque architecture. Speyer's interior (FIG. 9-6) shows the same striving for height and has the same compartmentalized effect as that of St. Sernin. By virtue of the use of the alternate-support system, the rhythm of the Speyer nave is a little more complex, a little richer perhaps, and since each compartment is individually vaulted, the effect of a sequence of vertical blocks of space is even more convincing.

From Carolingian times, Rhineland Germany and Lombardy had been in close political and cultural contact, and it is generally agreed that the two areas cross-fertilized each other artistically. But no such agreement exists as to which source of artistic influence was dominant—the northern or the southern. The question, no doubt, will remain the subject of controversy until the date of the central monument of Lombard architecture—the church of Sant' Ambrogio in Milan—can be established unequivocally. Dates ranging from the tenth to the early twelfth century have been advanced for the present building (preceded by an earlier church that dated back to the fourth century), with the late eleventh and early twelfth centuries apparently most popular with architectural historians today.

9-5 Plan of Speyer Cathedral.

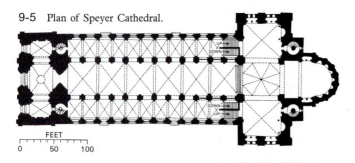

FEET
0   50   100

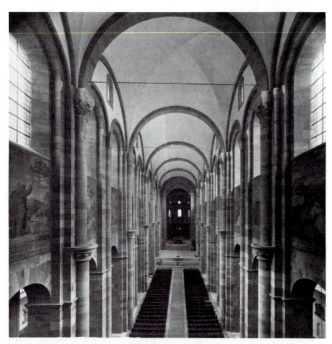

9-6 Interior of Speyer Cathedral.

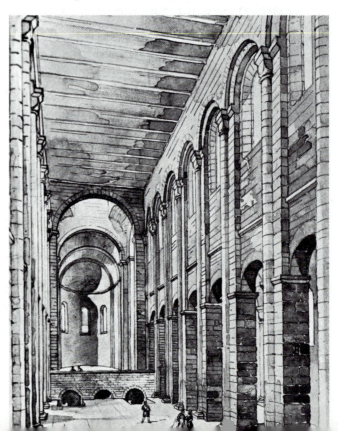

9-7 Reconstruction of the original nave of Speyer Cathedral, c. 1030–60.

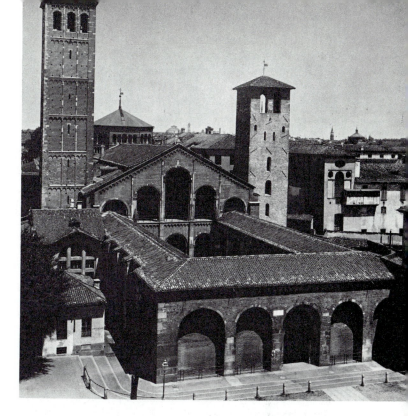

9-8 Sant' Ambrogio, Milan, late
eleventh to early twelfth centuries.

9-9 Plan of Sant' Ambrogio.

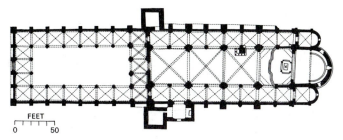

Whether or not a prototype, Sant' Ambrogio remains a remarkable building. As shown in FIG. 9-8, it has an atrium (one of the last to be built); a two-story narthex pierced by arches on both levels; two towers joined to the building; and, over the east end of the nave, an octagonal tower that recalls the crossing towers of German churches. Of the façade towers, the shorter one dates back to the tenth century, while the taller north tower was built during the twelfth. The latter is a sophisticated and typical example of Lombard tower design; it is articulated by pilasters and shafting and divided, by means of corbel tables (horizontal projections resting on corbels), into a number of levels, of which only the topmost (the bell chamber) has been opened by arches.

In plan (FIG. 9-9) Sant' Ambrogio is three-aisled and without a transept. The square schematism has been applied with consistency and greater precision than at Speyer, each bay consisting of a full square in the nave, which is flanked by two small squares in each aisle, all covered with groin vaults. The main vaults are slightly domical, rising higher than the transverse arches, and the last bay is covered by an octagonal dome that provides the major light source (there is no clerestory) for the otherwise rather dark interior (FIG. 9-10). The geometric regularity of the plan is perfectly reflected in the emphatic alternate-support system, in which the light supports are interrupted at the gallery level while the heavy ones rise to support the main vaults. These ponderous vaults have supporting arches along their groins and are sometimes claimed to be the first examples of rib-vaulting (see p. 318); in fact, however, these vaults are solidly constructed groin vaults that have been strengthened by diagonal ribs.

The dating of the Sant' Ambrogio vaults remains controversial. Most scholars seem to feel that they were not built until after 1117, when a severe earthquake caused great damage to the existing building. If so, the Speyer vaults would be earlier than those of Sant' Ambrogio, and the inspiration and technical knowledge for the construction of groin vaults of this size would seem, then, to have come from the north. But such possible influence did not affect the proportioning of the Milanese building, which does not

aspire to the soaring height of the northern churches. Sant' Ambrogio's proportions are low and squat and remain close to those of Early Christian basilicas. As we will see, Italian architects never—not even during the height of the Gothic period—accepted the verticality found in northern architecture.

The fame of German architecture rests on its achievements in the eleventh and early twelfth centuries. After the mid-twelfth century it made no major contribution to architectural design. The architectural statements at

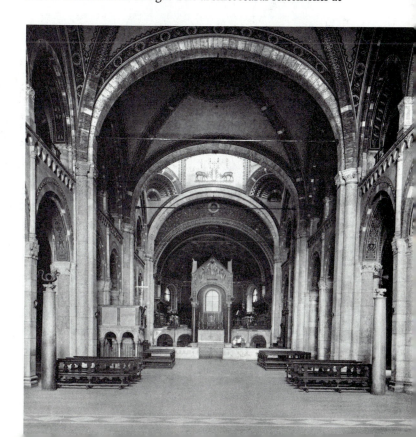

9-10 Interior of Sant' Ambrogio.

Speyer were repeated at Worms and Mainz and other, later churches. German builders were content with refining their successful formula; beyond that, they tended to follow the lead of the more adventurous and progressive Franks and Normans.

Normandy-England

The predatory pagan Vikings settled in northwest France after their conversion to Christianity in the tenth century and almost at once proved themselves skilled administrators and builders. With astounding rapidity they absorbed the lessons to be learned from Ottonian architecture and went on to develop the most progressive of the many Romanesque styles and the one that was to become the major source in the evolution of Gothic architecture. The church of St. Étienne at Caen in Normandy is generally

9-11 West façade of St. Étienne, Caen, begun c. 1067.

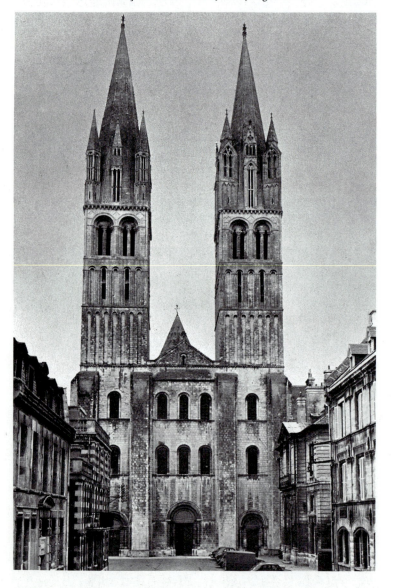

considered to be the master model of Norman Romanesque architecture. It was begun by William of Normandy ("the Conqueror") in 1067 and must have been completed when he was buried there in 1087. The west façade (FIG. 9-11) is a striking design that looks forward to the two-tower façades of later Gothic churches. Four large buttresses divide it into three bays that correspond to the nave and aisles in the interior. There is also a triple division of the towers above their buttresses and a progressively greater piercing of their walls from lower to upper stages. The spires are a later (Gothic) feature. The tripartite division is employed throughout the façade, both vertically and horizontally, organizing it into a close-knit, well-integrated design that reflects the careful and methodical planning of the entire structure. Like the cathedral of Speyer, St. Étienne was originally planned to have a wooden roof, but from the beginning the walls were articulated in an alternating rhythm (simple half-columns alternating with shafts attached to pilasters) that mirrors the precise square schematism of the building's plan (FIGS. 9-12 and 9-13). This alternate-support system was effectively utilized some time after 1110—significantly later than at Speyer or Milan—when it was decided to cover the nave with vaults. Its original installation, however, must have been motivated by esthetic rather than structural concerns. In any event, the alternating compound piers soar all the way to the springing of the vaults, and their branching ribs divide the large, square vault compartments into six sections, making a so-called sexpartite vault (FIGS. 9-12). These vaults, their crowns slightly depressed to avoid the "domed-up" effect of those at Sant' Ambrogio, rise high enough to make an efficient clerestory; they are also viewed as some of the earliest true *rib vaults*, in which the diagonal and transverse ribs compose a structural skeleton that partially supports the as yet fairly massive paneling between them. Rib-vaulting was to become universal practice during the Gothic period, and its development by Norman builders must be rated as one of the major structural innovations of the Middle Ages. There are other elements in St. Étienne that point to the future: The complex piers, their nuclei almost concealed by attached pilasters and engaged columns, forecast the Gothic "cluster-pier"; and the reduction in interior wall surfaces that resulted from use of very large arched openings anticipates the bright curtain walls of Gothic architecture. In short, St. Étienne at Caen is not only a very carefully designed structure but a highly progressive one in which the Romanesque style begins to merge into the Early Gothic.

The conquest of Anglo-Saxon England in 1066 by William of Normandy began a new epoch in English history; in English architecture it signaled the importation of Norman building and design methods. The cathedral of Durham in northern England, begun in 1093, was apparently designed for vaulting at the outset. As with most Romanesque churches in England, it was subjected to many later

9-12 Interior of St. Étienne, vaulted *c.* 1115–20.

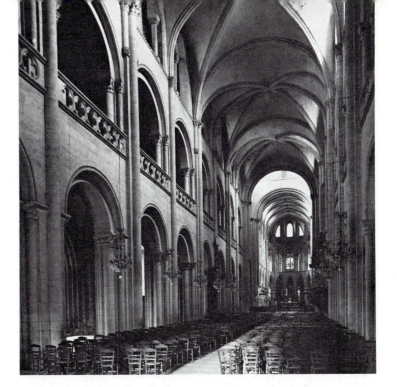

9-13 Plan of St. Etienne.

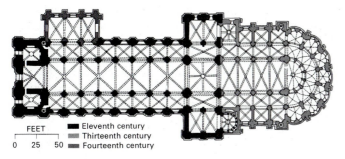

FEET
0   25   50

■ Eleventh century
■ Thirteenth century
■ Fourteenth century

alterations that, in this case, fortunately were largely confined to the exterior; the interior (FIG. 9-14) has its original severe Romanesque appearance. Ambitious in scale—comparable to both St. Sernin at Toulouse and St. Étienne at Caen—its 400-foot length compares favorably with that of the great imperial cathedral of Speyer. With the latter it also shares its reliance upon mass for stability. But unlike Speyer, this building was conceived from the very beginning as a completely integrated skeleton in which the vaults stood in intimate and continuous relation to the vertical elements of the compound piers that support them. At Durham the alternate-support system is interpreted with blunt power and more emphasis, perhaps, than in any other Romanesque church. Large, simple pillars ornamented with abstract designs—diamond, chevron, and cable patterns descended from the metalcraft ornamentation of the migrations—alternate with compound piers that carry the transverse arches of the vaults. The pier-vault relationship could scarcely be more visible or the structural rationale of

the building better expressed. The plan (FIG. 9-15), typically English in its long, slender proportions and the strongly projecting transept, does not develop the square schematism with the same care and logic as that of Caen. But the rib vaults of the choir (1104) are the earliest in Europe, and, when they were combined with slightly pointed arches in the western parts of the nave (before 1130), the two key elements that were to determine the structural evolution of Gothic architecture were brought together for the first time. Only the rather massive construction and the irregular division into seven panels prevent these vaults from qualifying as Early Gothic structures.

Among the numerous regional Romanesque styles of architecture it is the northern—more specifically, the Nor-

9-14 The nave of Durham Cathedral, England, begun *c.* 1093 (view facing east).

9-15 Plan of Durham Cathedral.

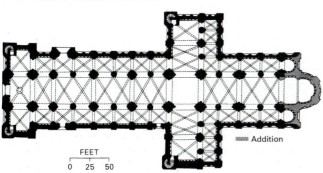

FEET
0   25   50

▨ Addition

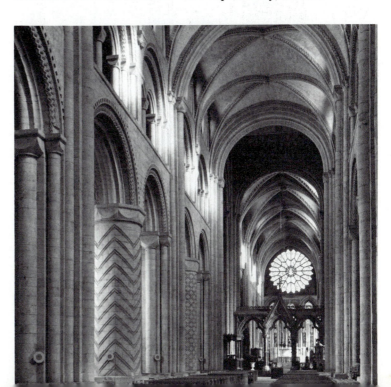

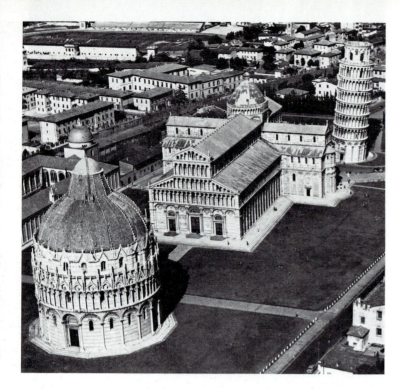

man—style that will indirectly influence the development of the Gothic; no other style had as great a potential for evolution.

Tuscany

Italy south of the Lombard region retained its ancient traditions and for the most part produced Romanesque architecture less structurally experimental than that of Lombardy. The buildings of Tuscany seem to adhere more

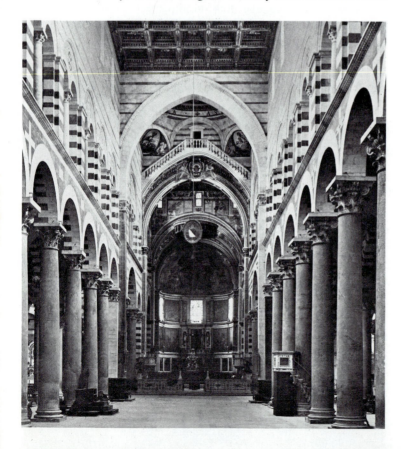

closely than those of any other region to the traditions of the Early Christian basilica. The cathedral group of Pisa (FIG. 9-16) manifests, in addition to these conservative qualities, those of the great classical "renaissance" of the late eleventh and twelfth centuries, when architects, craftsmen, poets, and philosophers again confronted classical-Christian prototypes and interpreted them in an original yet familiar way. The cathedral is large, five-aisled, and one of the most impressive and majestic of all Romanesque churches. At first glance, it resembles an Early Christian basilica, but the broadly projecting transept, the dome over the crossing, the rich marble incrustation, and the multiple arcade galleries of the façade soon distinguish it as Romanesque. The interior (FIG. 9-17) also at first suggests the basilica, with its timber roof rather than vault (originally the rafters were exposed as in Early Christian basilicas), nave arcades, and classical (imported) columns flanking the nave in unbroken procession. Above these columns is a continuous, horizontal molding on which rest the gallery arcades. The gallery, of course, is not a basilican feature but is of Byzantine origin. There are other divergences from the basilica, such as the relatively great verticality and, at the crossing, the markedly unclassical pointed arch, which was probably inspired by Islamic architecture. The striped incrustation, produced by alternating dark green and cream-colored marble, provides a luxurious polychromy, which becomes a hallmark of Tuscan Romanesque and Gothic buildings. The leaning campanile, the result of a settling foundation, tilted from the vertical even while it was being built and now inclines some sixteen perilous feet out of plumb at the top. Round, like the Ravenna campaniles, it is much more elaborate, and its stages are marked by graceful, arcaded galleries that repeat the motif of the cathedral's façade and effectively relate the tower to its mother building. Although the baptistry, with its partly remodeled Gothic exterior, may strike a slightly discordant note, the whole composition of the three buildings, with the adjacent Campo Santo (cemetery), makes one of the handsomest ensembles in the history of architecture and expresses dramatically the new building age that was made possible by the prosperity enjoyed by the busy maritime cities of the Mediterranean.

Another Tuscan church, San Miniato al Monte (FIG. 9-18) in Florence, recalls Early Christian architecture, although the wall arcading and its elaborate, geometrical incrustation in colored marbles make for a rich ornamental effect foreign to the austere exteriors of the earlier buildings. Retrospective as San Miniato may appear externally, the interior (FIG. 9-19) is another matter. Though the church is timber-roofed, as are most Tuscan Roman-

9-17 The nave of the cathedral of Pisa.

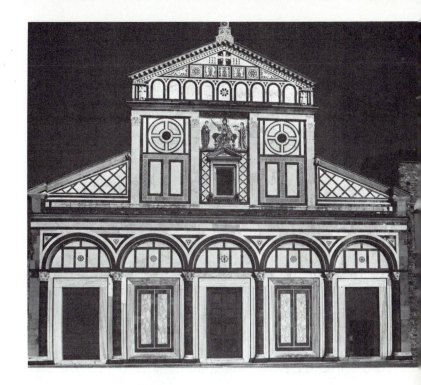

esque churches, the nave is divided into three equal compartments by *diaphragm arches* that rise from compound piers. The piers alternate with simple columns in a–b–b–a rhythm that recalls St. Michael's in Hildesheim. The diaphragm arches, which appear here for the first time (before 1060), have multiple functional and esthetic purposes: They brace the rather high, thin walls; they provide fire-breaks within the wooden roof structure; and they compartmentalize the basilican interior in the manner so popular with most Romanesque builders. Antique, or neo-Antique, motifs appear in the capitals as well as in the incrustation, expressing again the persistence of the classical tradition in Tuscany.

Aquitaine

Influences criss-crossed in Romanesque architecture, helping to diversify it and creating exotic hybrids. In the region of Aquitania in southwest France, for instance, it became customary to roof the churches with domes, reflecting the influence of Byzantium, Armenia, and Cyprus, the crusaders' bridge between East and West. Curiously, most of these Aquitanian churches mate the dome with a longitudinal plan to which, at first glance, it seems ill suited. In the typical Aquitanian church, a longitudinal, aisle-less nave is covered by a sequence of domes, which, in turn, are usually covered by a pitched wooden roof. The result turns out to be highly practical, as the pendentive-supported domes require much less buttressing than, for instance, continuous barrel vaults. Also, the system automatically produces the cherished compartmentalized effect mentioned above. Although they never aimed at the soaring height of northern Romanesque structures, these Aquitanian domed churches not only represent an almost perfect fusion of geometric plan with elevation, but also are visually most effective, clearly exhibiting the functions of all their structural parts (FIG. 9-20).

From about 1050 on, the old dependence of the pre-Romanesque—Carolingian and Ottonian—upon Late Antique and Early Christian design concepts fades gradually, though never completely. Romanesque architecture develops a number of clear characteristics: the square schematism, the alternating-support system, and the increased relief and depth of walls and piers as they connect with the vaults above. The Romanesque architect conceives a building in terms of the geometric relation of its parts, a view basically different from that of the Early Christian architect, who never thought of large units as related geometrically and who thought of the wall not as essentially a structural element, but as a surface to receive applied decoration.

SCULPTURE

For Medieval art the first definite relation of architecture and sculpture appears in the Romanesque style. Figurative sculpture, confined for centuries to small art, flowers again in the new Romanesque churches of the mid-eleventh century. The rich profusion of sculpture and something of its nature may be guessed from Bernard of Clairveaux's famous tirade against it, written in 1127:

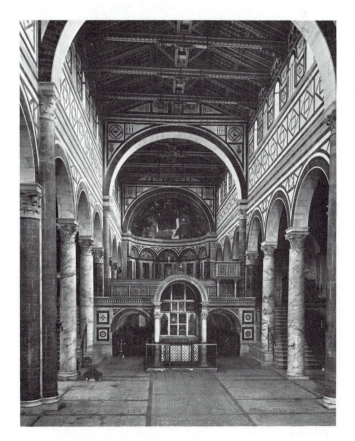

9-19 Interior of San Miniato al Monte.

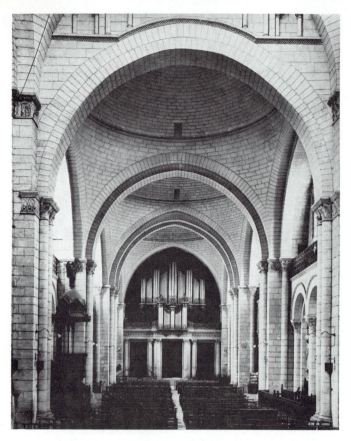

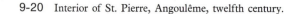

important Romanesque achievements. As stone buildings began to rise again, so did the impulse to decorate parts of the structure with relief carving in stone. It was to be expected that the artists should turn for inspiration to surviving Roman sculpture and to sculptural forms such as ivory carving or metalwork; it is obvious that they also relied upon painted figures in manuscripts. But these Romanesque artists developed their own attitude toward ornamental design and its relation to architecture. At first this relation was somewhat random and haphazard; one put the sculpture wherever there seemed to be a convenient place. A little later, the portals of the church seemed the appropriate setting, both for religious reasons and for the practical matter of display. As Romanesque sculpture turns into Gothic the statuary of the portals becomes integrated with the design of the whole façade, following the lines of the architecture. An example of the earlier, random placement is a figure of Christ in majesty, set into the wall of the ambulatory of St. Sernin at Toulouse (FIG. 9-21). It clearly shows that its source is some prototype made of metal, perhaps a book cover like that of the Codex Aureus of St. Emmeram) (FIG. 8-10). The figure has the bulge of

I say naught of the vast height of your churches, their immoderate length, their superfluous breadth, the costly polishings, the curious carvings and paintings . . . . [Men's] eyes are feasted with relics cased in gold, and their purse-strings are loosed. They are shown a most comely image of some saint, whom they think all the more saintly that he is the more gaudily painted. Men run to kiss him, and are invited to give; there is more admiration for his comeliness than veneration for his sanctity. Hence the church is adorned with gemmed crowns of light . . . . candelabra standing like trees of massive bronze, fashioned with marvellous subtlety of art, and glistening no less brightly with gems than with the lights they carry. . . . O vanity of vanities, yet no more vain than insane! The church is resplendent in her walls, beggarly in her poor; she clothes her stones in gold and leaves her sons naked . . . . in the cloister, under the eyes of the Brethren who read there, what profit is there in those ridiculous monsters, in that marvellous and deformed comeliness, that comely deformity? To what purpose are those unclean apes, those fierce lions, those monstrous centaurs, those half-men, those striped tigers, those fighting knights, those hunters winding their horns? Many bodies are there seen under one head, or again, many heads to a single body. . . . For God's sake, if men are not ashamed of these follies, why at least do they not shrink from the expense?[2]

As we have noted, stone sculpture had almost disappeared from the art of western Europe during the eighth and ninth centuries. The revival of the technique is one of the most

[2]Holt, *Literary Sources of Art History* pp. 17-18.

9-21 *Christ in Majesty,* late eleventh century, from the ambulatory of St. Sernin, Toulouse.

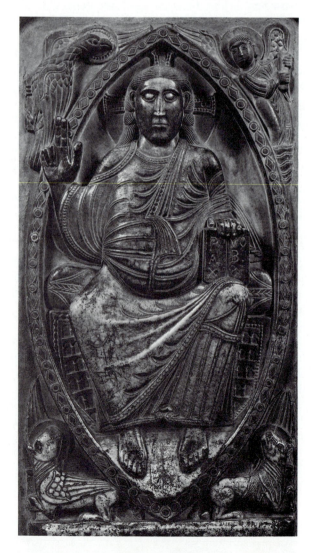

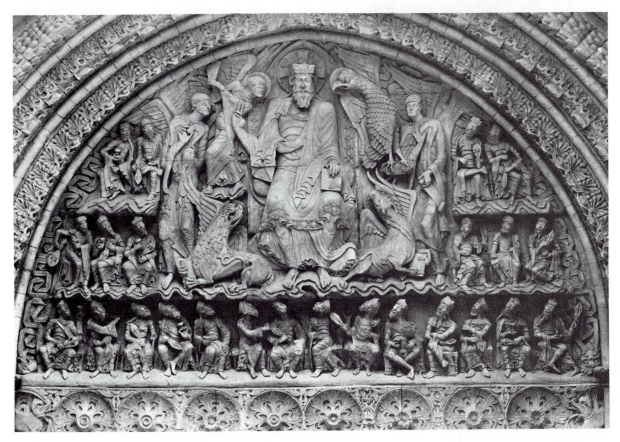

9-22 Tympanum of the south portal of St. Pierre, Moissac, c. 1115–35.

metal hammered out from behind, as in the *repoussé* method, and even here in stone one senses the gloss of smooth metal. The signs of the Evangelists at the four corners square off the book-cover-like design and remind one of the corner screws that fix the plate to the book. As yet there is no relation between the relief and its architectural setting; it is "portable," like a work of craft art, and could find its place on any wall. In the later mode the architectural limits of the parts of a portal or the shape of a capital were respected as frames to which the sculptors accommodated their work. A typical Romanesque portal can be seen in the façade of St. Trophime at Arles in the south of France (FIG. 9-27). Architectural elements of such a portal are: jambs, lintel, semicircular tympanum (beneath the arches or archivolts) and in some instances a pier, or *trumeau*, in the middle of the doorway.

The stirring of the peoples in Romanesque Europe, the Crusades, the pilgrimages, and the commercial journeyings brought a slow realization that Europeans were of the same religion, even if of different ethnic stock. The reception of hitherto unknown documents of Greek thought and learning strongly influenced theology, bringing to it, along with new and deep challenges, a kind of order and concentration. There can be little doubt that theologians dictated the subjects of the Romanesque portals; it was just as important to have the right subjects carved in the right places as to have the right arguments rightly arranged in a theological treatise. The apocalyptic vision of the Last Judgment,

appalling to the imagination of twelfth-century man, was represented conspicuously at the western entrance portal as an inescapable reminder to all who entered.

The semicircular tympanum of the portal of Moissac shows the Second Coming of Christ as King and Judge of the World (FIG. 9-22). As befits his majesty, Christ is centrally enthroned, reflecting a rule of composition we have seen followed since Early Christian times. The signs of the Evangelists flank him: on his right side the angel of Matthew and the lion of Mark; on his left, the eagle of John and the ox of Luke. To one side of each pair of signs is an attendant angel holding scrolls upon which to record the deeds of mankind for judgment. The figures of crowned musicians are the twenty-four music-making elders who accompany Christ as the kings of all this world and make music in his praise; each turns to face him, much as would the courtiers of a Romanesque monarch in attendance on their lord. The central group, reminiscent of the heraldic groupings of ancient Mesopotamian art, is set among the elders, who are separated into three tiers by two courses of wavy lines that symbolize the clouds of heaven.

There are as many variations within the general style of Romanesque sculpture as in Romanesque architecture, and the figures of the Moissac tympanum constitute no exception. Yet there are elements here familiar in painting and sculpture throughout western Europe in the eleventh and twelfth centuries. The extremely elongated figures of the recording angels; the curious, cross-legged, dancing pose

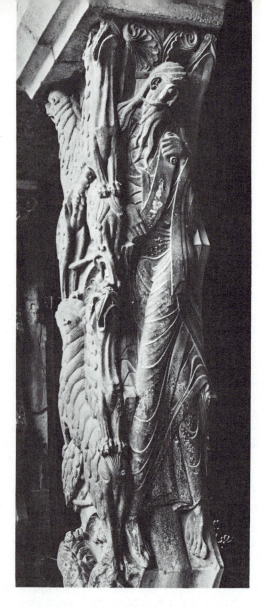

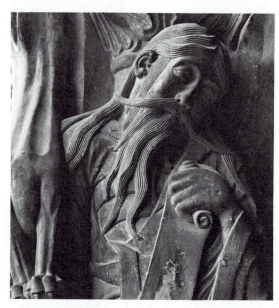

of the angel of Matthew; and the jerky, hinged movement are characteristic in general of the emerging vernacular style of representing the human figure. Earlier Carolingian, Ottonian, and Anglo-Saxon manners diffused and interfused to produce the now sure, unhesitating style-languages of the Romanesque. The zigzag and dovetail lines of the draperies (the linear modes of manuscript painting are everywhere apparent), the bandlike folds of the torsos, the bending back of the hands against the body, and the wide cheekbones (reminiscent of the ancient Archaic mask) are also common features of this new, cosmopolitan style.

A triumph of the styles is the splendid figure of the prophet Jeremiah (by some identified as Isaiah) carved in the trumeau of the Moissac portal (FIG. 9-23). His position below the apparition of Christ as the apocalyptic Judge is explained by his prophecy—recalled by his scroll—of the end of the world, when "ruin spreads from nation to nation." He is compressed in the mass of the trumeau behind roaring, interlaced lions of the kind familiar not

only in barbarian art but in the art of ancient Mesopotamia and Persia and Islamic Spain. (The totemistic animal is never far from the instinct and imagination of the Medieval artist and certainly not far from Medieval man in general; kings and barons are often named by association with animals thought the most fiercely courageous—for example, Richard the Lion-heart, Henry the Lion, and Richard III of England, whose heraldic animal was the wild boar. It is not unthinkable that the Medieval artist, with millennia of animal lore and ornament in his background, would associate animal strength with architecture, the animal body being thought of as providing support and symbolizing the very forces locked in the architectural fabric. The sphinxes and winged monsters at the palace gates in the ancient world—at Boghazköy, Khorsabad, Persepolis, and Mycenae—are the ancestors of the interlaced lions at Moissac.) The figure of Jeremiah is very tall and thin, in the manner of the angels of the tympanum, and, like the angel of St. Matthew, he executes a cross-legged step that repeats the criss-crossing of the lions. There is as yet no representation of movement in terms of the actual structure of the body or its natural proportions. At this beginning of a new epoch in the history of sculpture, movement is a kind of grotesque, mechanical dance. The placing of the parts of the body is dependent upon the architectural setting, the sculptor's interpretation of his carved or painted model, or the vocabulary of the prevailing vernacular styles; the artist's originality could also play a large part, as in this case. The folds of the drapery are incised in flowing, calligraphic line that ultimately derives from manuscript illumination and here plays gracefully around the elegant figure.

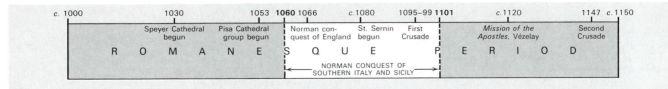

c. 1000	1030	1053	**1060** 1066	c. 1080	1095–99	**1101**	c. 1120	1147	c. 1150	
	Speyer Cathedral begun	Pisa Cathedral group begun	Norman conquest of England	St. Sernin begun	First Crusade		Mission of the Apostles, Vézelay	Second Crusade	

R O M A N E S Q U E P E R I O D

NORMAN CONQUEST OF SOUTHERN ITALY AND SICILY

A detail of the head and shoulders (FIG. 9-23) reveals the artist's striking characterization of his subject. The long, serpentine locks of hair and beard (familiar in the vocabulary of French Romanesque details) frame an arresting image of the dreaming mystic. The prophet seems entranced by his vision of what is to come, his eyes wide but unseeing the light of ordinary day; there is an expression slightly melancholy, at once pensive and wistful. For the man of the Middle Ages there were two alternative callings, one to the active life (*vita activa*), the other to the religious life of contemplation (*vita contemplativa*), the pursuit of the beatific vision of God. The sculptor of the Moissac *Jeremiah* has given us the very image of the *vita contemplativa*. It has been said that in Greek sculpture the body becomes "alive" before the head (as in the *Fallen Warrior* from Aegina, FIG. 5-31); in the epoch that begins in the eleventh century, the head becomes humanly expressive well before the body is rendered as truly corporeal. The *Jeremiah* is a remarkable instance of this.

Romanesque sculpture is not confined to the portals but appears in delightful variety in the carved capitals within the church and in the cloister walk; it was such sculpture that Bernard complained distracted the monks from their devotions; we are distracted, too, by its ingenuity and decorative beauty. The capitals of the Moissac cloister (FIG. 9-24)—some of which are historiated and some purely decorative—are excellent examples. The capital in the foreground of the view at the left has an intricate leaf-and-vine pattern with volutes, an echo of the Corinthian capital. The abacus carries rosettes, and its upper edge the fish-scale motif. The capital just beyond has figures seated at a table, probably a representation of the Marriage Feast

at Cana. The other capitals shown reveal the richness and color of the Romanesque sculptor's imagination; monsters of all sorts—basilisks, griffins, lizards, gargoyles—cluster and interlace and pass grinning before us. We have the Medieval bestiary in stone.

Yet for all its distinctive stylistic characteristics and exotic look, Romanesque art reveals its debt to ancient Roman, Early Christian, and Byzantine art, and to their classical heritage. For example, the beautifully carved rosettes on the lintel beneath the tympanum at Moissac (FIG. 9-22) derive from ancient Roman types. It is likely that some very late, still classicizing work—perhaps of the seventh century—served as model for the rosettes. Other rosettes closely resembling those of the Moissac lintel survive. At the same time, there are unmistakable indications of Islamic influence in other decorative motifs of the portal.

The relatives of the monsters of the Moissac capitals appear as the demons of hell in the awesome tympanum of the church of St. Lazare at Autun in Burgundy (FIG. 9-25). At Moissac we saw the apparition of the Divine Judge before he has summoned man; at Autun the Judgment is in progress. The detail shows the weighing of souls, while below in the lintel, the dead are rising, one plucked from the earth by giant hands. Mankind's pitiful weakness and littleness are distilled in these terror-stricken, weeping dolls, whom an angel with a trumpet summons to judgment. Angels and devils contest at the scales where souls are being weighed, each trying to manipulate the beam for or against a soul. Hideous demons guffaw and roar; their gaunt, lined bodies, with legs ending in claws, writhe and bend like long, loathsome insects. A devil leaning from the dragon-mouth of hell drags souls in, while above him a

9-24 Capitals from the cloister of St. Pierre, Moissac.

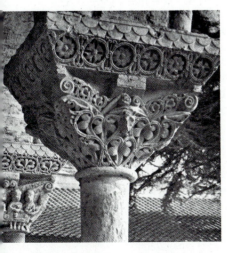
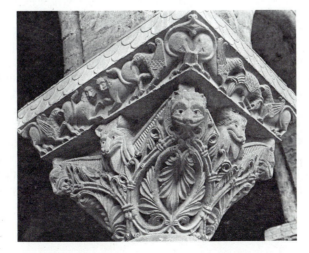
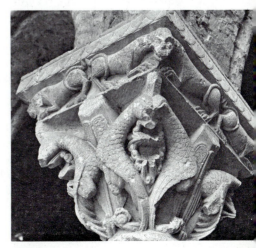

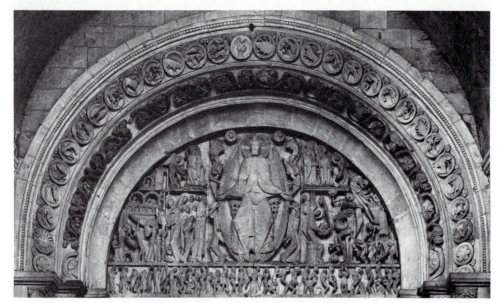

9-25 West tympanum of St. Lazare, Autun, *c.* 1130.

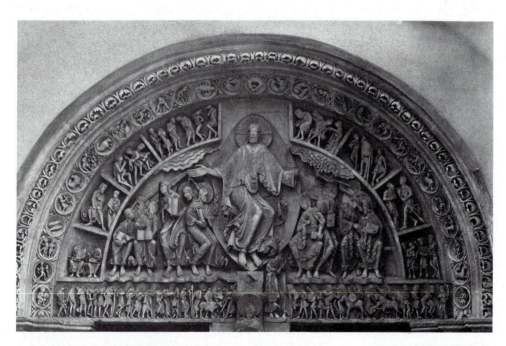

9-26 *The Mission of the Apostles,* tympanum of the center portal of the narthex of La Madeleine, Vézelay, 1120–32.

howling demon crams souls head first into a furnace. The resources of the Romanesque imagination, heated by a fearful faith, provide an appalling scene; one can appreciate the terror the Autun tympanum must have inspired in the believer who passed beneath it as he entered the cathedral.

Another great tympanum, this one at the church of La Madeleine at Vézelay, not far from Autun, varies the theme of the apocalyptic Last Judgment, representing the Ascension of Christ and the Mission of the Apostles (FIG. 9-26). As related in scripture (Acts 1:4-9), Christ foretold that the apostles would receive the power of the Holy Ghost and become the witnesses of the truth of the gospels throughout the world. The rays of light emanating from his hands represent the promise of the coming of the Holy Ghost. The apostles, holding the gospel books, receive

their spiritual assignment. Christ had assigned three specific tasks to the apostles and given them the power to perform them: to save or to condemn; to preach the gospel to all nations; to heal the sick and drive out devils. The task of saving or condemning is indicated in the central scene and in the lower four of the compartments surrounding it. The task of preaching the gospel to all nations (some at the very edge of the world) is represented on the lintel. The task of healing the sick and driving out devils is indicated in the upper four compartments. The outer archivolt has a repeated ornamental device, and the inner, medallions with the signs of the zodiac, the seasons, and the works of the months.

The Vézelay tympanum reflects, like a vast mirror, religious and secular writings and the influence of antiquity and the Byzantine East. It is a complete, encyclopedic Mission of the Apostles, in which the mission and the power to perform it are merged in a single subject. The theme has its sources in the Acts and in the gospels, in the prophecies of Isaiah, and in writings of antiquity and of the Middle Ages. The crowding, agitated figures reveal wild deformities. We find people with the heads of dogs, enormous ears, fiery hair, snoutlike noses; there are hunchbacks, mutes, blind men, lame men—a whole lexicon of human defects and ailments. Mankind, still suffering, awaits the salvation to come. The whole world is electrified by the promise of the ascended Christ, whose great figure, seeming to whirl in a vortex of spiritual energy, looms above human misery and deformity. Again, as in the Autun tympanum, we are made emphatically aware of the greatness of God and the littleness of man.

Vézelay is more closely associated with the Crusades than any other church in Europe. Pope Urban II had intended to preach to the First Crusade at Vézelay in 1095, about thirty years before the tympanum was carved. In 1146, some fifteen years after the tympanum was in place, Bernard preached to the Second Crusade, and King Louis VII of France took up the cross. In 1190 it was from Vézelay that King Richard the Lion-heart of England and King Philip Augustus of France set out upon the Third Crusade. Doubtless the spirit of the Crusades determined the iconography of the Vézelay tympanum, for it was believed that the Crusades were a kind of second mission of the apostles to convert the infidel: "When the tympanum was created the crusaders had already fulfilled the most important part of their mission. They had recaptured Jerusalem on the 15 July, 1099. Contemporary writers stress the fact that this is the day on which the apostles had dispersed throughout the world to fulfill their mission."[3]

Stylistically, the figures of the Vézelay tympanum display characteristics similar to those of Moissac and Autun: abrupt and jerky movement (strongly exaggerated at Vézelay), rapid play of line, wind-blown drapery hems, elongation, angularity, and agitated poses, gestures, and silhouettes. The figure of the Vézelay Christ is a splendid essay in calligraphic theme and variation, and is almost a summary of the Romanesque skill with decorative line. The lines of the drapery shoot out in rays; break into quick, zigzag rhythms; and spin into whorls, wonderfully conveying a spiritual light and energy flowing from Christ over and into the animated apostles. The technical experience of centuries of working with small art—with manuscripts, ivories, and metalcraft—is easily read from this monumental translation of such work into stone.

In Provence, rich in the remains of Roman art and architecture, the vivid linear style of Languedoc (Moissac)

[3] Adolf Katzenellenbogen, "The Central Tympanum at Vézelay: Its Encyclopedic Meaning and Its Relation to the First Crusade," *Art Bulletin*, vol. 26, no. 3 (Sept. 1944), pp. 141–51.

and Burgundy (Autun and Vézelay) is considerably modified later in the twelfth century by the influence of the art of antiquity. The quieting influence of this art is seen at once in the figures of the façade of St. Trophime at Arles and in the design of the portal, which reflects the artist's interpretation of a Roman triumphal arch (FIG. 9-27). The tympanum shows Christ surrounded by the signs of the Evangelists. On the lintel, directly below him, appear the twelve apostles at the center of a continuous frieze that depicts the Last Judgment; the outermost parts of the frieze depict the saved (on Christ's right) and the damned (on his left) in the flames of hell. Below this, in the jambs and the front bays of the portals, stand grave figures of saints draped in classical garb, their quiet stance contrasting with the spinning, twisting, dancing figures seen at Autun and Vézelay. The stiff regularity of the figures in the frieze also contrasts with the animation of the great Burgundian tympana and reminds us of the "lining up" seen in Early Christian sarcophagus sculpture. Their draperies, like those of the large statues below, are also less agitated and show nothing of the dexterous linear play familiar at Moissac, Autun, and Vézelay. The rigid lines of the architecture of the façade as a whole (rather than just an enframing element such as a tympanum) are now determining the placement and look of the sculpture, and the freedom of execution appropriate to small art is sacrificed to a simpler and more monumental adjustment to the architecture. In the north of France, in the area around Paris, a new system of portal sculpture was developing some thirty years earlier than that at St. Trophime. In the Royal Portal of the cathedral of Chartres we shall see the expansion of the whole portal design into a magnificent frontispiece in which the architectural and sculptural elements are in balanced relation, the sculptural style firmly determined by the lines of the building (FIG. 10-13).

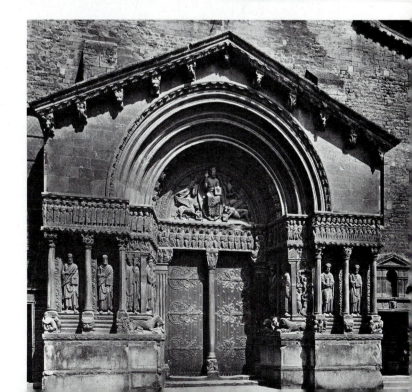

9-27 Portal on the façade of St. Trophime, Arles, late twelfth century.

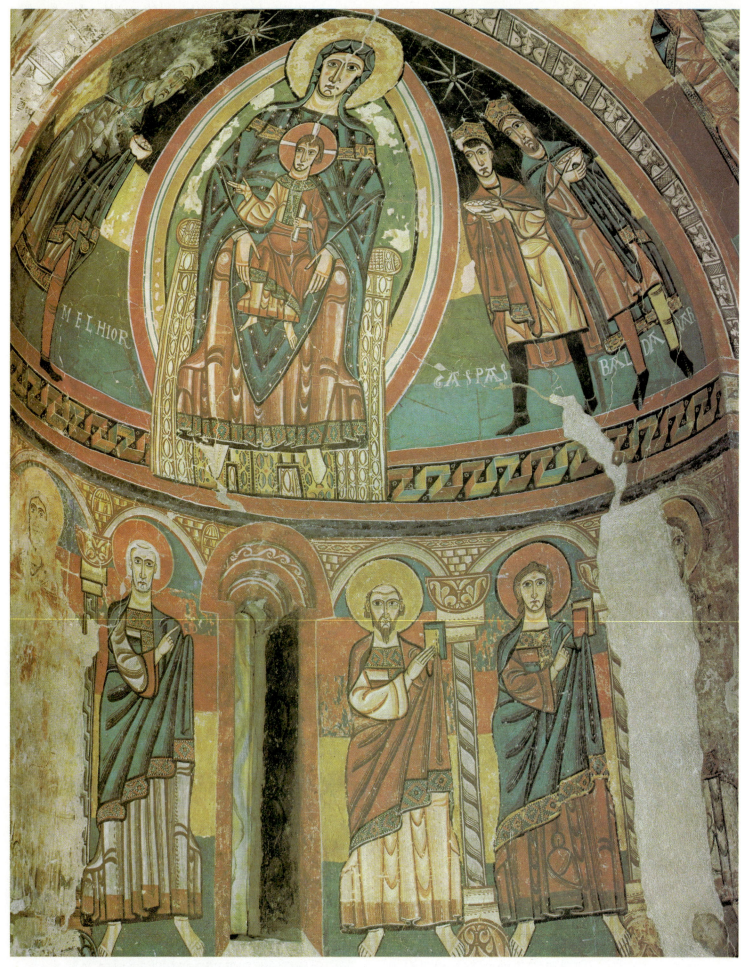

9-28 *Adoration of the Magi*, apse fresco from Santa Maria, Tahull, Catalonia, eleventh century.

PAINTING
AND ILLUMINATION

Monumental mural painting, like monumental sculpture, comes into its own once again in the eleventh century. Although we have examples of it from Carolingian and Ottonian times, and although there is an unbroken tradition of it in Italy, it blossoms in the Romanesque period. As with architecture and sculpture there are many regional styles and many degrees of sophistication. Sometimes a provincial style—that is, a style that appears at some distance from its origin, in an artistic "province" rather than at an artistic "capital"—can reveal more clearly than its sophisticated source the elements common to both. Such is the case in the mural painting in the apse of the little church of Santa Maria, at Tahull in Catalonia in the extreme northeast corner of Spain. This painting (FIG. 9-28) could be called provincial Byzantine, as, for that matter, could much Romanesque painting. If we compare it with a Byzantine mosaic like that at Daphne (FIG. 7-52) or the apse mosaic at Monreale (FIG. 7-54), we find that its distance from the Byzantine source—much greater than the distance from Venice or Sicily to Byzantium—results in a loss of subtlety and refinement and some misunderstanding of motifs in the original style. On the other hand, the Tahull painting has a simple and strong directness, even bluntness, that gives it a peculiarly expressive force. One emphatic feature is the partitioning of the draped figures into separate decoratively modeled segments that almost break the figure itself into independent parts. (Note the similarity to the modulation and articulation of Romanesque architecture.) This is especially well seen in the pattern made by the pipelike legs and the ladderlike folds between them. This decorative banding of the surface serves to keep the figures flat and contributes to the effect of stiff formality. The drapery, also with decorative partitioning, is scarcely distinguished from the body. Even the hands of the Madonna are subdivided, as are the heads and necks of other figures. This technique, which had begun to appear in Ottonian painting (FIG. 8-22), is almost universal in Romanesque; it may be seen beneath the whirling linear draperies of Autun and Vézelay and in the angels of the Moissac tympanum. Here the sharp patterning of the figures is assisted by bold coloring, and the whole effect is one of rude strength, not a little of which derives from the architectural planes to which the patterned figures are masterfully adjusted.

The vernacular Romanesque style can be seen almost in exaggeration in a manuscript illumination from northern France illustrating the life of St. Omer (FIG. 9-29). Here the figures are cut into patterns by hard lines, and the action is remote from even an approximation of organic motion. St. Omer (bound and pulled by the beard) and his captors seem to be performing some bouncing ritual ballet. The frame creates no sense of containment as it did in Anglo-Saxon and Carolingian manuscripts, and bodies and feet move arbitrarily in and out of and across it. Locally different from the Tahull mural, the St. Omer illumination shares its fundamental vocabulary.

9-29 *The Life and Miracles of St. Audomarus (Omer)*, illuminated manuscript, eleventh century. Bibliothèque Municipale, Saint-Omer, France.

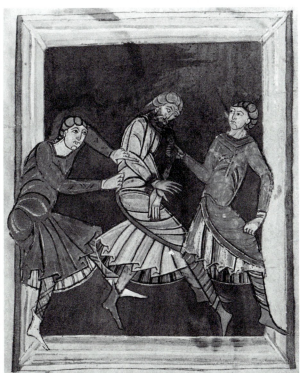

9-30 *St. George and the Dragon*, from the *Moralia in Job* illuminated manuscript, early twelfth century. 13¾″ × 9¼″. Bibliothèque Municipale, Dijon.

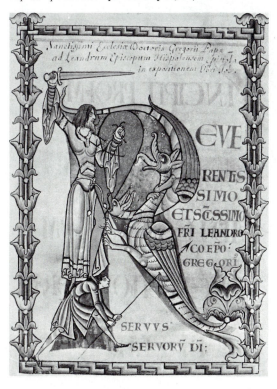

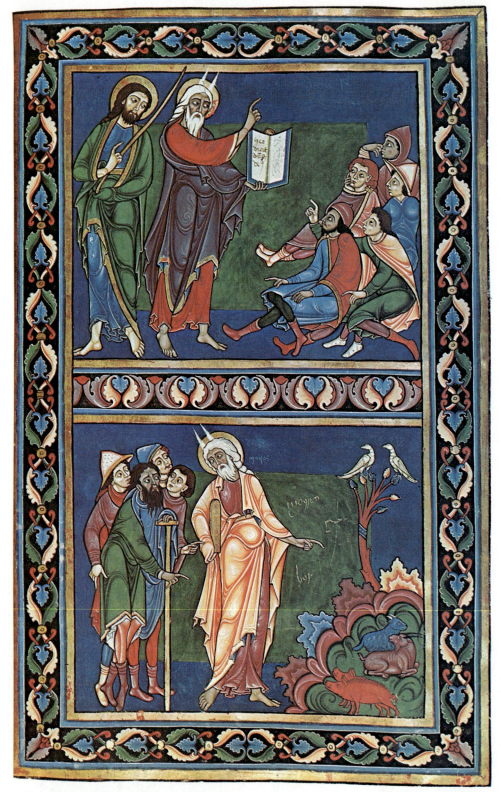

9-31 MASTER HUGO, *Moses Expounding the Law,* frontispiece of the Book of Deuteronomy of the Bury Bible, the abbey of Bury St. Edmunds, early twelfth century. Illuminated manuscript, approx. 20″ × 14″. Reproduced by permission of the Master and Fellows of Corpus Christi College, Cambridge, England.

The vocabulary, richly applied and gracefully modulated, appears in what surely must be one of the masterpieces of Medieval art, a manuscript illuminated in Bernard's great abbey of Cîteaux, the motherhouse of the Cistercian order. Cîteaux, and its sister abby, Clairvaux, where Bernard was abbot, produced magnificent illuminated manuscripts throughout the twelfth century, among which was Gregory's *Moralia in Job,* painted before 1111. A splendid example of Cistercian illumination, the historiated initial from this manuscript (FIG. 9-30) represents St. George, his squire, and the roaring dragons intricately composed to make the letter "R." St. George, a slender, regal figure, raises his shield and sword against the dragons, distinguished representations of the age-old animal style so often encountered, while the squire, crouching beneath St. George, runs a lance through one of the monsters. (An image of status, the greater and the lesser dragons correspond to the lord and his man.) The ornamented initial goes back to the Hiberno-Saxon eighth century; the inclusion of a narrative within the initial is a practice that will have an important future in Gothic illumination. The banding of the torso, the fold partitions (especially evident in the skirts of the servant), and the dovetail folds—all part of the Romanesque manner—are done here with the skill of a master who deftly avoids the stiffness and angularity that result from less skillful management of the vocabulary. Instead, he makes a virtue of stylistic necessity; the partitioning accentuates the verticality and elegance of the figure of St. George, as it does the thrusting action of his servant. The flowing sleeves add a spirited flourish to St. George's gesture. The knight, handsomely garbed, cavalierly wears no armor and aims a single stroke with proud disdain. This miniature may be a reliable picture of the costume of a Medieval baron and of the air of nonchalant gallantry he cultivated.

An illumination of exceeding refinement of execution, exemplifying the sumptuous illustration common to the large Bibles produced in the wealthy Romanesque abbeys, is the frontispiece to the Book of Deuteronomy from the Bury Bible (FIG. 9-31). Produced at the abbey of Bury St. Edmunds in England toward the middle of the twelfth century, the work shows two scenes from Deuteronomy enframed by symmetrical leaf motifs in softly glowing, harmonized colors. The upper register shows Moses and Aaron proclaiming the Law to the Israelites; the lower, Moses pointing out the clean and unclean beasts. The gestures are slow and gentle and have quiet dignity; the figures of Moses and Aaron seem to glide. This is quite different from the abrupt emphasis and spastic movement of the earlier Romanesque; here, as the patterning softens, the movements of the figure become more integrated and smooth. Yet the patterning does remain in the multiple divisions of the draped limbs, the lightly shaded volumes being connected with sinuous lines and ladder-folds; the drapery and body are still thought of as somehow the same. The frame now has a quite definite limiting function, and the figures are carefully fitted within it.

The transition from the Romanesque vernacular style to something new seems to reach a midpoint in a work of great expressive power, the portrait of the scribe Eadwine in the *Eadwine Psalter* (FIG. 9-32), made in Canterbury about the same time as the Bury Bible. Particularly noteworthy is the fact that the portrait represents a living man, a priestly scribe, not some sacred person or King David, who usually dominated the Psalter. While it is true that Carolingian and Ottonian manuscripts included portraits of living men, they were of reigning emperors, whose right to appear in sacred books was God-given, like the right of Justinian and Theodora and their court to be depicted in

the sanctuary of San Vitale. Here, the inclusion of his own portrait sanctified the scribe's work, marking a change in attitude that points to the future emergence of the artist as a person and a name.

The style is related to that of the Bury Bible, but, though the patterning is still firm—notably in the cowl and the thigh—the drapery has begun to fall softly, to wrap about the frame, to overlap parts of it, and to follow the movements beneath. The arbitrariness of the Romanesque vernacular style is yielding, slightly but clearly, to the requirements of a more naturalistic representation. The artist's instinct for decorative elaboration of his surface remains, as is apparent in the whorls and spirals of the gown, but it is significant that these are painted in very lightly and do not conflict with the functional lines that contain them.

With the distinction of body and drapery finally achieved in the Gothic art of the thirteenth century, an epoch of increasing naturalism will begin. As did Exekias' billowing sail (FIG. 5-7), the Eadwine figure marks a turning point—in this case, in the history of Medieval representation. The Late Romanesque and Early Gothic "feel" of body and drapery as surfaces that interact forcefully implies not only a sense of their materiality but also a sense of depth. That sense will sharpen and deepen into the representational art of the Renaissance.

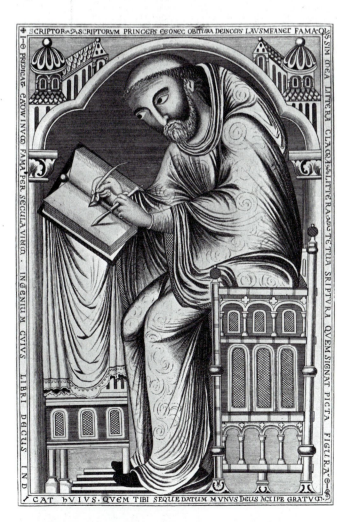

9-32 Nineteenth-century engraving of *The Scribe Eadwine* from the *Eadwine Psalter*, c. 1150, Trinity College, Cambridge, England.

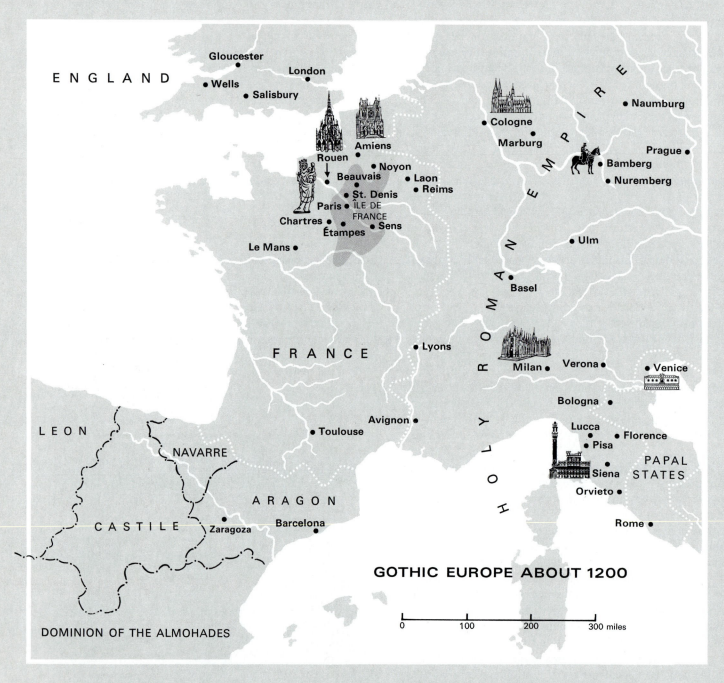

ENGLAND

Gloucester
London
Wells
Salisbury

Rouen
Amiens
Noyon
Beauvais
Laon
Reims
St. Denis
Paris   ÎLE DE
FRANCE
Chartres   Sens
Étampes
Le Mans

FRANCE

Lyons

Toulouse
Avignon

LEON
NAVARRE

ARAGON

CASTILE
Zaragoza
Barcelona

DOMINION OF THE ALMOHADES

Cologne
Marburg

Naumburg

Prague
Bamberg
Nuremberg

Ulm

Basel

Milan   Verona
Venice

Bologna
Lucca
Florence
Pisa
Siena
Orvieto

PAPAL
STATES

Rome

HOLY ROMAN EMPIRE

GOTHIC EUROPE ABOUT 1200

0   100   200   300 miles

chapter ten

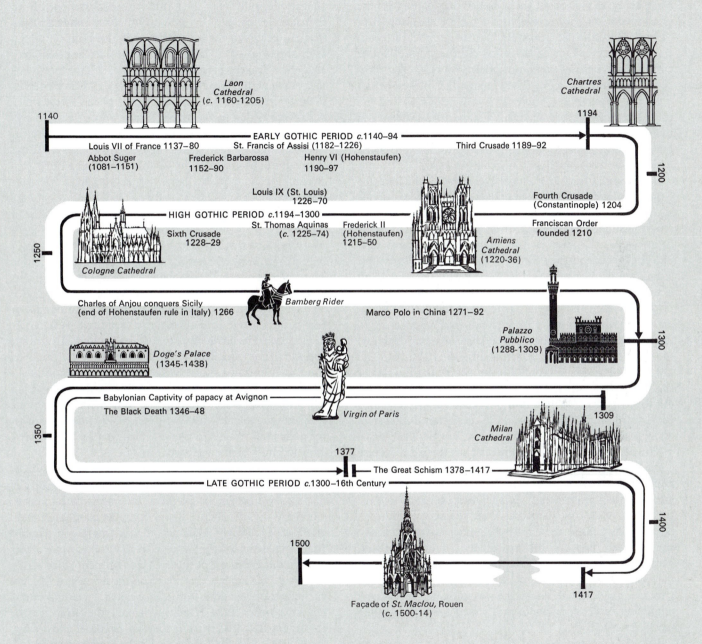

Laon Cathedral (c. 1160-1205)

Chartres Cathedral

1140

EARLY GOTHIC PERIOD c.1140–94

1194

Louis VII of France 1137–80   St. Francis of Assisi (1182–1226)   Third Crusade 1189–92

Abbot Suger (1081–1151)   Frederick Barbarossa 1152–90   Henry VI (Hohenstaufen) 1190–97

1200

Louis IX (St. Louis) 1226–70   Fourth Crusade (Constantinople) 1204

HIGH GOTHIC PERIOD c.1194–1300

St. Thomas Aquinas (c. 1225–74)   Frederick II (Hohenstaufen) 1215–50   Franciscan Order founded 1210

1250   Sixth Crusade 1228–29

Cologne Cathedral   Amiens Cathedral (1220-36)

Charles of Anjou conquers Sicily (end of Hohenstaufen rule in Italy) 1266   Bamberg Rider   Marco Polo in China 1271–92

Palazzo Pubblico (1288-1309)

1300

Doge's Palace (1345-1438)

Babylonian Captivity of papacy at Avignon

The Black Death 1346–48   Virgin of Paris

1309

1350   Milan Cathedral

1377

The Great Schism 1378–1417

LATE GOTHIC PERIOD c.1300–16th Century

1400

1500

1417

Façade of *St. Maclou,* Rouen (c. 1500-14)

Gothic Art

GOTHIC WAS FIRST used as a term of derision by Renaissance critics who scorned the lack of conformity of Gothic art to the standards of classical Greece and Rome: "May he who invented it be cursed," wrote one of them. Mistakenly, they thought the style had originated with the Goths, who thus were responsible for the destruction of the good and true classical style. The men of the thirteenth and fourteenth centuries, however, referred to the Gothic cathedrals as *opus modernum* (modern work) or *opus francigenum* (Frankish work). They recognized in these structures that towered over their towns a style of building and of decoration that was original. It was with confidence in their own faith that they regarded their cathedrals as the real image of the City of God, the Heavenly Jerusalem, which they were privileged to build on earth.

There are strong contrasts between the Gothic and the Romanesque environment and point of view. Romanesque society was dominated by the uncertainties inherent in the anarchical tendencies of feudalism. The great barons of the countryside and the great abbeys enjoyed an almost total independence, and the conflict of their claims to privilege led to constant warfare. Gothic society was also feudal, but it was a comparatively ordered feudalism. Here and there powerful barons had been able to make themselves kings, and monarchy, especially in England and France, asserted itself strongly to limit the independence of lesser lords and the Church. Centralized government was established, and law and order instilled confidence in people of all walks of life. The cities, entirely new or built on the foundations of old Roman ones, began to thrive and become strong; allied for common defense, they were very often powerful enough to defy kings and emperors. Within their walls men who had escaped from the land could find freedom: "The air of the city is the breath of freedom," one slogan had it. City life took on a complex but ordered form; craft guilds, resembling strong unions, were formed to give protection and profit to artisans of the same specialties. A middle class, made up of the craftsmen, merchants, and professionals (lawyers, doctors, teachers, and many others) came to constitute a new and puissant force to check and balance the feudal aristocracy. The fear and insecurity that pervaded the Romanesque world was mitigated by the new alignment of economic and social forces, and the Gothic world emerged.

Romanesque society had been dominated by men. In Gothic society women took on a new importance. Wandering minstrels sang less of the great deeds of heroes in war and more of love, beauty, and springtime. Eleanor of Aquitaine, wife to Louis VII of France and Henry II Plantagenet of England and mother of Richard the Lionheart and John, was one of the first to rule over a "court of love," where respect for the lady was prerequisite and from which was to emanate the code of chivalry that so decided social relations in the later Middle Ages. The monastic prejudice against women no longer determined the representation of them in art. In the twelfth century *luxuria*, sensual pleasure, is represented at Moissac as a woman with serpents at her breasts; in the thirteenth century it is represented as a pretty girl looking into a mirror. It is almost with relief that the Gothic upper classes turn from the *chansons de geste* to the new amorous songs and romances, in which the lover adores his lady and in which such immortal lovers as Tristan and Isolde are celebrated. Marie de France, herself a noblewoman, introduced this tale, along with many others of the new Arthurian legends, to northern French feudal society. The poetry of the times nicely illustrates the contrast between Romanesque and Gothic taste and mood: While in the Romanesque *Song of Roland* the dying hero waxes rhapsodic over his sword, the German minnesinger of the Gothic period, dreaming in a swooning ecstasy of his lady, is "woven round with delight."

The love of woman, celebrated in art and formalized in life, received spiritual sanction in the cult of the Virgin Mary, who, as the Mother of Heaven and of Christ and in the form of Mother Church, loved all her children. It was Mary who stood compassionately between the judgment seat and the horrors of hell, interceding for all her faithful. The later twelfth and thirteenth centuries sang hymns to her, put her image everywhere, and dedicated great cathedrals to her. Her image was carried on banners into battle, and her name sounded in the battle cry of the king of France: "Sainte Marie . . . Saint Denis . . . Montjoie!" Thus, Mary became the spiritual lady of chivalry, and the Christian knight dedicated his life to her. The severity of Romanesque themes stressing the Last Judgment yields to the gentleness of the Gothic, in which Mary is represented crowned by Christ in Heaven.

It was not alone the new position of women, the lyrical and spiritual exaltation of love, or the cult of the Virgin that softened barbarous manners. In concert with the new mood was the influence of one remarkable man, St. Francis of Assisi, who saw Christ not as the remote and terrible Judge but as the loving Savior who had walked among and had himself been one of the "rejected of men." The series of reform movements that make up the history of Medieval monasticism culminates in St. Francis' founding of the religious order that bears his name, the Franciscans. St. Francis felt that the members of his order must shun the cloistered life and freely walk the streets of the busy cities as mendicants, preaching the original message of Christ—the love of oneself and one's neighbor. Shortly after Francis' death and against his wish that his followers never settle in monasteries, they commenced the great basilica in his name at Assisi. The historical importance of the Franciscan movement lies in its strengthening of religious faith, its stimulating of the religious emotion among people in cities, and its weakening of the power and influence of the old, Romanesque, countryside abbeys.

St. Francis could be said to have brought a kind of democracy to religion in Europe at the expense of its feudal establishment.

Courtly love, the development of chivalry, the cult of the Virgin Mary, and the teaching and example of St. Francis could not, of course, nullify, though they could mitigate, the cruel realities of Medieval life. While St. Francis was still living, the Fourth Crusade sacked Christian Constantinople, visiting atrocities upon it that would outdo those of the later conquest by the Ottoman Turks. The papacy and king of France collaborated in the annihilation of the peoples of Languedoc and Provence in the south of France, the so-called Albigensians, who were accused of heresy but who also stood in the way of the territorial ambitions of royal France. It was this region that had fostered the new poetry of the troubadours and produced the Romanesque sculpture examined earlier. The Albigensian "crusade" produced also that grim and fateful instrument of heretic-hunting, the Inquisition, or "Holy Office," instituted by St. Dominic. The Dominicans, called in fearful derision *Domini Canes* ("dogs of the Lord"), were in many ways rivals of the Franciscans and saw themselves as rooting out unbelievers and heretics and guarding the purity of orthodox dogma. The Dominicans' concern for theology led them to be teachers, and they produced one of the great Christian theologians and philosophers, St. Thomas Aquinas, who at mid-thirteenth century was the leading light of the University of Paris.

The institution of the university begins to appear in the early Gothic period, its natural setting the city. The monastic and cathedral schools of the earlier Middle Ages had sought to keep the learning of the fathers of the Church alive and to reassess these teachings in the light of developing Christian thought. From these schools the universities, communities of scholars and their pupils, evolved in the twelfth and thirteenth centuries at Bologna and Padua, Oxford, and Paris. The most important study at the university was theology, but several other subjects were taught, among them mathematics, astronomy, music, grammar, logic, law, and medicine. Ancient Greek philosophy, principally that of Aristotle, was recovered from Arabic translations and had an enormously stimulating effect upon theology. Here appeared a reasoned, systematic method of argument and a treasury of lore and observation of natural things. The philosophers set to work to find some way to adjust this new authoritative knowledge to Christian belief; they sought, in short, to rationalize religion. Their method was to arrive at proofs for the central dogmas of the faith by argument, or disputation. This method, taught in the schools and universities, came to be called scholasticism, and its proponents schoolmen. Scholastic philosophy is still the official philosophy of the Roman Catholic Church. The greatest exponent of this systematic procedure was St. Thomas Aquinas. Typical of the method is his treatise, the *Summa Theologica*, which was laid out into Books, the Books into Questions, the Questions into Articles, each Article into objections with contradictions and responses, and, finally, answers to the objections.

Within this framework the shrewdest and subtlest arguments of the Middle Ages were advanced. The habit of mind it created lasted for centuries, an obstacle to the rise of what we call empirical thought and science; yet much of value is still found in it today. It is quite possible that the scholastic habit of disputation is reflected in the thought processes of Gothic architects, as Erwin Panofsky suggested.

St. Thomas wrote his summary of Christian theology at a time when the great cathedrals were manifesting a kind of architectural "summation" of the Christian universe. At the time, the papacy ruled supreme in Europe, not only spiritually but temporally. At the beginning of the thirteenth century, Pope Innocent III, who took England away from King John, could claim: "Single rulers have single provinces, and single kings single kingdoms; but Peter . . . is pre-eminent over all, since he is the Vicar of Him whose is the earth and the fulness thereof, the whole wide world and all that dwell therein."

The thirteenth century represents the summit of achievement for unified Christendom. It represents the triumph of the papacy; a successful and inspiring synthesis of religion, philosophy, and art; and the first firm formation of the states that will make modern history. The scene of this great but brief equilibrium of forces favoring religion is the Gothic city; within the city, the soaring cathedral, "flinging its passion against the sky," asserts the nature of the Gothic spirit.

EARLY GOTHIC

Architecture

On June 11, 1144, Louis of France, Eleanor of Aquitaine (his queen), members of the royal court, and a host of distinguished prelates, including five archbishops, as well as a vast crowd, converged on the royal abbey of St. Denis, just a few miles north of Paris, for the dedication of the new choir. This choir, with its crown of chapels radiant with stained-glass windows, set a precedent that the builders in the region surrounding Paris, the Île-de-France, were to follow for the next half century.

Two eminent persons were particularly influential in the formation of the Gothic style: Bernard of Clairvaux and Suger, abbot of St. Denis. Bernard held the belief that faith was mystical and intuitive rather than rational. In his battles with Abelard, a contemporary scholastic philosopher whose views were a basis for the dialectical method of Aquinas, he upheld this position with all the persuasiveness of his powerful personality and eloquence and by the

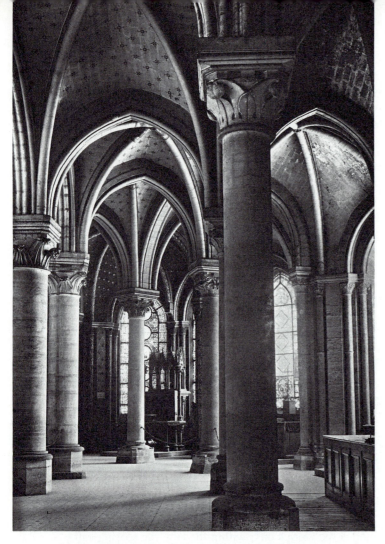

10-1 Choir (including ambulatory) of the abbey church of St. Denis, near Paris, 1140-44.

building role were one: to construct a kingdom and an architectural expression of it. In 1122 he was elected abbot of St. Denis and within fifteen years was at work rebuilding the old monastery, which had been in use for almost 300 years. As he made his plans for the new building, he must have recalled many of the churches seen during his travels, and the workmen and artists who labored to raise the church were summoned from many regions. St. Denis, one of the last great abbey churches to be built, became the monastic inspiration for the city cathedrals and is known as the cradle of Gothic art.

Suger described his new choir at St. Denis (FIG. 10-1) as follows:

Moreover, it was cunningly provided that—through the upper columns and central arches which were to be placed upon the lower ones built in the crypt—the central nave of the new addition should be made the same width, by means of geometrical and arithmetical instruments, as the central nave of the old [Carolingian] church; and, likewise, that the dimensions of the new side-aisles should be the same as the dimensions of the old side-aisles, except for that elegant and praiseworthy extension . . . a circular string of chapels, by virtue of which the whole [church] would shine with the wonderful and uninterrupted light of most luminous windows, pervading the interior beauty.[1]

The abbot's description is a key to the understanding of Early Gothic architecture. As he says, the major dimensions of the structure were dictated by an older church, but it was the "elegant and praiseworthy extension," the "string of chapels" with "luminous windows," that proclaimed the new style.

Although the crypt at St. Denis served as a foundation for the choir above it, a comparison of their respective plans and structures reveals the major differences between Romanesque and Gothic building (FIG. 10-2). The thick walls of the crypt create a series of separate volumes—careful Romanesque "partitioning" into units—whereas the absence of walls in the choir above produces a unified space. The crypt is essentially a wall construction, and it is covered with groin vaults; the choir, on the other hand, is a skeletal construction, and its vaults are Gothic rib vaults (FIG. 10-3).

The ancestors of the Gothic rib vault (at Caen and Durham) were discussed above. A rib vault is easily identified by the presence of crossed, or diagonal, arches under the groins of a vault. These arches form the armature, which serves as the framework for Gothic skeletal construction. The Gothic vault may be distinguished from other rib or arched vaults by its use of the pointed, or broken, arch as an integral part of the skeletal armature; by the presence of thinly vaulted webs, or severies, between the arches; and by the fact that, regardless of the space to

example of his own holiness. The Cistercian architecture that was being built under Bernard's influence reflected his theology, stressing purity of outline, simplicity, and a form and light peculiarly conducive to meditation.

Although Bernard denounced lavish decoration and elaborate architecture, the Gothic style was initiated by a fellow-abbot who, accepting Bernard's admonitions to reform his monastery, built his new church in a style that surpassed the Romanesque in splendor. The fellow-churchman was the Abbot Suger, who had risen from humble parentage to become the right-hand man of both Louis VI and Louis VII, and, during the latter's absence in the Second Crusade, the regent of France. From his youth, Suger wrote, he had dreamed of the possibility of embellishing the church that had nurtured him, the royal Church of France, within whose precincts its kings had been buried since the ninth century. It was in fact his intention to confer authority on the claims of the kings of royal France to the territory we recognize as France today, for in Suger's time the power of the French king, except for scattered holdings, was confined to an area not much larger than the Île-de-France. Thus, Suger's political role and his

[1]Erwin Panofsky, trans., *Abbot Suger on the Abbey Church of St. Denis and its Art Treasures* (Princeton, N.J.: Princeton Univ. Press, 1951), p. 101.

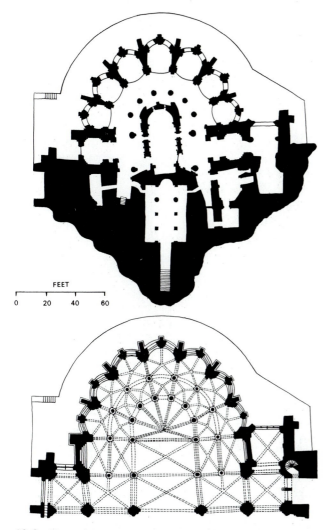

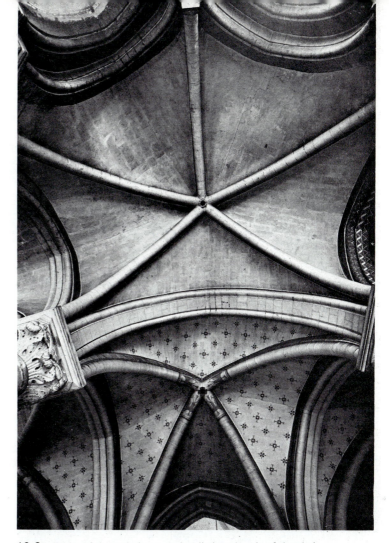

10-2 Plans of the crypt (top) and choir of St. Denis. (After Sumner Crosby.)

10-3 Vaults of the ambulatory and radiating chapels of the choir of St. Denis.

be vaulted, all the arches have their crowns at approximately the same level—something the Romanesque architects could not achieve with their semicircular arches (FIG. 10-4). Thus, flexibility is a major advantage of the Gothic vault, permitting the vaulting of compartments of varying shapes, as may be readily seen in the plan of the choir of St. Denis and in many other Gothic choir plans. Moreover, although it does not entirely support the webs, the Gothic armature allows predetermining of the alignment and concentration of thrusts to be buttressed.

10-4 The Gothic rib vault and the domical vault differ in ways that derive from the fact that they are based on the pointed arch and the semicircular arch, respectively. The diagram (1) illustrates this: *ABCD* is an oblong bay to be vaulted; *AC* and *BD* are the diagonal ribs; *AB* and *DC*, the transverse arches; and *AD* and *BC*, the wall arches. If semicircular arches (the dotted arcs) are used, their radii, and therefore their heights (*EF, GH,* and *IJ*), will be different. The result will be a domical vault (2), irregular in shape and difficult to light. If pointed arches are used, the points (and hence the ribs) can have the same heights (*IK* and *GL*). The result will be a Gothic rib vault (3), a lighter, more flexible system than the domical, affording ample space for large clerestory windows.

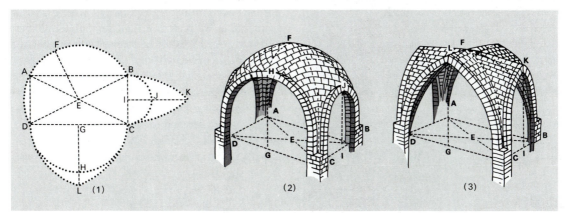

319

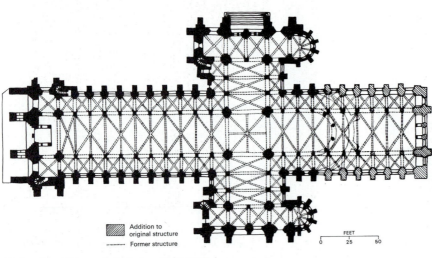

10-5 Plan of Laon Cathedral, *c.* 1160–1205. Choir extended after 1210. (After E. Gall.)

Addition to original structure
Former structure

FEET
0   25   50

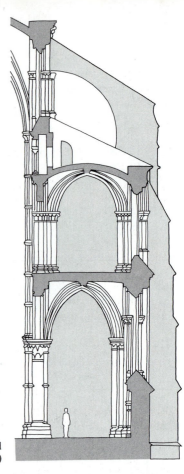

10-6 Section through the aisle, gallery, triforium, and clerestory of Laon Cathedral. (After E. Gall.)

10-7 Nave of Laon Cathedral.

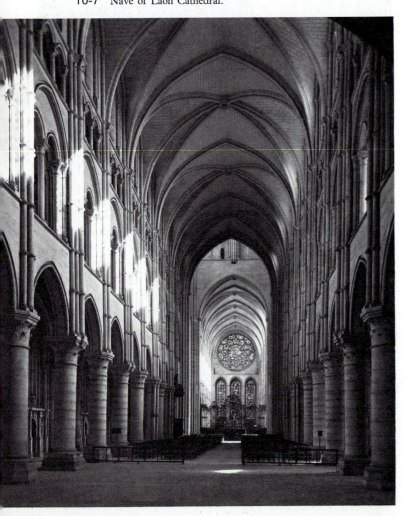

Although the Medieval mason unquestionably derived great satisfaction from his mastery of these technical problems and at times must have been preoccupied with them, he did not permit them to be an end in themselves. The ambulatories and chapels at St. Denis are proof that the rib vault was exploited, as Suger wrote, so that the whole church "would shine with wonderful and uninterrupted light." This was, in Medieval terms, the *scientia*—the theory—that motivated the creation of the Gothic style; and it was *ars*—technical knowledge and practical skill—that made it possible. The difference between the two was akin to that between modern physics and engineering; when a Medieval architect spoke of the "art of geometry," he meant not the abstract nature of geometrical forms, but the practical uses to which mathematical formulations might be put in designing a piece of sculpture or in erecting a building. An understanding of Gothic architecture will not be reached, however, by trying to decide whether it was predominantly concerned with *ars* or with *scientia* but rather by realizing that the cathedrals were the result of both. And it is in the stones themselves, in the extraordinary sensitivity of the Gothic mason for stone as a building material, that the spirit of Gothic architecture is to be discovered. The fact is that procedure was often hit or miss and rule of thumb; buildings often collapsed and were rebuilt with very large margins of safety. There was no one sure way and certainly no fundamental agreement about method. The certainties of modern engineering—themselves sometimes not so certain—were centuries beyond the Gothic reach. Even so, what still stands of Gothic architecture is a monument to the supreme skill, persistence, and vision of the Gothic architects.

It was the *scientia* of light that led Suger to the invention of the Gothic building, the slender skeletal structure that permitted the flooding of the interior with light. This "theory" came from the writings of a fifth-century mystic called the pseudo-Dionysius the Areopagite because of his claim to be the true Dionysius, a first-century Athenian follower of St. Paul. This "pseudo-Dionysius" had become confused with the patron saint of royal France, St. Denis, making it natural for Suger to take the former's mystical identification of light with the divine as a kind of prescription for any building dedicated to St. Denis. When Suger, steeped in the theology of the Areopagite, envisioned the new St. Denis, he saw it as a mystic radiance. This is another example of the significance of religious authority in the Middle Ages. Not only scripture, but the works of the fathers of the Church were the key to reality, and things had to be interpreted in terms of their authority.

The evolution of Gothic architecture is a continuing adjustment of scale, proportion, buttressing, vault arrangement, and wall and façade design that, in Panofsky's image, is like the steps of a complex scholastic argument. Only the choir of St. Denis was completed in the twelfth century; for a fairly complete view of the Early Gothic style of the second half of the century, one must turn to the cathedral of Laon (FIGS. 10-5 to 10-8). Begun about 1160 and completed shortly after 1200, the building retains many Romanesque features but combines them with the new Gothic structural devices—the rib vault and the pointed arch. Shortly after the building's completion the choir was enlarged and the present plan, relatively long and narrow with a square east end, has a decidedly English flavor. Among the plan's easily discernible Romanesque features are the strongly marked-off crossing square and the bay system composed of a large unit in the nave flanked by two small squares in each aisle (FIG. 10-5). The nave bays are defined by sexpartite rib vaults and an alternate-support system that, in combination, continue the Romanesque tradition of subdividing the interior into a number of separate compartments. Both features, as well as the gallery above the aisles, have been derived from Norman Romanesque architecture, which enjoyed great prestige in northern France throughout the twelfth century (FIGS. 9-12 and 9-13). A new feature of the interior, however, is the *triforium*, the band of arcades below the clerestory that occupies the space corresponding to the exterior strip of wall covered by the sloping timber roof above the galleries. The triforium expresses a growing desire to break up and eliminate all continuous wall surfaces. Its insertion produces the characteristic Early Gothic nave-wall elevation of four parts: nave arcade, gallery, triforium, and clerestory (FIGS. 10-6 and 10-7).

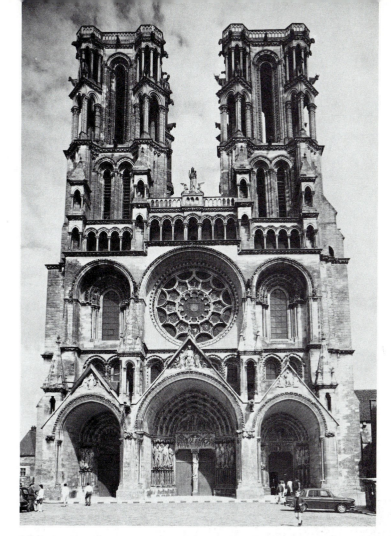

10-8 Façade of Laon Cathedral, begun c. 1190.

At Laon the alternate-support system is treated less emphatically than in other Early Gothic churches (for example, Sens, Noyon). It is not reflected in the nave arcade (although colonnettes were added to a few of the columns as an afterthought), as alternating bundles of three and five shafts have their origin above the level of the main wall supports (FIG. 10-7). It appears that the Laon architect was no longer completely happy with the compartmentalized effect of Romanesque interiors, which tend to make the visitor pause as he advances from unit to unit. Gothic builders aim, as yet rather timidly at Laon, to create an integrated, unified interior space that sweeps uninterruptedly from west to east. The alternate-support system, hugging the ground in Ottonian times and rising to dominate nave walls in northern Romanesque, has lost its footing at Laon and, like the solid masonry of Romanesque walls, is about to evaporate.

Important changes in the design of the church exterior were also part of the Early Gothic experience. At Laon the doorways, under protective porches, and the towers have been treated as integral parts of the mass of the building (FIG. 10-8). The interior stories are reflected in the levels into which the façade is divided. (A noticeable discontinu-

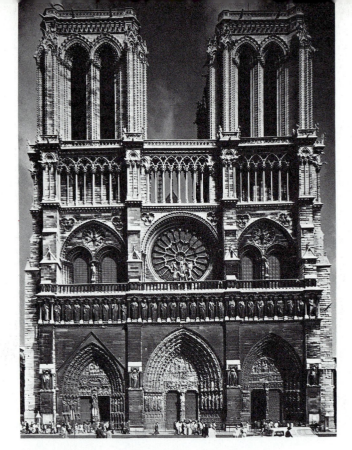

10-9 Façade of Notre Dame, Paris, 1163–1250.

of Laon and St. Étienne at Caen (FIG. 9-11) reveals how deep the penetration of the mass of the wall has become. Here, as in Gothic generally, there is operating a kind of principle of reduction of sheer mass by its replacement with intricately framed voids.

Laon has a pair of towers flanking each arm of the transept (only two completed) and a lantern tower over the crossing, which, with the two western towers, gives a total of seven, the perfect mystic number. (Composed of three and four, it represents the Trinity and the Evangelists or the gospels.) This complement of towers was the Early Gothic ideal and continues the German Romanesque tradition of multiple integrated towers. Rarely, however, did building funds suffice for the completion of all towers. Even the façade towers of French cathedrals were seldom finished, most, including those of Laon, lacking the crowning spires planned for them. Eventually the massed towers of the east end were omitted from building plans and the Norman two-tower façade became the French High Gothic standard.

Transept towers were not part of the plan for the cathedral of Paris, the renowned Notre Dame (FIG. 10-9). Thus, this essentially Early Gothic building has a High Gothic silhouette in which only the slender crossing spire interrupts the long horizontal roof line that extends eastward behind the massive façade towers (FIG. 10-10). Notre Dame of Paris was begun in 1163, only a few years after Laon, and embodies a fascinating mixture of conservative and progressive ideas. Choir and transept were completed by 1182, the nave by 1225, and the façade by 1250. The plan (FIG. 10-11) shows an ambitiously scaled, five-aisled

ity between the central and flanking portions of the façade was to be regulated in later designs.) Typically Gothic are the deep embrasures of the doorways and windows and the open structure of the towers. A comparison of the façades

10-10 South flank of Notre Dame, Paris.

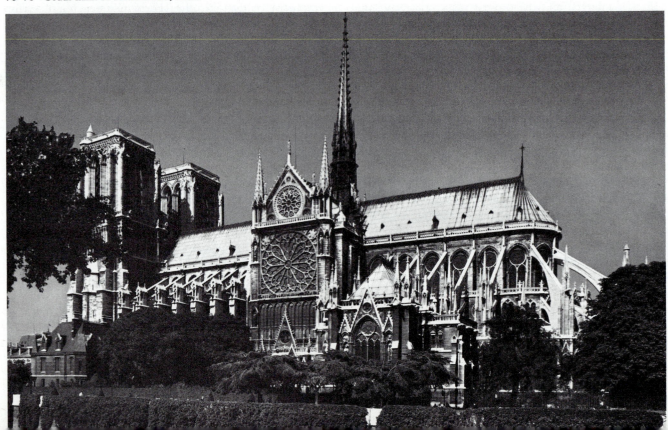

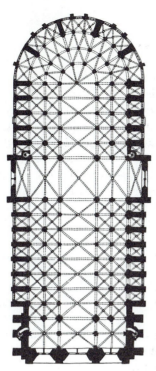

10-11 Plan of Notre Dame, Paris. (After Frankl.)

10-12 East end and part of the nave of Notre Dame, Paris, begun c. 1180, modified 1225–50.

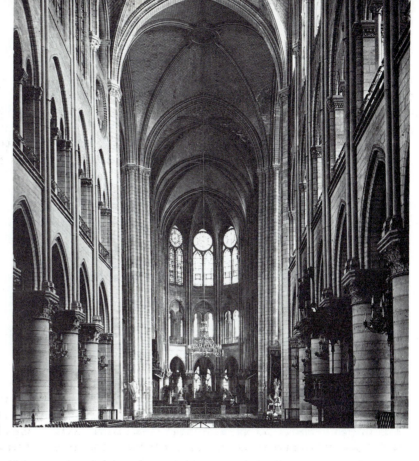

structure in which a Romanesque bay system is combined with Early Gothic six-part nave vaulting. The original transept was short and did not project beyond the outer aisles. The original nave wall was four-part, in the Early Gothic manner, with a triforium in the form of a series of rosettes.

Barely completed, the building was extensively modified. Between 1225 and 1250, chapels were built into the spaces between buttresses, and in 1250 the transept arms were lengthened. At the same time, perhaps as the result of a fire (according to Viollet-le-Duc, the cathedral's nineteenth-century restorer), but probably to admit more light into the nave, changes were made in the nave wall, although the bays adjacent to the crossing were left in their original form (FIG. 10-12). By this time the nave of the cathedral of Chartres had been completed (see below) and had rendered Early Gothic galleries and four-level wall elevations obsolete. Since the galleries had already been built at Paris, the "modernization" of the nave had to be a compromise. The clerestory windows were lowered to the top of the gallery by suppressing the rosettes of the triforium. This, in turn, required that the gallery roof be lowered and redesigned. The solution, a pitched roof with one of its slopes inclined toward the nave wall, created a difficult drainage problem that was solved only in the nineteenth century, when Viollet-le-Duc designed a single-slope roof that throws the water outward.

Like the interior, the façade seems to waver between the old and the new (FIG. 10-9). Begun after the Laon façade

had been completed, it appears much more conservative and, in the preservation of its "mural presence," more closely related to Romanesque than to High Gothic façades. From the modern observer's point of view, this may be one of its great assets. Less perforated and more orderly than Laon's, Notre Dame's façade exudes a sense of strength and permanence that is lacking in many contemporary and later designs. Careful balancing of vertical against horizontal elements has achieved a quality of restful stability that makes this façade one of the most satisfying and memorable in Gothic architecture.

Sculpture

Gothic sculpture first makes its appearance in the Ile-de-France and its environs with the same dramatic suddenness as Gothic architecture, and, it is likely, in the very same place, the abbey church of St. Denis. Almost nothing of the sculpture of the west façade of St. Denis remains to be studied, but it was there that sculpture emerged completely from the interior of the church and dominated the western entrances, which were regarded as the "gateways to Heavenly Jerusalem" and as the "royal portals." These royal portals, so called because of the statues of kings and queens on the embrasures flanking the doorways, are typified by the west portals of the cathedral of Chartres (FIG. 10-13), carved between 1145 and 1170. This west façade and its portals are the only surviving parts of an Early Gothic cathedral that was destroyed in a disastrous fire in

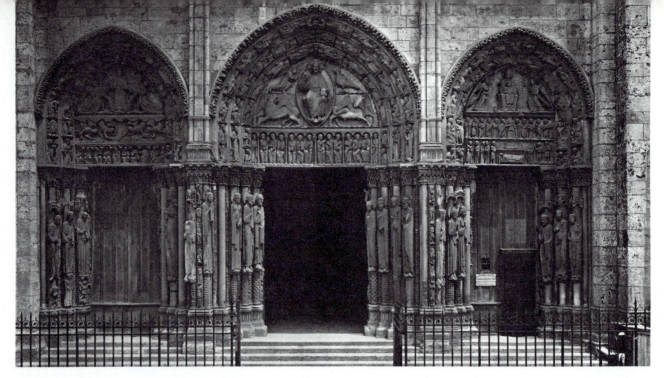

10-13　West ("royal") portals of Chartres Cathedral, *c.* 1145–70.

1194 before it had been completed. The cathedral was reconstructed immediately, but in the High Gothic style (see below). The portals, however, constitute the most complete and impressive corpus of Early Gothic sculpture.

The three west portals of Chartres, treated as a unit, proclaim the majesty and omnipotence of Christ. His birth, the Presentation at the Temple, and Christ in Majesty with his Virgin Mother are shown on the right portal, and his Ascension into heaven on the left. Scenes from his life and from the passion are vividly carved on the capitals, which continue as a frieze from one portal to the next. On the central portal is depicted the Second Coming, surrounded by the symbols of the four Evangelists, with the apostles below, seated as representing the corporate body of the Christian Church. The Second Coming, in essence the Last Judgment theme, remains, as in the Romanesque works we have seen (and which are only some twenty years older than the west portals of Chartres), centrally important. Here, however, it has become a symbol of salvation rather than damnation. It is, moreover, combined with other scenes and symbolic figures as part of a larger theme rather than as symbol of the dogma itself. In the archivolts of the right portal are shown the seven liberal arts, the core of Medieval learning, and therefore symbolic of man's knowledge, which will lead him to the true faith. The signs of the zodiac and scenes representing the various labors of the months of the year are carved into the left-portal archivolts as symbols of the cosmic and of the terrestrial worlds; and around the central tympanum are the twenty-four elders of the Apocalypse, accompanying the Second Coming. Decorating the multiple jambs flanking each doorway are the most striking figures, the great statues of the kings and queens of the Old Testament, the royal

ancestors of Christ (FIG. 10-14). It is almost certain that the Medieval observer also regarded them as the figures of the kings and queens of France, symbols of secular as well as of biblical authority. The unity of the triple portal in its message and composition complements the unity of the cathedral itself, which in its fluent, uninterrupted, vast and soaring space compounds earth and heaven in a symbol of the spiritually perfected universe to come.

The jamb statues are among the few original forms of architectural sculpture to have appeared in any age. At first glance they seem—in their disregard of normal proportions and their rigid adherence to an architectural frame—to follow many of the precepts of Romanesque architectural sculpture. Yet the differences are striking and important. The statues stand out from the plane of the wall; they are not cut back into it. They are conceived and treated as three-dimensional volumes. They move into the space of the observer and participate in it with him. Most significant of all is the first trace of a new naturalism: drapery folds are no longer calligraphic exercises translated into stone; they now either fall vertically or radiate naturally from their points of suspension. Although carefully arranged in regular patterns, these folds suggest that the artist is no longer copying painted images, but that actual models have become his guides. This is true particularly of the figures flanking the central doorway (some shown in left foreground of FIG. 10-14), which are the work of the anonymous HEADMASTER, the artist in charge of the overall design and decoration of the portals. The advanced nature of his style becomes particularly noticeable when his figures are compared with those on the outside jamb of the lateral portal (right background in FIG. 10-14), which evidently were carved by a different, perhaps older, certainly more conservative artist. The latter's approach is still deeply rooted in the Romanesque tradition. His figures seem more agitated, their silhouettes curvilinear and broken. The drapery folds are treated decoratively and, here and there, continue to rotate in abstract swirls. Only the windblown lower garment edges, characteristic of much Romanesque sculpture, have come to rest—reluctantly it seems and, perhaps, at the Headmaster's insistence. Even so, the figures fail to adjust themselves as neatly and consequently to their architectural setting as do the Headmaster's. The latter's statues, although they have stepped out of the wall and have become corporeal, are severely disciplined and have been rigorously subordinated to their architectural background. Seen from a distance, they appear to be little more than vertical decorative accents within the larger designs of portals and façade. And yet, within and despite its architectural strait jacket, the incipient naturalism has softened the appearance of the figures. This is particularly noticeable in their faces, in which the masklike features of the Romanesque are being converted into human likenesses. Here is the faint beginning of a personalizing naturalism that will become transformed first into idealized portraits of the perfect Christian and finally into the portraiture of specific individuals.

At this time, the early twelfth century, great changes were taking place in Western man's view of himself, especially with respect to the relation of body and soul. Previously, the old Augustinian view had prevailed: that the essence of the soul is completely unlike that of the body, the soul being spiritual and immortal, the body material and subject to corruption. With the rediscovery of the main works of Aristotle, it came to be gradually believed that the soul and the body were closely interrelated, that the soul had the *form* of the body, and that, therefore, the body was no longer to be despised as merely the corruptible prison of the soul from which the latter is released when the body dies. One scholastic philosopher saw the soul and the body as meeting, and the combination as responsible for the personality of the individual. Another saw the soul as ruling the body but also cherishing its prison. These views, in which the body is seen as coming into its own, reflect a universally changing outlook. John of Salisbury, the great English humanist, took the perhaps radical view that the soul is stimulated and acted upon by sensations from the world, rather than directly inspired and moved by entirely spiritual principles. He even declared that some of the principal problems of scholastic philosophy could be solved by psychological examination of the way we think. The West was now speaking with a new voice: Souls must be manifested through bodies, the individual bodies of men and women. Thus, the new individualized heads of Chartres herald an era of artistic concern with the realization of personality and individuality that may only now, in our times, be terminating. The

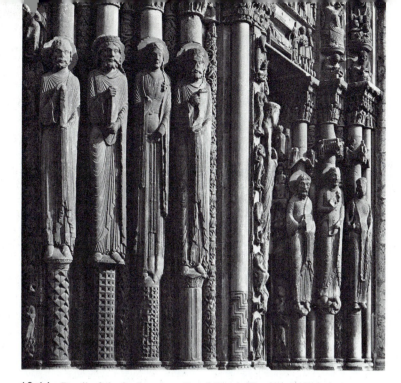

10-14   Detail of the jamb statues, Royal Portal, Chartres Cathedral.

figures of the Royal Portal hold a place analogous to the works of Greek artists in the late sixth century B.C.; they turn the corner into a historical avenue of tremendous possibility.

HIGH GOTHIC

Architecture

On June 10, 1194, a great fire consumed the town of Chartres. Its cathedral, which had only recently been completed, was again destroyed, except for the crypt, the western towers, and the Royal Portal between them. A new cathedral was begun almost immediately, to be completed for the most part by 1220. This new cathedral of Chartres is usually considered the first of the High Gothic buildings, the first to have been planned from the beginning for the use of flying buttresses.

The flying buttress, that exceedingly useful and characteristic Gothic structural device, seems to have been employed by about 1180 for the bracing of the nave of Notre Dame in Paris, and shortly thereafter at Laon. A section through the latter church (FIG. 10-6) shows how the flying buttress reaches across the lower vaults of aisle and gallery and abuts the nave walls directly at those points where the vaults exert their major thrusts. Similar methods to strengthen the walls of vaulted naves had already been used in Romanesque architecture, but there the buttresses had been concealed under the aisle roofing. Now, however, they are left exposed in a manner that has been either condemned as "architectural crudity" or praised as "structural honesty." An aerial view of the cathedral of Chartres

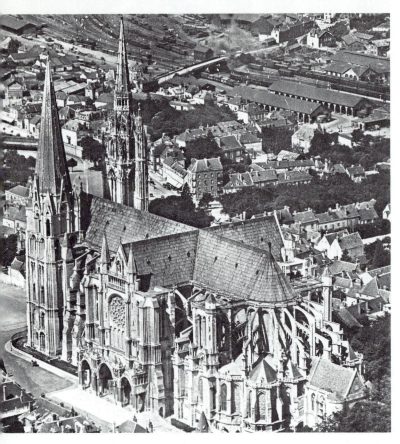

(FIG. 10–15) shows that a series of these highly dramatic devices has been placed around the *chevet* (the east end of the church), supporting the vaults with permanent arms, like scaffolding left in place. With the mastery of this structural form, the technical vocabulary of Gothic architecture is complete. The buttress eliminates the need for Romanesque walls and permits the construction of a skeletal structure that is self-consistent and self-supporting. The Chartres architect was the first to arrive at this conclusion and to design his building accordingly.

At Chartres, after the great fire, the overall dimensions of the new structure were determined by the towers left standing at the west and by the masonry of the crypt to the east. The crypt was the repository of the most precious relic of Chartres, the mantle of the Virgin, and for reasons of piety, but also of economy, was used as foundation for the new structure. The earlier forms did not limit the plan (FIG. 10-16), however, and it shows an unusual equilibrium between chevet, transept, and nave, which are almost equal in dimension; more important, perhaps, the plan shows a new kind of organization. The last remnants of square schematism, still present in Early Gothic Churches, have been replaced by a "rectangular bay system" that will become the High Gothic norm. Now a rectangular unit in

10-15   Aerial view of Chartres Cathedral, begun 1194.

10-16   Plan of Chartres Cathedral. (After Frankl.)

10-17   Nave of Chartres Cathedral.

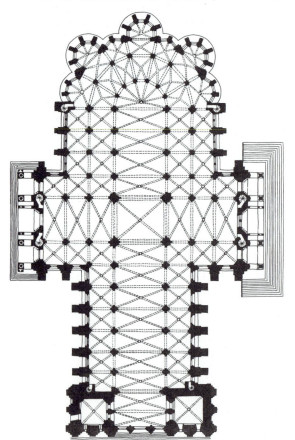

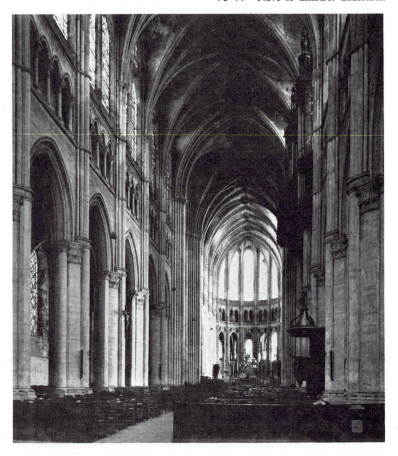

the nave, defined by its own vault, is flanked by a single square in each aisle. This new bay arrangement is accompanied by a change in vault design. The new High Gothic vault, covering a relatively smaller area and more easily braced than its Early Gothic predecessor, has only four panels. The visual effect of these changes is of an interior that has been decompartmentalized (FIG. 10-17), identical units having been so aligned that they are seen in too rapid a sequence to be discriminated as individual volumes of space. The alternate-support system, of course, is gone, and the nave, though richly articulated, has become a vast, continuous hall.

The organic, "flowing" quality of the High Gothic interior was enhanced by a new nave wall elevation, which admitted more light to the nave through greatly enlarged clerestory windows. The use of flying buttresses made it possible to eliminate the tribune gallery above the aisle, which had partially braced Romanesque and Early Gothic naves. The new High Gothic tripartite nave elevation, consisting of arcade, triforium, and clerestory, emphasizes the large clerestory windows; those at Chartres are almost as high as the main arcade. A comparison of the elevations of Laon and Chartres (FIG. 10-18) illustrates what radical changes could be achieved by the logical application of the new structural device—the flying buttress—that had been used only tentatively at Laon.

Despite the vastly increased size of the clerestory windows, some High Gothic interiors remain relatively dark, largely because of the light-muffling effects of their colored glass. Chartres has retained almost the full complement of its original stained glass (see below), and though it dims the interior, it sheds a color-shot light of great beauty that has helped to make the cathedral of Chartres the favorite church of lovers of Gothic architecture.

Whatever the glory of Chartres, it had a contemporary rival in the cathedral of Bourges (FIG. 10-19), which,

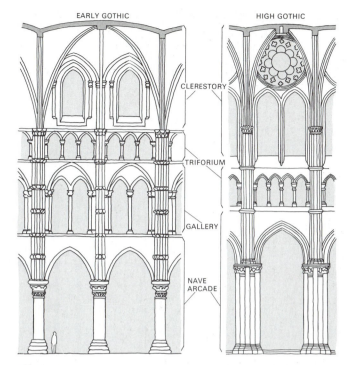

10-18 Elevations of the nave walls of the cathedrals of Laon (left) and Chartres (right). The latter is drawn to a smaller scale than the Laon elevation. Umschau-Verlag, Frankfurt/Main.

though perhaps without the esthetic power of Chartres, may have been to a degree its superior in structural ingenuity, stability, and economy of means. The two buildings, begun about the same time, were completely different yet satisfactory solutions to the problems of Gothic architectural design. As such, they offered to architects two alternative models to follow: At Amiens and Reims the design of Chartres was perfected, and at Beauvais the first master architect conceived a kind of synthesis of Chartres and Bourges.

The plan of Bourges is strikingly different from that of Chartres, resembling more that of Notre Dame in Paris (FIG. 10-11). At Chartres there is an equilibrium among the

10-19 Bourges Cathedral from the southeast, 1195–1255.

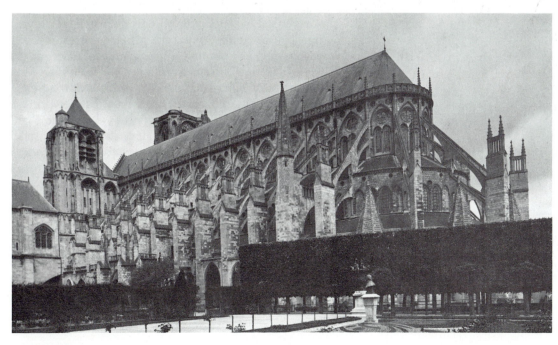

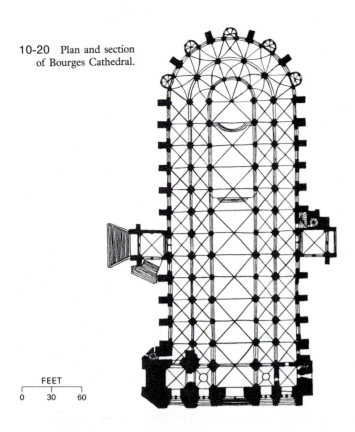

10-20 Plan and section
of Bourges Cathedral.

FEET
0   30   60

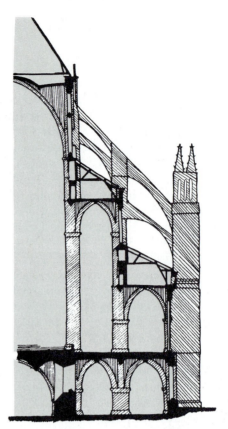

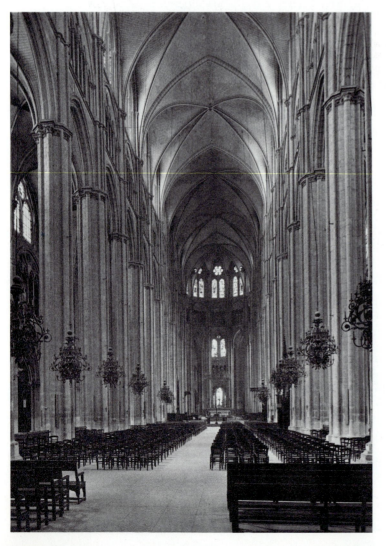

choir, transept, and nave, which are of almost equal dimension. At Bourges the plan is a continuous one (FIG. 10-20), eliminating the transept entirely, so that the side-aisles continue without interruption from the western façade around the choir to the east. The unity and sweeping continuity of the plan was furthered by the unusual elevation (FIG. 10-21). Instead of one aisle on each side of the nave, there are two, one (the inner) being higher and having its own clerestory, triforium, and arcade, all clearly visible through the nave arcade. The stepping upward of the side-aisles to a climax in the nave vaults, and the restatement in the inner aisle—albeit on a smaller scale— of the nave's three-part wall elevation, provides a rhythmic, vertical repetition of the distinctive High Gothic arrangement. At the same time, windows at three levels enhance the fluent opening of the space of the nave into the aisles, by saturating the interior with a form-dissolving permeation of light—the ideal of Gothic architecture.

The retention of older, Romanesque features like the six-part vaults, the alternating system (seen in the slight differentiation in membering of alternate piers), and small clerestory, do not reflect structural uncertainty. Modern engineering analysis of wind load and dead-load stresses (the kind necessary for the high-rise structures of today) shows that the lighter and more open buttresses of Bourges transfer structural forces to the foundations more efficiently than the massive ones at Chartres. Nevertheless, the Chartres design, with its balanced, additive, and logical arrangements of plan and elevation became the more influential of the two. At Bourges the relationships of the

10-21 Nave of Bourges Cathedral, 1225-50.

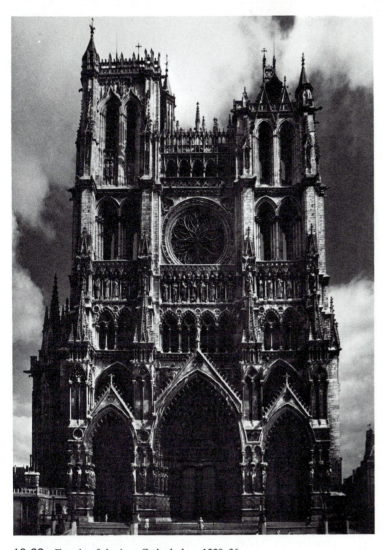

10-22 Façade of Amiens Cathedral, c. 1220-36.

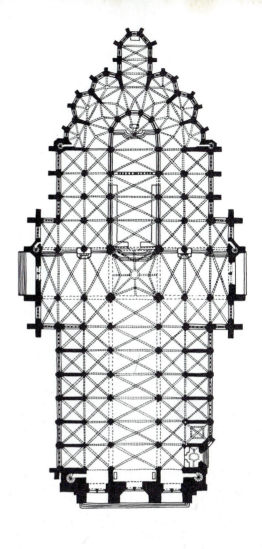

10-23 Plan of Amiens Cathedral. (After Frankl.)

parts were perhaps too elusive and individual to be readily grasped and widely applied as a standard.

The cathedral of Amiens (FIGS. 10-22 to 10-25) continues the Chartrian manner, gracefully refining it. Amiens was begun in 1220 according to designs of ROBERT DE LUZARCHES. The nave was finished in 1236 and the radiating chapels in 1247, but work on the choir continued until almost 1270. The façade (FIG. 10-22), slightly marred by uneven towers (the shorter dates from the fourteenth, the other from the fifteenth century), was begun at the same time as the nave (1220). Its lower parts seem to reflect the influence of the Laon façade in the spacing of its funnel-like and gable-covered portals. Unlike Laon's, the Amiens portals do not project from the façade, but are recessed behind the building's buttress-defined frontal plane. The upper parts of the façade, on the other hand, seem to be related to Notre Dame in Paris, the rose window (with fifteenth-century tracery) being placed above the "king's gallery" and between double-arched openings in the towers. But the Amiens façade goes well beyond its apparent models in the richness and intricacy of its surface decoration. The deep piercing of walls and towers seems to have

left few continuous surfaces to be decorated, to be sure, but the remaining ones have been covered with a network of articulating colonnettes, arches, pinnacles, rosettes, and other decorative stone work that screens and nearly dissolves visually the structure's solid core. Despite its decorative intricacy, the façade retains its monumental grandeur and is one of the first to achieve full integration with the building behind it. The cavernous portals correspond in width and placement to the nave and aisles and, although in slightly different proportions, the façade's three-part elevation reflects that of the nave, the rose window corresponding to the clerestory.

The plan of Amiens (FIG. 10-23), like the façade, is exemplary of the grand High Gothic style. Derived from Chartres and perhaps even more elegant in its proportions, it reflects the builder's unhesitating and confident use of the complete Gothic structural vocabulary: the rectangular bay system, the four-paneled rib vault, and a buttressing system that permits almost complete dissolution of the heavy masses and thick bearing walls of the Romanesque. The concept of a self-sustaining skeletal architecture has reached full maturity; what remains of the walls has been

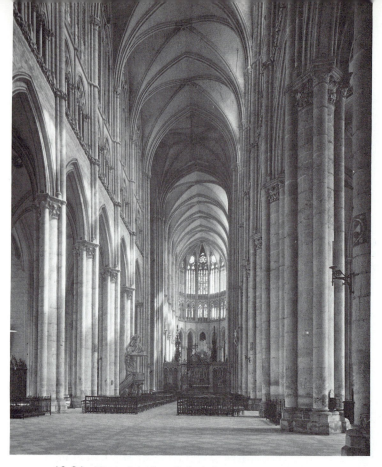

10-24 Nave of Amiens Cathedral.

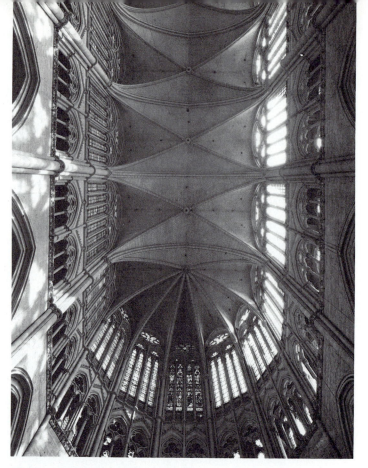

10-25 Choir vault of Amiens Cathedral.

stretched like a skin between the piers and seems to serve no purpose other than to provide a weather screen for the interior (FIG. 10-24). From a height of 144 feet the tense, strong lines of the vault ribs converge to the colonnettes and speed down the shell-like walls to the compound piers, almost each part of the superstructure having its corresponding element below—the only exception being the wall rib (the rib at the junction of the vault and the wall). There is an appearance of an effortless strength (that counters the fact of great weight), of a buoyant lightness one would never associate with the obdurate materiality of stone. Viewed directly from below, the vaults of the choir seem like a canopy, tentlike and suspended from bundled masts (FIG. 10-25). The light flooding in from the clerestory imparts even more "lift" and at the same time blurs structural outlines. The effect is visionary, and we are reminded of another great building, utterly different from Amiens, in which light plays an analogous role—Hagia Sophia in Constantinople. Not only is the physical mass of the building reduced by structural ingenuity and daring, but what remains is further dematerialized visually by light. As with scholastic philosophy, the logic of the structure is here in the service of mystery. While philosophy might prove the existence of God with reason, the experience of the beatific vision gave the believer a mystical proof, like Dante's experience in Paradise as he gazed, rapt, into the "heart of Light, the heart of Silence."

In examining the interior of Amiens it may be useful to reconsider Panofsky's abovementioned suggestion of a connection between Gothic architecture and Scholastic philosophy and the description of the method as typified in Aquinas' *Summa Theologica*. Most striking in the propositions of Aquinas and in the structure of Amiens is an insistence upon an order and unity made up of clearly distinguished and clearly related parts, the philosopher aiming at logical consistency, and the architect at structural coherence. In neither is the order intended to be less than total. Aquinas' *Summa* was designed to treat *all* possible questions where faith and reason touch; in Amiens all individual elements are subordinated to the whole, unlike the case of the sharply subdivided—often opposed—units of Romanesque design. This principle of *manifestatio* ("manifestation," "transparency") determines the look of the philosophic system as it does the look of the cathedral. As Panofsky wrote:

A man imbued with the Scholastic habit [of thought] . . . would look upon the mode of architectural presentation, just as he looked upon the mode of literary presentation, from the point of view of *manifestatio*. He would have taken it for granted that the primary purpose of the many elements that compose a cathedral was to ensure stability, just as he took it for granted that the primary purpose of the many elements that constitute a *Summa* was to ensure validity.

← to c.1140	1144	c.1160	1194	c.1200	1215	c.1220	1226	1233	c.1250	to c.1300 →
	St. Denis completed	Laon Cathedral begun		Chartres Cathedral Nave begun	Façade design, Notre Dame, Paris		Salisbury Cathedral begun	St. Elizabeth, Marburg, begun	Ekkehard and Uta	

EARLY GOTHIC HIGH GOTHIC

FREDERICK II
LOUIS IX (SAINT LOUIS) — to 1270

But he would not have been satisfied had not the membrification of the edifice permitted him to re-experience the very processes of architectural composition just as the membrification of the *Summa* permitted him to re-experience the very processes of cogitation. To him, the panoply of shafts, ribs, buttresses, tracery, pinnacles and crockets was a self-analysis and self-explication of . . . architecture much as the customary apparatus of parts, distinctions, questions and articles was, to him, a self-analysis and self-explication of reason. . . . the Scholastic mind demanded a maximum of explicitness. It accepted and insisted upon a gratuitous clarification of function through form, just as it accepted and insisted upon a gratuitous clarification of thought through language.[2]

The other principle Panofsky saw at work in philosophy and architecture is that of *concordantia* ("harmony"), whereby contradictory possibilities are accepted and ultimately reconciled. This is achieved by careful debate, the *disputatio*, in which a possibility is stated, one authoritative view is cited, another authoritative view is cited in objection, the solution (a reconciliation of positions) is given, and finally a reply is given to each of the original arguments now rejected. Panofsky saw this process in the resolution of three "questions" in Gothic architecture: the placement and design of the rose window in the west façade, the design of the interior wall beneath the clerestory, and the conformation of the pier. (Very likely the development of the Gothic plan could also be seen as an evolved "solution" to a "question.") Evidence that the habit of mind reflected in the *disputatio* was not exclusive with the scholastics in the universities, but was more broadly shared, is found in a page from the "album" of drawings by the thirteenth-century architect VILLARD DE HONNECOURT. According to the inscription, an ideal plan for a chevet was drawn by Villard and another architect, PIERRE DE CORBIE, the design being arrived at after a discussion—that is, a *disputatio*.

THE RAYONNANT STYLE

From the grand style of the first half of the thirteenth century came a period of great refinement, the so-called *rayonnant* ("radiant") style, which dominated the second half of the century and was associated with the royal Paris court of Louis IX (St. Louis), famed throughout Europe

[2]Erwin Panofsky, *Gothic Architecture and Scholasticism* (Latrobe, Pa.: Archabbey Press, 1951), pp. 58–60.

for his justice, chivalry, and piety, and the Medieval ideal of the "saint-king." Royal France, growing increasingly wealthy, powerful, and prestigious, radiated its art and culture through Europe. The king was lavish in embellishing the realm, especially with religious architecture.

A handsome and characteristic example of the new rayonnant style is the Sainte-Chapelle in Paris (FIGS. 10-26 and 10-27). The building, joined to the royal palace, was intended to be a repository for relics of the Passion of Christ brought back by Louis IX after the ill-fated Sixth Crusade, so that its resemblance to an intricately carved reliquary is intentional. Here the dissolution of the wall

10-26 Sainte-Chapelle, Paris, 1243–48. The rose window was installed after 1485.

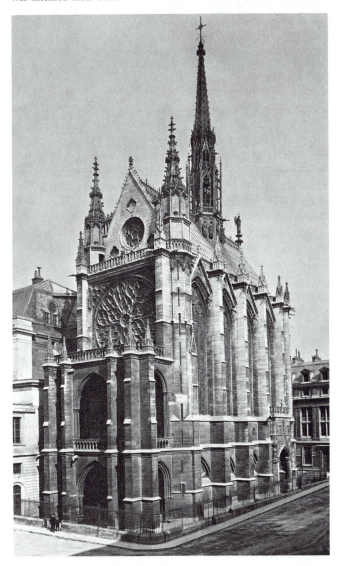

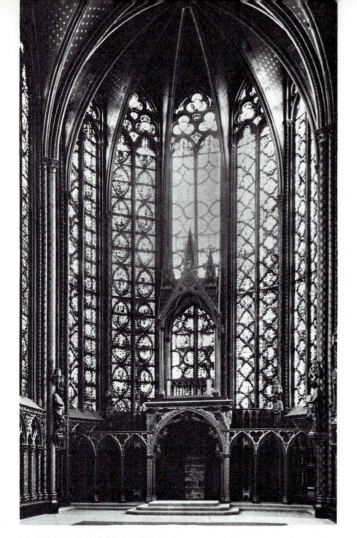

10-27 Interior of Sainte-Chapelle.

The rayonnant manner can be appreciated also in the transepts of Notre Dame in Paris (FIG. 10-10), especially if they are compared with those parts of the building that are some sixty years older. The whole wall seems to open into glass; in the south transept the spectacular rose window, echoed by a smaller window in the gable, contrasts strikingly with the earlier rose in the west façade, which still is framed by massive wall. The south transept rose is the wall become transparent, a filigree of bar tracery seeming as fragile and insubstantial as lace.

The choir of the unfinished cathedral of Beauvais (FIG. 10-28) is an example of the Gothic "rush" into the skies. That skyward impulse, seen first in the height of the nave at Paris (at the turn of the century), became an obsession with Gothic builders. With their new skeletal frames of stone, they attempted goals almost beyond limit, pushing with ever slenderer supports to new heights, aiming always at effects of insubstantial visions floating far beyond the reach of man. The nave vaults at Laon had risen to a height of about 80 feet; at Paris, to 107 feet; at Chartres, to 118 feet; and at Amiens, to 144 feet. In 1272 the builders of the choir of Beauvais planned a height of 157 feet. (Only the choir and transepts were built; the building remains without a nave.) In 1284 the vaults collapsed; the cause of the failure is still a matter of scholarly debate. The

and the reduction of the bulk of the supports has been carried to the point where more than three-quarters of the structure is composed of stained glass. The supporting elements have been so reduced that they are hardly more than large mullions that separate the enormous windows, which measure approximately 49 by 15 feet and are the largest designed up to their time. Although the chapel was heavily restored during the nineteenth century (after being damaged in the French Revolution), it has retained most of its original thirteenth-century glass, which filters the light and fills the interior with an unearthly rose-violet atmosphere. Amid richly colored stone surfaces and shimmering strips of decorative mosaic stand statues of the Apostles. Multicolored also, they stand on soffits almost independent of the architecture, and their related poses, with multiple axes, foreshadow the graceful rhythms of later thirteenth- and fourteenth-century sculpture. Here are technical and esthetic refinements that would have upset the solemn harmonies and monumentality of the art of the earlier part of the century. The emphasis upon extreme slenderness of the architectural forms and upon linearity in general, with exquisite color and precise carving of details, does indeed recall the richly ornamented reliquaries of the time.

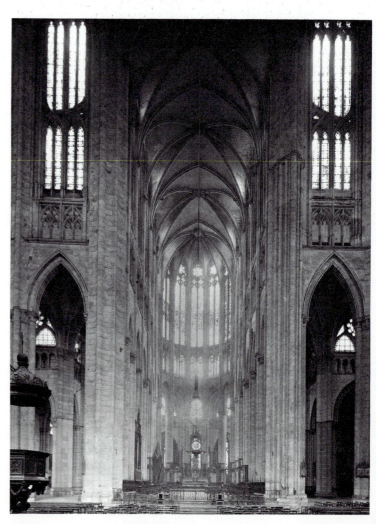

10-28 Choir of Beauvais Cathedral, 1272; vaults rebuilt after 1284.

original design of the first master architect had been brilliant, audacious, and stable; the parts of the choir hemicycle completed by him remained standing. Modern engineering analysis, of the kind we have mentioned in the discussion of Chartres and Bourges, indicates that succeeding builders seem to have miscalculated wind and dead-load stresses, particularly those on the external intermediate piers. The choir, rebuilt with a broad margin of safety, has additional piers and old-fashioned, six-part vaults, not unlike those at Bourges. Unfortunately, the rebuilt vaults and piers disfigure the original design, for it was exactly those former features of wide-spread piers and slender buttresses that the rayonnant architects had sought in their effort to make an architecture seemingly out of nothing but line and light. Henceforth, the great structural innovations of the High Gothic, and the vast scale in which they were worked out, would be things of the past. Late Gothic architecture, born of the linear rayonnant, would be confined to buildings of quite modest size, conservative in structure and ornamented with restless designs of intricately meshed pointed motifs.

Sculpture

Sculpture was subservient to architecture during the High Gothic period, as it had been since the Romanesque. But rapid changes were taking place. The unity of idea that controls the design of the Royal Portal of Chartres expanded to embrace the whole cathedral (see the façade of Amiens, FIG. 10-22). The sculptural program came to include not only the huge portals but the upper levels of the building as well. This was at the height of Gothic art, the cathedral-building and cathedral-adorning age, covering the years 1210 to 1260. The range of the iconography of the sculpture is as vast and complex as the building. Most of the carved figures are symbolic, but many, particularly the grotesque gargoyles, used as rain-spouts, and other details of the upper portions, are purely decorative and show the vivacity and charm of the Medieval spirit of this moment, when it was confident in its faith. The iconographic program, no longer (as in Romanesque art) confined almost entirely to the letter of the dogma, is extensive enough to embrace all the categories of Medieval thought. Indeed Émile Mâle showed that many iconographic schemes are based upon the *Speculum majus* ("Great Mirror") of Vincent of Beauvais, a comprehensive summary of Medieval knowledge in which accounts of natural phenomena, scriptural themes, and moral philosophy serve a didactic religious purpose.

Nature begins to come forward as important, and man comes forward with it. Two figures from the Porch of the Confessors in the south transept of the cathedral of Chartres illustrate how much the incipient realism of the Royal Portal has advanced (FIG. 10-29). The figures represent St. Martin and St. Jerome, and date from the period

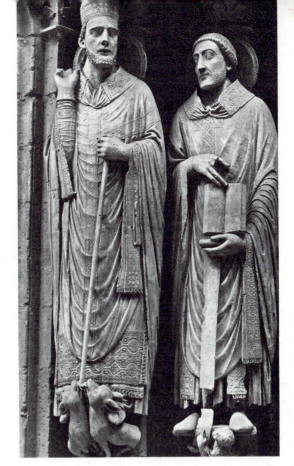

10-29 *St. Martin and St. Jerome, c.* 1220-30, from the Porch of the Confessors, Chartres Cathedral.

1220-30. Although attached to the architectural matrix, their poses are not determined by it as much as formerly. The setting now allows the figures to communicate quietly with one another, like dignitaries waiting for some solemn procession to begin; they turn slightly toward each other, breaking the rigid vertical lines that, on the Royal Portal, fix the figures immovably. Their draperies are no longer described by the stiff and reedy lines of the figures of the Royal Portal; they fall and lap over the bodies in soft, if still regular, folds.

The faces are most remarkable; they show for the first time since the ancient world the features of specifically Western men, with no admixture whatever of the denatured mask that had come down through a thousand years. Moreover, they seem to have been taken from particular persons as models, and we have no difficulty characterizing them. St. Martin is tall, ascetic, the intense priest with the gaunt features of the Gothic visionary (compare the spiritually moved but not particularized face of the Moissac *Jeremiah* of FIG. 9-23); he may have been a saintly canon of Chartres, reluctantly become a bishop; in any event— another realistic touch—his vestments are the liturgical costume of the time. His companion, St. Jerome, appears the humorous, kindly, practical administrator-scholar, who holds his Vulgate translation of the Scriptures. Thus, the two men are not simply contrasted by their poses, gestures,

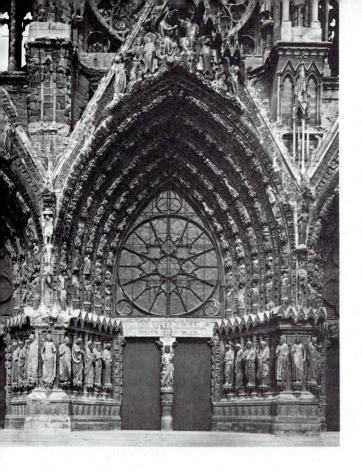

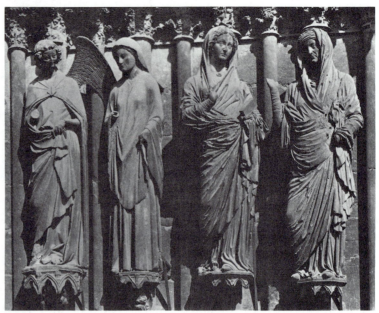

10-30 Central portal of the west façade of Reims Cathedral, c. 1225-90.

10-31 *The Annunciation* and *The Visitation,* detail of FIG. 10-30.

and attributes but most particularly and emphatically as *persons,* so that personality, revealed in human faces, makes the real difference—something that had been rare even in classical art. In another century or so the identifiable portrait will emerge.

The fully ripened Gothic style appears in the west portals of the cathedral of Reims (FIG. 10-30), built in the mid-thirteenth century. At first glance, the jamb statues appear completely detached from their architectural background. The columns to which they are attached have shrunk into insignificance and in no way impede the free and easy movement of the full-bodied figures. (On the Royal Portal of Chartres the background columns occupy a volume equal to that of the figures; see FIG. 10-14.) However, two architectural devices limit the statues' spheres of activity and tie them to the larger design of the portal—the pedestals upon which they stand and the canopies above their heads. Less submissive than their predecessors from the Royal Portal of Chartres, these Reims figures create an electric tension within the portal design; they were designed for this portal, however, and would look incongruous in any other setting. Gothic portal statues placed in museums to protect them from weathering look, without exception, forlorn and out of place.

On the right jamb of the central portal, four figures (FIG. 10-31) represent the Annunciation (left) and the Visitation (right). In their different styles they show the hands of several anonymous masters. The master of the *Visitation* group, quite original in his manner, manifests a classicizing

bent startlingly unlike anything seen since Roman times. The group illustrates the impact on its master carver of either actual classical statuary he had seen or of manuscripts or ivories from Late Antiquity or Byzantium. Whatever the artist's source, the facial types, costumes, and drapery treatment are an astonishing approximation of the naturalistic style traits of ancient figure sculpture. He has even tried to represent the classical contrapposto stance, although the only partially successful result betrays the sculptor's ignorance of human anatomy. The two figures of the *Annunciation* group evidently were carved by different masters. The *Virgin* is by a sculptor who may have worked at Amiens before he came to Reims and whose style is characterized by a weighty, massive quality. Drapery resembling a thick, flannel-like material heavily falls from the figure's shoulders to her feet and, by stressing mass and verticality, imparts an aspect of grave solemnity.

The *Angel* of the *Annunciation* group differs strikingly from the *Virgin.* It is tall and slender, animated by a kind of swaying curve, the head quite small, the face bright with a winsome smile. This almost dainty figure, contrasting with the still and somber *Virgin,* represents the new, courtly style—corresponding to the rayonnant in architecture—that comes in with the reign of Louis IX and the cultural dominance of the Île-de-France after mid-century. The influence of these great cathedral statues must have been widely felt by those who contemplated them. John of Garland, writing in the thirteenth century on how univer-

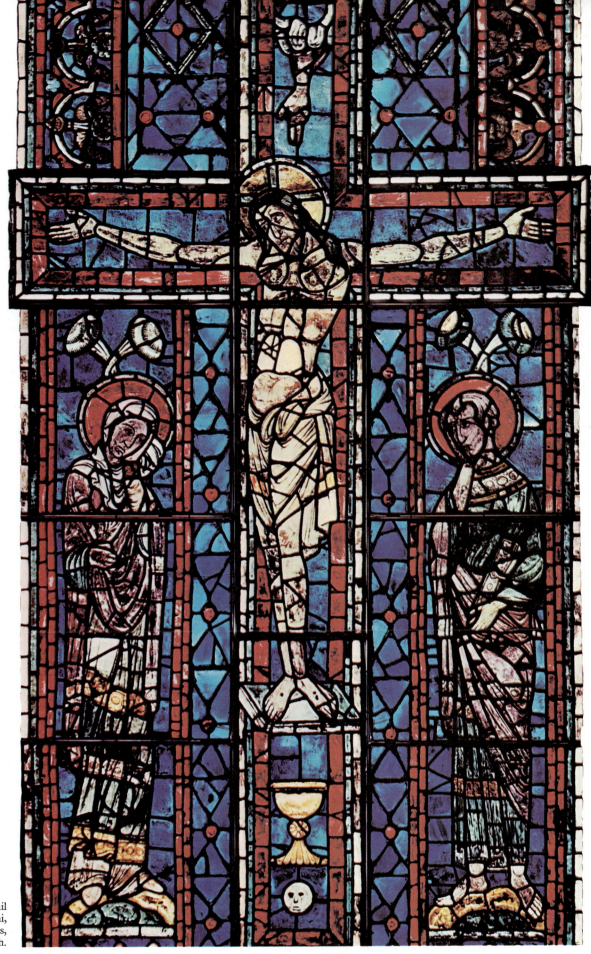

10-32 *Crucifixion,* detail of a window from St. Remi, Reims, *c.* 1190. Stained glass, approx. 12′ high.

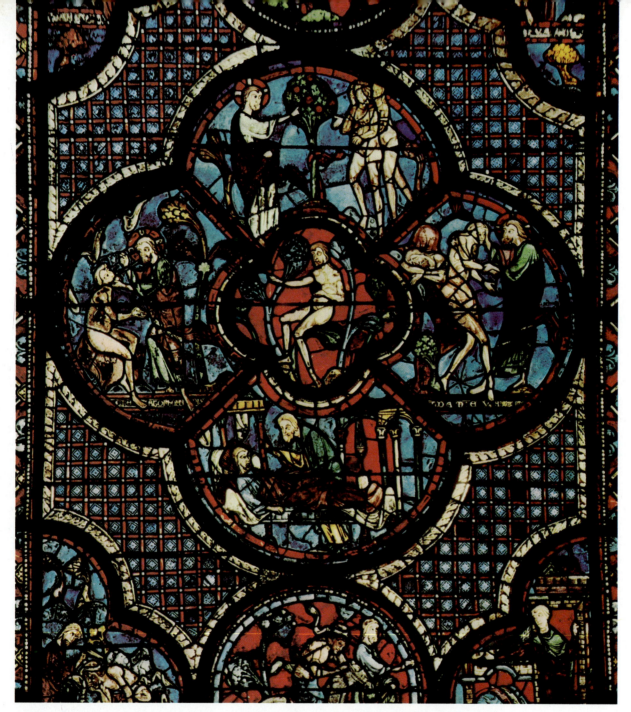

10-33 Detail of the *Good Samaritan* window, Chartres Cathedral, early thirteenth century. Stained glass.

sity students should conduct themselves, advises: ". . . regard as models of deportment the graven images of the churches, which you should carry in your mind as living and indelible pictures."

Certainly their influence upon artists must have been great, as for example, in the case of the painter of the St. Louis Psalter (p. 338 and FIG. 10-35). Though the degree and the progress of that influence has not yet been worked out in all detail, it is certain that by the fourteenth century Gothic sculpture was widely naturalized in Italy, as elsewhere outside of France. In Italy, by the beginning of the fifteenth century, the native Gothic sense for realism

had fused with a new classicizing impulse—partly generated from Byzantine art, partly from the discovery of the art of ancient Rome—to form the first distinctive styles of the Renaissance.

Stained Glass and Illumination

The Gothic accomplishment in architecture and sculpture is matched by the magnificent stained glass of the time. This medium is almost synonymous with the Gothic style; no other age has managed it with such craft and beauty. The mysticism of light that induced Suger to design an architecture that would allow for great windows is widespread in Gothic theology. "Stained glass windows," writes Hugh of St. Victor, "are the Holy Scriptures . . . and since their brilliance lets the splendor of the True Light pass into the church, they enlighten those inside." St. Bernard compares the manner in which light is tinted by a stained-glass window to the process of the Incarnation and virgin birth of Jesus. The Gothic mood seems almost to take its inspiration from the Gospel of John: "In him was life; and the life was the light of men. And the light shineth in darkness."

The difference between these words and the sonorous verses of Revelation, which provide the program of the Romanesque "Last Judgments," reflects the difference between the shining walls of colored light, which change with every passing hour or cloud, and the painted walls of Romanesque churches or the shimmering mosaics of the Byzantine.

Colored glass was used as early as the fourth century to decorate the windows of churches. Perfection of the technique must have been gradual, with the greatest advances during the tenth and eleventh centuries. The first accurately dated windows, those of the choir of St. Denis in 1144, show a high degree of skill; Suger states that they were "painted by the exquisite hands of many masters from different regions," proving that the art was widely known at that time. Yet the stained-glass window may be said to be the hallmark of the Gothic style, particularly in northern Europe, where the almost total dissolution of walls left few surfaces that were suitable for decoration with frescoes.

Imperfections or unexpected results in making colored glass were frequent; yet this was not an art left entirely to chance. The different properties of colors were well understood and carefully controlled. The glass was blown and either "spun" into a "crown" plate of varying thickness or shaped into a cylindrical "muff," which was cut and rolled out into square pieces. These pieces were then broken or cut into smaller fragments and assembled on a flat table, on which a design had been marked with chalk dust. Many of the pieces were actually "painted" with a dark pigment so that details, as of a face or clothing, could be rendered. The fragments were then "leaded," or joined by strips of lead that were used to separate colors or to heighten the effect of the design as a whole (FIGS. 10-32 and 10-33). The completed window was strengthened with an armature of iron bands, which in the twelfth century had the form of a grid over the whole design (FIG. 10-32), but in the thirteenth century was shaped to follow the outlines of the medallions and of the surrounding areas (FIG. 10-33).

The technical difficulties of assembling a large stained-glass window and fixing it firmly within its frame were matched by compositional problems. Illuminated manuscripts, which had been the painter's chief vehicle during the earlier Middle Ages, had little instructional value for artists who had not only to work on an unprecedented scale, but who had to adjust their designs to the larger whole of the church building and its architecture. Sculptors, of course, had already solved these problems and it may not be too surprising to find that painters turned to them for instruction. Certainly the saints flanking the cross in the Reims window (FIG. 10-32) seem vaguely familiar. Their erect poses, the straight, almost unbroken silhouettes, and the rather precarious manner in which they perch upon their hilltop pedestals stamp them as not too distant relatives of the jamb statues from the Royal Portal at Chartres. Here the Romanesque process has been reversed, and the sculptors, the former students who had found their inspiration in paintings, have now become the teachers.

Like the architects and sculptors with whom they worked in close collaboration, the stained-glass artists relied heavily on the *ars de geometria* for their designs, layouts, and assemblies. The sketchbook of Villard de Honnecourt, the mid-thirteenth-century architect referred to earlier, was intended as a text for Villard's students. But he does not confine his instruction to architecture alone. In addition to details of buildings, plans of choirs with radiating chapels, and church towers, he also presents information on lifting devices, a saw mill, and stained-glass windows. Sprinkled liberally through the pages are drawings of figures, religious and worldly, and animals—some surprisingly realistic, others purely fantastic. In the page shown (FIG. 10-34) Villard is evidently informing his stu-

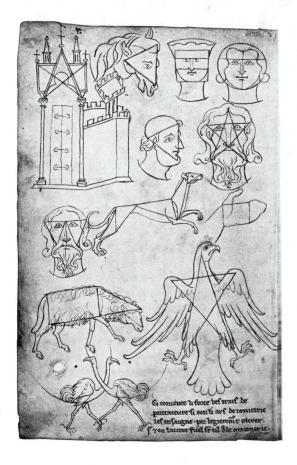

10-34 VILLARD DE HONNECOURT, page from a notebook, c. 1240. Bibliothèque Nationale, Paris.

dents of the usefulness of the *ars de geometria* in designing human heads and animals. In some instances Villard claims to have drawn his animals from nature, but even these appear to have been composed around a skeleton not of bones but of abstract geometrical figures. It seems likely that the designers of stained-glass windows proceeded in a similar manner. No matter how arrived at, the effect of these glowing, translucent paintings, which often seem to be suspended in space, is as spellbinding today as it must have been to the Medieval churchgoer. For the first time in centuries the art of painting had been made accessible to the common man—painting in a form so compelling that the desire to have more and more of it, from pavement to vault, may well have influenced the development of Gothic architecture. By the middle of the thirteenth century, architectural techniques were so advanced that the space of cathedrals seems to be defined by the burning intensity of the stained-glass windows rather than the stone structure.

The radiance of stained glass must have inspired the glowing color of illuminated manuscripts; in some cases, glass and book must have been produced by masters in the same shop, perhaps by one master who was expert in both arts. The *Psalter of St. Louis* (FIG. 10-35) is believed to have been one of a number of books produced in Paris in the late thirteenth century for King Louis IX of France ("St. Louis") by craftsmen associated with those who made the stained glass for the Sainte-Chapelle (FIGS. 10-26 and 10-27). Certainly the figures of this illumination express the same aristocratic elegance as the "court style" in architecture—the rayonnant—favored by royal Paris. The painted architectural setting reflects the pierced-screen-like lightness and transparency of royal buildings like the Sainte-Chapelle and the new work at St. Denis. The intense colors, especially the blues, emulate glass; the borders resemble glass partitioned by leading; and the gables pierced by rose windows are almost portraits of rayonnant architectural features. The subject is Abraham and the Three Angels. (See Andrei Rublëv's version of essentially the same theme, FIG. 7-58.) Two episodes are included, separated by the Tree of Mamre: In one, Abraham greets the three angels; in the other, he entertains them while Sarah peers at them from the tent. The figures, compared with those in Romanesque illumination (FIGS. 9-29 to 9-32), are quieter in pose and attitude and have a firmness of stance and a sense of weight suggestive of sculpture. The busyness of the drapery lines has greatly slowed, moreover, making us less mindful of the flat areas that encourage decorative line-play and more of the modeling tones that suggest plastic form and contour.

While these figures owe much to stained glass for their color, the influence of sculpture is also evident. The lead angel in the group at the left closely resembles the angel of the *Annunciation* group at Reims (FIG. 10-31); and if we look at the general arrangement of the portal (FIG. 10-30), we see that the illuminator thinks of the sacred personages as framed, canopied, and backed by architecture, and their placement determined by it—like the actual sculptures of the portal.

It may be that the artist's response to the monumental, over-life-size sculptures of the cathedral portals led him to a new sense of the possibilities of representation—the function of light and shade, for example, and of volume, contour, and silhouette. These imposing figures could have had a new, awesome authority compared with the traditional prototypes—ivory carvings, say, or painted pages. The impulse to naturalism and pictorial illusionism endemic in the Greco-Roman world, and by no means lost in Early Christian and Byzantine art, could here be receiving a new and powerful impulse from monumental sculpture. Here the illusionistic effect of sculpture may have caught and held the Gothic artist's attention.

Byzantine artists will go a different way, working within received conventions, disdaining sculpture and the pictorial form built upon it, respecting the flat surface, and unfriendly to the more or less systematic pursuit of three-dimensional illusionism widely favored in the West from this time till the twentieth century. We read of a Byzantine priest in the sixteenth century rejecting some paintings by Titian, the great Venetian master of the Renaissance (pp. 571–75 and FIG. 17-62 to 17-66), because "the figures stand quite out from the canvas" and therefore look "as bad as a group of statues."[3] The Byzantine artist did not find in his environment monumental sculpture like that of the Gothic portals. Would Byzantine painting and mosaic have been different if he had? The Gothic painter could not help but be struck by these majestic figures of great scale. The attention he paid them is evident in the figures of the Psalter of St. Louis.

LATE GOTHIC

The collapse of the vaults of Beauvais would seem to have brought the great thirteenth-century architectural debate to an unarguable conclusion. Analogously, the followers of Aquinas came to believe that his accommodation of faith and reason was impossible and that both must go their separate ways. It was the beginning of the dissolution of the Medieval synthesis, which would lead to the eventual destruction of the unity of Christendom. The resolution of opposites could not be achieved; the conflict must now begin that would reshape western Europe.

Villard de Honnecourt has left us a record of these years when so much was expected of art since so much had been achieved. The search for an ideal solution for a building and the codification of artistic—as well as philosophic—procedures were essentially academic in spirit, conscious

[3] Edward Gibbon, *Decline and Fall of the Roman Empire.* Quoted with citation in Ernst Kitzinger, *Byzantine Art in the Making* (Cambridge, Mass.: Harvard Univ. Press, 1977), p. 107.

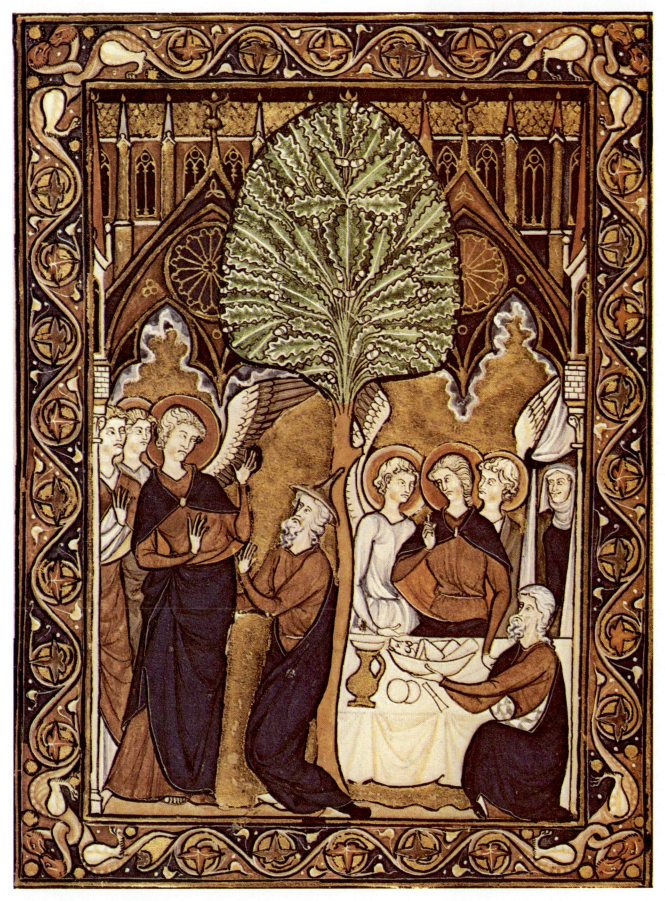

10-35 *Abraham and the Three Angels*, illuminated page from the Psalter of St. Louis, 1253–70. Bibliothèque Nationale, Paris.

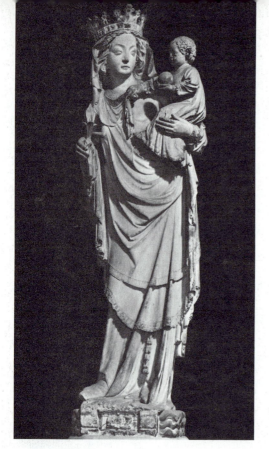

10-36 *The Virgin of Paris,* Notre Dame, early fourteenth century.

enterprises. Both were to be concerned with elaborations of surface forms rather than innovations in structure.

By the early fourteenth century the monumental and solemn sculpture of the High Gothic portals was replaced by the courtly style developed from the *Angel* of Reims (FIG. 10-31), a quite rarefied example of which may be seen in the statue of the Virgin and Child within Notre Dame in Paris (FIG. 10-36). The curving sway of the figure, emphasized by the bladelike sweeps of drapery that converge to the child, has a mannered elegance that will mark Late Gothic sculpture in general. This is the famed Late Gothic S-curve that one encounters again and again during the fourteenth and fifteenth centuries. Superficially it may resemble another S-curve seen much earlier—that of Praxiteles in the fourth century B.C. But, unlike its classical predecessor, the Late Gothic S is not organic, coming from within the figure, nor is it the result of a rational, if pleasing, organization of the figure's anatomical parts; it is an artificial form imposed upon the figure, a decorative device that may produce the desired effect of elegance but which has nothing to do with the figure's structure. In fact, in our example, the body is quite lost behind the heavy drapery, which, deeply cut and hollowed, would almost deny the figure solid existence. The ornamental line created by the flexible fabric is analogous to the complex, restless tracery of the flamboyant style in architecture, which dominated northern Europe in the fourteenth and fifteenth centuries; and the emphasis upon ornament for its own sake is in harmony with the artificial prettiness the artist contrives in the Virgin's doll-like face, large-eyed and tiny-mouthed under her heavy, gem-encrusted crown.

evaluations of a style that had already reached and passed its complete definition. Artistic practice and scholastic method would now spend a long time going over ground already covered but would no longer attempt grandiose

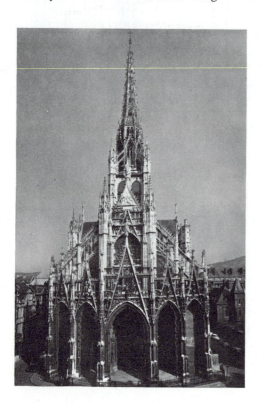

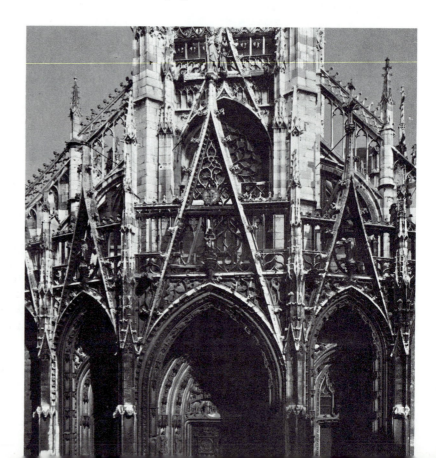

10-37 St. Maclou, Rouen, *c.* 1500–14; right: Detail of façade.

The change from rayonnant architecture to the Late Gothic or flamboyant (so called because of the flamelike look of its pointed tracery) took place in the fourteenth century; the style reached its florid maturity toward the end of the fifteenth. This period was a difficult one for royal France; long wars against England and Burgundy sapped its economic and cultural strength, and building projects in the royal domain were either halted or not begun. And so the new style found its most fertile soil in regions outside the Ile-de-France. Normandy is particularly rich in flamboyant architecture, and its close ties with England suggest that the Anglo-Norman school of "decorated" architecture may have had much to do with the development of the flamboyant style. The church of St. Maclou (FIG. 10-37), in Rouen, the capital of Normandy, presents a façade widely different from those of the thirteenth century. St. Maclou, some 180 feet long and 75 feet high, is almost diminutive compared with the great cathedrals. The five portals, two blind, bend outward in an arc and are crowned by five gables pierced through and filled with sinuous, wiry, flamboyant tracery. Pierced galleries of spidery arcades climb steeply to the center bay, marching along behind the transparent gables. The overlapping of all features, pierced as they are, confuses the structural lines and produces a bewildering complexity of views. It is almost as if the Celtic-Germanic instinct for intricate line, expressed in works like the *Book of Lindisfarne,* was manifesting itself once again against the form and logic newly abstracted from the traditions of the Mediterranean. Yet the Renaissance is not far off, and, within a generation or two of St. Maclou, France will have adopted a new classical style from Italy.

NON-FRENCH GOTHIC

Around 1269 the prior of a German monastery "hired a skilled architect who had just come from the city of Paris" to rebuild his monastery church. The architect reconstructed the church *opere francigeno,* "in the Frankish manner"—that is, in the Gothic style of the Ile-de-France. In 1268, Pope Clement IV, stipulating the conditions for the building of a new cathedral at Narbonne, wrote that the building was "to imitate the noble and magnificently worked churches. . . . which are built in the kingdom of France." The diffusion of the French Gothic style had begun even earlier, but it was in the second half of the thirteeth century that the new style became dominant and that European architecture, in many different ways, turned Gothic. Because the old Romanesque traditions lingered on in many places, each area, marrying its local Romanesque to the new style, developed its own brand of Gothic architecture.

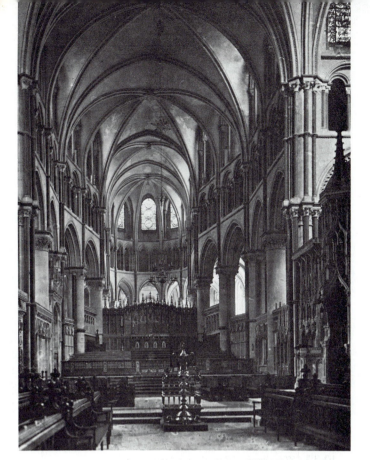

10-38   WILLIAM OF SENS, choir of Canterbury Cathedral, 1175-1184.

10-39   Plan of Canterbury Cathedral.

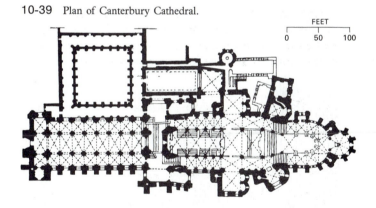

FEET
0   50   100

England

French Gothic came early to England—in the last quarter of the twelfth century. As was so often the case with the great cathedrals, the new style was inaugurated by a devastating fire (in 1174) that swept away an older Romanesque structure in the ancient see of Canterbury, merely creating a new architectural opportunity. (We know of the fire and what followed from a contemporary chronicler, Gervais of Canterbury, who describes the events in dramatic and informative detail.) William of Sens, a master builder commissioned to build the new cathedral, brought to it the Early Gothic manner of the cathedral in Sens (his home city in France), which was closely related to the design of Laon. The choir of Canterbury (FIGS. 10-38 and 10-39)

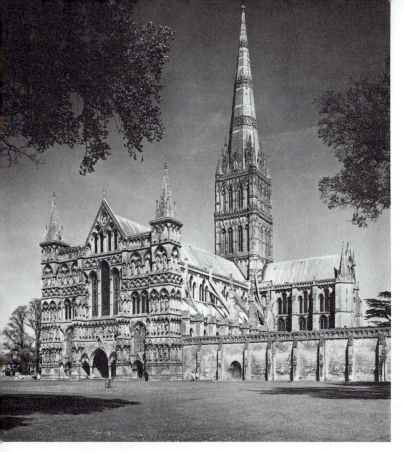

10-40 West façade of Salisbury Cathedral, begun *c.* 1220.

either Paris or Amiens. Also different is the emphasis on the great crossing tower (built c. A.D. 1320), which dominates the silhouette. The height of Salisbury is modest compared with that of the almost contemporary cathedral of Amiens; and since height in the English building is not a decisive factor, the flying buttress is used sparingly—as a rigid prop rather than as an integral part of the armature of arches. The exterior of the building, were it not for its pointed features, would look more like an "additive" Romanesque than a Gothic building.

Equally distinctive is the long rectilinear plan (FIG. 10-41), with its double transept and flat eastern end, the latter a characteristic of Cistercian churches and favored in England since Romanesque times. The interior (FIG. 10-42), though Gothic in its three-story elevation, in its pointed arches and rib vaults, and in its compound piers (actually a combination of columnar piers with detached monolithic shafts or colonnettes), shows conspicuous differences from French Gothic. The pier colonnettes do not ride up the wall to connect with the vault ribs; instead, the vault ribs rise from corbels in the triforium, producing a strong horizontal emphasis. There is rich detail in the moldings of the arches and the tracery of the triforium, which, enhanced by the contrasts of colored stone, gives a peculiarly crisp and vivid sparkle to the interior. The structural craft of the English stonemason is at its best in the Lady Chapel (dedicated to the Virgin Mary) of Salisbury Cathedral (FIG. 10-43). Incredibly slender piers composed of unattached shafts of Purbeck marble seem to tether the billowing vaults to the ground, rather than support them. Not only is this daring construction, but its linearity and slender forms are analogous to the rayonnant style on the continent.

English architecture early finds its native language in the elaboration of architectural pattern for its own sake; structural logic, expressed in the building fabric, is secondary. The pier, wall, and vault elements become increasingly complex and decorative in the fourteenth century, and English Gothic of that period has been described as "decorated." The choir of the cathedral of Gloucester (FIG. 10-44), built about a century after Salisbury, illustrates the passage from the "decorated" to the last English Gothic style, the "perpendicular" or "Tudor," named after the line

resembles Sens and Laon and is essentially French, much more so than most of the mature English Gothic churches that follow it. They will retain features familiar in the older Norman style in balance with importations from France. In the end they will be distinctively English.

The characteristics of English Gothic architecture are admirably embodied in the cathedral of Salisbury (FIGS. 10-40 to 10-43), built for the most part between 1220 and 1260, the tower and buttresses being erected in the fourteenth century. Its location in a park (or close), surrounded by lawns and stately trees, contrasts markedly with that of continental churches, around which the city dwellings nestle closely. The screenlike façade (FIG. 10-40) reaches beyond and does not correspond to the interior; with its dwarf towers, horizontal tiers of niches, and small entrance portals, it is emphatically different from the façades of

10-41 Plan of Salisbury Cathedral.

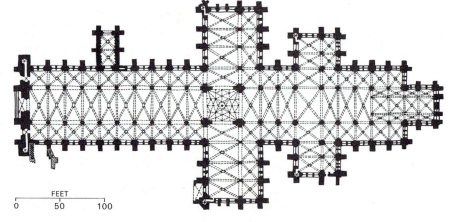

FEET
0   50   100

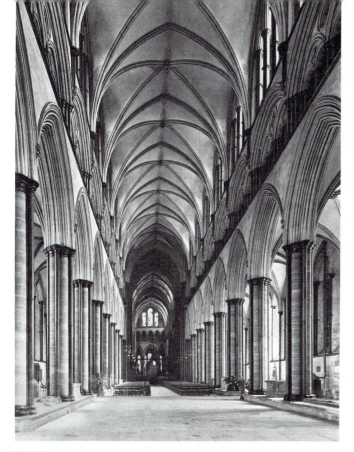

10-42 Nave of Salisbury Cathedral.

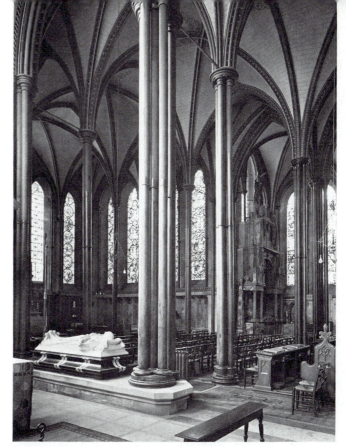

10-43 Lady Chapel of Salisbury Cathedral, *c.* 1225.

10-44 Choir of Gloucester
Cathedral, 1332–57.

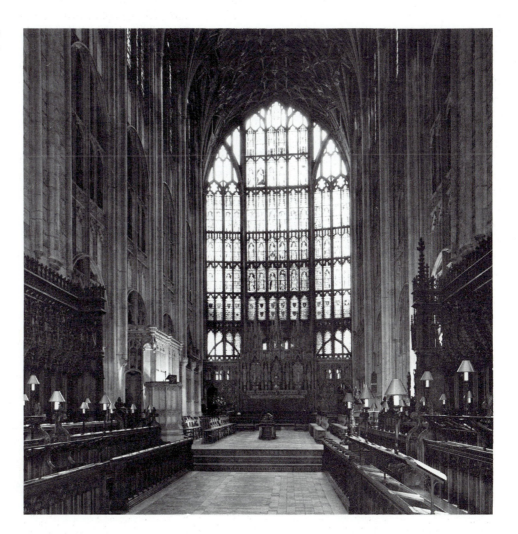

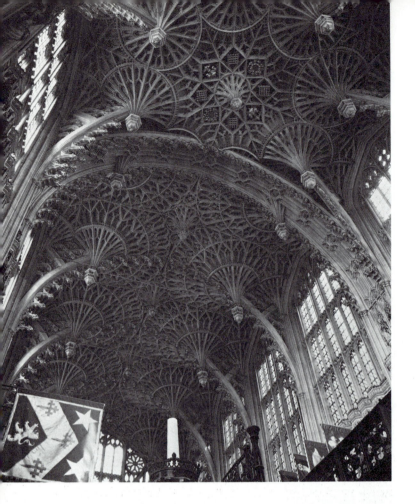

of English kings beginning with the accession of Henry VII to the throne in 1485.

The characteristically flat east end at Gloucester is opened in a single, enormous window divided into horizontal tiers of "transom" windows of like shape and proportion, reminiscent of the screen façade of Salisbury. In the nave wall, however, the strong horizontal accents of Salisbury have been erased, as the vertical wall elements, the *responds,* lift directly from the floor to the vaulting, pulling the whole elevation into a fluent unity. The vault ribs, which had begun to multiply soon after Salisbury, have now become a dense thicket of entirely ornamental strands having no structural function. This vault, in fact, is no longer a rib vault, but a continuous barrel vault with applied decorations.

The culmination of the English perpendicular style, and the flowering of Tudor, can be seen in the vault of the Chapel of Henry VII, which adjoins Westminster Abbey (FIG. 10-45) and was built in the first two decades of the sixteenth century. The linear play of ribs has become a kind of architectural embroidery pulled into "fan vault" shapes with pendent keystones resembling stalactites. The vault looks like something organic that has been petrified in the process of melting. The chapel represents the dissolution of structural Gothic into decorative fancy, its original lines being released from function and multiplying,

10-45   Detail of the vault of the Chapel of Henry VII, 1503–19, Westminster Abbey, London.

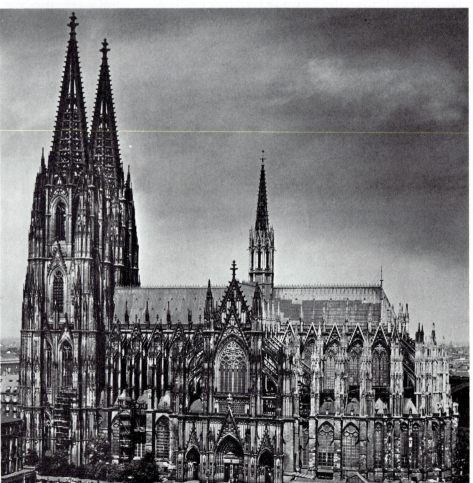

10-46   Cologne Cathedral, 1248– nineteenth century.

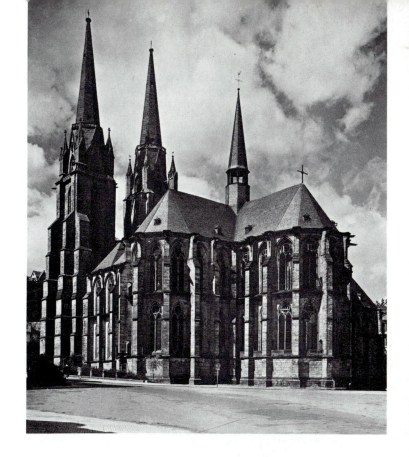

10-47 St. Elizabeth, Marburg, 1233-83.

variegating, and flowering into uninhibited architectural virtuosity and theatrics. The "perpendicular" style in this Tudor structure expresses peculiarly well the precious, affected, even dainty style of life codified in the dying etiquette of chivalry at the end of the Middle Ages. Life was, of course, as violent as ever—indeed, we are here at the threshold of the boisterous English Renaissance—but the description and expression of it in art comes in forms that are delicate rather than robust.

Germany

The architecture of Germany remained conservatively Romanesque well into the thirteenth century. The plan and massing of German churches include the familiar Rhenish double-apse system, with towers flanking both apses, and in many of these the only Gothic feature is the rib vault, which is buttressed, however, by the heavy masonry of the walls. By mid-century, though, the French influence became strongly felt, and the great 150-foot-high choir of the cathedral of Cologne (FIG. 10-46), is a skillful and energetic interpretation of Amiens. Cologne Cathedral has one of the longest building histories on record. Begun in 1248, it stood without a nave and with only its chevet, transept, and lower parts of the façade towers completed for some five centuries. Only in the early nineteenth century, when the original designs for the building were discovered, was it decided to finish the structure.

A design, probably of French origin, that met with great favor and was broadly developed in Germany is that of the *Hallenkirche,* or hall church. The term applies to those buildings in which the aisles rise to the same height as the nave (FIG. 10-48). An early and successful example of this type is the church of St. Elizabeth at Marburg (FIGS. 10-47 to 10-49), built between 1233 and 1283. Since the aisles provide much of the bracing for the central vault, St. Elizabeth's exterior is without the dramatic parade of flying buttresses that circle French Gothic chevets and appears rather prosaic. But the interior (FIG. 10-49), lighted by double rows of tall windows, is more unified and free-flowing, less narrow and divided, than those of

10-48 Plan and section of St. Elizabeth.

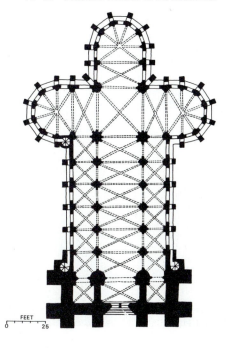

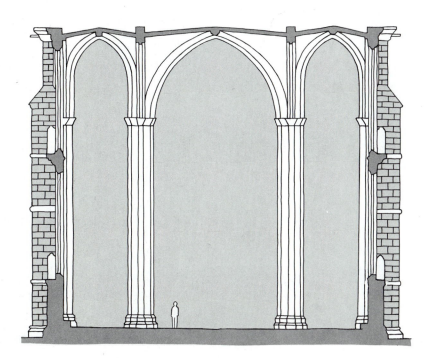

other Gothic churches. The hall church, widely used by later Gothic architects, heralds the age of the Protestant Reformation in Germany, when the old ritual that focused on the altar will be modified by the new emphasis on preaching, which will center attention on the pulpit.

French sculpture, like architecture, had its effect abroad. Two stately statues from the choir of the German cathedral at Naumburg (FIG. 10-50) show the quiet, regal deportment of the French statuary of the High Gothic portals, but with a stronger tincture of realism. *Ekkehard* and *Uta* represent persons of the nobility who, in former times, had been patrons of the church; the particularity of costume and visage almost make these figures portrait statues, though the subjects lived well before the sculptor's time. *Ekkehard*, blunt and teutonic, contrasts with the charming *Uta*, who with a gesture wonderfully graceful draws the collar of her gown partly across her face while she gathers up a soft fold of drapery with a jeweled, delicate hand. The drapery and the body it enfolds are now understood as distinct entities. The shape of the arm that draws the collar is subtly and accurately revealed beneath the drapery, as is the full curve of the bosom. The drapery folds are rendered with an accuracy that indicates the artist's use of a model. We have before us an arresting image of Medieval people—a feudal baron and his handsome wife—as they may well have appeared in life. By mid-thirteenth century

images not only of sacred but of secular personages had found their way into the cathedral.

The equestrian figure of a Gothic nobleman mounted against a pier in the cathedral of Bamberg (FIG. 10-51) is familiarly known as the *Bamberg Rider*. Like *Ekkehard* and *Uta*, it has the quality of portraiture; some believe it represents the German emperor Conrad III. The artist carefully describes the costume of the rider, the high saddle, the caparison of the horse. The proportions of horse and rider are real, though the anatomy of the animal is not quite comprehended, and thus its shape is rather stiffly schematic. An ever present pedestal and canopy firmly establish the group's dependence upon its architectural setting and manage to hold the horse in strict profile. The rider, however, is turning easily toward the observer, as if presiding at a review of troops, and is beginning to break away from the pull of the wall. The stirring and turning of this figure seem to reflect the same impatience with subordination to architecture as did the portal statues at Reims.

Along with the gradual growth of naturalism during the thirteenth century was its modification during the fourteenth by an impulse toward charmingly ornamental effects and courtly convention, as seen in the *Virgin of Paris* (FIG. 10-36). Also rising was a new intensity of expression, which concentrated on such themes as the Crucifixion, the Man of Sorrows, and the Sorrows of the Virgin Mary. The

10-49 Interior of St. Elizabeth.

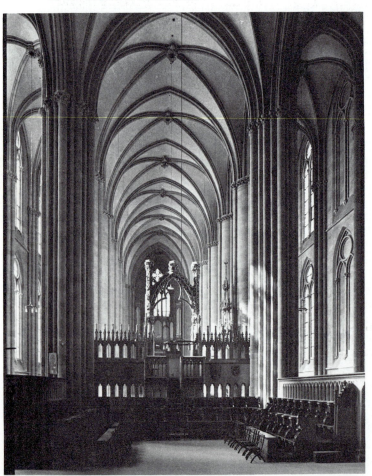

10-50 *Ekkehard* and *Uta, c.* 1250-60, Naumburg Cathedral.

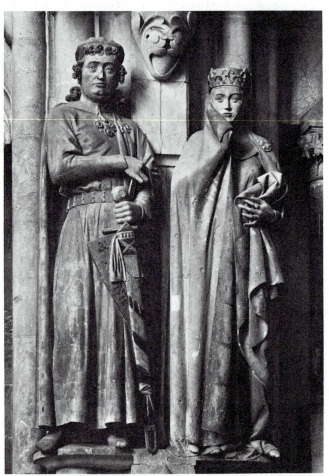

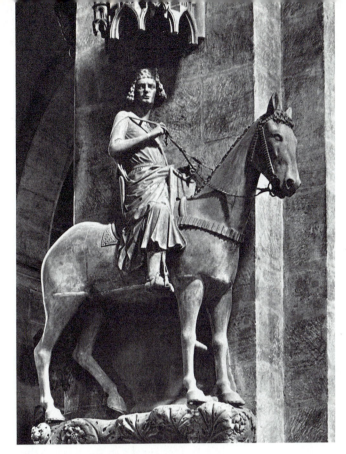

10-51 *The Bamberg Rider,* late thirteenth century, Bamberg Cathedral.

head of a crucifix in St. Maria im Kapitol in Cologne (FIG. 10-52), the features wrenched with pain and sorrow, shows the new preference for interpretations of sacred story in terms of human feeling rather than of dogma and mystery. The humanizing that began in the twelfth century is here accelerated. The anguish of the suffering Christ is represented with such force that it could not fail to stir the emotions powerfully, to arouse deep empathy in the observer. As motion is introduced into portal sculpture, so motion, which reads as emotion, activates the human face. Increasingly, images reach out to the observer, not only into his physical space, but into his emotions. The artist wants to do more than simply present the theological tenet in terms of some impersonal symbol; the mystery is brought back to earth once more, incarnate in the image of physical and psychic suffering.

Italy

Few Italian architects accepted the northern Gothic style, and the question has been raised whether it is proper to speak of buildings like the cathedral of Florence (FIGS. 10-53 to 10-55) as Gothic structures. Begun in 1296 by ARNOLFO DI CAMBIO and so large that it seemed to Alberti to cover "all of Tuscany with its shade," the cathedral looks scarcely Gothic at all. Most of the familiar Gothic features are missing: There are no flying buttresses, no

stately clerestory windows, and the walls are pierced only here and there by relatively small openings. Like San Miniato's (FIG. 9-18), the building's surfaces are ornamented, in the old Tuscan fashion, with marble-incrusted geometric designs to match it to the eleventh-century Romanesque baptistry nearby. Beyond an occasional ogival window and the fact that the nave is covered by rib vaults, there is very little that identifies this building as Gothic. The vast gulf that separates this Italian church from its northern European cousins is strikingly evident when the former is compared with a full-blown German representative of the High Gothic, the cathedral of Cologne (FIG. 10-46).

In Cologne Cathedral an emphatic stress on the vertical produces an awe-inspiring upward rush of almost unmatched vigor and intensity. The building has the character of an organic growth shooting heavenward, its toothed upper portions engaging the sky, the pierced, translucent stone tracery of the spires merging with the atmosphere. The cathedral of Florence clings to the ground and has no aspirations to flight. All emphasis is on the horizontal elements of the design, and the building rests firmly and massively on this earth. Simple geometric volumes are clearly defined and show no tendency to merge either into each other or into the sky. The dome, although it may seem to be rising because of its ogival section, has a crisp, closed silhouette that sets it off emphatically against the sky behind it. But, since this dome is the monument with which architectural historians usually introduce the Renaissance (it was built by Brunelleschi between 1420 and 1436), a comparison of the campanile with the Cologne towers may be somewhat more appropriate. Designed by the painter Giotto in 1334 (and completed with some minor modifications after his death), the Florence campanile stands apart from the cathedral in the Italian tradition. In fact, it could stand anywhere else in Florence without looking out of place; it is essentially self-sufficient. This can hardly be said of the northern towers; they are essential

10-52 Head of a crucifix, 1301. Wood. St. Maria im Kapitol, Cologne.

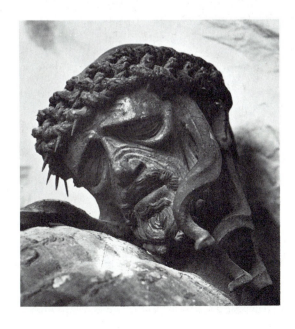

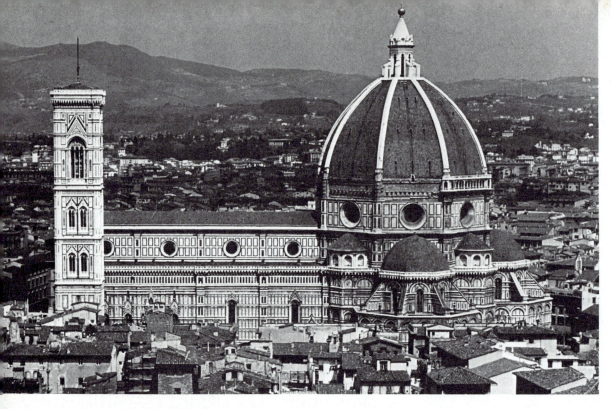

elements of the building behind them and it would be unthinkable to detach one of them and place it somewhere else. Heinrich Wölfflin has compared buildings of this kind to a flame, from which no single tongue can be separated. This holds true for every part of the structure, down to its smallest details; no single element seems to be capable of an independent existence; one form merges into the next, in an unending series of rising movements that pull the eye upward and never permit it to rest until it reaches the sky.

This structure's beauty is of an amorphous rather than a formal kind; it is a beauty that speaks to the heart rather than to the intellect.

How different the Italian tower! Neatly subdivided into cubic stages, Giotto's tower is the sum of its clearly distinguished parts. Not only could this tower be removed from the building without adverse effects, but each of the component parts, cleanly separated from each other by continuous, unbroken moldings, seems capable of continued, independent existence as an object of considerable esthetic appeal. This compartmentalization is reminiscent of the Romanesque, but it also forecasts the ideal of Renaissance architecture, which was to express itself in clear, logical relationships of a structure's component parts and which aimed for works that were self-sufficient and could exist in complete independence. Compared to the northern towers, Giotto's campanile has a cool and rational quality that appeals more to the intellect than the emotions.

From the plan of the cathedral of Florence (FIG. 10-54) it would seem that the nave was added to the crossing complex as an afterthought; in fact, the nave was built first, pretty much according to Arnolfo's original plans, and the crossing was redesigned in mid-fourteenth century to increase the cathedral's interior space. In its present form the area beneath the dome is the focal point of the design, and the nave leads to it, as Paul Frankl says, "like an introduction of slow chords, to a goal of self-contained finality." To the visitor from the north, the nave seems as strange as the plan; neither has a northern European counterpart. The cathedral dimensions are about the same as those of Amiens, but there the similarity ends. The Florence nave bays (FIG. 10-55) are three times as deep as those of Amiens; the

FEET
0   50   100

10-54 Plan of Florence Cathedral. (After Sir Banister Fletcher.)

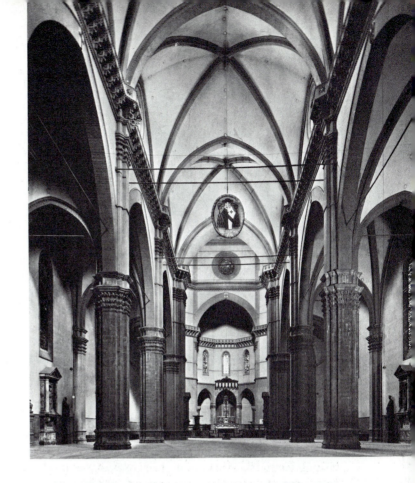

wide arcades permit the shallow aisles to become part of the central nave; the result is an interior that has an unmatched spaciousness. The accent here, as in the exterior, is on the horizontal elements. The substantial capitals of the piers prevent them from soaring into the vaults and emphasize their function as supports. While this interior may lack the mystery of northern naves, Nikolaus Pevsner observed that its serene calm and clarity tell the visitor that the Tuscan architects had never entirely rejected nor forgotten their classical heritage, and that it is indeed only here, in central Italy, that the Renaissance could have been born.

The façade of the cathedral of Florence was not completed until the nineteenth century, and then in a form much altered from its beginnings. In fact, Italian builders seemed little concerned with the façades of their churches, dozens being left unfinished to this day. One of the reasons for this may be that the façades were not conceived as integral parts of the structures but rather as screens that could be added to the fabric at any time. The façade of the cathedral of Orvieto (FIG. 10-56) is a typical and handsome example. Begun in the early fourteenth century, it pays a graceful compliment of imitation to some parts of the French Gothic repertory of ornament, especially in the four large pinnacles that divide the façade into three bays; but these pinnacles—the outer ones serving as miniature substitutes for the big northern west-front towers—grow up, as it were, from an old Tuscan façade and ultimately from the Early Christian. The rectilinearity and triangularity of the old Tuscan marble incrustation, here enframing and pointing to the precisely wrought rose window, is clearly seen behind the transparent Gothic overlay. The whole effect of the Orvieto façade is that of a great altar screen, its single plane covered with carefully placed carved and painted ornament. In principle, Orvieto belongs with San Miniato al Monte or the cathedral of Pisa, rather than Amiens or Notre Dame of Paris.

Since Romanesque times, northern European influences had been felt more strongly in Lombardy than in central Italy. When the citizens of Milan, in 1386, decided to build their own cathedral (FIG. 10-57), they invited and consulted experts not only from Italy, but also from France, Germany, and England. These experts must have carried on a rough *disputatio* about the strength of the foundations and the composition and adequacy of the piers and the vaults—the application of the true geometric *scientia* in working out plan and elevation. The result was a compromise; the proportions of the building, particularly those of the nave, became Italian (that is, wide in relation to height), and the surface decorations and details, Gothic. But even before the cathedral was half finished, the new classical style of the Renaissance had been well launched

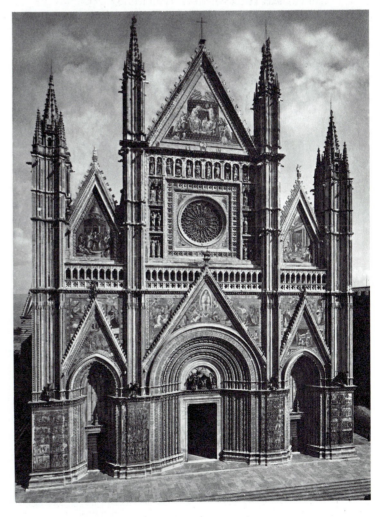

10-56   Façade of Orvieto Cathedral, begun c. 1310.

← to c.1194	1296	c.1300	1309	c.1322	c.1345	1377	1378	1386	1417	to 16th C.→
Florence Cathedral begun	Palazzo Pubblico completed, Siena	Façade of Cologne Cathedral begun	Doge's Palace begun, Venice			Milan Cathedral begun	
HIGH GOTHIC	L A T E G O T H I C									
	←——————— BABYLONIAN CAPTIVITY ———————→				←——— GREAT SCHISM ———→					

and the Milan design had become anachronistic. The elaborate façade represents a confused mixture of late Gothic with classical elements, and stands as a symbol of the waning of the Gothic style.

The city churches of the Gothic world were monuments of civic pride quite as much as they were temples or symbols of the spiritual and natural world. To undertake the construction of a great cathedral a city had to be rich, its commerce thriving; the very profusion of large churches during the period attests to the affluence of those who built and maintained them, as well as to the general revival of the economy of Europe in the thirteenth century.

The secular center of the community, the town hall, was almost as much the object of civic pride as the cathedral. A building like the Palazzo Pubblico of Siena (FIG. 10-58), the proud commercial and political rival of Florence, must have drawn the admiration of Siena's citizens as well as of visiting strangers, inspiring in them respect for the city's power and success. More symmetrical in its design than most buildings of its type and period, it is flanked by a lofty tower, which, along with Giotto's campanile in Florence, is one of the finest in Italy. It served as lookout over the city and the countryside around it and as a bell tower from which signals of all sorts could be rung to the populace. The Medieval city, a political unit in itself, had to defend itself against its neighbor cities and often against kings and emperors; but in addition it had to be secure against internal upheavals, in which the history of the Italian city-republics abounds. Feuds between rich and powerful families, class struggle, as well as uprisings of the whole populace against the city fathers were constant threats to a city's internal security. The heavy walls and battlements of the Italian town hall eloquently express the frequent need of city governors to defend themselves against their own citizens. The high tower, out of reach of most missiles, is further protected by machicolated galleries, built out on corbels around the top of the structure to provide openings downward for a vertical defense of the tower's base. But in many cases the battlements simply symbolize authority, or allegiance to a political party—flat-topped merlons indicating adherents of the Guelphs (pro-papacy); notched merlons, those of the Ghibellines (pro-emperor).

The secular architecture of the Italian mainland tends to have this fortified look. But Venice, some miles out in the Venetian lagoon, was secure from land attack and could

10-57   Milan Cathedral, begun 1386.

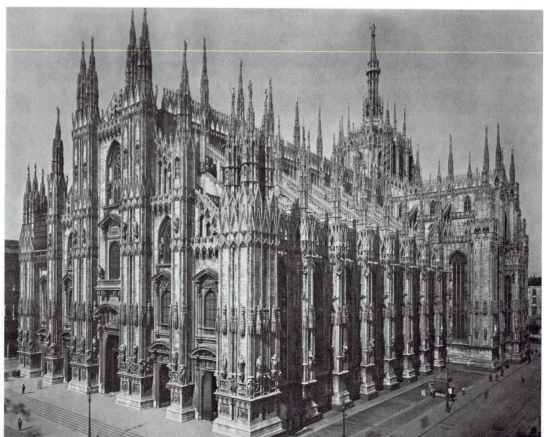

rely on her powerful navy to protect her against attacks coming from the sea. Internally, she was a tight corporation of ruling families that for centuries provided an unshakable and efficient establishment, free from disruptive tumults within. This stable internal structure made possible the development of an unfortified, "open" architecture like that of the Doge's Palace (FIG. 10-59), the seat of government of the Venetian republic. This, the most splendid public building of Medieval Italy, seems to invite the passerby to enter rather than to ward him off. In a stately march, the short and heavy columns of the first level support low-pointed arches and look strong enough to carry the weight of the upper structure. Their rhythm is doubled in the upper arcades, where taller and more slender columns carry ogival arches, which terminate in flamelike tips between medallions pierced with quatrefoils. Each story is taller than the one beneath it, the topmost being as high as the two lower arcades combined. And yet the building does not look top-heavy, a fact that is due in part to the complete absence of articulation in the top story and in part to the delicate patterning, in cream and rose-colored marbles, of its walls, which somehow makes them appear paper-thin. The Doge's Palace is the monumental representative of a delightful and charming variant of the Late Gothic. Its slightly exotic style reminds us of Venice's strategic position at the crossroads of the West and the Orient, where it could synthesize artistic stimuli received from either direction. Colorful, decorative, light and airy in appearance, and never overloaded, Venetian Gothic is ideally suited to the lagoon city, which floats between water and air.

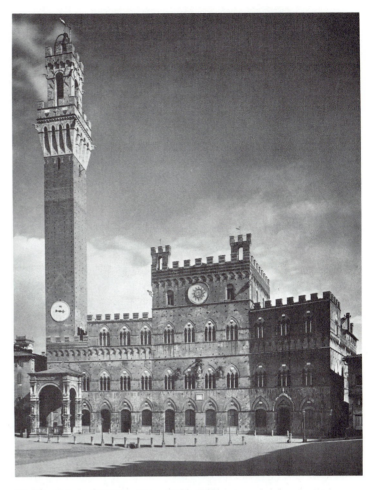

10-58   Palazzo Pubblico, Siena, 1288–1309.

10-59   Doge's Palace, Venice, c. 1345–1438.

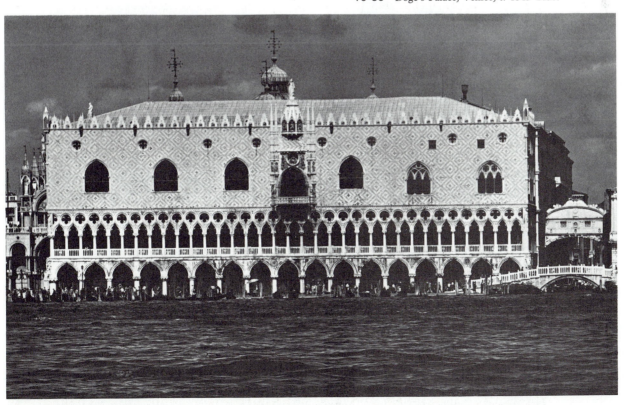

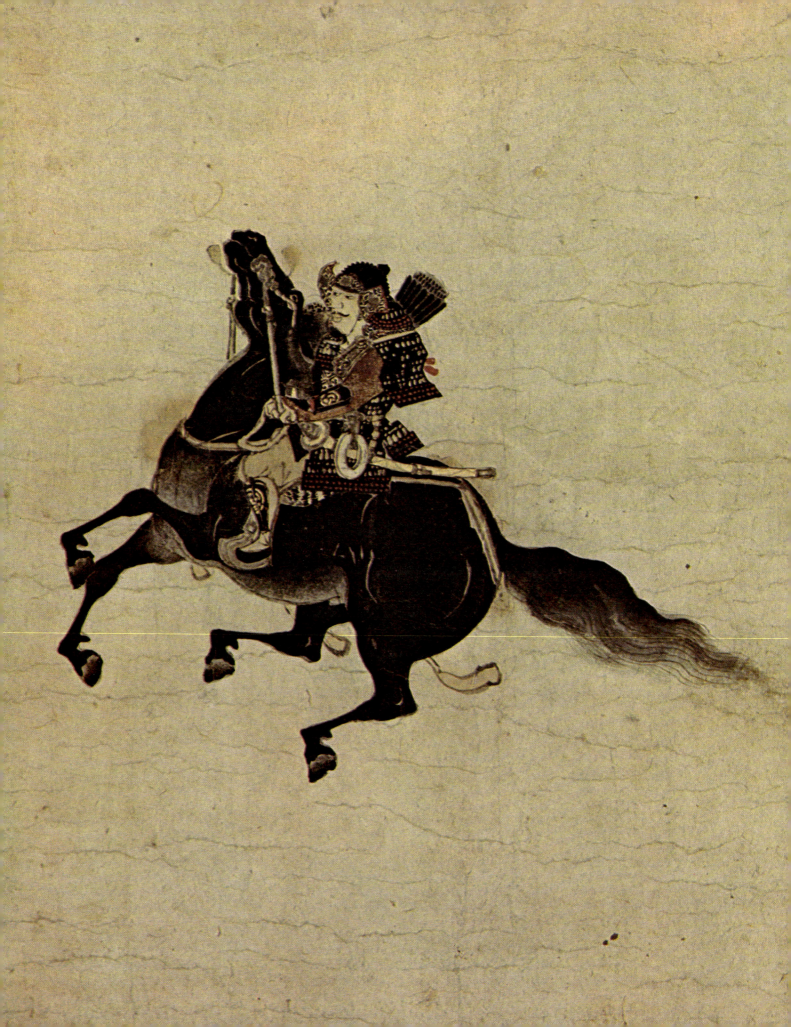

part three

The Non-European World

The art of non-European civilizations is introduced at this point in our survey because much of it is more closely related to the art of the prehistoric period and of the Middle Ages than to that of the Renaissance and of subsequent times. In these latter periods the Western artist moves from a dominantly religious and conceptual approach toward an ever more secular and perceptual one. This drive toward optical realism, and the persistent search for a rational, if not scientific, basis for the objectivization of natural appearances, was not shared by the numerous cultures outside the mainstream of European history. Thus, non-European art is more akin to Byzantine and other art of the Middle Ages, although its forms, based upon non-Western cultural and spiritual precepts, are, of course, very different.

There had been sporadic contacts between Africa and the Far East and the West since antiquity. The Phoenicians are said to have circumnavigated Africa as early as 600 B.C., and Alexander the Great, bent upon exploration as much as conquest, took his armies beyond the Indus River deep into India. Nomadic peoples from central Asia made repeated incursions into the

Portion of the scroll *The Burning of the Sanjo Palace*, thirteenth century.

353

Near East and Europe, the Huns, under Attila, reaching France in the fifth century. In the later Middle Ages the search for trade routes to the East inspired the exploratory journeys of such enterprising merchants as the Polo brothers, Nicolo and Maffeo, and Nicolo's famous son, Marco, who reached Peking in the late thirteenth century.

Yet all these contacts were transient and, even when given permanence through the establishment of sea routes during the Renaissance and Baroque periods, served commercial rather than cultural interests. Imported objects were admired as exotic curiosities, and even the eighteenth-century fascination with things Chinese was little more than a superficial and passing fashion. Only toward the end of the nineteenth century, when Western art had exhausted itself in its persistent drive toward realism and was beginning to search for alternative approaches, did non-Western art begin to have a more serious impact on the West.

Even though conquests, colonization, and missionary activity after the Middle Ages carried Christianity well beyond the boundaries of western Europe, we may identify the non-European world as the non-Christian world. This vast region, which dwarfs the area of Europe, produced a great variety of artistic styles and ideas. Of these the art of Islam has already been surveyed (Chapter Seven). The enormous remainder can be roughly subdivided into Oriental art and "Third World" art. The former embraces Southeast Asia, China, and Japan, and the latter, the essentially tribal arts of the North and South American Indian, of Africa, and of the South Pacific.

The earliest art works from the great Eastern civilizations in India, China, and Japan are from paleolithic and neolithic times. Buddhism was the common denominator of the later arts of these different countries, although each developed a distinctive style, or, rather, series of styles. Indian sculpture from its beginnings has been characterized by a pulsating vigor in reproducing the living body. Early Chinese bronzes display amazing technical virtuosity in the use of highly symbolic, though abstract, decorative motifs. In later dynasties, in sculpture and particularly in painting, carefully observed details are lyrically rendered and produce a haunting image of nature. Japanese art, in spite of being subject to recurring waves of foreign influence, especially from China, insistently returns to native traditions. Painting and, above all, architecture show a sensitivity to the relationship between decorative designs and natural forms.

In pre-Columbian Mexico, Central America, and the Andean region of South America, highly cultured peoples using a Stone Age technology erected great temple complexes elaborately decorated with reliefs and practiced the crafts of weaving and pottery with great skill. About A.D. 500 the North American Indian began to settle in agricultural communities. Some tribes, such as the Pueblo of the United States' southwest, reached a highly developed state in the eleventh, twelfth, and thirteenth centuries. Their stylized arts reflect an extraordinary understanding of the decorative qualities of abstract design.

The peoples native to Africa and the South Sea Islands produced a distinguished and individual art until contact with Europeans either modified it or brought it to a halt. This art, far from being technically or esthetically crude, is sophisticated in its presentation of conceptual rather than naturalistic images and has asserted itself in the West with ever stronger effect and ever more respectful recognition and appreciation. As we shall see in subsequent chapters, its rhythmical, abstract forms have become a valuable resource and inspiration for many modern artists of great distinction and originality.

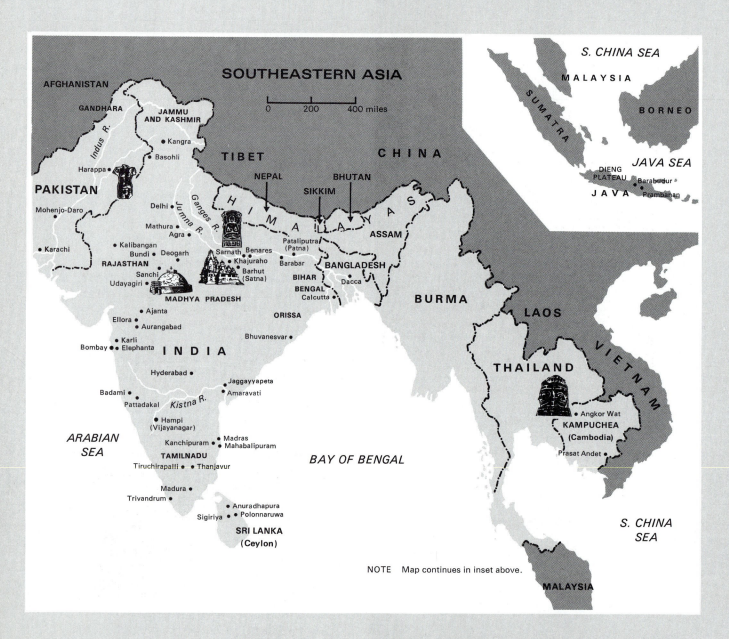

SOUTHEASTERN ASIA

0   200   400 miles

AFGHANISTAN
GANDHARA
JAMMU AND KASHMIR
TIBET
CHINA
• Kangra
• Basohli
Harappa •
PAKISTAN
NEPAL
BHUTAN
SIKKIM
H I M A L A Y A S
Mohenjo-Daro •
Delhi •
Jumna R.
Ganges R.
ASSAM
• Karachi
Mathura •
Agra •
Pataliputra (Patna)
• Kalibangan
Bundi • Deogarh
• Sarnath • Benares
Khajuraho
BANGLADESH
RAJASTHAN
Sanchi •
Barabar
Barhut (Satna)
• Dacca
Udayagiri •
BIHAR
BENGAL
Calcutta •
MADHYA PRADESH
BURMA
• Ajanta
ORISSA
Ellora •
LAOS
• Aurangabad
Bhuvanesvar •
• Karli
THAILAND
VIETNAM
Bombay • • Elephanta
INDIA
Hyderabad •
Jaggayyapeta •
• Angkor Wat
Badami •
• Amaravati
KAMPUCHEA (Cambodia)
Pattadakal •
Kistna R.
• Hampi (Vijayanagar)
Prasat Andet •
• Madras
ARABIAN SEA
Kanchipuram • • Mahabalipuram
TAMILNADU
BAY OF BENGAL
S. CHINA SEA
Tiruchirapalli • • Thanjavur
• Madura
Trivandrum •
• Anuradhapura
Sigiriya • • Polonnaruwa
SRI LANKA (Ceylon)

NOTE   Map continues in inset above.

MALAYSIA

S. CHINA SEA
MALAYSIA
SUMATRA
BORNEO
JAVA SEA
DIENG PLATEAU
• Barabudur
JAVA
• Prambanan

chapter eleven

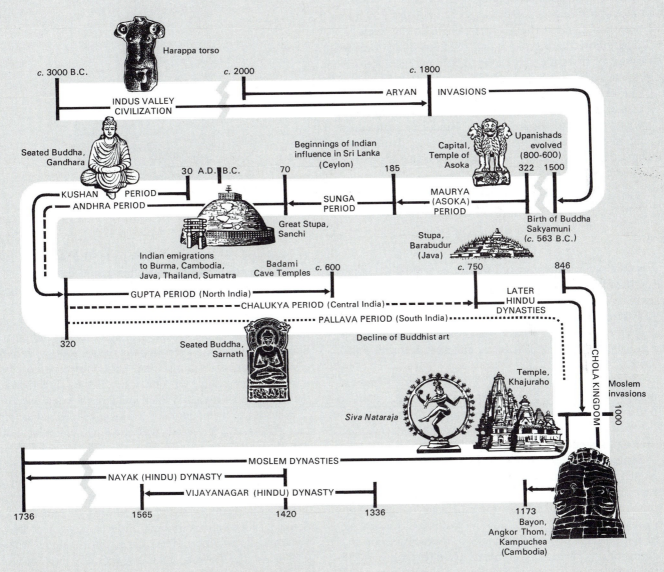

Harappa torso

c. 3000 B.C.　　　*c.* 2000　　　*c.* 1800

INDUS VALLEY
CIVILIZATION　　　ARYAN　INVASIONS

Seated Buddha,
Gandhara

Beginnings of Indian
influence in Sri Lanka
(Ceylon)

Capital,
Temple of
Asoka

Upanishads
evolved
(800–600)

30　A.D.　B.C.　　70　　185　　322　1500

KUSHAN　PERIOD
ANDHRA PERIOD

SUNGA
PERIOD

MAURYA
(ASOKA)
PERIOD

Birth of Buddha
Sakyamuni
(*c.* 563 B.C.)

Great Stupa,
Sanchi

Indian emigrations
to Burma, Cambodia,
Java, Thailand, Sumatra

Badami
Cave Temples

c. 600

Stupa,
Barabudur
(Java)

c. 750　　　846

GUPTA PERIOD (North India)
CHALUKYA PERIOD　(Central India)
PALLAVA PERIOD (South India)

LATER
HINDU
DYNASTIES

320

Seated Buddha,
Sarnath

Decline of Buddhist art

Temple,
Khajuraho

Siva Nataraja

CHOLA KINGDOM

Moslem
invasions

1000

MOSLEM DYNASTIES
NAYAK (HINDU) DYNASTY
VIJAYANAGAR (HINDU) DYNASTY

1736　　　1565　　　1420　　　1336　　　1173

Bayon,
Angkor Thom,
Kampuchea
(Cambodia)

The Art of India

THE SUBCONTINENT OF INDIA, contiguous with the Asian mainland on its northern boundaries, has three distinct geographical areas: the northeast, where the massive Himalayas, the traditional home of the gods, rise as a barrier; the fertile, densely populated area to the northwest and to the south of the Himalayas, where the valleys of the Indus and the Ganges rivers lie; and peninsular India, composed of tropical tablelands separated from the northern rivers by mountains and forests. In these areas are great extremes of climate, from tropical heat to perpetual snow and glaciers; from desert conditions to the heaviest rainfall in the world.

The ethnic characteristics and religions of the peoples vary as much as the geography. The most common language of north central India is Hindi, a Sanskrit derivative. Urdu, closely related, is spoken by most of the Moslem population. In the south, several Dravidian languages, unrelated to Sanskrit, are spoken. Hinduism is the main religion of India, as Islam is of Pakistan, but Jainism and Christianity have many adherents, and Buddhism and Judaism, a few.

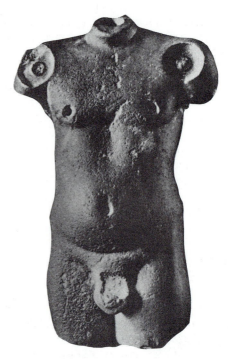

11-1 Male nude, Harappa, third to second millenium B.C. Red sandstone, 3½″ high. National Museum, New Delhi.

BEGINNINGS

The first major culture of India centered around the upper reaches of the Indus River valley during the late third and early second millennium B.C. Mohenjo-Daro and Harappa in Pakistan were the chief sites. Recently other important centers of this culture have been found farther south at Kalibangan, in Rajasthan, India, and near Karachi, Pakistan.

The architectural remains of Mohenjo-Daro suggest a modern commercial center, with major avenues along a north-south orientation; streets as wide as forty feet; multistoried houses of fired brick and wood; and elaborate drainage systems.

Some sculptures from this Indus civilization reflect Mesopotamian influences, while others indicate the presence of a thoroughly developed Indian tradition. The latter is exemplified by a miniature torso from Harappa (FIG. 11-1), which, at first glance, appears to be carved according to the precepts of Greek naturalism. (Some question the dating of this piece.) The emphasis given (by polishing) to the surface of the stone and to the swelling curves of the abdomen, however, reveals an interest, not in the logical anatomical structure of Greek sculpture, but in the fluid movement of a living body. This sense of pulsating vigor and the emphasis on sensuous surfaces remain chief characteristics of Indian sculpture for four thousand years.

Great numbers of intaglio steatite seals, found at Mohenjo-Daro, exhibit a blend of Indian and Near Eastern elements (FIG. 11-2). Indeed, it was the finding of a Mohenjo-Daro seal at a datable Mesopotamian site that enabled scholars to assign dates to the Indus valley cultures. The script on the seals has not been deciphered. Varied devices worked into the stone, such as trees (sometimes associated with animals and humanoid figures), are represented as objects of worship. The beasts most common on the seals are various kinds of bull (including the humped variety), the water buffalo, the rhinoceros, and the elephant. Fantastic animals and anthropomorphic deities are also represented. On one seal a seated three-headed figure appears in what is later known as a yoga position. The heads are surmounted by a trident-shaped device that two thousand years later was used to symbolize both the Buddhist community and the Hindu deity Siva. Around the deity are various animals, including the bull and the tiger, which were also to become symbols of Siva. Given its date, this seal probably represented a prototype of that god. Such continuity of iconography indicates the deep roots of religious tradition in India. Style, too, shows a continuous tradition. The animals on the Indus valley seals have the flowing contours and sensuous surfaces mentioned above (with reference to the Harappa figure) as being characteristic of sculpture through most of Indian history. This artistic continuity is remarkable, not only because of the time spanned, but because, for the period between the disappearance of the Indus civilization (about 1700 B.C.) and the rise of the Maurya empire (third century B.C.), there are virtually no remains of the visual arts. The Aryan invasions, which began about 1800 B.C., may account for the break in the sequence of Indian art. It is even more amazing, then, in view of the Aryans' profound effect on Indian culture, that so many indigenous traits persisted. Destruction by the invaders, as well as the perishability of the materials used, undoubtedly account for the disappearance of many of the objects by which Indian traditions were passed on during those two thousand years following the collapse of the Indus civilization.

The Aryans brought with them to India the Vedic religion. The term derives from the hymns (Vedas), which have survived to this day. These are addressed to the gods, who are personified aspects of nature. The warrior god Indra is thunder, Surya, the sun, and Varuna, the sky. There are many others. All were worshiped by means of hymns and sacrificial offerings in conformity to strict laws of ritual. There were no temples, but fire altars, built according to prescribed formulas, served as the focus of devotion. So important was the act of ritual that in time Agni, the sacrificial fire, and Soma, the sacrificial brew, became personified as gods in their own right. The rather simple form of religion and propitiation so beautifully expressed in the Vedic hymns was greatly elaborated in the Upanishads (800–600 B.C.), a series of treatises on the nature of man and the universe that introduced a number of concepts alien to the simple nature worship of the northern invaders. Chief among the new ideas were those of *samsara* and *karma*. Samsara meant the transformation of the soul into some other form of life upon the death of the body. The type of existence into which the reborn soul entered depended upon karma, the consequence of actions in all previous lifetimes. A bad karma meant a dark future, rebirth in a hell or in this world as a lower animal—a reptile, for example, or an insect. A good karma meant that the soul might go into the body of a king, a priest, or even a god, for gods also were subject to eventual death and to the endless cycle of rebirth. The goal of religion therefore became the submersion of individual life in a world soul. This was attainable only after an individual's karma had been perfected through countless rebirths. Penance, meditation, and asceticism were believed to speed the process.

During the sixth century B.C. two major religions developed in India. One, Buddhism, exerted a profound influence on the culture and art of India as a whole from the third century B.C. to the sixth or seventh century A.D. (In some parts, like Bengal and Bihar, it was influential to the eleventh century, and, in the south, to an even later date.) Although Jainism, the other major religion, never achieved Buddhism's dominance, it continues to the present day as a small but distinct religion in India, while Buddhism is practically extinct there.

The arts of many Asian countries derive from Indian Buddhism, which began with the birth of the Buddha Sakyamuni about 563 B.C. The son of a king who ruled a small area on the border of Nepal and India, the child, according to legend, was miraculously conceived and sprang from his mother's side. Named Siddhartha, and also known as Gautama, the child displayed prodigious abilities. A sage predicted that he would become a Buddha—an "enlightened" holy man destined to achieve nirvana. After a series of confrontations with old age, sickness, and death, Siddhartha renounced courtly luxury. While meditating under a pipal tree in the city of Gaya, Gautama obtained illumination—the complete understanding of the universe that is Buddhahood. His teaching may be summed up as follows: All existence implies sorrow; the cause of existence is attachment to work and the self; this attachment can be dissolved through the elimination of desires, which also bind the self to a countless succession of rebirths; the cessation of rebirth can be accomplished by following the Eightfold Path, which prescribes simple practices of right thought, right speech, and right action. This initial formulation of Buddhism, in which salvation was achieved by individual efforts, was later known as Hinayana Buddhism.

The religion of Buddhism, so conceived, was not opposed to basic Hindu thought, but was rather a minor heresy deriving from certain speculations in the Upanishads. What Buddhism did was to offer a specific method for solving the ancient Indian problem of how to break the chain of existence so that the individual could find ultimate peace.

11-2 Seals, Mohenjo-Daro, third millenium B.C. Steatite. National Museum, New Delhi.

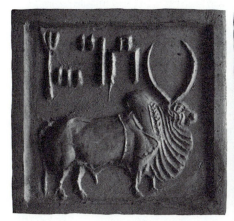 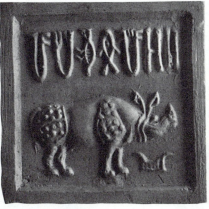 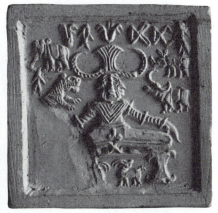

EARLY ARCHITECTURE AND SCULPTURE: BUDDHIST DOMINANCE

The earliest known examples of art in the service of Buddhism (from the middle of the third century B.C.) are both monumental and sophisticated.

Emperor Asoka (272–232 B.C.), grandson of Chandragupta, founder of the Maurya dynasty (c. 322–184 B.C.), was converted to Buddhism after witnessing the horrors of the brutal military campaigns by which he himself had forcibly unified most of northern India. His palace at Pataliputra (the modern Patna in Bihar) was designed after the Achaemenid palace at Persepolis (FIG. 2-32). Megasthenes, a Greek ambassador at Asoka's court, has left a glowing report of Pataliputra. Only parts of columns, the foundations of buildings, and remnants of a wood palisade now remain, but we may draw some idea of the architectural details from a series of commemorative and sacred columns that Asoka raised through much of northern India. These monolithic pillars were of polished sandstone, some as high as sixty or seventy feet. The capital of one (FIG. 11-3) now in the Sarnath Museum near Benares typifies the style of the period. It consists of a lotiform capital upon which rests a horizontal disk sculptured with a frieze of four animals alternating with four wheels. Seated on the disk are four addorsed lions that originally were surmounted by another huge wheel. All the forms are symbolic. The lotus, traditional symbol of divinity, also connoted man's salvation in Buddhism. The wheel repre-

sented the cycle of life, death, and rebirth. This "wheel of life" often had other levels of meaning. In this instance it was the teaching of Buddha—the "turning of the wheel of the law." The wheel itself (probably developed from ancient sun symbols), and the four animals (the four quarters of the compass), with which it is here associated, imply a cosmological meaning in which the pillar as a whole symbolizes the world axis. The lions also had manifold meanings but were here specifically equated with Sakyamuni Buddha, who was known as the lion of the Sakya clan.

The pillars are noteworthy not only for their symbolism but also because they exemplify continuity of style. Although the stiff heraldic lions are typical of Persepolis, the low-relief animals around the disk are treated in the much earlier fluid style of Mohenjo-Daro. So too are the colossal figures of *yakshas* and *yakshis* sculptured during Asoka's time or somewhat later. These male and female divinities, originally worshiped as local nature spirits, gods of trees and rocks, were now incorporated into the Buddhist and Hindu pantheons.

The Cave Temple

The Mauryan period also witnessed the beginnings of a unique architectural form—sanctuaries cut into the living rock of cliffs. Parts of the exteriors (and, later, interiors) of these caves were carved to imitate in accurate detail the wooden constructions of their period. The Lomas Rishi cave, hollowed out during Asoka's reign, has an entrance (FIG. 11-4) of a type that was to be perpetuated for a thousand years. The faithful replica of a wooden façade has

11-3 Lion capital of column erected by Emperor Asoka (272–232 B.C.). Polished sandstone, 7′ high. Pataliputra. Archaeological Museum, Sarnath.

11-4 Entrance to the Lomas Rishi Cave, Barabar Hills, third century B.C.

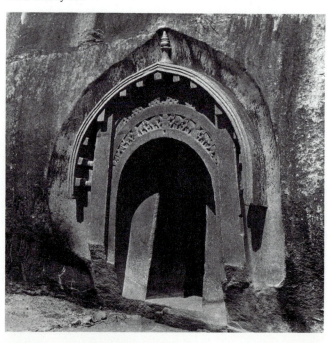

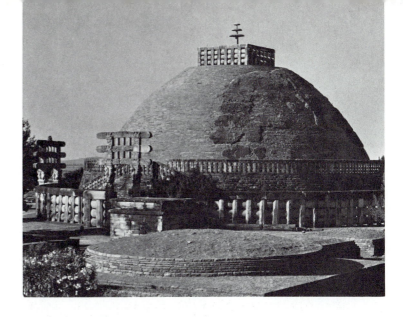

11-5 The Great Stupa, Sanchi, completed first century A.D. Shown are the west and south gateways.

a doorway with a curving eave that mimics a flexible wood roof bent over rectangular beams. A decorative frieze of elephants over the doorway carries on the indigenous sculptural traditions.

The fall of the Mauryan dynasty around the beginning of the second century B.C. led to the political fragmentation of India.

The Stupa

Under the Sungas and the Andhras, who were the chief successors of the Mauryas, numerous *chaitya* (Buddhist assembly halls) and *viharas* (monasteries) were cut into the hills of central India from the west to the east coast. At the same time, the *stupa*, which was originally a small burial or reliquary mound of earth, evolved as an important architectural program. (Asoka is supposed to have built thousands of stupas throughout India.) By the end of the second century B.C. they had grown to huge proportions. Sculptured fragments from early stupas have been found at Mathura, at Bharhut (near modern Satna), and elsewhere in India, but the grandeur of this type of structure can be seen best at Sanchi in the state of Madhya Pradesh. There, on a hill overlooking a wide plain, several stupas containing sacred relics were built over a period of centuries. Of these, the Great Stupa (FIG. 11-5), the tallest and finest, was originally dedicated by Asoka. Enlarged and finally completed about the middle of the first century A.D., it stands now as the culminating monument of an era.

A double stairway at the south leads from the base to a drum about twenty feet high and permits access to a narrow railed walk around the solid dome, which rises to fifty feet above the ground. Surmounting the dome is the *harmika*, a square enclosure from the center of which arises the *yasti* or mast. The yasti is itself adorned with a series of *chatras* (umbrellas). Around the whole structure is a circular stone railing with ornamented *toranas* (gateways, FIG. 11-6) at the north, east, south, and west.

The stupa, like most Indian structures, has more than one function. As a receptacle for relics it is an object of adoration, a symbol of the death of the Buddha, or a token of Buddhism in general. Devotion is given the stupa by the believer, who circumambulates its dome. But, in another sense, the stupa is a cosmic diagram, the world mountain with the cardinal points emphasized by the toranas. The harmika symbolizes the heaven of the thirty-three gods, while the yasti, as the axis of the universe, rises from the mountain-dome and through the harmika, thus uniting this world with the paradises above.

The railings and domes of some stupas were decorated with relief sculpture. The toranas at Sanchi are covered with Buddhist symbols, deities, and narrative scenes, but the figure of the Buddha never appears. Instead, he is symbolized by such devices as an empty throne, the tree under which he meditated, the wheel of the law, his footprints.

The awe expressed in this iconographic restraint— echoed by the quiet mass of the dome itself—is strikingly and paradoxically contradicted by the sculptural luxuriance that crowds the toranas. Lush foliage mingles with the flowing forms of human bodies, and warm vitality pervades both animal and man. Sensuous yakshis hang like ripe fruit from tree brackets. This almost hedonistic expression is alien to the Buddhist renunciation of life. It is an assertion, rather, of a basic Indian attitude that at all times unites and dominates almost all of Buddhist, Hindu, and Jain art.

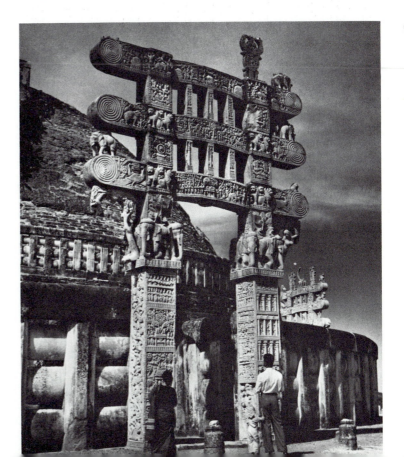

11-6 Eastern gateway, the Great Stupa, Sanchi, front view, completed first century A.D.

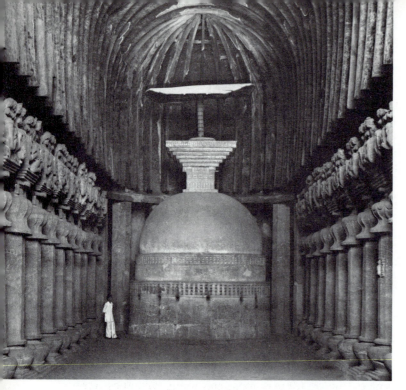

11-7 Interior of carved chaitya hall, Karli, c. A.D. 100.

monolithic stupa in the apse, and on either side of the nave is an aisle formed by a series of massive columns crowned with male and female riders on elephants (FIG. 11-7). These great columns follow the curve of the apse, thus providing an ambulatory behind the stupa (FIG. 11-8). The inner wall of the narthex, despite some later additions, is almost intact, and today it functions as a magnificent façade. On each side of the entrance massive elephants, like atlantes, support a multistoried building, while flanking the central doorway are male and female pairs (related to yakshas and yakshis) that enhance the rich surfaces with heroic and voluptuous forms. These undulant figures contrast with the immobile severity of the stupa within and, like the yakshis of Sanchi, speak of life, not death (FIG. 11-9).

THE BUDDHA IMAGE

As Sanchi is the greatest constructed monument of early Buddhism, so the chaitya at Karli is the finest of the sculptured cave temples. During the second and first centuries B.C. the cave sanctuaries had developed complexities far beyond the simple beginnings in the Lomas Rishi cave. Splendid façades reproducing wood architecture in exact detail were given permanence in stone. Around A.D. 100 at Karli, in the Western Ghats near Bombay, a cliff was hollowed out and carved into an apsidal temple nearly 125 feet long and 45 feet high. The nave of the hall leads to a

For four hundred years before the second century A.D., the Buddha was represented, as we have noted, by symbols only. Then, at the end of the first century, simultaneously in Gandhara and Mathura, he was suddenly depicted in anthropomorphic form. The explanation is partly to be found in the development of the Buddhist movement, which, during the first century, was divided by two conflicting philosophies. The more traditional believers regarded the Buddha as a great teacher who had taught a method by which man might ultimately attain nirvana. The newer thought, called Mahayana (the Great Vehicle) as opposed to the older Hinayana (the Lesser Vehicle), deified the Buddha and provided him with a host of divin-

11-8 Ground plan and elevation of chaitya hall, Karli, c. A.D. 100.

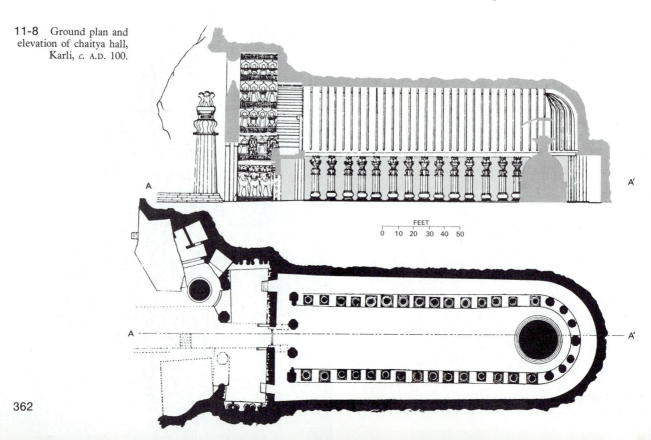

FEET
0 10 20 30 40 50

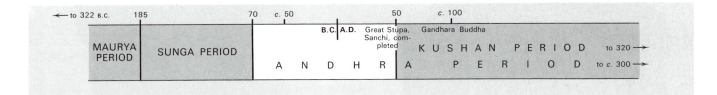

←to 322 B.C.	185		70	c. 50		50		c. 100			
					B.C. A.D.	Great Stupa, Sanchi, completed		Gandhara Buddha			
MAURYA PERIOD	SUNGA PERIOD				A N D H R A			K U S H A N P E R I O D		to 320 →	
								P E R I O D		to c. 300 →	

ities (Bodhisattvas) to aid him in saving mankind. According to the older belief, Sakyamuni was the last of seven Buddhas to have existed on earth. The Mahayanists peopled the universe with thousands of Buddhas, of whom Amitabha, Lord of the Western Paradise, and Maitreya, a messiah who is to appear on this earth, soon rivaled Sakyamuni in popular favor. Symbols of the Buddha were too cold and abstract to appeal to great masses of people and were not suited to the pageantry of the new faith. In addition, Buddhism had borrowed from a reviving Hinduism the practice of *bhakti* (the adoration offered a personalized deity), which demanded the human figure as its focus. Thus Buddhism, out of emulation of its rival, produced its most distinct symbol, the Buddha image.

Gandhara, where one of the two versions of the anthropomorphic Buddha had appeared, may be loosely taken to include much of Afghanistan and part of modern Pakistan, the westernmost section of northern India. In 327 B.C. it had been conquered by the armies of Alexander the Great. Although the Greek occupation lasted only a short time, it led to continued contact with the Classic West. It is not

surprising, then, that the Buddha image that developed at Gandhara had Hellenistic and especially Roman sculpture as its model (FIG. 11-10). Indeed, the features of the Master often suggest those of a marble Apollo, while many details—such as drapery patterns and coiffures—recall successive styles in contemporaneous Roman carving. While the iconography was Indian, even the distinguishing marks of the Buddha (*lakshanas*) were sometimes translated into a Western idiom. Thus the *ushnisha*, a knot of hair on the head, took on the appearance of a Classic chignon. At times even the robe of the Indian monk was replaced by the Roman toga, and minor divinities were transformed into Western water gods, nymphs, or atlantes.

While this intrusion of Western style was dominating the northwest, the purely Indian version of the anthropomorphic Buddha was evolving in the holy city of Mathura, a hundred miles south of Delhi. This image derived directly from the yaksha of popular art and, like the yaksha, it was draped in a mantle so thin and clinging that at first glance it seems to be nude (FIG. 11-11). The Mathura Buddha also has broad shoulders, a narrow waist, and a

11-9 Amorous couple, entrance of chaitya hall, Karli, *c.* A.D. 100.

11-10 Seated Buddha, Gandhara, late third century A.D. Stone. Yale University Art Gallery.

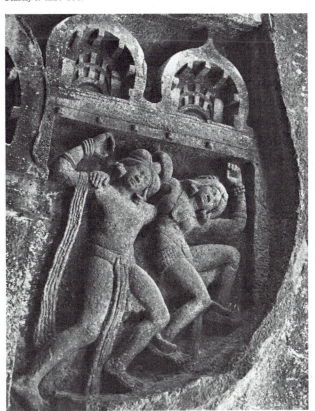

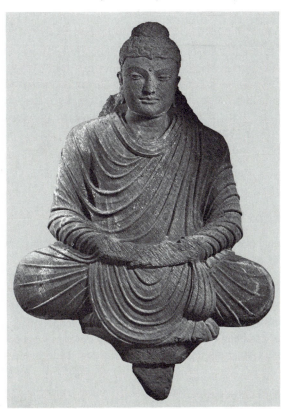

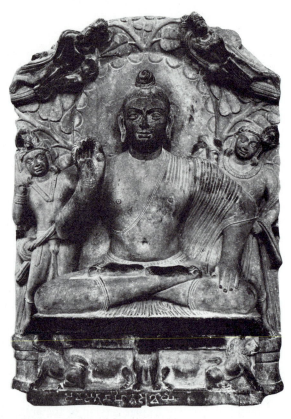

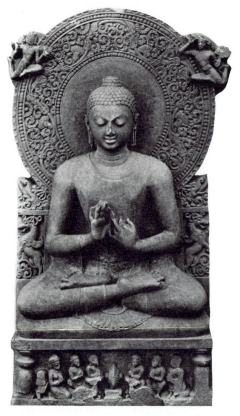

11-11 Seated Buddha, from Mathura, second to third centuries A.D. Red sandstone, 27¼″ high. Archaeological Museum, Muttra.

11-12 Seated Buddha Preaching the First Sermon, Sarnath, fifth century A.D. Stele, sandstone, 63″ high. Archaeological Museum, Sarnath.

supple grace. Only such iconographic details as the ushnisha, the *urna* (a whorl of hair between the brows, represented as a dot), the long-lobed ears, and the *mudra*, a symbolic hand gesture, distinguish the Buddha from the earlier yaksha.

By the third century A.D. the two anthropomorphic Buddha types began to coalesce into a form that served as a model for the earliest Chinese versions. But it is the Buddha at Sarnath (FIG. 11-12), from the end of the fifth century A.D., that conveys both the abstract idealism of the religion and the sensuousness of Indian art, the first in the simplified planes of the face, the second in the clinging drapery, which reveals the human form.

HINDU RESURGENCE

Architecture and Sculpture

While Buddhism was at its height, Hinduism was slowly gathering the momentum that was eventually to crush its heretical offspring. Buddhism owed its original victory to the clearness of its formula for achieving salvation. About the first or second century B.C., Hinduism's answer appeared in the *Bhagavad-Gita,* a poetic gospel that, ever since, has been fundamental to Hindu doctrine. According to the *Gita,* meditation and reason can lead to ultimate

absorption in the godhead; so too can the selfless fulfillment of everyday duties. Since the *Gita* also stressed bhakti, which focused on adoration of a personalized deity as a means of achieving unity with it, and since this answered a fundamental emotional need, the *Gita* swept Hinduism to final supremacy in the sixth and seventh centuries.

Sporadic examples of Hindu art dating from the last centuries B.C. have been found, but we know of no great monuments before the fourth century A.D. At that time the Hindus began to emulate the Buddhist cave temples, at first by carving out monumental icons in shallow niches. One such is the *Boar Avatar of Vishnu* (FIG. 11-13)[1] at Udayagiri near Sanchi. Here, a twelve-foot figure of Varaha, a manlike creature with a boar's head, is shown raising the earth goddess from the ocean—an act symbolic of the rescuing of the earth from destruction. The powerful form of Varaha, first formulated by the Kushans, served as a model for innumerable later sculptures of this popular theme. Within a few decades, other, more developed caves at the same site acquired sculptural doorways, interior columns, and central icons.

To the south during the sixth century, in the rock hillsides at Badami, the Chalukyans carved out rectangular

[1] An Avatar is a manifestation of a deity in which the deity performs a necessary function on earth; the number varies, Vishnu usually having ten, sometimes twenty-nine.

temples that had pillars, walls, and ceilings ornamented with figures of their favorite deities. Porches and interiors were defined by the embellished columns, which were so ordered as to focus attention on the shrine in the center of the rear wall. In a temple dedicated to Siva—with Vishnu one of the two chief divinities of the Hindu pantheon—the god is shown in his cosmic dance, with numerous arms spread fanlike around his body (FIG. 11-14). Some of the god's hands hold objects while others are represented in prescribed gestures (*mudra*), each object and each mudra signifying a specific power of the deity. The arrangement of the limbs is so skillful and logical that it is hard to realize that the sculptor conceived of the figure as a symbol and not as an image of a many-armed being.

Perhaps the supreme achievement of Hindu art is at Elephanta, where, in the sixth century, craftsmen excavated a hilltop and carved out a huge pillared hall almost a hundred feet square. On entering this sanctuary, the visitor peers through rows of heavy columns, until, adjusting to the dark, he sees, emerging from the end wall, the gigantic forms of three heads (FIG. 11-15). These represent Siva as Mahadeva, Lord of Lords and incarnation of the forces of creation, preservation, and destruction. The concept of power is immediately transmitted by the sheer size of the heads, which, rising nearly fourteen feet from the floor, dwarf the onlooker. Each of the three faces expresses a different aspect of the eternal. The center one, neither harsh nor compassionate, looks beyond humanity in the supreme indifference of eternal meditation. The other two faces, one soft and gentle, one angry and fearsome, speak of the sequence of birth and destruction that can be ended only in union with the godhead. The assurance of the

period is manifest in the guardians of the shrine, who stand tall and relaxed in the certainty of their power. On the surrounding walls, deeply cut panels illustrating the legends of Siva carry on the robust and sensuous traditions of both Harappa and Karli.

During the fourth to sixth centuries Buddhism in turn borrowed heavily from Hindu doctrine. Elaborate rituals and incantations, inspired by similar Hindu practices, replaced the simple activities the Buddha had prescribed. Esoteric sects sprouted, and the popular Hindu worship of Sakti, the female power of the deity, was adapted for Buddhist usage. A sixth-century relief in a Buddhist cave temple at Aurangabad depicts worship of the Buddha through music and dance (FIG. 11-16) in a scene that might have been taken from a Hindu temple, for the volatile and rapturous figures of the musicians and dancer represent an Indian, rather than Buddhist, way of life. With little to distinguish it from Hinduism, Buddhism and its art gradually withered and, within a few centuries, virtually disappeared.

In the same burst of creativity that produced cave temples, other innovative Hindu architects were building the first stone structural temples. One of the earliest that remains is the Vishnu temple built in the early sixth century—during the Gupta period (320–c. 600)—at Deogarh in north central India (FIG. 11-17). All later developments of the Hindu temple were in many ways elaborations upon the principles embodied in Deogarh.

The Hindu temple is not a hall for congregational worship; it is the residence of the god. The basic requirement is a cubicle for the cult image or symbol. This most holy of places, called the *garbha griha*, or womb chamber, has

11-13 *Boar Avatar of Vishnu,* Cave V at Udayagiri, Madhya Pradesh, *c.* 400 A.D. Vishnu is 12′ 8″ high.

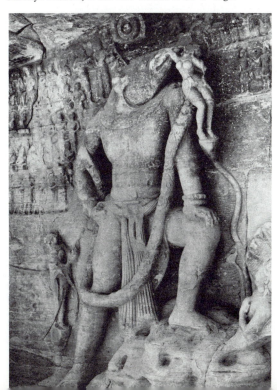

11-14 Dancing Siva, relief from cave temple, Badami, sixth century A.D.

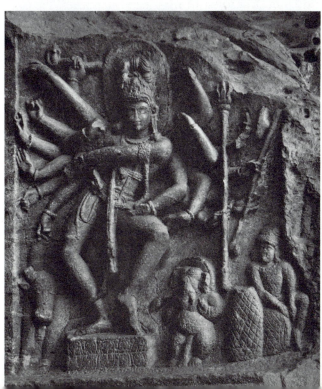

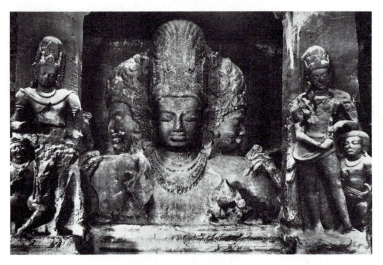

11-15   Siva as Mahadeva in rock-cut temple, Elephanta, sixth century A.D. Siva 10′ 10″ high.

thick walls and a heavy ceiling to protect the deity. A doorway through which the devotee may enter is the only other architectural necessity. As with the stupa, the temple has other meanings, for it is also the symbol of the *purusa*, or primordial man. In addition, in its plan it is a *mandala*, or magic diagram of the cosmos, and its proportions are based on modules that have magical reference. Thus the temple itself is a symbol to be observed from the exterior. Contemporary Western theories of architecture as dealing with space-enclosing form within which man carries on his activities do not apply to the Hindu temple, which is to be appreciated as sculpture rather than as architecture.

In early temples such as Deogarh, decoration is limited and restrained and the form is a simple cube, which origi-

nally was surmounted by a tower (*sikhara*). All the walls, save that of the entrance, are solid but include sculptured panels like false doorways framed in the walls. On these panels are scenes from Hindu mythology, with relaxed and supple figures that carry on the Indian tradition of ease and poise.

In striking contrast to the robust plasticity of northern sculpture are the carvings on the Buddhist monuments situated at the mouth of the Kistna River on the Bay of Bengal. The major sites, in chronological order (roughly from the second century B.C. to the third A.D.), are Jaggayyapeta, Amaravati, and Nagarjunakonda. Little remains from the first, but many reliefs from the other two are extant. These are elaborately ornamented and filled with hosts of figures that, particularly in the later Amaravati scenes (FIG. 11-18), are slender, attenuated, and in graceful movement—rendered almost as if by brush.

The record of Indian art farther to the south begins with a cave temple at Mandagapattu (early seventh century) that was commissioned by the first great ruler of the Pallavas, Mahendravarman I, and dedicated to the Hindu trinity. He was soon surpassed by his immediate successors at Mahabalipuram, on the coast not far from the city of Madras. Here, near a miscellany of monuments—including cave shrines, carved cliffsides, and a masonry temple—is a unique group of five small, free-standing temples (known as *rathas*) that were sculptured, perhaps as architectural models, from some of the huge boulders that litter the area (FIG. 11-19). One of the temples is apsidal, another has a long vaulted shape with a barrel roof, the ends of which reproduce the bentwood curves of the ancient chaitya halls. The smallest is a square shrine with a pyramidal roof that mimics in stone the thatch of primitive shrines as they

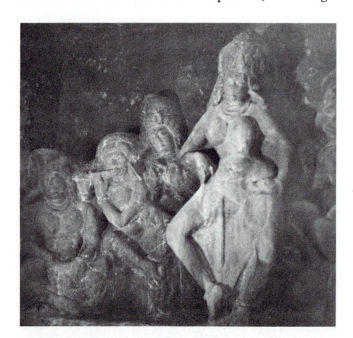

11-16   Relief with dancers and musicians, Aurangabad, sixth century A.D.

11-17   Vishnu temple, Deogarh, side view, early sixth century A.D.

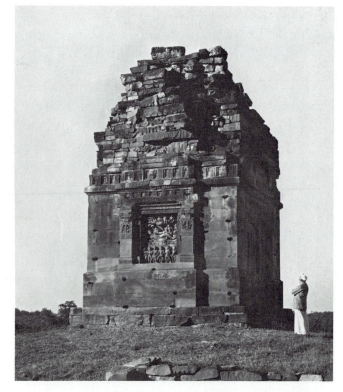

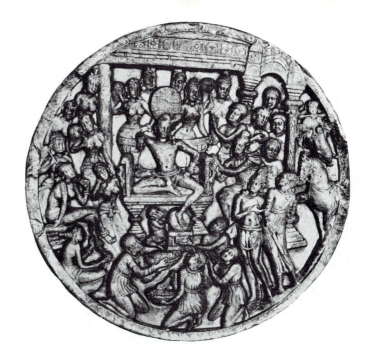

11-18 Relief from stupa, Amaravati, second century A.D.
Musée Guimet, Paris.

appear in reliefs on the rails of early stupas. The Dharma-raja, largest of the rathas, has a simple cubic cella, as at Deogarh. But the *vimana* (composed of the garbha griha and the sikhara) ascends, in typical southern style, in pronounced tiers of cornices decorated with miniature shrines. Spaced along the walls are niches containing figures of the major deities; these niches were to become a regular feature of the southern temple.

The south Indian temple was further developed at the beginning of the eighth century in nearby Kanchipuram and by the artists of the Chalukya dynasty in the Virupaksha Temple (*c.* 740) at Pattadakal near Badami. The vimana here is related to the Dharmaraja ratha, but porches and an assembly hall (*mandapa*) have been added in front of the garbha griha. The interior of this shrine consists of a dimly lighted ambulatory surrounding the cella, which is entered through a large columned assembly hall and two subsidiary shrines. Light entering the mandapa through narrow windows and two projecting porches plays over elaborate relief carvings on the columns and walls. The devotee, who entered through an open porch, walked from the blazing light through a cool, softly lighted, and spacious area until he reached in darkness the enigma of the garbha griha itself. There, in the austere chamber, he came face to face with the barely visible symbol of his deity. The sense of mystery offered the worshiper in such a setting was as satisfactory to the Hindu as was the soaring exultation of the Gothic cathedral to the Christian.

In the following few centuries in north India a different architectural order evolved, characterized by a smoother integration of halls and porches with the main shrine and tower and by an increased vertical emphasis in all parts. The problem of creating a unified exterior was solved in separate stages. The first step, adding height to the mandapa to mitigate the disparity between the vertical vimana and the horizontal mandapa, is illustrated in the immense Kailasa Temple (*c.* 750), the extraordinary rock-cut monument at Ellora. A second step is exemplified by the lovely Muktesvar Temple at Bhuvanesvar, Orissa (FIG. 11-20), where a high pyramidal superstructure over the mandapa brought what had been disproportionately horizontal into complete harmony with the tall sikhara. This evolution culminated during the tenth to eleventh

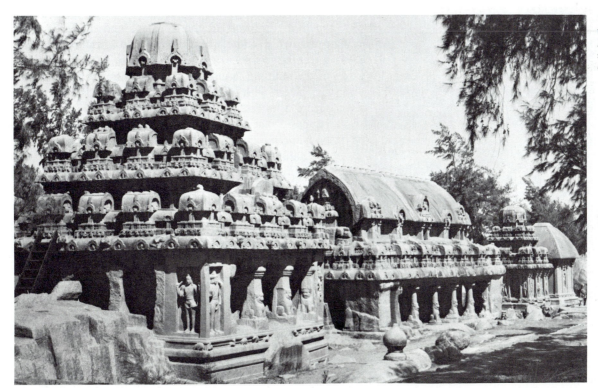

11-19 Rock-cut temples, Mahabalipuram, seventh century A.D.

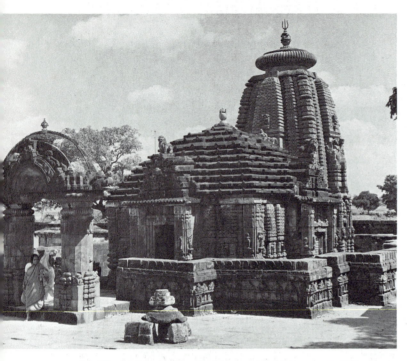

11-20　Muktesvar Temple, Bhuvanesvar, Orissa, c. A.D. 950.

11-21　Visvanatha Temple, Khajuraho, c. A.D. 1000.

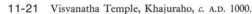

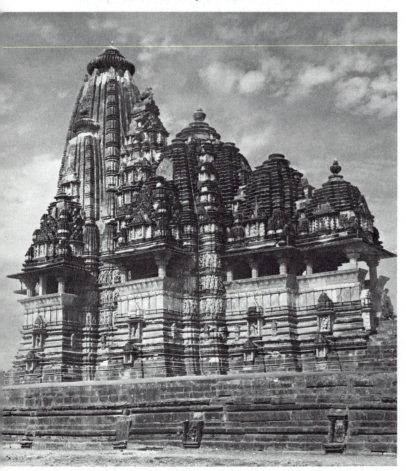

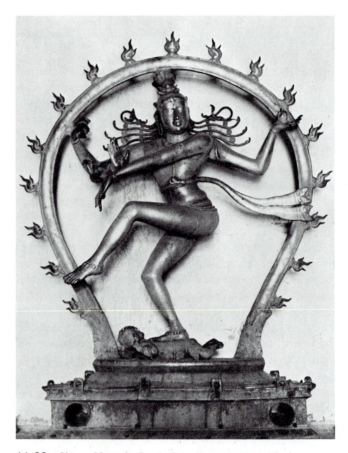

11-22　Siva as Nataraja, Lord of the Dance, Naltunai Isvaram Temple, Punjai, Tamilnadu, c. A.D. 1000. Bronze.

centuries at Khajuraho (FIG. 11-21) in north central India. There the temples, numbering over twenty, became larger, more elaborate, and, by virtue of their high plinths, even more prominent. Two and sometimes three mandapa were put before the cella. The greatest esthetic advance was made in the roofs of the mandapa and their pyramidal eaves, which unite with the sikhara to create a rapid and torrential sequence of cascading forms. The lower sections of the building, bound by a series of horizontal registers, are laden with sculptured deities, legends, and erotic scenes. Elongated figures are often set in complexly twisting poses that emphasize the sinuously curved lines of the body. Although the rendering of living forms has become less natural and at times even disturbingly contorted, the sculptures function superbly in leading the eye around the shifting planes of the sides of the temple.

In the year 1000 the first of a series of Moslem invasions sounded the knell of Hindu architecture in northern India. But in the south—first under the Chola kingdom (846–1173) and later under the Hoysala (1022–1342), the Vijayanagar (1336–1565), and Nayak (1420–1736) dynasties—sculpture and architecture continued to flourish.

Of particular beauty are the small early Chola temples scattered throughout Tamilnadu. Many are incomparable in their architectonic order, sensitive detail, and sculp-

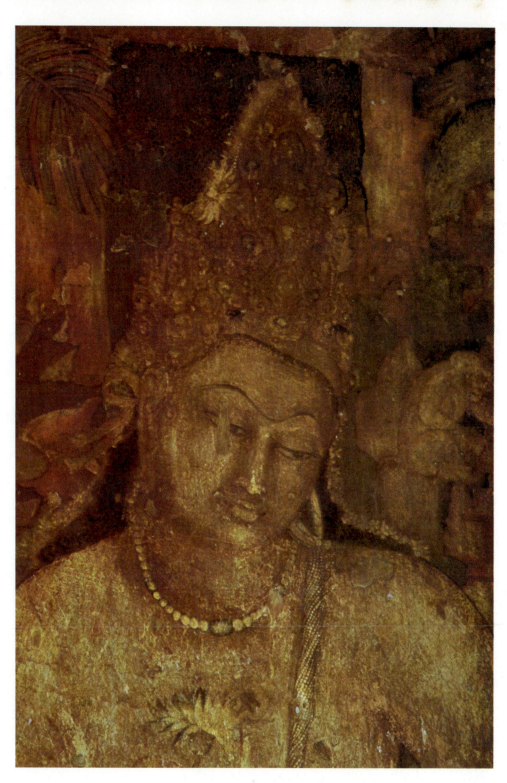

11-23 *Beautiful Bodhisattva Padmapani*, fresco from Cave I, Ajanta, *c.* A.D. 600–650.

ture. A trend toward larger buildings, reflecting the impe-rial grandeur of the Chola, led to the great Brihadesvara Temple (*c.* 1000), at Thanjavur, which is 160 feet high and replete with architectural elements and figures. On its walls are represented many deities although there are fewer than at Khajuraho and most are in niches spaced with restraint at ordered intervals.

Bronze images were made to grace the shrines and to be carried in processions during important ceremonies. Some of the world's most superb bronzes were produced in the Chola kingdom, the figures of Siva as Nataraja, Lord of the Dance, reaching their high point by the tenth century. The Nataraja (*c.* 1000) at the Naltunai Isvaram Temple at Punjai (FIG. 11-22) shows the god, represented in an ideal human form, dancing vigorously within a flaming nimbus, one foot on the Demon of Ignorance. His flying locks terminate in rearing cobra heads, and at one side they support a tiny figure of the river goddess, Ganga. One of

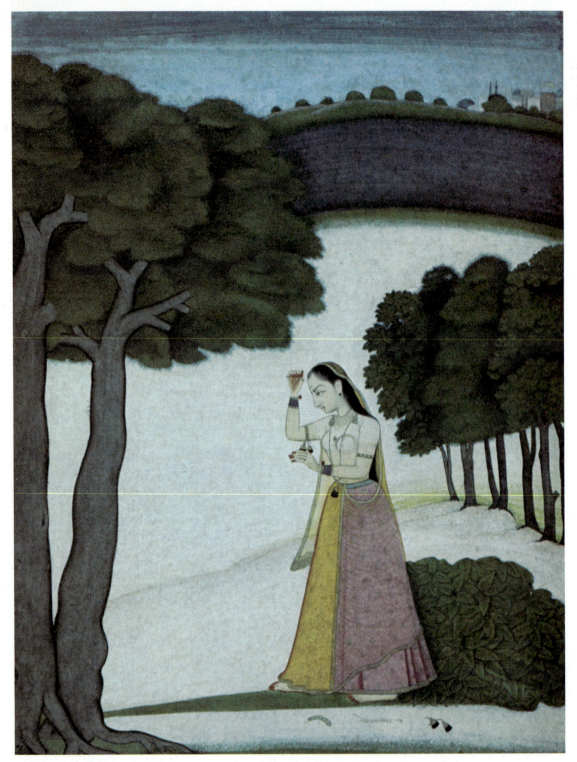

11-24 *The Disappointed Mistress,* c. 1740. Gouache, 8¼″ x 6″. Private collection, Los Angeles.

his four hands sounds a drum, while from another a flame flashes. Dancing thus, Siva periodically destroys the universe so that it may be reborn again. Exquisitely balanced, yet full of movement, this bronze is a triumph of three-dimensional sculpture and the art of bronze casting.

Enormous temple compounds grew around the nucleus of earlier temples. The Minakshi temple at Madura and the Srirangam temple at Tiruchirapalli eventually covered acres of ground. "Thousand-pillared" halls were built almost one beside the other, acquiring the aspect of a continuous structure interrupted only by courtyards and sacred water tanks for ritual bathing. Elaborate monolithic columns, carved with high- and low-relief figures, evoke a solemn mood, the stone sculpture giving the effect of iron castings. The original walled enclosure came to be surrounded by other walls as the temple expanded and the gateways (*gopuram*) at each of the four cardinal points grew progressively higher with each additional wall. The fully developed gopuram is multi-storied and crowded with sculpture; with many over 150 feet high, they dominate the landscape of south India.

The spread of Moslem domination gradually sapped the Indian tradition, even in the south. By the seventeenth century the harmonious proportions of earlier figures were lost, and even the metal castings had become inferior.

Painting

The art of painting was probably as great in India as the art of sculpture but, unfortunately, less of it survives. The earliest traces are a few fragments in Cave X at Ajanta that date from approximately the first century B.C. Like the ornamentation on the toranas at Sanchi (above), to which they are related in style, they illustrate scenes from the past lives of the Buddha.

At Ajanta, again, in Caves I and XVII, are found the next and most magnificent examples of Indian painting. These murals, from the fifth to seventh centuries A.D., embody all the clarity, dignity, and serenity of Gupta art; they must rank among the great paintings of the world. The *Beautiful Bodhisattva Padmapani* in Cave I moves with the subtle grace of the Deogarh sculptures, while the glow of color imparts an even more spiritual presence (FIG. 11-23). The Ajanta paintings, however, are more than the manifestations of Buddhist devotion. Their genre-like scenes and worldly figures, although illustrating Buddhist texts, reflect a sophisticated and courtly art.

The Ajanta painting tradition, in all its colorful vitality, was continued under the Chola rule, as witnessed by the paintings in the Brihadesvara Temple at Thanjavur. The dancing figures in these—though drawn in the vivacious postures familiar in the Chola bronzes—retain some of the modeling and the soft tonality of the Gupta style.

The Moslem conquests inhibited the evolution of Hindu sculpture and architecture in northern India after the thirteenth century, but they revitalized the art of painting. In the sixteenth century, especially under the reign of Akbar, who was sympathetic to Hinduism and Christianity as well as Islam, traditional Indian painters were exposed to the delicate and conventionalized miniatures of the great Persian artists. During the seventeenth and eighteenth centuries, painting responded vigorously to what was an interplay between foreign modes at the imperial capital and autochthonous idioms at isolated feudal courts. Many delightful hybrids and innovations resulted—some delicate and lyrical, as at Bundi, and Kishangarh (Rajasthan); some stark and bold, as at Basohli in the Himalayan foothills. Among others, the hill schools in Guler and Kangra developed their own idiom, emphasizing such subjects as elegant figures in serene landscapes, portraits of rulers, *ragamalas* (interpretations of musical modes), and religious themes. The joyous exuberance of these new styles was particularly well suited to newer Hindu cults, which were dedicated to the worship of Krishna, an avatar of Vishnu whose praises were sung in the erotic poetry of the *Gita-Govinda*. The love of the lush and the sensuous, which the earliest sculptures had expressed, thus found an entirely new medium in exquisitely colored, often tender paintings (FIG. 11-24).

THE SPREAD OF INDIAN ART

The vigorous culture that generated the great achievements of art in India overflowed its borders. The great tide of Buddhism in the early centuries of the Christian era carried Mahayana beliefs and the art of Gandhara-Mathura through Afghanistan, across the desert trade routes of Turkestan into China, and eventually into Japan.

The path of Hinayana Buddhism (pages 357 and 362), which was opened in the third century B.C. by the son of the Emperor Asoka, led in another direction—south from Amaravati to Sri Lanka (Ceylon) across the straits. From that time on Sri Lanka became a little India, its arts influenced first by Amaravati, then successively by the Guptas, the Pallavas, and the Cholas. The largest concentration of art was at two royal centers: Anuradhapura (virtually an extension of Amaravati), where most of what remains is from the second and third centuries A.D., and Polonnaruwa (eleventh to twelfth century), best known for the colossal 46-foot-long sculpture of the expiring Buddha (FIG. 11-25). Here also are many famous stupas that basically adhere to the Amaravati tradition but are simpler; an innovation is the carvings of guardian figures on stelae placed at stupa entrances. While there are some paintings at Polonnaruwa, the earliest (fifth century) and most exquisite are the heavenly maidens on the escarpment of the fortress at Sigiriya.

By the fifth century, a series of emigrations from India was bringing the impact of Indian culture to Burma, Thailand, Cambodia, Sumatra, and Java. There, Buddhism and Hinduism continued their struggle for supremacy, with each introducing and fostering its arts. While Buddhism was under siege in India, one of its greatest monuments was rising at Barabudur in Java (FIG. 11-26). There, around 800 A.D., a huge stupa, basically square and over 400 feet across the base, was built of stone in nine terraced levels, with a central stairway in each of the four sides. The base and the first four tiers are rectilinear and signify the terrestrial world of sensation; the upper four are circular and symbolize the heavens.

On the base, mostly covered by earth, 160 reliefs depict people trapped in the karmic cycle of life, death, and rebirth. Abundantly decorating the walls along the corridors of the next four tiers are over 1000 cautionary scenes from the *jatakas* and different *sutras*. But above, on the circular terraces, no narratives intrude. Here, ringing the pathways in solitary dignity, are latticed stupas, in each of

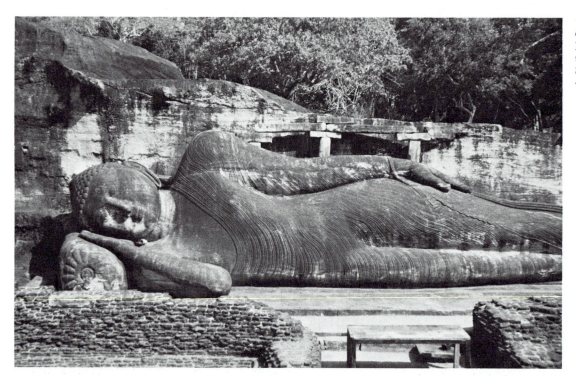

which, barely visible, is a seated Buddha of gentle beauty. (Originally there were 72). Rising at the pinnacle is a single larger stupa, which may have enclosed a single Buddha, symbol of the ultimate.

This architectural orchestration of sculptures is a mandala, a cosmic diagram perhaps representing the three spheres of Buddhist cosmology—the Human Sphere of Desire (didactic narratives crowded with figures and foliage), the Bodhisattva Sphere of Form, and the Buddha Sphere of Formlessness, where the simplicity and isolation of the individual stupas effect a serene release. The scheme uses 505 Buddha figures. In all, it is an eloquent statement

11-26 Stupa, Barabudur, Java, *c.* A.D. 800.

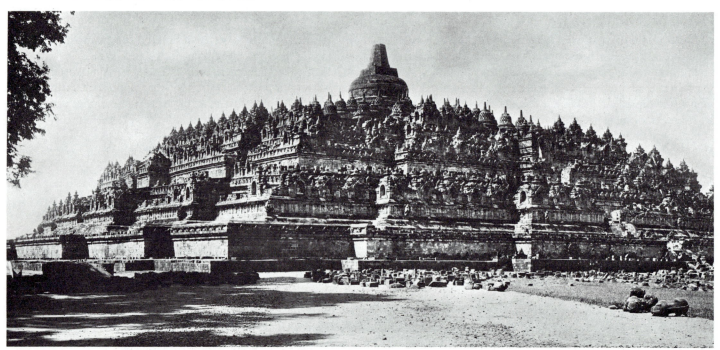

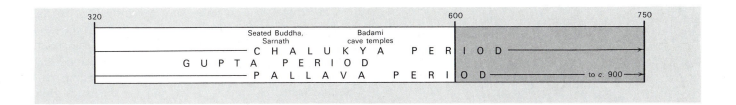

320	600	750

Seated Buddha,   Badami
Sarnath   cave temples

C H A L U K Y A   P E R I O D

G U P T A   P E R I O D

P A L L A V A   P E R I O D   to c. 900 →

of proto-Esoteric Buddhism as developed from Mahayana in Java.

The Buddhists in Java also erected *chandis* (temples). Two such that are near the stupa of Barabudur and of the same date are Chandi Mendut and Chandi Pawon. Their dark sanctuaries, containing colossal Buddhist images, have the same awesome impact as the shrines of the Buddhist cave temples in northwest India. Indeed, those caves as well as other sacred sites throughout India were well known to Indonesian pilgrims, whose exposure to Indian monuments and texts influenced their island culture.

The Hindus were also active in Java. On the Dieng Plateau they erected single-celled Siva temples based on south Indian Pallava models. At Prambanan in central Java, where structures and motifs were rapidly Javanized, the Siva temple of Lara Jonggrang (ninth to tenth century), tall and narrow, is characteristically a studied aggregate of piled-up stones, terraced peaks, and sanctuaries, the whole a symbol of Mahameru, axis of the universe and mountain home of the gods. Reliefs on the temple balustrade illustrate the *Ramayana*, the great Hindu epic. Naturalistic yet decorative, these dramatic narratives are a har-mony of Indian forms and Javanese physical types (FIG. 11-27).

The mainland, in contact with India by the third century A.D., also reacted to the stimuli of Indian culture. In Thailand, the softly modeled figures of bronze and stucco that were produced during the Dvaravati period (sixth to tenth century) were inspired by the Gupta style. During the Pre-Angkor or Early Khmer period (fifth to ninth century), the Cambodians, too, borrowed the flowing planes and sensitive surfaces of Gupta. Around the seventh century, they also worked in the manner of the south Indian Pallavas, as we can see in the figure of Harihara (a combined form of Siva and Vishnu) from Prasat Andet (FIG. 11-28). The elegance of the Pallava prototypes at Mahabalipuram has been modified only slightly by the addition of a taut almost spring-like tension. Tall, broad-shouldered, full-bodied, and slender-legged, this is an idealized figure, more godly than human. We shall see how the classical configuration of the Pre-Angkor gods was gradually transformed into a distinctly more squat Cambodian type with a broad face composed of full lips (doubly outlined), continuous eyebrows, and flat nose.

11-27 Ramayana scene, Siva temple, Lara Jonggrang, Java, ninth to tenth centuries.

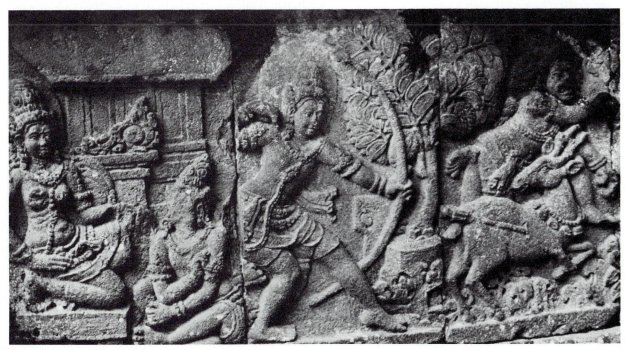

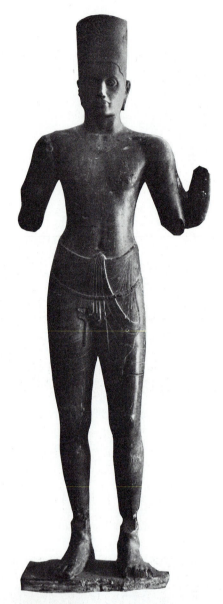

The temple in Cambodia was directly related to the Angkorian concept of kingship. Whereas in India the ideal king was the Universal Lord (*chakravartin*) who ruled through goodness, in Cambodia he was the God-King (*devaraja*) in life and after death. The temple the king built was dedicated to himself as the god. As the kings grew more powerful and ambitious, so grew the size of their temples and the multiplication of architectural and decorative elements.

A prime example of the colossal agglomerations typifying the fully developed Angkorean style is Angkor Wat (1100–75). A moat two and a half miles long surrounds this monument; one of its many corridors contains half a mile of sculptured reliefs; and the foundations of the central shrine alone are more than three thousand feet on each side. The temples comprising this great complex are set at the corners of two concentric walls that gird the central shrine. Each of the eight temple towers repeats the form of the main spire, which rises in the center from a raised platform like the apex of a pyramid. The towers themselves resemble in outline the sikhara of north Indian temples.

Angkor Wat was dedicated to Vishnu by its builder, the king Suryavarman II, and reliefs on the galleries illustrate the *Ramayana* and the ten incarnations of the god. These carvings express the Cambodian predilection for rhythmic design, the juxtaposition of two, three, or more identical figures, and the repetition of undulating contours. These graceful but stylized forms, thus locked together, move in a harmonious rhythm like their counterparts in Cambodian dance (FIG. 11-29).

The Bayon at Angkor Thom (FIG. 11-30), twelfth and thirteenth centuries, is in many ways the culmination of the Indian temple, particularly in its complete integration of sculpture and architecture. It also illustrates the syncretic relationship of Hinduism and Buddhism. The long impressive approach to the Bayon, a Buddhist temple, is lined in places with giant gods and demons holding onto the body of the serpent Vasuki, in enactment of a Hindu legend, the Churning of the Sea of Milk. But the uniqueness of the Bayon lies in the size and disposition of the

11-28 *Harihara*, Prasat Andet, seventh century. Musée Albert Sarraut, Pnompenh.

11-29 Dance relief, Angkor Wat, twelfth century. Musée Guimet, Paris.

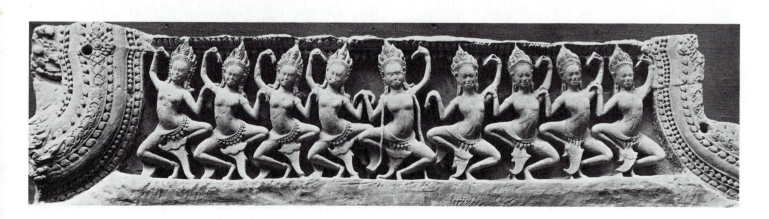

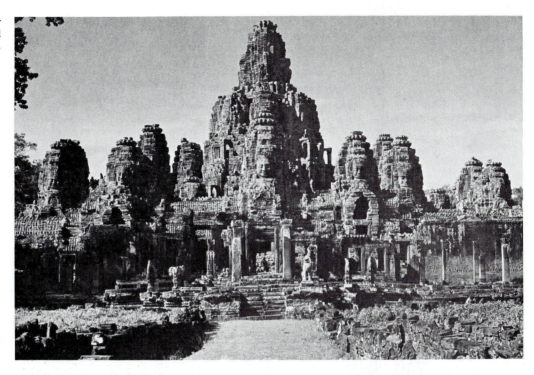

11-30 Bayon, Angkor Thom, twelfth and thirteenth centuries.

colossal heads, one on each side of the square towers (FIG. 11-31). These faces, their Cambodian features now fully stylized, smile enigmatically from a lofty height. They are the faces of the Bodhisattva Lokesvara, god form of the reigning king, symbol of the infinite powers of the devaraja-Bodhisattva, which extend to all points of the compass. The Bayon was conceived as the world mountain. On it and around it a tropical luxuriance of decorative and narrative carvings intensifies its magic. The creative force that had been India left its last great record abroad in these compassionate faces of Lokesvara surveying from eternity the legendary history carved on the walls below.

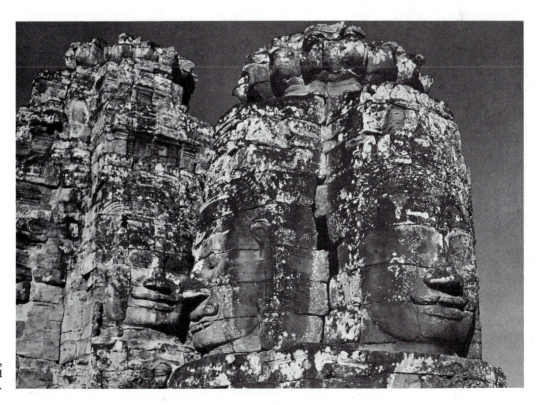

11-31 Tower of Bayon, Angkor Thom, twelfth and thirteenth centuries.

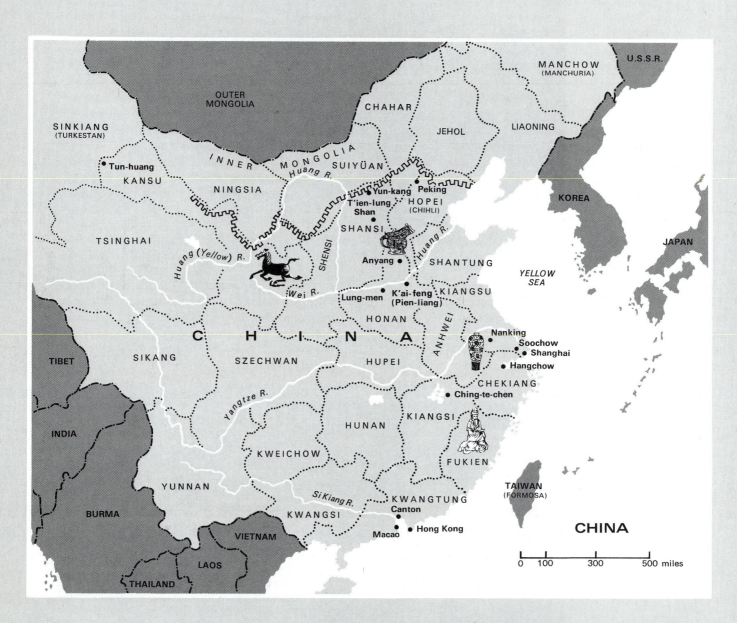

MANCHOW
(MANCHURIA)

U.S.S.R.

OUTER
MONGOLIA

SINKIANG
(TURKESTAN)

CHAHAR

JEHOL

LIAONING

INNER   MONGOLIA

SUIYÜAN

Huang R.

Tun-huang

KANSU

NINGSIA

Yun-kang Peking

T'ien-lung
Shan

HOPEI
(CHIHLI)

KOREA

JAPAN

SHANSI

Anyang

Huang R.

SHANTUNG

TSINGHAI

Huang (Yellow) R.

SHENSI

Lung-men

K'ai-feng
(Pien-liang)

KIANGSU

YELLOW
SEA

Wei R.

HONAN

ANHWEI

Nanking

C H I N A

Soochow

Shanghai

TIBET

SIKANG

SZECHWAN

HUPEI

Hangchow

CHEKIANG

Ching-te-chen

INDIA

Yangtze R.

KIANGSI

HUNAN

KWEICHOW

FUKIEN

TAIWAN
(FORMOSA)

YUNNAN

Si Kiang R.

KWANGTUNG

Canton

CHINA

BURMA

KWANGSI

VIETNAM

Macao Hong Kong

0   100   300   500 miles

LAOS

THAILAND

chapter twelve

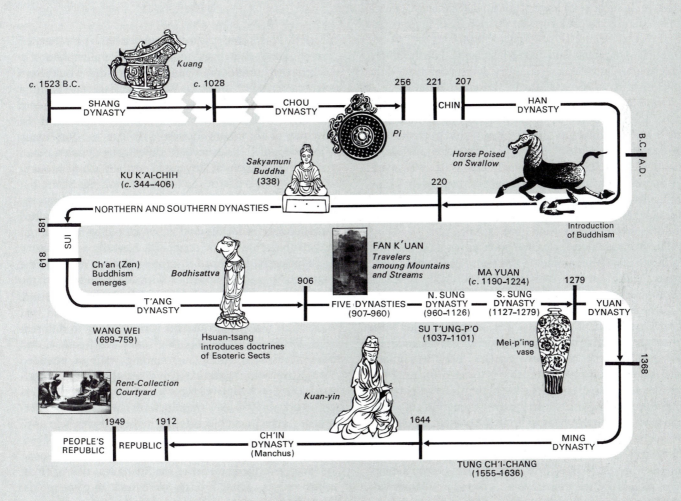

Kuang

c. 1523 B.C.   c. 1028   256   221   207

SHANG DYNASTY   CHOU DYNASTY   CHIN   HAN DYNASTY

B.C. | A.D.

Pi

KU K'AI-CHIH (c. 344–406)

Sakyamuni Buddha (338)

Horse Poised on Swallow

220

NORTHERN AND SOUTHERN DYNASTIES

Introduction of Buddhism

581

618

SUI

Ch'an (Zen) Buddhism emerges

Bodhisattva

FAN K'UAN *Travelers amoung Mountains and Streams*

MA YUAN (c. 1190–1224)

1279

906

T'ANG DYNASTY   FIVE DYNASTIES (907–960)   N. SUNG DYNASTY (960–1126)   S. SUNG DYNASTY (1127–1279)   YUAN DYNASTY

WANG WEI (699–759)

Hsuan-tsang introduces doctrines of Esoteric Sects

SU T'UNG-P'O (1037–1101)

Mei-p'ing vase

1368

Rent-Collection Courtyard

Kuan-yin

1949   1912   1644

PEOPLE'S REPUBLIC   REPUBLIC   CH'IN DYNASTY (Manchus)   MING DYNASTY

TUNG CH'I-CHANG (1555–1636)

The Art of China

OF THE GREAT non-Western civilizations, that of China was the first known and appreciated in Europe. But it is only in the past half-century or so that the achievements of Chinese art and culture have been progressively revealed and studied systematically. Still, many in the West who now realize the extent and continuity of Chinese civilization and who recognize the striking beauty of its art are not fully aware of the complexity of either. Our task here is to identify the spirit of Chinese art and to trace, at least in outline, its major developments and styles.

China is a vast and topographically varied country about the size of the United States. Its political and cultural boundaries have spread at times to double that area, encompassing Tibet, Chinese Turkestan (Sinkiang), Mongolia, Manchuria, and parts of Korea. The country includes great stretches of sandy plains, mighty rivers, towering mountains, and fertile farmlands. North China, centering around Peking, has a dry and moderate-to-cold climate, whereas south China is moist and tropical.

While the spoken language of China varies so much as to be unrecognizable in different areas, the written language has remained uniform and intelligible in all parts of the country, permitting literary, philosophic, and religious traditions to be shared by people thousands of miles apart. Distinct regional styles of art did appear, especially in the early eras and during times of political fragmentation, but a broad cultural unity also permitted an easy flow of artistic ideas and influence throughout China.

The primarily expressive function of Chinese painting during the last millennium has been gradually made more comprehensible to the Western mind, partly by developments in the modern art of the West. We have become more aware of fundamental differences between Chinese secular art and the traditional, premodern art of the West, differences determined by those between the philosophies of nature and man of the two cultures. For the Chinese, man is not dominant in nature; he is a part of it, responding like all living creatures to its rhythms. To be happy is to live in accord with nature; to be a painter is to be the instrument through which nature reveals itself. The painter's work is an expression of his immersion in the flow of life and of his attunement to all that changes and grows and, in so being, is also the expression of a personal character refined by the contemplation of nature. Moreover, because nature is not measured and classified according to space and time, the Chinese painter does not frame it off in perspective boxes with colors scaled in light and shade. He does not attempt by such means to duplicate and fix natural appearances. The asymmetry of growing things, the ceaseless and random movements of nature, the infinity of cosmic happenings—these forbid all enframements, rigid regularities, beginnings and ends. Appearance is always transformed by the artist's passage through it. He becomes part of the total expression of his art as his art is the total expression of his experience of nature.

This philosophical attitude of the Chinese toward secular painting can be seen even in the artist's almost ritualistic preparation of his medium, his materials. The best ink, for instance, was derived from soot or lampblack mixed with animal glue and pulverized clay, oyster shells or powdered jade, and various fragrances. From these ingredients, each of which had symbolic as well as physical properties, an ink stick (often carved) was formed that was treasured by the artist.

SHANG

A series of Neolithic cultures characterized by a variety of painted wares date back to the fourth millennium B.C. According to traditional Chinese history this would have been the period of the Hsia. While the Hsia state is still a matter of legend, the remains of a considerable kingdom discovered within the last fifty years have confirmed the existence of the Shang dynasty. As late as 1928 many scholars doubted the existence of the Shang dynasty, but in that year excavations at Anyang in northern China brought to light not only one of the last capitals of the Shang but also evidence of their earlier development. Among the astounding discoveries were large numbers of inscribed bones, once used for divination, which tell us much about the Shang people. Their script was basically pictographic but sufficiently developed to express abstract ideas. These fragmentary records, together with other finds from the excavations, reveal an advanced if barbaric civilization. They indicate that the king was a feudal ruler and that some of his wives were also his vassals, living in different cities. Warfare with neighboring states was frequent, and cities were protected by surrounding walls of pounded earth. Royal tombs were extensive, and the beheaded bodies of servants or captives accompanied the deceased rulers to the grave. Chariots, trappings of horses buried alive, weapons, and ritual objects found in these graves help us to describe the art of this period.

Although sculpture in marble and small carvings in bone and jade exist, the great art of the Shang was that of ritual bronze vessels. These bronzes were made in piece molds. They show a casting technique as advanced as any ever used in the East or West, which indicates that this art must have been practiced for some centuries before the period of Anyang. The bronze vessels were intended to hold wine, water, grain, and meat used in sacrificial rites. The major elements of decoration are zoomorphic, but usually the background and sometimes the animals themselves are covered with round or squared spirals. Conventions, which obviously evolved over a long period, rigidly governed the

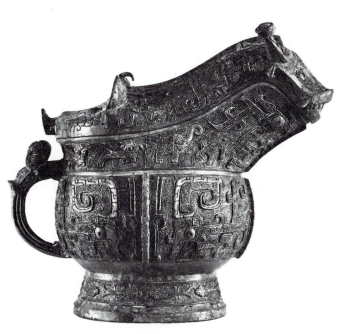

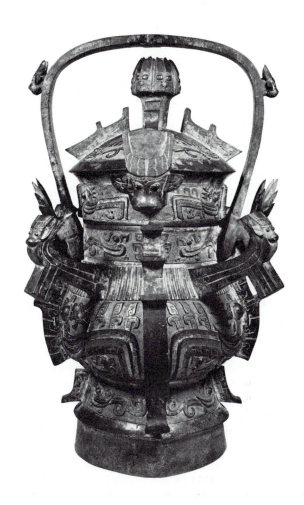

12-1 *Kuang*, Shang dynasty, twelfth century B.C. Bronze, 6½″ high.
Smithsonian Institution, Freer Gallery of Art, Washington, D.C.

12-2 *Yu*, Early Chou dynasty, *c.* tenth century B.C. Bronze.
Smithsonian Institution, Freer Gallery of Art,
Washington, D.C.

stylistic representation of animals, so that images or symbols are often involved and difficult to decipher. A major zoomorphic motif is that of an animal divided in half lengthwise, with the two halves spread out on the vessel body in a bilaterally symmetrical design. The two head parts, meeting in the center, can often also be read as a complete frontal animal mask with vestigial bodies at both sides. Such ambiguity of design occurs frequently on Shang vessels, where fragmentary parts of bodies take on a life of their own.

Such an animal is shown in FIG. 12-1, a covered libation vessel, or *kuang*. In this complex design, the representation (on the vessel's side) may be of eyes of a tiger and horns of a ram. (On other such Shang vessels the eyes may be of a sheep; the horns, of a bull, water buffalo, or deer.) The front of the lid is formed of a horned animal; the rear, of a horned head with a bird's beak in its mouth. Another horned head is on the handle. Fish, birds, elephants, rabbits, and more abstract, composite creatures swarm over the surface against a background of spirals. Specific combinations of such animal motifs may have defined certain concepts; for example, the animal or bird in the mouth of another animal perhaps signifies generation. The multiple designs and their enigmatic fields of spirals are so closely integrated with the form of the vessel that they are not merely an external embellishment but an integral part of

the sculptural whole. The tense outline of the bronze compactly encloses the forces symbolized on its surface. These vessels were not only ritual containers but also, in their very form and decoration, a kind of sculptural icon or visualization of the early Chinese attitude toward the powers of nature.

CHOU

About 1027 B.C. the Shang dynasty was overthrown by the Chou, whose dynasty endured until 256 B.C. Although the Chou were a more primitive people from the west, their culture apparently resembled that of the Shang.

The very earliest Chou bronzes are indistinguishable from those of the Shang. Indeed, they were probably made by the same craftsmen. But within a generation the new and bolder spirit of the conquerors was unmistakably imprinted on the ritual vessels. Where the Shang silhouette had been suave and compact, the Chou was explosive and dynamic (FIG. 12-2). Gradually this vitality diminished, and in a hundred years the shapes became more utilitarian and the zoomorphic designs more ornamental. The animal forms were distorted and twisted into interlaces until, by the beginning of the Late Chou period (600–256 B.C.), almost all evidence of the original awesome motifs was lost in an exuberance of playful rhythms over the surface of the bronzes. What had once expressed the power of magic and religion was transformed into a secular display of technical skill and fantasy.

During the sixth century B.C. the Chou empire began to dissolve into a number of warring feudal states. As old values were forgotten, Confucius and other philosophers strove to analyze the troubles of their day. While Confucius urged intelligent and moral action upon his followers, his famous contemporary, Lao-tzu, favored meditation, inaction, and withdrawal from society. Neither philosophy, however, was to affect the arts for several centuries.

The art of the Late Chou, whether in bronze, jade (FIG. 12-3), or lacquer, was produced to satisfy elaborate demands of ostentatious feudal courts that vied with each other in lavish display. Popular at this time were bronzes inlaid with gold and silver and mirrors highly polished on one side and decorated with current motifs on the other. About the fourth century B.C. ritual bronzes were embellished with an entirely new system of narrative designs. Scenes of hunting, religious rites, and magic practices, although small, nevertheless reveal subjects and compositions probably reflective of paintings lost but mentioned in literature of the period.

In the Late Chou, carvings of jade, a stone regarded with special reverence by the Chinese and found in neolithic tombs, reached a peak of technical perfection in jewelry and ritual objects entombed with the dead (FIGS. 12-3 and 12-6). At this time Confucius extolled the virtues of jade in which, he said, superior men in ancient times

12-3 *Pi*, disc, Late Chou dynasty, fifth to third centuries B.C. Jade. Nelson Gallery-Atkins Museum, Kansas City, Missouri (Nelson Fund).

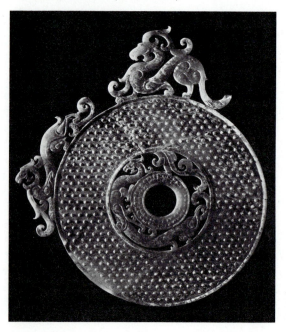

"found the likeness of all excellent qualities": It was soft, smooth, and glossy (when polished), like benevolence; fine, compact, and strong, like intelligence; angular, but not sharp and cutting, like righteousness; and (when struck) like music. Like loyalty its flaws did not conceal its beauty nor its beauty its flaws and, like virtue, it was conspicuous in the symbols of rank.[1]

The culture that had produced the great bronzes and jades of the Shang and Chou was being transformed. The political turbulence of the late Chou period, sometimes called the period of the Warring States, was accompanied by an intellectual and artistic upheaval that coincided with the rise of conflicting schools of philosophy and, in art, a new iconography and style combined with vestigial elements from the Shang and early Chou periods. During the next four hundred years, a radically different art developed.

CH'IN AND HAN

The political chaos of the last few hundred years of the Chou dynasty was temporarily halted by Shih Huang Ti, ruler of the state of Ch'in. In the third century B.C., in an attempt to eradicate old traditions, he ordered the burning of all historical books and established totalitarian control over most of China. At his death the people revolted, and in 206 B.C. a new dynasty, the Han, was founded. A powerful centralized government extended the southern and western boundaries of China. Chinese armies penetrated far into Turkestan, and indirect trade was maintained with distant Rome. Confucianists struggled with Taoists (followers of the mystic philosophy of Lao-tzu) for control of governmental powers. The Confucianists eventually won, though the formalized Confucianism that triumphed was far removed from the teachings of the master. The Confucian legends of filial piety and the folklore of Taoism together provided most of the subject matter of Han art.

The Han pictorial style is known from a few extant paintings and many stone reliefs as well as stamped pottery tiles. In some paintings the outlines of figures are rendered in the characteristic Chinese line, whose calligraphic elasticity conveys not only outline but depth and mass as well. Overlapping of arms and drapery further emphasizes the third dimension, while flat colors applied within contours accent the rhythmic relationship between figures. There is no background or any other indication of environment.

Numerous stone reliefs from the Wu family shrines in Shantung (c. A.D. 150) also reflect modes of Han pictorial representation. On the slabs are depicted scenes from history and folklore, mythological beings associated with

[1] From the *Li Chi* attributed to Confucius, translated by James Legge, *The Sacred Books of the East* (1968), vol. 28, p. 464.

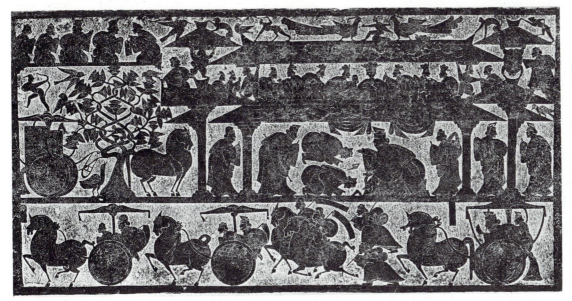

12-4 Mythological scenes, Wu family shrine, Shantung, Later Han dynasty, A.D. 147–168. Rubbing of stone relief, approx. 60″ long.

Taoism as well as exemplars of Confucian piety. The story unfolds in images of flat polished stone against an equally flat though roughly striated ground (FIG. 12-4). The rounded figures are related by the linear rhythms of their contours. In addition, buildings and trees now indicate a milieu. Space, though, is conceptual, as in Egyptian painting; and distance is suggested by the superposition of figures although, curiously enough, chariot wheels overlap. Individuals of importance are shown hieratically in larger size than their subordinates. Most interesting are the trees, which are highly stylized as masses of intertwined branches bearing isolated, overlarge leaves. Yet within this schematic form some accidental variation in a twisted branch or broken bough shows how the designer's generalization derived from observation of specific trees and how a detail of the particular could individualize the general. It is this subtle relationship between the specific and the abstract that became one of the most important esthetic attributes of later Chinese painting.

A group of reliefs from Szechwan, while similar to those of the Wu tombs and probably of the same date, are further advanced. Rhythms are more rapid, and space and the environment are more fully stated. Some subjects concern everyday life, in contrast to the earlier preoccupation with mythological or historical themes. There is also a figure of the Buddha, probably the earliest in China and therefore the first reference to the religion that was to dominate Chinese thought for the next thousand years.

A superb example of Han bronze craft in the tradition of Chinese mastery of that metal since Shang times is a recently discovered (1969) figure of a horse from a tomb (FIG. 12-5) in Kansu. Though its action is certainly that of a quick trot, it seems to be flying, one hoof lightly poised on its single point of attachment to its pedestal. The horse,

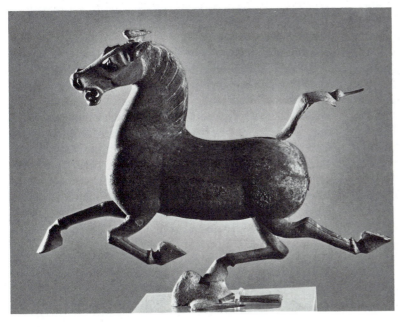

12-5 Flying horse poised on one leg on a swallow, from a tomb at Wu-wei, Kansu, Later Han dynasty, second century A.D. Bronze, 13½″ high, 17¾″ long. The exhibition of archeological finds of the People's Republic of China.

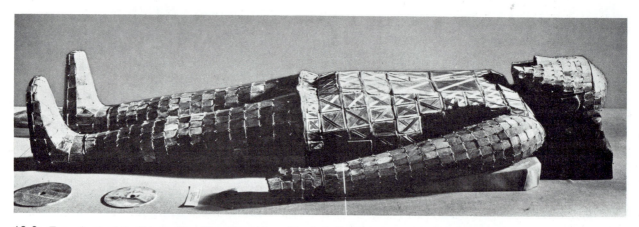

12-6   Funeral suit of the Princess Tou Wan, Man-ch'eng, Hopei, Earlier Han dynasty, late second century B.C. Jade tablets sewn with gold wire; suit is 68″ long. The exhibition of archeological finds of the People's Republic of China.

because it was revered for its power and majesty, has a prominence in Chinese art tantamount to that of the lion or bull in the art of the Near East.

A second-century B.C. Han tomb unearthed in 1968 appears to confirm our knowledge of the use of jade. As noted above with respect to the Late Chou *Pi* (FIG. 12-3), jade was believed to have magical properties protective of the dead. The tomb (in Hopei) contained the remains of a prince and princess, each of whom had originally been masked and completely outfitted in suits (FIG. 12-6) composed of over 2000 jade tablets expertly cut, fitted, and sewn together with gold wire—an extraordinary technical feat.

THREE KINGDOMS
THROUGH SUI

Buddhism (p. 359), whose spirit was one profoundly different from the ancient and native philosophies of China, was introduced by the first century of the Christian era. During the last hundred years of Han rule and the succeeding period of the Three Kingdoms, China, splintered by strife, grasped eagerly at a new ideal by which to live. The Confucian system of ethics had proved unable to adapt itself to the anarchy of the times, and Taoism, having degenerated into magic and superstition, no longer appealed to the philosophic mind. Buddhism offered the Chinese masses the promise of hope beyond the troubles of this world. In addition, it attracted the intellectuals by its fully developed logical system, whose refinements surpassed those of any previous Chinese system of thought. Buddhist missionaries from India, working at first with the ruling families, spread their gospel so successfully that their teachings ran like wildfire through China.

The arts flourished in the service of the imported religion. Following the brief Three Kingdoms period in the third century A.D., China entered an era of political con-

fusion, with many short-lived states, known as the period of the Northern and Southern Dynasties. Native Chinese dynasties, centered at Nanking, ruled in the south. Most of the Buddhist art surviving from this period, however, originated in the northern states, which were ruled by barbarian peoples who rapidly adopted Chinese ways and culture. A new esthetic was developed in imitation of Indian or central Asian models, in harmony with the prescribed formalism of Buddhist doctrine. The earliest important Buddhist image, a gilt-bronze statuette of Sakyamuni Buddha, dated by inscription in the year 338 (FIG. 12-7), is clearly related, in both style and iconography, to the prototype that had been conceived and developed at Gandhara (p. 363).[2] The heavy concentric folds of the robe, the *ushnisha* on the head, and the cross-legged position all derived ultimately from the Indian prototype, examples of which had been brought to China by pilgrims and priests who had made the hazardous journey along the desert trade routes of central Asia.

The Chinese artist transformed the basic Indian pattern during the following century or so. These changes may be observed in a series of great cave temples that were carved into the hillsides after the fashion of the early Buddhists in India. At Tun-huang, westernmost gateway to China, over three hundred sanctuaries were cut into the loess cliffs, the walls decorated with paintings, and the chambers adorned with images of clay. This site was dedicated in 366, but the earliest extant caves are from the late fifth century. About the same time, in 460, sculptors at Yun-kang, near Ta-t'ung in northern China, were carving temples in cliffs of sandstone. Although the materials are different, both sites have an archaic style similar to the sculpture of the sixth century B.C. in Greece and of the early twelfth century in

[2] Yet so new was the icon and its meaning that the Chinese craftsman, although endeavoring to make an image faithful to prescription, nevertheless erred in representing the canonical *mudra* of meditation: the Buddha's hands are clasped across his stomach, whereas they should be turned palms upward, with thumbs barely touching.

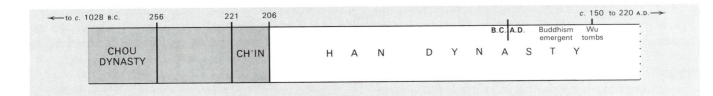

←to c. 1028 B.C.	256	221	206		c. 150 to 220 A.D. →
CHOU DYNASTY		CH'IN	H A N D Y N A S T Y	B.C. A.D.	Buddhism emergent Wu tombs

France. Like their Western counterparts, the cave figures have faces carved in sharp planes and drapery conventionalized into angular patterns, and, as a whole, they too express the intense and noble dignity of a deeply felt religion (FIG. 12-8). The Buddhist concept of divinity may be seen in the caves of Yun-kang, where the image of the Buddha, a blend of conventional restraint and religious fervor, became human enough for popular recognition while remaining sufficiently idealized to carry the worshiper beyond the image to the abstraction it symbolized.

In 494 the Wei Tatars, staunch Buddhists who had supported the colossal program at Yun-kang, moved their court southward to Lo-yang in Honan. Near there, in the limestone cliffs of Lung-men, another series of caves was started where work continued, in the first phase, until the first part of the sixth century. The new carvings reveal elongated body and facial types and a fluid elegance in rendering drapery folds that reflect the influence of native

Chinese styles, including those of painting. An air of courtly sophistication appears, especially in some of the secular figures of imperial donors. The new linearity and elongation, combined with pure body volumes and balanced poses, resulted in many images that harmonized religious sincerity with extraordinary grace of design.

While the Lung-men caves were being worked on, the people's imagination was captured by a new form of Buddhism, promoted by various "Paradise Sects," that gave promise of rebirth in a Buddhist paradise rich in the material pleasures that are denied to most in this world. As an idyllic existence in this paradise could be gained merely by faith in the word of the Buddha, many who might have failed to appreciate the goal of nirvana and the ultimate extinction of personality were won over to Buddhism by the more tangible and attractive goal of the Paradise Sects. Glories beyond those even of the imperial court were thus offered to every man who put his trust in the Buddha. The

12-7 *Sakyamuni Buddha,* Northern and Southern Dynasties, A.D. 338. Gilt bronze. Asian Art Museum of San Francisco, The Avery Brundage Collection.

12-8 Colossal Buddha, from Cave XX, Yun-kang, Shansi, Northern and Southern Dynasties, c. A.D. 460. Sandstone, 45' high.

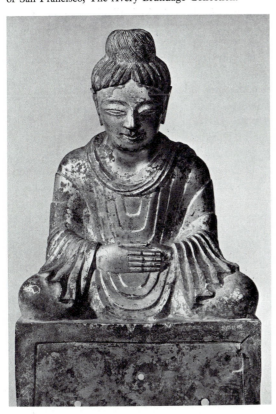

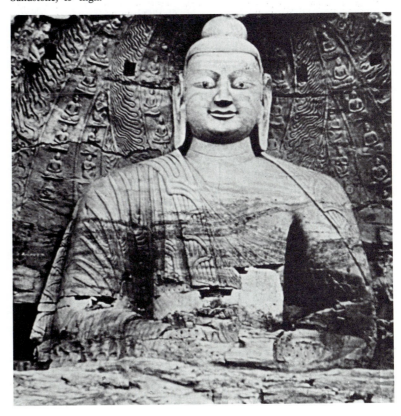

pleasant aspirations of these Buddhists were reflected in the greater naturalism of their arts, particularly in the humanization of the deity. Thus, it is no wonder that, when the Paradise Sects reached their peak in the Sui dynasty, the Buddha was gradually transformed from an archaic image of divine perfection into a gentle and human saviour. The transition is manifest in the gilt-bronze shrine shown in FIG. 12-9, which also reflects the attenuated Lung-men style. Prabhutaratna, Buddha of the remote past, listens to the sermon by Sakyamuni, the most recent Buddha. Seated within flamelike aureoles, their graceful, slender figures are almost absorbed into the rhythmic fall and flow of linear drapery beginning to acquire the character of cloth. The humanization is manifest in the gentle, suave beauty of attitude and gesture; the faces retain the characteristics of archaic formulae.

A comparable development of Buddhist images can be observed in the richly painted walls of the Tun-huang sanctuaries, which were calculated to inspire in the worshiper the splendor of Buddhism and (like Medieval paintings) to instruct the illiterate. Hieratic figures of the Buddha were surrounded by illustrations of stories about past lives (*jataka*). The formalized patterns of the individual Buddhas are like those of the sculptured images at Yun-kang and Lung-men. But the narrative scenes carried on the traditions of Han painting, especially in the cell-like composition, in the leaping rhythms, and in the disproportionate relationship of figures to diminutive, conventionalized settings.

By 539 most traces of central Asian influence had disappeared. Like sculpture of the time, Buddhist painting responded to the happy credo of the Paradise Sects with increasing naturalism and grace. Although the Buddha groups retained the strict frontality and rigid balance of ritualistic art, the jataka tales expanded haphazardly over the temple walls, and their figures, now slim, elegant, and emancipated from their compartmental designs, move freely over the plane surface. By the end of the century the abstract environment of the painted figures began to be three-dimensional. Overlapping was used to create depth, and a sense of reality was further heightened by the surrounding of the celestial groups with such earthly phenomena as trees, pavilions, lotus ponds, and bridges.

It was especially at the courts of the Southern Dynasties that painting flourished during this period. Taoist nature cults and a new appreciation of landscape themes in poetry provided the background for the early development of landscape painting. No scrolls from the hands of individual masters have survived from this early era, but descriptive texts indicate that the almost magical potential of landscape painting to re-create and organize the experience of nature, or to transport the viewer to an imaginary realm, was already well appreciated. When the painter TSUNG PING (373–443), for example, became too old to continue his mountain wanderings, he re-created favorite landscapes on the walls of his studio in order to take imaginary journeys. Of the representational power of painting, he wrote:

> Nowadays, when I spread out my silk to catch the distant scene, even the form of the K'un-lun [Mountain] may be captured within a square inch of space; a vertical stroke of three inches equals a height of several thousand feet . . . . By such means as this, the beauty of the Sung and Hua Mountains and the very soul of the *Hsuan-p'in* [Dark Spirit of the Universe] may all be embraced within a single picture . . . .[3]

Another fifth-century painter, WANG WEI, elaborated on the re-creative potential of landscape painting.

> I unroll a picture and examine it, and reveal mountains and seas unfamiliar to me. The wind scatters in the verdant forests, the torrent overflows in bubbling foam. Ah, how could this be achieved merely by the skilful use of hands and fingers? The spirit must also exercise control over it. For this is the essence of painting.

The painter and essayist KU K'AI-CHIH (c. 344–406) is one of the few individual artists from this period to whom extant paintings have been seriously attributed. In an essay on landscape painting couched in Taoist terms, he describes "crags, fang-like and tapering" and "rocks, split with fissures as though torn by lightning." But for Ku K'ai-chih and others of his time the crucial aspect of painting was not mere imitation of appearance but transmission of "spiritual quality." Indeed, late in the fifth century the critic Hsieh Ho gave as the first of the "Six Principles" of painting "spirit-consonance engendering movement"—a sense of animation through transmission of the vital spirit that pervades both artist and object—which was to remain the cardinal principle for artists and critics until modern times.

Something of this vital spirit appears in a horizontal scroll attributed to Ku K'ai-chih called *Admonitions of the Instructress to the Court Ladies,* perhaps an early copy of a painting of Ku's era. Scrolls in this format were meant to be viewed slowly and in sections; in this case, scenes are illustrated between passages of explanatory text. One of the sections depicts a well-known act of heroism in which the Lady Feng saved the life of her emperor by placing herself between him and an attacking bear (FIG. 12-10). There is no background and only a minimal setting for the scene, but fluid poses and fluttering ribbons of drapery in concert with individualized facial expressions convey the quality of animation called for in texts of the period.

---

[3] For this and other excerpts from essays on painting quoted below, see Michael Sullivan, *The Birth of Landscape Painting in China* (Berkeley: Univ. of California Press, 1962).

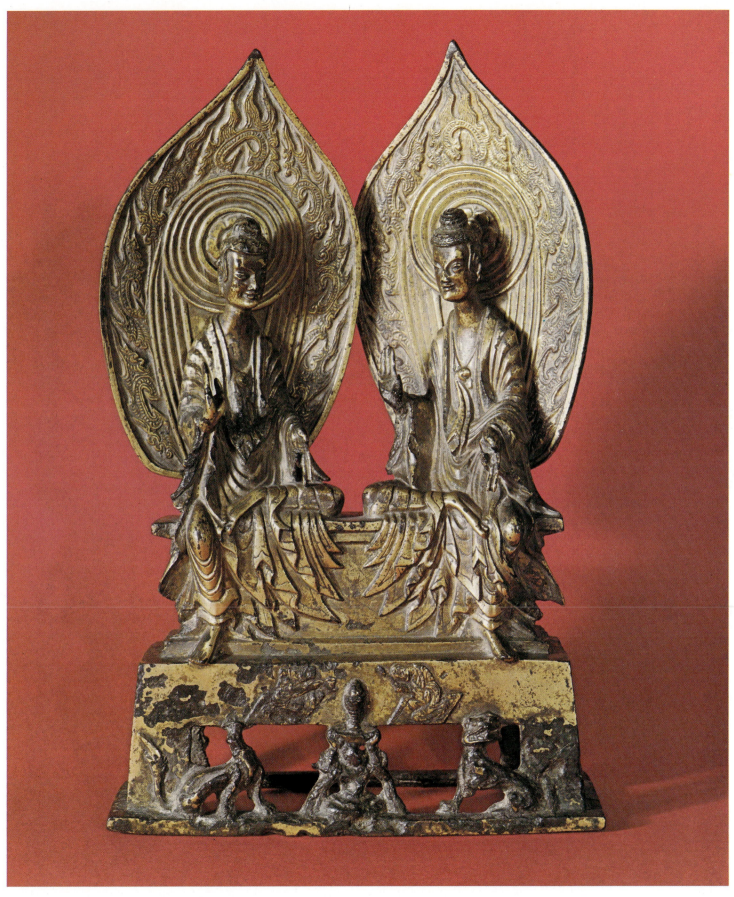

12-9 *Prabhutaratna and Sakyamuni*, Northern and Southern Dynasties, *c*. A.D. 518. Gilt bronze, 10½" high. Musée Guimet, Paris.

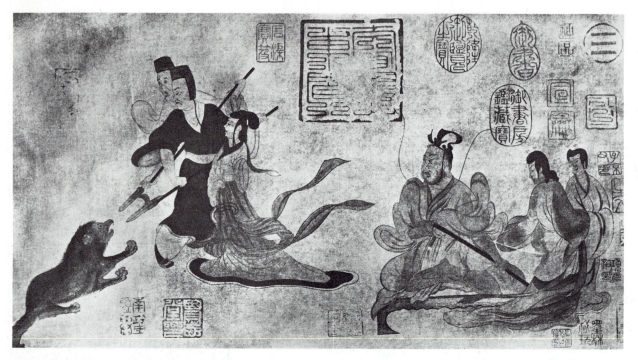

12-10 Attributed to KU K'AI-CHIH (c. A.D. 344–406), *Lady Feng and the Bear*, section of the *Admonitions of the Instructress to the Court Ladies*. Horizontal scroll, ink and colors on silk, 7⅝″ high. British Museum, London.

T'ANG

The short-lived Sui dynasty (581–618) was followed by the T'ang empire, under which China entered a period of unequaled magnificence. Chinese armies marched to the ends of central Asia, opening a path for the flow of wealth, ideas, and foreign peoples. Arab traders, Nestorian Christians, and other travelers journeyed to the cosmopolitan capital of the T'ang, and the Chinese in turn adventured westward. During the middle of the seventh century, Hsuan-tsang, a Chinese monk, visited India, as had some earlier devotees, and returned from the mother country of Buddhism with revolutionizing doctrines of the recently developed Esoteric Sects. It was a critical moment for Buddhism, which was being brought into disrepute by a lax court and a corrupt clergy. Under the notorious Empress Wu, who had usurped the throne, the religion was used as an instrument for political power and as a cloak for personal excesses. The material rewards promised in heaven by the Paradise Sects offered no effective antidote to the troubles of the time. But the elaborate and mysterious rituals of the new Esoteric Sects attracted worshipers by giving them in their daily life many of the sensory pleasures that the Paradise Sects had promised in heaven. As the new cult spread, the Chinese craftsman again looked to India, where he found appropriate models in the sculpture of the time.

The fluid style of art developed during the Gupta dynasty in India (p. 365, Chapter Eleven) had already affected Chinese sculpture during the late sixth century, and by the end of the next century Buddhist sculpture in China had lost much of its own character in its borrowing from the sensuous carvings of India. Fleshiness increased even more, and drapery was made to cling as if wet against the bodies. The new wave of influence from India brought not only stylistic changes but also the iconography of the Esoteric Sects, which we see in figures with multiple arms and heads, symbolizing various aspects of the deities as described in the new gospels.

The early T'ang style under Indian influence is admirably exemplified by the *Bodhisattva* in FIG. 12-11. The sinuous beauty of this figure has been accented by the hipshot pose and revealing drapery, as in Gupta sculpture. Executed at almost the same time as the Bodhisattva—around 700—were carvings in the caves of T'ien-lung Shan, which anticipated the style of later T'ang. These cave figures might seem gross were it not for the graceful postures and the soft drapery that falls in rhythmic patterns over the plump bodies.

Esoteric Buddhism, with its emphasis on detailed and complicated ritual, placed the deity in a formal relationship to the worshiper. The followers of Amitabha Buddha—one of the most important Buddhas of the Paradise Sects—in stressing salvation by faith, had visualized a warm and human deity, but by the ninth century the arduous discipline of the Esoteric Sects had inspired an austere, heavy-set, almost repellent icon. At times fleshiness was exaggerated almost to the point of obesity, and yet sufficient restraint lent the figures a somber dignity.[4]

[4] Few sculptures survived the terrible persecutions of Buddhism during a revival of Confucianism in 845. Many wooden temples were destroyed by fire and their bronze images melted down. Fortunately, we are able to reconstruct the style of the period from Buddhist art in Japan, which was then under direct Chinese influence (see pp. 401–02).

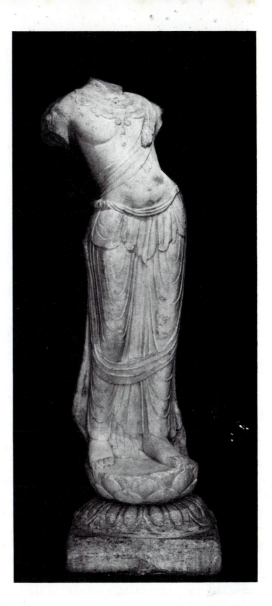

12-11 *Bodhisattva*, early T'ang dynasty, seventh to eighth centuries. Marble. Private collection, New York.

The westward expansion of the T'ang empire increased the importance of Tun-huang. Here the desert routes converged and the cave temples profited from the growing prosperity of the people. By the eighth century wealthy donors were demanding larger and more elaborately decorated caves. The comparatively simple Buddha group in paintings of the previous century was enlarged to include crowds of attendant figures, lavish architectural settings, and minor deities who worshiped the resplendent Buddha with music and dance. The opulence of the T'ang was reflected in the detailed richness of the brilliantly colored *Paradise Paintings* (FIG. 12-12). Vignettes flanking the Buddha group illustrate incidents from specific *sutras*. These little scenes, like the jataka tales in earlier caves, are usually set in landscapes painted in an altogether different style from that of the hieratic groups. Mountains, for example, are stacked one behind the other and painted in graded washes to give the impression of distance. (Yet, although each mountain is related to the adjacent peak through this device of atmospheric perspective, there is still no continuous perspective to give a sense of recession into the distance.)

The persecutions of 845 did not affect Tun-huang, which was then under Tibetan rule. Numerous paintings—murals and scrolls—were produced, but in this region, isolated from the mainstream of Chinese culture, they remained static in style from the middle of the ninth

12-12 *Paradise of Amitabha*, Cave 139A, Tun-huang, T'ang dynasty, wall painting, ninth century.

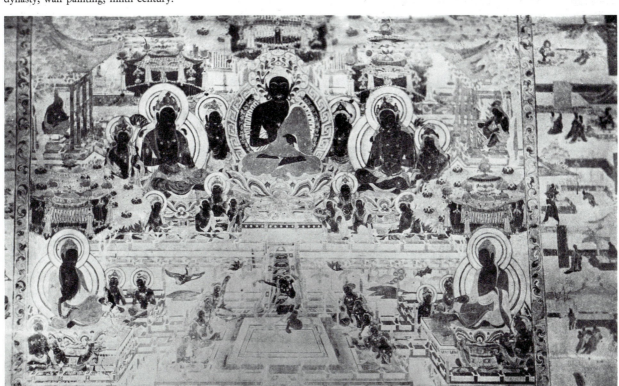

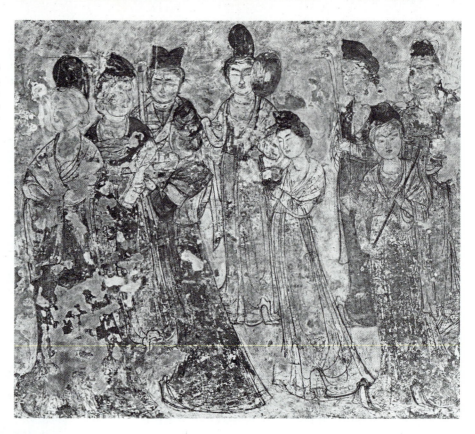

12-13 *Palace Ladies*, from the tomb of Princess Yung-t'ai, near Sian, Shensi. Wall painting, T'ang dynasty, A.D. 706.

to the beginning of the eleventh century. Meanwhile during the seventh and eighth centuries at the T'ang court in Ch'ang-an, perhaps the greatest city in the world during this period, a brilliant tradition of figure painting developed that, in its variety and balance, reflected the worldliness and self-assurance of the T'ang empire. Indeed, Chinese historians regard the early T'ang dynasty as their golden age of figure painting. Glowing accounts by poets and critics and a few remaining examples of the paintings themselves permit us to understand this enthusiasm.

Wall paintings from the tomb of the T'ang princess Yung-t'ai (built in 706) allow a view of court painting styles unobscured by problems of authenticity and reconstruction (FIG. 12-13). The figures of palace ladies are arranged as if on a shallow stage; although there are no indications of background or setting, intervals between the two rows and the grouping of figures in an oval suggest a consistent ground plane. The women are shown full-face and in three-quarter views from the front and back. The device of paired figures facing into and out of the space of the picture in a near mirror-image—an effective means of creating depth—appears often in paintings attributed to this period. Thick, even contour lines describe full-volumed faces and suggest solid forms beneath drapery, all with the utmost economy. This simplicity of form and drawing, along with the measured cadence of the poses, results in an air of monumental dignity befitting a daughter of the ruling house of the T'ang.

In perfect accord with descriptions of the robust T'ang style are the unrestored portions of *Portraits of the Emperors*, masterfully drawn in line and in colored washes by

YEN LI-PEN, celebrated painter and statesman of the seventh century. Each emperor is represented as standing in undefined space, his eminence clearly indicated by his great size relative to that of his attendants. Yen Li-pen also made designs for a series of monumental and spirited stone horses that once flanked the approach to the tomb of the T'ang emperor T'ai-tsung.

The horse in Chinese art reflected the importance the emperors placed on the quality of their stables. Even in Han times emperors had sent missions westward to Bactria for blooded stock. Paintings of the finest among his 40,000 steeds were commissioned by the emperor Ming Huang (713–756), and one of these may be the picture of a tethered horse attributed to HAN KAN, Ming Huang's favorite painter of horses. The fiery stallion (FIG. 12-14) evokes the dynamic "inner vitality" so stressed by Chinese critics.

Two of the most famous artists of the T'ang period were WANG WEI (699–759), who is not to be confused with Wang Wei of the fifth century, and WU TAO-TZU (active *c*. 725–*c*. 750), both of whom are now almost legendary figures although none of their paintings has survived. Wang was not only a painter; like so many Chinese artists he was also a poet. His poems are mellow and lyrical, as his paintings are said to have been. Although none of his painting survives, numerous imitations have the peaceful lyricism of his poems. Many of these copies are of snow scenes, a favorite subject of Chinese artists, probably because of its adaptability to monochrome painting, an art of infinite variation and contrast in black and white. Wu's work, according to reports of his time, was very different. He painted with such speed and "ferocious energy" and

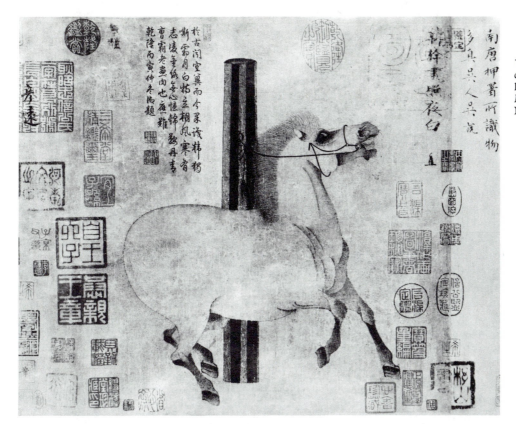

12-14 HAN KAN, *Horse,* T'ang dynasty, eighth century. Album leaf, ink on paper, 11$\frac{13}{16}$" high. Metropolitan Museum of Art, New York.

over such large surfaces that people would watch with awe the rapid appearance of astonishingly real images. His bold brushwork and expansive forms were frequently copied, and rubbings made from engraved replicas. Later artists looked to Wu's virtuoso brushwork and to Wang's subtle harmonies for their models.

The T'ang rulers embellished their empire with extravagant wooden structures, all of which have disappeared. Judging from records, however, they were of colossal size and colorfully painted. Bronze mirrors with decorations in strong relief added to T'ang luxury and to the furnishings of a court already enriched by elaborate gold and silver ornaments.

The potter met the demand for display by covering his wares with colorful lead glazes and by inventing robust shapes with clearly articulated parts—base, body, and neck. Earlier potters had imitated bronze models, but the T'ang craftsman derived his directly from the character of clay. Ceramic figures of people, domesticated animals, and fantastic creatures were also made by the thousands for burial in tombs (FIG. 12-15). The extraordinarily delicate grace and flowing rhythms of these figures have a charm and vivacity seldom equaled in ceramic design. Their subject matter, which included such diverse figures as Greek acrobats and Semitic traders, is proof of the cosmopolitanism of T'ang China.

12-15 T'ang tomb figurines, seventh to ninth centuries: Left: Peddler. Portland Art Museum, Portland, Oregon. Middle: Dancer. Nelson Gallery-Atkins Museum, Kansas City, Missouri. Below: Horse. Fogg Art Museum, Harvard University.

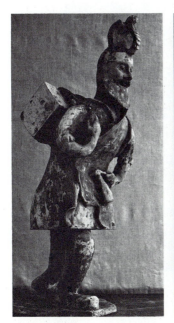
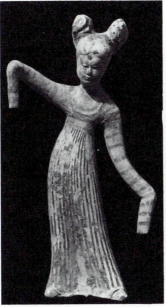
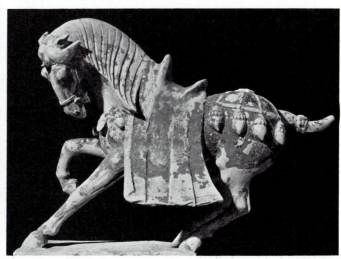

FIVE DYNASTIES AND NORTHERN SUNG

The last century of T'ang rule witnessed the gradual dis-integration of the empire. When in 906 the dynasty finally fell, China was once more left to the ravages of civil war. Conflicting claims between rival states were not resolved until the country was consolidated under the Sung, whose court was at Pien-liang (modern K'ai-feng in Honan). During the interim of internal strife known as the Five Dynasties (906–960) there was a marked development in the styles and techniques of landscape painting. An analogy with events of the period of the Northern and Southern Dynasties (pp. 382–84) may be justified; that earlier period of political and social turmoil also witnessed a turning away from society toward an involvement with nature and an accompanying development of landscape art.

CHING HAO, who flourished during the first half of the tenth century, left an essay in which he listed his criteria for judging paintings. Under the classification of "divine" he grouped the greatest paintings. In these, he wrote, "there appears no trace of human effort; hands spontaneously reproduce natural forms." In the lowest category he placed the "skillful" artist who "cuts out and pieces together fragments of beauty and welds them into the pretense of a masterpiece. . . ." "This," he added, "is owing to the poverty of inner reality and to the excess of outward form." Although these ideas were not original with Ching Hao, his restatement of them shows the continuity of thought underlying Chinese painting regardless of changing styles. The artist who painted the truth beneath surface appearances had to be imbued with ch'i, the "divine spirit" of the universe. The man who achieved this had done so through years of self-cultivation. Ching Hao and his equally famous contemporary LI CH'ENG, through the inherent power of their personalities, departed from T'ang landscape formulas, breathing life into every twig and rock they painted. Succeeding generations went to their works for inspiration—great artists to catch the spirit, lesser painters to copy tricks for drawing trees and hills.

We know enough about the art of this period to be able to distinguish the styles of some individual masters, such as TUNG YUAN and CHU-JAN, of the mid-tenth century, and FAN K'UAN and KUO HSI, active early and late, respectively, in the eleventh century. Paintings by these latter two artists, which exemplify the maturity of landscape painting styles in the Northern Sung period, express very different personalities and yet exhibit a common feeling for monumentality. A characteristic painting in this style presents a vertical landscape of massive mountains rising from the distance (FIG. 12-16). Human figures, reduced to minute proportions, are dwarfed by overwhelming forms in nature. Paths and bridges in the middle region vanish only to reappear in such a way as to lead the spectator on a journey through the landscape—a journey facilitated by shifting perspective points. No single vanishing point organizes the entire perspective, as in many Western paintings, and as a result the observer's eye moves with freedom. But in order to appreciate these paintings fully one must focus on intricate details and on the character of each line.

The full development of the horizontal handscroll occurred during this period. The scroll, which might measure as long as fifty feet, had to be unrolled from right to left; only a small section could be seen at a time and then, properly, by only two or three persons. The organization of these paintings has been compared to the composition of a symphony because of the way in which motifs are repeated and moods are varied in the different sections. The temporal sequence of the scroll involved memory as well as vision; it was an art of contemplation and leisure.

12-16 FAN K'UAN, *Travelers Among Mountains and Streams*, Northern Sung dynasty, early eleventh century. Hanging scroll, ink and colors on silk, 81" × 29". Collection of the National Palace Museum, Taipei, Taiwan.

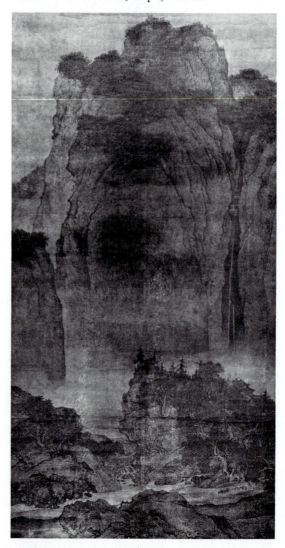

Among the versatile figures clustered around the court at this time was SU TUNG-P'O (SU SHIH, 1036–1101), one of China's greatest poets, a celebrated painter and statesman. Another was LI KUNG-LIN (1040–1106), who was famous for his original Buddhist compositions and for his outline drawings of horses. These, along with the antiquarian and landscapist MI FU (1052–1109), were the leading figures in a group of scholar-gentlemen painters who created an alternative to the emphasis on skillful representation of nature then prevailing among professional and academy artists. The amateurs, by contrast, saw painting as primarily expressive of the moods and personality of the artist. Representational accuracy was deemphasized, even derided, in favor of learned allusions to antique styles, sometimes couched in deliberately awkward or naive forms. Many paintings in this style concentrate on qualities inherent in the medium of brush and ink. In this they were close to the expressiveness of calligraphy, which depended for its effects on the controlled vitality of individual brushstrokes and the dynamic relationships of strokes within a character and among the characters themselves. Training in calligraphy was a fundamental part of the education and self-cultivation of scholars and officials; with Su Shih and Mi Fu, ranked among the greatest of Northern Sung calligraphers, calligraphic qualities and effects became part of the repertory of many painters as well.

The emperor HUI-TSUNG (ruled 1101–1125), an avid collector and patron of art, was himself an important painter. He is known particularly for his meticulous pictures of birds in which almost every feather was carefully drawn in sharp lines. Lesser artists attached to the imperial court functioned as a sort of academy and in general followed the detailed and colorful style of the emperor. Illustrating some lines of poetry in painting often served as an examination for court office. Fans painted by master artists were treasured in albums. But while the court spent its energy on esthetic refinements, less cultured neighbors were assaulting the frontiers of China.

SOUTHERN SUNG

In 1127, because of increasing pressure from the Tatars and Mongols in the west and north, the capital of China was moved to the south. From then until 1279 the Southern Sung court lived out its days amid the tranquil beauties of Hangchow. Neo-Confucianism, a blend of traditional Chinese thought and some Buddhist concepts, became the leading philosophy. Accordingly, orthodox Buddhism declined. Buddhist art continued to develop in the north, where a Tatar tribe had established itself as the Chin dynasty, but it stagnated in the south. Buddhist sculpture in the Southern Sung period merely added grace and

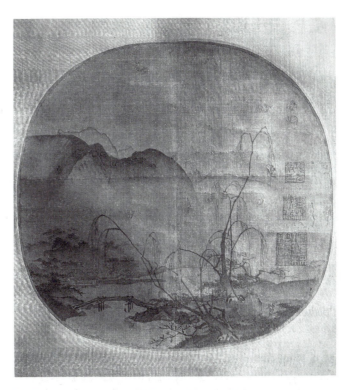

12-17   MA YUAN, *Bare Willows and Distant Mountains*, Southern Sung dynasty, thirteenth century. Album leaf, ink and colors on silk, 9½″ × 9½″. Museum of Fine Arts, Boston.

elegance to the T'ang style. Secular paintings and those associated with Ch'an, a meditative school of Buddhism, however, reflected a new and more intimate relationship between man and nature.

A typical Southern Sung landscape is basically asymmetrical. It is composed on a diagonal and consists of three parts—foreground, middle distance, and far distance—separated from each other by a field of mist. The first is marked by a rock, which, by its position in the foreground, emphasizes the distance of the other parts; the middle distance may be marked by a flat cliff or given over entirely to mist or water, and in the far distance mountain peaks, which are usually tinted in pale blue, suggest the infinity of space. The whole composition illustrates the manner in which the Sung artists used great voids to hold solid masses in equilibrium. The technique is one of China's unique contributions to the art of painting. To this basic composition, of which there were many variations, the artist frequently added the figure of a scholar meditating under a gnarled pine tree and accompanied by an attendant. Such paintings were expressions of the artists' ideal of peace and pantheistic unity.

The chief painters in the Southern Sung style were MA YUAN (*c.* 1190–1224) and HSIA KUEI (*c.* 1180–1230). Ma was a master of suggestion, as is demonstrated by a small fan-shaped album leaf—a picture of tranquility stated in a few sensitively balanced and half-seen shapes (FIG. 12-17).

Hsia Kuei's misty landscapes were often so like those of Ma Yuan—though sometimes more delicate and sometimes bolder—that the Chinese refer to them and their followers as the Ma-Hsia school. But the Ma-Hsia tradition, despite its gentle beauty, could not be maintained. It perpetuated an ephemeral, classic moment, but the serenity of its beliefs was soon threatened by political realities.

As orthodox Buddhism lost ground under the Sung, the new school of Buddhism, called Ch'an in China but better known by its Japanese name, Zen, gradually gained importance, until it was second only to Neo-Confucianism. The Zen sect traced its semilegendary origins to Bodhidharma, an Indian missionary of the sixth century A.D. By the time of the Sixth Patriarch, who lived in early T'ang, the pattern of the school was already established, and Zen remains an important religion in Japan today.

The followers of Zen repudiated texts, ritual, and charms as instruments of enlightenment. They believed, instead, that the means of salvation lay within the individual, that meditation was useful, and that direct personal experience with some ultimate reality was the necessary step to enlightenment. Zen enlightenment was conceived as a sudden, almost spontaneous act. These beliefs shaped a new art.

LIANG K'AI, a Zen painter of the thirteenth century, has left us two portraits of Hui Neng, the Sixth Patriarch. In one, the patriarch is a crouching figure chopping bamboo (FIG. 12-18); in the other, he is tearing up a Buddhist sutra. Both are informal sketches that look as though they were caricatures of the revered figure. The brush strokes are staccato and splintery like the spontaneous process of Zen enlightenment. They probably were painted in a few minutes, but, like enlightenment, they required years of training. Their impact can be a shock, much like the shock of Zen understanding.

Southern Sung artists also produced superb ceramics with monochrome glazes. The most famous of the single-glaze wares are known as *celadon*, *Ying-ch'ing*, and *Ting*. The first is a mat gray-green, the second a subtle pale blue, and the last a fine white protoporcelain. There was also the heavier *Chun* ware, in which a blue glaze, splashed with red and purple, flowed over a stoneware body. A quite different kind of pottery, loosely classed as *Tz'u-chou*, is a type of northern Chinese ceramic in which, during the Sung period, the subtle techniques of under-glaze painting and incision of the design through a colored slip were developed. The *Mei-p'ing* vase shown (FIG. 12-19) has an

intricate black-white design produced by cutting through a black to a white slip. Here the tightly twining vine and petal motifs closely embrace the high-shouldered vessel in a perfect accommodation, so common in Chinese pottery in its great periods, of surface design to vase shape. These shapes were generally more suave than those of T'ang; some, however, reflecting the prevailing interest in arche-

12-18 LIANG K'AI, *The Sixth Ch'an Patriarch Chopping Bamboo*, Southern Sung dynasty, thirteenth century. Hanging scroll, ink on paper, 29¼" high. Tokyo National Museum, Tokyo.

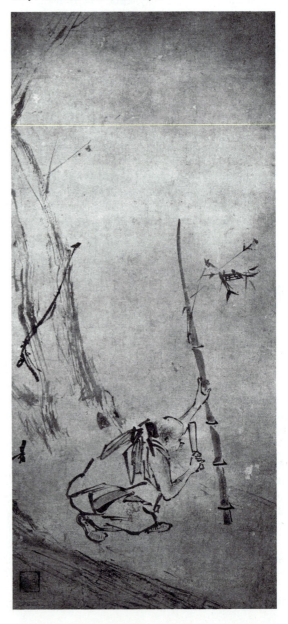

YUAN

The artistic vitality of Southern Sung was not a reflection of the political condition. In 1279 the dynasty crumbled beneath the continued onslaughts of Kublai Khan. Yuan, the dynasty of the Mongol invaders, dominated China only until 1368, and yet it profoundly affected the culture of the country and particularly the art of painting. Many of the scholar-painters chose exile in the provinces rather than service to the barbarian usurpers in Peking. Forced by their exile to reappraise their place in the world, the artists no longer looked at a landscape as an idyllic retreat, but as part of a formidable environment. The new austerity is evident in a painting (FIG. 12-20) by one of the great masters of Yuan, HUANG KUNG-WANG (1269–1354). Here the misty atmosphere of the Southern Sung landscapes has been replaced by textureful, massive forms. The inner structure and momentum of the landscape is rendered by a rhythmic play of brush and ink.

Another leader of the Yuan scholar-artist movement was CHAO MENG-FU (1254–1322), whose paintings contain knowing allusions to old styles. The landscapes of his grandson WANG MENG (d. 1385) reached a high level of dynamic, expressive intensity. Most of these painters rejected the mellow harmonies of Southern Sung as no longer valid; for their sources they went back to the more monumental works of the tenth century. The degree to which styles could become personalized in this period is shown in the spare, almost brittle landscapes and bamboo-and-rock paintings of NI TSAN (1301–74), which reveal an aloof and fastidious personality. They contrast with the paintings of WU CHEN (1280–1354), done in a softer

12-19   Mei-p'ing vase, Sung dynasty. Tz'u-chou stoneware, carved black slip over white, 19½″ × 7¾″. Asian Art Museum of San Francisco, The Avery Brundage Collection.

ology, imitated the powerful forms of Shang and Chou bronzes. Other crafts, particularly jade carving, were also subjected to the influence of archeological or antiquarian interests.

12-20   HUANG KUNG-WANG, *Dwelling in the Fu-ch'un Mountains,* Yuan dynasty, A.D. 1347–50. Section of a horizontal scroll, ink on paper, 13″ high. National Palace Museum, Taipei, Taiwan.

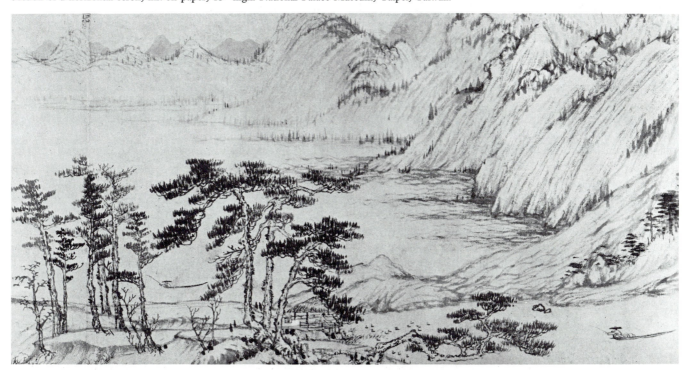

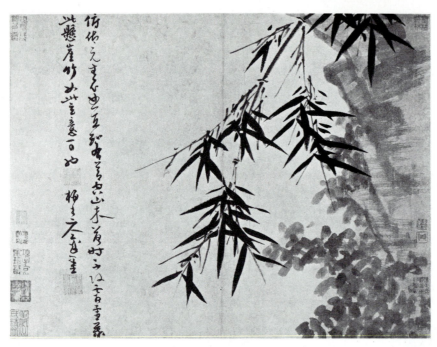

12-21 WU CHEN, *Bamboo*, Yuan dynasty, A.D. 1350. Album leaf, ink on paper, 16″ × 21″. Collection of the National Palace Museum, Taipei, Taiwan.

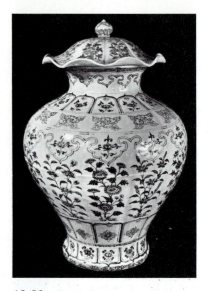

12-22 Covered vase, excavated at Peking, late Yuan or early Ming dynasty, late fourteenth century. White porcelain with underglaze decoration, 26½″ high. The exhibition of archeological finds of the People's Republic of China.

and more relaxed manner. Paintings of bamboo, for which Wu Chen is famous (FIG. 12-21), were particularly favored at this time, for that plant is a symbol of the ideal Chinese gentleman, who in adversity bends but does not break. Moreover, the pattern of leaves, like that of calligraphic script, provided an excellent opportunity for the display of brushwork.

The Mongol regime apparently did little to disturb the Chinese potters in their increasing mastery of porcelain. A late Yuan or early Ming vase of white porcelain, discovered in 1961 (FIG. 12-22), exhibits brilliance in the use of under-glaze decoration that was so successful in the Sung period.

MING, CH'ING, AND LATER

In 1368 a popular uprising drove out the hated Mongol overlords, and from that time until 1644 China was ruled by the native Ming dynasty. Many of the fifteenth-century Ming masters, such as TAI CHIN (1388–1452), reverted to Sung models. The court, where Tai Chin worked, was one center of patronage and activity; local schools of painting, such as those centered in Nanking and in Soochow, also became important. The Soochow school, under the leadership of SHEN CHOU (1427–1509) and WEN CHENG-MING (1470–1559), included a number of highly educated amateur painters who concentrated on refined re-creations of the styles of masters of the preceding Yuan dynasty. Professional artists active in Soochow and elsewhere executed works that displayed great skill and spontaneity.

The distinction between scholar-amateur and academic-professional traditions was codified, rather artifi-

cially, in the writings of the influential critic, statesman, and artist TUNG CH'I-CH'ANG (1555–1636) at the end of the Ming period. Tung's glorification of the amateur or literati school reflected his own voracious study and collecting of old paintings. Tung's theories promoted the creation of an orthodoxy in later art that could be stifling, but his own works were true to his ideal of the transformation of old styles rather than the sterile imitation of them. In Tung's landscapes there is often a radical reorganization of forms that attempts to reveal the inner structure and momentum of nature (FIG. 12-23). Ground planes are allowed to tilt or shift; this, and the bold arrangement of rocks and trees to emphasize repeated abstract shapes and textures, heedless of natural scale and surface qualities, may seem arbitrarily distorted or even crude. What is lost in harmony of surface or representational accuracy, however, is more than made up in qualities of monumentality and power. Paintings by Tung and other masters during the period of social and intellectual readjustment at the end of the Ming dynasty created an atmosphere of artistic freedom; the artists who lived into the next dynasty were its beneficiaries.

The internal decay of Ming bureaucracy permitted another group of invaders, the Manchus, to overrun the country. Established as the Ch'ing dynasty (1644–1912), the northerners quickly adapted themselves to Chinese life. The early emperors cultivated a knowledge of China's arts, but their influence seems merely to have encouraged academic work. While the Yuan style continued to be fashionable among the conservatives, other painters experimented with extreme effects of massed ink or individualized patterns of brushwork. Bold and freely manipulated compositions appear that have a new expressive force.

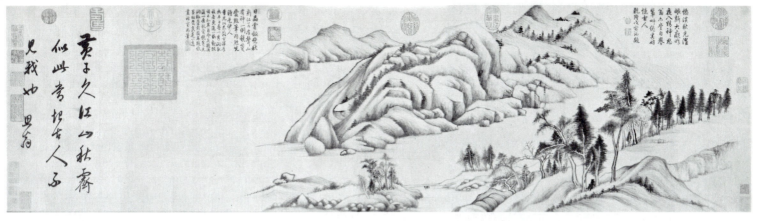

12-23 TUNG CH'I-CH'ANG, *Autumn Mountains*, Ming dynasty, early seventeenth century. Horizontal scroll, ink on paper, 15⅛″ × 53⅞″. Cleveland Museum of Art (purchase from the J. H. Wade Fund).

Two artists with intensely personal styles stand out against a mass of lesser painters. The sketchy brush and wet-ink technique of CHU TA (1625–c. 1705) derived from sixteenth-century forerunners, but his subjects—whimsical animals or petulant birds tensely balanced on an album page—demonstrated his discontent with conventional themes. The theoretical writings of Chu Ta's great contemporary TAO-CHI (1641–c. 1717) called for a return to wellsprings of creativity through use of the "single brushstroke" or "primordial line" that was the root of all phenomena and representation. The figure in a hut in one of his album leaves (FIG. 12-24) is surrounded by the surging energy of free-floating colored dots and multiple, sinuous contour lines that suggest the vital arteries of an organism. What is depicted is not so much the appearance of the landscape as the animating, molding forces that run

through it—from the earliest times the prime focus of Chinese landscape art.

Some twentieth-century artists, such as CH'I PAI-SHIH, found the free brush expressive, and maintained the calligraphic tradition with vitality. HSU PEI-HUNG, known for his boldly brushed pictures of horses, imbued his work with social content, in keeping with China's political developments. The coming decades will reveal whether a popular art assimilates the traditions of aristocratic painting that dominated Chinese art for over a thousand years.

In ceramics the technical ingenuity of the Ming and Ch'ing potters exceeded the skill of even those of the Sung. In general, porcelain was favored over pottery, with the exception of Ming stonewares, which were broadly decorated in "three-color" enamels. More delicate designs were painted on "five-color" wares, with enamels and under-

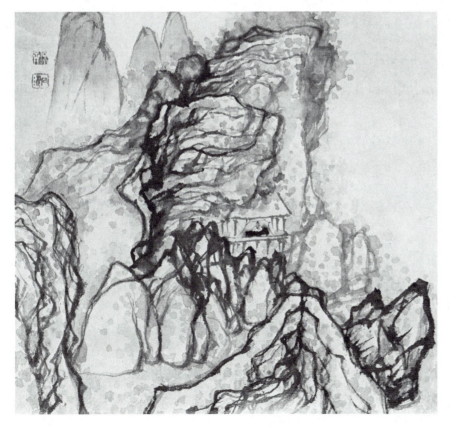

12-24 TAO-CHI, *Landscape*, Ch'ing dynasty, late seventeenth century. Album leaf, ink and colors on paper, 9½″ × 11″. C. C. Wang Collection, New York.

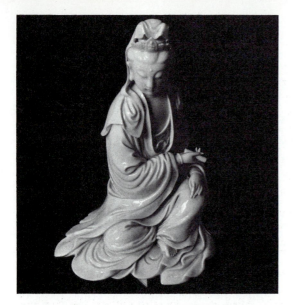

12-25 *Kuan-yin*, early Ch'ing dynasty, seventeenth to eighteenth centuries. Fukien ware, white porcelain, 8⅞″ × 6¼″. Trustees of the Barlow Collection, University of Sussex.

glaze painting on fine clay. The celebrated blue-and-white porcelains (FIG. 12-27) owed their quality as much to the distinction of their painted decoration as to the purity of the imported cobalt pigments. Craftsmen also devised a "secret," or barely visible decoration that was carved into porcelain as thin as paper.

When the Manchus came into power in 1644, they continued to support the great kilns at Ching-te-chen, where enormous quantities of excellent porcelains were made until the destruction of the kilns during warfare in the middle of the nineteenth century. In the K'ang-hsi period (1662–1722) delicate glazes known as clair de lune (a silvery blue) and peachbloom (pink dappled with green) vied with the polychrome wares. Experiments with glazes led to the invention of the superb imperial yellow and oxblood monochromes. A brief revival of Sung simplicity occurred during the reign of Yung-cheng (1723–35), but under Ch'ien-lung (1736–95) a reaction led to a style that was sometimes more elaborate than artistic.

Fine embroidered and woven textiles, created for lavish court ceremonies, followed the general style of the age, becoming more intricate and at the same time more delicate.

During this long period, from mid-seventeenth to late eighteenth century, sculpture consisted primarily of charming but inconsequential porcelain bibelots and jade and ivory carvings of an almost unbelievable technical perfection. An example of this work is the white porcelain *Kuan-yin*, goddess of compassion, from the early Ch'ing dynasty (FIG. 12-25), which completes that long process of humanization of the sacred Buddhist images that began even before the T'ang. (See FIG. 12-9.) The lovely statuette, reflecting the culmination of technical achievement of Chinese ceramists, embodies the Bodhisattva's quality of mercy in its softness of form. An easy play of line betrays the influence of painting upon ceramics. This "white china ware" (*blanc-de-Chine*) was widely exported to Europe in the eighteenth century, and in the West to this day fine ceramic wares, especially porcelain, are called "china."

As the eighteenth century waned, huge workshops, much like our own production-line factories, continued to provide masses of materials for imperial use. Specialists, instead of designer-craftsmen, worked on each stage of manufacture. By the middle of the nineteenth century this system had drained all vitality from the crafts.

The establishment of the People's Republic of China in 1949 has produced a social realism in art familiar to the world of the twentieth century (see pp. 833–36), breaking drastically with the Chinese art of tradition. Though some carry on creative work based on the old traditions, for most, the purpose of art now is, as the People's Republic would claim, to serve the people in the struggle to liberate and elevate the masses. In the work shown in FIG. 12-26, a life-sized tableau, the old times are grimly depicted in a scene common enough before the revolution. Peasants worn and bent by toil are bringing in their taxes in produce to the courtyard of their merciless plundering landlord. The message is clear: This kind of thing must not happen

12-26 ANONYMOUS SCULPTORS, *The Rent Collection Courtyard*, detail of a tableau, 1965. Clay-plaster, life-size.

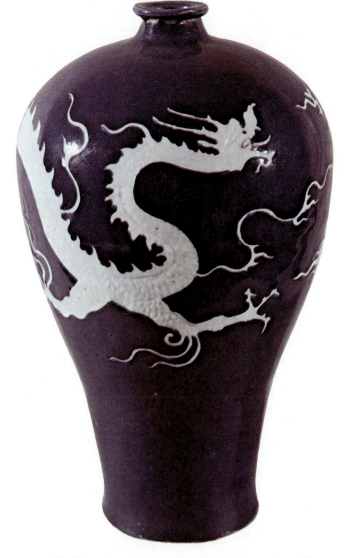

12-27 Vase, Ming dynasty, fifteenth century. Porcelain with blue underglaze decoration. Musée Guimet, Paris.

again. Significantly, the artists who depict the event are an anonymous team. The "name" artist also belongs to the past; only collective action, say its theoreticians, can bring the transformations the People's Republic hopes for.

ARCHITECTURE

Little has been said about Chinese architecture, partly because few early buildings exist and partly because Chinese architecture over the centuries did not display distinctive changes in style. The modern Chinese building closely resembles its prototype of a thousand years ago. Indeed, the dominating silhouette of the roof, which gives Chinese architecture much of its specific character, may go back to Chou or Shang times. Even the simple buildings depicted on Han stone carvings reveal a style and a method of construction still basic to China. The essentials consist of a rectangular hall, dominated by a pitched roof with projecting eaves supported by a bracketing system and wooden columns. Walls served no bearing function but acted only as screening elements.

Within this limited formula the Chinese architect focused his attention on the superstructure. As early as the Han dynasty, combinations of brackets, impost blocks, and columns were devised to support the weight of massive tiled roofs. The architects gave the exterior animation by varying the shapes of the brackets. From these simple beginnings later architects developed very intricate systems of support. Some brackets were placed parallel to the walls, while others reached outward to support a beam or other brackets, until the multiplication of units created a rich pattern of light and shade. The effect was intensified by decorations in red and gold lacquer. Function was often subordinated to ornament; complicated bracket systems were sometimes introduced for decoration where only minimal support was required.

On the exterior the coloristic interplay of the supports formed a pleasing contrast to the uninterrupted sweep of the pitched roof. The overhanging eaves became even wider during the T'ang period and builders began to turn up the corners. These slightly curving eaves were exaggerated in later buildings, especially in south China, where they produced a riotous fantasy of upswept lines. But in most areas the gentle curves of the roofs give an air of grace to the otherwise severe rectangular form and rigid symmetry that were imposed by the plans of the buildings and by various systems of arrangement. For centuries the orientation of buildings, even of whole cities, had been ordered on a strict north-south axis. Houses, palaces, temples, and official buildings all fell within one formal pattern. Even the seeming randomness of the varied bridges and pavilions in the informal gardens was carefully devised.

Buddhist architecture contributed a specific form, the pagoda, which to many has become a symbol of China. These towers, which dot the countryside and seem so native to the land, were derived from the Indian stupa (p. 361). Most of the wooden pagodas, with their multiplicity of winged eaves, bear little resemblance to the solid domes of Sanchi or Amaravati; but their origin, like that of the Chinese Buddha, is to be found in Gandhara, where terraced and towering variants of the stupa had once impressed Chinese pilgrims with their grandeur. So quickly was the stupa structure assimilated by the Chinese that even the earliest pagodas (sixth to eighth century) show only a few traces of their Indian origin. In the Chinese wooden idiom all that remained of the Indian stupa was the *yasti* and parasols, which crowned that structure. Instead of a circular plan the Chinese preferred a four-, six-, or eight-sided one, and story was piled upon story to form towers as much as three hundred feet high. Each story was marked by its own projecting eaves, the curved lines of which soared into the sky.

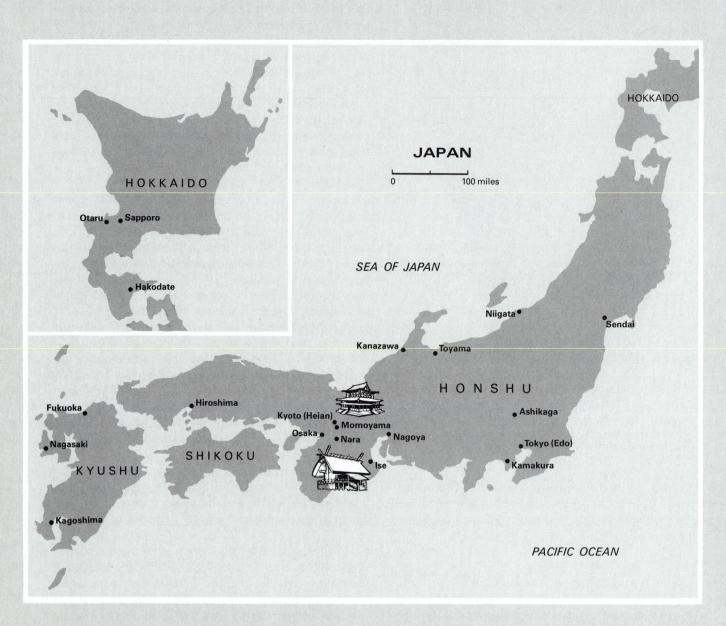

JAPAN

0 _____ 100 miles

SEA OF JAPAN

PACIFIC OCEAN

HOKKAIDO

Otaru • Sapporo

Hakodate

HOKKAIDO

Niigata

Sendai

Kanazawa • Toyama

HONSHU

Fukuoka

Hiroshima

Ashikaga

Nagasaki

Kyoto (Heian)
Momoyama

Osaka • Nara

Nagoya

Tokyo (Edo)

KYUSHU

SHIKOKU

Ise

Kamakura

Kagoshima

chapter thirteen

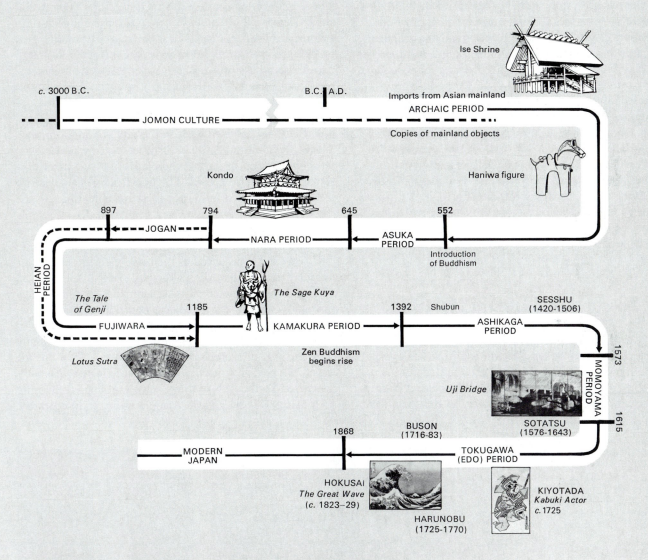

Ise Shrine

c. 3000 B.C.

B.C. A.D.

Imports from Asian mainland

ARCHAIC PERIOD

JOMON CULTURE

Copies of mainland objects

Kondo

Haniwa figure

897 794 645 552

JOGAN NARA PERIOD ASUKA PERIOD

Introduction
of Buddhism

The Sage Kuya

HEIAN PERIOD

*The Tale
of Genji* 1185 1392 Shubun

SESSHU
(1420-1506)

FUJIWARA KAMAKURA PERIOD ASHIKAGA
PERIOD

Zen Buddhism
begins rise

Lotus Sutra

1573

Uji Bridge

MOMOYAMA PERIOD

SOTATSU
(1576-1643)

1615

BUSON
(1716-83)

1868

MODERN
JAPAN

TOKUGAWA
(EDO) PERIOD

HOKUSAI
The Great Wave
(*c.* 1823–29)

HARUNOBU
(1725-1770)

KIYOTADA
Kabuki Actor
c. 1725

The Art of Japan

THE ARTS OF JAPAN have neither the progressive stylistic continuity of those of India nor the wide variety of those of China. A series of foreign influences sporadically affected the course of Japan's artistic evolution. Yet, no matter how overwhelming the impact of new forms and styles, the indigenous tradition invariably reasserted itself. Hence, the artistic pattern evolved in a rhythmic sequence of marked periods of borrowing, of absorption, and of return to native patterns.

Because Japan and its nearby islands are of volcanic origin, there is little stone suitable for carving or building. In architecture, this lack led to the development of wooden construction carefully devised to withstand the frequent earthquakes and tempests. In sculpture, figures were modeled in clay, which was often left unfired, cast in bronze by the *cire perdue* process familiar to many other cultures, or constructed of lacquer. Although the lacquer technique probably originated in China, Japanese artists excelled in creating large, hollow lacquer figures by placing hemp cloth soaked in the juice of the lacquer tree over wooden armatures. The surfaces were gradually added to and finished, but the technique remained one of modeling rather than carving. Such figures were not only light but very durable, being hard and resistant to destructive forces. Hollow lacquer was gradually superseded by sculpture carved in wood with unusual sensitivity for grain and texture.

NATIVE TRADITIONS

The first artifacts known in Japan are pottery vessels and figurines from a culture designated Jomon, which apparently flourished as early as the fourth millennium B.C. These objects are associated with Neolithic tools, although they persisted in northern Japan as late as the fourth or fifth century A.D., even while a metal culture was being fully developed in the south.

Japanese objects from about the beginning of the Christian era are of three kinds—those imported from the Asian mainland, those copied from imported articles, and those of Japanese invention. There are, for instance, bronze mirrors from Han China as well as replicas of these made in Japan. Some of the replicas are adorned with a Japanese innovation—spherical rattles attached to the perimeter. From Korea, another source of continental influence, came a gray pottery known as *sue*, which was soon copied, and small comma-shaped stones (*magatama*) used in necklaces. A third area—Indo-China—was the source of motifs used on bell-shaped bronzes known as *dotaku*. Houses and boats depicted on these bronzes are similar to those on contemporaneous drums from Annam (modern Vietnam), in Indo-China.

Within this heterogeneous culture, a specifically Japanese creativity asserted itself in the production of *haniwa*. These are sculptured tubes made of pottery and placed fencelike around burial mounds, possibly to control erosion or to protect the dead. The upper parts of the haniwa are usually modeled in human form but sometimes in the shape of a horse, a bird, or even a house (FIG. 13-1). Simple pottery cylinders were used similarly in Indo-China, but the sculptural modeling of haniwa is uniquely Japanese. The arms and legs as well as the mass of the torso in most instances recapitulate the cylindrical base of the haniwa. The tubelike character of some later monumental sculpture and even of a particular wooden doll common in Japan may derive from these remote ancestors.

Architecture was first limited to pit dwellings and simple constructions of thatched roofs on bamboo stilts, but we learn from some haniwa that wooden architecture was fully developed by the fifth century, some buildings containing such features as two stories, saddle roofs, and decorative

13-1 Haniwa figures, horse and peasant, fifth to sixth centuries A.D. Clay. Horse, Cleveland Museum of Art (gift of The Norweb Collection); peasant, Cleveland Museum of Art (purchase, James Parmelee Fund).

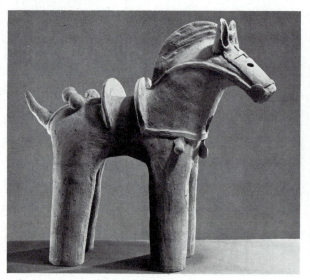
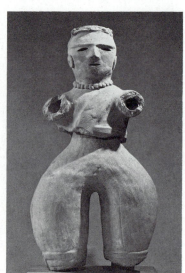

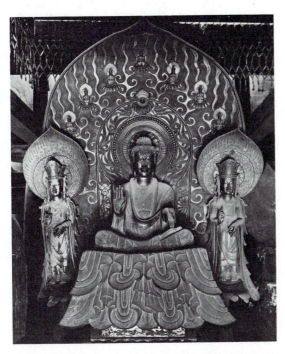

13-2 TORI BUSSHI, *Shaka Triad*, Asuka Period, A.D. 623. Bronze, 69½″ high. Horyu-ji Temple, Nara.

gables. There may have been monumental constructions of wood, but nothing remains from this early period except colossal mounds, which were the tombs of rulers.

ADVENT OF BUDDHISM

The native traditions, which were being established at this time, were interrupted in 552 by an event of paramount importance to Japan. In that year the ruler of Kudara (Korean: Paikche), a kingdom in Korea, sent a gilt bronze figure of the Buddha to Kimmei, emperor of Japan. With the image came the gospels. For half a century the new religion met with opposition, but at the end of that time Buddhism and its attendant arts were firmly established in Japan. Among the earliest examples of Japanese art serving the cause of Buddhism is a bronze sculpture of Shaka (Sanskrit:Sakyamuni) and attendant Bodhisattvas (FIG. 13-2) made in 623 by TORI BUSSHI, a third-generation Korean living in Japan. Tori's style is that of the mid-sixth century in China. His work proved how tenaciously the formula for a "correct" representation of the icon had been maintained since the introduction of Buddhism almost a century earlier. Yet at the same time a new influence was coming from Sui China. This may be seen in the cylindrical form and flowing draperies of the wood sculpture known as the Kudara Kannon (Chinese: Kuan-yin). The two styles were blended, and in the middle of the seventh century they coalesced in one of Japan's finest sculptures,

the *Miroku* (Sanskrit: Maitreya) of the Chugu-ji nunnery at Nara (FIG. 13-3). In this figure the Japanese artist combined a gentle sweetness with formal restraint in a manner unknown in Chinese sculpture.

Within a little more than half a century, however, all the archaisms of the fused style (loosely called Suiko after the empress who reigned from 593 to 628, or Asuka after the site of the capital) were swept aside by a new influence from T'ang China. The T'ang style, which found its way to Japan at the end of the Hakuho period (645–710), dominated Japanese art during the following periods of Late Nara (710–794) and Early Heian (794–897). Chinese models were followed not only in sculpture and painting but also in architecture, literature, and even in etiquette.

The mature style of T'ang appeared suddenly in Japan in the bronze *Shrine of Lady Tachibana* (FIG. 13-4). This consists of three full-round figures, the Buddha Amida seated on a lotus between the smaller figures of Kannon and Dai Seishi, each standing on a lotus and all three rising from a platform representing the stylized waters of the Sukhavati lake in the paradise of the Buddha. Behind them is a threefold screen on which are modeled in low relief the graceful forms of *apsaras* (heavenly nymphs) seated on lotuses and the tiny figures of souls newly born into heaven. The upswept scarves of the apsaras and the petals,

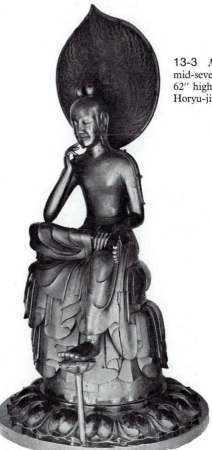

13-3 *Miroku*, Asuka period, mid-seventh century. Wood, 62″ high. Chugu-ji Nunnery, Horyu-ji, Nara.

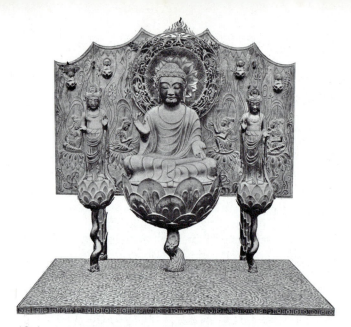

13-4 *Amida Triad*, from the *Shrine of Lady Tachibana*, Nara period, early eighth century. Gilded bronze; Amida, 11″ high, attendants, 10″ high. Horyu-ji temple, Nara.

tendrils, and pads of the lotuses create an exquisite background for the three divinities, while a detached openwork halo of delicate design frames the head of the Buddha. The ensemble gives some idea of the glorious T'ang bronzes

13-5 *Tamamushi Shrine*, Horyu-ji, Asuka period, seventh century. Lacquer on wood, 7′ 8″ high. Horyu-ji Museum, Nara.

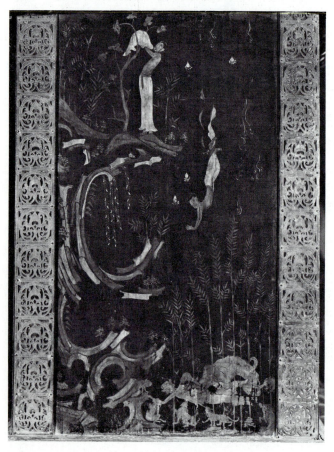

that were melted down in China during the Buddhist persecutions of 845. It also demonstrates the remarkable adaptability of the Japanese artist, which permitted him to seize upon a new art form and make it his own.

The development of painting in Japan paralleled that of Buddhist sculpture. Among the earliest surviving examples are those on the *Tamamushi* (Beetle-Wing) *Shrine* (so-called because its base was decorated with the iridescent wings of beetles), which dates from the first half of the seventh century (FIG. 13-5). The sides and doors of the shrine, which is a wooden cabinet, are decorated with scenes from the jataka in the style of the Tun-huang caves of a century earlier, as may be seen in the cell-like composition, the crystalline rock formations, the attenuated figures, and the free linear movement. There is also the same delight in surface pattern to the disregard of naturalism in scale and spatial relationships.

The many treasured articles in the Shosoin (storehouse for the belongings of Emperor Shomu after his death in 756) also illustrate the dependence of eighth-century Japan on the arts of China, although the wooden building itself is purely Japanese in style.

This Japanese dependence on China during the seventh and eighth centuries is not confined to sculpture and painting. Buddhist architecture adhered so closely to Chinese models that the lost style of the T'ang can be reconstructed from such temple complexes as the Horyu-ji or the Todai-ji, which still stand in Japan. The Kondo (Golden Hall) of the Horyu-ji (FIG. 13-6), which dates from shortly after A.D. 670, is one of the oldest wooden buildings in the world. Although periodically repaired and somewhat altered (the covered porch was added in the eighth century, the upper railing in the seventeenth), it retains the light and buoyant quality that had been characteristic of the Northern and Southern Dynasties style in China.

For a more typically Japanese structure we must refer to the shrines of Shinto, the indigenous faith of the Japanese people.[1] These shrines were customarily destroyed every twenty years and then replaced by exact duplicates, a process that has been repeated since the third century. Thus, we may assume that such a construction as the Ise shrine (FIG. 13-7) (last rebuilt in 1973), reproduces with a great measure of accuracy the original method of building. This, the greatest of all Shinto shrines, covers an area 55 by 127 yards and is enclosed by four concentric fences. The Shoden, the main building, rests on piles and has a thatched roof. Massive golden-hued columns, once the great trunks of cypress trees, and planks of the same wood are burnished to mellow surfaces, their color and texture contrasting with the white gravel that covers the ground of the sacred precinct. In the characteristic manner of the

[1]Shinto or "the Way of the Gods," was based on love of nature, of the family, and, above all, of the ruling family, as direct descendents of the gods. Extremely nationalistic in character, Shinto was embodied in symbolic forms and shunned pictorial representation.

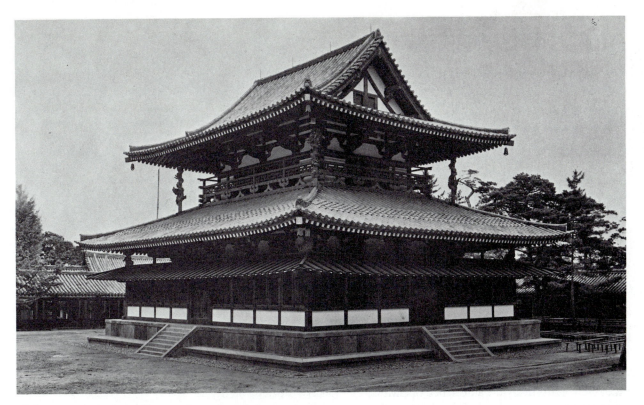

13-6   Kondo (Golden Hall), Horyu-ji, Asuka period, seventh century.

Japanese artist, the thatched roof was transformed from a simple functional element into one that established the esthetic of the entire structure. Browned by a smoking process, the thatch was sewn into bundles that were carefully laid in layers that gradually decreased in number from the eaves to the ridgepole. The entire surface was then sheared smooth, and a gently changing contour resulted. The roof line was further enhanced by decorative elements that once had been structural—the *chigi* or crosspiece at the gables, and cylindrical wooden weights placed at right angles across the ridgepole. The repeats and echoes of the various parts of the main building and of the related structures are a quiet study in rhythmic form. The shrine, in its setting, is an expression of purity and dignity, effectively emphasized by the extreme simplicity of carefully planned proportions, textures, and architectural forms.

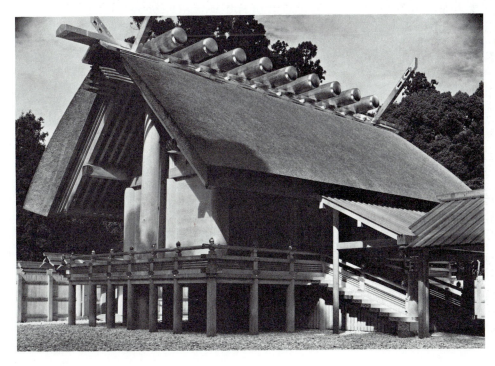

13-7   Shoden, main building of the Ise Shrine. Rebuilt in 1973, reproducing third-century type. © Grand Shrine of Ise.

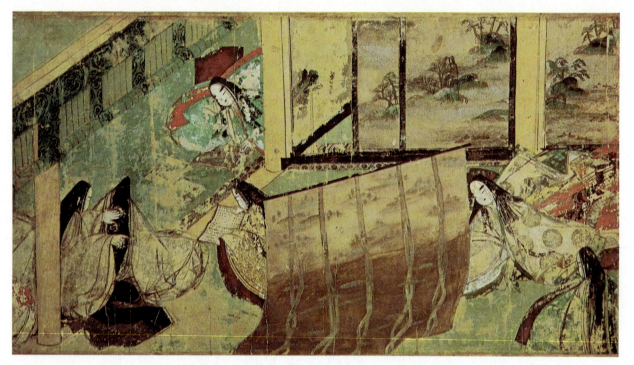

13-8 TAKAYOSHI, detail of *The Tale of Genji*. Late Heian period, twelfth century. Scroll, color on paper, $8\frac{1}{2}'' \times 15\frac{3}{4}''$. Tokugawa Museum, Nagoya.

HEIAN PERIOD AND OTHER INDIGENOUS INNOVATIONS

A new style in representation made its way into Japan at the beginning of the ninth century. Under the influence of Esoteric Buddhism (p. 386), a heavier image with multiple arms and heads was introduced—a type which in China was then replacing the earlier classic grace of T'ang. The bloated forms of the new style, though they may be repellent, have the merit of somber dignity. In paintings these bulky figures, often cut off at the sides, give the effect of a mighty force expanding beyond the pictorial format.

From the middle of the ninth century, relations between Japan and China deteriorated so rapidly that by the end of that century almost all intercourse had ceased. No longer able to reflect the fashions of China, the artists of Japan began to create their own forms during the Later Heian or Fujiwara period (897–1185). At this time court practices at Heian (Kyoto) were refined to the point of preciosity. A vivid and detailed picture of the period appears in Lady Murasaki's eleventh-century novel, *The Tale of Genji*, a work of superb subtlety. The picture is of a court in which etiquette overwhelmed morality, a society in which poor taste—in such matters as the color of a robe, the paper used in the endless writing of love letters, or the script itself—was considered a cardinal sin. The very essence of this court is reflected in a set of scrolls (illustrating *The Tale of Genji*) attributed to the twelfth-century court artist TAKAYOSHI (FIG. 13-8). Painted in the horizontal-scroll (*makimono*) format, the small pictures here alternate with sections of text. The artist uses a distinctly Japanese tech-

nique for representing space, the scenes viewed as from an elevation, ceilings removed to expose the interiors, and the ground plane sharply tilted toward a high horizon or one that is often excluded altogether. Thus the area of representation was expanded in terms of content and abruptly contracted by the resulting diminution of a sense of depth. Flat fields of unshaded color emphasize the painting's two-dimensional character, as do strong diagonal lines, which direct the eye more along the surface than into the picture space. Human figures have the appearance of being constructed of stiff layers of contrasting fabrics, and although they represent specific characters, their features are scarcely differentiated. A formula for such aristocratic faces, which produced a depersonalizing effect, called for a brush stroke for each eye and eyebrow, one for the nose, another (sometimes omitted) for the mouth. Paintings in this purely Japanese style, known as Yamato-e,[2] reflect the sophisticated taste of the Fujiwara nobility for whom they were created.

From about the same period are a series of fan paintings (FIG. 13-9) illustrating, with text, the *Hokke-kyo* (*Lotus Sutra*). The high perspective and lavish sprinkling of cut gold and mica to ornament the paper are related to the courtly style of the *Genji* scrolls. But the scenes of lower-class life and the printing of the under-drawing by wood blocks suggest that the fans may be an early example of that blending of sophisticated taste with popular subjects and modes that was one of the great and persistent themes of Japanese art.

[2]Yamato is the area around Kyoto and Nara regarded as the cradle of Japanese culture. The suffix -*e* means, in effect, "painting of."

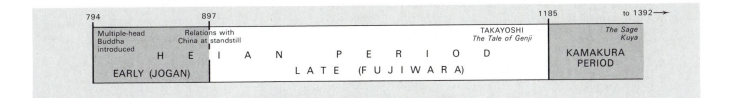

794   897   1185   to 1392 →

| Multiple-head Buddha introduced | Relations with China at standstill | | TAKAYOSHI *The Tale of Genji* | *The Sage Kuya* |

H E I A N   P E R I O D   KAMAKURA PERIOD

EARLY (JOGAN)   L A T E   (F U J I W A R A)

A different facet of Yamato-e is represented by the *Shigisan Engi* (the Legends of Mount Shigi), painted at the end of the Fujiwara period (FIG. 13-10). One of the first Japanese scrolls designed as a continuous composition, it illustrates the story of a Buddhist monk and his miraculous golden bowl. Our episode—called "The Flying Storehouse"—depicts the bowl lifting the rice-filled storehouse of a greedy merchant and carrying it off to the monk's hut in the Wakayama mountains. The gaping merchant, his attendants, and several onlookers are shown in various poses, some grimacing, others wildly gesticulating and scurrying about in frantic astonishment. The Fujiwara aristocracy felt that only the crude and ill-bred would display such feelings and that it was therefore an appropriate subject for humorous caricature. The faces—so unlike the generalized masks in the Genji scrolls—are drawn with

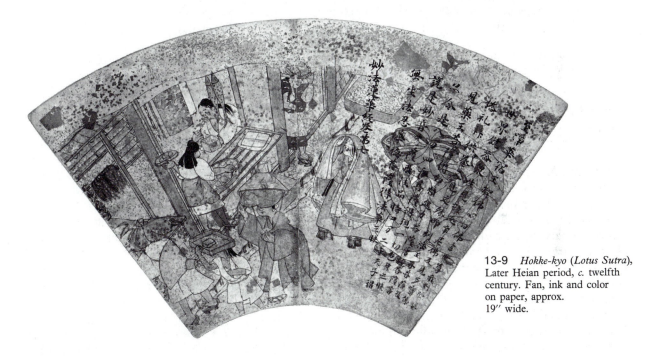

13-9 *Hokke-kyo* (*Lotus Sutra*), Later Heian period, *c.* twelfth century. Fan, ink and color on paper, approx. 19″ wide.

13-10 *The Flying Storehouse,* detail of the *Shigisan Engi,* Fujiwara period, late twelfth century. Horizontal scroll, ink and color on paper, 12½″ high. Chogosonshi-ji, Nara.

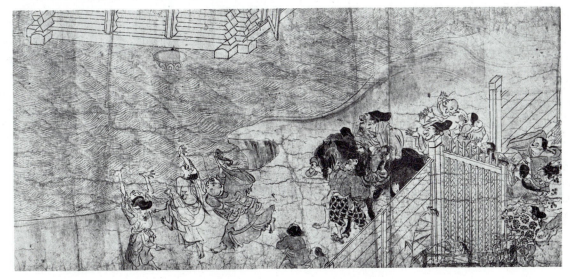

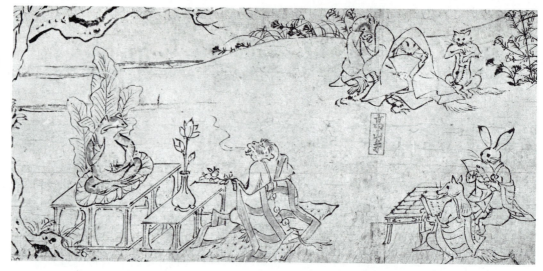

13-11 Animal caricatures, detail of a horizontal scroll attributed to Toba Sojo, later Heian period, *c.* late twelfth century. Ink on paper, approx. 12″ high. Kozan-ji.

each feature exaggerated, thus conforming to a convention of the period to distinguish the lower classes from the nobility. Cartooning of this kind became an important element in Japanese pictorial art.

From the same general period (but of disputed date) are four horizontal scrolls of animal caricatures, painted in monochrome with a free calligraphic brush more typical of Chinese Zen painting than of the refined style of Yamato-e. One of these scrolls, often attributed to the Buddhist Abbot Toba (TOBA SOJO), depicts a medley of frogs, monkeys, and hares in a hilarious burlesque of Buddhist practices. In one section a monkey dressed as a priest pays homage to a Buddha in the shape of a frog seated pompously on a lotus throne with a nimbus of luxuriant banana leaves (FIG. 13-11). In another, more animated, passage, the animals tumble and frolic while washing each other in a river. Throughout this whimsical satire the Japanese predilection for decoration asserts itself in charming clumps of foliage that play a delicate counterpoint to the vigorous movement of the animals.

A more conservative style of Buddhist art continued through the Later Fujiwara period, but a new subject was added. This subject, known as Raigo, portrayed the Buddha Amida descending through clouds amid a host of Bodhisattvas welcoming deceased believers to his paradise. Such paintings were products of the Paradise Sects (p. 383), which eased the rigors of religion for the luxurious courtiers in Kyoto. A remarkable sculptural rendering of the Raigo theme is housed at the Hoodo (Phoenix Hall) of the Byodoin temple at Uji, near Kyoto (FIG. 13-12). The light and sweeping design of the building, suggesting a bird in flight, recalls at once aristocratic palace pavilions and the Chinese architecture depicted in Paradise paintings at Tun-huang (FIG. 12-12). Inside the hall, the gilded wood figure of Amida by the sculptor JOCHO embodies a serene grace through the expanding curves of face and torso, stabilized into a triangular composition by the elongated legs below. The smaller figures of angels and celestial musicians, floating on clouds as they accompany Amida on his descent, complete the impression of courtly elegance.

13-12 Hoodo (Phoenix Hall), Byodoin temple at Uji, Heian period, eleventh century. Left: exterior; right: interior with *Amida* by JOCHO, 1053, gilded wood, 9′ 4″ high.

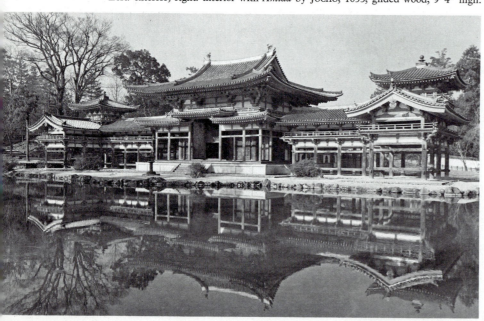

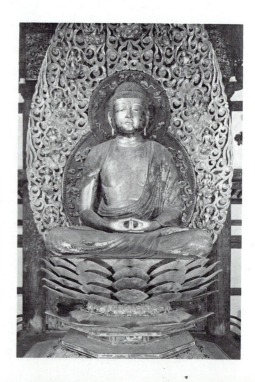

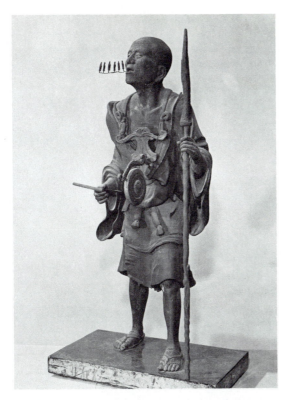

13-13 *The Sage Kuya Invoking the Amida Buddha*, Kamakura period, thirteenth century. Painted wood. Rokuharamitsu-ji Temple, Kyoto.

KAMAKURA REALISM

A series of civil wars led to the downfall of the decadent Fujiwara rulers, and their successful rivals established a new capital at Kamakura, the city that gave its name to the period from 1185 to about 1392. The new rulers, reacting against what they considered to be the effeteness of the Fujiwaras, supported an art emphasizing strength and realism. The style of the Nara period (710–794) was revived by UNKEI (d. 1223), perhaps the greatest sculptor of Japan. Unkei and his followers went even further than the earlier realists by carefully reproducing their observations of every accidental variation in the folds of drapery and by using crystal for the eyes of their sculptures. That they were able, nonetheless, to keep a sensitive balance between the spiritual and the realistic is shown by the superb figure of Kuya, a priest who is represented as he walked about invoking the name of Amida Buddha (FIG. 13-13). Not only is every detail meticulously rendered, but six small Buddha images issue from the saint's mouth, as if in a comic strip balloon, to represent the words Amida, Amida, Amida. . . . Realism was thus carried to the point at which the sculptor attempted to invest his figures with speech.

Painting during the Kamakura period is most interesting for the advances made in the Yamato-e style, although all the different types of Fujiwara art were also continued. Perhaps the greatest Yamato-e of this time is *The Burning of the Sanjo Palace*, one of a series of horizontal scrolls illustrating tales of the Heiji insurrection (*Heiji Monogatari*). Here, the artist, perfecting the symphonic composition of the Chinese landscape scroll, has added drama with swift and violent staccato brushwork and vivid flashes of color. At the beginning of the scroll (read from right to left) the eye is caught by a mass of figures rushing toward a blazing building—the crescendo of the painting—then led at a decelerated pace through swarms of soldiers, horses, and bullock carts, finally, it seems, to be arrested by a warrior on a rearing horse (FIG. 13-14). But the horse and rider are positioned to serve as a deceptive cadence (false ending), for they are a prelude to the single figure of an archer, which picks up and completes the mass movement of the soldiers and so draws the turbulent narrative to a quiet close.

13-14 *The Burning of the Sanjo Palace*, Kamakura period, thirteenth century. Section of a horizontal scroll, ink and color on paper, 22′ 10″ long. Fenollosa-Weld Collection, Museum of Fine Arts, Boston.

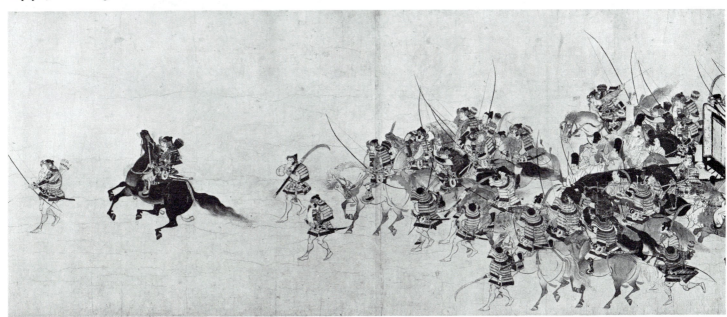

ASHIKAGA: RENEWED CHINESE INFLUENCE

The power of the Kamakura rulers ceased in 1333, after which internal warfare persisted until 1392, when the Ashikaga shoguns (military dictators) imposed a brief peace. Civil war soon broke out again, though the shoguns managed to maintain control amid almost continuous insurrections, and lasted until 1573. The arts, nevertheless, flourished. New painting styles imported from China coexisted with conventional Buddhist pictures and with paintings in the Yamato-e style carried on by artists of the Tosa family. The monochrome landscape style of the thirteenth-century Sung masters Ma Yuan and Hsia Kuei was adopted by the painter-monk SHUBUN at the beginning of the fifteenth century. Shubun created evocative, idealized landscapes, sometimes with subjects and associated poems based on Chinese themes, which reflects the deep involvement with Chinese culture at Japanese monasteries of this period. MINCHO (1352–1431) and other painters went directly to Yuan dynasty models. But the most powerful current to come from China was that which accompanied Zen Buddhism and which accounts largely for the efflorescence of art despite the troubled times of the Ashikaga period. The new philosophy appealed to the samurai, a caste of professional warriors composed of men who held a relatively high position in society and who were supporters of the feudal nobility. They lived by rigid standards that placed high values on such virtues as loyalty, courage, and self-control. The self-reliance required of its adherents made Zen the ideal religion for the samurai.

Because the samurai found Zen attractive, the arts that had been associated with it in China swept Japan. Sculpture, as in China under Ch'an, lost importance, and painting widely imitated the bold brush of the Sung masters of Ch'an. Early in the Ashikaga period the artist KAO worked in the style of the thirteenth-century Chinese artist Liang K'ai, while his contemporary MOKUAN painted almost indistinguishably from a Chinese predecessor, Mu-ch'i. Of all the Zen artists in Japan at this time SESSHU (1420–1506) is the most celebrated. He had several different styles, but is best known for paintings in the Ma-Hsia manner (p. 392). He greatly admired Sung painting and, although he studied in China, he decried the work of contemporary Ming painters. Nevertheless he was affected by the Ming style, for one of his masterpieces, an ink-splash landscape in the National Museum, Tokyo (FIG. 13-15), contains elements basic to the Ming style as well as to the Sung. Although the landscape recalls the wet style characteristic of Ch'an painters of the Sung, the brushwork is more abstract and the tonal contrasts more startling, after the Ming manner.

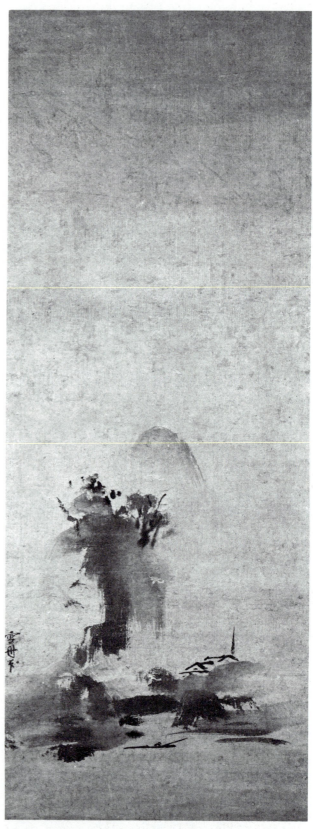

13-15 SESSHU, *Landscape*, Ashikaga period, 1495. Detail of a hanging scroll, ink on paper. Tokyo National Museum.

The Tea Ceremony

The influence of Zen went considerably beyond painting. It gave rise during the Ashikaga period to the tea ceremony, a unique custom that, among other things, provided a new outlet for the products of the Japanese artist-craftsman. This ceremony soon became a major social institution of the aristocracy. Special teahouses were built in the subtly arranged gardens of the period. The teahouse itself was small and was designed to give the appearance of refined simplicity. Even its exterior was carefully planned to blend with the calculated casualness of the garden. A flagstone path usually led past moss-covered stone lanterns to an entrance where the guests, after washing at a "natural" spring, entered through a low doorway. There the host and a group of four guests sat in an atmosphere of almost unadorned simplicity. Scaled to create a feeling of intimacy, the room was a rectangle broken only by an alcove (*tokonoma*), which held one painting—most appropriately one in the free monochrome style of Zen—and perhaps a stylized flower arrangement. The ritual of tea drinking in this setting imposed on all the participants a set of mannered gestures and even certain topics of conversation. Every effort was made to prevent any jarring note that might shatter a perfectly planned occasion.

Each object employed in the ceremony was selected with the utmost discrimination. The connoisseur preferred a tea bowl, a flower container, a lacquer tray or other ritual utensil—all of which had to appear to have been made without artifice. The same effect was sought in the room itself, which was constructed of unpainted wood. Although the supporting posts were fashioned so as to keep their natural appearance and thus remained rounded and knotty as tree trunks, all the surfaces were painstakingly rubbed and burnished to bring out the beauty of grains and textures. Potteries used in the ceremony were covered with heavy glazes seemingly applied in a casual manner, belying the skill that had controlled the colors and textures (FIG. 13-16). The irregular, sometimes battered or flawed shapes of many Japanese tea wares provide an extreme contrast with the technical perfection common in Chinese ceramics (FIG. 12-25). Many wares of this type were given individual names based on literary or historical associations of their decor or the visual and tactile qualities of the entire piece. Conferring such attention and importance on an individual object at this stage foreshadows the entrance into ceramics of major artists, who would sign, paint, and even inscribe poems on their wares as part of the development of a craft into a self-conscious and sophisticated art.

The Tosa and Kano Schools

The artistic understatement of the tea ceremony was counterbalanced by the continuing Yamato-e style of decorative painting. TOSA MITSUNOBU (1434–1525), the foremost exponent of the latter during the Ashikaga period, retained the coloristic patterns of his native style, but also emphasized ink outline after the fashion of Chinese painting. The new manner of painting resulting from this combination is most apparent in pictures of the Kano school. MOTONOBU (1476–1559), who was probably the grandson of the founder of the Kano school, worked so closely in the Sung tradition that some of his paintings have been mistaken for those of Hsia Kuei (p. 391). He had, however, a more personal style in which we find a new emphasis on brushed outlines and strong tonal contrasts—features that became distinctive of the Kano school. In addition Motonobu often used Tosa coloring and at times even painted in a purely Tosa manner. As a result the Tosa and Kano schools became less distinguishable after the sixteenth century.

13-16 Tea ceremony water jar, named *Kogan* ("ancient stream bank"), Momoyama period, late sixteenth century. Shino ware with underglaze design, 7″ high. Hatakeyama Memorial Museum, Tokyo.

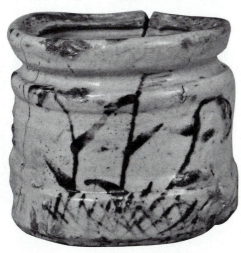

MOMOYAMA AND EDO: THE DECORATIVE STYLE

In the Momoyama period (1573–1615), which followed the stormy Ashikaga, a succession of three dictators finally imposed peace on the Japanese people. Huge palaces were erected, partly as symbols of power, partly as fortresses. The grand scale of the period is typified by the Nagoya Castle, built about 1610. This castle also exemplifies how well the new style of painting suited the tastes of the Momoyama nobility. The sliding doors and large screens within the mammoth structure were covered with gold leaf on which were painted a wide range of romantic and historic subjects, even exotic portrayals of Dutch and

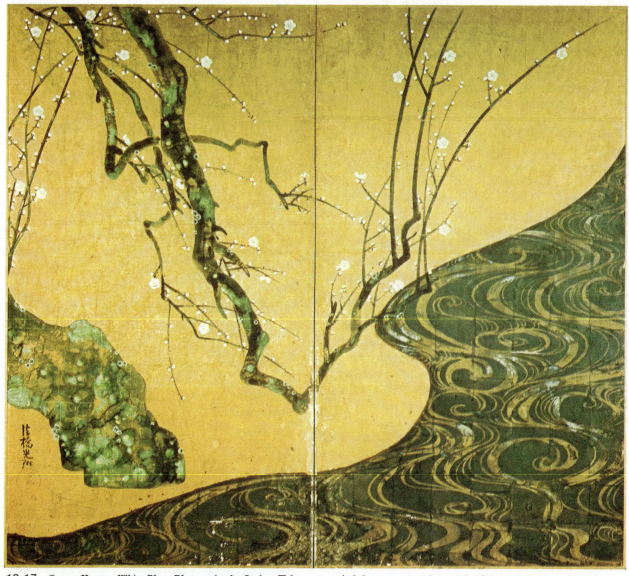

13-17 OGATA KORIN, *White Plum Blossoms in the Spring*, Tokugawa period, late seventeenth to early eighteenth century. Screen, color on gold paper, 62″ high. Tokyo National Museum.

13-18 *Uji Bridge*, Momoyama period, sixteenth to seventeenth centuries. Six-fold screen, color on paper. Tokyo National Museum.

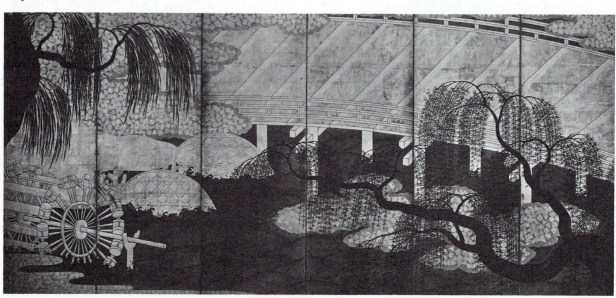

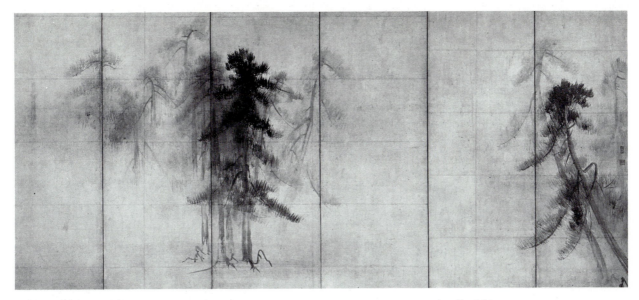

13-19 HASEGAWA TOHAKU, *Pine Trees*, Momoyama period, sixteenth to seventeenth centuries. Six-fold screen, ink on paper, 61″ high. Tokyo National Museum.

13-20 TAWARAYA SOTATSU and HONAMI KOETSU, *Deer and Calligraphy*, Tokugawa period, early seventeenth century. Section of a horizontal scroll, ink and gold and silver on paper, 12½″ high. Seattle Art Museum (gift of Mrs. Donald E. Frederick).

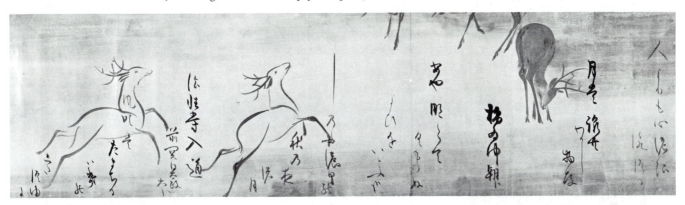

Portuguese traders. Traditional Chinese themes were frequent, as were commonplace subjects of everyday experience. But all were transformed by an emphasis on two-dimensional design and striking color patterns (FIG. 13-18). The anecdotal or philosophical content was almost lost in a grandiose decorative display.

Not every Momoyama artist worked exclusively in the colorful style exemplified by the Nagoya paintings. HASEGAWA TOHAKU (1539–1610), for instance, carried on the Zen manner of Mu-ch'i with brilliant success. His versatility, which was shared by most artists of the time, is evident in a brilliant monochromatic screen painting, *Pine Trees*, whose strong verticals and diagonals are distinctively Japanese (FIG. 13-19).[3]

In 1615 Ieyasu Tokugawa, last of the Momoyama rulers, consolidated his power as shogun of Edo (Tokyo) and established the Tokugawa or Edo rule, which lasted until 1857. (Printmaking, which emerged about this time as a popular art, is discussed on page 413). Screen painting was continued in all its Momoyama magnificence by such

artists as KANO SANRAKU (1561–1635), KOETSU (1558–1637), and TAWARAYA SOTATSU (1576–1643), whose lives spanned both periods. Koetsu and Sotatsu also composed numerous scrolls in which pictorial forms—those of flowers or of animals—were interlaced with strokes of a free-flowing calligraphy. One such collaborative effort is a deer scroll (FIG. 13-20), in which the shapes of the animals, painted in decorative gold and silver, are repeated with subtle variations in pose and interval to create an almost musical effect.

KORIN (1658–1716) and his brother KENZAN (1663–1743) carried the decorative tradition that characterized the Momoyama on into the eighteenth century. The first was primarily a decorative painter who also worked as a lacquer designer, the second a master potter, whose line of "natural" wares is still continued today by the ninth artist to take his name. Korin is famous largely for his dramatic renderings of rocks, tree-branches, and waves, which he combined in elegant and flowing compositions (FIG. 13-17). Both artists harmonized the decorative styles of Momoyama and early Edo with the studied simplicity required of art in the service of the tea ceremony.

[3] In Japan the decoration of screens was especially highly developed and often exemplifies the highest quality of painting.

Nanga and Realism

While the decorative style of the Sotatsu-Korin schools continued to flourish until the nineteenth century, it had to share its popularity with several other trends in later Japanese painting. One, Nanga ("Southern school painting"), was inspired by Chinese "literary" school painting (p. 391). The Nanga painters transformed the techniques of their Chinese models into one that combined virtuoso brushwork with decorative pattern and a strong sense of humor. Two outstanding early representatives of this style are IKENO TAIGA (1723–76) and YOSA BUSON (1716–83),

who jointly illustrated an album entitled *The Ten Conveniences and the Ten Enjoyments of Country Life*. On one of Buson's pages (FIG. 13-21) a bulbous-nosed figure peering from a hut at richly textured summer foliage is shown with wistful humor by this master of the brush.

Another main line of later Japanese painting, which has been called realistic or naturalistic, is represented by MARUYAMA OKYO (1733–95). His studies of animals, insects, and plants (FIG. 13-22) combine an almost Western objectivity with an unusual handling of the brush to produce a style that follows the observed forms rather than established conventions. This kind of realism may well be

13-21   YOSA BUSON, *Enjoyment of Summer Scenery,* from *The Ten Conveniences and the Ten Enjoyments of Country Life,* Tokugawa period, 1771. Album leaves, ink and color on paper, 7″ high. Yasunari Kawabata Collection, Kanagawa.

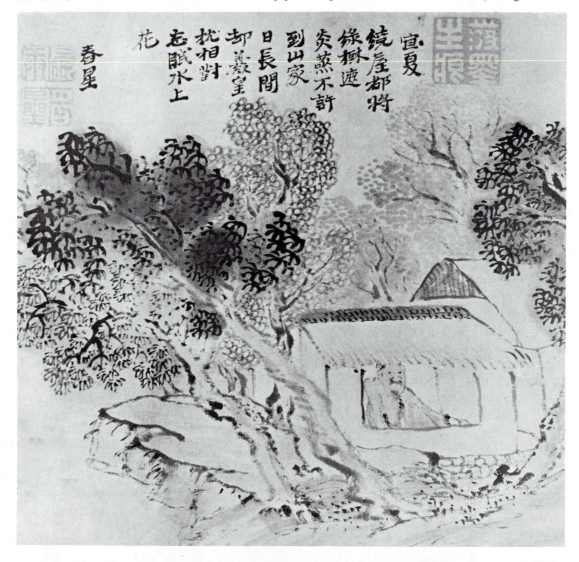

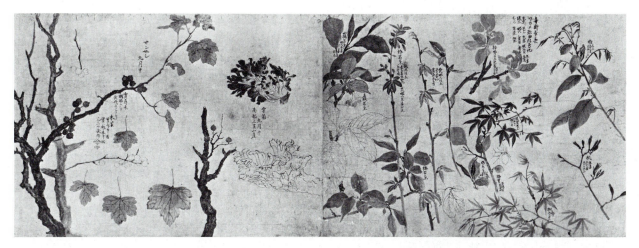

13-22 MARUYAMA OKYO, detail of *Nature Studies*, Tokugawa period, eighteenth century. Horizontal scroll, ink and color on paper, 12½″ high. Nishimura Collection, Kyoto.

due, in part, to Western influence. From the mid-sixteenth century on, Portuguese missionaries and Dutch traders visited Japan, bringing with them paintings that, despite the efforts of the Tokugawa shoguns to bar foreign influences, did not fail to have some effect on Japanese art.

Ukiyo-e and Printmaking

The Tokugawa shoguns maintained a static and stratified society and, as a result, each class developed its own distinctive culture. The center of the plebeian culture was the Yoshiwara entertainment area of Edo, where the popular idols were the talented courtesans of the teahouses and the actors of the Kabuki theater. Kabuki itself was a popular and lusty form of drama that developed in response to a demand for a more intelligible and more easily enjoyed theater than that of the highly stylized No plays, the latter patronized exclusively by the nobility and a small number of the *nouveau riche.* The former eventually provided endless subjects for a new art form, a style of genre painting, beginning around 1600, that was to have considerable influence on Western art in the nineteenth century (p. 779). This new art, known as *ukiyo-e,* or "pictures of the floating (or passing) world," was largely centered in Kyoto. Toward the end of the seventeenth century the center of production shifted to Edo, and the medium became predominantly that of the woodblock print, which reflected the tastes and pleasures of a bourgeoisie emerging in a feudal society.

The woodblock as a device for printing had been invented in China during the T'ang dynasty. The technique was introduced into Japan during the eighth century, when it was employed chiefly to reproduce inexpensive religious souvenirs or charms. In the seventeenth century, Chinese woodblock book illustrations inspired the production of low-priced illustrated guidebooks of the Yoshiwara district.

The art of block printing as it ultimately developed in the eighteenth century was a triumph of collaboration. The artist, having been selected and commissioned by a publisher, prepared his design in ink, merely adding color notations. Next, a specialist in woodcutting transferred the lines to the blocks. A third man did the printing. The quality of the finished picture depended as much on the often anonymous cutter and printer as on the painter of the original design.

MORONOBU (*c.* 1625–1694) was probably the first to employ the woodblock print to illustrate everyday subjects in books and for individual prints, which he began to produce about 1673. The woodblock quickly evolved as a medium for cheap reproduction and wide distribution. Moronobu's woodblocks were simply in black outline against a plain white paper, as were the prints produced for the next fifty years, but often they were hand-colored by their purchasers. Moronobu's designs of large and simple forms had the exuberance of a young art. The same vitality was expressed in prints of the Torii school by such artists as KIYONOBU I (1664–1729), KIYOMASU I (active 1694–1716), and KIYOTADA (active in the early eighteenth century) (FIG. 13-23). These artists specialized in portraying Kabuki actors. (Kiyonobu I was an actor's son.) They worked with a broad rhythmic outline, and, for emphatic pattern, used the bold textile designs of the actors' robes.

At about the same time, members of the Kaigetsudo family were painting pictures and making designs for woodblocks of elegant courtesans. The Kaigetsudo figures had more grace but somewhat less power than those of the Torii painters. In general the print style gradually acquired more delicacy during the eighteenth century. The invention of a process of printing in color directly from blocks brought the "primitive" period of ukiyo-e printmaking to an end about 1741.

MASANOBU (1686–1764) had earlier experimented with what is called "lacquer technique" in an effort to increase

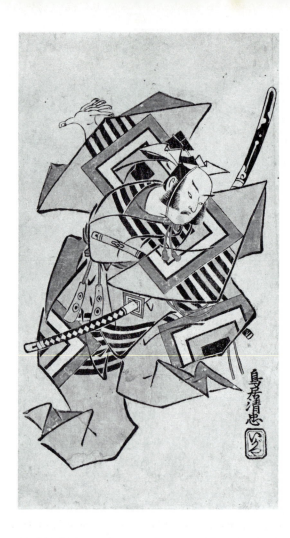

13-23 KIYOTADA, *Dancing Kabuki Actor*, Tokugawa period, *c.* 1725. Print, 11¼″ × 6″. Metropolitan Museum of Art, New York (Harris Brisbane Dick Fund, 1949).

the luster of the ink in his black-and-white prints. He later used a new two-color method for printing in pink and green (*benizuri-e*) in which the dominant pink contrasts with patches of pale green and still smaller areas of black to produce a strong color vibration despite the very limited palette. Coincident with the use of color printing the artists began to work in smaller, more delicate scale. In 1765 a device was introduced that gave more accurate register and permitted the successful use of even smaller color areas. This led to the development of the *nishiki-e* or "brocade picture," which was a true polychrome print. The new technique encouraged greater refinement and delicacy, evident in prints by the two leading print masters of the time, the incomparable HARUNOBU (1725–70) and KORYUSAI (active 1764–88). Their work (FIG. 21-68) shows a new loveliness replacing the monumentality of earlier compositions. The figures are of slighter proportions, the colors more muted, the line lyric rather than dramatic.

After the death of Harunobu, prints changed rapidly in style, shape, subject, and color. KIYONAGA (1752–1815) and UTAMARO (1753–1806) revived the taste for tall, willowy figures. Utamaro, who later concentrated on half-length figures, was fortunate in having the services of craftsmen skilled enough in woodcutting to allow him to

13-24 HOKUSAI, *The Great Wave*, from *Thirty-Six Views of Mt. Fuji*, Tokugawa period, early nineteenth century. Print, 14¾″ wide. Museum of Fine Arts, Boston.

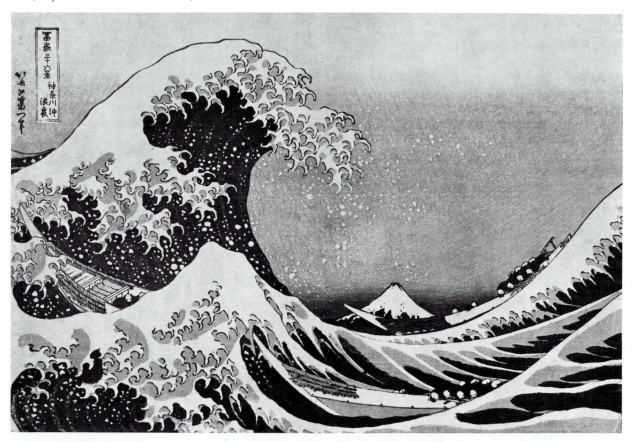

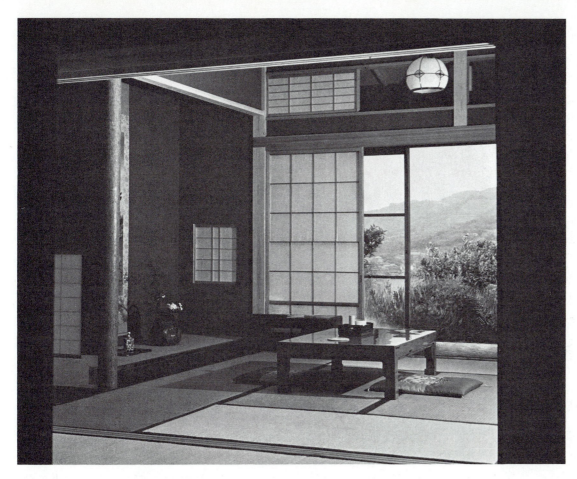

create extraordinary nuances in color, texture, and line. BUNCHO (active 1766-90), working in another vein, made many striking portraits of well-known figures. Even more dramatic are the prints of SHARAKU, who, active for a brief ten months during 1794 and 1795, was a unique and enigmatic figure among print artists. About one hundred and sixty of his prints survive, all of them piercing, rather acid, psychological studies of actors, wrestlers, or managers. TOYOKUNI I (1769-1825) followed in a similar, less biting manner, but the strength of this style was dissipated in the hands of later artists.

Dozens of other artists contributed to the popular art of printmaking, but during the nineteenth century HOKUSAI (1760-1849) and HIROSHIGE (1797-1858) were outstanding. Increasing political and moral censorship, which was to contribute to the decline of this art, led Hokusai to landscape for his ukiyo-e subjects. His brilliant and ingenious compositions, such as his *Thirty-Six Views of Mt. Fuji,* make use of striking juxtapositions and bold linear designs (FIG. 13-24). Nature was his primary subject, but in its setting he also included genre and anecdote as minor themes. Hiroshige, too, specialized in landscape and, like Hokusai, painted birds, flowers, and legendary scenes. In general, however, his prints did not evoke the sense of grandeur implicit in Hokusai's work.

These prints, although sometimes influenced by European art, show the Japanese attitude toward nature, which regarded natural forms in their utmost simplicity as a point of departure for an interpretation of reality and which, in turn, led to abstract pictorial design.

DOMESTIC ARCHITECTURE

Until recently, the Japanese home—modest or pretentious—has been designed according to what are basically the same structural and esthetic principles as those discussed with respect to the Shinto shrine and the tea ceremony house. The Japanese dwelling almost invariably is intimately related to the land around it, and wherever possible it is set in a garden closed off by a bamboo fence (a thing of beauty in itself), providing a sense of privacy and intimacy even in the most crowded environment. Uniformity and harmony of proportions are achieved by the use of the conventional mat (*tatami*) as a module for the dimensions of the rooms (FIG. 13-25).

The structure is essentially a series of posts supporting a roof. The walls, which are thus screens rather than supports, slide—to open onto the outside or from one room into another. Space is treated as continuous yet harmoniously divisible—a concept that revolutionized architectural theory in the West. Adoption of the Japanese traditions of painstaking craftsmanship is more difficult for the West.

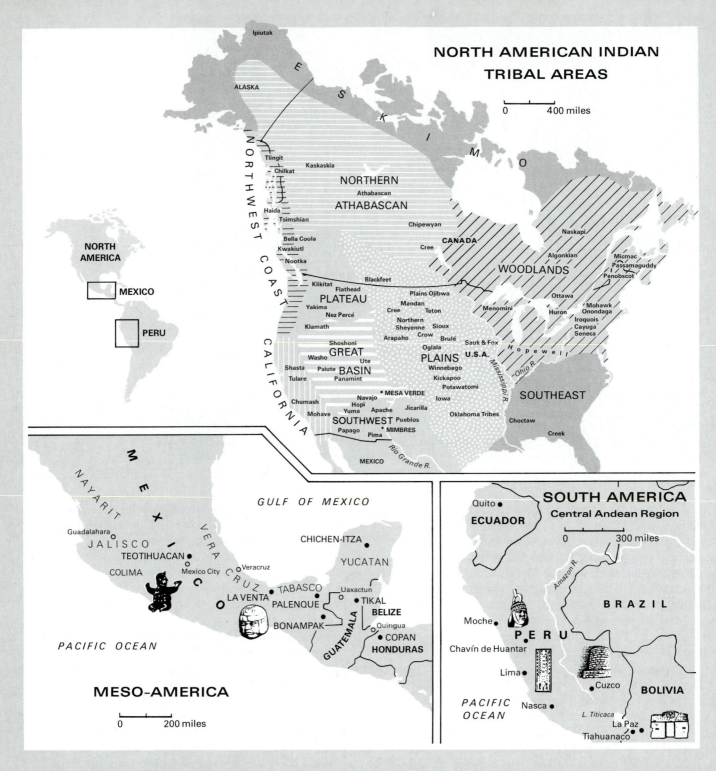

NORTH AMERICAN INDIAN TRIBAL AREAS

0   400 miles

E S K I M O

Ipiutak

ALASKA

Tlingit
Chilkat
Haida
Tsimshian
Bella Coola
Kwakiutl
Nootka

N O R T H W E S T   C O A S T

Kaskaskia

NORTHERN
ATHABASCAN

Athabascan

Chipewyan

Naskapi

CANADA

Cree

Algonkian

Micmac
Passamaguddy
Penobscot

WOODLANDS

Klikitat
Blackfeet
Flathead
Plains Ojibwa
Mandan

Ottawa

Mohawk
Onondaga
Iroquois
Cayuga
Seneca

PLATEAU

Yakima
Nez Percé
Klamath

Cree
Northern
Sheyenne
Arapaho
Crow
Teton
Sioux
Brulé

Menomini

Huron

C A L I F O R N I A

Shoshoni
Washo
Ute
GREAT
BASIN

Oglala

Sauk & Fox

H o p e w e l l

Shasta   Paiute
Tulare   Panamint

Winnebago
Kickapoo
Potawatomi

PLAINS

Ohio R.

U.S.A.

M
i
s
s
i
s
s
i
p
p
i   R.

SOUTHEAST

Chumash
Mohave

Navajo
Hopi
Yuma   Apache
SOUTHWEST   Pueblos
Papago   Pima

• MESA VERDE

Jicarilla

• MIMBRES

Iowa

Oklahoma Tribes

Choctaw

Creek

MEXICO

Rio Grande R.

NORTH AMERICA

MEXICO

PERU

GULF OF MEXICO

M   E   X   I   C   O

NAYARIT

Guadalajara
JALISCO
TEOTIHUACAN
COLIMA
Mexico City

V
E
R
A

C
R
U
Z

Veracruz

TABASCO
LA VENTA
PALENQUE
BONAMPAK

CHICHEN-ITZA

YUCATAN

Uaxactun
• TIKAL

BELIZE

G
U
A
T
E
M
A
L
A

Quirigua
• COPAN
HONDURAS

PACIFIC OCEAN

MESO-AMERICA

0   200 miles

SOUTH AMERICA
Central Andean Region

Quito •
ECUADOR

0   300 miles

Amazon R.

B R A Z I L

Moche •

P E R U

Chavín de Huantar

Lima •

• Cuzco

BOLIVIA

Nasca •

L. Titicaca

La Paz •

PACIFIC OCEAN

Tiahuanaco

---

chapter fourteen

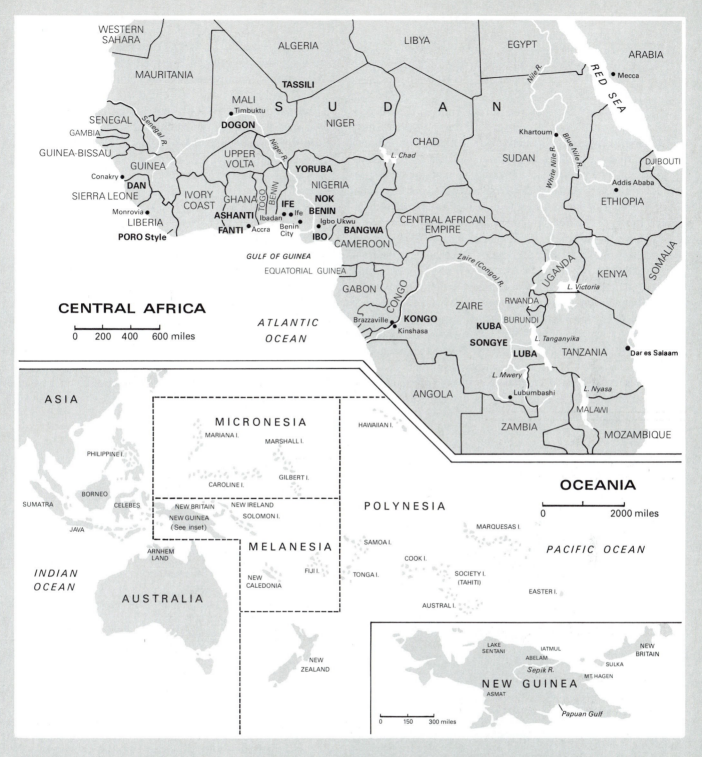

The Native Arts of the Americas, Africa, and the South Pacific

Though rich and varied and coming from three continents and numerous historical backgrounds of great diversity, the art traditions dealt with in this chapter are more like one another than they are like those of Europe and Asia. An exception is the pre-Columbian art of Central and South America, some phases of which are characterized by monumental architecture, which is not found in the other regions. This, and the preference for working in stone, gives pre-Columbian art a quality of permanence not shared by that of the other native cultures. (The arts of the North American Indian, of Africa, and of the South Pacific give greater emphasis to transient, impermanent works.) Perhaps the rigidity implied by this preference for enduring materials was partly responsible for the abrupt and complete collapse of late pre-Columbian cultures under the onslaught of Spanish conquerors. In other parts of the colonized world, native arts tended to survive conquest, declining slowly to extinction or, more frequently, living on to today, albeit in forms modified by Western influence.

In its broadest sense, "pre-Columbian" refers to all the peoples indigenous to the New World as they existed prior to the advent of the Europeans. In practice, however, the term is used to designate the pre-European-contact cultures of Meso-America and South America. Although the Aztecs and the Incas are the two groups most commonly associated with the pre-Columbian world, in actuality they represent only a final brief flicker of a flame of cultural development that had been kindled thousands of years before the arrival of Columbus. This development began with a series of migrations, primarily, it seems, via a land bridge from Asia at what is now the Aleutian Island chain.

Perhaps as early as 4000 B.C. some of these wandering peoples had developed the food plant maize, and, with agriculture established and a constant food supply assured, these early Americans were able to turn from the time-consuming necessities of hunting and gathering to developing the complex civilizations that were marveled at by the Spanish conquistadors. Their civilizations were impressive not only in grandeur and complexity, but as well in the vastness of time and of area in which they developed.

MESO-AMERICA

Meso-America (primarily an ethnographic term) includes most of central and southern Mexico and the northern section of Central America. Within this vast area one encounters geographic and climatic conditions (ranging from the temperate central highlands to the hot, humid southern coast of Veracruz) of a variety that is paralleled in the art styles found in it. Those discussed in this brief section are representative of only four of the many distinct periods and areas of the Meso-American realm.

Olmec

The Olmecs were the first to display a number of artistic and social features considered typical of the peoples of Meso-America. For this reason, they are often referred to as the "mother culture" of that region. Although their heartland was principally in the area of La Venta and San Lorenzo (northern Tabasco and southern Veracruz) their influence was felt in many parts of Mexico. La Venta itself was a ceremonial center with earthen platforms and columns of basalt marking out two large courtyards. Facing out from the courtyard were four huge human heads of basalt (FIG. 14-1). The supple modeling of these heads reflects the Olmecs' ability to manipulate extremely hard materials such as basalt and jadeite. An equal achievement was the transportation of these huge pieces of stone, the closest known source of which is separated from La Venta by over sixty miles of swampland.

Although the colossal heads may be the best known examples of Olmec stone sculpture, this culture also produced small-scale stone carvings and relief sculpture. The former frequently depicted a creature combining the features of a human infant with those of a jaguar. So numerous are these figures that it is believed that the creature was a principal figure in the Olmec pantheon. Numerous relief sculptures on Olmec themes are found at the highland site of Chalcacingo, apparently an Olmec ceremonial center. One, a 9 × 10-foot relief (FIG. 14-2), depicts an important personage seated in a stylized niche, while from clouds

14-1 Colossal head, Olmec, La Venta, Mexico, 1500–800 B.C. Basalt, 8′ high and 21′ in circumference. © Courtesy National Geographic Society.

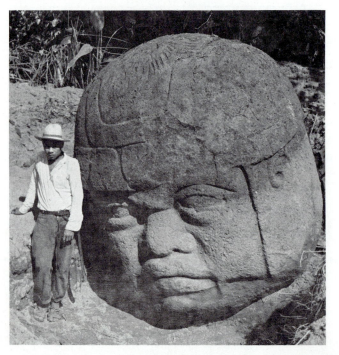

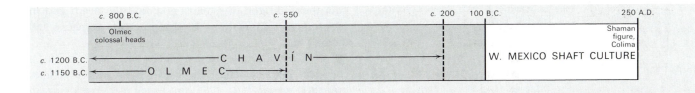

c. 800 B.C.		c. 550		c. 200	100 B.C.		250 A.D.
Olmec colossal heads							Shaman figure, Colima
c. 1200 B.C. ←	———— C H A V Í N ———→				W. MEXICO SHAFT CULTURE		
c. 1150 B.C. ←	——— O L M E C ———						

above, phallic shapes rain downward. The scene appears to refer to agricultural fertility and related rites practiced by local Olmec people.

Although there is growing evidence that the Maya (below) may have had an Olmec origin, the sculpture styles of the two cannot be confused. Mayan stone sculpture was predominantly architecture-related, while the Olmec emphasized free-standing forms modeled in the full round.

West Mexico

The pre-Columbian peoples of West Mexico produced neither massive architecture nor large-scale stone sculpture and in general did not share in the cultural achievements of the central and southern zones of Meso-America. In fact, the West Mexico areas of Jalisco, Nayarit, and Colima have frequently been referred to as cultural backwaters relative to the "high" cultures for which Meso-America is most famous.

Yet West Mexico had a long and rich artistic tradition, principally in the medium of clay sculpture. Effigy figures of humans, animals, and mythological creatures have been encountered in distinctive tombs consisting of shafts (as

much as fifty feet deep) with chambers at their bottom end. Unfortunately, this area was long neglected by archeologists, and our limited knowledge of the tomb contents derives primarily from the operations of grave robbers.

Large, hollow ceramic effigy figures for which the area is noted exhibit—particularly in the swollen torsos and limbs of the figures—a distinct sense of volume. The Colima figures are consistently a highly burnished red-orange, in contrast with the distinctive variegated surfaces of the majority of other west coast ceramics. The area is also famed for small-scale clay scenes that include modeled houses or temples and numerous solid figurines, the latter shown in a variety of lively activities some of which have been interpreted as festivals and battles.

It has frequently been observed that the sculpture from this area exhibits a secular quality seldom encountered in the arts of Meso-America. To some degree this viewpoint may have been a result of our inability to discriminate religious from nonreligious objects. Many figures have been identified, for example, as "warriors" *or* as "shamans." For our figure (FIG. 14-3) the latter seems the correct identification, especially since it is becoming increasingly clear that the arts of this area, with few exceptions, were largely connected with religion and ritual.

14-2 Important personage seated in a stylized niche, Olmec, Chalcacingo, Morelos, Mexico, c. 1100–800 B.C. Relief sculpture, approx. 9′ high. (Drawing by Frances Pratt.)

14-3 "The Drinker," seated shaman figure, Colima, Mexico, c. A.D. 250. Ceramic, 13″ high. Collection of Proctor Stafford, Los Angeles.

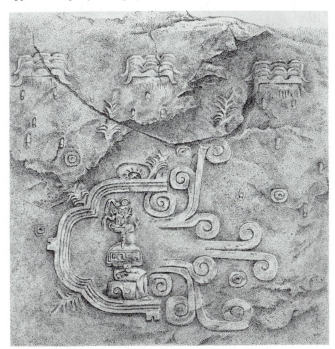

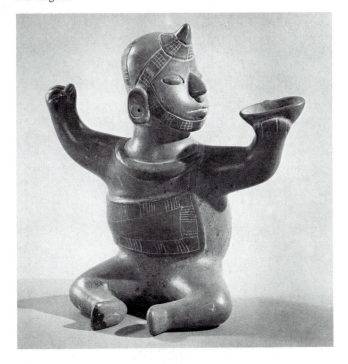

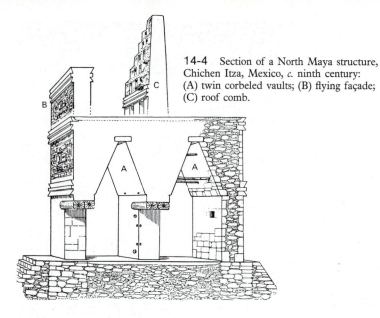

14-4 Section of a North Maya structure, Chichen Itza, Mexico, c. ninth century: (A) twin corbeled vaults; (B) flying façade; (C) roof comb.

Maya

By the early centuries of the Christian era the Maya Indians, who occupied the moist lowlands of what is now Guatemala, British Honduras, and Yucatan, had reached a stage of cultural advancement that presupposes development for many centuries. Like all Meso-American cultures, the Maya possessed only tools of stone, wood, and bone, even during their classic period (c. A.D. 250–600), when they erected huge limestone structures with richly carved decorations at such centers as Copan, Tikal, Uaxactun, Yaxchilan, and Palenque. Metal was not used on a large scale in Meso-America until after about A.D. 800.

Priests, astronomer-priests, and nobles are believed to have constituted a theocratic government that dominated the mass of the people, who were farmers and artisans. Agricultural activities were probably regulated by religious precept, and people traveled far to visit the ceremonial centers for festivals and markets. The intricate Maya calendar expresses the interaction of such gods as the sun god, the wind god, the maize god, and the death god in astrological combinations for purposes of prophesy and divination.

In building durable stone enclosures the Mayans used a corbeled vault structure in which the masonry courses projected inward (FIG. 14-4) until they met, producing an interior space whose upper part was triangular in section. Rooms so constructed were never more than about fifteen feet wide but might be of any length. Temples, constructed in this manner, consisted of one or more long, narrow compartments. In some buildings a pierced roof crest or decorative comb rose above the roof.

A representative temple group (FIG. 14-5) stands at Uaxactun. It was part of a larger assembly of temples and buildings on hilltops, all connected by roadways and covering many square miles. Its base consisted of a series of terraces with stairways leading up to the temple court. The massive temple roofs were surmounted by ornate and towering roof combs. Both roofs and combs were polished and painted so that their surfaces shone brilliantly.

Wealth of ornament is characteristic of Maya sculpture. This is seen in the stelae, commemorative or calendrical stone shafts five to twenty-five feet high, erected in the temple plazas. Many bear dates, often recording the day of the erection of the stone. Such stelae were carved from about the first to the seventh or eighth century A.D., so that a stylistic sequence can be accurately charted. Most are crowded with relief carvings, usually consisting of a figure in ceremonial dress surrounded by hieroglyphs and other motifs in low relief.

The huge boulder at Quirigua (FIG. 14-6), which may have been an altar, is entirely covered with intricate carvings in both high and low relief. The most conspicuous part of the design on the north face is a human figure dressed in rich garments, wearing an enormous, elaborate headdress, and seated in the mouth of a great dragon. Such placing of a human figure in the jaws of a reptile is quite

14-5 Temple group, Maya, Uaxactun, Mexico. Reconstruction drawing by T. Proskouriakoff as of c. A.D. 700. Carnegie Institute, Washington, D.C.

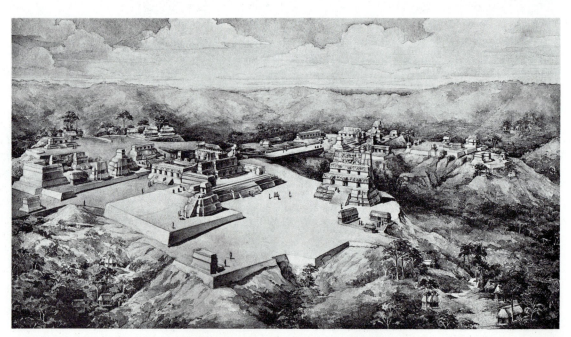

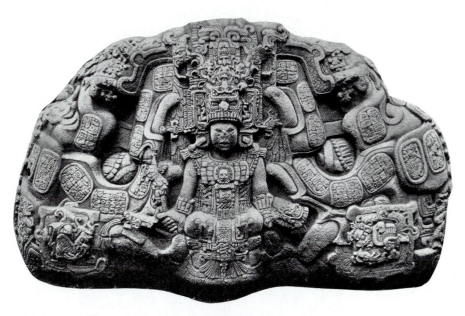

14-6   *Great Dragon*, Maya, Quirigua, Mexico, sixth century A.D. 7'3" high.

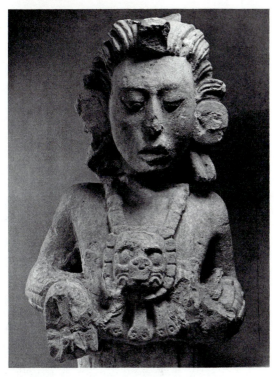

14-7   Maize God, Maya, Copan, Honduras, sixth century A.D. Limestone. American Museum of Natural History, New York.

14-8   Temple mural of warriors surrounding captives on a terraced platform, Maya, Bonampak, Mexico, *c.* sixth century A.D. Watercolor copy by Antonio Tejeda. Carnegie Institute, Washington, D.C.

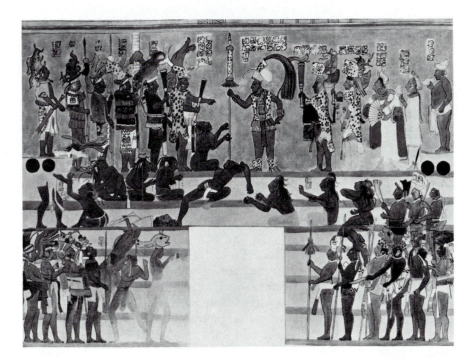

common in Maya art, and in view of the fact that serpent forms often symbolize the sky, perhaps indicates the supernatural or godlike character of the human represented.

Maya stone sculpture in the round, or in high relief, is rare, and it is usually closely associated with architecture, as in the case of the head and torso of the Maize God (FIG. 14-7) from Copan. Sculpture is often found on lintels, jambs, and entire façades.

The work of the Maya painter, like that of the sculptor, was closely coordinated with building and can hardly be considered separately, for most of the reliefs were colored.

Most other painting occurs on the inside of temple walls. The painter outlined his figures in red, filled them in with flat colors, and finally outlined the figures again in black.

In the temple discovered in Bonampak in 1947, narrative murals in scenes of rich color cover the walls of the three chambers. In each chamber, lower, middle, and upper registers correspond respectively to the people, to priests and nobles, and to celestial symbols. The principal scenes deal with preparations for a ritual dance, a raid on a town and capture of prisoners, the sacrifices of prisoners (FIG. 14-8), and the dance.

Teotihuacan

Contemporaneous with the period of early classic Maya art was the civilization called Teotihuacan, from the name of the great city and ritual center just north of Mexico City. The site was the largest city in the pre-contact New World, with a possible population of 100,000 at its height. The builders of its temples were an agricultural people who created a distinctive art style during the first centuries of the Christian era. They worshiped many nature gods and made innumerable clay figurines of humans to place in their fields, perhaps to ensure fertility.

Teotihuacan ("place of the gods") was laid out so that all its temples were in symmetrical groupings flanking a broad avenue. The largest and most imposing was the so-called Pyramid of the Sun. This massive pyramidal substructure, which once supported a temple, consists of five tiers and one broad stairway, alternately single and double, leading from the ground level to the top. A smaller shrine, the Temple of Quetzalcoatl (a major hero of the Meso-American mythos), lay at the center of a great quadrangle marked by terraced mounds. Its sculptured panels, because they were covered by subsequent building, are excellently preserved. The temple (FIG. 14-9) consists of six terraces, each decorated with massive projecting heads of the feathered serpent Quetzalcoatl, which alternate with heads of the goggle-eyed rain god, Tlaloc. Linking these alternating heads are low-relief depictions of feathered serpent bodies and seashells, the latter indicating contact with the coast.

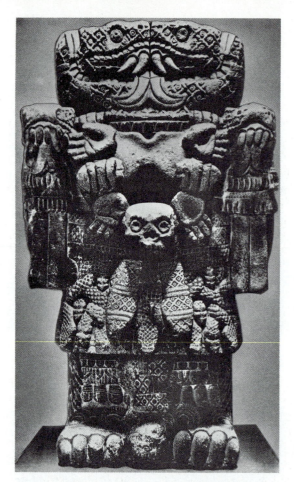

14-10 Coatlicue, goddess of earth and death, Aztec, fifteenth century. Andesite, approx. 8½' high. Museo Nacional de Antropologia, Mexico City.

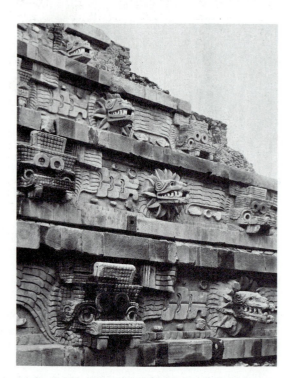

14-9 Detail of Temple of Quetzalcoatl, Teotihuacan, Mexico, third century A.D. (?).

Aztec

The Aztecs, a small and warlike tribe from the north, established their capital, Tenochtitlan (now the site of Mexico City), in the Valley of Mexico about 1325. This was to become the center of an extensive empire. The Aztecs, fierce in their religious as in their military life, practiced human sacrifice, believing that since the sun god had sacrificed himself to create man, man was obliged to repay him with the nourishment of human blood. The ritual required not only a splendid temple setting, but magnificent costumes and accessories, which, like much of Aztec culture, continued customs already established by their predecessors.

Aztec sculpture is famous for its massive, monumental quality, as exemplified in the figure of Coatlicue (FIG. 14-10), earth goddess and mother of the gods. Her identifying features include a skirt composed of intertwining snakes, as well as features symbolic of sacrificial death—a necklace of human hands and hearts, and a skull pendant. The quality of overwhelming monumentality of Aztec sculpture is also present in a variety of realistic large-scale representations of organic forms, including such diverse entities as snakes, rabbits, grasshoppers, squash, and cacti.

CENTRAL ANDES

Of the three zones (jungle, highlands, and coast) that make up the Central Andean region in South America, two—the coast and the highlands—served as homes for highly developed Andean cultures. The coastal zone is a narrow desert plain (transected by fertile valleys) whose dryness resulted in the preservation of organic burial offerings to a degree rarely encountered in the New World. The highland zone lies in the Andean Cordillera, whose massive ranges are occasionally broken by habitable high-altitude valleys. Both zones lie in the area composing modern Peru.

Chavín

There is evidence that in the first millennium B.C. a cult began to grow that at its height prevailed in great portions of the coast and highland areas. The cult is called Chavín after the ceremonial center Chavín de Huantar, which is located in the northern highlands and consists of a number of stone-faced pyramidal platforms penetrated by narrow passageways and small chambers and associated with a sunken court.

Chavín de Huantar is famed too for its stone sculpture. Associated with the architecture and consisting of much sunken relief on panels, lintels, and columns and some rarer instances of sculpture in the round, this sculpture has a linear quality. Free-standing sculpture is represented by an immense cult image in the center of the oldest structure, as well as heads of mythological creatures that were tenoned into the exterior walls. Although at first glance the subject matter of Chavín stone carving appears to exhibit considerable variety, most consistently the emphasis is upon composite creatures that combine feline, avian, reptilian, and human features. The Raimondi stone (named after its discoverer) is representative of the late variant of Chavín stone carving (FIG. 14-11). On the lower third of the stone is a figure called the Staff God (for it is always depicted holding staffs), versions of which have been encountered from Columbia to northern Bolivia, but seldom with the degree of elaboration found at Chavín. In this instance, the squat, scowling deity is depicted with his gaze directed upward. An elaborate headdress dominates the upper two-thirds of the slab. Inverting the image reveals that the headdress is composed of a series of fanged, jawless faces, each emerging from the mouth of the one above it. Snakes abound, extending from the deity's belt, forming part of the staffs, serving as whiskers and hair for the deity himself and the headdress creatures, and, finally, forming a guilloche at the apex of the composition.

The ceramic vessels of the northern Chavín area are easily identified by their massiveness of chamber, spout, and surface relief. The stirrup-spout became popular at this time and continued to be a commonly used north-coast form until the advent of the Spanish.

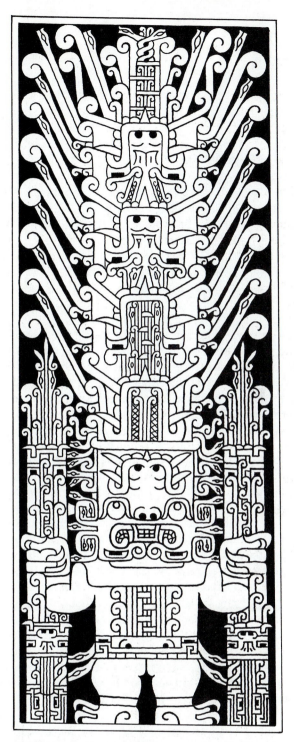

14-11   Drawing of the Raimondi stone, from principal pyramid, Chavín de Huantar, Peru, first millennium B.C. Incised green diorite, 6′ high. Instituto Nacional de Cultura, Lima.

Moche

The great variations occurring within Peruvian art styles is exemplified by two coastal traditions that developed during the period between about 200 B.C. and A.D. 600 in the cultures of the Moche on the south coast.

The Moche concern with ritual is clearly reflected in their ceremonial architecture and ceramic vessels. The

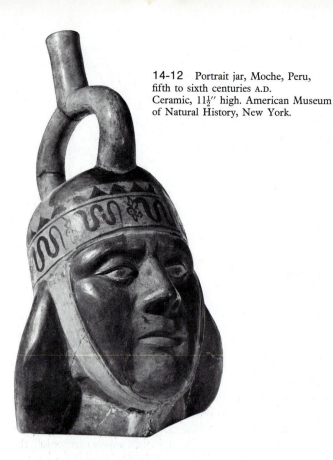

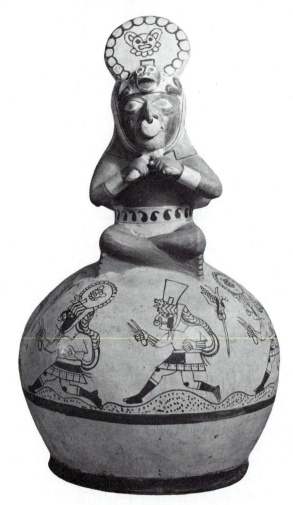

14-12 Portrait jar, Moche, Peru, fifth to sixth centuries A.D. Ceramic, 11½″ high. American Museum of Natural History, New York.

14-13 Messenger and runner figures, Moche, Peru, fifth to sixth centuries A.D. Ceramic, 10⅝″ high. Art Institute of Chicago.

former consisted of immense pyramidal supporting structures for temples that, because of the scarcity of stone, were constructed of sun-dried brick or adobe. Their scale may be surmised from the remains of the so-called Temple of the Sun in the lower Trujillo Valley, which utilized millions of adobes. The temple atop it had already disappeared by the advent of the Spaniards. As a result of persistent treasure-hunting by early colonial residents, only a remnant of the original pyramid remains.

Probably the most famous art objects produced by the ancient Peruvians are the ceramic vessels of the Moche, which were predominantly flat-bottomed, stirrup-spout jars produced without the aid of a potter's wheel and generally decorated with a bichrome slip. (Their abundance can be credited to the ancient Peruvians' practice of seeing that their dead were accompanied in the grave by many offerings.) The Moche potters continued to employ the stirrup-spout, making it an elegant tube much more slender than the Chavín prototype. This may be seen in FIG. 14-12, which shows one of the famous Moche portrait bottles, believed to be either a warrior or a priest. In early bottles of this type, the sculptured form was dominant; in time, however, linear surface decoration came to be employed equally. The Moche pot illustrated in FIG. 14-13 has, on its top, a messenger figure, seated and holding the ties of his headdress. Below him a painted frieze depicts human runners carrying bags. The piece combines realistic modeling with a fine linear style of painting that offers a striking contrast to the bold stylization of the decor on the Nasca vessel shown in FIG. 14-14.

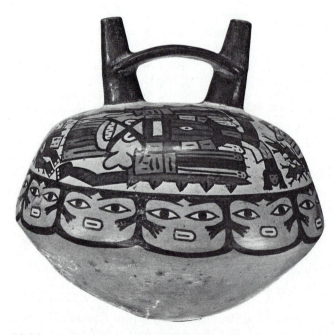

14-14 Bridge-spouted vessel, Nasca, Peru, c. fifth and sixth centuries. A.D. Ceramic with slip, 5½″ high. University of California, Los Angeles, Museum of Cultural History.

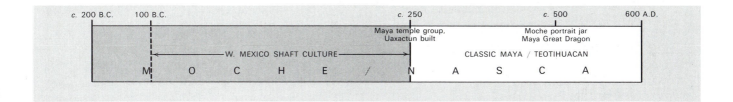

c. 200 B.C. 100 B.C.   c. 250   c. 500   600 A.D.

                                                    Maya temple group,   Moche portrait jar
                                                    Uaxactun built   Maya Great Dragon

                    ←———— W. MEXICO SHAFT CULTURE ————→   CLASSIC MAYA / TEOTIHUACAN

                  M   O   C   H   E   /   N   A   S   C   A

Nasca

Although the Nasca rarely produced large-scale ceremonial architecture as was done in the north, they did create a comparable art form in their ceramic vessels, which, unlike their north-coast counterparts, had round bottoms, double spouts connected with bridges, and—most distinctive—smoothly burnished polychrome surfaces. The subject matter is of great variety, with particular emphasis on plants, animals, and mythological creatures. The initially elegant simplicity of their depiction evolved into a style exhibiting a marked complexity (FIG. 14-14).

Tiahuanaco

The bleak highland country around Lake Titicaca in southeastern Peru contrasts with the warm valleys of the coast. Isolated in these mountains, another culture, named for Tiahuanaco, the principal archeological site on the southern shores of the lake, developed semi-independently of the coastal cultures until A.D. 1000, when the style of its art spread to the adjacent coastal area as well as to the highland areas, extending from southern Peru to northern Chile.

At Tiahuanaco an imposing center was built of massive stones, some of which were joined with copper cramps. The gateway (FIG. 14-15) is monolithic, with a sculptured frieze above the doorway. In the center of the frieze is the image of the Staff God, a deity who was part of the ancient Chavín pantheon. During the Tiahuanaco period the Staff God is frequently associated with smaller-scale attendant figures—in this instance, rows of winged and sometimes bird-headed men. The importance of the Staff God is conveyed not only by the dominance of its scale, but also by its central position and its high relief, which contrasts strongly with the low-relief of the attendant figures.

Best known of the Tiahuanaco-style textiles are polychrome tapestries of extremely fine weave, in which the principal motif is frequently a single figure repeated at regular intervals but with varying details (FIG. 14-16). Specific features consistent in this style include a bifurcated "eye" (generally a rounded octagon with one half black, the other white), N-shaped canine teeth, and blunt-ended, limb-like forms.

14-15 Below: Detail of monolithic gateway shown at right. Tiahuanaco, Bolivia, ninth century (?).

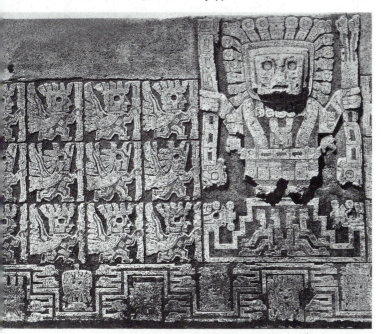

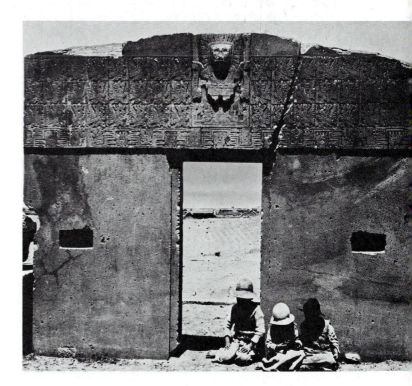

Inca

The Inca, a small tribe in the southern highlands of Peru, embarked about 1438 upon a course of expansion that did not cease until the area from northern Ecuador to central Chile was under their rule.

Although the Inca aimed at imposition of their art style throughout their realm, objects of pure Inca style were confined to areas that came under the power of the southern capital, Cuzco. The Inca were concerned not so much with annihilation of local traditions as with subjugation of them to those of the empire. Thus local styles, although they sometimes came to employ a few Inca features, continued to be produced in areas marginal to the centers of Inca power.

Imperial Inca architecture is famous for its dry-masonry techniques. Though stone (in the walls of temples or administrative buildings) was occasionally laid in regular horizontal courses, a dramatic polygonal pattern was more common. One of the most striking aspects of this mortarless masonry is the extreme precision with which stones were fitted together. A prime example of this precision is the Temple of the Sun (FIG. 14-17) in Cuzco, the remains of which now support the apse of a Dominican church.

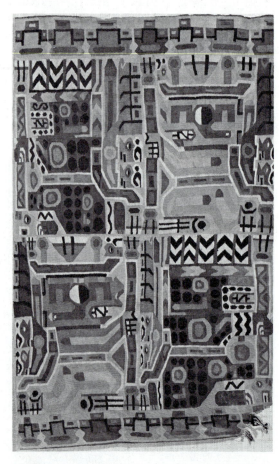

14-16 Textile, Coastal Tiahuanaco style, *c.* A.D. 800. Alpaca, wool, cotton, 21″ long. Metropolitan Museum of Art, New York.

14-17 Temple of the Sun (now church of Santo Domingo), Inca, Cuzco, Peru, fifteenth century.

NORTH AMERICAN INDIAN AND ESKIMO

The styles and objects of the North American cultures are well known for the period beginning with prolonged contact with Europeans. However, there is also quite extensive knowledge of much earlier forms and styles. There have been discovered in many parts of the United States and Canada "prehistoric" cultures that reach back as much as 12,000 years, although most of the finer art objects come from the last 2000 years. "Historic" cultures, designated as such beginning with the earliest date of prolonged contact with Europeans (varying from the sixteenth to the nineteenth century), have been widely and systematically recorded by anthropologists and usually reflect profound changes wrought by the impact of alien tools, materials, and values.

Scholars divide the vast and varied territory involved into a number of areas on the basis of relative homogeneity of language and culture patterns. Both prehistoric and historic art forms from most of these culture areas are discussed briefly below.

Prehistoric Era

Eskimo sculpture, often severely economical in the handling of form, is at the same time refined, even elegant, in the placement and precision of incised designs, both geometric and representational. The carved ivory burial mask (FIG. 14-18) is from the Ipiutak culture of about A.D. 300 and is composed of nine carefully shaped parts that are interrelated so as to produce several faces, both human and animal, in the manner of a visual pun. It is a confident,

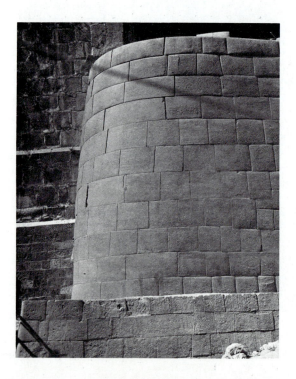

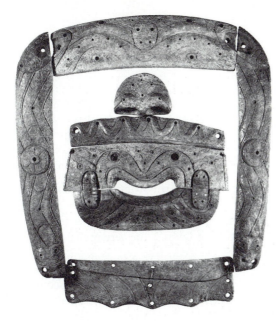

14-18 Set of burial carvings, Ipiutak, *c.* A.D. 300. Ivory, greatest width 9½″. American Museum of Natural History, New York.

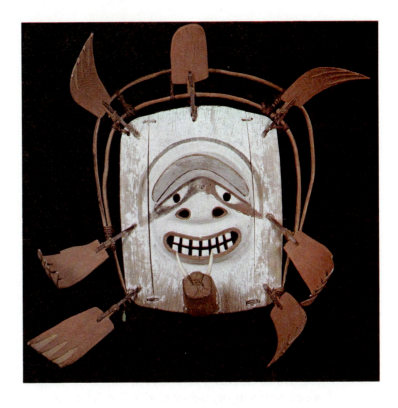

14-19 Eskimo shaman mask representing a sea mammal spirit, before 1900. 17″ high. Lowie Museum, Berkeley, Calif.

subtle composition in shallow relief, a tribute to the artist's imaginative control over the materials. Over the centuries Eskimos have also carved hundreds of small figures and animals, usually in ivory, and highly imaginative "mobile" masks (ones with moving parts), used by shamans (FIG. 14-19), that, because of their fanciful forms and odd juxtapositions of images and materials, were much appreciated by Surrealists in the 1920s.

Early American Indian craftsmen also excelled in working stone into a variety of utilitarian and/or ceremonial objects. The quite realistic handling of the so-called Adena pipe (1000–300 B.C.)—a figural pipe bowl (FIG. 14-20)—provides an interesting contrast to the two-dimensional, more animated composition (FIG. 14-21) found at a Mississippian culture site in Tennessee and dating from the Temple Mound II Period of about A.D. 1200–1500. The

14-20 *Adena Pipe*, Adena, *c.* 1000 B.C. to A.D. 300. Stone, 8″ high. Ohio Historical Society.

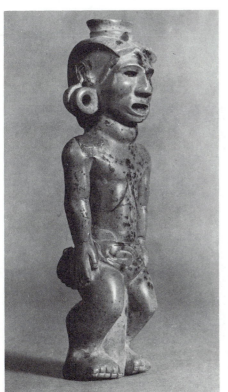

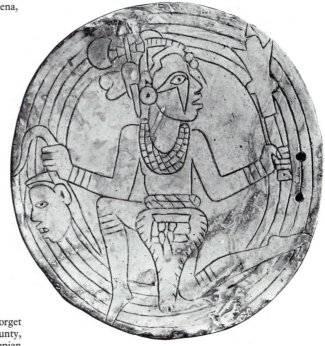

14-21 Incised shell gorget from Sumner County, Tennessee. Mississippian culture, *c.* A.D. 1200–1500. 4″ wide. Museum of the American Indian, New York.

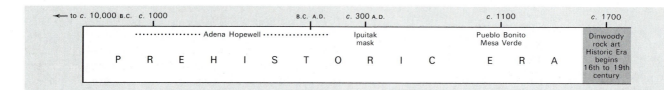

← to c. 10,000 B.C.	c. 1000	B.C. A.D.	c. 300 A.D.	c. 1100	c. 1700
	·········· Adena Hopewell ··············		Ipuitak mask	Pueblo Bonito Mesa Verde	Dinwoody rock art Historic Era begins 16th to 19th century

P R E H I S T O R I C   E R A

incised shell gorget depicts a kneeling personage with elaborate headdress, carrying a mace in his left hand and a severed human head in his right. The standing pipe figure, although simplified, has naturalistic joint articulations and musculature, a lively flexed-leg pose, and an alert facial expression, all combining to suggest movement. Most Adena and Mississippian objects come from burial and temple mounds and are thought to have been gifts to the dead to ensure safe, prosperous arrival in the land of the spirits. Other art objects found in such contexts include fine mica and embossed-copper cut-outs of hands, bodies, snakes, birds, and other presumably symbolic forms.

One of the larger Indian creations—the Serpent Mound (FIG. 14-22) in Adams County, Ohio—is an artistic trans-

formation of the natural environment. Undoubtedly made for spiritual purposes, this monument is a spectacular prehistoric example of the universal practice of creating visually impressive settings for ceremonial activities. The serpent, which has been restored, is about a quarter of a mile long. Other effigy mounds are known, and complex platformed temple mounds have been discovered. The latter, along with small, incised shell reliefs, such as the above-mentioned Mississippian shell (FIG. 14-21), show strong influence from pre-Columbian Meso-America.

Engravings and paintings on rock are found widely distributed across North America. It is supposed that many of these are sacred sites used for communal rituals or the recording of personal spiritual experiences, which were very important in traditional American Indian religions. Rock arts vary from lively naturalistic or schematic renderings of humans and animals to complex convoluted compositions of yet-undeciphered symbols. Both the symbolic complex in black, white, and red (FIG. 14-23) shown in its cave setting near Santa Barbara and the processions of linear, geometric, human (or spirit) figures (FIG. 14-24) picked into rock surfaces near Dinwoody, Wyoming, have overlays suggesting successive visits, probably for ritual purposes. Precise dating of rock art is often impossible, and although the examples shown were probably made prior to white contact, others depict horses and guns and have more naturalistic renderings, indicating a later date of execution.

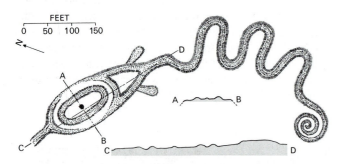
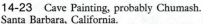

14-22 *Serpent Mound.* Approx. 1400' long. Adams County, Ohio.

14-23 Cave Painting, probably Chumash. Santa Barbara, California.

14-24 Human figures engraved on a sandstone cliff, attributed to prehistoric Shoshone. Size of panel, 18' × 8'2″. Dinwoody, Wyoming.

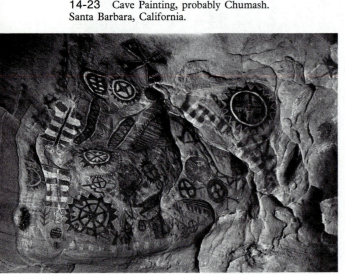

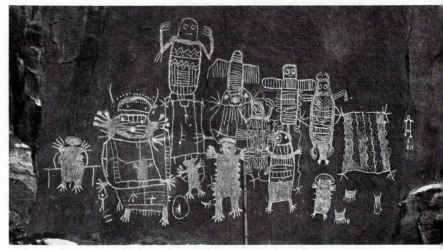

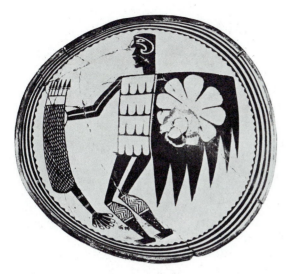

14-25 Bowl, Mimbres, thirteenth century. Ceramic, 9″ in diameter. Peabody Museum, Harvard University.

The thirteenth-century bowl illustrated here (FIG. 14-25) has an animated, graphic rendering of a warrior with a shield in a composition that creates a dynamic tension between the black figuring and the white ground. Thousands of different compositions are known from Mimbres, from lively and often complex geometric patterns to fanciful, often whimsical pictures of humans and animals; almost all are imaginative creations of artists who seem to have been bent on not repeating themselves. Designs are created by linear rhythms balanced and controlled within the clearly defined border. Because the potter's wheel was unknown in the Southwest, the countless sophisticated shapes of varied size—always characterized by technical excellence—were built by the coiling method.

In the later centuries of the prehistoric era, Indians of the Southwest constructed many architectural complexes that reflect masterful building skills and impressive talents of spatial organization. Of the many ruins of such complexes, Pueblo Bonito and the "Cliff Palace" at Mesa Verde are among the best known. The Cliff Palace (FIG. 14-26) occupies a sheltered ledge above a valley floor and has about two hundred rectangular rooms—mostly communal dwellings—in several stories of carefully laid stone or adobe and timber. Twenty larger circular underground structures, called *kivas*, were the spiritual and ceremonial centers of Pueblo life. Pueblo Bonito (FIG. 14-27) contains similar rooms but contrasts with Mesa Verde in its siting in the open and, especially, in its superbly unified plan. The whole complex is enclosed by a wall in the shape of a giant

Most Indian art forms—rock painting, pottery, architecture—span great periods. Detailed chronological sequences of pottery styles are, in fact, the historian's major tool in dating and reconstructing the cultures of the distant past, especially in the Southwest, since there were no written records. There are many fine specimens of Southwest ceramics dating from before the Christian era until the present day, but after about A.D. 1000 pottery becomes especially fine, and its decoration most impressive.

14-26 Cliff Palace, *c.* A.D. 1100. Mesa Verde National Park, Colorado.

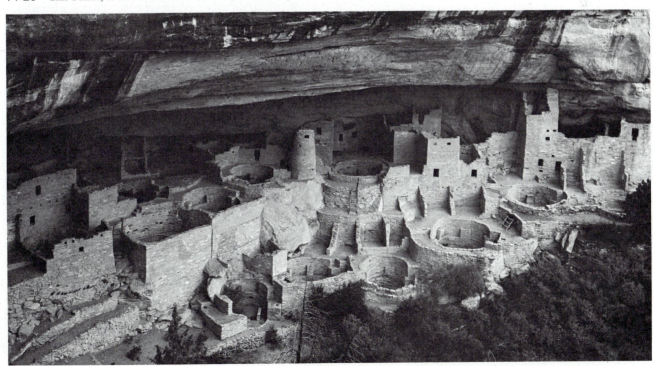

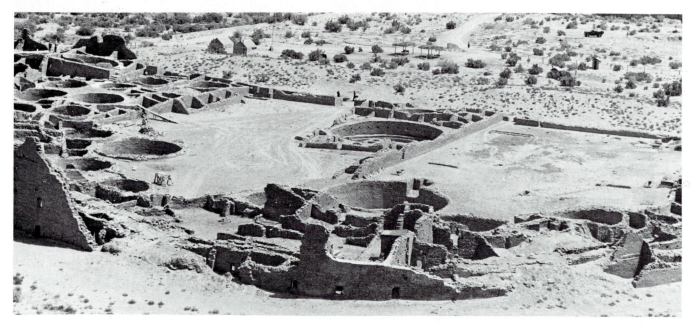

14-27 Pueblo Bonito, *c.* A.D. 1100. New Mexico.

"D." The careful planning suggests it was designed by a single architect or master builder and constructed by hundreds of workers under a firm directing hand. Modern terraced pueblos, like Taos in New Mexico, though impressive, reflect neither such unified design nor such a massive, well-organized building effort.

Between 1200 and 1400 A.D., long before Europeans arrived in the New World, the ancestors of the present-day Hopi and Zuñi people decorated their kivas with elaborate mural paintings representing deities associated with agricultural fertility. The detail of the Kuaua mural shown in FIG. 14-28 depicts a "lightning man" on the left side, and fish and eagle images (associated with rain) and the partial figure of a "blue corn maiden" on the right side. All of these are associated with the fertility of the earth and the life-giving properties of the seasonal rains.

Historic Era

SOUTHWEST

Obviously the motivations, functions, and means of art forms from the historic period are better known than those of forms (surveyed above) from earlier eras. Thus, the complex prehistoric religious murals from the Southwest are hard to interpret, while Navajo sand painting, an art that still survives, is susceptible of detailed elucidation. These paintings, highly transient, are constructed by artist-priests to the accompaniment of prayers and chants as an essential part of ceremonies for curing disease. (In the healing ceremony the patient sits in the center of the painting so as to absorb the healing, life-giving powers of the gods and their representations.) Similar rites are used

14-28 Detail of an Anasazi kiva painting from Kuaua Pueblo (Coronado State Monument), New Mexico, *c.* A.D. 1300–1500. Museum of New Mexico, Santa Fe.

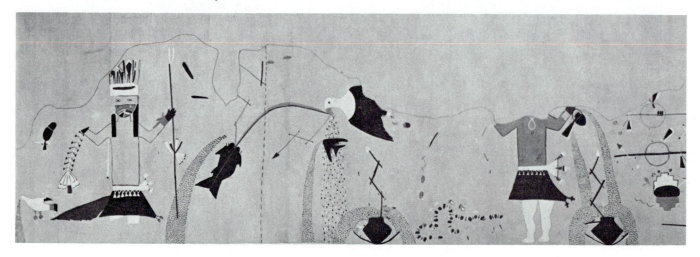

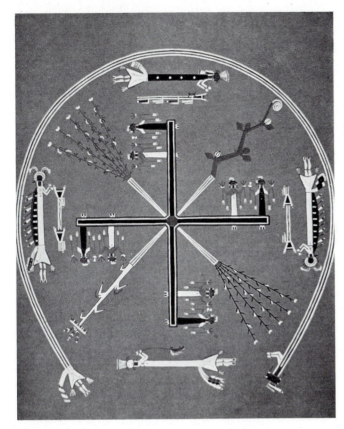

14-29 Yei-bet-chai ceremony dry painting, Navajo, 1952.

14-30 Kachina spirit mask, Hopi people, late 1890s,
22″ high. Museum of the American Indian, New York.

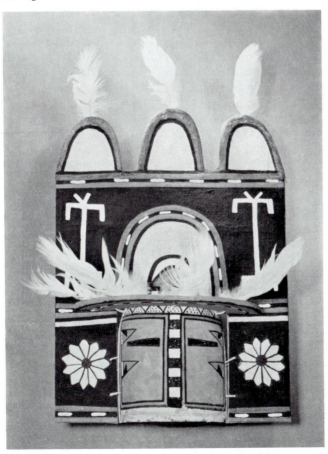

to assure success in hunting and to promote fertility in man and nature alike. The natural materials used—corn pollen, charcoal, varicolored powdered stones—have a symbolic role reflecting the Southwestern Indians' preoccupation with the spirits and forces of nature. The paintings, which depict the gods and mythological heroes whose help is sought, are destroyed in the process of the ritual, so no models exist; still, the traditional prototypes, passed on from artist to artist, must be adhered to as closely as possible, since mistakes can render the ceremony ineffective. Navajo dry-painting style is rigid, composed of simple curves, straight lines, and serial repetition, despite the potential freedom of free-hand drawing (FIG. 14-29). Navajo weaving and silver jewelry-making are later developments and, until very recently, have been made to high technical and artistic standards.

Another art form from the Southwest, the Kachina mask (FIG. 14-30) contrasts markedly with masks from the Northwest Coast (FIG. 14-31) and the Eastern Woodlands (FIG. 14-39). The Hopi spirit mask shown here, that of a rain-bringing deity, is painted in geometrical patterns based on rainbow, cloud, and flower forms—quite different from the more expressionistic handling of human physiognomy in the masks of Northwest Coast and Eastern Woodlands peoples.

NORTHWEST COAST

Working in a highly formalized, subtle style, the Indians of the Northwest Coast have produced a wide variety of art objects—totem poles, masks, rattles, chests, bowls, clothing, charms, and decorated houses and canoes. Masks were carved for use by shamans in their healing rites and by

14-31 Mask, Kwakiutl, c. 1890. Approx. 13¼″ high.
Denver Art Museum.

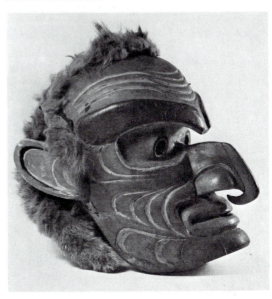

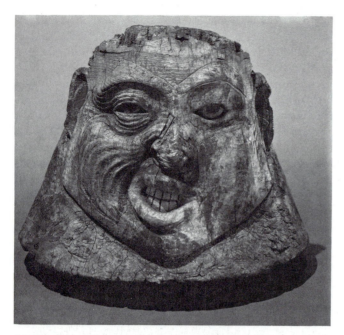

14-32 Helmet, Tlingit. Wood, 12″ high. American Museum of Natural History, New York.

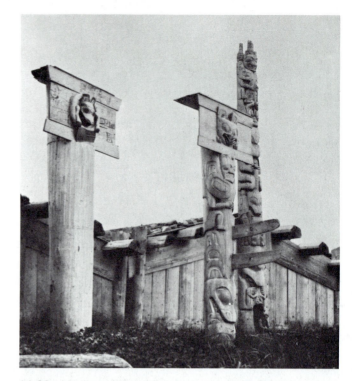

14-33 Haida mortuary poles and house frontal poles at Skedans Village, British Columbia, 1878. After a photograph by George M. Dawson, National Archives, Canada.

others in public reenactments of "spirit quests." The animals and mythological creatures encountered on such quests were in turn represented in masks and a host of other carvings. The mask shown in FIG. 14-31, from the Kwakiutl people, owes its dramatic character to the exaggeration of facial parts and to the deeply undercut curvilinear depressions, which give strong shadows. It is a refined yet forceful carving typical of the more expressionistic styles of the area. Others are more subdued, and some, like the Tlingit headdress shown in FIG. 14-32, are

exceedingly naturalistic, probably actual portraits, almost as if the artist were proving that he could represent whatever he chose to. Inherited motifs and styles were usually preferred, however, above radical new departures. Although Northwest Coast arts have a spiritual dimension, they are more important as expressions of social status, in that the art form one uses and, indeed, the things one may depict, are functions of that status. Haida mortuary poles and house frontal poles (FIG. 14-33), used where totemic crest emblems of clan groups are displayed before the clan

14-34 Blanket with bear design, Chilkat. Wild goat's wool and cedar bark in bright colors. American Museum of Natural History, New York.

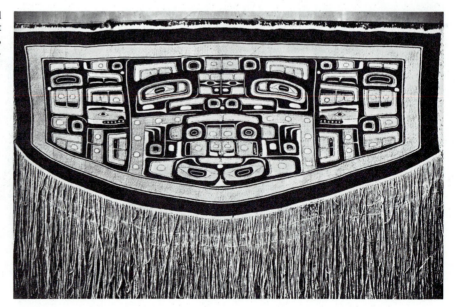

chief's house, are striking expressions of this interest in social status.

Another characteristic Northwest Coast art form is the Chilkat blanket (FIG. 14-34), the designs for which were provided by male artists in the form of pattern boards from which the female weaver worked. These blankets, which became widespread prestige items of ceremonial dress during the nineteenth century, display several recurrent characteristics of Northwest Coast style: symmetry and rhythmic repetition, schematic abstraction of animal motifs (in the blanket illustrated, a bear), eye designs, a regularly swelling and thinning line, and a tendency to round off corners.

Elegant, precise, and highly accomplished technically, the art of the Northwest Coast is held by many to be one of the sophisticated high points of North American Indian artistic accomplishment.

Indians of the Great Plains worked in materials and styles quite different from those of the Northwest Coast. Much artistic energy went into decoration of leather garments, first with compactly sewn quill designs and later with beadwork patterns. Tipis, tipi linings, and buffalo-skin robes were painted with geometric and stiff figural designs prior to about 1830; after that there was a more or less gradual introduction of naturalistic scenes, often of war exploits, in styles adapted from those of visiting white artists. The tipi lining illustrated (FIG. 14-35) is of that later style, when realistic action and proportions, careful detailing, and a variety of colors were employed. An example of the earlier type of Plains art is a finely quilled buckskin shirt (FIG. 14-36), which belonged to the Dakota chief Spotted Tail. With attached hair locks and six red and

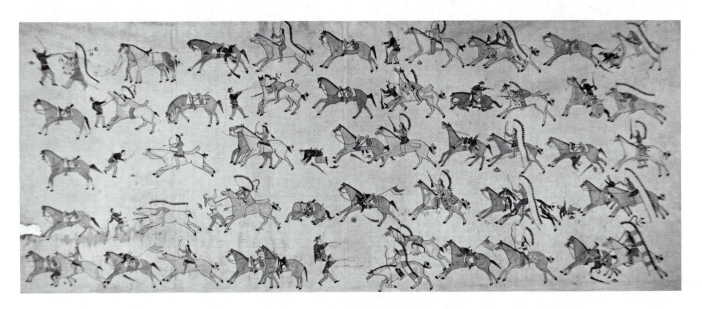

14-35 Tipi lining with pictograph of war scenes, Crow, late nineteenth century. Painted muslin, 85″ × 35″. Smithsonian Institution, Washington, D.C.

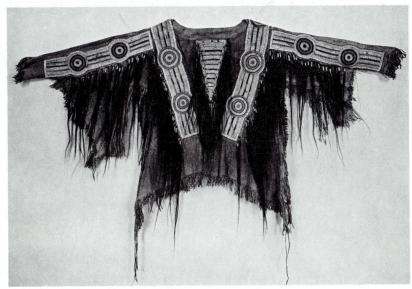

14-36 Shirt, Brulé, early nineteenth century. Buckskin with quillwork, beads, and hair locks, 58″ arm spread. Museum of the American Indian, Heye Foundation, New York.

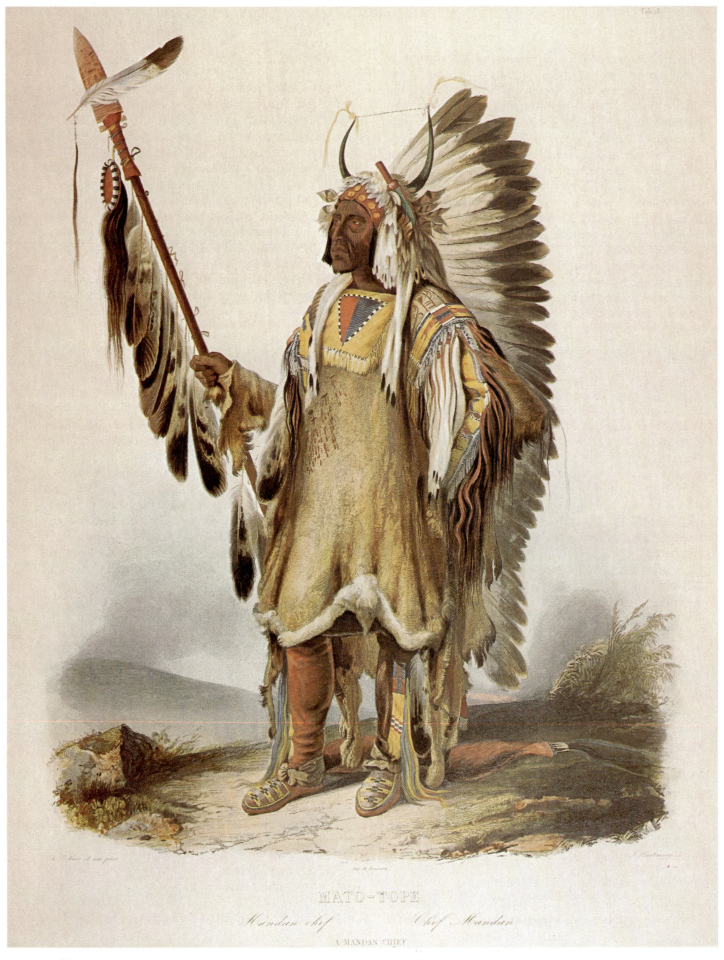

MATÓ-TOPE

Mandan chief   *Chef Mandan*

A MANDAN CHIEF

14-37   KARL BODMER, *Mandan Chief Mato-Tope*, 1840. Lithograph, 10″ × 14″. Thomas Gilcrease, Institute of American History and Art, Tulsa.

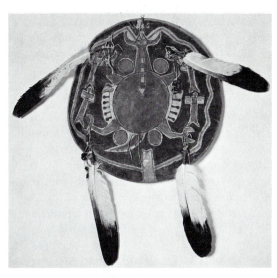

14-38 Shield, Mandan, North Dakota. Buffalo hide, deerskin, black and green paint, feathers, and bells. Museum of the American Indian, Heye Foundation, New York.

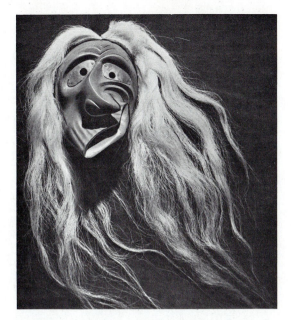

14-39 ELON WEBSTER, False Face mask, Iroquois, 1937. Wood. (The artist was an Onandaga of Tonawanda Reservation.) Courtesy of Cranbrook Institute of Science, Bloomfield Hills, Michigan.

yellow bull's eye patterns connected by parallel lines, such a garment, especially in motion, would have a dramatic impact.

Since, at least in later periods, most Plains peoples were nomadic, their esthetic attention was focused largely on their clothing and bodies and on other portable objects such as shields, clubs, pipes, tomahawks, and various containers. Transient but important Plains art forms can sometimes be found in the paintings and drawings of visiting white artists. The Swiss Karl Bodmer, for example, accurately portrayed the personal decoration (FIG. 14-37) of Chief Four Bears, a Mandan warrior and chief. His body paintings and feather decorations, all symbolic of his affiliations and military accomplishments, may be said to be his biography—a composite artistic statement in several media—which could be easily "read" by other Indians. Plains men also made shields and shield covers that were at once art works and "power images." Shield paintings often derive from religious visions; their symbolism, the pigments themselves, and added materials—such as feathers—provided their owners with magical protection and supernatural power. The Mandan example illustrated in FIG. 14-38 has a central, schematic view of a turtle whose legs, head, and tail radiate outward. This and two smaller motifs are encircled by an undulating line that repeats but varies the round format. The drawing is rough but vigorous.

EASTERN WOODLANDS

Artists of the Eastern Woodlands made quilled and beaded objects and items of clothing often decorated with curvi-

linear floral motifs. Iroquois peoples also carved compelling, expressionistic masks for use by the False Face Society, whose ceremonies healed physical and psychological sickness and cleansed whole communities of destructive impurities (FIG. 14-39). The spirit "faces" portray legendary supernaturals whose exploits are recounted in mythology. Bold in conception, these masks rely on a dramatizing distortion and exaggeration of facial features for their strong effects. Like others used in Africa and Oceania, these masks must be hidden when not in use lest their power inadvertently cause injury.

Whether secular and merely decorative or spiritual and highly symbolic, the diverse styles and forms of North American Indian art testify to the ancient and continuing artistic sensibility of the native Americans. Their creative use of local materials and pigments constitutes an artistic reshaping of nature that in many cases reflects the Indians' reliance on and reverence toward the environment that they considered it their privilege to inhabit.

AFRICA

The huge continent of Africa has a population of millions that is subdivided into several racial and linguistic groups. Though nearly all African peoples have produced artists—dancers, musicians, storytellers, rock painters, architects, and adepts at personal decoration—only those peoples dwelling in the vast areas drained by the great Niger and Congo rivers—essentially, tropical Africa—produced

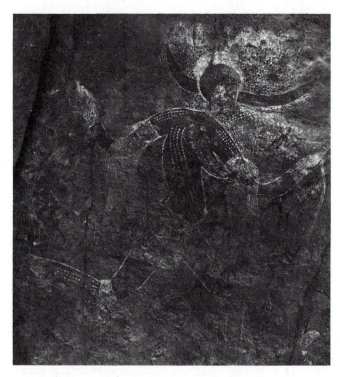

14-40 Rock painting, Inaouanrhat, *c.* 3000 B.C. Tassili region, Algeria.

the great numbers of sculptures, primarily in wood, that have become deservedly famous as "African art." It is this area that will be surveyed below.

Africa is as widely varied artistically as it is sociopolitically, geographically, ecologically, linguistically, and racially. Divine rulers head great kingdoms, and groups of elders govern small tribal groups; forest regions along the coast give way inland to grassy savannas and highlands and in turn to semi-arid lands south of the Sahara.

Like North America, Africa has hundreds of Neolithic rock painting sites that contain the earliest examples of its art. These paintings and engravings, considerably more recent than the Paleolithic works found in Spain and Southern France, are equally accomplished renderings of humans, animals, and a host of nonrepresentational patterns thought to be symbolic. One very sensitively executed human figure (FIG. 14-40) is a "dancing" woman from Inaouanrhat in the Tassili region. She is actively posed and has varied types of body decoration done in several colors and with delicate precision.

The dancing figure dates from roughly 3000 B.C., but here, as with many rock paintings, dating is somewhat speculative. From a number of archeological sites collectively labeled Nok, however, we have more precise radiocarbon dating (*c.* 500 B.C.–A.D. 200). Here is found the earliest African evidence of sculpture in the round. Because they are so confidently handled, Nok terra-cotta heads and figures of humans (FIG. 14-41) and animals

suggest wooden or other clay prototypes, now lost. No "formative" prototypes are known. Volumes are full and surfaces smoothly modeled in these terra-cotta sculptures, which some authorities believe to be direct ancestors of Ife terra-cottas and bronzes found 150 miles southwest of the Nok area and dated from A.D. 1000 to 1200.

By about the ninth century A.D., at Igbo Ukwu in tropical Africa, sophisticated lost-wax casting techniques had evolved, and, by the twelfth century, the most naturalistic style known for any tropical African era had appeared. Woodcarvings were certainly made in the latter period too, but no examples have survived. The bronze figure illustrated here (FIG. 14-42) is undoubtedly an ancient divine king of Ife, the city in western Nigeria that is still the spiritual capital of the numerous Yoruba peoples. The king figure, unlike most African wood sculpture, shows realistic, fleshlike modeling that attempts a realistic rendering of the human form. The idealized naturalism of the flesh and head in this figure approaches portraiture, although its proportions, which exaggerate the head, are not lifelike. The casting is fine, although somewhat weathered, and accurately records precise details of costume and jewelry worn by ancient Ife kings.

There are numerous historical and ritual ties between the divine kings of Ife and those who presided over the kingdom of Benin, ascendant from the fifteenth to the eighteenth century. Many finely cast, complex bronzes, as well as ivory, wood, terra-cotta, and wrought-iron sculptures, are known from Benin, where bronze casting and ivory carving were royal prerogatives carried out by guilds of highly trained professionals. Most are rendered in a

14-41 Head, Nok, fifth century B.C. to second century A.D. Terracotta, 9″ high. Jos Museum, Nigeria.

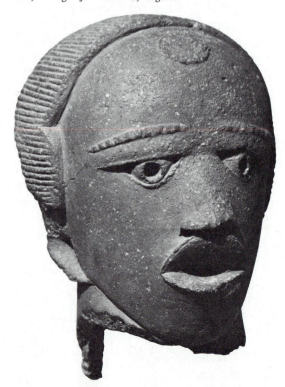

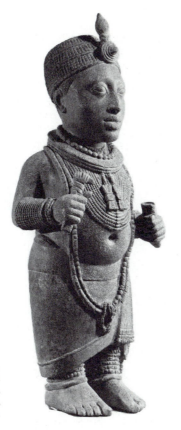

14-42 Ife king figure, Yoruba, tenth to twelfth centuries A.D. Bronze, 18½″ high. Ife Museum, Nigeria.

distinctive style of simplified, somewhat rigid naturalism, far more conventionalized than Ife works. Much Benin art, like the gilded objects of the Ashanti further west and the altarpiece illustrated (FIG. 14-43), glorifies the office and trappings of the divine king, who is central and most prominent in this casting, as in many others. As in the Ife figure (FIG. 14-42), the head is greatly exaggerated, reflecting the view that it is the center of being and the source of power and intelligence. Taken together with the hieratic arrangement of the group, this distortion clearly affirms the importance of symbolism to the artist.

The Ijo Iphri sculpture (FIG. 14-44) manifests the symbolism of power in a less centralized culture than that of Benin. The owner himself is seen sitting atop a monstrous animal (symbolic of his own aggressiveness) and holding a fan and libation vessel. This Ijo piece seems more expressionistic in form and freer in invention than the more court-regulated style at Benin (FIG. 14-43).

In understanding the range and quality of African art, customary definitions must be broadened to include more than monuments, more than objects that can be displayed in museums. This is especially true of the art of masquerade, which depends on music, dance, and costuming for its real vitality. Although many of the wooden masks used in such performances are dramatic carvings in their own

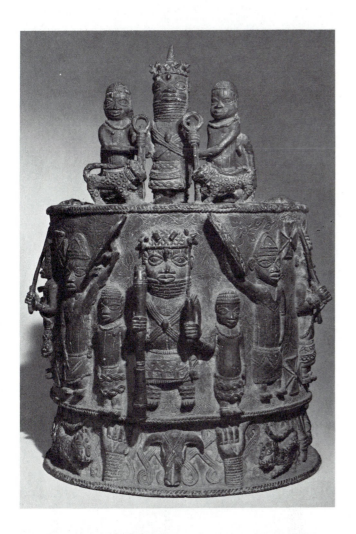

14-43 Altar of the Hand, Benin, Nigeria. Bronze, 17½″ high. British Museum, London.

14-44 Iphri figure, Ijo people, Nigeria, twentieth century. Wood, 25½″ high. Metropolitan Museum of Art, New York (Michael C. Rockefeller Memorial Collection of Primitive Art, gift of the Matthew T. Mellon Foundation).

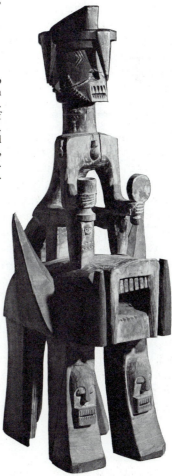

right, they should be seen as single important elements in a complex of interacting artistic media that occupy time as well as space.

The Yoruba *Gelede* masquerader (FIG. 14-47), photographed in full costume and caught in motion, is a case in point. Gelede is a cult devoted to the propitiation and entertainment of powerful senior women and deities associated with witchcraft in Yoruba communities. The masqueraders perform in pairs, their rich appliqué-panel costumes activated by vigorous dance movements. Theater and ritual combine in the dance, and the masked characters present a bewildering array of traditional and modern types: a motorcyclist, cloth-seller, hunter, leopard, king, white man, prostitute, policeman. Performances involve much social criticism of the community at large expressed in song and gesture as well as dance, and in the masks themselves.

The Yoruba, Africa's most prolific artists, have created an abundance of art forms other than masks: cult figures in wood, bronze, terra-cotta, and iron, beaded objects and garments, as well as palace houseposts and doors designed to enhance the dignity and prestige of leaders. One such door (FIG. 14-45), which stood at the king's palace at Ikerre, was carved by the master sculptor AREOGUN of Osi. It records the historic visit of an early British colonial as

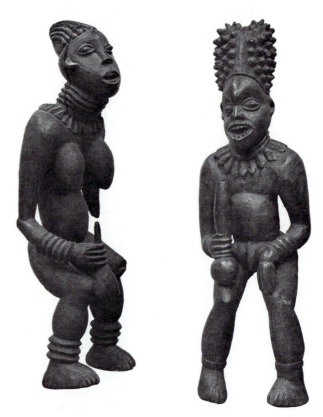

14-46 Dancing royal couple, Bangwa, nineteenth century. Wood, female 33½″ high, male 35½″ high. Collection of Mr. and Mrs. Harry A. Franklin, on loan to the Los Angeles County Museum of Art.

14-45 AREOGUN, door from palace at Ikerre, Yoruba. Wood, approx. 6′ high. Trustees of the British Museum, London.

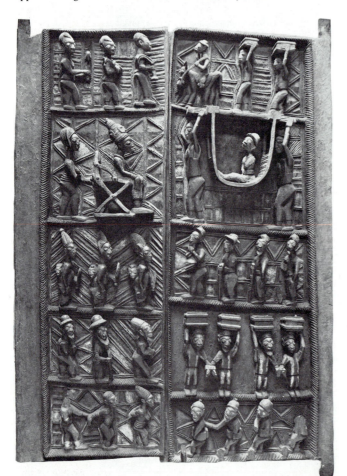

well as genre scenes and anecdotes of Yoruba life. Like many African artists, Areogun had a clearly recognizable personal style—figures are elongated and rather expressionistic—and many other artists were locally famous, although individuality and personal, idiosyncratic style are of less concern here than, for example, in the modern West.

As the prevalence of the multimedia art of masquerade suggests, dance may be the artistic medium most important and expressive to native Africans. Many sculptures are used in dance contexts, and many others depict people dancing. The vital, energetic figures (FIG. 14-46) from the Bangwa kingdom of the Cameroon Grasslands express the vigor of dance in several complementary ways: by active, asymmetrical posing, a thrust-back head with open mouth, constrictions at the joints, which rhythmically energize the figure, and by the use of rough textures—surfaces faceted with tool marks. The female figure is believed to portray a priestess and finder of witches. Both stood among dozens of royal carvings depicting ancestors, chiefs, and priests—those, whether living or dead, who were responsible for the continuity of life itself. Such figures were gathered for rituals, given food and drink, and at the same time served to display the wealth, power, and taste of the ruler who presided over them. The importance of artistic

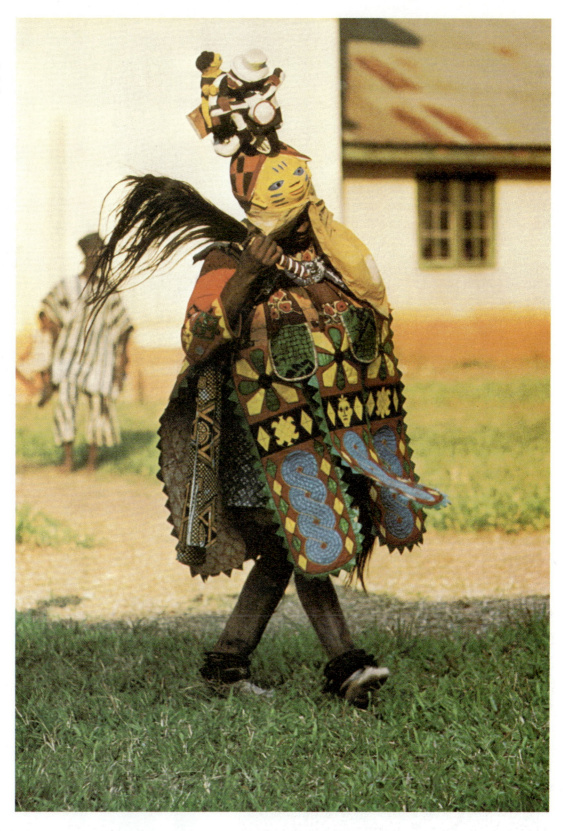

14-47 Dancer of the gelede society of Meko, Yoruba, 1969.

display to Cameroon leaders made them major patrons of the arts and critics as well.

Ibo *mbari* houses, like the Yoruba door discussed above, are complex works of art. Groupings of clay sculptures (often with more than a hundred pieces in one mbari) and paintings in a specially designed architectural setting, these elaborate, unified complexes are built to honor principal community deities, often the goddess of the earth. In the illustration (FIG. 14-48) the goddess is seated with dignity in the center of the front side, her children close by, her servants, in high relief, standing guard behind. The sculptor has enlarged and extended her torso, neck, and head to

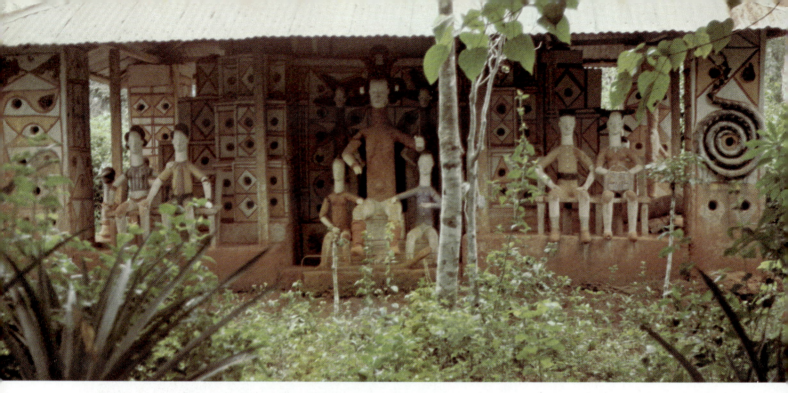

14-48 Mbari house at Ndiama Obube, Ibo, Nigeria.

express her aloofness and power. She is the apex of a formalized, hieratic composition balanced on either side by seated couples. More informally posed figures and groups are found on the other sides of the house—beautiful, amusing, or frightening figures of animals, humans, and gods taken from history, mythology, and everyday life. The complex, secret mbari construction rituals, as well as the sculptural program, suggest that each house is in fact a cosmic symbol and the building process itself a stylized world-renewal ritual. Ceremonies of opening the house to public view indicate that the god has accepted the offering (of the house) and for a time, at least, will be benevolent. The mbari is never repaired; instead it is allowed to disintegrate and return to the earth from which it is made and to which it often is dedicated. The mbari, then, is a relatively transient art form, as are the arts of masquerade, personal ornamentation, and festivals. (The last three are best seen on film, which preserves the movement inherent in their design.)

Ancestral or power images from Zaire (formerly the Belgian Congo), such as the two shown in FIGS. 14-49 and 14-50, are more conventional sculptural forms that were often carefully preserved by their owners for generations. The commemorative ancestral mother-and-child carving from the Kongo peoples has a smooth, refined delicacy,

while the composite power figure from the Songye, a people living several hundred miles east, deals with the human form more abstractly, in abrupt and forceful carving. The functions of the two are comparable, both being visible manifestations of ancestral power, which can so materially affect men's lives. The Kongo piece, probably a

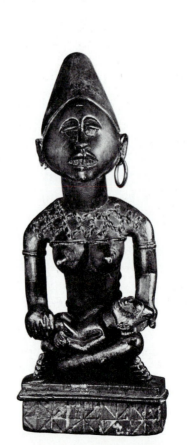

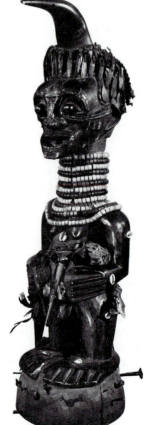

14-49 Ancestral figure, Kongo people. Wood and brass, 16″ high. Musée Royal de l'Afrique Centrale, Tervuren, Belgium.

14-50 Power figure, Songye people, Congo. Wood, iron, copper, horn, fibers, cowrie shells, feathers, and glass beads, 35″ high. Musée Royal de l'Afrique Centrale, Tervuren, Belgium.

symbolic repository of the soul of a deceased noblewoman, received prayers invoking her continuing care and beneficence, while the Songye figure directed (for the benefit of the community) specific ancestral powers that were activated by (and to some extent contained in) various "medicines" placed inside and on the figure. Of the purposes of such power figures, protection in warfare, promotion of human and crop fertility, curing disease, and ending drought were among the most common.

The dramatic contrast between the style of the Songye image and that of the Kongo mother and child suggests the wide range and variety of carving conventions present in Africa. Indeed, tendencies toward realism or toward abstraction are not easily charted on the African map; deviations sometimes occur between neighboring tribes, within a tribe, and occasionally in the work of a single artist. This latter is the case among the Dan and related peoples of Liberia, Sierra Leone, and the Ivory Coast. Like many African peoples the Dan have evolved a great variety of masks representing judges, policemen, priests, and a host of other people, both harmful and helpful. In many cases the role conferred by the mask was functionally real. A person wearing a judge or executioner mask, for example, actually judged cases or executed criminals. Members of the men's masking society, armed with the spirit power of the bush spirits and clothed in anonymous masking costumes, regulated the behavior of the community. The society also held masked entertainments, impersonating secular personages whose behavior was held up for public scrutiny, or performing spectacular acrobatic and stilt dances.

Dan woodcarvers, required to make representations of these varied spiritual and secular types, became skilled in several contrasting styles. The same man could carve a refined, polished mask depicting a beautiful woman, such as that shown in FIG. 14-51, and a rougher, highly abstracted mask called *Kagle* (FIG. 14-52). In fashioning the female mask the carver has simplified facial planes and brought their smooth surfaces to a high polish, while retaining naturalistic shapes and the placement of features. The carver of *Kagle*, on the other hand, simplifies and abstracts, creating a series of forceful thrusting and receding positive and negative shapes with great dramatic impact.

The royal Kuba sculptors of the central Congo (Zaire) created an entirely different type of mask to represent a primordial ancestor who helps to oversee the ritual passage of boys into adulthood. (Many other African peoples have masks used in analogous ceremonies.) Several of these, like the Mboom mask illustrated here (FIG. 14-53), employ a rich combination of beads, feathers, copper, fur, and raffia—all attached to a carved wooden helmet. Thus a strong basic head shape with a bulging forehead is overlaid with visually complex textural effects that are Kuba symbols of royalty.

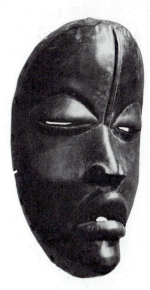

14-51 Mask, Dan people, Sierra Leone. Wood, 8½″ high. Metropolitan Museum of Art, New York.

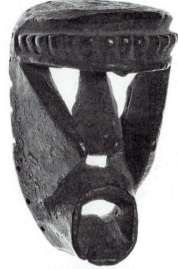

14-52 *Kagle* (mask), Dan people. Wood, 9″ high. Yale University Art Gallery, gift of Mr. and Mrs. James M. Osborn for the Linton Collection of African Art.

14-53 Mboom helmet mask, Kuba, Central Congo (Zaire). Wood, brass, cowrie shells, beads, seeds, 13″ high. Musée Royal de l'Afrique Centrale, Tervuren, Belgium.

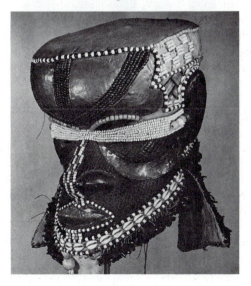

The seated male and female sculpture shown in FIG. 14-54 is an example of another well-known African style, that of the Dogon people of Mali. Depicting mythical ancestors of the human race, this group is a masterfully integrated composition of vertical forms enclosed by tubular shapes, with geometric incised decorations on the surfaces of both. Rejecting naturalistic rendering in this

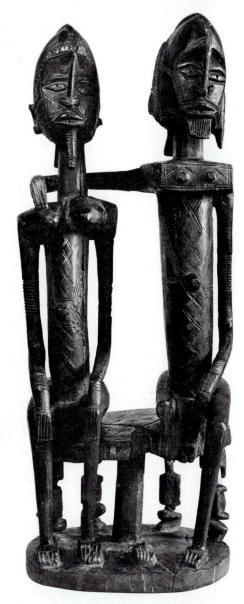

14-54 Couple, Dogon people, Mali. Wood, 30″ high. Photograph Copyright 1975 by The Barnes Foundation.

ures that represent wild bush spirits (*asie usu*) (FIG. 14-55). The main distinction is found in the surface. The *asie usu* have a "sacrificial patina"—a surface thickly encrusted with matter accumulated when they are "fed" during sacrificial ritual; the spirit marriage partners, on the other hand, are rubbed and polished, so that, in time, they acquire a smooth and shiny surface.

African arts also include beautifully decorated utilitarian objects such as stools, chairs, pipes, spoons; a host of sculptural as well as decorated buildings; body painting and scarification; miniature objects such as the well-known Ashanti gold weights; finely crafted textiles and leatherwork and countless forms of pottery and basketry. Subdivision of the arts into "fine," "decorative," and "crafts" is in fact a barrier to the understanding of African artistic sensibilities; for African arts often play a role in everyday affairs, as well as in the life-crisis rituals such as initiations, funerals, and the countless other events that punctuate human existence.

14-55 Wild bush spirit, Baule people, Ivory Coast. Wood, male figure approx. 22″ high. Metropolitan Museum of Art, New York (Michael C. Rockefeller Memorial Collection of Primitive Art, gift of Nelson A. Rockefeller, 1969).

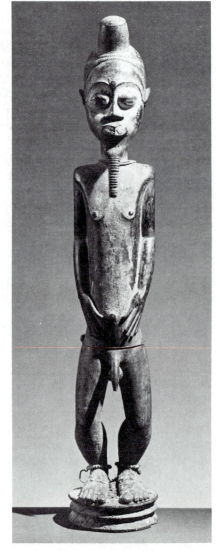

instance (though he was capable of it) the Dogon sculptor seems here to have dismantled the human body, straightening, simplifying, and distorting its parts before reassembling them. Body parts are present but often sharpened, attenuated, or reduced to suggestions. Perhaps it was this primordial couple's remoteness from life that prompted the artist to work in such a schematic style. In any case, the group remains one of the great monuments of African creative genius, a strong and complex statement about human values—indeed, about the very origins of the human race itself.

Recent research among the Baule people of the Ivory Coast has led to new information regarding the male and female figures so popular in European and American private and public collections. Figures that represent spirit "marriage partners" (*blolo bla*, the male, and *blolo bia*, the female) differ neither formally nor conceptually from fig-

OCEANIA

Relative to the abundant records associated with Western art, there is little historical depth to the arts of Oceania even though archeologists, linguists, and others have gone far in sorting out migration routes, language and racial distributions, and early aspects of stone age technology and social organization. The thousands of islands that make up Oceania are conventionally divided into three culture areas—Polynesia, Melanesia, and Micronesia.

Polynesia was the last area in the world to be settled. Its inhabitants seem to have brought complex sociopolitical and religious institutions with them, and there is a general homogeneity of style (lacking in Melanesia) despite the relative isolation of various island groups during the several centuries prior to European exploration. Polynesian societies are typically aristocratic, with ritual specialists and elaborate political organizations headed by chiefs. Polynesian art forms often served as one of the means of upholding spiritual power, *mana*, which was vested in the nobility and channeled by ancestral and state cults.

Melanesia was certainly settled early, and its art forms seem to suggest varied overlays of style and symbolism brought with a series of migrations. Art styles are both numerous and extremely varied. Typical Melanesian societies are more democratic than the Polynesian and relatively unstratified. Their cults and art forms address a host of nature and legendary ancestral spirits. Masks, absent in Polynesia, are central in many Melanesian spirit cults, and elaborate festivals, in which masks and other art forms are displayed, occur with some frequency.

Micronesia, in contrast to the other two areas, has little visual material and will not be discussed. The rich arts of Australia, though quite distinct from those of other areas, are often included in discussions of Oceanic art and will be mentioned briefly here.

Polynesia

Polynesian artists excelled in carving figural sculptures in wood, stone, and ivory in sizes ranging from the gigantic fabled stone images of Easter Island to tiny ivory Marquesan ear plugs an inch long. These sculptures were generally full-volumed, monochromatic human figures, often dynamic in pose. Polynesians were also adept in making decorative bark cloth, called *tapa*, and the art of tattoo was highly developed.

Polynesian carving at its most dramatic is represented by the Hawaiian figure of the war god, Kukailimoku (FIG. 14-56). Huge wooden images of this deity were erected on stone temple platforms that, in varied forms, were part of the apparatus of all Polynesian state religions. Although relatively small, the figure illustrated here is majestic in scale and forcefully carved to convey vigorous tensions—

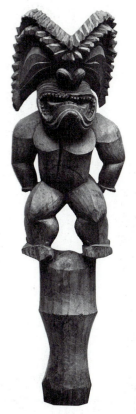

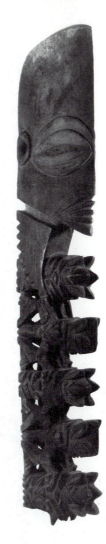

14-56 Kukailimoku, Hawaii. Wood, 30″ high. British Museum, London.

14-57 District God, Cook Islands. Wood. Peabody Museum, Harvard University.

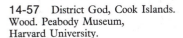

in short, the ferocity attributed to the deity. Flexed limbs and faceted, conventionalized muscles combine with the aggressive, flaring mouth and serrated headdress to achieve a tense dynamism seldom rivaled in any art. This is the work of a master sculptor supremely confident of his materials and technique—a work that speaks forcefully across cultural barriers.

Even though Polynesians were skillful navigators, various island groups remained isolated enough from one another to allow the development of distinct regional styles within a recognizable general Polynesian style. Thus, the arts of central Polynesia, represented here by the contrasting art forms of a wooden district god (FIG. 14-57) and a skeletalized double-headed male figure from Easter Island (FIG. 14-58), are quite different from the Hawaiian figures. The highly polished district god from the Cook Islands has a blade-shaped head and schematized features. Instead of a body there appear numerous tiny abstracted figures—the god's progeny—carved in the same geometric, angular style as the head above. Such carvings probably represented clan ancestors revered for their protective and procreative powers. Analogous images are known (from Mangaia in the Cook Islands and Rurutu in the Austral Islands) that also have multiple figures attached to their

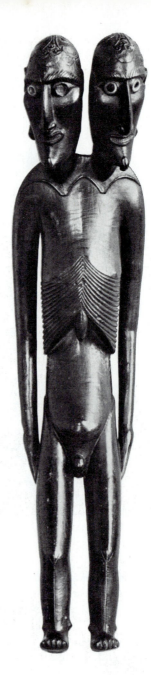

14-58 Double-headed male figure (*moai kava-kava*) from Easter Island, before 1860. Wood, approx. 16″ high. Museum of Natural History, La Rochelle, France.

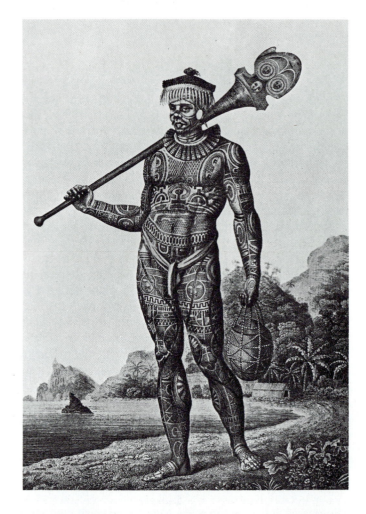

14-59 Tattooed Marquesan warrior. (Nineteenth-century engraving.)

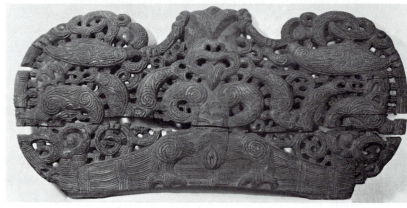

14-60 Door lintel, Maori. Wood, 45″ × 19″. Peabody Museum of Salem, Massachusetts.

bodies. All such images refer ultimately to creator deities revered for their central role in human fertility. The Easter Island double-headed figure may represent a mythological ancestor or deity of the early inhabitants of the island. Its bent posture and the emphasis on skeletal structure reflect an esthetic quite different from that of the massively aggressive sculpture of the Hawaiian war god (FIG. 14-56).

Polynesians developed the painful but prestigious art of tattoo more fully than other Oceanic peoples. Nobles and warriors, especially, were concerned with increasing their status, mana, and personal beauty by accumulating such patterns over the years. An early nineteenth-century en-

graving (FIG. 14-59) shows Marquesan tattoo patterns covering most of the body with divided and subdivided geometric motifs. Such a multiplication of small, repetitive abstract forms—also seen in the "children" on the above-mentioned Cook Islands figure—is in fact one major tendency in much Polynesian art. The other main tendency—toward bold, full-volume, large-scale figural sculptures—is manifest in the Hawaiian war god figure (FIG. 14-56).

The highly distinctive arts of the Maori peoples of New Zealand merge these two stylistic currents in images that are at once dynamic and intricate, bold in major forms but with surfaces covered and interconnected by minute curvi-

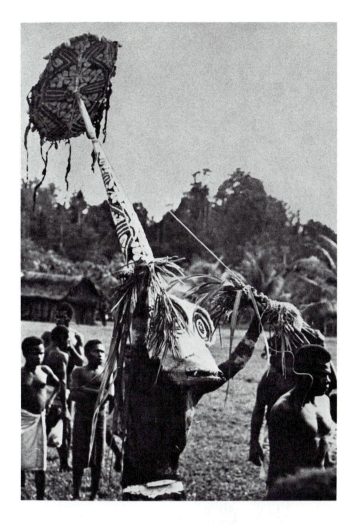

14-61 Composite day dance helmet and mask from the Northwest Baining of New Britain. Bark cloth and bamboo, approx. 9' long. George A. Corbin, New York.

linear detailing. The door lintel shown in FIG. 14-60 comes from a council house generously decorated, inside and out, with technically refined, complex imagery. The subjects are real and mythological ancestors whose advice and protection were sought for the political, war-making, and ritual deliberations that took place in their midst. Countless prestige items and weapons of the Maori nobility displayed this unique style, as did the tattooing on their faces and bodies.

Melanesia

Despite the aggressive poses of the figural art of Hawaii and the lively surface convolutions of that from New Zealand, Polynesian art is generally characterized by compactness, solidity, and restraint, as exemplified in the Cook Islands district god shown in FIG. 14-57. Melanesian art, on the other hand, has an insubstantial, colorful, flamboyant aspect epitomized in bark-cloth masks from the Baining of New Britain (FIG. 14-61) and woodcarving from New Ireland (FIG. 14-66). The mask of the Baining is made of bark-cloth and bamboo painted with charcoal and plant-derived pigments. It is used only once—for a day-long, night-long ceremony to celebrate the harvest and to commemorate the dead—then discarded. Similar forms are made anew the following year at harvest time, only to be discarded again after use. The black-and-white designs that cover the mask are symbols of the growth of garden plants, while the long, protruding, cone-shaped form refers to the growth of coconut trees. The woodcarvings in FIG. 14-66, called *malanggan* and used in display ceremonies of the same name, have a bewildering intricacy that stems from generous use of openwork and sliverlike projections and from over-painting in minute geometric patterns that further subdivide the image. The result is a "splintered" or fragmented and airy effect. This style is the more remarkable in view of the fact that most of these forms are carved from a single block of wood, a characteristic of all woodcarving considered in this chapter. In the scene shown in FIG. 14-66 several malanggan showpieces were set up in a special house dramatically opened to the public; the associated rituals served both to commemorate ancestors and initiate youths into adulthood. A variety of intricate masks was also danced during these rites.

The Melanesian penchant for color and drama in art is reflected too in the New Guinea Abelam cult sculptures and paintings found on and inside the monumental Men's Houses (FIG. 14-62). The gable paintings on these buildings show row upon row of mythological creatures intricately painted in contrasting bright colors. This kind of repetition and almost compulsive space-filling is common to many art areas considered in this chapter and can be

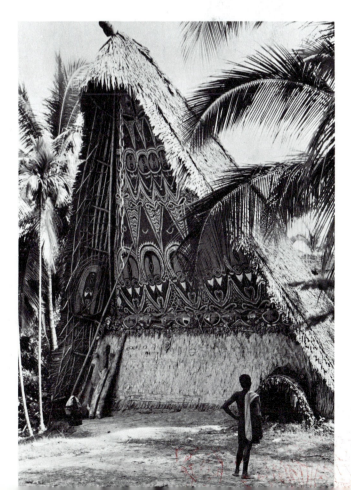

14-62 Ceremonial Men's House, Abelam, New Guinea.

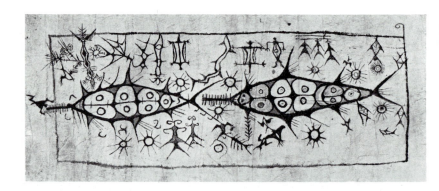

14-63 Banner, Lake Sentani, New Guinea. Bark cloth, tapa, black and red paint, 52″ long. Collection of Paul Wingert, New York.

seen in the bark-cloth banner from Lake Sentani, near the North Coast of New Guinea (FIG. 14-63). These banners, display cloths for funeral and other ritual occasions, are painted in a lively and, to us, somewhat whimsical style displaying a variety of aquatic creatures and symbols that may well refer to myths.

In other Melanesian art forms, from the Papuan Gulf and Asmat areas of New Guinea's South Coast, the artists distort human forms according to local preferences, which here, as elsewhere, are not attuned to realistic proportions or modeling. The fact that remote spirits (Papuan Gulf— FIG. 14-64) and ancestors (Asmat—FIG. 14-65) are portrayed accounts partially for the lack of naturalism, as do the long traditions of repeating and renewing such spiritual images—a repetition that seems to give rise in conservative societies to highly conventionalized styles. The Papuan Gulf figure is a Melanesian version of the power image whose in-dwelling spirit is invoked to protect and otherwise benefit its owner, while the Asmat pole is erected in ceremonies that prepare the participants to avenge the death of a community member in war. Such poles represent ancestors; the openwork "flags" are penises exaggerated in a reflection of the Asmat male's aggressive roles in sex and headhunting.

These and many other Oceanic peoples were headhunters until early in the twentieth century, and many of their art forms were created for rituals concerned with headhunting and attendant beliefs about the loss and gain of

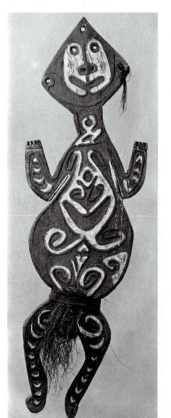

14-64 Spirit figure, Papuan Gulf, New Guinea. Wood, fibers, bark, red and white paint, 51″ long. Tropenmuseum, Amsterdam.

14-65 Ancestral poles, Asmat, New Guinea. Wood, paint, sago palm leaves, approx. 18′ high. Metropolitan Museum of Art, New York.

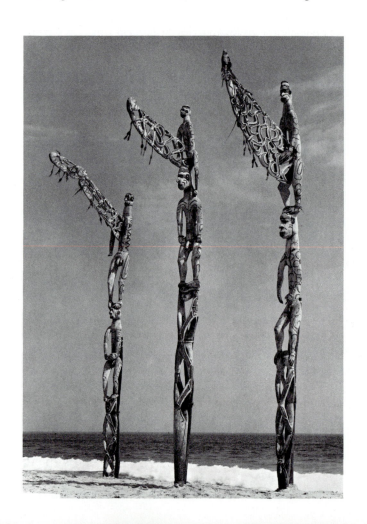

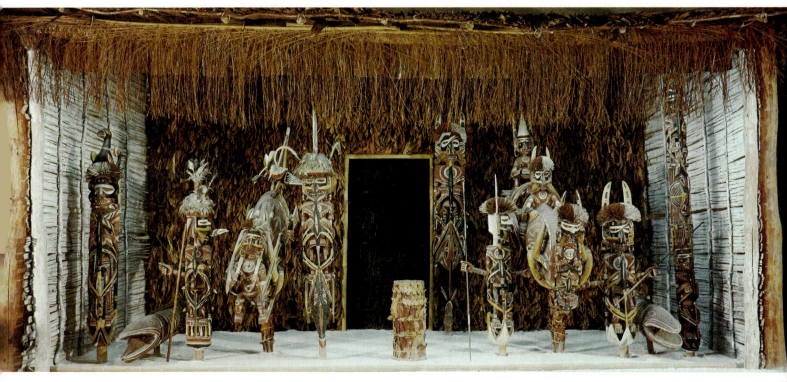

14-66 Malanggan tableau, New Ireland. Bamboo, palm and croton leaves, painted wood, approx. 8′ × 16½′ × 10′. Museum für Völkerkunde, Basel.

life-force. In several cultures, as among the Iatmul of the Sepik River, artists cleaned actual human skulls and reworked them into art objects (FIG. 14-67) by modeling over the skull with a claylike paste and painting the result with the kinds of flowing facial decoration worn in life, particularly on ritual occasions. These graphic images (a fascinating parallel to the "reconstructed" prehistoric skulls found at Jericho, FIG. 2-2) were held to contain the life-force or power men sought to increase by headhunting; they were displayed in ceremonies preparing for war or celebrating its success, and at funerals.

Face and body decoration are still important art forms in several parts of New Guinea. Although of course extremely transient, such embellishments were often highly complex, colorful, multimedia assemblages of pigments, feathers, fur, leaves, shells, and other materials, which gain both in symbolic significance and artistic impact from their combination. Both men and women decorated themselves in this fashion to display their idealized beauty and to compete with rivals similarly embellished.

Varied types and styles of masks were worn in Iatmul ceremonies as well as those of the peoples of New Britain, New Ireland, Abelam, the Papuan Gulf, Asmat, and other areas. As in Africa and America, such masks were used in ceremonies to materialize spirits whom man felt the need to entertain and propitiate. Elaborate festivals sometimes included over a hundred such "spirit impersonators," who

danced to entertain the human community and at the same time to remind it of its obligations to supernatural ancestors and culture-bringers. Many of the same masked spirits played an important role in initiating and educating youths to be fully socialized, productive members of the group. Especially in the design of the heads and bodies of spirits, Melanesian artists seem to have given free rein to their creativity and imagination. A bizarre, flamboyant Sulka

14-67 Skull, Iatmul, New Guinea. Human skull, clay, paint, human hair, cuscus fur, 10″ high. Gift of Mr. and Mrs. John J. Klijman, Metropolitan Museum of Art, New York

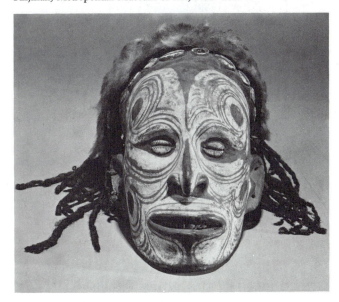

mask (FIG. 14-68), but one example, is of a kind made by stretching and sewing vegetable fibers over a light framework. These and other Melanesian masks were thus quite perishable; indeed, in some areas the masks were ritually destroyed at the end of a ceremony, an act that banished the spirits until their next "invitation" to intervene in human affairs.

Some Melanesian styles, like that of the Solomon Islands, are more restrained than those discussed above. In the protective canoe-prow carving shown (FIG. 14-69) the emphasis is on strong modeling, the enlarging of facial features, and very precise inlay patterns of seashell fragments that contrast with the solid dark color of the head itself. In several Melanesian areas there are styles that combine high-contrast, intricate surface patterns with bold sculpture, and in some, masks are not used, which suggests that these cultures may be transitional between those in which the wilder, less restrained Melanesian style prevails and those of the Polynesian, with its more solid, full-volumed sculpture.

Australia

Australia has a number of varied styles, as well as object types, that bear little relationship to the arts of neighboring New Guinea. Most objects are ceremonial aids in project-

ing the people into the legendary past—called "Dream Time"—when their world, its creatures, and its institutions were created. For the native Australian, the fertility of nature and man and the continuity of life itself depended on reenactment of the primordial events of Dream Time. Cosmogonic myths were recited in concert with songs and dances, and many art forms—body painting, decorated stones, carved figures, rock and bark paintings—were essential props in these dramatic re-creations. A bark painting entitled *The Djanggawul Sisters* (FIG. 14-70) describes in schematic form the birth of the human race along with other mythical episodes from Dream Time, the Djanggawul sisters and brothers being the mythological progenitors of the Yirrkala people of Arnhem Land. Symbolic motifs include trees and pole emblems, the rising and setting sun, a Djanggawul brother, and, on the right, the artist himself. Its intricate style is representative of the main features of Yirrkala art: rhythmic repetition, subdivision into crowded panels, fine detailing, and lack of a groundline, perspective, or modeling.

Australian art is well-known, too, for its "X-ray" style, which simultaneously depicts the insides (backbone, heart, and other organs) as well as the outsides of human beings and animals (FIG. 14-71). This style of painting is common to the area of Arnhem Land called Oenpelli. Our example shows a hunter and his quarry, a black kangaroo, at the moment a spear is about to strike the startled animal. In

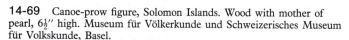

14-68 Mask, Sulka, Melanesia, 1900–10. Fiber structure covered with pitch, feathers, and pieces of wood, 27″ high, without leaf skirt. Übersee-Museum, Bremen.

14-69 Canoe-prow figure, Solomon Islands. Wood with mother of pearl, 6½″ high. Museum für Völkerkunde und Schweizerisches Museum für Volkskunde, Basel.

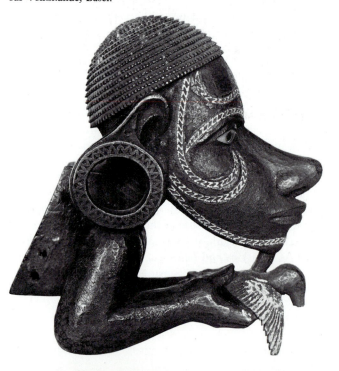

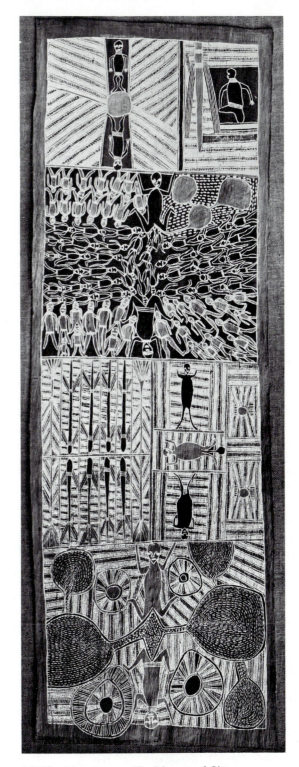

14-70 MUNGARAWAI, *The Djanggawul Sisters*, Yirrkala, Arnhem Land, Australia. Bark and paint. Art Gallery of New South Wales, Australia.

contrast to the rather static order of the Yirrkala composition, the Oenpelli painting has a fluid and dynamic quality. The figures are large in relation to the surface on which they have been placed and, unlike the distant "bird's-eye view" of the Yirrkala painting, the immediacy of the depicted action tends to draw the viewer into its orbit.

AFTERWORD: THE PRESENT

The traditional arts of North America, Africa, and Oceania, surveyed above, are, for the most part, not now being practiced, for they no longer have critical roles in cultural continuity and survival. Ironically it is only now that we are coming to acknowledge the variety and richness of earlier art traditions—at a time when most of them may no longer be accessible for study and preservation.

Although each area still produces artifacts of various sorts, some of high quality, the advent of modern mechanized life—bringing schools, missions, inexpensive clothing, plastic utensils—has changed artistic motivations and needs. Today one finds "tourist" arts, poor copies of earlier works, and some frankly modern works that draw inspiration from current European styles.

In earlier times, artistic energies were released on countless occasions and for hundreds of reasons, all bearing on the social and spiritual well-being of men and women. Some artifacts took their places in the daily rhythms of existence; others emerged only at climactic individual or community events—initiations, funerals, festivals, for example—when they often served as symbols of higher, guiding powers. In nearly all cases, the wealth and prestige of the people were involved, and art works were a focus of spiritual energy, activated in performance and display. As in all times and all places, art served to dramatize and intensify life itself, and life without art was virtually unknown.

14-71 Hunter and kangaroo, from Oenpelli, Arnhem Land, Australia. Paint on bark, 51" × 32". National Museum of Victoria, Melbourne, Australia.

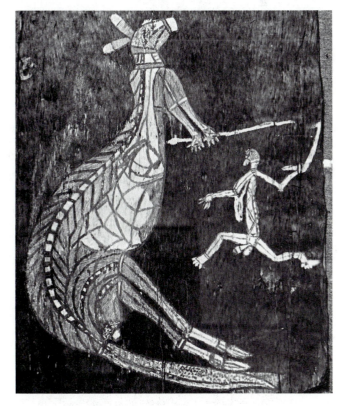

glossary

Italicized terms are themselves defined in the glossary.

abacus (ab′a·kus) The uppermost portion of the *capital* of a *column*, usually a thin slab.

abstract In painting and sculpture, emphasizing a derived essential character having little visual reference to objects in nature.

academy A place of study, derived from the name of the grove where Plato held his philosophical seminars. Giorgio Vasari founded the first academy of fine arts, properly speaking, with his Accademia di Disegno in Florence in 1563.

Achaean (a·kee′an) Of or pertaining to *Achaia*.

Achaia (a·ka′va) An ancient section of the northern Peloponnesos; loosely, Greece in general.

acroterium or **acroterion** In classical buildings, a figure or ornament usually at the apex of the *pediment*.

addorsed Set back-to-back, especially as in heraldic design.

adobe (a·do′bee) The clay used to make a kind of sun-dried brick of the same name or a building made of such brick.

aerial perspective See *perspective*.

agora (ag′e·ra) An open square or space used for public meetings or business in ancient Greek cities.

alabaster A variety of gypsum or calcite of dense, fine texture, usually white, but also red, yellow, gray, and sometimes banded.

alla prima (a′la pree′ma) A painting technique in which pigments are laid on in one application, with little or no drawing or underpainting.

altarpiece A panel, painted or sculptured, above and behind an altar.

ambulatory A covered walkway, outdoors (as in a *cloister*) or indoors, especially the passageway around the *apse* and *choir* of a church.

amphora (am′fe·ra) A two-handled, egg-shaped jar used for general storage purposes.

apadana (ap·a·dan′a) The great hall in ancient Persian palaces.

apse A recess, usually singular and semicircular, in the wall at the east end of a Roman *basilica* or Christian church.

arabesque Literally, Arabian-like. A flowing, intricate pattern derived from stylized organic motifs, usually floral, often arranged in symmetrical *palmette* designs; generally an Islamic decorative motif.

arcade A series of *arches* supported by *piers* or *columns*.

arch A curved structural member that spans an opening and is generally composed of wedge-shaped blocks (*voussoirs*) that transmit the downward pressure laterally. See also *thrust*.

architectonic Having structural or architectural qualities (usually as elements of a non-architectural object).

architrave (ark′i·trayv) The *lintel* or lowest division of the *entablature*, sometimes called the epistyle.

archivolt (ark′i·volt) One of a series of concentric *moldings* on a Romanesque or Gothic arch.

armature In sculpture, a skeletonlike framework to support material being modeled.

aspara In India, a nymph of the sky or air; in Chinese Buddhism, a heavenly maiden.

atlantes (at·lan′teez) (*pl. of* **atlas**) Male figures that function as supporting columns. See *caryatid*.

atmospheric perspective See *perspective*.

atrium (ay′tree·um) The court of a Roman house, near the entrance and partly open to the sky. Also, the open colonnaded court in front of and attached to a Christian *basilica*.

Aurignacian (o′rig·nay′shun) Of or pertaining to the first epoch of Upper *Paleolithic* culture, remains of which were found at Aurignac (Haute-Garonne), France.

avant-garde (a·vahn·gard′) Artists whose work is in (or work that reflects) the latest stylistic direction.

avatar (ah′vuh·tar) In Hinduism, an incarnation of a god.

axial plan See *plan*.

axis An imaginary line, or lines, about which a work, a group of works, or part of a work is visually or structurally organized, often symmetrically.

baldacchino (bal·da·kee′no) A canopy on columns, frequently built over an altar.

barrel vault See *vault*.

bas (bah) **relief** See *relief*.

basilica (ba·sil′i·ka) In Roman architecture, a public building for assemblies (especially tribunals), rectangular in plan and having an entrance on a long side. In Christian architecture, an early church somewhat resembling the Roman basilica, usually entered from one end and with an *apse* at the other, creating an *axial plan*.

batter To slope inward, often almost imperceptibly, or such an inward slope of a wall.

bay A subdivision of the interior space of a building. In Romanesque and Gothic churches the transverse *arches* and *piers* of the *arcade* divide the building into bays.

beehive tomb A beehive-shaped type of subterranean tomb constructed as a *corbeled vault* and found on prehistoric Greek sites.

ben-ben A pyramidal stone; a *fetish* of the Egyptian god Re.

blind arcade (wall arcade) An *arcade* having no actual openings, applied as decoration to a wall surface.

bodhisattva (bo·dee·sot'vuh) In Buddhism, a being who is a potential *buddha*.

bottega (but·tay'ga) A shop; the studio-shop of an Italian artist.

bouleuterion In ancient Greece, an assembly hall or council chamber.

broken color A painting technique using short, thick strokes laid over a ground color to create rich textures and vibrant effects of light.

broken pediment A *pediment* in which the *cornice* is discontinuous at the apex or the base.

Buddha The supreme enlightened being of Buddhism, an embodiment of divine wisdom and virtue.

burin (byoor'in) A pointed steel tool for *engraving* or *incising*.

buttress An exterior masonry structure that opposes the lateral thrust of an *arch* or *vault*. A **pier buttress** is a solid mass of masonry; a **flying buttress** consists typically of an inclined member carried on an arch or series of arches and a solid buttress to which it transmits lateral *thrust*.

calligraphy Handwriting or penmanship, especially elegant or "beautiful" writing as a decorative art.

campanile (kam·pa·neel'eh) A bell tower, usually free-standing.

capital The upper member of a *column;* it serves as a transition from the *shaft* to the *lintel*.

cardo The north-south road in Etruscan and Roman towns, intersecting the *decumanus* at right angles.

cartoon In painting, a full-size drawing from which a painting is made. Cartoons were usually worked out in complete detail and the design then transferred to the working surface by coating the back with chalk and going over the lines with a stylus, or by pricking the lines and "pouncing" charcoal dust through the resulting holes.

cartouche (kar·toosh') A scroll-like design or medallion, purely decorative or containing an inscription or heraldic device; also, in ancient Egypt, an oval device containing such elements as *hieroglyphic* names of Egyptian kings.

caryatid (kar·ee·at'id) A female figure that functions as a supporting *column*. See also *atlantes*.

casting In sculpture, duplication of a clay original in plaster or metal by use of a mold.

cella (sel'a) An enclosed chamber, the essential feature of a Classical temple, in which the cult statue usually stood.

centering A wooden framework to support an *arch* or *vault* during its construction.

central plan See *plan*.

ceramics The art of making objects such as pottery of clay; also, the objects themselves.

chaitya (chight'yuh) An Indian shrine, especially a Buddhist assembly hall having a votive *stupa* at one end.

chalice A cup or goblet, especially that used in the sacraments of the Christian Church.

chamfer The surface formed by cutting off a corner of a board or post; a bevel.

champlevé (shahn·le·vay') A process of enameling in which a design is cut into a metal plate in such a way as to leave thin raised lines that create compartments to hold the enamel.

chandi A Javanese temple.

chevet (sheh·vay') The eastern end of a Romanesque church, including *choir, ambulatory,* and radiating chapels.

chevron A zigzag or V-shaped motif of decoration.

chiaroscuro (kee·ar'eh·skoor'o) In painting or drawing, the treatment and use of light and dark, especially the gradations of light that produce the effect of modeling.

chinoiserie (shee·nwaz·eh·ree') Chinese motifs used as decorations for furniture, in wallpaper, etc., applied largely to eighteenth-century Rococo style.

chiton (kite'en) A Greek tunic, the essential (and often only) garment of both men and women, the other being the mantle (*himation*).

choir The space reserved for the clergy in the church, usually east of the *transept*, but in some instances extending into the *nave*.

ciborium (sih·bor'ee·um) A canopy, usually free-standing and supported by four columns, erected over an altar; also, a covered cup used in the sacraments of the Christian Church. See *baldacchino*.

cinquecento (cheenk·way·chain'toh) The sixteenth century in Italian art.

cire-perdue (seer-pair·dew') The "lost-wax" process. A bronze-casting method in which a figure is modeled in wax and covered with clay. The whole is fired, melting away the wax and hardening the clay, which then becomes a mold for molten metal.

clerestory (kleer'sto·ry) The part of a building that rises above the roofs of the other parts and whose walls contain openings for light.

cloison (klwa·zohn') Literally, a partition. A cell made of metal wire or a narrow metal strip, usually gold, soldered edge-down to a metal base to hold enamel or other decorative materials.

cloisonné (klwa·zoh·nay') A process of enameling employing *cloisons*.

cloister A court, usually with covered walks or *ambulatories* along its sides.

closed form A form, especially in painting, whose contour is not broken or blurred.

clustered pier See *compound pier*.

coffer A sunken panel in a *soffit, vault,* or ceiling, often ornamental.

coin type The pattern or design used to decorate a coin.

collage (kul·lahzh') A composition made by pasting together on a flat surface various materials such as newspaper, wallpaper, printed text and illustrations, photographs, and cloth. See *montage*.

colonnade A series or row of *columns,* usually spanned by *lintels*.

colonnette A small *column*.

color See *hue, saturation,* and *value*.

color solid A conceptual device in which the principal variables of *color* are visualized as having a three-dimensional relationship in the form of two cones set base to base. The vertical *axis* (running from apex to apex) is *value,* the *hues* are arranged around the axis, and *saturation* is the distance from the surface of the solid to the axis.

column A vertical, weight-carrying architectural member, circular in cross section, and consisting of a base (sometimes omitted), a *shaft,* and a *capital*.

complementary after-image The image, in a *complementary color,* that is retained briefly by the eye after the stimulus is removed.

complementary colors Those pairs of colors, such as red and green, that together embrace the entire spectrum. Thus the complement of one of the three *primary colors* is a mixture of the other two. In pigments they produce a neutral, or gray, when mixed in the right proportions.

compound or **clustered pier** A pier composed of a group or cluster of members, especially characteristic of Gothic architecture.

connoisseur (kon·nuh·ser') An expert on works of art and the individual styles of artists.

contour A visible border of a *mass* in space; a *line* that creates the illusion of *mass* and *volume* in space.

contrapposto (kon·tra·poh'stoh) The disposition of the human figure in which one part is turned in a direction opposite that of the other (usually hips and legs one way, shoulders and chest another)—thus, a counter-positioning of the body about its central *axis*. Sometimes called "weight-shift," since the weight of the body tends to be thrown to one foot, creating tension on one side and relaxation on the other.

cool color Blue, green, or violet. Psychologically, cool colors are calming, unemphatic, depressive; optically, they generally appear to recede. See *warm color*.

corbel (kor'bel) A projecting wall member used as a support for some element in the superstructure. Also, courses of stone or brick in which each course projects beyond the one beneath it. Two such structures, meeting at the topmost course, create an archlike form.

cornice The projecting, crowning member of the *entablature;* also, any crowning projection.

cosmati (koz·ma'tee) Cut-stone *mosaic* inlay decoration in geometric patterns.

cramp A device, usually metal, to hold together blocks of stone of the same course. See *dowel*.

crenelated Notched or indented, usually with respect to tops of walls, as in battlements.

crocket A projecting foliate ornament of a *capital, pinnacle, gable, buttress,* or *spire*.

Cro-Magnon (kro-mag'non) Of or pertaining to the *homo sapiens* whose remains, dating from the *Aurignacian* period, were found in the Cro-Magnon cave of Dordogne, France.

cromlech (krom'lek) A circle of monoliths.

crossing The space in a cruciform church formed by the intersection of the *nave* and *transept*.

crown The topmost part of an *arch,* including the *keystone;* also, an open *finial* of a tower.

crypt A *vaulted* space under part of a building, wholly or partly underground; in Medieval churches, normally the portion under an *apse* or *chevet*.

cuneiform (kyoo·nee'ih·form) Literally, wedge-shaped; thus a system of writing used in Babylonia-Assyria, the characters of which were wedge-shaped.

cyclopean (sike·lo·pee'an) Gigantic; vast and rough; massive. Cyclopean architecture is a style of stone construction using large irregular blocks without mortar.

dado (day′doh) A horizontal band, often decorated, at the base or lower part of a wall or pedestal.

decumanus (dek·yoo·man′us) The east-west road in an Etruscan or Roman town, intersecting the *cardo* at right angles.

diptych (dip′tik) A two-paneled *altarpiece;* also, an ancient Roman and Early Christian two-hinged writing tablet, or ivory memorial panels.

dolmen (dohl′men) Several large stones capped with a covering slab, erected in prehistoric times.

dome A hemispherical *vault;* theoretically, an *arch* rotated on its vertical *axis.*

donjon (don′jun) A massive tower forming the stronghold of a Medieval castle.

dowel In ancient architecture, wooden or metal pins placed between stones of different courses to prevent shifting. See *cramp.*

dromos The passage to a *beehive tomb.*

drum The circular wall that supports a dome; also, one of the cylindrical stones of which a non-monolithic *shaft* is made.

dry point An *engraving* in a soft metal such as copper in which the burr raised by the *burin* is retained to produce a soft, richly black effect in the print. See *etching, intaglio.*

duecento (doo·ay·chain′toh) The thirteenth century in Italian art.

earth colors Pigments, such as yellow ochre and umber, that are obtained by mining; they are usually compounds of metals.

echinus (eh·kee′nus) In architecture, the convex element of a *capital* directly below the *abacus.*

eclecticism (eh·klek′ti·sism) The practice of selecting from various sources, usually in order to form a new system or style.

écorché (ay·kor·shay′) A figure painted or sculptured to show the muscles of the body.

elevation In drawing and architecture, a geometric projection of a building on a plane perpendicular to the horizon; a vertical projection.

embrasure A flared frame around a doorway or window.

enamel A vitreous, colored paste that solidifies when fired. See *champlevé, cloisonné.*

encaustic An ancient method of painting with colored molten wax in which the wax is fused with the surface by application of hot irons.

engaged column A columnlike, nonfunctional form projecting from a wall and articulating it visually. See *pilaster.*

engobe (en·gohb′) A slip of finely sifted clay used by Greek potters; applied to a pot it would form a black *glaze* in firing.

engraving The process of *incising* a design in hard material, often a metal plate, usually copper; also, the print or impression made from such a plate. See *burin, dry point, etching, intaglio.*

entablature The part of a building, usually the *façade,* between the *capitals* of *columns* and the roof or upper story.

entasis (en·tay′sis) An almost imperceptible convex tapering (an apparent swelling) in the *shaft* of a *column.*

epistyle See *architrave.*

esthetic The distinctive vocabulary and theory of a given style.

etching A kind of *engraving* in which the design is *incised* in a layer of wax or varnish on a copper plate. The parts of the plate left exposed are then etched, or slightly eaten away, by acid in which the plate is immersed after incising. Because wax and varnish are relatively soft materials, the etcher is freed from the restrictions imposed upon the woodcutter and engraver by their media. Etching is thus one of the most facile of the graphic arts and the one most capable of subtleties of line and tone. See *dry point, engraving,* and *intaglio.*

extrados (eks·trah′dohs) The upper or outer surface of an *arch.*

façade Usually, the front of a building; also, the other sides when they are emphasized architecturally.

faïence (feye·ahnce′) Pottery (except porcelain) glazed with compounds of tin; also, any glazed earthenware.

fan vault See *vault.*

fenestration The arrangement of the windows of a building; by extension, the arrangement of all openings (windows, doors, *arcades*).

ferroconcrete See *reinforced concrete.*

fête galante (fet ga·lahnt′) An elegant and graceful celebration; applied to the works of Antoine Watteau and other Rococo painters.

fetish An object believed to possess magical powers, especially one capable of bringing to fruition its owner's plans; sometimes regarded as the abode of a supernatural power or spirit.

figure-ground The visual unity, yet separability, of a form and its background; usually with "relationship."

finial A knoblike ornament, usually with a foliate design, in which a vertical member such as a *pinnacle* terminates.

flamboyant Flamelike, flaming; applied to aspects of a late Gothic style, especially architectural tracery.

flute or **fluting** Vertical channeling, roughly semicircular in cross section and used principally on *columns* and *pilasters.*

flying buttress See *buttress.*

foreshortening Seeming visual contraction of an object viewed as extended in a plane not perpendicular to the line of sight; also, the representation of this phenomenon.

form In its widest sense, total organic structure; a synthesis of all the elements of that structure and of the manner in which they are united to create its distinctive character. The form of a work is what enables us to apprehend it. See *closed form* and *open form.*

formalism Strict adherence to, or dependence on, prescribed forms of execution and traditional rules of composition.

fresco Painting on plaster, either dry **(dry fresco)** or wet **(wet** or **true fresco).** In the latter method the pigments are mixed with water and become chemically bound to the plaster. Also, a painting executed in either method.

fret or **meander** An ornament, usually in bands but also covering broad surfaces, consisting of interlocking geometric motifs.

frieze (freez) The part of the *entablature* between the *architrave* and *cornice;* also, any sculptured or ornamented band in a building, on furniture, etc.

garbha griha The *cella* or inner sanctum of the Hindu temple.

gargoyle In architecture, a waterspout, usually carved, often in the form of a *grotesque.*

genre (zhahn′reh) A style or category of art; also, a kind of painting realistically depicting scenes from everyday life.

gesso (jess′oh) Plaster mixed with a binding material and used for *reliefs* and as a *ground* for painting.

glaze A vitreous coating applied to pottery to seal the surface and as decoration; it may be colored, transparent or opaque, and glossy or *matte.* In oil painting, a thin, transparent or semitransparent layer put over a color to alter it slightly.

golden mean or **golden section** A proportional relationship obtained by dividing a line so that the shorter part is to the longer as the longer part is to the whole. These proportions have an esthetic appeal that has led artists of varying periods and cultures to employ them in determining basic dimensions.

gopuram (go′poor·om) The massive, ornamented entrance structure of South Indian temples.

gouache (goo·ahsh′) *Watercolor* rendered opaque by the addition of a filler such as zinc white. It has more body and dries more slowly than the transparent watercolor and lends itself to bright color effects and meticulous detail. Also, a picture painted in this medium.

granulation In jewelry, a method of ornamenting in which small grains of metal, usually gold, are soldered to a flat surface.

graphic arts Those visual arts that are linear in character (such as drawing and *engraving*); also, generally, those that involve impression (printing and printmaking).

graver A cutting tool used by engravers and sculptors.

Greek cross A cross in which all the arms are the same length.

grisaille (greez·eye′) A monochrome painting done mainly in neutral grays to simulate sculpture.

groin The edge formed by the intersection of two *vaults.*

groin vault See *vault.*

grotesque In art, a kind of ornament—sometimes called (imprecisely) *arabesque*—used in antiquity and consisting of representations of medallions, sphinxes, foliage, and imaginary creatures.

ground A coating applied to a canvas or other surface to prepare that surface for painting; also, background.

guilloche (gi·lush′) An ornament consisting of interlaced curving bands.

hallenkirche (holl′en·keer·kheh) A hall church. In this variety of Gothic church, especially popular in Germany, the aisles are almost as high as the *nave.*

hammer-beam ceiling An English Gothic open-timber ceiling whose support elements resemble the claws of a hammer.

hatching A technique used in drawing, engraving, etc., in which fine lines are cut or drawn close together to achieve an effect of shading.

haunch The part of an *arch* (roughly midway between the *springing* and the *crown*) where the lateral *thrust* is strongest.

herringbone perspective See *perspective*.

heiroglyphic A system of writing using symbols or pictures; also, one of the symbols.

himation (him·mat′ee·on) A Greek mantle worn by men and women over the tunic and draped in various ways.

historiated Ornamented with representations—such as plants, animals, or human figures—that have a narrative, as distinct from a purely decorative, function. Historiated initial letters were a popular form of manuscript decoration in the Middle Ages.

hue The name of a color. The *primary colors* (blue, red, and yellow) together with the *secondary colors* (green, orange, and violet) form the chief colors of the spectrum. See also *complementary colors, cool color, saturation, value, warm color*.

hydria An ancient Greek three-handled water jar.

hypostyle hall A hall whose roof is supported by columns; applied to the colonnaded hall of the Egyptian *pylon* temple.

icon (eye′con) A portrait or image, especially in the Greek church, a panel with a painting of sacred personages that are objects of veneration. In the visual arts, a painting, a piece of sculpture, or even a building regarded as an object of veneration.

iconography (eye·con·og′ra·fee) The study dealing with the symbolic, often religious, meaning of objects, persons, or events depicted in works of art.

iconostasis (eye·con·os′ta·sis) In eastern Christian churches, a screen or partition, with doors and many tiers of *icons*, that separates the sanctuary from the main body of the church.

idealization The representation of things according to a preconception of ideal *form* or type; a kind of esthetic distortion to produce idealized forms. See *Realism*.

illumination Decoration with drawings, usually in gold, silver, and bright colors, especially the initial letters of a manuscript.

imagines (*pl. of* **imago**) (i·maj′i·nees) In ancient Rome, wax portraits of ancestors.

imam One who leads worshipers in prayer in Moslem services.

impasto (im·pah′stoh) A style of painting in which the pigment is applied thickly or in heavy lumps, as in many of Rembrandt's paintings.

impost block A stone with the shape of a truncated, inverted pyramid, placed between a *capital* and the *arch* that springs from it.

Impressionism A type of *Realism* whose aim is to render the immediate sense impression of the artist. It had its origins in nineteenth-century France with the work of Édouard Manet and was developed and altered by Claude Monet and others. A main concern of the Impressionists was the study and representation of light.

incising Cutting into a surface with a sharp instrument; also, a method of decoration, especially on metal and pottery.

in situ (si′too) In place; in original position.

intaglio (in·tal′yoh) A category of graphic technique in which the design is *incised*, so that the impression made is in *relief*. Used especially on gems, seals, and dies for coins, but also in the kinds of printing or printmaking in which the ink-bearing surface is depressed. Also, an object so decorated. See *dry point, engraving, etching*.

intarsia (in·tahr′sya) Inlay work, primarily in wood and sometimes in mother-of-pearl, marble, etc.

intercolumniation The space or the system of spacing between *columns* in a *colonnade*.

intrados (in·trah′dohs) The underside of an *arch* or *vault*.

isocephaly Arrangement of figures so that the heads are at the same height.

jataka (jah′tuh·kuh) Tales of the lives of the Buddha.

jube (joo′bee) A *choir* screen treated as an architectural ornament.

ka (kah) In ancient Egypt, immortal human substance, the concept approximating the Western idea of soul.

kakemono A Japanese hanging or scroll.

karma (kar′muh) In Buddhist and Hindu belief, the ethical consequences of a person's life, determinant of his or her fate.

keystone The central, uppermost *voussoir* in an *arch*.

khutbah (koot′buh) In Moslem worship, a sermon and a declaration of allegiance to a community's leader.

kiln A large stove or oven in which pottery is fired.

krater (or **crater**) (kray′ter) An ancient Greek wide-mouthed bowl for mixing wine and water.

kuang A Chinese covered libation vessel.

kylix (or **cylix**) (kye′liks) An ancient Greek drinking cup, shallow and having two handles and a stem.

lacquer A resinous spirit varnish such as shellac, often colored.

lantern In architecture, a small, often decorative structure with openings for lighting that crowns a *dome*, turret, or roof.

lapis lazuli (la′pis la′zyoo·lye) A rich ultramarine semiprecious stone used for carving and as a source of *pigment*.

Latin cross A cross in which the vertical member is longer than the horizontal member, through whose midpoint it passes.

lectionary A list, often illustrated, of lections, selections from the Scriptures that are read in church services.

lierné (lyair·nay′) A short *rib* that runs from one main rib of a *vault* to another.

line The mark made by a moving point and having psychological impact according to its direction and weight. In art it defines space and may create a silhouette or define a *contour*, creating the illusion of *mass* and *volume*.

linear perspective See *perspective*.

lintel A beam of any material used to span an opening.

lithography In graphic arts, a printmaking process in which the printing surface is a polished stone (or metal plate) on which the design is drawn with a greasy material. Greasy ink, applied to the moistened stone, is repelled by all surfaces but the lines of the drawing. The process permits linear and tonal values of great range and subtlety.

local color In painting, the actual color of an object.

loggia (luh′jee·uh) A gallery that has an open *arcade* or *colonnade* on a side or sides.

lunette A semicircular opening, with the flat side down, in a wall over a door, niche, or window.

luster A thin *glaze*, usually metallic, sometimes used on pottery to produce a rich, often iridescent color. Used particularly in Persian pottery and in *majolica*.

machicolation An opening (in the floor of an overhanging gallery) through which the defenders of a castle dropped stones and boiling liquids on attackers.

madrasah (muh·dros′uh) A combined Moslem school and *mosque*.

Magdalenian (mag·de·lee′nee·an) Of or pertaining to the climactic cultural stage of the Upper *Paleolithic* and named after archeological findings at La Madeleine (Dordogne), France.

majolica (ma·jah′lik·uh) A kind of Italian Renaissance pottery coated with a whitish tin-compound enamel, brilliantly painted and often *lustered*.

makimono A Japanese horizontal scroll.

malanggan Intricately carved Melanesian ceremonial masks.

mandala (man′duh·luh) In Hinduism and Buddhism, a magical geometric symbol of the cosmos.

mandapa (man·dop′uh) A Hindu assembly hall, part of a temple.

mandorla An almond-shaped nimbus, or glory, surrounding the figure of Christ.

mass The effect and degree of bulk, density, and weight of matter in space. As opposed to plane and area it describes *form* in three-dimensional space. See also *volume*.

mastaba (mah′sta·buh) A bench-shaped ancient Egyptian tomb.

matte (mat) In painting, pottery, and photography, a dull finish.

mbari Ceremonial houses filled with clay sculptures, honoring community deities of the Ibo tribe in Africa.

meander See *fret*.

medium The substance or agency in which an artist works; also, in painting, the vehicle, usually liquid, that carries the pigment.

megaron (meh′ga·ron) A large rectangular living hall, fronted by an open two-columned porch, traditional in Greece since Mycenaean times.

menhir (men′heer) A prehistoric monolith, uncut or roughly cut, standing singly or with others in rows or circles.

merlon The solid part of a battlement.

Mesolithic (Middle Stone Age) Of or pertaining to the period between the *Paleolithic* and *Neolithic*, characterized by food-gathering and incipient agriculture.

metope (met′a·pee) The space between *triglyphs* in a Doric *frieze*.

mihrab (mee′rob) In the wall of a *mosque*, the niche that indicates the direction of Mecca.

minbar (meen′bar) The pulpit in a *mosque*.

miniature A small picture illustrating a manuscript; also, any small portrait, often on ivory or porcelain.

modeling The shaping of three-dimensional forms in a soft material such as clay; also, the gradations of light and shade reflected from the surfaces of matter in space, or the illusion of such gradations produced by alterations of *value* in a drawing or painting.

module (mod'yool) A basic unit of which the dimensions of the major parts of a work are multiples. The principle is used in sculpture and other art forms, but it is most often employed in architecture, where the module may be the dimensions of an important part of a building, such as a column, or simply some commonly accepted unit of measurement such as the centimeter or the inch, or, as with Le Corbusier, the average dimensions of the human figure.

molding In architecture, a continuous narrow surface, either projecting or recessed, plain or ornamented, whose purpose is to break up a surface, to accent, or to decorate by means of the light and shade it produces.

monochrome A painting in one color; also, the technique of making such a painting.

montage (mohn'tahzh) A composition made by fitting together pictures or parts of pictures; also, motion-picture effects produced by superimposing images or showing them in rapid sequence. See *collage.*

monumental In art criticism, any work of art of unpretentious grandeur and simplicity, regardless of its size.

mosaic Patterns or pictures made by embedding small pieces of stone or glass (*tesserae*) in cement on surfaces such as walls and floors; also, the technique of making such works.

mosque A Moslem place of worship.

mudra (muh·drah') A stylized gesture of mystical significance, usually in representations of Hindu deities.

mullion A vertical member that divides a window or separates one window from another.

mural A painting on a wall; a *fresco* is a type of mural.

narthex A porch or vestibule of a church, generally colonnaded or arcaded and preceding the *nave.*

Naturalism The doctrine that art should adhere as closely as possible to the appearance of the natural world. Naturalism, with varying degrees of fidelity to appearance, recurs in the history of Western art.

nave The part of a church between the chief entrance and the *choir,* demarcated from aisles by *piers* or *columns.*

Neanderthal (nee·an'der·thal) A species of *Paleolithic* man.

necking A groove at the bottom of the Greek Doric capital between the *echinus* and the *flutes* that masks the junction of *capital* and *shaft.*

necropolis (neh·krop'o·lis) A large burial area; literally, a city of the dead.

Neolithic (New Stone Age) Of or pertaining to the period that saw the first elements of a farming economy and fixed settlements.

niello (nee·el'o) Inlay in a metal of an alloy of sulfur and such metals as gold or silver. Also, a work made by this process, or the alloy itself.

nirvana (neer·vah'nuh) In Buddhism and Hinduism, a blissful state brought about by absorption of the individual soul or consciousness into the supreme spirit.

obverse On coins or medals, the side that bears the principal type or inscription. See *reverse.*

odalisque (oh'de·lisk) An Oriental slave girl or concubine, a favorite subject of artists such as Ingres and Matisse.

oenochoe (eh·nuk'oh·ee) An ancient Greek wine pitcher.

oeuvre (uh'vreh) The whole of an artist's output; literally, his "work."

ogee (oh'jee) A *molding* having in profile a double, or *S*-shaped, curve. Also, an *arch,* each of whose sides has this form.—**ogival** *adj.*

oil color *Pigment* ground with oil.

open form A *mass* penetrated or treated in such a way that space acts as its environment rather than as its limit. See *closed form.*

order In Classical architecture, a style represented by a characteristic design of the *column* and its *entablature.* See also *superimposed order.*

Paleolithic (Old Stone Age) Of or pertaining to the period preceding the *Mesolithic* and characterized by stone implements and cave painting. Lower Paleolithic man (to 32,000 B.C.) was a nomadic hunter, while Upper Paleolithic man (32,000–8000 B.C.) was a specialized hunter.

palette (pal'it) A thin board with a thumb hole at one end upon which an artist lays and mixes his colors; any surface so used. Also, the colors or kinds of colors characteristically used by an artist.

palmette A conventional decorative ornament of ancient origin composed of radiating petals springing from a calyxlike base.

Panathenaea (pan'a·then·ee'a) The most ancient and important festival of Athens, held in honor of the goddess, Athena.

Pantheon All the gods of a people, or a temple dedicated to all such gods; especially, the Pantheon in Rome (though it is not certain that this was its function).

papyrus A plant native to Egypt and adjacent lands used to make a paperlike writing material; also, the material or any writing on it.

passage grave A burial chamber entered through a long tunnel-like passage.

pastel Finely ground *pigments* compressed into chalklike sticks. Also, work done in this *medium,* or its characteristic paleness.

patina (pa·teen'a) The green oxidized layer that forms on bronze and copper.

pediment In Classical architecture, the triangular space (gable) at the end of a building, formed by the ends of the sloping roof and the *cornice;* also, an ornamental feature having this shape.

pendentive (pen·den'tiv) A concave, triangular piece of masonry (a triangular section of a hemisphere), four of which support a *dome* erected over a square.

peripteral (per·ip'ter·al) A style of building in which the main structure is surrounded by a *colonnade.*

peristyle A *colonnade* surrounding a building or a court.

perspective A scheme or formula for projecting an illusion of the three-dimensional world on a two-dimensional surface. In **linear perspective,** the most common type, all parallel lines or lines of projection seem to converge on a single point on the horizon, known as the *vanishing point,* and associated objects are rendered smaller the further from the viewer they are intended to seem. **Atmospheric** or **aerial perspective** creates the illusion of distance by the greater diminution of color intensity, shift in color toward an almost neutral blue, and blurring of contours as the intended distance between eye and object increases. In **herringbone perspective** the lines of projection converge not on a vanishing point, but on a vertical *axis* at the center of the picture.

pi (bee) The Chinese symbol of heaven, a jade disk.

piano nobile (peea'no no'bee·lay) The principal story, usually the second, in Renaissance buildings.

pictograph A picture, usually stylized, that represents an idea; also, writing using such means. See *hieroglyphic.*

picture plane The surface of a picture.

pier A vertical, unattached masonry support.

Pietà (peeay·ta') A work of art depicting the Virgin mourning over the body of Christ.

pigment Finely powdered coloring matter mixed or ground with various vehicles to form paint, crayon, etc.

pilaster (pi·las'ter) A flat, rectangular, vertical member projecting from a wall of which it forms a part. It usually has a base and a *capital* and is often *fluted.*

pillar Usually a weight-carrying member such as a *pier* or a *column;* sometimes an isolated free-standing structure used for commemorative purposes.

pinnacle A tower, primarily ornamental, but functioning in Gothic architecture to give additional weight to a *buttress* or *pier.* See *finial.*

pithos (pith'oss) (*pl.* **pithoi**) A large clay storage vessel frequently set into the earth, and, therefore possessing no flat base.

plan The horizontal arrangement of the parts of a building, or a drawing or diagram showing such arrangement as a horizontal *section.* An **axial plan** is one in which the parts of a building are organized longitudinally, or along a given *axis;* a **central plan** is one in which the parts radiate from a central point.

plasticity In art, the three-dimensionality of an object.

plinth The lowest member of a base; also, a block serving as a base for a statue.

polychrome Done in several colors.

polyptych (pol'ip·tik) An *altarpiece* made up of more than three sections.

porcelain Translucent, impervious, and resonant *pottery* made in a base of kaolin, a fine white clay; sometimes any pottery that is translucent, whether or not made of kaolin.

portico A porch with a roof supported by *columns* and usually having an *entablature* and a *pediment.*

pottery Objects, usually vessels, made of clay and hardened by firing.

predella The narrow ledge on which an *altarpiece* rests at the back of an altar.

primary colors The *hues* red, yellow, and blue. From these three, with the addition of white, it is theoretically possible to mix the full color spectrum. The primary colors cannot be produced by mixing others.

program The architect's formulation of a

design problem with respect to considerations of site, function, materials, and aims (of the client); also, in painting and sculpture, the conceptual basis of a work.

pronaos (pro·nay'os) The enclosed space in front of the *cella* of a Greek temple.

provenance Origin, source.

psalter A book containing the Psalms of the Bible.

putto (*pl.* **putti**) A young child, a favorite subject in Italian painting and sculpture.

pylon (pie'lon) The *monumental* entrance of an Egyptian temple.

qiblah (keeb'lah) The direction (toward Mecca) in which Moslems face in prayer. (Often *kibla*.)

quatrefoil (kat're·foyl) An architectural ornament having four lobes or foils. See *trefoil*.

quattrocento (kwat'tro·chain'toh) The fifteenth century in Italian art.

quoin (koin) Large, sometimes *rusticated*, usually slightly projecting stone or stones that often form the corners of the exterior walls of masonry buildings.

raking cornice The *cornice* on the sloping sides of a *pediment*.

Ramayana A Sanskrit epic telling of Rama, an incarnation of the Hindu god Vishnu.

Realism The doctrine that art should represent nature without *idealization*.

reinforced concrete (ferroconcrete) Concrete whose tensile strength is increased by iron or steel mesh or bars embedded in it.

relief In sculpture, figures projecting from a background of which they are part. The degree of relief is designated high, low (or **bas**), or sunken (or hollow). In the last, the backgrounds are not cut back and the points in highest relief are level with the original surface of the material being carved. A kind of low relief that is hardly more than a scratching of the surface was originated by Donatello and is termed **stiacciata** or **sciacciata**. See *repoussé*.

reliquary A small receptacle for a sacred relic, usually of a richly decorated precious material.

repoussé (ruh·poo·say') Formed in relief by beating a metal plate from the back, leaving the impression on the face. The metal is hammered into a hollow mold of wood or some other pliable material and finished with a *graver*. See *relief*.

respond An engaged *column, pilaster,* or similar structure, either projecting from a *compound pier* or other supporting device, or bonded to a wall and carrying one end of an *arch*, often at the end of an *arcade*. A nave arcade, for example, may have nine pillars and two responds.

retable (ruh·tay'bl) An architectural screen or wall above and behind an altar, usually containing painting, sculpture, carving, or other decorations.

reverse On coins or medals, the side opposite the *obverse*.

rhyton (right'on) An ancient Greek ceremonial drinking vessel whose base is usually in the form of the head of an animal, woman, or mythological creature.

rib A relatively slender molded masonry *arch* that projects from a surface. In Gothic architecture the ribs form the framework of the *vaulting*.

ribbed vault See *vault*.

rinceau (ran·so') An ornamental design composed of undulating foliate vine motifs.

rose or **wheel window** The large circular window with *tracery* and stained glass frequently used in the *façades* of Gothic churches.

rusticate To bevel or rabbet the edges of stone blocks in order to emphasize the joints between them. The technique was popular during the Renaissance, especially for stone courses at the ground-floor level.

samsara (som·sah'ruh) In Hindu belief, rebirth of the soul into a succession of lives.

sarcophagus A stone coffin.

saturation The purity of a *hue;* the higher the saturation, the purer the hue. *Value* and saturation are not constantly related: For example, high-saturation yellow tends to have a high value, while high-saturation violet tends to have a low value.

satyr (sat'er) In Greek mythology, a kind of demi-god or deity, a follower of Dionysos, wanton and lascivious and often represented with goatlike ears and legs and a short tail.

scale The dimensions of the parts or totality of a building or object in relation to its use or function. In architectural *plans,* the relation of the actual size of a structure to the size of its representation.

sculpture in the round Free-standing figures, carved or modeled in three dimensions.

secondary colors The colors (green, orange, purple) that result from mixture of pairs of the *primary colors.*

section In architecture, a diagram or representation of a part of a structure or building along an imaginary plane passing through it vertically.

seicento (say·chain'toh) The seventeenth century in Italian art.

serdab A small concealed chamber in a pyramid for the statue of the deceased.

sfumato (sfoo·ma'toh) A smokelike haziness that subtly softens outlines in painting, particularly applied to the painting of Leonardo.

sgraffito (zgra·fee'toh) Decoration produced by scratching through a surface layer of plaster, glazing, etc., to reveal a different colored ground; also, pottery or other ware so decorated.

shaft The part of a *column* between the *capital* and base.

shaft grave A grave in the form of a deep pit, the actual burial spot being at the base of the shaft or in a niche at the base.

sikhara (shih'kuh·ruh) In Hindu temples of Vishnu, the tower above the shrine.

silver point A drawing technique involving use of a silver-tipped "pencil" on a paper with a white *matte* coating; also, the delicate drawings so made.

sinopia Reddish-brown earth color; also, the *cartoon* or underpainting for a *fresco;* often spelled **sinopie.**

sistrum An instrument of metal rods loosely held in a metal frame, which jingle when shaken. Peculiarly Egyptian, it was used especially in the worship of Isis and is still used in Nubia.

Siva or **Shiva** (shee'vuh) Hindu god of destruction and creation.

slip Potter's clay dispersed in a liquid and used for *casting,* decoration, and to attach parts of clay vessels such as handles.

socle (soh'kel) A molded projection at the bottom of a wall or *pier,* or beneath a pedestal or *column* base.

soffit The underside of an architectural member such as an *arch, lintel, cornice,* or stairway. See *intrados*.

Solutrean Of or pertaining to a period of the Upper *Paleolithic.* Named after the site of Solutré, France, the culture appears to have been intrusive between the *Aurignacian* and *Magdalenian.*

spandrel The roughly triangular space enclosed by the curves of adjacent arches and a horizontal member connecting their vertexes; also, the space enclosed by the curve of an arch and an enclosing right angle.

splay A large bevel or *chamfer.*

splayed opening An opening (as in a wall) that is cut away diagonally so that the outer edges are farther apart then the inner. See also *embrasure.*

springing The lowest stone of an *arch,* resting on the *impost block.*

square schematism A church plan in which the crossing square is used as the *module* for all parts of the design.

squinch An architectural device used to make a transition from a square to a polygonal base for a *dome.* It may be composed of *lintels, corbels,* or *arches.*

stele (stee'lee) A carved stone slab or pillar used especially by the ancient Greeks for grave or site markers and similar purposes.

still life A painting representing inanimate objects such as flowers and household articles.

stoa In ancient Greek architecture, an open building whose roof is supported by a row of columns parallel to the back wall.

stringcourse A horizontal *molding* or band in masonry, ornamental but usually reflecting interior structure.

stucco Fine plaster or cement used as a coating for walls or for decoration.

stupa (stoo'puh) A large mound-shaped Buddhist shrine.

style A manner of treatment or execution of works of art that is characteristic of a civilization, a people, or an individual; also, a special and superior quality in a work of art.

stylobate The upper step of the base of a Greek temple, which forms a platform for the *columns.*

superimposed orders *Orders* of architecture placed one above another in an *arcaded* or *colonnaded* building, usually in the following sequence: Doric (the first story), Ionic, and Corinthian. Superimposed orders are found in Greek *stoas* and were used widely by Roman and Renaissance builders.

sutra (soo'truh) In Buddhism, an account of a sermon by or dialogue involving the Buddha.

swag A kind of decoration for walls, furniture, etc., done in *relief* and resembling garlands and gathered drapery. It was particularly popular in the eighteenth century.

symmetry Esthetic balance, usually achieved by disposing forms about a real or imaginary *axis* so that those on one side correspond more or less with those on the other. The correspondence may be in terms of shape, color, texture, etc.

tectiforms Rooflike shapes found painted on the walls of *Paleolithic* caves.

tell In Near Eastern archeology, a hill or mound, usually ancient sites of habitation.

tempera A technique of painting using as a *medium pigment* mixed with egg yolk, glue, or casein; also, the medium itself.

Tenebrists A group of seventeenth-century European painters who used violent contrasts of light and dark.

terra-cotta Hard-baked clay used for sculpture and as a building material. It may be *glazed* or painted.

tesserae (tess′er·ee) Small pieces of glass or stone used in making *mosaics.*

tholos (thoh′los) A circular structure, generally in Classical Greek style; also, an ancient circular tomb.

thrust The outward force exerted by an *arch* or *vault.* It must be counterbalanced by *buttresses.*

tondo A circular painting or piece of *relief* sculpture.

torana (tor′uh·nuh) Gateways in the stone fence around a *stupa,* located at the cardinal points of the compass.

torus A convex *molding* or part of a molding, usually the lowest in the base of a *column.*

totem An animal or object and its representation or image considered a symbol of a given family or clan.

trabeated Having horizontal beams or *lintels.*

tracery Branching ornamental stonework, generally in a window, where it supports the glass. It is particularly characteristic of Gothic architecture.

transept The part of a cruciform church whose *axis* crosses, at right angles, the axis running from the chief entrance through the *nave* to the *apse.*

trecento (tray·chain′toh) The fourteenth century in Italian art.

trefoil An architectural ornament having three lobes or foils. See *quatrefoil.*

triforium In a Gothic cathedral, the gallery between the principal *nave* arcades and the *clerestory* and opening on the nave through an *arcade.*

triglyph A projecting grooved member of a Doric *frieze* that alternates with *metopes.*

triptych A three-paneled *altarpiece.*

trompe l'oeil (trohmp loy′) A form of illusionistic painting that attempts to represent an object as though it existed in three dimensions at the surface of the painting; literally, "eye-fooling."

trumeau (troo·moh′) A *pillar* in the center of a Romanesque or Gothic portal.

tympanum The space enclosed by a *lintel* and an *arch* over a doorway; also, the recessed face of a *pediment.*

ushnisha Stylized protuberance of the Buddha's forehead, emblematic of his superhuman consciousness.

value The amount of light reflected by a *hue;* the greater the amount of light, the higher the value. See also *saturation.*

vanishing point In *linear perspective,* that point on the horizon toward which parallel lines appear to converge and at which they seem to vanish.

vault A masonry roof or ceiling constructed on the *arch* principle. A **barrel vault,** semi-cylindrical in cross section, is in effect a deep arch or an uninterrupted series of arches, one behind the other. A **fan vault** is a development of *lierné* vaulting characteristic of English Perpendicular Gothic, in which radiating *ribs* form a fanlike pattern. A **groin vault** is formed at the point where two barrel vaults intersect at right angles. A **ribbed vault** is one in which there is a framework of ribs or arches under the intersections of the vaulting sections.

veduta (veh·doo′ta) A painting of a view.

vignette Originally, a decorative element of vine leaves and tendrils. Hence, any rather small decorative design in a book or manuscript that has no definite boundaries or frame.

vimana (vih·mah′nuh) In Hindu and Buddhist temples, the pyramidal tower above the shrine.

Vishnu Hindu god, called "The Preserver," one of whose incarnations is Krishna.

volute A spiral scroll-like form characteristic of the Greek Ionic *capital.*

voussoir (voo·swahr′) A wedge-shaped block used in the construction of a true *arch.* The central voussoir, which sets the arch, is the *keystone.*

wainscot A wooden facing for an interior wall, usually paneled.

wall arcade See *blind arcade.*

warm color Red, orange, or yellow. Psychologically, warm colors tend to be exciting, emphatic, and affirmative; optically they generally seem to advance or project. See *cool color.*

wash In *watercolor* painting especially, a thin, transparent film of color.

watercolor A painting technique using as a *medium, pigment* (usually prepared with gum) mixed with water and applied to an absorbent surface. The painting is transparent, with the white of the paper furnishing the lights. See *gouache.*

westwork A multistoried mass, including the *façade* and usually surmounted by towers, at the western end of a Medieval church.

woodcut A wood block from whose surface those parts not intended to print are cut away to a slight depth, leaving the design raised; also, the printed impression made with such a block.

yaksha (*f.* **yakshi**) A divinity in the Hindu and Buddhist pantheon.

yu A covered Chinese libation vessel.

Zen A Buddhist sect, and its doctrine, that emphasizes enlightenment through intuition and introspection rather than the study of scripture. In Chinese, *Ch'an.*

ziggurat (zig′oor·at) Roughly pyramidal structures built in ancient Babylonia and Assyria and consisting of stages, each succeeding stage stepped back from the one beneath.

zoomorphism The representation of gods in the form or with the attributes of animals; the use of animal forms in art or symbolism.

bibliography

As a convenience to those who use libraries catalogued in the Library of Congress system, the call numbers for that system are shown at the end of each entry in this bibliography. Final digits may vary slightly from library to library according to differences in local shelving policies. The information supplied comes from two computer-generated search systems—the Ohio College Library Classification (OCLC) system and the Research Libraries Information Network (RLIN).

Reference Books

Encyclopedia of World Art. 15 vols. New York: McGraw-Hill, 1959–68, revised 1972. N31 .E4833

Fielding, Mantle. *Dictionary of American Painters, Sculptors and Engravers.* New York: James F. Carr, 1965. N6536 .F5

Fleming, John; Honour, Hugh; and Pevsner, Nikolaus. *Penguin Dictionary of Architecture.* Baltimore: Penguin, 1966. NA31 .F55

Hall, James. *Dictionary of Subjects and Symbols in Art.* London: J. Murray, 1974. N7560 .H34

Hind, Arthur M. *A History of Engraving and Etching from the Fifteenth Century to the Year 1914.* 3rd rev. ed. New York: Dover, 1963. NE400 .H66

Huyghe, René, ed. *Larousse Encyclopedia of Byzantine and Medieval Art.* New York: Prometheus Press, 1963. Reprint. New York: Hamlyn/American (paperbound), 1976. N5970 .H813

———— *Larousse Encyclopedia of Renaissance and Baroque Art.* New York: Prometheus Press, 1964. Reprint. Hamlyn/American (paperbound), 1976. N6350 .H813

Kronenberger, Louis. *Atlantic Brief Lives: A Biographical Companion to the Arts.* Boston: Little, Brown, 1971. CT105 .K765

Murray, Peter, and Murray, Linda. *A Dictionary of Art and Artists.* New York: Penguin, 1972. N31 .M8

Myers, Bernard Samuel, ed. *Encyclopedia of Painting: Painters and Painting of the World from Prehistoric Times to the Present Day.* 3rd rev. ed. New York: Crown, 1970. ND30 .E5

Myers, Bernard S., and Myers, Shirley D., eds. *Dictionary of 20th Century Art.* New York: McGraw-Hill, 1974. N6490 .M89

Pevsner, Nikolaus. *An Outline of European Architecture.* 8th rev. ed. Baltimore: Penguin, 1974. NA950 .P4

Quick, John. *Artists' and Illustrators' Encyclopedia.* New York: McGraw-Hill, 1977. N33 .Q5

Stierlin, Henri. *Encyclopedia of World Architecture 1978.* New York: Facts on File, 1978. NA202 .S76

chapter 1   The Birth of Art

Bandi, Hans, and Breuil, Henri, et al. *The Art of the Stone Age: Forty Thousand Years of Rock Art.* New York: Crown, 1961. N5310 .S683

Bataille, Georges. *Lascaux: Prehistoric Painting or the Birth of Art.* Lausanne: Skira, 1955. N5310 .B38

Breuil, Henri. *Four Hundred Centuries of Cave Art.* Montignac: Centre études et de documentation préhistoriques, 1952. N5310 .B643

Graziosi, Paolo. *Paleolithic Art.* New York: McGraw-Hill, 1960. N5310 .G663

Leroi-Gourhan, A. *Treasures of Prehistoric Art.* New York: Abrams, 1967. N5310 .L5313

Windels, Fernand. *The Lascaux Cave Paintings.* New York: Viking, 1950. N5310 .W72

chapter 2   The Ancient Near East

Braidwood, Robert J. *The Near East and the Foundations for Civilization.* Eugene, Ore.: Oregon State System of Higher Education, 1952; Ann Arbor, Mich.: University Microfilms, 1974. CB301 .B63

Culican, William. *The Medes and Persians.* London: Thames & Hudson, 1965; New York: Praeger, 1965. D5275 .C8

Frankfort, Henri. *The Art and Architecture of the Ancient Orient.* Baltimore: Penguin, 1971. N5345 .F7

Garbini, Giovanni. *The Ancient World.* London: Hamlyn, 1976. N5345 .G3

Ghirshman, Roman. *Persia from the Origins to Alexander the Great.* London: Thames & Hudson, 1964. N5390 .G48

Kenyon, Kathleen M. *Digging Up Jericho.* New York: Praeger, 1974. D5704 .K39

Kramer, Samuel N. *History Begins at Sumer.* Garden City, N.Y.: Doubleday, 1959. DS72 .K7

———— *The Sumerians: Their History, Culture, and Character.* Chicago: University of Chicago Press, 1963. DS72 .K73

Lloyd, Seton. *The Art of the Ancient Near East.* New York: Praeger, 1969. N5345 .L55

Mellaart, James. *The Earliest Civilizations of the Near East.* New York: McGraw-Hill, 1965. CB301 .M38

———— *Çatal Hüyük: a Neolithic Town in Anatolia.* New York: McGraw-Hill, 1967. DS49.3 .M4

Oppenheim, A. Leo. *Ancient Mesopotamia.* Rev. ed. Chicago: University of Chicago Press, 1977. DS69.5 .O6

Parrot, André. *The Arts of Assyria.* New York: Golden Press, 1961. N5370 .P333

———— *Sumer: The Dawn of Art.* New York: Golden Press, 1961. N5370 .P343

Perkins, Ann Louise. *The Art of Dura-Europos.* Oxford: Clarendon Press, 1973. N5873.6 .S92D876

Porada, Edith, and Dyson, R. H. *The Art of Ancient Iran: Islamic Cultures.* Rev. ed. New York: Greystone Press, 1969. N5390 .P62

Woolley, Charles L. *The Art of the Middle East, Including Persia, Mesopotamia and Palestine.* New York: Crown, 1961. N5343 .W613

———— *The Development of Sumerian Art.* London: Faber & Faber, 1935. N5370 .W6

chapter 3   The Art of Egypt

Aldred, Cyril. *The Development of Ancient Egyptian Art from 3200 to 1315 B.C.* 3 vols. London: Academy Edition, 1973. N5350 .A6

Badawy, Alexander. *A History of Egyptian Architecture.* 3 vols. Berkeley: University of California Press, 1954–68. NA215 .B3

Breasted, James. *History of Egypt.* 1909. Reprint. New York: Scribner's, 1956. DT83 .B782

Emery, Walter B. *Archaic Egypt.* Baltimore: Penguin, 1962. DT61 .E4

Lange, Kurt, with Hirmer, Max. *Egypt: Architecture, Sculpture and Painting in Three Thousand Years.* 4th ed. London and New York: Phaidon, 1968. N5351 .L313

Mekhitarian, Arpag. *Egyptian Painting.* New York: Skira, 1978. ND2863 .M4413

Smith, William Stevenson. *The Art and Architecture of Ancient Egypt.* Harmondsworth, England: Penguin, 1965. N5350 .S65

Smith, E. Baldwin. *Egyptian Architecture as Cultural Expression.* Watkins Glen, N.Y.: American Life Foundation, 1968. NA215 .S6

Woldering, Irmgard. *Gods, Men and Pharaohs: The Glory of Egyptian Art.* New York: Abrams, 1967. N5350 .W5613

chapter 4   The Art of the Aegean

Blegen, Carl W., and Rawson, Marion. *The Palace of Nestor at Phylos in Western Messenia.* 2 vols. Princeton: Princeton University Press, 1966. NA277 .B55

Demargne, Pierre. *Aegean Art: The Origins of Greek Art.* London: Thames & Hudson, 1964. N5630 .D413

Evans, Arthur. *The Palace of Minos.* 4 vols. 1921–35. Reprint. New York: Biblo & Tannen, 1964. DF221 .C8E75

Graham, James W. *The Palaces of Crete.* Princeton: Princeton University Press, 1969. NA279 .C7G7

Marinatos, Spyridon, with Hirmer, Max. *Crete and Mycenae.* London: Thames & Hudson, 1960. N5660 .M35

Matz, Friedrich. *The Art of Crete and Early Greece.* New York: Crown, 1962. N5630 .M313

Pendlebury, John. *The Archeology of Crete.* London: Methuen, 1967. DF221 .C8P38

Schliemann, Heinrich. *Ilios.* 1881. Reprint. New York: B. Blom, 1968. (Other reprints available.) DF221 .T8S3

—— *Mycenae.* 1880. Reprint. New York: Arno Press, 1976. DF221 .M9S35

—— *Tiryns.* 1885. Reprint. New York: Arno Press, 1976. DF221 .T5S3

Vermeule Emily. *Greece in the Bronze Age.* Chicago: University of Chicago Press, 1964. DF220 .V4

Wace, Alan. *Mycenae, an Archeological History and Guide.* New York: Biblo & Tannen, 1964. DF221 .M9W33

chapter 5 The Art of Greece

Arias, Paolo. *A History of One Thousand Years of Greek Vase Painting.* New York: Abrams, 1962. NK4645 .A69

Ashmole, Bernard. *Architect and Sculptor in Classical Greece.* New York: New York University Press, 1972. NA270 .A8

Beazley, John D. *The Development of Attic Black-Figure.* Berkeley: University of California Press, 1964. NK4648 .B42

—— *Potter and Painter in Ancient Athens.* London: G. Cumberledge, 1944. NK4645 .B41

Beazley, John D., and Ashmole, Bernard. *Greek Sculpture and Painting to the End of the Hellenistic Period.* Cambridge: Cambridge University Press, 1932, 1966. N5630 .B35

Berve, Helmut. *Greek Temples, Theatres, and Shrines.* New York: Abrams, 1963. NA275 .B413

Blumel, Carl. *Greek Sculptors at Work.* London: Phaidon, 1969. NB90 .B552

Brilliant, Richard. *Arts of the Ancient Greeks.* New York: McGraw-Hill, 1973. N5630 .B74

Bruno, Vincent J., ed. *The Parthenon.* New York: Norton, 1974. NA281 .B78

Buschor, Ernst. *Greek Vase Painting.* Reprint. New York: Hacker, 1978. NK464 .B9

Carpenter, Rhys. *Greek Sculpture: A Critical Review.* Chicago: University of Chicago Press, 1960. NB90 .C26

Charbonneaux, Jean; Martin, Roland; and Villard, François. *Hellenistic Art.* New York: Braziller, 1973. N5630 .C46513

Cook, Robert M. *Greek Art: Its Development, Character and Influence.* Harmondsworth, England: Penguin, 1976. N5630 .C77

Lawrence, Arnold W. *Greek Architecture.* 2nd ed. Baltimore: Penguin, 1967. NA270 .L36

Lullies, Reinhard, and Hirmer, Max. *Greek Sculpture.* Rev. ed. New York: Abrams, 1960. NB90 .L813

Pfuhl, Ernst. *Masterpieces of Greek Drawing and Painting.* 2nd ed. New York: Macmillan, 1955; Chicago: Argonaut, 1967. ND110 .P43

Pollitt, Jerome G. *Art and Experience in Classical Greece.* Cambridge: Cambridge University Press, 1972. N5630 .P54

Richter, Gisela M. *Attic Red-Figure Vases: A Survey.* New Haven: Yale University Press, 1958. NK4649 .R5

—— *A Handbook of Greek Art.* 6th ed. New York: Phaidon, 1969. N5630 .R49

—— *The Sculpture and Sculptors of the Greeks.* 4th ed. New Haven: Yale University Press, 1970. NB90 .R54

Robertson, Donald S. *Greek and Roman Architecture.* 2nd ed. Reprint. Cambridge: Cambridge University Press, 1969. NA260 .R6

Robertson, Martin. *Greek Painting.* Geneva: Skira, 1959. ND110 .R6

—— *A History of Greek Art.* 2 vols. Cambridge: Cambridge University Press, 1976. N5630 .R63

Robertson, Martin, and Frantz, Alison. *The Parthenon Frieze.* New York: Oxford University Press, 1975. NB91 .A7R62

Scranton, Robert L. *Greek Architecture.* New York: Braziller, 1962. NA270 .S3

Scully, Vincent J. *The Earth, the Temple and the Gods: Greek Sacred Architecture.* Rev. ed. New York: Praeger, 1969. NA275 .S3

Swindler, Mary H. *Ancient Painting.* New Haven: Yale University Press, 1929. ND70 .S8

chapter 6 Etruscan and Roman Art

Brilliant, Richard. *Roman Art, from the Republic to Constantine.* New York: Praeger, 1974. N5760 .B74

Brown, Frank Edward. *Roman Architecture.* New York: Braziller, 1961. NA310 .B75

Goldscheider, Ludwig. *Roman Portraits.* London and New York: Phaidon, 1940. NB164 .G6

Hanfmann, George. *Roman Art.* Greenwich, Conn.: New York Graphic Society, 1964. N5740 .H3

Kraus, Theodor. *Pompeii and Herculaneum: The Living Cities of the Dead.* New York: Abrams, 1975. N5769 .K7213

MacDonald, William L. *The Architecture of the Roman Empire.* Vol. I. New Haven: Yale University Press, 1965. NA310 .M2

Maiuri, Amedeo. *Pompeii.* 14th ed. Rome: Istituto poligrafico dello Stato, 1970. DG70 .P7M26

—— *Roman Painting.* Geneva: Skira, 1953. ND120 .M25

Mansuelli, Guido. *The Art of Etruria and Early Rome.* New York: Crown, 1965. N5750 .M34

Richardson, Emeline. *The Etruscans: Their Art and Civilization.* Chicago: University of Chicago Press, 1976. DG223 .R5

Rivoira, Giovanni. *Roman Architecture and Its Principles of Construction Under the Empire.* New York: Hacker, 1972. NA310 .R52

Robertson, Donald S. *Greek and Roman Architecture.* 2nd ed. Reprint. Cambridge: Cambridge University Press, 1969. NA260 .R6

Strong, Donald. *Roman Art.* Harmondsworth, England: Penguin, 1976. N25 .P4V.39

Strong, Eugenie. *Art in Ancient Rome.* Reprint. Westport, Conn.

Ward-Perkins, John. *Roman Architecture.* New York: Abrams, 1977. NA310 .W32

Wickhoff, Franz. *Roman Art: Some of Its Principles, and Their Application to Early Christian Painting.* London: W. Heinemann; New York: Macmillan, 1900. N5761 .W6

chapter 7 Early Christian, Byzantine, and Islamic Art

Anthony, Edgar W. *A History of Mosaics.* Reprint. New York: Hacker, 1968. NA3750 .A55

Arnold, Thomas W. *Painting in Islam.* New York: Dover, 1965. ND198 .A7

Aslanapa, Oktay. *Turkish Art and Architecture.* London: Faber & Faber, 1971. N7161 .A87

Baynes, Norman, and Moss, Henry, eds. *Byzantium.* Oxford: Clarendon Press, 1961. DF521 .B28

Beckwith, John. *The Art of Constantinople: An Introduction to Byzantine Art (330–1453).* New York: Phaidon, 1968. N6250 .B4

—— *Early Christian and Byzantine Art.* New York: Penguin, 1979. N7832 .B3

Chatzidakis, Manolis. *Byzantine and Early Medieval Painting.* New York: Viking, 1965. ND142 .C5

Creswell, K. A. C., and van Berchem, Marguerite.

Early Muslim Architecture. 2nd ed. Oxford: Clarendon Press, 1969. NA381 .C72

Dalton, Ormonde M. *Byzantine Art and Archaeology.* New York: Dover, 1961. N6250 .D2

Demus, Otto. *Byzantine Mosaic Decoration.* London: Paul, Trench & Trubner, 1948. NA3780 .D39

Ettinghausen, Richard. *Arab Painting.* Geneva: Skira, 1962. ND198 .E8

—— *From Byzantium to Sasanian Iran and the Islamic World.* Leiden: Brill, 1972. N7429 .E88

Grabar, André. *The Beginnings of Christian Art, 200–395.* London: Thames & Hudson, 1967. N7832 .C6813

—— *Byzantine Painting.* Geneva: Skira, 1953. ND142 .G7

—— *The Golden Age of Justinian: From the Death of Theodosius to the Rise of Islam.* New York: Odyssey Press, 1967. N6250 .G713

Grabar, André, and Chatzidakis, Manolis. *Greek Mosaics of the Byzantine Period.* New York: New American Library, 1964. NA3780 .G7

Grabar, Oleg. *The Formation of Islamic Art.* New Haven: Yale University Press, 1973. N6260 .G69

Grunebaum, Gustave von. *Classical Islam: A History, 600–1258.* Chicago: Aldine, 1970. D538 .3 .V6413

Hamilton, George H. *The Art and Architecture of Russia.* 2nd ed. New York: Viking, 1975. N6981 .H34

Hamilton, John A. *Byzantine Architecture and Decoration.* 1933. Reprint. Freeport, N.Y.: Books for Libraries/Arno, 1972. NA4829 .B9

Hawley, Walter A. *Oriental Rugs, Antique and Modern.* 1936. Reprint. New York: Dover, 1970. NK2808 .H3

Huyghe, René, ed. *Larousse Encyclopedia of Byzantine and Medieval Art.* See Reference Books.

Kitzinger, Ernst. *Early Medieval Art in the British Museum.* London: British Museum, 1969. N5963 .K5

Krautheimer, Richard. *Early Christian and Byzantine Architecture.* Harmondsworth, England: Penguin, 1975. NA4817 .K7

Kühnel, Ernst. *Islamic Art and Architecture.* London: Bell, 1966. N6260 .K7783

Lane, Arthur. *Early Islamic Pottery, Mesopotamia, Egypt and Persia.* New York: Van Nostrand, 1948. NK3880 .L3

Levey, Michael. *The World of Ottoman Art.* New York: Scribner's, 1975. N7164 .L48

Lowrie, Walter S. *Art in the Early Church.* New York: Norton, 1969. N7832 .L58

MacDonald, William L. *Early Christian and Byzantine Architecture.* New York: Braziller, 1962. NA360 .M3

Meyer, Peter. *Byzantine Mosaics: Torcello, Venice, Monreale, Palermo.* London and New York: Batsford, 1952. NA3780 .M4

Morey, Charles R. *Early Christian Art.* Princeton: Princeton University Press, 1953. N7832 .M67

Pope, Arthur, and Ackerman, Phyllis. *A Survey of Persian Art from Prehistoric Times to the Present.* London and New York: Oxford University Press, 1977. N7280 .S96

Rice, David T. *The Appreciation of Byzantine Art.* London: Oxford University Press, 1972. N6250 .R45

—— *The Art of Byzantium.* New York: Abrams, 1959. N6250 .R46

—— *Byzantine Art.* Harmondsworth, England: Penguin, 1968. N6250 .R47

—— *Islamic Art.* London: Thames & Hudson, 1975. N6260 .R53

Simson, Otto von. *Sacred Fortress: Byzantine Art and Stagecraft in Ravenna.* Chicago: University of Chicago Press, 1976. NA5621 .R3S5

Smith, Earl Baldwin. *Architectural Symbolism of Imperial Rome and the Middle Ages.* Princeton: Princeton University Press, 1956. NA310 .S6

—— *The Dome, a Study in the History of Ideas.*

Princeton: Princeton University Press, 1950. NA2890 .S6

Swift, Emerson H. *Hagia Sophia*. New York: Columbia University Press, 1940. NA5870 .S3S9

Volbach, Wolfgang. *Early Christian Mosaics, from the Fourth to the Seventh Centuries.* New York: Oxford University Press, 1946. NA3780 .V62

Volbach, Wolfgang, and Hirmer, Max. *Early Christian Art*. New York: Abrams, 1962. N7832 .V63

Weitzmann, Kurt. *Ancient Book Illumination*. Cambridge: Harvard University Press, 1959. ND2910 .N4

————— *Illustrations in Roll and Codex*. Princeton: Princeton University Press, 1970. ND2900 .W4

chapter 8   Early Medieval Art

Arnold, Bruce. *A Concise History of Irish Art.* Rev. ed. London: Thames & Hudson, 1977. N6782 .A8

Beckwith, John. *Early Medieval Art: Carolingian, Ottonian, Romanesque.* New York: Oxford University Press, 1974. N5970 .B42

Conant, Kenneth. *Carolingian and Romanesque Architecture 800-1200*. 2nd integrated rev. ed. Harmondsworth, England and New York: Penguin, 1978. NA365 .C6

Finley, Ian. *Celtic Art, an Introduction.* London: Faber & Faber, 1973. N5925 .F56

Goldschmidt, Adolf. *German Illumination.* New York: Hacker, 1970. ND3151 .G613

Grabar, André, and Nordenfalk, Carl. *Early Medieval Painting from the Fourth to the Eleventh Century.* New York: Skira, 1957. ND140 .G7

Henderson, George. *Early Medieval.* Pelican Style and Civilization Series. New York: Penguin, 1972. N5975 .H35

Henry, Françoise. *Irish Art in the Early Christian Period, to 800 A. D.* Rev. ed. London: Methuen, 1965. N6784 .H4213

————— *Irish Art During the Viking Invasions, 900-1200 A. D.* Ithaca, N.Y.: Cornell University Press, 1970. N6784 .H4413

Hinks, Roger P. *Carolingian Art.* Ann Arbor: University of Michigan Press, 1966. N6245 .H5

Laszlo, Gyula. *The Art of the Migration Period.* London: Allen Lane, 1974. N6814 .L313

Leeds, Edward T. *Early Anglo-Saxon Art and Archaeology.* Westport, Conn.: Greenwood Press, 1970. DA155 .L43

Nordenfalk, Carl. *Celtic and Anglo-Saxon Painting: Book Illumination in the British Isles 600-800.* New York: Braziller, 1977. ND2940 .N67

Simons, Gerald. *Barbarian Europe.* New York: Time-Life Books, 1968. D117 .S55

Taylor, Harold M., and Taylor, Joan. *Anglo-Saxon Architecture.* 2 vols. Cambridge: Cambridge University Press, 1965. NA963 .T3

Wilson, David M., and Klindt-Jensen, Ole. *Viking Art.* London: Allen & Unwin, 1966. N7003 .W5

chapter 9   Romanesque Art

Anthony, Edgar W. *Romanesque Frescoes.* Princeton: Princeton University Press, 1951. ND2580 .A5

Baum, Julius. *Romanesque Architecture in France.* 2nd ed. London: Country Life, 1928. NA397 .B3

Bevan, Bernard. *History of Spanish Architecture.* London: Batsford, 1938. NA1301 .B4

Brooke, Christopher. *The Monastic World, 1000-1300.* London: Elek, 1974. BX2470 .B76

Clapham, Alfred W. *English Romanesque Architecture After the Conquest.* Oxford: Clarendon Press, 1964. NA5463 .C54

————— *Romanesque Architecture in Western Europe.* Oxford: Clarendon Press, 1936. NA390 .C6

Conant, Kenneth. *Carolingian and Romanesque Architecture 800-1200*. Baltimore: Penguin, 1959. NA365 .C6

Crichton, George H. *Romanesque Sculpture in*

Italy. London: Routledge & Paul, 1954. NB613 .C7

Decker, Heinrich. *Romanesque Art in Italy.* New York: Abrams, 1959. N6913 .D413

Deschamps, Paul. *French Sculpture of the Romanesque Period—Eleventh and Twelfth Centuries.* 1930. Reprint. New York: Hacker, 1972. NB175 .D4

Evans, Joan. *Art in Medieval France 987-1498.* Oxford: Clarendon Press, 1969. N6843 .G8

Focillon, Henri. *The Art of the West in the Middle Ages.* 2nd ed. London and New York: Phaidon, 1969. N6280 .F613

Gantner, Joseph; Pobé, Marcel; and Roubier, Jean. *Romanesque Art in France.* London: Thames & Hudson, 1956. NB543 .G3

Gibbs-Smith, Charles H. *The Bayeux Tapestry.* London: Phaidon, 1973. NK3049 .B3G44

Grabar, André, and Nordenfalk, Carl. *Romanesque Painting.* New York: Skira, 1958. ND140 .G683

Kuback, Hans E. *Romanesque Architecture.* New York: Abrams, 1975. NA390 .K7913

Kuenstler, Gustav, ed. *Romanesque Art in Europe.* New York: Norton, 1973. N6280 .K8

Leisinger, Hermann. *Romanesque Bronzes: Church Portals in Mediaeval Europe.* New York: Praeger, 1957. NB1282 .L413

Michel, Paul H. *Romanesque Wall Paintings in France.* Paris: Éditions Chêne, 1949. ND2746 .M56

Morey, Charles R. *Medieval Art.* New York: Norton, 1970. NN5970 .M6

Porter, Arthur K. *Medieval Architecture.* 2 vols. 1909. Reprint. New York: Hacker, 1969. NA350 .P8

————— *Romanesque Sculpture of the Pilgrimage Roads.* 1923. Reprint. New York: Hacker, 1969. NB175 .P6

Ricci, Corrado. *Romanesque Architecture in Italy.* London: W. Heinemann, 1925. NA405 .R5

Rivoira, Giovanni. *Lombardic Architecture: Its Origin, Development, and Derivatives.* 1933. Reprint. New York: Hacker, 1975. NA1119 .L8R613

Saalman, Howard. *Medieval Architecture: European Architecture 600-1200.* New York: Braziller, 1962. NA350 .S2

Schapiro, Meyer. *Romanesque Art: Selected Papers.* London: Chatto & Windus, 1977; New York: Braziller, 1976. NB175 .S28

Stoddard, Whitney. *Monastery and Cathedral in France.* Middletown, Conn.: Wesleyan University Press, 1966. N6843 .S7

Stone, Lawrence. *Sculpture in Britain in the Middle Ages.* Baltimore: Penguin, 1955. NB463 .S8

Swarzenski, Hanns. *Monuments of Romanesque Art.* Chicago: University of Chicago Press, 1974. N6280 .S9

Webb, Geoffrey F. *Architecture in Britain: The Middle Ages.* Harmondsworth, England: Penguin, 1956. NA963 .W4

chapter 10   Gothic Art

Adams, Henry. *Mont-Saint-Michel and Chartres.* Reprint. New York: Doubleday/Anchor, 1959. (Other reprints available.) DC801 .M83A44

Arnold, Hugh. *Stained Glass of the Middle Ages in England and France.* London: A. & C. Black, 1939. NK5308 .A7

Arslan, Edoardo. *Gothic Architecture in Venice.* London: Phaidon, 1971. NA1121 .V4A813

Aubert, Marcel. *The Art of the High Gothic Era.* New York: Crown, 1965. N6310 .A833

————— *Gothic Cathedrals of France and Their Treasures.* London: N. Kay, 1959. NA5543 .A923

Branner, Robert. *Chartres Cathedral.* New York: Norton, 1969. NA5551 .C5B7

————— *Gothic Architecture.* New York: Braziller, 1961. NA440 .B68

Duby, Georges. *The Europe of the Cathedrals.* Geneva: Skira, 1966. NA4830 .D7813

Dupont, Jacques, and Gnudi, Cesare. *Gothic Painting.* Geneva: Skira, 1954. ND140 .D85

Evans, Joan. *Art in Medieval France 987-1498.* Oxford: Clarendon Press, 1969. N6843 .G8

————— *The Flowering of the Middle Ages.* New York: McGraw-Hill, 1966. CB351 .E9

Fitchen, John. *The Construction of Gothic Cathedrals.* Chicago: University of Chicago Press, 1977. NA440 .F5

Focillon, Henri. *The Art of the West in the Middle Ages.* Vol. 2. New York: Phaidon, 1969. N6280 .F613

Frankl, Paul. *Gothic Architecture.* Baltimore: Penguin, 1963. NA440 .F683

————— *The Gothic Literary Sources and Interpretations.* Princeton: Princeton University Press, 1960. NA440 .F7

Harvey, John H. *The Gothic World.* New York: Harper & Row, 1969. N6310 .H3

Huizinga, Johan, *The Waning of the Middle Ages.* London: E. Arnold, 1970. DC33 .2 .H83

Jantzen, Hans. *The High Gothic: The Classic Cathedrals of Chartres, Reims, and Amiens.* New York: Pantheon, 1962. NA453 .J23

Johnson, James. *The Radiance of Chartres.* New York: Random House, 1965. NK5349 .C5J6

Katzenellenbogen, Adolf. *The Sculptural Programs of Chartres Cathedral.* Baltimore: Johns Hopkins Press, 1959. NA5551 .C5K3

Male, Émile. *The Gothic Image: Religious Art in France of the Thirteenth Century.* New York: Harper & Row, 1958. N7949 .M313

Panofsky, Erwin. *Abbot Suger on the Abbey Church of St. Denis and Its Art Treasures.* 2nd ed. Princeton: Princeton University Press, 1979. NA5551 .S2S8

————— *Gothic Architecture and Scholasticism.* Latrobe, Penn.: Archabbey Press, 1951. NA2563 .P3

Robb, David M. *The Art of the Illuminated Manuscript.* Cranbury, N.J.: A. S. Barnes, 1973. ND2900 .R63

Sheridan, Ronald, and Ross, Anne. *Gargoyles and Grotesques: Paganism in the Medieval Church.* Boston: New York Graphic Society, 1975. NB170 .S47

Simson, Otto von. *The Gothic Cathedral.* 2nd rev. ed. Princeton: Princeton University Press, 1974. NA4830 .S5

Stoddard, Whitney. *Monastery and Cathedral in France.* Middletown, Conn.: Wesleyan University Press, 1966. N6843 .S7

Thompson, Daniel. *The Materials and Techniques of Medieval Painting.* New York: Dover, 1956. ND1500 .T5

Ward, Clarence. *Medieval Church Vaulting.* 1915. Reprint. New York: AMS Press, 1973. NA5253 .W3

chapter 11   The Art of India

Archer, William G. *Indian Miniatures.* Greenwich, Conn.: New York Graphic Society, 1960. ND3247 .A7

————— *Indian Paintings from the Punjab Hills.* 2 vols. London and New York: Sotheby Parke Bernet, 1973. ND1337 .I5A72

Bachhofer, Ludwig. *Early Indian Sculpture.* 1929. Reprint. New York: Hacker, 1972. NB1002 .B3

Balasybrahmanyan, S. R. *Early Chola Art—Part I.* New York: Asia Publishing House, 1966. NA6002 .B3

————— *Early Chola Temples: Parantakat to Rajaraja I, A.D. 907-985.* Bombay: Orient Longman, 1971. NA6002 .B32

Barrett, Douglas E. *Early Cola Bronzes.* Bombay: Bhulabhai Memorial Institute, 1965. NB1002 .B37

Barrett, Douglas E., and Gray, Basil. *Painting of India.* Geneva: Skira, 1963. ND1002 .B3

Basham, Arthur L. *The Wonder That Was India.* 3rd rev. ed. Paris: Arthaud, 1976. DS425 .B33

Bhattacharji, Sukumari. *The Indian Theogony, a*

Comparative Study of Indian Mythology. London: Cambridge University Press, 1970. BL20012 .B48

Coomaraswamy, Ananda K. *History of Indian and Indonesian Art.* New Delhi: Munshiram Manaharlal, 1972. N7260 .C65

―――― *Yaksas.* New Delhi: Munshiram Manaharlal, 1971. BL1215 .Y3C62

Dehijia, Vidya. *Early Buddhist Rock Temples.* Ithaca, N.Y.: Cornell University Press, 1972. NA6002 .D37

Ghosh, Amalananda. *Ajanta Murals.* New Delhi: Archaeological Survey of India, 1967. ND2827 .G5

Gopinatha Rao, T. A. *Elements of Hindu Iconography.* 2nd ed. 4 vols. New York: Paragon, 1968. BL1201 .G7

Groslier, Philippe, and Arthaud, Jacques. *The Arts and Civilization of Angkor.* New York: Praeger, 1957. DS558 .A6G73

Harle, James C. *Gupta Sculpture: Indian Sculpture of the Fourth to the Sixth Centuries A.D.* Oxford: Clarendon Press, 1974. NB1002 .H33

Kramrisch, Stella. *The Art of India.* 3rd ed. London: Phaidon, 1965. N7301 .K68

―――― *The Hindu Temple.* 2 vols. Delhi: Motilal Banarsidass, 1976. NA6002 .K72

―――― *Indian Sculpture.* The Heritage of India Series. London and New York: Oxford University Press, 1933. NB1001 .K67

Krishna Deva. *Temples of North India.* New Delhi: National Book Trust, 1969. NA6007 .N6K7

Lee, Sherman E. *Ancient Cambodian Sculpture.* New York: Intercultural Arts Press, 1970. NB1015 .L42

Rawson, Philip. *The Art of Southeast Asia.* New York: Praeger, 1967. N5877 .A8R3

Rosenfield, John. *Dynastic Arts of the Kushan.* Berkeley: University of California Press, 1967. N5899 .K8R6

Rowland, Benjamin. *The Art and Architecture of India: Buddhist, Hindu, Jain.* Harmondsworth, England: Penguin, 1977. N7301 .R68

Sivaramamurti, C. *South Indian Bronzes.* New Delhi: Lalit Kala Akademi, 1963. NB1002 .S58

―――― *South Indian Paintings.* New Delhi: National Museum, 1968. ND1007 .S6S5

Srinivasan, K. R. *Temples of South India.* New Delhi: National Book Trust, 1972. NA6007 .S6S67

chapter 12   The Art of China

Cahill, James. *Chinese Painting.* New ed. Geneva: Skira, 1977; New York: Rizzoli, 1977. ND1043 .C28

Davidson, J. Leroy. *The Lotus Sutra in Chinese Art: A Study in Buddhist Art to the Year 1880.* New Haven: Yale University Press, 1954. N7343 .D35

Gray, Basil, and Vincent, John B. *Buddhist Cave Paintings at Tun-Huang.* Chicago: University of Chicago Press, 1959. ND2850 .T8G7

Honey, William B. *The Ceramic Art of China and Other Countries of the Far East.* New York: Beechhurst Press, 1954. NK4163 .H6

Lee, Sherman E. *Chinese Landscape Painting.* 2nd ed. Cleveland: Cleveland Museum of Art, 1962. ND1366 .L43

Loehr, Max. *Ritual Vessels of Bronze Age China.* New York: Asia Society, 1968. NK7983 .L57

Mizuno, Seiichi. *Bronzes and Jades of Ancient China.* Tokyo: Nihon Keizai, 1959.

Mizuno, Seiichi, and Nagahiro, Toshio. *A Study of the Buddhist Cave Temples at Lung-Men, Honan.* Tokyo: Zanho Press, 1941. BL1430 .M5

Rudolph, Richard. *Han Tomb Art of West China.* Berkeley: University of California Press, 1951. NB1043 .R8

Sickman, Lawrence C., and Soper, Alexander. *The Art and Architecture of China.* Baltimore and London: Penguin, 1956. N7340 .S46

Siren, Oswald. *A History of Later Chinese Paint-*

ing. 1938. Reprint. London: Medici Society, 1978. ND1040 .S52

―――― *Chinese Painting: Leading Masters and Principles.* Reprint. New York: Hacker, 1973. ND1040 .S492

―――― *Chinese Sculpture from the Fifth to the Fourteenth Centuries.* 4 vols. 1925. Reprint. New York: Hacker, 1970. NB1043 .S5

Sullivan, Michael. *The Birth of Landscape Painting in China.* Berkeley: University of California Press, 1962. ND1366 .S9

―――― *A Short History of Chinese Art.* Berkeley: University of California, 1970. N7340 .S92

Sullivan, Michael, and Darbois, Dominique. *The Cave Temples of Maichishan.* London: Faber & Faber, 1969. NB1043 .S77

Weber, Charles D. *Chinese Pictorial Bronze Vessels of the Late Chou Period.* Ascona: Artibus Asiae, 1968. NK7983 .W4

chapter 13   The Art of Japan

Akiyama, Terukazu. *Japanese Painting.* Geneva: Skira; New York: Rizzoli, 1977. ND1050 .A413

Cahill, James F. *Scholar Painters of Japan: The Nanga School.* Reprint. New York: Arno Press, 1976. ND10535 .C3

Drexler, Arthur. *The Architecture of Japan.* Reprint. New York: Arno Press, 1966. NA1550 .N4

Fontein, Jan, and Hickman, M. C., eds. *Zen Painting and Calligraphy.* Greenwich, Conn.: New York Graphic Society, 1970. N7262 .B61

Hirano, Chie. *Kiyonaga: A Study of His Life and Works.* Cambridge, Mass.: Harvard University Press, 1939. NE1325 .K6H5

Kidder, J. Edward. *Early Japanese Art.* London: Thames & Hudson, 1969. GN796 .J3

―――― *Japanese Temples: Sculpture, Painting, and Architecture.* Tokyo: Bijutsu Shuppansha, 1964. N7350 .K44

Lee, Sherman E. *A History of Far Eastern Art.* London: Thames & Hudson, 1975. N7336 .L43

―――― *Japanese Decorative Style.* New York: Harper & Row, 1972. N7350 .L43

Paine, Robert, and Soper, Alexander. *The Art and Architecture of Japan.* Baltimore: Penguin, 1955. N7350 .P3

Rosenfield, John M. *Japanese Art of the Heian Period, 749-1185.* New York: Asia Society, 1967. N7353 .R6

Rosenfield, John M., and Shimada, Shujiro. *Traditions of Japanese Art.* Cambridge, Mass.: Fogg Art Museum, Harvard University, 1970. N7352 .R67

Soper, Alexander. *The Evolution of Buddhist Architecture in Japan.* 1942. Reprint. New York: Hacker, 1978. NA1550 .S6

Stern, Harold P. *Master Prints of Japan: Ukiyo-e Hanga.* New York: Abrams, 1969. NE1315 .S7

chapter 14   The Native Arts of the Americas, Africa, and the South Pacific

PRE-COLUMBIAN ART

Bennett, Wendell C. *Ancient Arts of the Andes.* New York: Museum of Modern Art and Arno Press, 1966. F2230 .1 .A7B4

Bernal, Ignacio. *The Olmec World.* Berkeley: University of California Press, 1977. F1219 .B51713

Coe, Michael D. *The Jaguar's Children: Pre-Classic Central Mexico.* New York: Museum of Primitive Art, 1965. F1219 .3 .A7C56

Coe, William R. *Tikal: A Handbook of the Ancient Maya Ruins.* 3rd ed. Philadelphia: University Museum, University of Pennsylvania, 1970. F1465 .1 .T5C6

Emmerich, André. *Sweat of the Sun and Tears of the Moon: Gold and Silver in Pre-Columbian Art.* Reprint. New York: Hacker, 1977. E59 .A7E6

Heyden, Doris, and Gendrop, Paul. *Pre-Columbian Architecture of Mesoamerica.* New York: Abrams, 1975. F1219 .3 .A6H4913

Kubler, George. *The Art and Architecture of An-*

cient America: The Mexican, Maya, and Andean Peoples. 2nd ed. Harmondsworth, England and Baltimore: Penguin, 1975. E59 .A7K8

Lapiner, Alan C. *Pre-Columbian Art of South America.* New York: Abrams, 1976. F2230 .1 .A7L36

Lehmann, Walter, with Heinrich Doering. *The Art of Old Peru.* Reprint. New York: Hacker, 1975. F3429 .3 .A7L3313

Los Angeles County Museum of Art. *Sculpture of Ancient West Mexico: Nayarit.* Los Angeles: Los Angeles County Museum of Art, 1970. F1219 .3 .A7L6

Mason, John Alden. *The Ancient Civilizations of Peru.* Rev. ed. Harmondsworth, England: Penguin, 1975. F3429 .M36

Morley, Sylvanus G. *The Ancient Maya.* 3rd rev. ed. Stanford: Stanford University Press, 1973. F1435 .M75

Paddock, John, ed. *Ancient Oaxaca: Discoveries in Mexican Archeology and History.* Stanford: Stanford University Press, 1970. F1219 .1 .O11P25

Peterson, Frederick. *Ancient Mexico.* New York: Capricorn Books, 1962. F1219 .P42

Pettersen, Carmen L. *The Maya of Guatemala: Their Life and Dress.* Guatemala City and Seattle: University of Washington Press, 1976. F1465 .3 .C8P47

Proskouriakoff, Tatiana Avenirovna. *A Study of Classic Maya Sculpture.* Washington, D.C.: Carnegie Institute of Washington, 1950. AS32 .A5 no. 593

Robertson, Donald. *Pre-Columbian Architecture.* New York: Braziller, 1963. E59 .A7R6

Robertson, Merle G.; Rands, Robert L.; and Graham, John A. *Maya Sculpture from the Southern Lowlands.* Berkeley: Lederer, Street & Zeus, 1972. F1435 .3 .A7R63

Rowe, John H. *Chavin Art: An Inquiry into Its Form and Meaning.* New York: Museum of Primitive Art, 1962. F3429 .1 .C48R6

Steward, Julian H. *Handbook of the South American Indians.* 7 vols. New York: Cooper Square Publishers, 1963. E51 .U6 no. 143

Thompson, John E. S. *Maya History and Religion.* Norman, Okla.: University of Oklahoma Press, 1972. F1435 .T496

Wauchope, Robert, ed. *Handbook of Middle American Indians.* 16 vols. Austin: University of Texas Press, 1964-76. F1434 .H3

NORTH AMERICAN INDIAN AND ESKIMO ART

Boas, Franz. *Primitive Art.* 1927. Reprint. Magnolia, Mass.: Peter Smith, 1962. N5310 .B6

Collins, Henry, et al. *The Far North: Two Thousand Years of American Eskimo and Indian Art.* Bloomington, Ind.: Indiana University Press in association with the National Gallery of Art, Washington, D.C., 1977. E99 .E7F28

Curtis, Edward S. *The North American Indian.* 30 vols. Cambridge: Cambridge University Press, 1907-30. E77 .C97

Dockstader, Frederick. *Indian Art of the Americas.* New York: Museum of the American Indian, Heye Foundation, 1973. E98 .A7D57

―――― *Indian Art in America: The Arts and Crafts of the North American Indian.* Greenwich, Conn.: New York Graphic Society. E59 .A7D6

Ewers, John C. *Plains Indian Painting.* Stanford: Stanford University Press, 1939. E98 .A7E93

Feder, Norman. *Two Hundred Years of North American Art.* New York: Praeger, 1972. E98 .A7F43

Fraser, Douglas. *The Many Faces of Primitive Art.* Englewood Cliffs, N.J.: Prentice-Hall, 1966. N5310 .F68

Grant, Campbell. *Rock Art of the American Indian.* 1967. Reprint. New York: Promontory Press, 1974. E98 .P6G7

Gunther, Erna. *Art in the Life of the Northwest Coast Indians.* Portland, Ore.: Portland Art Museum, 1966. E78 .N78G8

Harding, Anne D., and Boling, Patricia. *Bibliog-*

raphy of Articles and Papers on North American Indian Arts. 1938. Reprint. New York: Kraus, 1969. Z1209 .H26

Murdock, George P., and O'Leary, Timothy. Ethnographic Bibliography of North America. 4th ed. New Haven: Human Relations Area Files Press, 1972. Z1209 .M8

Ray, Dorothy J. Artists of the Tundra and the Sea. Seattle: University of Washington Press, 1961. E99 .E7R25

Ritchie, Carson I. A. The Eskimo and His Art. New York: St. Martin's Press, 1976. E99E7 .R56

Scully, Vincent J. Pueblo Architecture of the Southwest: A Photographic Essay. Austin: University of Texas Press, 1971. Published for the Amon Carter Museum of Western Art, Fort Worth. E99 .P9C85

Walker Art Center and Minneapolis Institute of Arts. American Indian Art: Form and Tradition. New York: Dutton, 1973.

Whiteford, Andrew H. North American Indian Arts. New York: Golden Press, 1973. E98 .I5W45

AFRICAN ART

Bascom, William R. African Art in Cultural Perspective: An Introduction. New York: Norton, 1973. NB1080 .B37

Brentjes, Burchard. African Rock Art. London: Dent, 1967. N5310 .B6253

Cornet, Joseph. Art of Africa: Treasures from the Congo. London: Phaidon, 1971. N7399 .C6C613

D'Azevedo, Warren L., ed. The Traditional Artist in African Societies. Bloomington, Ind.: Indiana University Press, 1973. NX589 .T82

Elisofon, Eliot, and Fagg, William. The Sculpture of Africa. Reprint. New York: Hacker, 1978. NB1097 .6 .S73E44

Fagg, William B. Nigerian Images: The Splendor of African Sculpture. New York: Praeger, 1963. NB1097 .N5F2

Forman, Werner. Benin Art. London: Hamlyn, 1960. N7397 .N5F63

Fraser, Douglas F., and Cole, H. M., eds. African Art and Leadership. Madison, Wis.: University of Wisconsin Press, 1972. N7398 .A35

Gaskin, L. J. P. A Bibliography of African Art. London: International African Institute, 1965. Z5938 .A3I5

Laude, Jean. The Arts of Black Africa. Berkeley: University of California Press, 1973. N7398 .L313

Lieris, Michel, and Delange, Jacqueline. African Art. New York: Golden Press, 1968. N7380 .L3513

Thompson, Robert F. Black Gods and Kings: Yoruba Art at U.C.L.A. Bloomington, Ind.: Indiana University Press, 1976. N7399 .N52Y66

Trowell, Kathleen M. Classical African Sculpture. London: Faber & Faber, 1970. NB1098 .T7

Walker Art Center. Art of the Congo. Minneapolis: Walker Art Center, 1967. NB1097 .C75W3

Wassing, René S. African Art: Its Background and Traditions. New York: Abrams, 1968. N7397 .A3W33

Willett, Frank. African Art: An Introduction. London: Thames & Hudson, 1971. N7380 .W5

——— Ife in the History of West African Sculpture. New York: McGraw-Hill, 1967. NB1097 .W4W5

OCEANIC ART

Barrow, Tui T. Art and Life in Polynesia. Rutland, Vt.: Charles E. Tuttle, 1973. N7411 .P64B37

——— Maori Wood Sculpture of New Zealand. Rutland, Vt.: Charles E. Tuttle, 1970. NK9793 .B32

Batterberry, Michael, and Ruskin, Ariane. Primitive Art. New York: McGraw-Hill, 1973. N5311 .B3

Bernot, Ronald M. Australian Aboriginal Art. New York: Macmillan, 1964. N7401 .B4

Buck, Peter H. Arts and Crafts of Hawaii. Honolulu: Bishop Museum Press, 1964. DU6246 .B75

Dodd, Edward H. Polynesian Art. New York: Dodd, Mead, 1967. N7410 .D6

Firth, Raymond. Art and Life in New Guinea. 1936. Reprint. New York: AMS Press, 1977. N7411 .N4F5

Fraser, Douglas. Primitive Art. London: Thames & Hudson, 1962. N5310 .F7

Guiart, Jean. Arts of the South Pacific. New York: Golden Press, 1963. N7410 .G813

Kooijman, S. The Art of Lake Sentani. New York: Museum of Primitive Art, 1959. N7326 .N453

Linton, Ralph, and Wingert, Paul. Arts of the South Seas. 1946. Reprint. New York: Arno Press, 1972. N7410 .L5

Newton, Douglas. Art Styles of the Papuan Gulf. New York: Museum of Primitive Art, 1961. N7411 .N4N43

——— Crocodile and Cassowary: Religious Art of the Upper Sepik River, New Guinea. New York: Museum of Primitive Art, 1971. GN473 .N48

——— New Guinea Art in the Collection of the Museum of Primitive Art. New York: Museum of Primitive Art, 1967. N620 .M94A3 no. 2

Rockefeller, Michael C. The Asmat of New Guinea: The Journal of Michael Clark Rockefeller. Greenwich, Conn.: New York Graphic Society, 1967. DU744 .R52

Schmitz, Carl A. Oceanic Art; Myth, Man and Image in the South Seas. New York: Abrams, 1971. N7410 .S13

Stubbs, Dacre. Prehistoric Art of Australia. New York: Scribner's, 1975. N5310 .A83S85

Taylor, Clyde R. H. A Pacific Bibliography: Printed Matter Relating to the Native Peoples of Polynesia, Melanesia, and Micronesia. 2nd ed. Oxford: Clarendon Press, 1965. Z4501 .T3

Wingert, Paul. Primitive Art: Its Traditions and Styles. Cleveland: World Publishing, 1970. N5310 .W766

chapter 15 The "Proto-Renaissance" in Italy

Antal, Frederick. Florentine Painting and Its Social Background. London: Regan Paul, 1948. N6921 .F7A4

De Wald, Ernest T. Italian Painting: 1200-1600. New York: Holt, Rinehart & Winston, 1961. ND615 .D44

Fremantle, Richard. Florentine Gothic Painters from Giotto to Masaccio: A Guide to Painting in and near Florence. London: Martin Secker and Warburg, 1975. ND621 .F7F72

Marle, Raimond van. The Development of the Italian Schools of Painting. 19 vols. 1923-38. Reprint. New York: Hacker, 1970. ND611 .M272

Meiss, Millard. Painting in Florence and Siena After the Black Death. Princeton: Princeton University Press. ND621 .F7M4

Panofsky, Erwin. Renaissance and Renascences in Western Art. New York: Harper & Row, 1969. N6370 .P28

Pope-Hennessy, John. Introduction to Italian Sculpture. 2nd ed. 3 vols. New York: Phaidon, 1970-72. NB614 .P6

Schevill, Ferdinand. The Medici. New York: Harper, 1960. DG737 .42 .S3

Stubblebine, James, ed. Giotto: The Arena Chapel Frescoes. New York: Norton, 1969. ND623 .G6S7

Venturi, Lionello, and Skira-Venturi, Rosabianca. Italian Painting: The Creators of the Renaissance. 3 vols. Geneva: Skira, 1950-52. ND622 .V4

White, John. Art and Architecture in Italy, 1250 to 1400. Baltimore: Penguin, 1966. N6915 .W45

chapter 16 Fifteenth-Century Italian Art

Berenson, Bernard. The Drawings of the Florentine Painters. 3 vols. 1938. Reprint. Chicago: University of Chicago Press, 1970. NC256 .B4

——— Italian Pictures of the Renaissance. London: Phaidon, 1968. ND615 .B56

Borsook, Eve. The Mural Painters of Tuscany. London: Phaidon, 1960. ND2756 .T9B6

Burckhardt, Jacob. The Civilization of the Renaissance in Italy. 1867. Reprint. New York: Harper & Row, 1958. (Other reprints available.) DG533 .B85

Chastel, André. The Age of Humanism. New York: McGraw-Hill, 1964. CB361 .C473

Decker, Heinrich. The Renaissance in Italy: Architecture, Sculpture, Frescoes. New York: Viking, 1969. N6915 .D413

De Wald, Ernest T. Italian Painting, 1200-1600. New York: Holt, Rinehart & Winston, 1961. ND615 .D44

Edgerton, Samuel Y., Jr. The Renaissance Rediscovery of Linear Perspective. New York: Harper & Row, 1976. NC748 .E33

Ferguson, Wallace K., et al. The Renaissance. New York: Henry Holt, 1940. CB361 .F37

Gadol, Joan. Leon Battista Alberti: Universal Man of the Early Renaissance. Chicago: University of Chicago Press, 1969. NA1123 .A5G3

Godfrey, F. M. Early Venetian Painters, 1415-1495. London: Tiranti, 1954. ND621 .V5G6

Hale, John R. Italian Renaissance Painting from Masaccio to Titian. New York: Dutton, 1977. ND615 .H38

Helton, Tinsley, ed. The Renaissance: A Reconsideration of the Theories and Interpretations of the Age. Madison, Wis.: University of Wisconsin Press, 1964. CB361 .S93

Holt, Elizabeth B. A Documentary History of Art. Vol. 1. 2nd ed. Garden City, N.Y.: Doubleday, 1957. N5303 .H762

Huyghe, René. Larousse Encyclopedia of Renaissance and Baroque Art. See Reference Books.

Lowry, Bates. Renaissance Architecture. New York: Braziller, 1962. NA510 .L6

Marle, Raimond van. The Development of the Italian Schools of Painting. 19 vols. 1923-38. Reprint. New York: Hacker, 1970. ND611 .M272

Murray, Peter. The Architecture of the Italian Renaissance. New York: Schocken Books, 1966. NA1115 .M8

Murray, Peter, and Murray, Linda. The Art of the Renaissance. London: Thames & Hudson, 1974. N6370 .M97

Panofsky, Erwin. Renaissance and Renascences in Western Art. New York: Harper & Row, 1969. N6370 .P28

Pope-Hennessy, John. An Introduction to Italian Sculpture. 3 vols. 2nd ed. New York: Phaidon, 1970-71. NB611 .P6

——— Sienese Quattrocento Painting. New York: Oxford University Press, 1947. ND6211 .S6P6

Schevill, Ferdinand. The Medici. New York: Harper & Row, 1960. DG737 .42 .S3

Seymour, Charles. Sculpture in Italy, 1400-1500. Baltimore: Penguin, 1966. NB615 .S45

Symonds, John Addington. The Renaissance in Italy. 7 vols. 1875-86. Reprint. New York: Modern Library, 1935. (Other reprints available.) DG533 .S945

Vasari, Giorgio. The Lives of the Most Eminent Painters, Sculptors, and Architects. 1550-68. 4 vols. New York: Dutton, 1963. N6922 .V48

Werkmeister, William H., ed. Ferguson, Wallace, et al. Facets of the Renaissance. New York: Harper & Row, 1963. CB361 .F25

Wittkower, Rudolf. Architectural Principles in the Age of Humanism. New York: Random House, 1965. NA520 .W5

——— Art and Architecture in Italy, 1600 to 1750. 3rd rev. ed. Baltimore: Penguin, 1973. N6916 .W57

chapter 17 Sixteenth-Century Italian Art

Ackerman, James S. The Architecture of Michelangelo. London: Zwemmer, 1966. NA1123 .B9A63

——— Palladio. New York: Penguin, 1978. NA1123 .P2A65

Blunt, Anthony. *Artistic Theory in Italy, 1450–1600.* London: Oxford University Press, 1975. N6915 .B55

Briganti, Giuliano. *Italian Mannerism.* London: Thames & Hudson, 1962. ND615 .B732

Castiglione, Baldassare. *The Courtier.* 1528. Reprint. New York: National Alumni, 1907. (Other reprints available.) BJ1604 .C43

Cellini, Benvenuto. *Autobiography.* Reprint. New York: Grolier, 1969. (Other reprints available.) NB623 .C3S9

Einem, Herbert von. *Michelangelo.* London: Methuen, 1976. N6923 .B9E413

Freedberg, Sydney J. *Painting of the High Renaissance in Rome and Florence.* 1961. Reprint. New York: Harper & Row, 1972. ND615 .F67

Friedlaender, Walter, *Mannerism and Anti-Mannerism in Italian Painting.* New York: Schocken Books, 1965. ND615 .F7

Holt, Elizabeth B. *A Documentary History of Art.* Vol. 2. 2nd ed. Garden City, N.Y.: Doubleday, 1957. N5303 .H762

Murray, Linda. *The High Renaissance and Mannerism.* New York: Oxford University Press, 1977. N6374 .M87

——— *The Late Renaissance and Mannerism.* London: Thames & Hudson, 1967. N6915 .M98

Partner, Peter. *Renaissance Rome, 1500–1559: A Portrait of a Society.* Berkeley: University of California Press, 1977. DG812 .P37

Pope-Hennessy, John. *Italian High Renaissance and Baroque Sculpture.* 3 vols. Greenwich, Conn.: Phaidon, 1963.

Shearman, John K. G. *Mannerism.* Baltimore: Penguin, 1967. N6370 .S78

Venturi, Lionello. *The Sixteenth Century: From Leonardo to El Greco.* New York: Skira, 1956. ND170 .V43

Wölfflin, Heinrich. *The Art of the Italian Renaissance.* New York: Schocken Books, 1963. N6915 .W6

——— *Classic Art.* London and New York: Phaidon, 1968. N6915 .W6413

Würtenberger, Franzsepp. *Mannerism: The European Style of the Sixteenth Century.* New York: Holt, Rinehart & Winston, 1963. N6370 .W813

chapter 18   The Renaissance Outside of Italy

Benesch, Otto. *Art of the Renaissance in Northern Europe.* Rev. ed. London: Phaidon, 1965. N6370 .B37

——— *German Painting from Dürer to Holbein.* Geneva: Skira, 1966. ND565 .B413

Blunt, Anthony. *Art and Architecture in France 1500–1700.* 2nd ed. Harmondsworth, England: Penguin, 1970. N6844 .B6

Conway, William M. *The Van Eycks and Their Followers.* 1921. Reprint. New York: AMS Press, 1979. ND669 .F5C66

Cuttler, Charles P. *Northern Painting from Pucelle to Brueghel.* New York: Holt, Rinehart & Winston, 1968. ND454 .C8

Friedlaender, Max J. *Early Netherlandish Painting.* New York: Praeger, 1967. ND645 .F723

——— *From Van Eyck to Bruegel.* 3rd ed. London: Phaidon, 1969. ND635 .F713

Hind, Arthur M. *History of Engraving and Etching from the Fifteenth Century to the Year 1914.* 3rd rev. ed. New York: Dover, 1963. NE400 .H66

——— *An Introduction to a History of Woodcut.* New York: Dover, 1963. NE1030 .H55

Huizinga, Johan. *The Waning of the Middle Ages.* 1924. Reprint. New York: Doubleday/Anchor, 1970. DC33 .2 .H83

Lassaigne, Jacques, and Delevoy, Robert. *Flemish Painting.* New York: Skira, 1957. ND665 .L33

Mather, Frank J. *Western European Painting of the Renaissance.* New York: Cooper Square Publishers, 1966. ND170 .M3

Meiss, Millard. *French Painting in the Time of Jean de Berry.* New York: Braziller, 1974. ND3147 .M38

Panofsky, Erwin. *Early Netherlandish Painting.* Cambridge, Mass.: Harvard University Press, 1953. ND635 .P35

——— *The Life and Art of Albrecht Dürer.* 4th ed. Princeton, N.J.: Princeton University Press, 1971. ND588 .D9P28

Puyvelde, Leo van. *The Flemish Primitives.* London: Collins, 1948. ND665 .P84

Reau, Louis. *French Painting in the Fourteenth, Fifteenth, and Sixteenth Centuries.* New York: Hyperion Press, 1939. ND545 .R43

Stechow, Wolfgang, ed. *Northern Renaissance Art, 1400–1600.* Englewood Cliffs, N.J.: Prentice-Hall, 1966. N6370 .S66

Waetzold, Wilhelm. *Dürer and His Time.* Enl. ed. London: Phaidon, 1955. ND588 .D9W132

Wilenski, Reginald H. *Flemish Painters, 1430–1830.* 2 vols. London: Faber & Faber, 1960. ND672 .W5

chapter 19   Baroque Art
and
chapter 20   The Eighteenth Century: Rococo and the Rise of Romanticism

Bacou, Roseline. *Piranesi: Etchings and Drawings.* Boston: New York Graphic Society, 1975. NE2052 .5 .P5B3213

Bazin, Germain. *Baroque and Rococo Art.* New York: Praeger, 1974. N6410 .B36b

Blunt, Anthony. *Art and Architecture in France, 1500–1700.* 2nd ed. Harmondsworth, England: Penguin, 1970. N6844 .B6

Chatelet, Albert, and Thuillier, Jacques. *French Painting from Fouquet to Poussin.* Geneva: Skira, 1963. ND544 .C433

——— *French Painting from Le Nain to Fragonard.* Geneva: Skira, 1964. ND546 .T5

Fokker, Timon H. *Roman Baroque Art: The History of a Style.* London: Oxford University Press, 1938. N6920 .F6

Gerson, Horst, and ter Kuile, E. H. *Art and Architecture in Belgium 1600–1800.* Baltimore: Penguin, 1960. N6966 .G43

Hayes, John T. *Gainsborough: Paintings and Drawings.* London: Phaidon, 1975. NJ18 .G16A395

Hempel, Eberhard. *Baroque Art and Architecture in Central Europe.* Baltimore: Penguin, 1965. N6756 .H413

Herrmann, Luke. *British Landscape Painting of the Eighteenth Century.* New York: Oxford University Press, 1974. ND1354 .4 .H47

Hibbard, Howard. *Bernini.* New York: Penguin, 1965. NB623 .B5H5

——— *Carlo Maderno and Roman Architecture, 1580–1630.* London: Zwemmer, 1971. NA1123 .M3H5

Hinks, Roger P. *Michelangelo Merisi da Caravaggio.* London: Faber & Faber, 1953. ND623 .C26H5

Holt, Elizabeth B. *A Documentary History of Art.* Vol. 2. 2nd ed. Garden City, N.Y.: Doubleday, 1957. N5303 .H762

Kahr, Madlyn Millner. *Dutch Painting in the Seventeenth Century.* New York: Harper & Row, 1978. ND646 .K26

——— *Velázquez: The Art of Painting.* New York: Harper & Row, 1976. ND813 .V4K24

Kalnein, Wend, and Levey, Michael. *Art and Architecture of the Eighteenth Century in France.* New York: Viking/Pelican, 1973. N6846 .K2613

Kimball, Sidney F. *The Creation of the Rococo.* New York: Norton, 1964. N6410 .K5

Kitson, Michael. *The Age of Baroque.* London: Hamlyn, 1967. N6410 .K5

Lees-Milne, James. *Baroque in Italy.* New York: Macmillan, 1960. N6916 .L4

Martin, John R. *Baroque.* New York: Harper & Row, 1977. N6415 .B3M37

Millon, Henry A. *Baroque and Rococo Architecture.* New York: Braziller, 1961. NA590 .M5

Portoghesi, Paolo. *The Rome of Borromini.* London: Phaidon, 1972. NA1121 .R6P613

Powell, Nicolas. *From Baroque to Rococo: An Introduction to Austrian and German Architecture from 1580 to 1790.* London: Faber & Faber, 1959. NA1006 .P6

Rosenberg, Jakob; Slive, Seymour; and ter Kuile, E. H. *Dutch Art and Architecture, 1600–1800.* 3rd ed. New York: Penguin, 1977. ND646 .R59

Rosenblum, Robert. *Transformations in Late Eighteenth Century Art.* Princeton: Princeton University Press, 1970. N6410 .R66

Spear, Richard E. *Caravaggio and His Followers.* New York: Harper & Row, 1975. ND182 .B3S65

Stechow, Wolfgang. *Dutch Landscape of the Seventeenth Century.* 2nd ed. London: Phaidon, 1968. ND13593 .S73

Summerson, John. *Architecture in Britain, 1530–1830.* 4th rev. and enl. ed. Baltimore: Penguin, 1969. NA964 .S85

Tapié, Victor L. *The Age of Grandeur: Baroque Art and Architecture.* New York: Praeger, 1961. N6410 .T313

Waterhouse, Ellis K. *Italian Baroque Painting.* 2nd ed. London: Phaidon, 1969. ND616 .W38

——— *Painting in Britain, 1530–1790.* 4th ed. New York: Penguin, 1978. ND464 .W37

Whinney, Margaret D. *Sculpture in Britain, 1530–1830.* Baltimore: Penguin, 1964. .W5

Whinney, Margaret D., and Millar, Oliver. *English Art, 1720–1830.* London: H. M. Stationery Office, 1971. NB1305 .G7W45

Wittkower, Rudolf. *Art and Architecture in Italy, 1600–1750.* 3rd rev. ed. Baltimore: Penguin, 1973. N6916 .W5

——— *Gian Lorenzo Bernini: The Sculptor of the Roman Baroque.* 2nd ed. London: Phaidon, 1966. NB623 .B5W55

Wölfflin, Heinrich. *Principles of Art History.* 7th ed. New York: Dover, 1950. N5300 .W82

chapter 21   The Nineteenth Century: Pluralism of Style

Arnason, H. Harvard. *The Sculptures of Houdon.* New York: Oxford University Press, 1975. NB533 .H8A83

Aslin, Elizabeth. *The Aesthetic Movement: Prelude to Art Nouveau.* New York: Praeger, 1969. NK1175 .A8

Baudelaire, Charles. *The Mirror of Art, Critical Studies.* Garden City, N.Y.: Doubleday, 1956. N6847 .B362

Brion, Marcel. *Art of the Romantic Era: Romanticism, Classicism, Realism.* New York: Praeger, 1966. ND457 .B713

Brunhammer, Yvonne, et al. *Art Nouveau—Belgium, France: Catalogue of an Exhibition.* Houston: Institute for the Arts, Rice University, 1976. N6465 .A7A72

Canaday, John. *Mainstreams of Modern Art.* New York: Holt, 1959. N6450 .C33

Clark, Kenneth. *The Gothic Revival: An Essay in the History of Taste.* New York: Humanities Press, 1970. NA610 .C5

Courthion, Pierre. *Romanticism.* Geneva: Skira, 1961. N6450 .C65

Delacroix, Eugène. *The Journals of Eugène Delacroix.* New York: Phaidon, 1951. ND553 .D33A318

Friedlaender, Walter. *From David to Delacroix.* New York: Schocken Books, 1968. ND547 .F7613

Hamilton, George H. *Nineteenth and Twentieth Century Art.* Englewood Cliffs, N.J.: Prentice-Hall, 1972. N6450 .H29

Hanson, Anne Coffin. *Manet and the Modern Tradition.* New Haven: Yale University Press, 1977. ND553 .M3H33

Hawley, Henry. *Neo-Classicism, Style and Motif.* Cleveland: Cleveland Museum of Art, 1964. N6410 .H34

Hilton, Timothy. *The Pre-Raphaelites.* New York: Praeger, 1974. ND4675 .P7H5

Hitchcock, Henry-Russell. *Architecture: Nine-*

teenth and Twentieth Centuries. 2nd ed. Baltimore: Penguin, 1963. NA645 .H55

Holt, Elizabeth B. *From the Classicists to the Impressionists: Art and Architecture in the Nineteenth Century.* Garden City, N.Y.: Doubleday/Anchor, 1966. N5303 .H74

Leymarie, Jean. *French Painting in the Nineteenth Century.* Geneva: Skira, 1962. ND547 .L533

Licht, Fred. *Sculpture—Nineteenth and Twentieth Centuries.* Greenwich, Conn.: New York Graphic Society, 1967. NB197 .L5

Macaulay, James. *The Gothic Revival, 1745-1845.* Glasgow: Blackie, 1975. NA966 .M32

Martinell, César. *Gaudi: His Life, His Theories, His Work.* Cambridge, Mass.: MIT Press, 1975. NA1313 .G3M2813

Newton, Eric. *The Romantic Rebellion.* New York: Schocken Books, 1964. N6350 .N4

Nochlin, Linda. *Gustave Courbet: A Study of Style and Society.* New York: Garland, 1976. ND553 .C9N62

——— *Impressionism and Post-Impressionism 1874-1904: Sources and Documents.* Englewood Cliffs, N.J.: Prentice-Hall, 1966. ND1265 .N58

——— *Realism and Tradition in Art.* New York: Penguin, 1976. N6465 .R4N6

Novotny, Fritz. *Painting and Sculpture in Europe 1780-1880.* 2nd ed. Harmondsworth, England: Penguin, 1978. N6756 .N68

Pelles, Geraldine. *Art, Artists and Society: Origins of a Modern Dilemma, Painting in England and France 1750-1850.* Englewood Cliffs, N.J.: Prentice-Hall, 1963. ND466 .P4

Pevsner, Nikolaus. *Pioneers of Modern Design.* Harmondsworth, England: Penguin, 1964. N6450 .P4

Rewald, John. *The History of Impressionism.* New York: Museum of Modern Art, 1946. ND1265 .R4

——— *Post-Impressionism from Van Gogh to Gauguin.* New York: Museum of Modern Art, 1956. ND1265 .R43

Roberts, Keith. *The Impressionists and Post-Impressionists.* New York: Dutton, 1977. ND192 .I4I46

Sambrook, James, ed. *Pre-Raphaelitism: A Collection of Critical Essays.* Chicago and London: University of Chicago Press, 1974. NX543 .P73

Sloane, Joseph C. *French Painting Between the Past and the Present: Artists, Critics, and Traditions from 1848 to 1870.* Princeton: Princeton University Press, 1973. ND547 .S55

Sypher, Wylie. *Rococo to Cubism in Art and Literature.* New York: Random House, 1960. N6350 .S9

Vaughan, William. *Romantic Art.* London: Thames & Hudson, 1978. N6465 .R6V38

chapter 22   The Twentieth Century

Amaya, Mario. *Pop Art and After.* New York: Viking, 1972. N6490 .A62

Andersen, Wayne. *American Sculpture in Process 1930/1970.* Boston: New York Graphic Society, 1975. NB212 .A43

Apollinaire, Guillaume. *The Cubist Painters: Aesthetic Meditations, 1913.* New York: Wittenborn, 1970. ND1265 .A62

Arnason, H. Harvard. *History of Modern Art: Painting, Sculpture, Architecture.* 2nd rev. and enl. ed. Englewood Cliffs, N.J.: Prentice-Hall, 1977. N6490 .A713

Arp, Hans. *On My Way: Poetry and Essays, 1912-1947.* New York: Wittenborn, Schultz, 1948. PQ2601 .R633O5

Baldwin, John. *Contemporary Sculpture Techniques: Welded Metal and Fiberglass.* New York: Reinhold, 1967. NB1170 .B22

Banham, Reyner. *Guide to Modern Architecture.* Princeton: D. Van Nostrand, 1962. NA680 .B248

——— *Theory and Design in the First Machine Age.* 2nd ed. New York: Praeger, 1967. NA680 .B25

Battcock, Gregory, ed. *The New Art: A Critical Anthology.* New York: Dutton, 1973. N6490 .B37

Blake, Peter. *The Master Builder.* New York: Norton, 1976. NA680 .B52

Breton, André. *Surrealism and Painting.* New York: Harper & Row, 1972. ND196 .S8B7313

Burnham, Jack. *Beyond Modern Sculpture: The Effects of Science and Technology on the Sculpture of this Century.* New York: Braziller, 1968. NB198 .B84

Canaday, John. *Mainstreams of Modern Art.* New York: Holt, 1959. N6450 .C33

Carter, Peter. *Mies van der Rohe at Work.* London: Pall Mall Press, 1974. NA1088 .M65C37

Cassou, Jean, and Pevsner, Nikolaus. *Gateway to the Twentieth Century.* New York: McGraw-Hill, 1962. N6490 .C268

Collins, Peter. *Changing Ideals in Modern Architecture, 1750-1950.* London: Faber & Faber, 1971. NA500 .C6

Condit, Carl W. *The Rise of the Skyscraper: Portrait of the Times and Career of Influential Architects.* Chicago: University of Chicago Press, 1952. NA712 .C65

Cummings, Paul. *Dictionary of Contemporary American Artists.* 3rd ed. New York: St. Martin's Press, 1977. N6536 .C8

Diehl, Gaston. *The Moderns: A Treasury of Painting Throughout the World.* Milan: Uffizi, 1961. ND195 .D513

Duthuit, Georges. *The Fauvist Painters.* New York: Wittenborn, Schultz, 1950. ND1265 .D8

Elderfield, John. *The "Wild Beasts": Fauvism and Its Affinities.* New York: The Museum of Modern Art and Oxford University Press, 1976. N6494 .F3E42

Ernst, Max. *Beyond Painting and Other Writings by the Artist and His Friends.* New York: Wittenborn, Schultz, 1948. N6888 .E7A25

Giedion, Siegfried. *Space, Time and Architecture: The Growth of a New Tradition.* 4th enl. ed. Cambridge, Mass.: Harvard University Press, 1962. NA203 .G5

Giedion-Welcker, Carola. *Contemporary Sculpture: An Evaluation in Volume and Space.* New York: Wittenborn, 1961. NB198 .G513

Golding, John. *Cubism: A History and an Analysis, 1907-1914.* Rev. ed. Boston: Boston Book & Art Shop, 1968. ND196 .C8C6

Gray, Christopher. *Cubist Aesthetic Theories.* Baltimore: Johns Hopkins Press, 1953. ND1265 .G695

Haftmann, Werner. *Painting in the Twentieth Century: A Pictorial Survey.* London: Lund Humphries, 1965. ND195 .H323

Hamilton, George H. *Painting and Sculpture in Europe 1880-1940.* Rev. and enl. ed. Baltimore: Penguin, 1972. N6757 .H3

Hamlin, Talbot F., ed. *Forms and Functions of Twentieth-Century Architecture.* 4 vols. New York: Columbia University Press, 1952. NA680 .H3

Hanson, Anne Coffin. *Manet and the Modern Tradition.* New Haven: Yale University Press, 1977. ND553 .M3H33

Hitchcock, Henry-Russell. *Architecture—Nineteenth and Twentieth Centuries.* New York: Penguin, 1977. NA642 .H56

Hunter, Sam. *American Art of the Twentieth Century.* New York: Abrams, 1973. N6512 .H78

——— *Modern American Painting and Sculpture.* New York: Dell, 1965. N6512 .H8

——— *Modern French Painting, 1855-1956.* New York: Dell, 1966. ND547 .H8

Jacobus, John. *Twentieth-Century Architecture: The Middle Years, 1940-1964.* New York: Praeger, 1966. NA680 .J3

Janis, Sidney. *Abstract and Surrealist Art in America.* 1944. Reprint. New York: Arno Press, 1969. N6512 .5 .A2J36

Kahnweiler, Daniel H. *The Rise of Cubism.* New York: Wittenborn, Schultz, 1949. ND1265 .K315

Kaprow, Allan. *Assemblage, Environments, and Happenings.* New York: Abrams, 1966. NX458 .K3

Kepes, Gyorgy. *The Visual Arts Today.* Middletown, Conn.: Wesleyan University Press, 1960. N6490 .K4

Kirby, Michael, ed. *Happenings: An Illustrated Anthology.* New York: Dutton, 1966. PN3203 .K5

Lake, Carlton, and Maillard, Roger, eds. *Dictionary of Modern Painting.* 3rd rev. enl. ed. New York: Tudor, 1964. ND30 .D515

Licht, Fred. *Sculpture of the Nineteenth and Twentieth Centuries.* Greenwich, Conn.: New York Graphic Society, 1967. NB197 .L53

Lippard, Lucy R. *Pop Art.* New York: Praeger, 1966. N6490 .L53

Luci-Smith, Edward. *Symbolist Art.* New York: Oxford University Press, 1972. N6465 .S9L8

Lynton, Norbert. *The Modern World.* New York: McGraw-Hill, 1965. N6450 .L9

Martin, Marianne W. *Futurist Art and Theory.* Oxford: Clarendon Press, 1968. N6494 .F8M3

Mondrian, Pieter Cornelius. *Plastic Art and Pure Plastic Art.* 3rd ed. New York: Wittenborn, Schultz, 1952. N6490 .M6

Motherwell, Robert, ed. *The Dada Painters and Poets.* New York: Wittenborn, Schultz, 1951. ND1265 .M7

Nochlin, Linda. *Realism.* Baltimore: Penguin, 1976. N6465 .R4N6

Pehnt, Wolfgang. *Encyclopedia of Modern Architecture.* New York: Abrams, 1964. NA680 .E5

Raymond, Marcel. *From Baudelaire to Surrealism.* London: Methuen, 1970. PQ437 .R314

Raynal, Maurice. *History of Modern Painting.* 3 vols. Geneva: Skira, 1949-50. ND190 .R38

Read, Herbert. *A Concise History of Modern Painting.* 3rd ed. New York: Praeger, 1975. ND195 .R4

——— *A Concise History of Modern Sculpture.* Rev. and enl. ed. New York: Praeger, 1964. ND198 .R4

Read, Herbert, ed. *Surrealism.* New York: Praeger, 1971. NX600 .S9R42

Ritchie, Andrew C. *Abstract Painting and Sculpture in America.* New York: Arno Press, 1969. ND212 .N395

——— *Sculpture of the Twentieth Century.* New York: Arno Press, 1972. NB198 .R5

Rose, Barbara. *American Art Since 1900.* Rev. ed. New York: Praeger, 1975. N6512 .R63

Rosenblum, Robert. *Cubism and Twentieth-Century Art.* New York: Abrams, 1976. ND1265 .R63

Rubin, William S. *Dada, Surrealism and Their Heritage.* New York: Museum of Modern Art, 1977. N6490 .R77

Schapiro, Meyer. *Modern Art: Nineteenth and Twentieth Centuries.* New York: Braziller, 1978. N6447 .S33

Schiee, Gert, ed. *Picasso in Perspective.* Englewood Cliffs, N.J.: Prentice-Hall, 1976. ND553 .P5P477

Schlenoff, Norman. *Art in the Modern World.* New York: Bantam, 1965. N6450 .S29

Schneede, Uwe M. *Surrealism.* New York: Abrams, 1974. NX600 .S9S2813

Schwarz, Arturo. *Marcel Duchamp.* New York: Abrams, 1974. ND553 .D774S31813

Scully, Vincent. *Modern Architecture: The Architecture of Democracy.* New York: Braziller, 1961. NA680 .S395

Selz, Peter. *German Expressionist Painting.* 1957. Reprint. Berkeley: University of California Press, 1974. ND568 .S4

Sotriffer, Kristian. *Expressionism and Fauvism.* New York: McGraw-Hill, 1972. N6434 .E9S613

Tuchman, Maurice. *American Sculpture of the Sixties.* Los Angeles: Los Angeles County Museum of Art, 1967. NB212 .T8

Whittick, Arnold. *European Architecture in the Twentieth Century.* Aylesbury, England: Leonard Hill Books, 1974. NA958 .W49

Wilmerding, John. *The Genius of American Painting.* London: Weidenfeld & Nicolson, 1973. ND205 .W52

index

Page numbers in italics indicate illustrations.

El Greco (Domeniko Theotokopoulos), 625-27; *Burial of Count Orgaz, The, 626,* 627; *Fray Félix Hortensio Paravicino,* 627, *627*
Eliot, T. S., 17, 829, 836, 873, 876
Embryo in the Womb (Leonardo), 530, *531*
Encaustic painting technique, 117, 184
English art: architecture, 300-02, 341-45, 683-85, 690-91, 702-05, 727-28; Baroque, 683-85, 690-91; Gothic, 341-45; painting, 700-01, 708-09, 714-16, 749-50, 871-72; political background, 316, 580, 688; Romanesque, 300-02; Romantic, 702-05, 709, 714-16, 727-28, 749-50
Engobe: in Attic pottery, 112, *112,* 113
Engraving: African, 436; German, 603-04, 608, 610, 612; Italian, 512-13, 523, 604; Later Old Stone Age, 29-30; North American Indian, 428; Polynesian, 444; Renaissance, 512-13, 523, 603-04, 608, 610, 612
Enjoyment of Summer Scenery, detail of *The Ten Conveniences and the Ten Enjoyments of Country Life* (Buson), 412, *412*
Ensor, James, 812; *The Entry of Christ into Brussels,* 793, *794*
Entry of Christ into Brussels, The (Ensor), 793, *794*
Epidaurus: theater at, 150, *150, 151*
Equitable Building, New York, 801
Erased de Kooning by Robert Rauschenberg (Rauschenberg), 873
Erasmo da Narni, equestrian statue of ("*Gattamelata*") (Donatello), 488, *488,* 510-11
Erasmus of Rotterdam, 608, 613
Erechtheum, Acropolis, 129, 135, *135,* 136; Porch of the Maidens, 136, *136*
Ernst, Max, 829-30, 857; *Two Children Are Threatened by a Nightingale,* 830, *830*
Escorial (Herrera), 624, *624,* 625; church, 625, *625*
Escorial Deposition (Rogier van der Weyden), 593, *593*
Eskimo art, 426-27
Esoteric Buddhism, 386, 404
Estes, Richard: *Nedick's,* 875, *875,* 876
Esther Adorning Herself (Chassériau), 745, *745*
Estheticism, 791, 793
Et in Arcadia Ego (1630) (Poussin), *674,* 675
Et in Arcadia Ego (1655?) (Poussin), 675, *675*
Etching: Baroque period, 666-67, 674; Romantic period, 705, 716-17, 732
Étienne Chevalier and St. Stephen (Fouquet), 601, *601*
Etruscan art, 158-65; architecture, 158-60; craft art, 164-65; painting, 159-61; sculpture, 162-65
Etruscan bronze mirror, 164, *164*
Etruscan Room, Osterley Park House (Adam), *704,* 705
Euphronios, 114; *Herakles Strangling Antaios,* 113, *113*
Euripides, 140, 154, 253, 738
Euthymides, 113-114; *Revelers,* 113; *113,* 114
Evans, Arthur, 90-91
Evening Glow of the Andon, The (Harunobu), 779, *779*
Exekias, 113; *Dionysos in a Sailboat,* 112, *112,* 145
Expressionism, 855-56, 859; Abstract, 856-60, 865, 871; figural, 856-57, 860; in painting, 811-16, 856-60; in sculpture, 836-38
Expulsion from Eden, The (Masaccio), 496, *496, 497*
Expulsion from the Garden of Eden, The (Jacopo della Quercia), 482, *482*
Eyck, van. *See* Van Eyck, Hubert; Van Eyck, Jan

F

Fabriano, Gentile da. *See* Gentile da Fabriano
Faiyum portraits, 184-85, *185*
Fallen Warrior (pediment sculpture), Temple of Aphaia, 125-26, *126,* 145

"Falling Water" (Kaufmann House) (Wright), 852, *852,* 853
Family of Charles IV (Goya), 731, *731*
Family of Country People (Le Nain), 673, *673,* 674
Fan K'uan: *Travelers Among Mountains and Streams,* 390, *390*
Fan paintings, Japanese, 404
Fantasy in art, 791-93
Farnese Palace, Rome (Antonio da Sangallo), *534,* 535, *535,* 536; ceiling frescoes, *643,* 644, *644,* 645
Faun, House of the, Pompeii: mosaic from, 174, *182,* 183
Fauves, 809-16, 859
Feast of Herod, The (Donatello), 485, *485,* 487
Feast of the Gods, The (Bellini), 569, *569,* 570, 572
February, from *Les Très Riches Heures du Duc de Berry* (Limbourg Brothers), 584, *584*
Federal Reserve Bank Building, Minneapolis (Birkerts), 881, *881*
Feeding of Oryxes (Egyptian fresco), 75, *75*
Feininger, Lyonel, 853
Feuerbach, Anselm, 771; *Medea,* 771, *773*
Fibula (Early Medieval), 275, *275*
Ficino, Marsilio, 480, 517, 545
Ficoroni Cist, The (Novius Plautius), 165, *165*
Fiedler, Konrad, 789
Fifteenth-century art. *See* Renaissance
Figural Expressionism, 856-57, 860
Figurines. *See* Statuettes
Finding and Proving of the True Cross, The (Piero della Francesca), 500, *501*
Finding of the Body of St. Mark, The (Tintoretto), *576,* 577
Fiorentino, Rosso. *See* Rosso Fiorentino
Five Dynasties, China, 390-91
Flamboyant style, 340-41
Flaxman, John, 714-15; *Electra Leading Procession to Agamemnon's Tomb,* 715, *715*
Flemish art: Baroque, 655-60; illumination, 583-85; painting, 523, 586-601, 615-20; political background, 655-56; Renaissance, 580-600, 615-20; sculpture, 581-83
Flight into Egypt (A. Carracci), 648, *650*
Florence, 271, 454, 460, 464-65; in Renaissance, 480-518, 526
Florence Cathedral (Arnolfo di Cambio), 347-48, *348,* 349, *349,* 484; baptistry doors of, 463-64, *464,* 480-81, *486,* 487; campanile of (Giotto), 347-48; dome of (Brunelleschi), 347, 489, *489,* 490
Fluting of columns, 124
Flying horse poised on one leg on a swallow, Wu-Wei, 381, *381*
Flying Storehouse, The, detail of *Shigisan Engi* (Fujiwara period), 405, *405,* 406
Fontainebleau school, 621, 623
Font-de-Gaume, cave art, 25; *Reindeer,* 29, 30
Form, 6, 46; in modern art, 809, 811, 817-23, 839-42, 860, 863-71
Formalism, 98; in Egyptian art, 66, 81, 85-86, 87; in Mesopotamian art, 45-46, 48, 53-55, 56, 59. *See also* Abstract Formalism
Fortuna Primigenia, Sanctuary of, Praeneste, 170, *170,* 171, *171*
Fortuna Virilis, Temple of, Rome, 169, *169,* 217
Forums, Roman, *172,* 173, 188, 189, *189,* 190
Fossati, Chevalier, 241
Fountain of the Innocents, Paris: *Nymphs* from (Goujon), *622,* 623
Fouquet, Jean: *Etienne Chevalier and St. Stephen,* 601, *601*
Four Apostles, The (Dürer), 612, *612,* 613
Four Darks on Red (Rothko), 860, *862*
Four Horsemen of the Apocalypse, The (Dürer), 610, *610*
Fourteenth-century art. *See* Proto-Renaissance
Fowling Scene (Egyptian wall painting), *18,* 82, *82*
Fragonard, Jean-Honoré, 700; *The Swing, 698,* 699

Francesca, Piero della. *See* Piero della Francesca
Francis I (Clouet), 620, *620*
François Marius Granet (Ingres), 743, *743*
François Vase, The, 111, *111,* 112
Frankfort, Henri, 40
Frankish ornaments, *275*
Frankl, Paul, 348
Fray Félix Hortensio Paravicino (El Greco), 627, *627*
French Ambassadors, The (Holbein), 613, *613,* 614
French art: architecture, 5, 296-97, 300, 303, 317-23, 325-33 621-22, 677-83, 691-93, 705-06, 726; Baroque, 672-83, 696-700; Fauves, 809-16; Gothic, 5, 317-41, 460; illumination, 311-12; painting, 601-02, 620-21, 673-77, 696-700, 710, 711-14, 732-49, 755-64, 775-88, 809-12, 817-23; political background, 316-17, 580, 600, 620, 672, 674, 688, 693, 712-14, 735, 738-39, 757, 759-60; Realism, 755-64; Renaissance, 560, 600-02, 620-23; Rococo, 689, 691-93, 696-700; Romanesque, 296-97, 300, 303, 304-09; Romantic, 705-06, 707-10, 711-14, 726, 730, 732-49; sculpture, 304-09, 323-25, 333-34, 622-23, 683, 707-08, 730; twentieth-century, 809-12, 817-23
Fresco secco technique, 74
Frescoes: Byzantine, 249; in catacombs, 215; Egyptian, 73-74; Etruscan, 139, 161; Italian, *see* Italian art, painting; Minoan, 95-98; in Sistine Chapel, 482, 519, 545-47, 553-54, 651; techniques used, 74, 98. *See also* Ceiling decoration; Murals; Wall painting
Freud, Sigmund, 792, 806, 816, 828, 829
Friedrich, Caspar David, 754; *Cloister Graveyard in the Snow,* 754, *755*
Froebel, Friedrich, 853
Fromentin, Eugène, 660, 760
Funeral mask (Mycenaean), 103, *105*
Fuseli, Henry, 715-16; *The Nightmare,* 715-16, *716*
Futurism, 822-23, 859

G

Gabo, Naum, 827, 842-43, 870; *Kinetic Sculpture: Standing Wave,* 843, *844; Linear Construction,* 843, *843*
Gaddi, Taddeo. *See* Taddeo Gaddi
Gainsborough, Thomas: *Honourable Mrs. Graham, The,* 708, *708; Mrs. Richard Brinsley Sheridan,* 708-09, *709*
Galatea (Raphael), 539, *539*
Galen, 138
Galerie des Glaces, Versailles (Hardouin-Mansart and le Brun), *680,* 681
Galerie des Machines, Paris International Exhibition (1889), 801, *801*
Galla Placidia, mausoleum of, Ravenna, 228, *228,* 229-30; mosaics from, *229,* 231
Garden of Earthly Delights, The (Bosch), 598-99, *599,* 600, *600*
Garden Scene (wall painting), House of Livia, Primaporta, 176, *178*
Garnier, J. L. Charles: Paris Opéra, 728, *729*
Gasulla gorge, rock paintings at: *Marching Warriors, 31,* 31-32
"Gates of Paradise" (Ghiberti), *486,* 487
Gateway Arch, Jefferson National Expansion Memorial, St. Louis (Saarinen and Associates), 888, *888,* 889
"*Gattamelata*" (Donatello), 488, *488,* 510-11
Gaudi, Antonio: Casa Milá, Barcelona, 848, *848*
Gauguin, Paul, 781, 787-88, 811, 856; *Spirit of the Dead Watching,* 788, *789*
Gautier, Théophile, 744-45, 760, 791
Geese of Medum (Egyptian frieze), 73-74, *74*
Gelede masquerader, 438, *439*
Gellée, Claude. *See* Lorraine, Claude
Gentile da Fabriano: *The Adoration of the Magi,* 494, *494,* 495
Gentileschi, Artemisia, 648; *Judith and*

Herakles and Telephos (Roman wall painting), 180-81, *181,* 184

Herakles Strangling Antaios (Euphronios), 113, *113*

Herculaneum, 159, 171, 175, *175,* 178, 180, *180, 181,* 184, 705

Hermes and Dionysos (Praxiteles), *140,* 141, 143

Hermes Bringing the Infant Dionysos to Papposilenos (Phiale Painter), 139, *139,* 140

Herodotus, 55, 64, 65, 158

Herrera, Juan de: Escorial, 624, *624,* 625, *625*

Herringbone perspective, 176

Hesperides, The (Von Marées), 771, *773*

Hiberno-Saxon style, 276-79

Hierakonpolis: *Palette of Narmer,* 66, 67-68; wall painting from, *65,* 67

Hieroglyphic writing, 32, 64, 68

Hieronymus Holzschuher (Dürer), 611, *611*

High Gothic period, 325-38

High Renaissance, 526-56

Hindu art, 364-71, 373

Hinduism, 358, 363, 374

Hippodameia and the Centaur (pediment sculpture), Temple of Zeus, 128, *128*

Hippodamos, 151

Hippopotamus Hunt (relief), tomb of Ti, 73, *73*

Hiroshige, 415

Hispano-America (Orozco), 834, *834*

Hofmann, Hans, 857-58; *Effervescence,* 857, *858*

Hogarth, William, 7, 700-01, 708; *Breakfast Scene,* from *Marriage à la Mode,* 700-01, *701*

Hokke-kyo (*Lotus Sutra*), 404, *405*

Hokusai, 415; *The Great Wave,* from *Thirty-Six Views of Mt. Fuji, 414,* 415

Holbein, Hans (the Younger), 613-15; *Christina of Denmark, 615,* 615; *French Ambassadors, The,* 613, *613,* 614

Holland, art of, 660-72. *See also* Flemish art

Hollar, Wenzel, *297*

Holy Sepulcher, Church of the, Jerusalem, 218

Holy Trinity, The (Masaccio), *496,* 497

Homage to New York (Tinguely), 871, *871*

Homer, Winslow, 764; *Right and Left,* 768-69, *769*

Honnecourt, Villard de. *See* Villard de Honnecourt

Honourable Mrs. Graham, The (Gainsborough), 708, *708*

Honthorst, Gerard van: *The Supper Party,* 661, *661,* 662

Hoodo (Phoenix Hall), Byodoin Temple, 406, *406*

Hopper, Edward: *Eleven A.M.,* 835-36, *836*

Horizontal Spines (Calder), 843-44, *844*

Horn, Walter, 284

Horse (Han Kan), 388, *389*

Horse Fair, The (Bonheur), 774, *775*

Horsemen (frieze), Parthenon, 133, *133*

Horta, Victor: Hotel van Eetvelde, Brussels, 847, *847*

Horus, Pylon Temple of, Edfu, 78, *79*

Hosios Loukas, Greece: monastery churches at, 244, *244,* 245, *245*

Hotel van Eetvelde, Brussels (Horta), 847, *847*

Houdon, Jean-Antoine, 707-08; *Count Cagliostro,* 708, *708; Diana,* 707, *707,* 708

House of Livia, Primaporta: wall painting from, 176, *178*

House of Neptune and Amphitrite, Herculaneum: Roman mosaic from, 184, *184*

House of Pansa, Pompeii, 174, *174*

House of the Dioscuri, Pompeii: wall painting from, 180, *181*

House of the Faun, Pompeii: mosaic from, 174, *182,* 183

House of the Silver Wedding, Pompeii, 175, *175*

House of the Vetii, Pompeii: wall painting from, 176, 178, *179,* 180-82

Houses: African, 439-40; Early Medieval, 282; Etruscan, 158-59; Hellenistic, 152-53; Japanese, 415; Roman, 158-59, 174-83, 186; twentieth-century, 849-53

Houses of Parliament, London (Barry and Pugin), 727, *727,* 728

Howe, George: Philadelphia Savings Fund Society Building (with Lescaze), 854, *854*

Hsia Kuei, 391-92, 408

Hsieh Ho, 384

Hsu Pei-hung, 395

Hsüan-Tsang, 386

Huang Kung-Wang: *Dwelling in the Fu-ch'un Mountains,* 393, *393*

Hugh of St. Victor, 337

Hughes, Robert, 889

Hugo van der Goes, 595-96; *Adoration of the Shepherds,* from *The Portinari Altarpiece,* 596, *597; Portinari Altarpiece, The,* 596, *596*

Hui-tsung, 391

Huizinga, Johan, 586

Hulme, T. E., 725

Hulten, Pontus, 865

Humanism: in Greece, 108-09, 110, 127, 150; in Renaissance, 452-56, 461, 471, 480, 483, 503, 507-08, 553, 615

Hunter, from *Lion Hunt* (Hellenistic mosaic), 155

Hunter and Kangaroo, Oenpelli, Arnhem Land, 448-49, *449*

Hunters in the Snow (Bruegel), 618, *618*

Hydria, *111*

Hyksos period, Egypt, 76

I

Iatmul skull, New Guinea, 447, *447*

Ibex, winged, Persia, 60, *61*

Ibo art, 439-40

Iconography, 5

Icons: Byzantine, 246, 249-51, 254; Chinese, 386; Hindu, 364; Russian, 4, 251-52. *See also* Buddha images

Ictinos, 130, *130*

Idol, Cycladic, 91, *91*

Ife king figure, 436, *437*

Il Gesù (Porta and Vignola), 632, *632,* 633

Illumination, 592; Early Christian, 221-23, 250; Early Medieval, 276-82, 290-91; Flemish, 583-85; French, 311-12; Gothic, 338; Islamic, 266; ornamented initial, 312-13; Romanesque, 311-13

Iltners, Edgards: *Strong Hands,* 863, *863*

Imhotep, 68

Impressionism, 760, 775-82, 787, 859

Improvisations (Kandinsky), 812, 815, *816*

Inca art, 418, 426

Incised shell gorget (Mississippian culture), 427, *427,* 428

Incrustation wall painting, 175, *175,* 178

Independent Group, 871-72

India, art of, 353-71; architecture, 360-62, 364-71; Buddha image, 362-64, 371; Buddhism, 354, 359-66, 371; Hindu resurgence, 363, 364-71; historical background, 212, 353-54, 358-59; painting, 371; sculpture, 354, 358, 360-71; spread of, 371-75

Indian, American, art of. *See* North American Indian art

Indo-Chinese art, 400

Ingres, Jean-Auguste-Dominique, 17, 714, 741-45, 780; *François Marius Granet,* 743, *743; Grande Odalisque,* 742, *743; Oedipus and the Sphinx,* 742, *742; Paganini,* 743-44, *744*

Insane Woman (*Envy*) (Géricault), 736, 737

Insulae, 153, 186, *186*

Interior of the Pantheon (Pannini), 192, *192*

International style: in proto-Renaissance painting, 473, 494, 497, 499, 519, 580, 583, 584-86; in twentieth-century architecture, 850-55, 878, 888-89

Intricate wall painting, 176, 178, *179,* 180-82

Invalides, Church of the (Hardouin-Mansart), 682, *682,* 683

Ionic order. *See* Orders, Ionic

Iphri figure, Ijo people, 437, *437*

Ipiutak burial mask, 426-27, *427*

Iron Age house, *284*

Iroquois art, 435

Ise shrine, Japan, 402-03, *403*

Isenheim Altarpiece (Grünewald): *Crucifixion* from, 606-07, *607,* 608; *Resurrection* from, 608, *609*

Ishtar Gate, 56, *57; Lion* from the *Processional Way* from, 16, *55*

Islamic art, 213, 254-66; architecture, 254-65; decorative style, 259-61, 266; illumination, 266; object art, 265; textiles, 265-66

Isle of the Dead, The (Böcklin), *790,* 792-93

Italian art: architecture, 5, 302-03, 347-51, 489-93, 504-07, 530-36, 547-53, 562-67, 632-42, 689-90; Baroque, 632-51, 689-90; engraving, 512-13, 523, 604; fifteenth-century, 480-523; Gothic, 5, 347-51; Mannerism, 556-64, 575-77; painting, 464-77, 494-503, 513-30, 536-41, 553-60, 567-77, 642-51, 822-23; political background, 452, 460, 464-65, 480; proto-Renaissance, 460-77; Renaissance, 480-577, 580; Romanesque, 302-03; sculpture, 462-64, 480-88, 507-12, 541-45, 547-48, 560-62, 637-38, 728-29; sixteenth-century, 524-77; twentieth-century, 822-23, 829

J

Jack-in-the-Pulpit IV (O'Keeffe), 824, *826*

Jacopo della Quercia, 482, 541; *The Expulsion from the Garden of Eden,* 482, *482*

Jacopo Robusti. *See* Tintoretto

Jade carvings, Chinese, 380, *380,* 382, *382,* 393, 396

Jaeger, Werner, 108 and n

Jaguar Devouring a Hare (Barye), 16, 730, *730*

Jamb statues: Chartres Cathedral, 324, *324,* 325, *325,* 484, *484;* Reims Cathedral, 334, *334*

Japanese art, 400-15; architecture, 354, 400-01, 402-03, 409, 415; Ashikaga period, 408-09; Buddhism, 371, 401-08; cartooning, 406; Chinese influence on, 400-04, 408-13; etiquette, 401, 404; Heian period, 401, 404-06; Kamakura realism, 407; Momoyama period, 409-15; native traditions, 400-01; painting, 354, 402, 404-08, 409-13; pottery, 400, 409; print-making, 411, 413-15, 809; sculpture, 400-02, 406-07; teahouses, 409; ukiyo-e, 413-15

Javacheff, Christo. *See* Christo

Javanese art, 371-73

Jeanneret-Gris, Charles Edouard. *See* Le Corbusier

Jefferson, Thomas, 706-07; Monticello, Charlottesville, 706, *706;* State Capitol, Richmond, *706,* 707

Jericho, 36-37; fortifications at, *36,* 37

Jesus: representations of, 215, 219-20, 224, 225, 229, 230

Jesus, Church of. *See* Il Gesù

Joan of Arc (Bastien-Lepage), 774-75, *775*

Jocho: *Amida,* 406, *406*

John of Garland, 334-36

John of Salisbury, 325

Johns, Jasper: *Painted Bronze,* 873, *873*

Johnson, Philip, 855, 886; Pennzoil Place, Houston, 886-87, *887*

Jones, Inigo, 535, 685, 691; Banqueting Hall, Whitehall, London, *684,* 685

Joseph Recognizes His Brothers, from *Vienna Genesis,* 222, *222,* 223

Juan de Pareja (Velázquez), 653, *653,* 654

Judd, Donald, 868; *Untitled,* 868, *868,* 870

Judgment of Paris, The (Cranach), 606, *606*

Judith and Maidservant with the Head of Holofernes (Gentileschi), 648, *648,* 649

Julii, mausoleum of the: mosaic from, *220*

Jumping Figure (Eakins), 764, *765*

Jupiter and Io (Correggio), 556, *557*

Jupiter and Semele (Moreau), 791, *793*

picture credits

The authors and publisher are grateful to the proprietors and custodians of various works of art for photographs of these works and permission to reproduce them in this book. Sources not included in the captions are listed below. Numerical references are to figure numbers.

KEY TO ABBREVIATIONS

ACL	Copyright A.C.L., Brussels
Al	Fratelli Alinari
AMNH	American Museum of Natural History, New York
An	D. Anderson
ARB	Art Reference Bureau
Bg	Giacomo Brogi
Br	F. Bruckmann K G Verlag
Bulloz	J. E. Bulloz, Paris
DAI	Deutschen Archäologisches Institut
EPA	Editorial Photocolor Archives, Inc.
Fototeca	Fototeca Unione, Rome
Gab	Gabinetto Fotografico Nazionale, Rome
Gir	Giraudon
Gun	L. Gundermann Photo-Verlag
Hir	Hirmer Fotoarchiv, Munich
Mansell	The Mansell Collection, London
Mar	Bildarchiv Foto Marburg
Mas	Ampliaciones y Reproducciones MAS, Barcelona
Met	Metropolitan Museum of Art, New York
NYPL	New York Public Library
OI	Oriental Institute, University of Chicago
PRI	Photo Researchers, Inc., New York
Scala	Scala Fine Art Publishers, Inc., New York

Paperbound covers Volume I: Madeline Grimoldi/G. Guidotti; Volume II: Felix Klee Collection, Berne. COSMOPRESS, Geneva/S.P.A.D.E.M., Paris.

Introduction Josef Albers: 6, 7; Al-EPA: 9a, 10; Bibliothèque Nationale: 13; Dr. Thomas Brachert, Courtesy of *Art Bulletin*, Dec. 1971, LIII, 4: 4; Bg-EPA: 9b; Fogg Art Museum, Harvard University, Bequest of Paul J. Sachs: 3; Hir: 12; Walter Steinkopf: 14; Wilhelm-Lehmbruck-Museum: 1.

Part I Opening illustration: The British Museum, London.

Chapter 1 Aerofilms Ltd., London: 14; AMNH: 8, 9, 12; Caisse Nationale: 6, 7; Colorphoto Hinz, Basle: 1, 3, 5; Mas: 13; Edwin Smith: 15; Studio Laboric, Bergerac: 4, 11.

Chapter 2 Al-EPA: 37; Hir: 9, 11, 18, 19, 20, 21, 22, 25, 29; Jericho Excavation Fund: 1, 2; Mansell: 26, 27; Arlette Mellaart: 2, 6, 8; James Mellaart: 7; Musées Nationaux, Paris: 30, 34; OI: 12, 13, 17, 32, 35, 36.

Chapter 3 Harvey Barad, PRI: 6; Egyptian Expedition, Met: 16, 18, 31; Eliot Elisofon: 22, 25; George Gerster, PRI: 7; Hir: 2, 3, 10, 11, 12, 13, 14, 15, 21, 28, 33; Mar-ARB: 23, 24, 36; Met: 20, 27; Musées Nationaux, Paris: 37; OI: 19.

Chapter 4 Courtauld Institute Galleries, London Univ.: 23; Alison Frantz: 21; Hir: 4, 5, 6, 7, 8, 9, 10, 11, 12, 13, 14, 15, 16, 17, 20, 24, 26, 27; TAP Service: 25; from Christian Zervos, *L'Art de la Crète*, Editions Cahiers d'Art, Paris: 3; from Christian Zervos, *L'Art des Cyclades*, Editions Cahiers d'Art, Paris: 1, 2.

Chapter 5 Al-EPA: 14, 25, 54, 59, 60, 62, 66, 75; Frederick Ayer III, PRI: 77; from Richard Brilliant, *Arts of the Ancient Greeks*, 1973, McGraw-Hill Book Co.: 80, 81, 83, 85; DAI, Athens: 12; Felbermeyer: 70, 71; Alison Frantz: 35, 36, 37, 47, 48; Walter Hege: 41; Hir: 2, 4, 6–8, 10, 17–19, 22, 28, 31–34, 38, 40, 43–46, 49, 51–53, 56–58, 61, 65, 72, 76; Herschel Levit: 23; Mar-ARB: 63, 64; Musées Nationaux, Paris: 9, 55; Leonard von Matt, PRI: 69; Rev. Raymond V. Schoder, S.J.: 86; Staatliche Museen zu Berlin, DDR (Antiken-Sammlung): 84; Dr. Franz Stoedtner: 27; TAP Service: 16.

Chapter 6 Al-EPA: 6, 10, 11, 17, 25, 32, 34, 35, 37, 41, 56, 59, 60, 63, 66, 72, 81, 82; An-EPA: 38, 57; DAI, Rome: 8, 14, 65, 67, 73, 78, 80; Walter Drayer: 2, 9, 12; Foto KLM: 45; Fototeca: 7, 15, 16, 18, 19, 20, 21, 46, 49, 52, 55; Gab: 3, 68; M. Grimoldi: 39; André Held: 30; John Johnston: 79; G. E. Kidder Smith: 76; Herschel Levit: 58; Mar-ARB: 65; from Amedeo Maiuri, *Roman Painting*, Editions d'Art Albert Skira: 26; Museo Nazionale, Naples: 31; Museo Nazionale, Rome (M. Grimoldi): 83; Leonard von Matt, PRI: 61, 62, 69; H. Roger-Viollet: 42; Charles Rotkin, PFI: 44; Scala-EPA: 5, 23, 28, 33, 36, 48; Rev. Raymond V. Schoder, S.J.: 6.

Chapter 7 Al-EPA: 11, 12, 25, 33, 34, 35, 48, 60; An-EPA: 15, 20, 23, 63; Arts et Metiers Graphiques, Paris (from G. Marçais, *L'Architecture Musulmane d'Occident*): 64; Bibliothèque Nationale: 56; Byzantine Institute, Inc.: 55; Clarendon Press: 69; from K. A. C. Creswell, *Early Muslim Architecture*, Clarendon Press: 62, 67; Dept. of Antiquities and Museums, Jerusalem: 71; Dumbarton Oaks, Washington, D.C.: 39; Fotocielo: 46; Alison Frantz: 42, 45; M. Grimoldi: 54; André Held, Lausanne: 17; Hir.: 1, 7, 8, 9, 16, 18, 19, 22, 27, 30, 31, 32, 38; Iraq Mission to the United Nations: 61, 68; G. E. Kidder Smith: 40, 74; Linares, Yale Photo Collection: 72; Mar-ARB: 57; Mas: 65, 66, 73; Leonard von Matt, PRI: 2; OI: 21; Pontificia Commissione Centrale per l'Arte Sacra in Italia: 3; Josephine Powell: 52, 53; Rev. Fabrica di San Pietro in Vaticano: 10; Scala-EPA: 24, 26, 28, 29, 36, 37; Staatliche Museen, Berlin: 70; Tass, Sovfoto; 58; Tiers, Monkmeyer Press Photo Service, N.Y.: 76; Turkish Ministry of Tourism: 77; Victoria and Albert Museum, London: 59; plan drawn by Christopher Wodward: 78.

Part II Opening illustration: Scala-EPA.

Chapter 8 Dr. Harald Busch: 13; Hir: 10, 23; Mar-ARB: 21; Wagner, Göttingen, Germany: 17; Hermann Wehmeyer: 19, 20.

Chapter 9 Al-EPA: 8, 10, 17, 19; Bulloz: 22, 26; Caisse Nationale: 23; Jean Dieuzaide: 21; Willie Fix: 6; Fotocielo: 16; Gir: 27, 29; J. Gudiol Archives Photographiques, Paris: 24; Evelyn Hofer: 18; A. F. Kersting: 14; Mansell: 32; Studio Remy: 30; Yan, Reportage Photographique, Toulouse: 1; Jean Roubier: 3, 11, 20, 25; Scala-EPA: 28; W. S. Stoddard: 12.

Chapter 10 Aero-Photo, Paris: 15; Al-EPA: 36, 56–58; An-EPA: 55; Belzeaux, PRI: 33, 37; P. Berger, PRI: 8; Dr. Harald Busch: 49; Pierre Devinoy: 1, 3; Theo Felten: 46; Gir: 29, 31; George Holton, PRI: 53, 59: A. F. Kersting: 44; Herschel Levit: 22; Mar-ARB: 28, 30, 47, 51; National Monuments Record, London: 38, 42, 43; Revue Française de l'Electricité: 32; Rheinisches Bilderarchiv, Cologne: 52; H. Roger-Viollet: 13, 26, 27; Jean Roubier: 9, 12, 14; Helga Schmidt-Glassner: 50; Edwin Smith: 40, 45; W. S. Stoddard: 7, 10, 17, 19, 21; Clarence Ward: 24, 25.

Part III Opening illustration: Courtesy Museum of Fine Arts, Boston. Fenollosa-Weld Collection

Chapter 11 Black Star: 30; J. LeRoy Davidson: 13, 16, 18, 19, 22, 24, 25, 27; Eliot Elisofon, TIME/LIFE Books, Time, Inc.: 28; Government of India, Archaeological Survey of India: 1–7, 9, 11, 12, 14, 15, 17, 20; India Tourist Office: 21; Elizabeth Lyons: 31; I. Job Thomas: 23.

Chapter 12 Chavannes: 4; Gir: 27; Robert Harding Associates, London: 22; Magnum: 5, 6; Musées Nationaux, Paris: 9; Scala-EPA: 8; Audrey R. Topping: 26; Charles Uht: 11; Courtesy Estate of Langdon Warner: 12.

Chapter 13 From *A History of Far Eastern Art* by Sherman E. Lee, Harry N. Abrams, Inc. Publisher: 6, 10, 21, 22; Japan Tourist Association: 25; National Commission for Protection of Cultural Properties of Japan: 3, 4, 9, 11, 13; Sakamoto Photo Research Lab, Tokyo: 5, 8, 12; Yoshio Watanabe: 7; Zauho Press: 17.

Chapter 14 *The American Anthropologist*, 1919: 22; Archaeological Institute of America, rep. from *Art and Archaeology*, IV, 6, copyright 1916: 6; Archive of Hispanic Culture, Library of Congress: 15a; from *Chalcacingo*, by Carlo Gay and illustrated by Frances Pratt, pub. by Akademische Druck: 2; Chicago Natural History Museum: 15b; H. M. Cole: 48; field photo by Dr. George A. Corbin, Oct. 1972: 61; Susan Einstein, Museum of Cultural History, Univ. of California, Los Angeles: 14; David Gebhard, The Art Galleries, Univ. of California, Santa Barbara: 24; from Campbell Grant, *Rock Art of the American Indian:* 23; Abraham Guillen M.: 17; Dr. George Kennedy, Univ. of California, Los Angeles: 62; from J. D. Lajoux, *The Rock Painting of Tassili:* 40; National Park Service, Dept. of the Interior, Wash., D.C.: 26, 27; Smithsonian Institution, Wash., D.C.: 1; from Karl von den Steinen, *Die Marquesaner und ihre Kunst,* I: 59; The Wheelwright Museum of the American Indian, Santa Fe, N.M.: 29; Frank Willett, Northwestern Univ.: 41, 42, 47.

Part IV Opening illustration: Al-EPA.

Chapter 15 Al-EPA: 2, 4, 5, 6, 8, 9, 12, 13, 14, 15, 16, 17, 18, 21; An-EPA: 1, 7, 10, 22, 23, 24, 25; Bg-EPA: 3, 20; Gab: 11; Scala-EPA: 14, 19.

Chapter 16 Al-EPA: 4–6, 8–10, 13–17, 20, 27–29, 32, 34–38, 42, 45, 47–49, 55, 58, 61–65, 68; An-EPA: 18, 22, 25, 30–32, 39, 41, 53; An-Gir: 54; Marcello Bertoni: 1, 2; Bg-EPA: 3, 11, 12, 24, 52; Farbenfotografie: 67; Rollie McKenna, PRI: 40, 44; La Photothèque: 60; Scala-EPA: 26, 33, 51, 66.

Chapter 17 Harry N. Abrams, Inc.: 53; Al-EPA: 1, 3, 17, 18, 19, 20, 22, 25, 26, 29, 30, 37, 38, 44, 45, 48, 49, 58, 59, 62, 63, 65, 67, 68, 70; An-EPA: 4, 27, 33, 40, 41, 51; British Architectural Library, London: 13; Fototeca: 32, 35; Gir: 24; M. Grimoldi: 6, 10, 14, 16; M. Grimoldi/Francesco del Priore: 27; Phylis Dearborn Massar: 47, 54, 56, 57; Met: 36; Charles Rotkin, PFI: 31; Harvey Barad, PRI: 23; Scala-EPA: 28, 39, 43, 47, 61, 64, 69; Edwin Smith: 52

Chapter 18 ACL: 8, 9, 10, 18, 21, 22; Al-EPA: 19, 49, 56; Jean Arland: 28; Br-EPA: 33; Bulloz: 55; Caisse Nationale: 1, 51; Gir: 5, 6, 26, 35, 50, 54; Gun-ARB: 29; Lauras-Giraudon: 2; Mas: 57, 58, 60, 61; Meyer Erwin Photo: 48; Rheinisches Bilderarchiv, Cologne: 27; Charles Rotkin, PFI: 52; Scala-EPA: 20; Walter Steinkopf: 25, 39; Studio Remy: 4; Yan-PRI: 62.

Chapter 19 Aero-Photo, Paris: 70; AGRACI-EPA: 62; Al-EPA: 9, 11, 13, 14, 16, 26, 27, 29, 34, 45, 46, 51, 73, 78; An-EPA: 4, 7, 25, 35, 37; Harry N. Abrams, Inc.: 22; © ARCH. PHOTO., Paris/S.P.A.D.E.M.: 77; Avery Library, Columbia Univ.: 1; Br-EPA: 41; British Crown Copyright, Reproduced with permission of the Controller of Her Britannic Majesty's Stationery Office: 80; EPA: 19; Gab: 21; Gir: 66, 79; M. Grimoldi: 31; Gene Heil, PRI: 72; Photo Henrot: 74; A. F. Kersting: 5, 69; G. E. Kidder Smith: 18, 20; Frank Lerner: 58; Mansell: 64, 65; Met, Isaac D. Fletcher Fund, Rogers Fund, and bequests of Adelaide Milton de Groot (1897–1967) and of Joseph H. Durkee, by exchange, supplemented by gifts of friends of the museum, 1971: 38; National Monuments Record, London: 81; Courtesy of NYPL (Astor, Lenox, and Tilden Foundations): 8, 71; Réunion des Musées Nationaux: 28; H. Roger-Viollet: 75; Charles Rotkin, PFI: 3; Scala-EPA: 10, 24, 32; Helga Schmidt-Glassner: 68; Walter Steinkopf: 48, 61.

Chapter 20 ACL: 38; Al-EPA: 1, 2, 8, 12, 18; Wayne Andrews: 6; British Crown Copyright, Reproduced with permission of the Controller of Her Britannic Majesty's Stationery Office: 5; Bulloz-EPA: 36; J. Allan Cash, PRI: 4; Gir: 17, 29, 37; Erich Müller: 9; H. B. Fleming & Co.: 23; Merisio, Pepi, Bergano, courtesy Art and Architecture Div., NYPL (Astor, Lenox, and Tilden Foundations): 3; Scala-EPA: 14; Helga Schmidt-Glassner: 10; Hir: 13; A. F. Kersting: 20, 25; Library of Congress: 26; V-Dia/Scala-EPA: 7; Va. Chamber of Commerce: 27.

Part V Opening illustration: Collection of the Whitney Museum of American Art. Gift of the Howard and Jean Lipman Foundation, Inc. Photograph by Geoffrey Clements.

Chapter 21 ACL: 83; AGRACI-EPA: 18, 45, 46; Al-EPA: 5, 8, 14, 20, 23, 24, 26, 29, 91; An-EPA: 9, 12; John R. Brownlie, PRI: 2; Braun & Cie: 28, 30; Bulloz-EPA: 7, 25, 40; Caisse Nationale des Monuments Historiques: 1; J. Camponogara: 17; Chicago Architectural Photographing Co.: 93; Courtesy of The Franklin Institute, Phila., PA: 49; Freer Gallery: 99; Deutsche Fotothek, Dresden: 43; Gir: 15, 16, 44, 66, 87; Ralph Kleinhempel: 50; Hedrich-Blessing: 95; A. F. Kersting: 3; Library of Congress: 88; Mar-ARB: 90; Musées Nationaux: 13; Courtesy of NYPL (Astor, Lenox, and Tilden Foundations): 11, 22; Novosti Press Agency: 52; Philadelphia Museum of Art: 48; H. Roger-Viollet: 4.

Chapter 22 Rudolph Burckhardt, N.Y.: 88; Leo Castelli Gallery: 95, 97; Chicago Architectural Photographing Co.: 61, 62; Geoffrey Clements: 77, 98; Colorphoto Hinz, Basle: 6, 21; Tom Ebenhoh, Black Star: 122; David Gahr: 93; Galerie Welz: 1; Gianfranco Gorgoni: 90, 91; The Solomon R. Guggenheim Museum: 106, 107; Hedrich-Blessing: 17; Lucien Hervé: 63, 65, 104, 105; Institute für Leichte Flackentragwerke: 109; G. E. Kidder Smith: 118; Ralph Kleinhempel: 7; Jim Knipe: 112; Knoedler Gallery: 86; Robert C. Lautman: 115; William Lescaze Associates: 69; Mas: 60; Pierre Matisse Gallery: 73; Museum of Modern Art: 67, 70, 75, 78; National Geographic Society: 114; Office du Film du Québec: 111a; Robert Phillips for Fortune Magazine: 110; Cervin Robinson: 117; Michel Proulx: 116; H. Roger-Viollet: 103; *Beyond Habitat*, © Moshe Safdie, MIT Press in the U.S., Tundra Books in Canada: 111b; Oscar Savio: 108; Sidney Janis Gallery, N.Y.: 83; © foto Stedelijk Museum, Amsterdam: 64; Dr. Franz Stoedtner: 68; Ezra Stoller, copyright ESTO: 71; Don Sudnik, *AIA Journal:* 119; James A. Sugar: 113; Walter Thiem: 109b; Tiofoto: 50; Malcolm Varon, N.Y.: 22; Venturi and Rauch: 120, 121; Wolfgang Volz, Essen: 102

Permission S.P.A.D.E.M. 1974 by French Reproduction Rights, Inc., for the following: 19-77; 20-24, 25; 21-1, 67, 69, 70; 22-3, 6, 7, 9, 10, 11, 12, 15, 17, 19, 20, 24, 27, 31, 37, 42, 43, 55, 65, 77, 79, 81, 103, 104.

Permission A.D.A.G.P. 1975 by French Reproduction Rights, Inc., for the following: 22-8, 14, 17, 30, 48, 53, 56, 58, 73.

Illustration Credits

3-4 Adapted from the "Later Canon" of Egyptian Art, figure 1 in Erwin Panofsky, *Meaning in the Visual Arts.* Copyright © 1955 by Erwin Panofsky. Used by permission of Doubleday and Company, Inc.

3-17, 26; 5-26; 6-24, 47, 49a, 53; 7-47; 10-54; 17-11 From Sir Banister Fletcher, *A History of Architecture on the Comparative Method,* 17th ed., rev. by R. A. Cordingly, 1961. Used by permission of the Athlone Press of the University of London.

4-6; 7-1, 31 Hirmer Fotoarchiv, Munich.

6-75 From Fiske Kimball, M. Arch, and G. H. Edgell, *A History of Architecture,* 1918. Used by permission of Harper & Row, Inc., publishers.

7-6 From Kenneth J. Conant, *Early Medieval Church Architecture.* Used by permission of The Johns Hopkins Press.

10-4, 5 From Ernst Gall, *Gotische Kathedralen,* 1925. Used by permission of Klinkhardt & Biermann, publishers.

10-18 Used by permission of Umschau Verlag, Frankfort.

11-8 From Benjamin Rowland, *The Art and Architecture of India,* 1953, Penguin Books.

16-43 From Nikolaus Pevsner, *An Outline of European Architecture,* 6th ed., 1960, Penguin Books, Ltd., © Nikolaus Pevsner, 1943, 1960, 1963.